HOSTAGE TO FORTUNE

The Troubled Life of Francis Bacon

LISA JARDINE AND ALAN STEWART

 HILL AND WANG

A division of Farrar, Straus and Giroux

New York

Hill and Wang
A division of Farrar, Straus and Giroux
19 Union Square West, New York 10003

Copyright © 1998 by Lisa Jardine and Alan Stewart
Preface copyright © 1999 by Lisa Jardine and Alan Stewart
All rights reserved
Distributed in Canada by Douglas & McIntyre Ltd.
Printed in the United States of America
First published in 1998 by Victor Gollancz, Great Britain, as
Hostage to Fortune: The Troubled Life of Francis Bacon 1561–1626
First American edition published in 1999 by Hill and Wang

Library of Congress Cataloging-in-Publication Data
Jardine, Lisa.
    Hostage to fortune : the troubled life of Francis Bacon / Lisa
Jardine and Alan Stewart. — 1st American ed.
        p.   cm.
    Includes bibliographical references (p.   ) and index.
    ISBN 0-8090-5539-2 (alk. paper)
    1. Bacon, Francis, 1561–1626.   2. Great Britain—History—
Elizabeth, 1558–1603—Biography.   3. Great Britain—History—James
I. 1603–1625—Biography.   4. Philosophers—Great Britain—Biography.
5. Statesmen—Great Britain—Biography.   6. Scientists—Great
Britain—Biography.   I. Stewart, Alan, 1967–   .   II. Title.
DA358.B3J37   1999
942.06′1′092—dc21
[B]   98-53482

Contents

Acknowledgements

This book started life as a twinkle in the eye of Sean Magee of Victor Gollancz. We are immensely grateful to him for realising that the world needed a modern biography of Francis Bacon, and for giving us the chance to write it. The finished article would be a far less elegant and polished affair without the wonderful copy-editing of Gillian Bromley. To Sean and Gillian, thank you.

Two eminent Bacon scholars, Graham Rees and William Sessions, read the manuscript in its entirety, and gave us invaluable advice (some of which we heeded). Their contribution went way beyond the call of duty. For further advice, references and ideas, our thanks go to Warren Boutcher, Patricia Brewerton, Mordechai Feingold, Anthony Grafton, Paul Hammer, Cynthia Herrup, Lorna Hutson, James Knowles, Michèle Le Doeuff, Julian Martin, Andrew Penman, Bill Sherman, Jane and Colin Stewart, and David Wootton. We would also like to thank the editorial board of the Oxford Francis Bacon Project for their support.

We are grateful to the librarians, archivists and staff of the following libraries: the British Library (the North Library and Manuscripts Reading Room), Gray's Inn Library, the Institute of Historical Research, Lambeth Palace Library, the Public Record Office, the University of London Library and the Warburg Institute, all in London; Cambridge University Library; the Bodleian Library, Oxford; Edinburgh University Library; the Folger Shakespeare Library, Washington, DC; and the Henry E. Huntington Library, San Marino, California – especially Alan Jutzi and Mary Robertson. For permission to quote from their unpublished papers at, respectively, Longleat and Hatfield House, we thank the Marquess of Bath and the Marquess of Salisbury. We owe our pictures to Hugo Cox.

This book was made possible by the support of our colleagues, and the leave policies of our departments at Birkbeck College and Queen Mary and Westfield College, University of London. We are particularly grateful to the Birkbeck College Research Fund for financing Alan Stewart's visit to US libraries in September 1996.

A Note on Dating

For most (but not all) purposes, the early modern English year began on 25 March. Throughout the book, we have 'modernised' dates so that the year begins on the previous 1 January. For example, Francis Bacon was born on 22 January 1560 by contemporary reckoning (with 1561 beginning on 25 March, two months later); in our text, Bacon was born on 22 January 1561.

A further complication arises when considering continental sources (as we do in chapters 2–5). In the late sixteenth century, the continental calendar was ten days 'ahead' of the English – so that 10 June in London was 20 June in Paris, and so on. Men like Anthony and Francis Bacon, well used to dealing with both calendars, would specify which they were using when dating their letters, which has allowed us to rationalise the dating to the English calendar. In the case of a few documents, the endnotes contain both the given date and our (assumed) English equivalent.

Preface to the American Edition

Francis Bacon (1561–1626) is best known today for his trailblazing work on scientific methodology – work that earned him the lasting title 'Father of Modern Science'. He certainly deserves to be remembered as an intellectual innovator. His wide-ranging writings cover almost every field of inquiry, from how to plant a garden to how to succeed in business. His greatest contribution was a systematic approach to the whole of knowledge, based on his conviction that it was possible to devise a single deductive system covering the entire range of empirical research in the natural world. His *New Organon* would, he believed, fulfil the biblical prophecy from the Book of Daniel that 'Many shall pass to and fro, and knowledge shall be increased'. As he wrote himself: 'Surely it would be disgraceful if, while the regions of the material globe, – that is, of the earth, of the sea, and of the stars – have been in our times laid widely open and revealed, the intellectual globe should remain shut up within the narrow limits of the old discoveries'.

Scientists ever since have adopted Bacon as an emblem and figurehead for their boldest aspirations. When the Royal Society (the 'Royal Society of London, for Improving of Natural Knowledge', to give it its full title) was founded in 1660, shortly after King Charles II returned to the throne, Sir Francis Bacon became its patron saint. The author of the Society's first *History*, Thomas Spratt, prefaced his 1667 work with a poem by Abraham Cowley containing the following eulogy to their founding inspiration:

> *Bacon* at last, a mighty Man arose
> Whom a wise King and Nature chose
> Lord Chancellor of both their Laws.

It is Sir Francis Bacon, Cowley goes on, who has rescued knowledge from its long captivity at the hands of ignorance and error:

> Bacon, like Moses, led us forth at last,
> The barren Wilderness he past,
> Did on the very Border stand

Of the blest promis'd Land,
And from the Mountain Top of his Exalted Wit,
Saw it himself, and shewed us it.

Such was the impact of Bacon upon the seventeenth-century 'scientific revolution' that modern scientists still regard Bacon as their intellectual forebear.

When we set out to write the present biography, it was this extraordinary reputation and enduring prominence whose detailed unfolding we expected to recount. In telling Bacon's story at length for the first time in very many years, we were able to take full advantage of modern electronic resources and of the great leaps forward they allow in gaining access to and processing archival material. We did, indeed, uncover new material and rich veins of previously unexplored areas of Bacon's activities, which confirmed that he led a rich and crowded life, packed with activity and impinging, like his writings, on many areas of interest.

Bacon was the youngest son of the Lord Keeper of the Great Seal (a high official in Queen Elizabeth's government). He was educated at Trinity College, Cambridge, and Gray's Inn, where he embarked on a lengthy legal career. In time, he became Learned Counsel to both Elizabeth and her successor, James I, then Solicitor-General, Attorney-General, and eventually Lord Chancellor, head of the Court of Chancery. An active parliamentarian in the House of Commons from the age of nineteen, Bacon eventually became a member of James's Privy Council, the King's innermost group of advisors, and was elevated to the House of Lords as Viscount St Albans. Only in his final five years, after he was accused of corruption in his capacity as Lord Chancellor, did he retire from public life to a secluded existence in the Hertfordshire countryside.

This thumbnail sketch of Bacon's career suggests a successful life, crowned by the highest rewards. We also found, however, that many of his ambitions were unrealised, and many opportunities were lost or botched. Bacon lived his entire life in the glare of public life; his every action was accompanied by a barrage of comment from friends and adversaries. Teasing out the truth from this kind of contemporary commentary turned out to be difficult, but unexpectedly rewarding. We discovered that a number of outrageous stories that circulated about the flamboyant Lord Chancellor during his lifetime and shortly after his death – stories traditionally judged to be apocryphal – were surprisingly accurate and illuminating. Bacon's personal and political life became more colourful and enthralling the more closely we were able to look at it.

For a man actively engaged in public life throughout his adult years, Bacon's written legacy is impressive. His major works cover a whole range of intellectual interests. The *Novum Organum* – an entirely new method of inquiry for the sciences – has absorbed the attention of philosophers of science continuously since it was published in 1620. The *De augmentis scientiarum* (the enlarged Latin version of his *Advancement of Learning*), completed during his period of disgrace, is still required reading for any student of intellectual history. The recreational *Essays* continue to be read and quoted from today, as exemplary thinking about human values and social responsibility. Bacon's utopian fiction, the *New Atlantis*, published posthumously in 1627, enshrines a set of aspirations for the relationship between science and civic life to which more recent inventors of ideal societies regularly defer.

We have not attempted here to do justice to the detail of Bacon's works. We offer the present book as a rich context for those works and urge readers to turn to Bacon's writings themselves. Brief summaries cannot capture either their complex argument or their characteristically ringing prose (several of Bacon's contemporaries commented on the eloquence of his speeches and admired the stylishness of his writing).

Researching a biography means getting to know one's chosen individual extremely well. On a number of occasions in the course of our collaborative efforts we asked each other whether we liked or disliked the Lord Chancellor. This turned out to be a pertinent question. Bacon's life was a bundle of contradictions. There is much in his life of which he could be justly proud and that contributed to the Lord Chancellor's enduring position as a landmark figure in European history. There is also material (some of which we include for the first time) that reveals him to be somewhat less worthy of our admiration. He lavished attention on his friends, but sometimes let them down. He was generally dismissive of women (including his wife), but took up the cause of the wronged Lady Hatton and pursued it devotedly. He regularly overspent on elaborate tailoring and on his personal household, but left us, in the *Essays*, a collection of unforgettable aphorisms about proper conduct in public and private life.

Too often in the past Bacon's biographers have set out with the prior resolve either to blame him for his misdemeanours (much publicised by his adversaries) or to exonerate him wholesale from that blame. Here we have tried hard to present Bacon's life to the reader candidly, warts and all, without attempting to resolve its contradictions. It should be clear that we consider him a man worthy of our attention and a figure of real importance. Our hope is that readers will, when they reach the end of the story, be able to determine for themselves the true greatness of Francis Bacon.

Lisa Jardine and Alan Stewart
London, October 1998

INTRODUCTION

A Life of Virtue and Mischief

He that hath wife and children, hath given hostages to
fortune; for they are impediments to great enterprises, either
of virtue or mischief.
Francis Bacon, 'Of Marriage and Single Life' (1612)

A T THE END of January 1594, two of the most powerful figures in
Queen Elizabeth I's government, Robert Devereux, earl of Essex,
and Sir Robert Cecil, the son of Lord Burghley, Elizabeth's Lord
Treasurer, quarrelled in the dark interior of a coach rattling out of London.
They had just finished interrogating the Queen's Portuguese Jewish doctor
Lopez, who was accused of conspiring with other aliens against her life
and would soon be executed on their orders. Lopez's treason, and the
danger to the realm which its discovery (revealed by Essex) had narrowly
averted, were the talk of London. But the two interrogators' minds were
on other kinds of plotting. Away from the court, in the privacy of the
shared coach, Sir Robert asked Essex who his candidate was for the key
vacant post of Attorney-General. Essex bridled, and affected astonishment.
'I wonder that you should ask me that question, seeing it could not be
unknown unto you that I stand resolutely against all whosoever for Francis
Bacon.'

Now it was Sir Robert's turn to affect amazement. 'Good Lord,' he
replied, 'I wonder your Lordship should go about to waste your strength
in so unlikely or impossible a matter.' It was out of the question, he
continued, that Francis Bacon should be raised to a position of such emi-
nence. Of course, it was well known that the earl was determined to reward
Bacon's service with as high an office as his patronage could procure. But
he challenged Essex to give him a single example of anyone so comparatively young and inexperienced as Francis attaining a position of such
seniority (Francis was thirty-three at the time).

Essex readily admitted that he could not think of a precedent for so youthful a candidate for the post of Attorney. But with a touch of malice he pointed out that youth and inexperience did not seem to be hindering Robert Cecil's own bid to become Principal Secretary of State, the most influential of all government posts: 'A younger than Francis, of lesser learning and of no greater experience, sueth and shoveth with all force for an office of far greater importance, greater charge and greater weight than the Attorneyship.'

The jibe was not lost on Sir Robert. As Lord Burghley's son he was sensitive to any suggestion that his swift rise was dependent upon his father's power and influence. He retaliated immediately. 'I know your lordship means myself. Although my years and experience are small, yet weighing the school I studied in and the great wisdom and learning of my schoolmaster, and the pains and observations I daily passed, yet I deem my qualifications to be sufficient. The added entitlement of my father's long service will make good the rest.' As for Essex's ostentatious bids for career opportunities for Francis Bacon – Cecil's first cousin – on every possible occasion, he would, Sir Robert suggested, stand more chance of success in his attempt to reward a loyal man for services rendered to him if he set his sights somewhat lower: 'I beg your lordship to consider of it, if at least your lordship had spoken of the Solicitorship, that might be of easier digestion to her Majesty.'

Essex exploded with characteristically ill-controlled anger. 'Digest me no digestions,' he roared, 'it is the Attorneyship that I must have for Francis, and in that I will spend all my power, mine authority, and amity, and with tooth and nails defend and procure the same for him against whomsoever, and whosoever getteth this office out of my hands for any other, before he have it, it shall cost him the coming by, and this be you assured of Sir Robert for now do I fully declare myself.

'And for your own part Sir Robert,' he continued, unable to resist a further dig at his well-connected political opponent, 'I find strange both of my Lord Treasurer and you that can have the mind to seek the preferment of a stranger before so near a kinsman as a first cousin.'[1]

In this ill-natured exchange between political rivals we encounter all the key components of what turned out to be the lifelong troubles in matters of political advancement of Francis Bacon, youngest son of Queen Elizabeth's earlier Lord Keeper, Sir Nicholas Bacon. Though dynastically well placed, his prospects were obstructed throughout his early career by Sir Robert Cecil, the equally ambitious son of his mother's sister (Mildred Cooke, wife of Lord Burghley). Rather than throw himself upon the mercy of his cousin, Francis hedged his bets between the two factions which between them controlled the Elizabethan court in the 1590s – the

Cecils and Essex. His preferred champion, the earl of Essex, was charismatic, charming and well educated – the kind of man for whom throughout his life Francis Bacon had a weakness. But this flamboyant patron with whom Bacon threw in his lot increasingly publicly was, in matters of state, headstrong and reckless, regularly ignoring the measured advice offered by those whose causes he supported, in his dealings with the Queen.

Francis Bacon's own view was that a man might mould his fortune in public life through his own efforts – '*faber quisque fortunae suae*' (every man is the architect of his own fortune), as he put it in *The Advancement of Learning* (1605). 'For there is a wisdom of counsel, and again there is a wisdom of pressing a man's own fortune,' he there continued. But the reality, as Bacon also conceded, was that a measure of mobility around the throne meant that the outcomes of planned political moves were even harder to anticipate than in more settled times. Strategies for self-advancement were fraught with uncertainty where so many competing interests jostled for position: public service and personal advancement 'do sometimes meet, and often sever'.[2] Bacon's own unashamed efforts to build a career in public office by a combination of shrewd pursuit of favour from a whole range of competing public figures and self-promotion through the intellectual and political advice he furnished those in power repeatedly came to grief. The best-laid plans were wrecked by the unpredictable outcomes of dirty political games being played with increasing deadliness in the shadow of the throne during Queen Elizabeth's declining years.

Among these strategies, attempts to exploit bonds of kinship proved particularly liable to let Francis Bacon down. In the episode upon which we have just eavesdropped, Sir Robert Cecil showed an understandable sensitivity at the slightest suggestion by Essex that his own political career depended on his father's prominent position in government ('the added entitlement of my father's long service'). Essex himself affected astonishment at the idea that Lord Burghley and his son might prefer a non-kin candidate for the attorney-generalship over a blood relation. Yet it is strikingly apparent that neither a famous father nor well-placed cousins seemed to do Francis Bacon much good. Though he was regularly accused of exploiting the fact that his father had been Elizabeth's Lord Keeper, comparisons tended to be made unfavourably between father and son; and since his father was dead, he could offer no practical help in the way of lobbying, nor simply by being someone to be reckoned with in contemporary political power games (as Lord Burghley undoubtedly was until the end of his long life).

Francis' mother Anne Bacon was closely related to significant figures in the court circle (including, again, Lord Burghley), but these connections seem to have been as much a hindrance as a help to her son's career. She had a reputation as an obstinate, determined and headstrong woman – that is to say, she was a woman with a mind of her own. She became accustomed early on to the fact that her husband's family by his first marriage obstructed her own children's prospects, and had to be opposed at every turn, so that she was inclined to protest as a matter of course against any course of action they proposed. She also held openly controversial doctrinal beliefs, and was widely admired by European religious reformers – enough in itself to make English orthodoxy suspicious of her.

We have a record of Lady Bacon's efforts on behalf of her son Francis shortly after the occasion in the mid-1590s when he came close to the coveted post of Attorney-General. In that January of 1594 the earl of Essex was not the only one pressing Robert Cecil to yield the attorneyship to Sir Nicholas' youngest son. Hearing that he was proving unhelpful, Lady Bacon herself paid a visit to Sir Robert Cecil at court. She entered his quarters unannounced, as was her privilege as beloved sister of Robert's mother, Mildred Cecil, Lady Burghley. Robert probably groaned when he saw her. Lady Bacon was sharp-witted and sharper-tongued. Above all, she pursued the interests of her two sons with a ferocity which earned her both admiration and scorn at court. Nor was she wrong to do so. In spite of their rank, Anthony and Francis Bacon were in constant danger of being sidelined politically by their family position, as the youngest of Sir Nicholas Bacon's five sons and those of his second, late marriage.

Having exchanged courtesies with her nephew, Lady Bacon broached the matter of her younger son's prospects with Sir Robert. Francis was acknowledged to be intelligent and gifted; the Queen herself had said he would go far. There was constant talk of his talents around the court, and it was understood that his counsel was valuable when intellectual intelligence was to be gathered or opinion sought on matters of state. Whereas his older brother Anthony seemed to have inherited only ill health from his distinguished father, Francis was his true intellectual heir. His maturity of judgement and political acumen fully equipped him for the legal posts to which he aspired. Yet somehow his rise was being blocked.

'Methinks he is but strangely used by man's dealings,' she added darkly, 'God knows by whom and why.'

Cecil reassured her: 'I dare say my father would gladly have had seen my cousin placed by now.'

'I hope so,' replied his aunt, 'but some think if Lord Burghley had been in earnest it would have been done.'

Cecil insisted – perhaps sincerely, perhaps simply to get rid of his determined and abrasive aunt – that both he and his father had urged the Queen to bestow some office of consequence upon Francis. Only last Tuesday, Lord Burghley had come from the Queen's presence and told his son he had sought appropriate employment for his nephew from her. And he, Cecil, was in just the same position as his cousin Francis. Both found themselves consigned to inaction, waiting on the whim of the Queen to decide their futures in public life. 'Let him not be discouraged but carry himself wisely. It may be that her Majesty was too much pressed by others at first, which she liketh not, and will decide finally as she sees fit.' With this inconclusive outcome Lady Bacon had to be content.[3]

Notwithstanding Cecil's protestations of concern and occasional promises of support, the offices of Attorney-General and then Solicitor-General continued to elude Francis Bacon, whereas Cecil himself rose steadily. Francis, in fact, never held an official position under Elizabeth, nor during the early years of James's reign. In other words, the plotting and lobbying of which these two occasions are instances were of no avail, and Francis Bacon's efforts to be architect of his own fortune came to naught.

Before leaving this episode we should note, however, that in all that is going on here Francis Bacon is not simply the passive victim of events beyond his control, and cannot be regarded as entirely beyond reproach.

In the earl of Essex's outburst − 'Digest me no digestions, it is the Attorneyship that I must have for Francis, and in that I will spend all my power, mine authority, and amity, and with tooth and nails defend . . .' − history preserves for us the passionate voice of a man who was sincerely and notoriously tireless in pursuit of due reward for those he believed to have served him faithfully. His close circle of friends, secretaries, information-gatherers and intelligencers (or spies) was made up of young men on the make, young men with political aspirations who knew that Essex would reward them as he could by assiduously promoting their individual causes. As long as Essex's star was rising, the Bacon brothers, Anthony and Francis, had no hesitation in throwing in their lot with him, publicly and without reservation.

In 1599, however, when the earl's relations with the Queen soured, it began to be widely rumoured that Francis Bacon was counselling her that Essex's activities in Ireland were potentially treasonable. In a letter to Henry Howard, later the earl of Northampton, a close friend and ally of Essex, Bacon vigorously protested his innocence on any such charge. He did, however, intimate that, faced with a conflict between loyalty to his old master and loyalty to the Queen, his allegiance to his sovereign must necessarily take precedence: 'For my Lord of Essex, I am not servile to him, having regard to my superior duty. I have been much bound unto him.'[4] Howard detected in the careful past tense of that last sentence some cooling in Bacon's commitment. His rebuke to Bacon was swift, and made clear his distaste for those who placed their own interests before those of someone who had shown himself a longstanding ally. In chastising Francis for disloyalty he preserves for us a sense of the kind of personal charisma that drew men to Essex. How, he asked indignantly, could Bacon dismiss as a casual, temporary bond an attachment which, as far as the earl was concerned, was total and sincere? When Bacon had needed a man of standing as a backer, Essex had taken the greatest pains on his behalf. He had always delighted in Francis' company. He had been personally devastated whenever he could not 'seal up assurances of his love by fruits, effects and offices, proportionable to an infinity'. Howard had himself seen the earl pondering ingenious ways to please Bacon, 'to engage your love by the best means he could devise'. All of which were 'so forcible persuasions and instances to make me judge that a gentleman so well born, a wise gentleman so well levelled, and a gentleman so highly valued by a person of his virtue, worth and quality, would rather have sought after all occasions of expressing thankfulness (so far as duty doth permit) than either omit opportunity or increase indignation'.[5]

In recalling the many occasions on which Essex had shown his personal generosity towards Bacon, beyond any obligations on grounds of services rendered, Howard was alluding to a dimension in their relationship which Bacon carefully and comprehensively erased in later life. After Francis' death, his amanuensis Thomas Bushell maintained that Essex had been instrumental in kindling, and then encouraging, Bacon's interest in natural philosophy, and in scientific ideas: 'Their first rise (as I have heard him say) was from the noble nature of the earl of Essex's affection.' Indeed, Essex's most substantial gift to Bacon had been made on such an occasion. 'Upon [Bacon's] presenting him with a secret curiosity of Nature, whereby to know the season of every hour of the year by a Philosophical Glass, placed (with a small proportion of water) in his chamber', Essex had given Bacon an estate at Twickenham, with 'its Garden of Paradise to study in'.[6] It was to Twickenham that Bacon retired whenever things got too hot politically in London, and there that he did much of his most important scientific work. Howard would have considered Bacon's omission of all reference to his intellectual benefactor where Twickenham was concerned as dishonourable.

As it turned out, Howard was right politically as well as on grounds of honour. Francis, as usual, had made the wrong strategic choice in publicly distancing himself from the earl's patronage as soon as Essex's favour with the Queen began to wane. In the course of the succession negotiations of the later 1590s, a particularly warm friendship had developed between Essex and James VI of Scotland, the most likely successor to the English throne. In 1598 the French ambassador noted that James entrusted all his negotiations at the English court to Essex.[7] Following Essex's abortive 'uprising' in 1601, and the indictment of the earl and his close advisers for treason and their execution, some prominent figures associated with Essex managed to keep their places at court. Howard was one of those who had managed to remain 'neuter' – in other words, who had built up enough support in the Robert Cecil camp to neutralise possible accusations in connection with Essex's fall.[8] Anthony Bacon, who was much closer to the earl than his younger brother, and who never abandoned his cause, was among those who managed to avoid prosecution, though he died in any event shortly after the earl was executed. When the Scottish King became James I of England in 1603, he remembered and rewarded those who had stayed true to his old friend the earl of Essex. What little favour he did show to Francis Bacon in those early years of his reign was a consequence not of Francis' detachment from Essex but of his brother Anthony's steady attachment to his patron.

In the last decade of Elizabeth's reign Henry Howard, like many of those who made a successful transition politically in spite of the royal dynastic change, apparently managed to balance both key factions – Cecil's and Essex's. Ironically, as 'family' Francis Bacon could not hedge his factional bets in quite the same way: either he belonged to his cousin Cecil's party or his non-participation identified him with Essex's opposition camp. But the kinship bond (deriving as it did from Francis' mother) was somehow not close enough to count for much with Burghley himself – as Lady Bacon intimated in attempting to pressure Robert Cecil into doing something for Francis. Thus, in an intensely factional climate, in a curious sense the family connection with the Cecils acted to Bacon's disadvantage.

One further theme crucial to our understanding of the life of Francis Bacon arises out of the intimate circle around the earl of Essex in which Bacon moved in the last decade of the sixteenth century. To Howard this circle stood for all that was most noble about close male friendship – that *amicitia* concerning which the Roman writer and politician Cicero had much to say, and which served as a model for the networks of mutually dependent gentlemen on which civic life in late Tudor and early Stuart England relied.[9] To others, however, the exclusively male, intense and passionate forms of service which surrounded Essex, in which both Anthony and Francis Bacon were implicated until the death of the earl, could readily be represented in a less respectable light as a world rife with male sexual intrigue and sodomy. Lampoons, letters and intelligence reports from the period contain frequent suggestions that one or other of the rising young men is involved in some homosexual sexual liaison or other. A few – Anthony Bacon among them – actually found themselves brought to court for alleged sodomitical activity.

★

Throughout his life, Francis Bacon himself alternated between believing that he would be successful in achieving the prominence in public life of a Burghley and imagining that he would lead a more retired existence, building a lasting reputation through his Great Renewal of learning – the *Instauratio magna*. It is clear that, given the choice, he would have preferred the latter. He yearned after the leisured life of the man of comfortable means, a life enjoyed by his two eldest half-brothers, Nicholas and Nathaniel, but one which permanently eluded him. He particularly resented the fact that his half-brothers failed to exploit their condition of ease; had he had their fortunate circumstances, he would have taken advantage of them to complete his grand intellectual project and rebuild knowledge from its foundations up.

Instead, Francis was obliged to make a working career for himself in the law – a career which constantly interfered with his beloved intellectual pursuits. As he told his uncle Burghley in a letter of 1592, 'I confess that I have as vast contemplative ends, as I have moderate civic ends.' Given half a chance, he went on, he would sell up his modest inheritance, and dedicate his life to 'profitable inventions and discoveries' – if, that is, Burghley was unable to find him a suitable household post, preferably one which made secretarial assistance available to him: 'place of any reasonable countenance doth bring commandment of more wits than of a man's own; which is the thing I greatly affect.'[10]

The ideal scenario, however, would have involved no demands of employment on Francis Bacon's time whatsoever. This freedom would have allowed him to pursue his ambitious intellectual plans, which would in turn have made him rich and world-famous. The first stage in this plan, as he explained it in *The Advancement of Learning*, was a ruthless overhaul of contemporary philosophical assumptions to 'remove the impediments of the mind' and put in place his new intellectual system. This would 'clear the passages of fortune', to allow 'wealth and means' to pour in, to be followed by great honours.[11] In the paragraph immediately following this grandiose statement of intent, Bacon ruefully accounts for his own failure to achieve this end. Such an exacting task, he explains, could be carried out only with utter single-mindedness. It is essential, then, 'not to embrace any matters which do occupy too great a quantity of time'. 'And that is the cause', he continues, 'why those which take their course of rising by professions of burden, as lawyers, orators, painful divines, and the like', do not succeed in their own fortunes, 'because they want the time to learn particulars, to wait occasions, and to devise plots'.

Eventually, Bacon did get the leisure he craved to devote himself to the life of the mind, but not in the way he would have wished. Only when decades of tireless striving after public office and the financial security that came with it culminated in his falling foul of the very system he had so assiduously exploited could he devote himself entirely to his intellectual pursuits.

In later years, Bacon was careful to separate his life into a 'before' period of political intrigue, treacherous behaviour of friends and social climbing, and an 'after' of austere scientific enquiry in a country retreat. As a way of glossing over his perpetual struggles with the competing demands of his two possible careers to create a plausible 'life', this worked. But it has left posterity with two clearly incompatible versions of Francis Bacon. All subsequent biography has struggled to resolve them.[12] In our own we have largely set aside the substantial body of posthumous apologetics and have elected to tackle the great Verulam from scratch, as he survives in archives and contemporary printed texts. This approach is, we believe, consistent with Bacon's own rendition of the treatment he hoped posterity might afford him, as he expressed it in his last will and testament: 'For my name and memory, I leave it to men's charitable speeches, and to foreign nations, and the next ages.'[13]

PART I

THE BOLD BIRTH OF
OPPORTUNITY

1561–1588

1

Much Hoped Imps

My father, though I think I had greatest part in his love of all
his children; yet in his wisdom served me as a last comer.
Francis Bacon to Sir Thomas Egerton (1597)

'THE MOULD OF a man's fortune, is in his own hands. *Faber quisque fortunae suae*', reiterates Bacon in the essay 'Of Fortune'. However, he continues, 'it cannot be denied, but outward accidents, conduce much to fortune; favour, opportunity, death of others.'[1] Of all the events in Francis Bacon's colourful career, the one which did most to shape the fortunes of himself and his brother Anthony, the two surviving children of Sir Nicholas Bacon by his second marriage, was their father's sudden and unexpected death in 1579.

In his inexorable rise from son of a Bury abbot's sheep-reeve to Lord Keeper of the Great Seal of England, Nicholas Bacon has served historians well as a model example of the possibilities of social advancement brought about by the dual innovations of humanistic learning and Reformation land transactions in Tudor England.[2] It might never have been thus if Nicholas had followed the original plan, as legend would have it, of a life in the cloisters. He could, it seems, have managed monastic discomfort, but the tonsure was too much for him: 'Being sent to be made a priest and perceiving that his crown must be shaven, rather than he would abide that which he so much misliked, he ran away and after he had hid himself a great while, at the length by an uncle (on the other side) of his that was a rich tailor, he was sent and maintained at the Inns of Court from whence he was admitted to the dignity which after he came into.'[3]

His actual career was a little less wayward, though no less striking. After attending the abbey school in Bury St Edmunds, the thirteen-year-old Nicholas won a Bible scholarship to Bene't College (now Corpus Christi), Cambridge, in 1523, entering Gray's Inn in 1532. This educational process – church school, Cambridge University and the Inns of Court – had a profound effect on Bacon. He expressed his commitment to it later in life in a series of educational benefactions, including the refounding of Bury St Edmunds Grammar School (he also drafted the orders for the establishment of the Redgrave and re-establishment of the St Albans grammar schools), the founding of six scholarships and a college chapel at Bene't College, and the donation of 200 books to the Cambridge University Library. In one respect, though, the traditional account is correct: in 1523 Nicholas Bacon matriculated at Cambridge a yeoman's son, but by the time he went on from there to the Inns of Court he considered himself a gentleman.[4]

The name of Nicholas Bacon first appears on a payroll, for the Court of Augmentations, in 1538, at the same time as he began undertaking paragovernmental work, in an advisory role. By the mid-1540s he was part of a distinguished social circle which included Henry VIII's sixth and last wife, Catherine Parr, Lord John Russell, William Cecil, the duchess of Suffolk, Roger Ascham, John Cheke and Sir Anthony Cooke – all intellectuals, heavily influenced by the new humanist learning. This was the circle which shaped the liberal intellectual atmosphere around Henry VIII's two younger children, Edward and Elizabeth, and their influence was later remembered and rewarded. In 1547, Nicholas Bacon took his own next step up the ladder of preferment to become Attorney of the Court of Wards and Liveries.

George Puttenham thought Sir Nicholas 'a most eloquent man, and of rare learning and wisdom, as I ever knew England to breed'. 'I have come', he wrote, 'to the lord keeper Sir Nicholas Bacon and found him sitting in his gallery alone with the works of Quintilian before him.'[5] For Guillaume de Salluste, le sieur Du Bartas, and Thomas Nashe he ranked alongside Sir Thomas More and Sir Philip Sidney as one of the 'chief pillars of our English speech'.[6] Ben Jonson (an admirer of both intellectual Bacons, father and son) went further, and compared Sir Nicholas to Cicero: 'Cicero is said to be the only wit, that the people of Rome had equalled to their empire. We have had many, and in their several ages (to take in but the former seculum) Sir Thomas More, the elder Wyatt; Henry, Earl of Surrey; Chaloner, Smith, Elyot, Bishop Gardiner, were for their times admirable: and the more, because they began eloquence with us. Sir Nicholas Bacon was singular and almost alone, in the beginning of Queen Elizabeth's time.'[7]

Nor is this mere flattery of a man in high office. There is evidence that Nicholas Bacon was something of a scholar, though his official duties presumably left him little time to indulge his intellectual leanings (just as would later prove to be the case for his scholarly son). Thomas Digges remembered Sir Nicholas discussing geometrical principles and their applications with his father, the mathematician Leonard Digges: 'Calling to memory the conference it pleased your honour to use with him touching the Sciences Mathematical, especially in Geometrical measurements.'[8]

For Nicholas Bacon, the social rise which had begun with his education in the liberal arts and the law was consolidated by marriage. His first wife was a Suffolk merchant's daughter named Jane Fernley, who was to provide him with an important family link to the influential London merchant banker (and financial agent to the Queen) Sir Thomas Gresham, who married her sister Anne. Jane bore him seven children, then died suddenly in late 1552. With six surviving offspring, all under twelve, to be cared for, a second marriage had to be arranged as a matter of urgency: Sir Nicholas took a new wife within weeks. In spite of the speed with which the marriage contract must have been negotiated, it was an equally shrewd move in terms of the bereaved Sir Nicholas' future prospects within the Tudor gentry.

Sir Nicholas' second bride, Anne Cooke, came from the intellectual milieu he took such pleasure in frequenting. The suspicion with which his first wife's family always regarded her suggests the possibility that she had already taken his fancy even before the ailing Jane died. Anne was one of the five daughters of Sir Anthony Cooke, widely esteemed from their youth for their erudition and piety. According to Thomas Fuller, 'they were all most eminent scholars, the honour of their own, the shame of our sex.'[9] The scholar Walter Haddon eulogised the Cooke household at Gidea Hall in an oration to the University of Cambridge: 'And what a house did I find there, yea, rather a small university, in truth while staying there I seemed to be living in a Tusculan villa, except only that in this Tusculum, the industry of the females was in full vigour.'

Sir Anthony, a man of great cultivation, had been chosen as tutor to Henry VIII's son Prince Edward, soon to become King Edward VI, to which post he owed his subsequent power and position at court (a position he forfeited for the period of Mary Tudor's reign). Like Sir Thomas More, Sir Anthony took great pride in the education he secured for his daughters, considering their success a reflection on his own intellectual standing. The girls' education was designed, in true humanist fashion, to enhance their virtuous image with decorative intellectual accomplishments, rather than to supply them with skills useful for public affairs or business. It therefore centred on Greek rather than Latin, and above all on New Testament Greek, and the Greek church fathers. We still have translations from the Greek by Mildred of St Basil's sermon on Deuteronomy 15, and Elizabeth's translation from the Latin of John Ponet's *Diallacticon*. Sir Henry Chauncey maintained that Anne was 'exquisitely skilled in the Greek, Latin and Italian tongues'. The more practical aptitudes of Cooke's four sons paled into insignificance by comparison.

Each Cooke daughter made an outstandingly successful match with a

man who would turn out to be a leading figure in the Elizabethan establishment. Margaret married the London goldsmith Sir Ralph Rowlett, but
died after only five weeks of marriage in August 1558; Elizabeth married
first Sir Thomas Hoby, best remembered for his translation of Castiglione's
Book of the Courtier, and then Lord John Russell, son of Francis, earl
of Bedford; Katharine married the diplomat Sir Henry Killigrew. Most
significantly, Anne's sister Mildred became the second wife of William
Cecil, who was later appointed Elizabeth's Principal Secretary of State as
Lord Burghley.[10]

Although these men represent a roll-call of the good and great of Elizabeth's reign, it could be argued that at the time of their marriages the
Cooke sisters were the more prominent figures, able to exert considerable
influence in the matter of their husbands' careers. As women, they had
the advantage over their menfolk that their political and religious beliefs
were either invisible or at least tended to be treated as harmlessly private.
Through their father's position they had grown up in the same milieu as
the royal children, and retained emotional ties to them, even when their
husbands risked imprisonment or exile for doctrinal dissidence. Throughout the reign of the Catholic Mary Tudor, the influence the Cooke women
could wield was critical for the safety of their immediate families. In spite
of her own devout Protestantism (presumably for the time being concealed), Anne Bacon was one of Mary Tudor's intimate inner circle of
ladies. When her brother-in-law William Cecil, the future Lord Burghley,
fell out of favour with the Queen over his apparent allegiance to John
Dudley, duke of Northumberland (who supported Lady Jane Grey's rival
bid for the throne), it was Anne Bacon who obtained a pardon for him.[11]

On Elizabeth's accession in 1558, when Charles V's ambassador Count
de Feria reported the key appointments the new Queen had made, he
attributed Nicholas Bacon's rise to Anne's position and connections: 'They
have given the seals to guard to Mr. Bacon who is married to a sister of
the wife of secretary Cecil, a tiresome prude, who belonged to the Bedchamber of the late Queen who is in heaven. He is a man who is not
worth much.' The insult of 'prude' mocks Lady Anne's learning and piety,
but the form of the report shows that she was the better-known of the
couple to an informed foreign observer in 1558.[12]

Formidable she may have appeared to outsiders, but there is no doubt
as to the fondness of Sir Nicholas for his second wife. An affectionate
poem he wrote for her in the last year of Mary's reign (1557–8) survives,
'made at Wimbledon in his Lordship's great sickness'. It suggests that Sir
Nicholas was fully aware how much his well-being depended upon his
supportive and talented wife:

Calling to mind my wife most dear
How oft you have in sorrows sad
With words full wise and pleasant cheer
My drooping looks turned into glad,
How oft you have my moods too bad
Borne patiently with a mild mind,
Assuaging them with words right kind.
. . .

Thinking also with how good will
The idle times which irksome be
You have made short through your good skill
In reading pleasant things to me,
Whereof profit we both did see,
As witness can if they could speak
Both your Tully and my Seneck [Cicero and Seneca].
. . .

Calling to mind these your kind deeds
And herewithal wishing there might
Such fruit spring out of these your sides
As you might reap store due of right
Strait want of power appeared in sight
Affirming that I sought in vain
Just recompense for so great gain.
. . .

Then reason to my comfort said
That want of power will should supply,
If endeavour gave his whole aid
To think and thank right heartily,
And said she knows as well as I
That *ultra posse non est esse* [it would be impossible to do more],
To do your best therefore address ye.
. . .

In doing this I had respect
As reason would to your delight,
And knowing that it doth reject
Such things as in most women's sight
Though vain indeed seems most of might,
Therefore for you I could not find
A more deep thing than fruits of mind.

When Nicholas wrote these words, the fruitful intellectual friendship –
the companionate marriage – between Nicholas and Anne, on which

contemporaries commented, was not matched in success by flesh-and-blood children. Nicholas' poem was probably offered to his wife as comfort for the death that summer of the second of their baby daughters. Nicholas felt he was failing his wife in furnishing her with 'fruits of mind' but not fruits of the body; perhaps he felt his sexual powers to be waning. Their first son, Anthony, was not born until 1558, when Nicholas and Anne Bacon had been married for five years. By this time, Nicholas was Sir Nicholas Bacon, Lord Keeper of the Great Seal of England, and the family was installed in the traditional residence of the Lord Keepers of England (leased from the Archbishop of York), York House on the Strand – on the site that is today to the immediate east of Charing Cross Station. It was here, on the direct route between the City and Westminster, a stone's throw from Whitehall, that Francis Bacon was born on 22 January 1561, and in the local church of St Martin-in-the-Fields that he was baptised.

The Bacon boys did not grow up in the city, however, but in the Hertfordshire countryside: for Sir Nicholas had capitalised once again on the considerable potential which the Cooke sisters' links by birth and marriage offered and acquired a country estate. He took advantage of the marriage negotiations under way between the Cooke family and the wealthy Sir Ralph Rowlett, who was to become the husband of Anne's sister Margaret, and negotiated the purchase from him of the manor of Gorhambury, near St Albans, in January 1557.[13] Francis spent most of his childhood at Gorhambury, in the new house Sir Nicholas built between 1563 and 1568 to replace the antique pile already on site, and it was here that he and his brother Anthony developed a closeness which lasted until Anthony's death in 1601. Indeed, throughout Francis Bacon's life, Gorhambury remained its emotional centre. After his father's death it was his mother's home, to which he returned, more or less reluctantly, when summoned or to escape pressure upon him in London. Formally, its ownership passed to him when Anthony died, but since his mother had taken up permanent residence there, it effectively became his only on her death in 1610.

Sir Nicholas designed the house to reflect his intellectual pursuits: Gorhambury was an exercise in self-conscious classicising, both architecturally and in the literary allusions strewn through the house's decoration. He chose the family motto, *mediocria firma* (moderate things endure), from a chorus in the Latin author Seneca's *Oedipus*. There was an italianate loggia, and a long pillared gallery in which each column was decorated with an erudite apophthegm out of the collection Sir Nicholas had made from classical texts. A magnificent painted, many-paned glass window survives today, reputedly part of the refurbishments undertaken in anticipation of Queen Elizabeth's visit during her progress of May 1577. Each pane of coloured glass represents an exotic fruit, a plant, bird or animal, including early representations of novelties from the new world – the tobacco plant, and a turkey. John Aubrey saw the painted windows in one of the galleries, 'and every pane with several figures of beast, bird or flower: perhaps his lordship might use them as topiques for local memory.'[14] (In other words, Bacon may have used the sequence of pictures as mnemonics when preparing a speech to deliver extempore, each paragraph recalled by the appropriate pane of glass pictured in his mind's eye.)

★

Nicholas Bacon's two families belonged to two separate generations. By the time Anthony was born his father was already well advanced in making financial settlements for the children of his first marriage. With the birth of Anne's children he had to begin the task of making suitable provision for his heirs all over again. Crucially, he had not completed the land purchases which would provide secure revenues for Francis when he died. Deprived of a secure income in the form of revenues from estates, Francis was obliged to combine the lifestyle and public image of the old Lord Keeper's son with the money-raising strategies of the newly established, or insufficiently endowed, from London's commercial classes. He was in any case inclined to extravagant living, and (according to his mother) over-generous with his friends and servants. Until well into middle age, the greatest day-to-day pressure on Francis Bacon was how he would find the funds to pay his household bills.

Land and family homes were the securities against which prominent figures in public life in sixteenth-century England borrowed the cash resources to finance the ostentatious lifestyles expected of them. As first-generation gentry, Sir Nicholas Bacon could not himself lay claim to the extensive land holdings of those whose pedigree ran back through several generations. On the other hand, unlike most of the gentry and nobility, Sir Nicholas was the recipient of considerable cash sums as part of the accepted Elizabethan process of doing business. Fees, receipts for services of all kinds, stipends, levies, retainers and straightforward backhanders made him, in the course of a successful career in public office, a very rich man. These were the resources which Sir Nicholas deployed to provide his heirs with the kind of properties and estates which would ensure the lasting reputation – the dynastic endurance – of the Bacon line.[15]

Sir Nicholas Bacon planned the futures of his sons and daughters meticulously. Having risen to become the holder of an office that generated vast sums in profits – estimated at about £2,600 in 1560 and rising to something over £4,000 per annum before his death in 1579 – the Lord Keeper systematically purchased lands which were entailed on his five surviving sons, to maximise the likelihood of their acquiring wealthy, though not necessarily titled, brides. At the age of nineteen, the eldest son, also named Nicholas, was part of an entail arrangement that gave him a life interest in seven manors, including Sir Nicholas' own first home and his eventual one, Redgrave Hall. Two years later Anne Butts, heiress to two estates, was selected as his wife. The marriage negotiations, which had to take into account six principal parties and three major estates, and included the heavy compensation of Anne's uncles, were complex and the arrangements thus constructed as near as possible to foolproof: it was put on record that, should Nicholas unfortunately die before the settlement was complete, his brother Nathaniel would be substituted as bridegroom. After all the Lord Keeper's planning and negotiations, Nicholas was provided with an estate worth almost £1,000 a year, positioning him securely as one of the leading gentlemen of Suffolk.[16]

Nathaniel, three years younger than Nicholas, was destined to lead Norfolk society from his estate at Stiffkey. His wife was another Anne, the young illegitimate daughter of Sir Nicholas' brother-in-law Sir Thomas Gresham. Acknowledged from birth by her father, she too brought a considerable fortune to her marriage. Building out from Stiffkey, Nathaniel's estate soon included four Suffolk manors settled on the couple by Gresham and two Norfolk manors bought up by his father.[17] The Bacon daughters, too, were well set up. The eldest, Elizabeth, married the courtier Sir Robert Doyly; Ann married Henry Woodhouse of Wraxham, son of a prominent Norfolk family; and the youngest (confusingly also named Elizabeth) married the recorder of Norwich, Sir Francis Wyndham, who later became a Judge of Common Pleas. Each had a substantial marriage portion (£800 in the case of the elder Elizabeth; one thousand marks each for the two younger sisters).[18]

And so Sir Nicholas' endeavours continued, with lands being bought and settled on his third and fourth sons, Edward and Anthony, and marriage arrangements sought for them. In the event, neither of the proposed matches – Edward's with a daughter of Sir Harry Gates, and Anthony's with one Dowsabell Paget – came to fruition, but Edward was left with significant holdings in Suffolk and London, and Anthony had various Hertfordshire lands worth some £360 a year.[19] With the four eldest boys settled, and his three daughters profitably married, Sir Nicholas set about saving for the future of his fifth and last son, Francis. Undoubtedly, if everything had gone to plan, Francis Bacon would have had sufficient lands to live off for the rest of his life. But Sir Nicholas Bacon died unexpectedly before those lands had been acquired; and the £2,500 in cash which remained uninvested at his death was inevitably consumed in paying his small cash legacies and reimbursing his debtors.

Sir Nicholas was not mistaken in believing that in economically unstable times a shrewdly planned marriage could provide an aspiring public figure with a more secure financial basis than other kinds of more obviously commercial investment. It was a model to which Francis himself was to return in middle life when, faced with the failure of his repeated bids for advancement in the public sphere, he selected himself a rich City heiress as his bride.

★

Lady Bacon's unannounced appearance in the court quarters of her nephew Sir Robert Cecil in 1594 typifies the ease with which she could gain access to those more powerfully placed than her own immediate family. The marriages of the Cooke sisters gave rise to an extensive network of connections and influence upon which their families could build lasting dynastic power. Thomas Twyne, dedicating a book to the Bacons in 1575, wrote that in marrying Anne Cooke Sir Nicholas Bacon was 'beautified with a loving lady, the offspring of an excellent race, niece to a rightworshipful grandsire, daughter to a worthy knight, scholar to a learned schoolmaster, sister to a right honourable lady, mother of much hoped imps, aunt to a peerless countess, wife to a noble counsellor, lady of a godly family, subject to a loving prince, a true worshipper of Almighty God'.[20] Anne Cooke's most significant and enduring contribution to the fortunes of her two sons, however, came not from her family connections, nor from her humanistic erudition, but from her deeply Protestant religious convictions. Her father Sir Anthony, a well-known Protestant figure, was one of the Marian exiles who, faced with the prospect of a Catholic queen on the throne, went into voluntary banishment in 1554. Well before she married Nicholas Bacon, Anne had translated into English and published sermons by the Siennese preacher Bernardino Ochino, dealing with predestination and the joys of the elect in their sense of enfolding divine love. Ochino, 'that sanctified Barnardine' as Anne dubbed him, enthralled Italian-speaking audiences in London when he was welcomed into Lambeth Palace during the reign of Edward VI. In Francis' infancy she translated John Jewel's *Apology in Defence of the Church of England*, one of the key books in the attempt to establish the Anglican church during the early Elizabethan years. Nor was Anne Bacon merely a dutiful translator. Her own clear-headed command of Protestant doctrine is audible in her versions of the often turgid originals, and the prefatory letter to the Jewel *Apology* contributed by Matthew Parker, Archbishop of Canterbury, commends her personal commitment.[21]

Throughout her marriage, and after her husband's death, Anne Bacon filled their house at Gorhambury and the neighbouring parishes with a succession of preachers with strong Puritan leanings: the Bacon household chaplains included Thomas Fowle and Robert Johnson, who were both deprived of the licence to preach on account of their Nonconformity.[22] Whereas Sir Nicholas consistently represented his faith as orthodox Anglicanism, pursuing the 'middle way' of the moderate reformed church just as he advocated *mediocria firma* in every walk of life, Lady Bacon was noted for her unconventional, not to say unorthodox conduct in matters religious: on several occasions she publicly attended sermons by Nonconformist radical preachers, and she laid out considerable sums of money to support individuals whose beliefs were patently not aligned with Church of England doctrine.

Nevertheless, for public purposes Lady Bacon's religious convictions were on the whole firmly subordinated to those of her husband. When the Archbishop of Canterbury, Matthew Parker, turned to Anne Bacon to sort out a quarrel that had arisen between himself and the Lord Keeper, he saw her as '*alter ipse*': another himself, another Nicholas Bacon.[23] But even before her husband's death, there are hints that her acquiescence was from time to time less than totally assured. In 1572, Anne united with her sisters to work on a set of verses as part of a campaign to help the preacher Edward Dering, who had insulted the Queen in a sermon two years earlier and subsequently lost his licence to preach. Her contribution is obscured, however, by her husband's subsequent prosecution of Dering in the Star Chamber.[24]

It was the independent-spirited Lady Bacon who saw to the early education of her two sons, selecting, hiring and supervising their tutors. Consequently, both Anthony and Francis were given a solid grounding in the severer sort of radical Protestantism. Their earliest home tutor (probably from June 1566 to 1569) was a scholar from Christ Church, Oxford, named John Walsall, who later recalled to Lady Bacon how, in the course of her and her husband's 'demeaning yourselves in the education of your children', he was 'called from the university to teach your two sons' and then 'called from teaching of children, to instruct men' in a series of livings provided by the Lord Keeper. He recalled Anthony and Francis as 'such children, as for the true fear of God, zealous affection to His word, obedience to their parents, reverence to their superiors, humility to their inferiors, love to their instructor, I never knew any excel them.'[25]

The importance for both sons in later life of a godly education, closely supervised by a devout, scholarly mother of the intellectual calibre of Anne Bacon, was considerable. Her competence as a spiritual and an intellectual guide was also clearly understood by contemporaries – not least because her own two sons were manifestly better disciplined and educated than their elder half-brothers, of whom Anne had not had the educational charge. In the summer of 1569, as noted above, Nathaniel Bacon married Anne, the illegitimate daughter of Sir Thomas Gresham by a Mistress Dutton, one of his household servants who had been married off by her master to Thomas Dutton, a factor employed by Gresham in Antwerp and Hamburg. Anne's education naturally left much to be desired, and as the bride of Sir Nicholas' son she had to be turned into a lady at speed. Nathaniel knew exactly how this was to be done. Immediately after the marriage he arranged for her to join his much younger half-brothers in the schoolroom at Gorhambury.

Sir Thomas Gresham's wife Anne was not entirely comfortable to see Anne Dutton-Gresham under Lady Bacon's roof. Nathaniel wrote first to one of Sir Thomas' servants, asking him to put the case to his parents-in-law: 'I require no great time for my wife to be with my Lady [Lady Bacon], half a year or a quarter, more or less as my father[-in-law] shall appoint the time certain, and within that space if upon any occasion he shall mislike of her usage, I will undertake it shall be so.'[26] To Lady Gresham herself he wrote reassuring her that the cost at least would be met elsewhere: 'In my talk had with your Ladyship I perceived you were not minded, if my wife were placed here, to be at any charge with her. I shall undertake that shall be so rather than any let [hindrance] shall thereby grow; only I require that you and my father[-in-law] will show a good liking of her coming hither, for otherwise I know my Lady [Lady Bacon] will not have her.'[27]

Some years later Nathaniel recalled the circumstances, and acknowledged his debt to his stepmother:

Your ladyship knoweth how, being matched in marriage as I am, it stood me upon to have some care of the well bringing up of my wife, for these words of Erasmus are very true: *plus est bene instrui quam bene nasci* [it is better to have been well instructed than well born]. If she should have had the want of both, I had just cause to fear what might befall. Hereupon, being not able to remedy the one, I did as much as in me lay to provide for the other, and therefore I sought by all the means I could to have her placed with your ladyship. This is it for which I think myself so greatly beholding to your ladyship, in that you were content to trouble yourself with having my wife, and not that alone, but during her being with you to have such care over her and better to use her than I myself could have wished. Yea, I often said, and yet say, a more strait manner of usage would have wrought a greater good. Yet such was your ladyship's goodwill, which I will not live to be unmindful of: for the care had of her, I account it had of me; the good done to her, I account it done to me, for I persuade myself it was done in respect of me.[28]

Anne Gresham Bacon herself was fulsome in her acknowledgement of the pains Lady Bacon had taken with her, and retained fond memories of those shared lessons, sending warm wishes, when she wrote to her mother-in-law, 'to my brother Anthony and my good brother Frank'.[29]

Such understanding between Nathaniel Bacon and his stepmother was exceptional; on the whole, neither her inevitable interference in his inheritance prospects nor her sharp tongue endeared her to him. He admitted to Lady Gresham that she might well 'marvel how it falleth out I have this great liking of my lady'. The reason for his approval in this case was directly linked to Lady Bacon's seriousness, godly discipline and piety: like her, Nathaniel was a zealous Puritan who actively sought out godly preachers to fill the rectory at Stiffkey. 'In this respect I have ever liked of [Lady Bacon], though in other things, as cause moveth me, it may be I have as great misliking of her.'[30]

We may surmise that Anne Gresham Bacon absorbed the same low church piety as Anthony and Francis. When her first child was born in 1573, she asked Lady Bacon to be the godmother. In family terms this was not at all a straightforward matter. Lady Gresham, Anne's mother in name if not in reality, was the sister of Sir Nicholas Bacon's first wife, Nathaniel's mother, and there had always been a certain amount of coldness between the families of the two wives on account of Sir Nicholas' overswift remarriage. But Anne Gresham Bacon placed the godly upbringing of her first-born above family squabbles.[31]

★

Nicholas, Nathaniel and Edward Bacon, Sir Nicholas' sons by his first marriage, showed little inclination towards learning (though Nathaniel was good with figures). Nicholas and Nathaniel attended Trinity College, Cambridge, briefly in 1561, but were withdrawn before they had been there a year; Edward lasted a little longer. Anne Bacon's two sickly boys, by contrast, were studious and serious.

In April 1573, at the age of fourteen, Anthony Bacon was sent in his turn to Trinity. Edward Tyrrell, one of Sir Nicholas' wards, who later married a Bacon cousin, went with him. Anthony's brother Francis went too, although he was barely twelve – under the customary age for boys other than choristers to join the university community. But the two brothers had always been very close, and their father thought that they would provide each other with suitable companionship. They would, in any case, be well cared for away from home: their father entrusted them to the personal safe keeping of the Master of Trinity, John Whitgift, later to be Archbishop of Canterbury.

Although Anthony and Francis notionally spent almost three years at the university, their period of residence was twice interrupted when plague broke out in the Cambridge area. The university was shut between August 1574 and March 1575, and the boys left Cambridge again in August 1575 – in which month their half-brother Edward wrote to Nathaniel Bacon: 'My brothers of Cambridge the next week come to Redgrave and there remain; the plague is about Royston and Cambridge.'[32] Accounts for their keep at Cambridge do not begin again until the following October.[33]

The boys were lodged in John Whitgift's own quarters, and he took care of their domestic arrangements, as well as supervising their studies. Sir Nicholas met all their expenses, paying over the money directly to Whitgift, who kept careful accounts of everything he spent. Compared to the austerity of college life for the ordinary student at Trinity, the Master's noble charges were housed and cared for in considerable comfort. However, Whitgift oversaw the day-to-day activities of his elite pupils and the college scholars together, and applied the same rigour to all: 'He held [them] to their public disputations, and exercises, and prayers which he never missed, chiefly for devotion, and withall to observe others absence, always severely punishing such omissions and negligences. He usually dined and supped in the common Hall, as well to have a watchful eye over the scholars, and to keep them in a mannerly and awful obedience, as by his example, to teach them to be contented with a scholler-like college diet.'[34] (In the case of the Bacon boys, though, Whitgift supplemented the meagre college fare with boiled mutton and other items – the excuse for such indulgence being the poor state of their health.)

When Anthony and Francis arrived, Whitgift purchased books for the boys' studies: Livy's *History of Rome*, Caesar's *Commentaries*, the *Orations* of the Greek writer Demosthenes, Homer's *Iliad* and the classical rhetoric handbook *Ad Herennium* (believed then to be by Cicero). Later he bought them Aristotle and Plato, Cicero's *Complete Works* and a commentary on his *Orations*, Sallust's *Roman History*, Hermogenes and Xenophon in a facing-page Greek and Latin edition. There were also Greek grammars, and a Latin bible. More standard textbooks were probably provided in-house, or borrowed. Whitgift usually used two elementary logic textbooks, by Seton and Caesarius, with his pupils.

In his 'Life of Bacon', William Rawley, Francis' chaplain, claimed that while at Cambridge Bacon 'first fell into the dislike of the philosophy of Aristotle; not for the worthlessness of the author, but for the unfruitfulness of the way [method]; being a philosophy (as his lordship used to say) only strong for disputations and contentions, but barren of the production of works for the benefit of the life of man.'[35] This suggestion of precocious philosophical insight ought perhaps to be taken with a pinch of salt. It is possible that Aristotle's stranglehold over the traditional curriculum came as a shock to an intelligent thirteen-year-old who in his classroom at home had been tutored by 'ordinary language' religious teachers from the reformed movement, and trained in humanist pedagogic methods grounded largely in Roman forensic techniques of argumentation; however, it is more likely that Bacon's hostility to the Aristotelians dates from his maturity and was superimposed on memories of those early years at Trinity.

As the architect of the new, humanistically oriented statutes for Trinity College, Whitgift was well qualified to offer a basic liberal arts education in Greek and Latin eloquence of the kind Sir Nicholas Bacon wanted for his two boys. The effectiveness of that early grounding may be detected in Francis Bacon's lifelong eloquence – in speech and writing – as well as in his easy reference to the major literary and historical works of Greece and Rome. The books Whitgift bought for his young charges suggest an education perfectly in line with Francis' and Anthony's anticipated futures as well-placed gentlemen of means, taking an active part in public affairs, though not necessarily as 'men of business' – cultivated patricians, rather than men employed to serve the state. At the end of his life, when Francis Bacon self-consciously fashioned an image of himself as the man of letters, retired from the hurly-burly of politics to a contemplative life in the country, he took as his models the authors who had shaped his outlook in these early years, Cicero and Demosthenes, along with the stoic philosophical writer Seneca.

Most of Whitgift's purchases for Francis and Anthony Bacon, however, were not scholarly at all. There were endless pairs of shoes and slippers, which they seemed to get through at a great rate; there were garters, silk points for doublets, dye for Francis' stockings, hats and linings for hats, and sums laid out for alterations to doublets and hose, as well as their mending and laundering. The Bacon brothers clearly developed their love of elegant dress early on in life. (After his marriage, when Francis finally had enough money to indulge his tastes, his extravagance and ostentation in matters of dress frequently occasioned comment.) There were lute strings, bows, quivers, arrows and shooting gloves for the boys' recreations; and there were household goods to make the boys' lodgings more comfortable – several desks, chairs, wall-hangings and maps, candlesticks and candles, and glass for windows (glazed windows were a considerable luxury in the 1570s). For the Bacon brothers the two years or so they spent in Cambridge took the form of a gentlemanly grooming, rather than an in-depth training in any particular discipline.

A good deal of money was paid out on account of one or other of the boys falling sick – so much, indeed, that Whitgift more than once overspent the funds he had been given, and had to ask Sir Nicholas for more. The pattern of recurrent illness which dogged both Anthony and Francis throughout their lives is already well established in their teens – as was the practice of taking addictive remedies (including mild opiates). Anthony's poor health in particular necessitated expensive purchases like large quantities of coal during the summer months – thirty shillings' worth on two separate occasions, out of a total budget of twenty-odd pounds for the period. Right at the end of Anthony's life, when he was as usual deeply in debt, his mother Lady Anne Bacon paid equivalent sums to send coal in summertime to Essex House, where Anthony was in residence.

Francis' first extant letter dates from the Trinity years, written 'to my very loving brother Mr Nicholas Bacon at Redgrave' in a fairly neat secretary hand.

After my hearty commendations unto you and to my sister. Sir sith [since] it is so that you have promised my cousin Sharpe[36] a buck [a deer] against [for] this Commencement [graduation], and the time draweth so near; I have to desire you because he now hath sent for it, and he must needs be at great charges if the messenger tarry there upon his own cost, that you will so use the messenger that he be at no cost either for lodging or meat and drink while he is with you. Besides this, if you will show my cousin at my request so much courtesy that he may pay the keeper no fees for the same buck, ye shall both pleasure him and me very much. Thus desiring you to do this for me I leave you to the tuition of God. At Cambridge this third day of July. 1574.

> Your loving brother
> Francis Bacon

My brother had written unto you if by reason of sore eyes he had not tarried at London.[37]

This letter charmingly confirms the impression that the thirteen-year-old Bacon had his mind somewhat more on the lifestyle of a young gentleman than on logic or Greek grammar. It also shows that even during the periods when the boys were technically resident in Cambridge, they often travelled back to London for health or other reasons. On this occasion the excuse is the state of Anthony's eyes (he had suffered from some damaging condition shortly before leaving home for university). Whitgift's accounts also include sums for the hire and maintenance of horses for a seven-day visit to the family home at Redgrave.

★

Whenever Francis later recalled his time at Cambridge it was as a period entirely detached from the worlds of politics, business or commerce. His lifelong dream of a new philosophy, a *scala intellectualis* or method of intellectual ascent, whereby a man might pass from fundamental cerebral principles to an understanding of the entire world system, was similarly theoretical and 'pure'. Yet until its very end Francis Bacon's own life was deeply immersed in politics, in business affairs, and in the commercial, practical world of Tudor and Stuart London.

Just as Bacon chose to 'forget' how closely involved the earl of Essex had been in his early formation as a philosopher, natural scientist and intellectual, so he chose to 'forget' his robust links with the busy technological and commercial world in which he grew up. This may have been because here again the early promises of wealth and success failed to materialise. Sir Nicholas Bacon expected to get more out of the marriage link to the Greshams than simply the settlement in the marriage contract. Sir Thomas Gresham became Francis' father's close colleague. At the time of his father's death, Francis Bacon was away in France, and unable to follow his father's coffin in the great pomp and ceremony of Sir Nicholas' sumptuous funeral – a funeral worthy in its magnificence of Elizabeth's Lord Keeper. His father's old friend Sir Thomas Gresham, however, was present. Amid what has been described as the 'recklessly' expensive finery specified in Sir Nicholas' will, Gresham walked behind the coffin with Bacon's sons and his three sons-in-law, the Master of the Rolls, the Attorney-General, the Solicitor-General and the Master of the Queen's Jewel House. Each of them had received six yards of top-quality black cloth, at 26s 8d a yard, for their funeral finery. They were preceded only by the Lord Treasurer (who was principal mourner, in twelve yards of blacks at 30s a yard), the earls of Leicester and Huntingdon (the same), and Mr Secretary Walsingham (eight yards of blacks).[38]

But when Gresham himself died six months later, it transpired that he had carefully tied up his entire estate, in order to keep it out of the hands of his wife's sons by her first marriage. At the time of his death his daughter Anne had produced three daughters from her marriage to Nathaniel Bacon, so that Sir Thomas was without a male heir in the first and second generations. The bequest of Gresham's entire estate to found Gresham College – a bequest finally realised only on the death of Lady Gresham, and after she had officially contested the will in the courts – also put paid to the inheritance expectations of the Bacon family.

2

A Protestant Abroad

Travel in the younger sort is a part of education.
Francis Bacon, 'Of Travel' (1625)

LOOKING BACK IN later life, Francis Bacon reckoned the years between 1576 and 1579 to have been among those most crucial for his development. Attempting to impress King James with his curriculum vitae in 1610, it was not to his Cambridge education, nor to his legal training, that he drew the monarch's attention, but – after his status as the son of Sir Nicholas Bacon – his early experience across the Channel. 'I was', he wrote, 'three of my young years bred with an ambassador in France.' His choice of that verb 'bred' suggests something of the crucial formative influence on him of his sojourn in France, and, more specifically, of the ambassador, Sir Amias Paulet – the lasting influence of a surrogate father figure.

It is tempting to imagine the young Francis setting out on some kind of early mind-enriching Grand Tour. A gentle peregrination around the antiquities, cultural sites and intellectual salons of the continent would have been an eminently suitable preparation for an erudite young gentleman. It would have fitted in well as a preamble to the broad sweep of his later intellectual range, the cultivation he went on to make so particularly his own. The truth is that Francis was sent to France primarily to bolster the somewhat parochial training in English common law he might expect to gain at Gray's Inn with an understanding of Roman law, as practised in France. In pursuit of this prosaic end, Francis spent months billeted in substandard village accommodation hundreds of kilometres from Paris, where his hosts extended to him only a guarded welcome, accompanied by a certain amount of downrightly hostile suspicion, as the son of a reputedly radical Protestant.

He set off, though, in the train of an English diplomat. By the mid-sixteenth century diplomacy had become a more sophisticated affair than simple 'service', or attendance, performed in the household of a prominent public figure. It now involved a set of elaborate public practices which had to be actively mastered by the would-be ambassador. The comparatively greater sophistication of intellectual life on the European mainland had created the need in England for public servants trained in a range of skills that neither the universities nor the Inns of Court could supply at home. In 1561, Bacon's uncle William Cecil sent his eldest son Thomas across the Channel specifically not to be 'scholarly learned, but civilly trained [in civil law], and to have either the French or Italian tongues', hinting at the increased value attached to vernacular languages, rather than merely the traditional *lingua franca* of Latin. In addition to languages and secretarial skills, the would-be diplomat required a firm grasp of the customs, social organisation and political systems of a number of emerging European nation-states, which needed to be observed in operation. Similarly, the state-of-the-art fortification and siege warfare techniques described in books like Machiavelli's *Art of War* were only available to be inspected in mainland Europe, where armed struggles for political and territorial supremacy were conducted almost continuously, and where specialists in munitions sold their expertise on the open market.[1]

The logistics of planning such an extended education, outside the more standard university and Inns of Court structure, were complicated. Just how complicated can be gauged from the experience of the scholar, poet and soldier Philip Sidney, who arranged for his younger brother Robert to be placed in Strasbourg in 1579. Despite the presence in Strasbourg of his old friend Hubert Languet, who was resident there, to make the arrangements, and the willingness of the esteemed humanist scholar Jean Sturm to provide the young man's accommodation (at a price), there remained the difficulty first of finding a suitable tutor and then of retaining him on the pittance that Sidney could afford. But such locally organised arrangements were necessary if the visit was to be a success. The young English gentleman student 'might live somewhat cheaper with a common citizen', according to Languet, but 'neither his meals nor his rooms would be so good; and as the townspeople are wont to admit many boards to the same table, and have no control over them, it happens sometimes that disputes arise among them; and strangers are always more liable to be insulted than natives of the place.'[2]

Continental travel was expensive. Lord North, in the 1570s, estimated that it cost £160 per annum to keep a gentleman abroad; at the more extravagant end of the market, Edward de Vere, earl of Oxford, contrived to spend £4,561 in fourteen months in 1575–6.[3] But, as Sir Nicholas noted cannily, if a young man were attached to the household of an ambassador, then the costs decreased considerably. No prospective ambassador could with impunity turn down the honour of having the Lord Keeper's son in his entourage, and in 1576 there was a prospective ambassador in sight – Sir Amias Paulet, whom the Queen had resolved by mid-April to appoint to succeed Dr Valentine Dale as her ambassador to the French King.[4]

To Sir Nicholas and Lady Bacon, Paulet looked like a very safe pair of hands into which to commit their youngest son. Although the Paulet family hailed originally from the Somerset town of Hinton St George, where they retained a power base, it was on the island of Jersey, the captaincy of which he inherited from his father in 1571, that Sir Amias had made his mark. In league with the Governor-General of Guernsey, Sir Thomas Leighton, Paulet had actively promoted the Protestant cause, welcoming Huguenot refugees to the island in large numbers, taking care to see that Jersey was fortified against any possible French attack and appointing a Huguenot minister to the island's most important benefice.[5] The call to France came just as the Church of the Channel Islands formally adopted its first 'Form of Discipline', a presbyterian form of worship largely taken from the Discipline of the Reformed Church of France.[6] Paulet's sense of control and religious security at home in Jersey was to be dashed by his experiences in France: two years later, he lamented to Leighton, 'I can now tell you by experience that it is a blessed life to live in those little Isles. When I consider the course of things in this world I persuade myself that God loveth those Isles and careth for them.'[7]

Even Lady Bacon approved of the man who would later (when assigned to guard Mary Queen of Scots) be described as 'a gentleman of an honourable family, a Puritan in religion, and very ambitious'. She was possibly less happy with the rumours about Paulet's wife Margaret, who had been a Catholic like her father until she married; or Paulet's uncle John, a Roman Catholic dean; or Paulet's stepmother, who was known to hold mass in her house in Clerkenwell. In a period in which it was a matter of importance to which precise sector of the Catholic or reformed churches an individual adhered, the uncertainty about the religious affiliations of Sir Amias' own household dogged his footsteps throughout his time in France.[8]

During the 1570s, the Low Countries were in the possession of the Spanish King Philip II (who had previously been married first to the English Queen Mary Tudor, and then to the daughter of the King of France). English diplomatic relations with France were determined by fluctuations in the level of anxiety caused by the threat of Habsburg (Catholic) expansion, rather than by any coherent policy. Elizabeth had a vague commitment to international Protestantism, and to encouraging the Huguenots (Protestants) in France against the ruling Catholics. At the same time, however, England's political interests lay in an alliance with Catholic France. When Paulet arrived in France in the autumn of 1576 a peace agreement had recently been reached between the new King, Henri III, and his opponents grouped around the Protestant Henri de Navarre. The

Huguenots had been granted minor concessions for the 'free, public and general exercise' of their religion, and a measure of political freedom. A vague but powerful Catholic League was born to coordinate protest against these moves, with the odd effect that the main threat to the stability of the (Catholic) throne was now perceived as Catholic.[9]

In such an atmosphere, the appointment of a new ambassador was a touchy matter. In a little treatise entitled *The Ambassador,* Jean Hotman (who later became a member of Paulet's household in Paris) advised that ambassadors should be appropriate to their postings – in other words, 'that one that is a Protestant should not be so fit to be about the Pope nor the King of Spain'.[10] Paulet, an active Huguenot sympathiser, was already regarded with suspicion by the French administration for his radical views, and to the Spanish ambassador in France, Bernardino de Mendoza, was 'not only a heretic ... but a terrible Puritan'. But this was the idea. Burghley urged Paulet: 'Change not your manners with the soil you go to; confirm by your actions abroad the good opinion you have at home, namely for your religion and discretion.'[11]

The original plan was that not only Francis but also Edward Bacon would accompany Paulet on this embassy, and Sir Nicholas accordingly obtained a Privy Council licence for them both to travel, 'for their increase in knowledge and experience'. Knowing, however, that Edward would baulk at the idea of chaperoning his fifteen-year-old half-brother, Sir Nicholas neglected to mention the plan. He also withheld the necessary passport to travel.[12] Edward finally worked out what was going on when one of his servants informed him that he would be obliged to accompany Francis on Paulet's embassy. 'A meaning there was I should have gone with my brother,' Edward commented wryly to his brother Nathaniel. Instead of falling in with this plan, Edward set out without his father's backing, accompanied by an unidentified 'Frenchman learned greatly' and 'a man to keep my horses which, all such as I could provide, I carry with me'.[13]

Francis later recalled his departure from England as one of the milestone moments in his life. Writing to Sir Robert Cecil in January 1595, he refers to having served Elizabeth 'for these one-and-twenty years (for so long it is that I kissed her Majesty's hands upon my journey into France)'; and at the same time he tells his friend and patron the earl of Essex of serving 'now these twenty years (for so long it is, and more, since I went with Sir Amias Paulet into France, from her Majesty's royal hand)'.[14] Putting to one side his erratic sense of time, there seems to be no good reason to doubt that Francis took his leave directly from the Queen, as ambassadors and their household were expected to do – Sir Amias felt obliged to apologise when his wife and children failed to pay their parting duty to the monarch, on account of their recent infection with the smallpox.[15] By his own account, Francis never forgot the thrill of being allowed to kiss Elizabeth's hand, the sign that royal favour had been extended to him. Ever afterwards he considered himself to have been actively in the Queen's service from that moment.

★

Preparations for the embassy started in earnest once the Privy Council had formally commissioned Paulet on 26 August 1576.[16] The journey was delayed ostensibly by the state of Sir Amias' legs, which, as he reported to Burghley on 8 September, so 'grieved' him that he had not been able to leave his house since the previous Friday.[17] The truth of the matter was that Sir Amias needed to stall for as long as possible in order to raise some cash, by selling off several of his manorial estates.[18] The life of a resident ambassador was an expensive one, for although the post was an official appointment, it was largely financed from the postholder's own pocket.[19] Jean Hotman's ideal ambassador was rich 'in the goods of fortune', because poverty was an obstacle to his having 'that dignity which he ought to represent', whereas the liberality of a wealthier ambassador reflected honourably upon the monarch he represented.[20]

However much Paulet managed to raise, it quickly turned out not to be enough. Arriving in the French capital on 3 October, after an eight-day journey including a nasty crossing (exacerbated by the 'utter ruin' of Dover harbour), Paulet soon felt 'the weight of his heavy train' and begged Burghley 'to use your reasonable goodwill in my allowance for my transportation, my charges (no doubt) being much increased by this extraordinary occasion'.[21] Paris proved to be a particularly expensive posting. All the necessary provisions, both for his household and for his horses, were excessively dear − notably the wines, suffering from the general failure of that year's crop − and Paulet soon discovered that his chargeable expenses did not include the cost of his wife's transportation, carriage and post-horses − expenses which he thought 'seemed very reasonable, because she is part of my train'.[22] Paulet tried to justify a heavy expenses claim by pointing out that 'my train hath been great by reason of divers gentlemen recommended unto me by the Queen's Majesty as Master Doctor Caesar, Mr Throckmorton and Mr Hilliard besides those of mine owne company'.[23] Coming as they did with the Queen's recommendation, he could not turn these companions away.[24]

The Queen's instructions to Paulet were, as was customary, detailed.[25] He was to negotiate on an international level, often in personal contact with sovereigns; adhere to all the complex protocol; provide a news and intelligence service; keep an eye on Anglo-French merchandise; complain loudly about alleged French piracy; make clear Elizabeth's goodwill towards the Huguenots; and run a household. But we should be cautious about taking this document entirely at face value as a personal briefing to Paulet. This list of instructions was designed to be circulated as the 'official version' (a successful strategy, if the number of copies surviving today is any indication), and was drafted by Sir Francis Walsingham using a good deal of the wording of the instructions he received as Elizabeth's ambassador to the French King in December 1570.[26]

Sir Amias' first days in Paris encapsulated the precarious position of the resident ambassador, simultaneously pursuing official and non-official activities. Meeting the French King and Queen Mother in a shared audience, he and the outgoing ambassador Dr Dale were well treated and dinner was provided for them in a special chamber at court. But while afternoons and evenings were spent in official splendour, nights were spent conducting secret interviews with Huguenot leaders such as François de la Noue and Philippe Du Plessis-Mornay, meetings aimed at building up and reinforcing Huguenot networks.

No clear distinction was made between legitimate diplomatic activity and undercover espionage. Much of the ambassador's most important work was done off the record. Paris was particularly valuable as a centre for information-gathering – both overt and covert – because of its strategic location, its proximity to open mainland routes and its relatively speedy access to London, and the embassy in Paris was the linchpin of an intelligence-gathering operation carefully constructed by Sir Francis Walsingham. Succeeding Burghley as Principal Secretary in 1573, Walsingham had inherited from him a system of spies and informers from which he built up an intelligence network. A great deal of his information did come through what we might see as 'normal' diplomatic channels; but in addition, each ambassador and agent was expected to build up his own personal intelligence service, drawing on servants and secretaries in great households. Walsingham also made considerable use of the Protestant communities across the Low Countries, Germany and France: after his death, it was discovered that he received regular reports from twelve locations in France, nine in Germany, four in Italy, four in Spain and three in the Low Countries, as well as from individuals in Constantinople, Algiers and Tripoli. Even within England, four Walsingham agents were tracking down Jesuit priests and seminarians.

As with the public ambassadorial duties, there was no official budget for any of this, and a large proportion of the operation was subsidised personally by Walsingham. There were various ways of gaining access to a country's secret affairs, the most obvious one being hard cash, 'which maketh the closest cabinets of princes to fly open'. But Hotman recommended another, 'more open, and less suspected', namely, 'entertainment at the table'. This hospitality obliged the ambassador's guests, especially those who thus became beholden to him, to 'smell out all the news and report them unto him, at his table, or in private' – though the ambassador should always take care to remember that intelligences were 'not always of a true stamp'.[27]

The resident ambassador's main job was to act as a gatherer and disseminator of news, but hitting the right balance between proper ambassadorial display and the real work took some time. Paulet complained that he had been so troubled with entertaining other ambassadors, and especially those of 'the religion', that he was forced to make his despatches at night.[28] Some of the results of those night-time labours are still available to us today: Paulet's 'copy-book' (a volume containing copies or drafts of letters to be sent) has survived, and is now lodged in the Bodleian Library, Oxford. It provides an extraordinary insight into the world which Francis Bacon inhabited for three years, revealing above all the sheer bulk of written work that the resident was expected to coordinate – work in which the members of his household certainly participated.

The ambassador had to provide the sovereign with a regular, full and lucid report of his activities in his host country, with meticulously detailed accounts of how he was received at court, over whom he took precedence, with whom he was permitted to speak, and so on. From this the Queen could gauge her present standing in the host nation, both absolutely and in relation to other countries sending ambassadors there. But the resident was also required to send another report, more bluntly worded, to the Secretary (or Secretaries) of State. Other senior ministers might also have demanded personalised accounts, as might now obscure but then influential clerks of the Privy Council. On top of this, the resident had to maintain cordial relations with his personal patrons, his country neighbours and his kinsmen, and also to forge new relations with potential sources of fresh and elusive intelligence. As Hotman notes, 'he shall do most wisely in establishing forthwith his intelligences from all parts following the order of his predecessor, adding thereunto, the correspondency which he can have with his friends, even to the remotest countries.'[29]

Everything had to be done to an immovable deadline – the departure of the post, by which time all letters had to be drafted, converted into the relevant cipher (there were different ciphers for each recipient of sensitive information), and then copied into the copy-book for future reference. Thus, for example, on 19 February 1578 Paulet wrote to the Queen, the Secretaries (Francis Walsingham and Thomas Wilson), Walsingham separately, Wilson separately, the earl of Warwick, Lord Treasurer Burghley, the earl of Leicester, his predecessor Dr Valentine Dale, the Treasurer (Mr Heneage), Edward Tremayne of Colocumb, an active officer in the west of England, the Privy Council clerk Thomas Wilkes, and Sir Thomas Leighton, the Puritan Governor-General of Guernsey). On 11 March (the next major post) the key figures – the Queen, the Secretaries together and separately, Warwick, Burghley and Leicester – were joined by the earl of Sussex, the earl of Hertford, the Lord Admiral, Mr Treasurer again, Mr Horsey, Wilkes and Tremayne again, the Privy Council clerk Robert Beale, and Nicasius Yetsweirt.[30] Letter-writing became so habitual that when, in November 1579, Paulet finally left France, he could not shrug it off, as he told Walsingham: 'I am Jack out of office, I thank God for it; yet I cannot forbear my wonted course, to write somewhat to Sir Francis Walsingham.'[31]

Often the post left so abruptly that some letters remained unwritten – or at least, it provided a good excuse that Paulet wore rather thin over the years.[32] Since it was expected that the letter ostensibly for the eyes of the Queen would be copied and shown around the court, there was somewhat less urgency about keeping individual courtiers fully informed. But the copy-book bears witness to miscalculations on occasions when Paulet assumed that Burghley or Leicester would be at court and sent only a cursory note directly to them. Their evident disapproval at being thus expected to get their news at second hand is witnessed by Paulet's multiplied efforts in his next letters to ensure the fullest coverage for his demanding patrons.

Much energy was spent on the tedious business of copying letters, often to make clear illegible handwriting or, conversely, to obscure an overly familiar hand – a task made the more difficult by the post deadlines and the occasional paucity of clerks, who may have been sent on missions elsewhere.[33] Unsurprisingly, then, Hotman regarded the ambassador's secretaries as among his 'most necessary' officers, and those 'in choice of whom he ought to be most careful'. Their duties were 'to assist and ease him in the businesses of his charge, and to dispatch causes that concern the same, and to hold a good register thereof, to keep faithfull the scrolls, ciphers, and other papers of importance (which nevertheless would be better under the master's lock)'.[34]

Throughout his life Bacon carried with him a set of habits and an approach towards textual work which he acquired during his time with Sir Amias. Paulet preferred to work methodically, stay late and get the business done. Bacon recalled Paulet in his essay 'Of Dispatch' (1612) as 'a wise man [that] had it for a by-word, when he saw men hasten to a conclusion, "Stay a little, that we may make an end the sooner"'. Under Paulet, Bacon learned that 'affected dispatch is one of the most dangerous things to business that can be. It is like that which the physicians called *predigestion*, or hasty digestion; which is sure to fill the body full of crudities and secret seeds of diseases. Therefore measure not dispatch by the times of sitting, but by the advancement of the business.'[35]

Besides providing a centre for intelligence, Paulet was well placed to be taken advantage of as a commodity broker, whether the commodity was a copy of Jean Bodin's *De imperio* for Sir Edward Dyer, 'four fair mulets for the litter' of the earl of Leicester (which got repeatedly waylaid), or silk for the Queen. Sadly, in the case of the last commission, plague in Italy adversely affected supplies, so Paulet had to send 'such as I can find' – satin or silk – and swear that the French Queen and all the court ladies in Paris were also forced to 'make all their new garments of coloured satin with gold and silver'.[36]

This Parisian networking, where Paulet, for all the demands on his time, found some semblance of a sympathetic audience, was rudely interrupted within weeks. In the autumn of 1576 the entire court decamped to Blois for a summit meeting of all the contending French political constituencies. Within two months of arriving in Paris the ambassador was obliged to leave the capital to follow, with his entourage. As far as Paulet was concerned, out of Paris was 'no where, wandering from place to place'.[37]

★

The ambassador was not the only one of the visiting English with financial problems. Francis Bacon was also finding living within his means (the licence for the Bacon brothers had allowed them 'their servants, six horses or geldings, and three score pounds in money') a severe strain. So Bacon wrote to his 'cousin' (a term used in the period affectionately for any close friend) Thomas Bodley, putting his data-gathering services at his disposal.

Thomas Bodley (whose lasting renown is as a book collector, the founder of the Bodleian Library in Oxford) was the ideal person for Francis Bacon to approach in this way. Now in his early thirties, he had spent much of his childhood, during the reign of Mary Tudor, with his Protestant family in exile on the continent. After spending time in Wesel and Frankfurt, the Bodleys had settled in Geneva. There, Thomas recalled, 'I was at that time of twelve years' age, but through my father's cost and care, sufficiently instructed to become an auditor of Chevalerius in Hebrew, of Beroaldus in Greek, of Calvin and Beza in Divinity, and of some other professors in that university, (which was newly then erected) besides my domestical teachers, in the house of Philibertus Saracenus, a famous physician in that city, with whom I was boarded: where Robertus Constantinus, that made the Greek lexicon, read Homer unto me.' Arriving back in England after Elizabeth's accession, Bodley senior had won the patent for the exclusive printing of the Geneva Bible. In 1576 Bodley junior set off again on his own travels, which were to take him to Italy, France and Germany. Ostensibly, it was his intellectual, religious and book-collecting interests that took him all over Europe, trawling for Protestant contacts and interesting publishing ventures. However, doubling up with these activities, Bodley was an intelligencer – in effect, an elite spy, gathering continental information for one or more paymasters back in England.[38]

Bodley replied a couple of months later, sending Bacon, with the letter, £30 'for your present supply': as much, he said, as he could spare. In exchange for this, Bodley described the 'manner of return your friends expect from you'. He expected Bacon to report meticulously back to him on whatever he met on his travels.

> Now, cousin, though I will be no severe exactor of the account, either of your money or time, yet for the love I bear you, I am very desirous, both to satisfy myself, and your friends how you prosper in your travels, and how you find yourself bettered thereby, either in knowledge of God, or of the World; the rather, because the days you have already spent abroad, are now both sufficient to give you light, how to fix yourself and end with counsel, and accordingly to shape your course constantly unto it. Besides, it is a vulgar scandal unto the travellers, that few return more religious than they went forth; wherein both my hope and request is to you, that your principal care be to hold your foundation, and to make no other use of informing yourself in the corruptions and superstitions of other nations, than only thereby to engage your own heart more firmly to the truth.

Thus, at this early point in his life, Francis Bacon was forced by shortage of cash into relinquishing thoughts of leisured contemplation of the world about him and taking up active employment as an information-gatherer. It was a foretaste of things to come, for throughout his entire life he was to be dogged by financial difficulties and the ever-present necessity of expending his energies on extricating himself from them. Now, he set about earning the £30 Thomas Bodley had sent him.

Bodley's instructions were extensive. France, he wrote, was 'a country of two several professions [faiths]', and Francis should learn the requisite skills for analysing them – indeed, 'you shall return a novice, if you be not able to give an account of the ordinances, strength, and progress of each, in reputation, and party, and how both are supported, balanced and managed by the state, as being the contrary humours, in the temper of predominancy whereof, the health or disease of that body doth consist.' Francis was to gather this intelligence from a double perspective: as an Englishman, 'whom it may concern, to what interest his country may expect in the consciences of their neighbours'; but more importantly, 'as a Christian, to consider both the beauties and blemishes, the hopes and dangers of the Church in all places.

Now for the world, I know it too well, to persuade you to dive into the practices thereof; rather stand upon your own guard, against all that attempt you thereunto, or may practice upon you in your conscience, reputation, or your purse. Resolve, no man is wise or false, but he that is honest: and let this persuasion turn your studies and observations from the impostures of the debased age, to more real grounds of wisdom, gathered out of the story of times past, and out of the government of the present state. Your guide to this, is the knowledge of the country and the people among whom you live: for the country, though you cannot see all places, yet if, as you pass along, you enquire carefully, and further help yourself with books that are written of the cosmography of those parts, you shall sufficiently gather the strength, riches, traffic, havens shipping, commodities, vent, and the wants and disadvantages of places. Wherein also, for your good hereafter, and for your friends, it will be fit to note their buildings, furnitures, their entertainments; all their husbandry, and ingenious inventions, in whatsoever concerneth either pleasure or profit.

For your people, your traffic among them, while you learn their language, will sufficiently instruct you in their habilities [customs], dispositions, and humours, if you a little enlarge the privacy of your own nature, to seek acquaintance with the best sort of strangers, and restrain your affections and participation, for your own countrymen of whatsoever condition.

In the story of France, you have a large and pleasant field in three lines of their kings, to observe their alliances and successions, their conquests, their wars, especially with us; their councils, their treaties; and all rules and examples of experiences and wisdoms, which may be lights and remembrances to you hereafter, to judge of all occurents [events] both at home and abroad.

The idea was to be, not a vulgar spy – not 'to spend all your time in fishing after the present news, humours, graces or disgraces of court, which haply may change before you come home' – but a source of more deep-seated intelligence, with a 'better and more constant ground': namely,

to know the consanguinities, alliances, and estates of their princes; proportion between the nobility and magistracy; the constitutions of their courts of justice; the state of their laws, as well for the making, as the execution thereof: how the sovereignty of the king infuseth itself into all acts and ordinances; how many ways they lay impositions and taxations, and gather revenues to the Crown. What be the liberties and servitudes of all degrees; what disciplines and preparations for wars; what invention for increase of traffic at home, for multiplying their commodities, encouraging arts and manufactures, or of worth in any kind. Also what good establishment, to prevent the necessities and discontentment of people, to cut off suits at law, and duels; to suppress thieves, and all disorders.

Francis was not to waste his 'spirits, and the precious time of your travel, in a captious prejudice and censuring of all things, nor in an infectious collection of base vices and fashions of men and women, or general corruption of these times, which will be of use only among humorists, for jests and table-talk'. Instead, he should endeavour to 'strain your wits and industry soundly to instruct yourself in all things between Heaven and Earth, which may tend to virtue, wisdom, and honour, and which may make your life more profitable to your country, and yourself more comfortable to your friends, and acceptable to God.' Francis should not rely on his memory, 'where time may lessen your stock', but entrust his observations to 'good writings, and books of account, which will keep them safe for your use hereafter'. And an incentive was offered: 'If in this time of your liberal traffic, you will give me any advertisement of your commodities in these kinds, I will make you as liberal a return from myself and your friends here, as I shall be able.'[39]

Although no evidence survives to prove conclusively that Francis entered into this arrangement, the information-gathering techniques described by Bodley were to become an integral part of Bacon's intellectual working practice in years to come.

★

The peripatetic arrangements of the French court did not make the ambassador's life any easier. Paulet complained that the ambassadors were deliberately 'lodged poorly',[40] in a small village named St Die outside Blois, so that they would not hear the 'many complaints, many quarrels, many accusations, yea, against the King himself'.[41] When the summit was abandoned in March 1577, Paulet and his retinue travelled from St Die to Tours to Poitiers. Meanwhile Sir Amias' explicit support for Henri de Navarre, together with Elizabeth's protests against persecution of Huguenots, made the ambassador's position increasingly awkward; by July 1577 Paulet was 'in very bad odour, and more especially because the policy of his Queen is daily shown to be more and more hostile to the Crown'.[42]

For Paulet there were further implications of being 'always lodged seven and ten leagues from the court': namely, that with 'my old acquaintance of the Religion being dispersed abroad, now my best friends are hired papists.'[43] As he explained to the Queen, 'this bad time' of civil war forced the resident to engage in 'marchandise' with 'bad fellows': there was no other way of discovering treasons 'than by corruption, these corrupted instruments, and especially such as we have credit with your rebels and other enemies are easy to be found, and therefore where they may be obtained, ought not to be refused for the price.'[44]

In Poitiers, where Paulet's household spent three months in the autumn of 1577, the French court met the diplomats and courtiers of Henri de Navarre's court, including Du Plessis-Mornay and Du Bartas, and Bacon became 'very intimate with a young Frenchman of great wit, but somewhat talkative, who afterwards turned out a very eminent man'. This man's party piece, Bacon recalled, was 'to inveigh against the manners of old men, and say that if their minds could be seen as well as their bodies, they would appear no less deformed.'[45] Francis also made the acquaintance of Jean la Jessée, secretary to the duc d'Alençon. Gascon by birth, la Jessée, ten years Francis' senior, had left the University of Bordeaux to become the protégé of Jeanne d'Albret. An early work, *Amours de Marguerite*, proclaimed his love for Charles IX's sister, Margaret, the future wife of Henri de Navarre. A convinced Protestant, and member of the Famille de la Charité, he fled Paris after the St Bartholomew's Day Massacre of 1572, but published precociously. Anthony Bacon's papers at Lambeth contain a French sonnet from la Jessée to 'Monsieur Françoys Bacon', elaborately complimenting the Queen, which includes the lines 'So (Bacon) if my Muse is led to celebrate the name of the divine Queen, it is not out of my own erudition or wisdom, even though your own wisdom makes me more knowledgeable.'[46]

On 25 September 1577, Henri III was forced to sign the Peace of Bergerac, confirmed by the Edict of Poitiers, which allowed public Huguenot worship only in Protestant-held towns and one place in each *bailliage* (district), and banned all leagues and associations. The outbreak of peace was hardly an improvement: to the Queen Paulet wrote, 'If at other times it hath been received for a maxim that France must always have some war in hand, how much more now when they have been unsettled as they cannot abide to live in peace?'[47] The move back to Paris in the closing months of 1577 was similarly a mixed blessing. The hand-to-mouth existence in the French countryside had had its disadvantages, but it had been a lot cheaper than life in the capital. Now, however, Paulet could start the serious work of establishing a Huguenot support and intelligence system from his prime location. And for Francis Bacon, the serious business of education for which he had come to France could finally commence.

★

The house of an ambassador, wrote Jean Hotman, 'is a sanctuary and place of retreat to his servants and followers, against all injuries and violence: provided that they do nothing against the laws of the country where they are, and against public honesty.'[48] It should therefore have been a relatively safe haven for a young man such as Francis Bacon – but limitless possibilities for disorder lurked within the house itself. The ambassador being occupied with his official duties, the house required a wife 'whose eye will stop infinite abuses amongst his people, and disorders in his house';[49] and Sir Amias accordingly brought with him his wife Margaret.

The nurturing Lady Paulet could hardly have been more unlike Francis' own mother, and he remembered her ministrations with particular affection. He recalled how she cured him of a wart on his finger, which had persisted since childhood, but which was suddenly joined by a multitude of new blemishes ('at least an hundred in a month's space') in Paris. Margaret Paulet was 'a woman far from superstition', who knew a way to cure warts: 'She got a piece of lard, with the skin on, and rubbed the warts all over with the fat side; and amongst the rest, that wart which I had had from my childhood: then she nailed the piece of lard, with the fat towards the sun, upon a post of her chamber window, which was to the south. The success was, that within five weeks' space all the warts went quite away: and that wart which I had so long endured, for company.'[50]

With Sir Amias and Lady Paulet came their six children – Hugh, Anthony, George, Joan, Sarah and Elizabeth. Hugh, at eighteen three years Francis' senior, and Anthony, a year his junior, must have been close companions. Thanks to his Jersey upbringing, Hugh was already fluent in French, precociously dedicating a manuscript volume of French translation – the story 'de la fille d'un Roy d'angleterre' – to his father, knowing, as he wrote, 'the great and fervent desire to see me advanced in the French language'.[51]

While Francis was enjoying Paulet family life, he also formed lasting friendships with some of the other young men in the ambassador's entourage. One of these was 'Master Doctor Caesar', one of five sons of Queen Mary's Paduan-born physician, Caesar Adelmare. Most likely this was Julius Caesar, who is known to have visited Paris between 1578 and 1581 to study civil law. Almost forty years later, Francis Bacon gave away his niece, Anne Woodhouse, in marriage to the now-knighted Sir Julius, and there is a tradition that Bacon died in Caesar's arms.[52]

The ambassador's trickiest charge was Arthur, son of Sir Nicholas Throckmorton. He was sent home at his own request, after only ten months in France, since 'having now got the French tongue in good perfection, he cannot make any other profit by his abode in France.' Paulet was not sorry to see the young Throckmorton go. 'To be plain with you,' he confided to Walsingham, 'I think myself very happy that I am honestly delivered of him.' Throckmorton's extreme youth (he was nineteen years old in 1576) had exacerbated his 'imperfections, which riper years and good counsel may remove from him'. So, presumably, had his open Catholicism. Arthur's immediate objective in returning to England was to obtain a licence to go into Italy: Paulet had foiled his attempts to use Paris as a launching pad for Italian travels, laying down the law that 'he may not go into Italy without the company of some honest and wise man, and so I have told him, and in many other things have dealt very plainly with him.' A profligate youth, Arthur had also contrived to run up expenses for his mother to meet, despite Paulet's provision of all the necessaries: the situation, he wrote, 'must be imputed to his folly, having had his meat and drink with me for himself and his man, and [I] have not only from his first coming to Paris provided him of a horse, but also have found his horse at my charges.'[53] Arthur was still borrowing money to pay off his debt to Sir Amias in May 1583.[54]

Also on the embassy was the miniaturist Nicholas Hilliard who, with his new wife Alice, had joined Paulet at the Queen's command – possibly to obtain the likeness of her latest French marriage hope, François duc d'Alençon.[55] Fluent in French as a result of his boyhood in Geneva, Hilliard quickly made his way into the employ of Alençon, but Paulet insisted to Walsingham (trying to appease his restive Queen) that 'Hilliard meaneth nothing less [i.e. has nothing further from his mind] than to leave Her Majesty's service, being repaired hither for no other intent as he saith than to increase his knowledge by this voyage, and upon hope to get a piece of money of the lords and ladies here for his better maintenance in England at his return.' Indeed, Hilliard would have been back in England by now 'if he had not been disappointed by some misfortunes, intending to repair thither very shortly, and carry his wife with him'.[56] In the event, held up by sickness, Nicholas had to send his pregnant wife home to England without him, and did not himself return until October 1578.[57]

This delay resulted in one of the few lasting images of the adolescent Francis Bacon, who posed for a Hilliard miniature in Paris. In the estimation of Roy Strong, the miniature is 'of superlative quality. The features are delicately rendered, the eyes turned out towards the spectator, the lips thin and compressed. The sitter is altogether a superior young man, and the inscription leaves us in no doubt as to his intelligence: *1578 Si tabula daretur digna / Animum mallem Æ[tatis] S[uae] 18* [If the face as painted is deemed worthy, yet I prefer the mind, in his eighteenth year].'[58] The relationship struck up between the ascendant artist and his young gentleman model lasted until Hilliard was in his eighties: an account-book kept by Bacon's steward records on 19 August 1618 a gift of £11 paid 'to old Mr. Hilliard'.[59]

The burden of responsibility for these young gentlemen made itself felt on the ambassador, and not only financially. For, standing *in loco parentis*, Paulet had to find appropriate tutors to continue the young men's education. Initially the Paulet boys and Francis had been taught by one Mr Duncumbe, who was, Paulet assured Sir Nicholas, 'worthy of the government of your Lordship's son, or of any gentleman in England, of what degree so ever. I cannot tell if your Lordship be more indebted unto him for his carefulness in your service than I am for his good and quiet behaviour in my house.'[60] When Duncumbe returned to England in October 1577, Paulet had to find a replacement, and complained publicly that his countrymen 'should do God and their country good service if either they would provide schoolmasters for their children at home, or else would take better order for their education here, where they are infected with all sorts of pollutions, both ghostly and bodily, and find many willing schoolmasters to teach them to be bad subjects.'[61]

Ignoring Hotman's advice that he should avoid taking in native servants, 'it being very certain, that they are so many spies,'[62] Paulet turned to a Frenchman to educate his children – appropriately enough, to Jean Hotman himself. Hotman's father, the controversial French Protestant and republican François Hotman, gratefully placed his eldest son with Paulet during the embassy's final year. Paulet wrote proudly to the Secretaries of his coup in gaining a Frenchman whose academic career (at Paris, Valencia and Caen) and religious credentials were above suspicion: ' "Ottoman," a professor of the civil law, not unknown to you as I think, has his eldest son dwelling with me, and is schoolmaster to my children.'[63] It was to be a long-lasting and successful arrangement, as Hotman returned to England with the Paulets, accompanying the boys to Christ Church, Oxford, before going into service with both Henri, King of Navarre, and the earl of Leicester.[64] Jean Hotman has been proposed as the author of the earliest French translation of Bacon's *History of the Reign of Henry VII*, published in 1627.[65]

Bacon also came under the influence of Paulet's household chaplain, Arthur Wake, as he recalled forty years later to Wake's son Isaac.[66] The chaplain's stay in France was, however, cut short when he discovered that his wife was pregnant and was forced to return home – 'You know how impossible it is for a woman in that state to follow a French progress, and especially in that troublesome time.' Faced with a winter in Paris without a chaplain, Paulet was 'very sorry that my great household should continue any longer without a shepherd', and ordered the search for a suitable replacement, taking certain precautions: 'It is of necessity that he must be unmarried, or at the most leave his wife in England.'[67]

It was in France that Francis had his first experience of ciphers and cryptography, which were to play such an important role not only in his later life, but also in his posthumous reputation as the shadowy figure whose authorial identity is cryptically contained in anything from the works of Shakespeare to the Rosicrucian manifesto. In this field, he was lucky to strike up an early relationship with the grand master of intelligence ciphers, Thomas Phelippes, a servant of Sir Francis Walsingham, who had been placed with the embassy to give it the benefit of his skills in languages and ciphering.[68] Bacon and Phelippes also remained close over the following years: Francis was a friend of Thomas' father, employed his younger brother as secretary and close companion during the early 1580s, and recommended Thomas himself to the attention of the earl of Essex in 1591. A letter from Sir Amias to Phelippes written in January 1586 sent 'hearty commendations' from himself and Lady Paulet to Phelippes 'and their good friend Mr. Francis Bacon'.[69]

Phelippes was described as being 'of low stature, slender every way, dark yellow haired on the head, and clear yellow bearded, eaten in the face with smallpox' and, perhaps unsurprisingly for a man who spent his life peering at fading manuscripts, 'of short sight'. Five years Francis' senior, Thomas had been at Trinity College, Cambridge, alongside the Bacon brothers, graduating as Bachelor of Arts in 1574, and Master of Arts in 1577. Still only in his early twenties, 'young Phelippes' had made a name for himself (with its own idiosyncratic spelling; his father and brother used the more conventional Philippes) as one of the leading cipherers of his day; Secretary Wilson even sent papers from London to Paris to make use of his skills.[70]

An integral element of Phelippes' prowess in cryptanalysis was his mastery of the various languages in which the European powers operated – at least French, Italian, Spanish, Latin and German. Working for Walsingham throughout the 1580s on the continent, notably in Paris, elsewhere in France and in the Netherlands, he was to become one of the most important personal centres of English intelligence, seeking out Roman Catholic threats both at home and abroad, an occupation that appealed particularly to his Puritanism. His enemies knew him as 'a severe Huguenot . . . greedy of honour and profit' and 'a notable knave'. Letters containing local intelligence were sent to him under various aliases such as 'John Morice' and 'Peter Halins, Merchant', pseudonyms with entire personalities attached to them. 'John Morice', for example, was a Catholic; informers writing to him also pretended to be Catholic, going so far as to slip in sly references to 'Phelippes, that enemy to the cause', to put possible interceptors off the scent. Matters of state were couched in less than elevated language: the Queen and her Privy Council appeared prosaically as 'Harry Jobson and his brokers'.

As a decipherer, Phelippes specialised in breaking difficult codes: on one occasion it took him twenty days to crack the cipher concerning a Spanish plan to invade England. He was also credited with having the ability 'to write any man's hand if he had once seen it as the man himself that writ it', a useful way of forwarding bogus intelligence and instructions. Sir Amias was to remember the skills of the young Thomas Phelippes when, almost a decade later, he was entrusted with the highly sensitive task of guarding Mary Queen of Scots through her final days. Phelippes was brought in to devise and operate a secret letter scam, whereby Mary was duped into placing ciphered messages into a barrel, from which they would be promptly removed and decoded by Phelippes.

What Francis learned under Thomas Phelippes remained with him for the rest of his life. In his later work *De augmentis scientiarum* (1623), Bacon introduces a 'contrivance, which I devised myself when I was at Paris in my early youth, and which I still think worthy of preservation': namely, a code whereby each letter of the alphabet (amounting to twenty-four, at a time when i and j, u and v were not distinguished) was made equivalent to one of twenty-four combinations of a and b, so that a = aaaaa, m = ababb, z = babbb.[71] Phelippes himself was to feature significantly more than once in Bacon's adult life.

★

The few letters that survive from Paulet to Sir Nicholas Bacon in the ambassador's copy-book – the originals have been lost – attest to his goodwill and loyalty towards the father, and to the son's continued good health. From Poitiers on 28 July 1577, for example, excusing himself 'that I have not troubled you more often of late with my letters', he jots 'these few lines . . . by the same to advertise you that your son thanks be to God is in good health, and other good news your Lordship may not look to hear out of these parts'. At some point, Sir Nicholas evidently questioned Sir Amias as to the good sense of Francis' remaining in France while the political situation was so volatile, and Sir Amias vouchsafed his son's safety. As peace was declared in September 1577, he wrote: 'This quiet time doth give me no occasion to trouble your Lordship with long letters, only I must tell you that I rejoice much to see that your son, my companion, hath, by the grace of God, passed the brunt and peril of this journey; whereof I am the more glad, because in the beginning of these last troubles it pleased your Lordship to refer his continuance with me to my consideration. I thank God these dangers are past, and your son is safe, sound, and in good health, and worthy of your fatherly favour.'[72]

Previous accounts of Bacon's early life have not been able to provide much information concerning Francis himself during the latter half of the embassy. At some point Paulet's manuscript copy-book fell apart or was split into two, and the printed version reproduced only the earlier part (to January 1578). However, the (unpublished) continuation of the copy-book has also found its way into the Bodleian Library. This 'second' copy-book and a previously overlooked letter in the British Library enable us to shed new and surprising light on Bacon's time in France.

Bacon's chaplain William Rawley later alleged that Bacon was 'after awhile held fit [by Paulet] to be entrusted with some message or advertisement to the queen', a mission that he 'performed with great approbation' before returning 'back into France again, with intention to continue for some years there,' a plan that was ultimately cut short by his father's death.[73] The choosing of the bearer of the post was an important decision, since many of the most sensitive portions of communication home were transmitted orally, under cover of the written document. It was standard for the ambassador to refer his correspondent 'for the state of things here to the report of this bearer, whose declaration by mouth shall be more effectual than if the same were set down in writing'. The mission had to be strictly confidential – even the identity of the messenger needed to be kept secret: 'no other man living is acquainted with the voyages of my messengers than the messengers themselves'.[74] Clearly, then, the bearer needed to be someone well educated, well informed, trustworthy and intimately acquainted with the business of the embassy. Although other bearers occasionally presented themselves – servants travelling abroad on behalf of their English masters, men making their way through France on other diplomatic business, merchants (who were 'likely to pass without suspicion') and men who made their livelihood from the occupation – Paulet tended to rely on his closest household servants, and on occasion his eldest son, to carry such despatches. The disadvantage of this arrangement, of course, was that while such servants were away for extended stretches of time – and the trip had to include not only the two journeys from France to the English court and back, but also all the waiting associated with the court, and if necessary trips to prominent courtiers in their country or London houses – they were not available to carry out their everyday jobs at the ambassador's residence. Paulet's correspondence is littered with complaints about understaffing, a problem he never solved.

Naturally, there were inconveniences and dangers to be taken into consideration on such a mission. The bearer would have to take care not to mislay letters, and hope that the weather held out. He would hope also to avoid the alarming experience of one of Paulet's servants who was arrested in Sably, imprisoned, 'stripped twice to his shirt, and the collar of his shirt [a traditional hiding place for clandestine letters] and all his other garments searched with all extremity' – to no avail, since he was carrying only personal mail destined for Jersey.[75] However, the dangers were offset by the personal advantages to the bearer in terms of guaranteed access to the presence of the Queen and her counsellors, during which access the bearer was, as we have seen, often called upon to enlarge on the letters' contents verbally. Such an opportunity would have been seized with alacrity by a young, ambitious man such as Francis Bacon; but aside from Bacon's own assertion as reported by Rawley, it was believed that no first-hand evidence survived to prove that Bacon undertook such a mission. However, a letter has come to light which recounts in detail how Francis came from France to Queen Elizabeth's court to deliver some letters, accompanied by the ambassador's man.[76] The letter is undated, but it mentions only Walsingham as Secretary of State, which suggests that the mission might possibly have taken place before Walsingham was joined as Secretary by Thomas Wilson on 12 November 1577 (Paulet was always careful to write to both Secretaries). The letter is valuable on two counts: it is one of the earliest known extant examples of Francis Bacon's writing, and it tells a vivid and surprising story of the way letters circulated at the Elizabethan court.

Francis left Paris one Friday afternoon, at about two o'clock, and arrived at court the following Tuesday, bearing various letters and a message to be delivered by word of mouth to Burghley. He made his way initially to Mr Secretary Walsingham, whom he found 'scant well at ease'; he was obliged to deliver his 'charge of letters' while the Secretary was 'laid upon his bed'. Walsingham opened the packet and handed two letters, both addressed to the earl of Leicester, back to Bacon, telling him to deliver them 'with mine own hands, saying that for the rest he could see them delivered himself'. Francis was accordingly dismissed 'with very favourable speech', and made his way to Leicester's chamber; but, finding the earl already occupied 'with the Queen', the young emissary wisely 'thought good' to head off instead to his uncle Burghley.

By chance, he ran into his uncle between the court and the Lord Treasurer's house. Burghley took the letter from Paulet, and informed Francis that he 'would speak with me further some other time'. An hour later, Francis attended him more formally at his chamber, but he was not there, so they met again in the park, where they spoke at greater length and Francis 'received of him many good words'. Burghley interrogated his nephew about several matters, pointing out to him 'how much I was bound' to Paulet, and conveyed 'her Majesty's meaning' that he should come into her presence that evening. All this while, the message had not been delivered: Burghley promised 'he would hear it at his first leisure'. Francis later located the Queen in the garden, 'where it pleased her Majesty to use unto me so many and so gracious words as could not be uttered in most ample and effectual sort'. Once again the Queen appears to have been accompanied by the earl of Leicester, who saluted Francis and accepted his letters. Francis then made another attempt to deliver Paulet's message to Burghley, but was 'put over as touching my message until some other time'.

Writing on the following morning, Francis had to admit to Paulet that he had still been unable to pass the verbal message to Burghley. He reasoned that the Lord Treasurer was more interested in conveying Paulet's letters to the Queen, while Francis was 'only to render a report for the rest', of probable interest to Burghley, but not of pressing urgency. Francis goes on to acknowledge Paulet's both bestowing on him 'your own good opinion' and – by allowing him to deliver these letters – being 'the cause of the good opinion of others'. He also particularly thanks Paulet for sending over his man with him. His gratitude was well placed. Like his initial departure to the embassy, it gave Francis an opportunity to serve the Queen directly. He was effectively being groomed to work as an intermediary or facilitator in the complex world of international politics.[77]

★

In Paris, Francis spent his spare time profitably. He visited Pont-Charenton one afternoon, and heard its famous echo 'return the voice thirteen several [separate] times' – others alleged that sixteen echoes were possible if you went in the evening. There he met 'an old Parisian who took it to be the work of spirits, and of good spirits. For (said he) call *Satan*, and the echo will not deliver back the devil's name; but will say *va-t'en*; which is as much in French as *apage* or *avoid*. And thereby I did hap to find that an echo would not return "S", being but a hissing and an interior sound.'[78]

Such leisure pursuits, although serving their turn as illustrative anecdotes later in Bacon's life, were not, however, what he had gone to France for. Indeed, the life he was living at the embassy was turning out to be not to his father the Lord Keeper's liking. Perhaps Sir Nicholas' idealised notions of what diplomacy entailed – the mastery of languages, mores and negotiation, and the intricacies of the civil law – were simply not to be had amid the hurly-burly of the overstretched and somewhat beleaguered Paulet embassy; in any event, Francis, Sir Nicholas decided, needed a more specific and practically based education. On 24 January 1578 Sir Amias wrote to the Lord Keeper to report a change in Francis' living arrangements.

Although I would have been glad to have enjoyed the company of Mr. Francis Bacon in my house during the time of his abode in this country, and to say truly did take great comfort of his person, yet being intended that he shall study the civil law I must confess that his absence from me shall be more profitable for him and especially being so happy as to be placed in the house of a civilian [civil lawyer] whose private conference shall stand him in great stead. Wheresoever he shall be, I will account of him as of your Lordship's son, and as I honour your Lordship so I will not fail to love him, to be careful for him, and to do him in all things all the pleasure that may lie in my little power. God bless him, and then your lordship shall be the happy father of a towardly son.[79]

Francis Bacon's removal from the embassy into the household of a civil lawyer was consistent with Sir Nicholas Bacon's own developed theories of a legal training appropriate to a future Elizabethan civil servant. Nicholas Bacon had long entertained the hope of setting up a training programme for those destined for civic office, in which both common and civil law would play a part, and which would introduce its students to the practicalities of diplomatic service. In the late 1530s he had joined Robert Cary and the Middle Temple veteran Thomas Denton in compiling a report on the Inns of Court, commissioned by the King. It proposed the foundation of a new, fifth Inn to provide the systematic training of statesmen and diplomats, and of lawyers with a strong orientation towards such professions. Students, handpicked from the existing Inns by the crown, were to be financially supported by the crown. French and Latin would be taught as spoken languages, and students would be expected to acquire a well-rounded knowledge of Greek and Latin classics. Eventually, one or two of these students would accompany each foreign embassy, in order that the students 'should be seen expert in all civil things'. Although these ideas were never implemented, they evidently took a profound hold on Nicholas Bacon's mind: echoes of them can be detected in his designs for reforming the common law, and for rationalising the finances of the crown, in his scheme for an academy for the wards of the crown, and in the statutes for Redgrave Grammar School. In his youngest son Sir Nicholas saw a final chance to put his ideas to the test.[80]

Civil lawyers had a great deal to contribute to embassies, given their fluency in Latin and their grasp of the international law, the *ius gentium*, that dealt with the rights of princes, the niceties of war, captivity and treaties. When Richard Bancroft was putting together a mission to Denmark in 1600, he demanded that a 'grounded civil lawyer' be included within the group, and refused to accept a doctor of divinity as a substitute. 'I can say some part of St Paul's Epistles by heart,' he remarked, 'but that will not serve to encounter in this case so much as with Bartolus.' Conversely, embassies could teach students of civil law a great deal.[81] Dr David Lewes, mentor to Bacon's friend Julius Caesar, urged that proficiency in foreign languages was essential to a civil lawyer, giving the advantage to an admiralty judge when pleadings and other court documents were couched in the native languages of foreign litigants. Fluency in these tongues provided the means 'whereby ye may con over the text before ye enter into the labyrinth of the lectors or intepreters'. Bacon himself remarked that 'he that travelleth into a country before he hath some entrance into the language, goeth to school, and not to travel.' It seems fair to assume that part of the reason for Bacon's being placed with a French civil lawyer was to immerse him in French, as Languet would try to immerse Robert Sidney in German, in order to gain this 'entrance into the language'. It worked: later, in April 1581, Francis was employed by his uncle Lord Burghley to interpret for the French dignitaries at a lavish banquet for a French commission to negotiate the proposed Alençon marriage.[82]

Bacon would no doubt have learned more in the household of a French civil lawyer than a working knowledge of the language. Even the doctorate in civil law at Oxford and Cambridge was almost entirely theoretical, providing no experience of court procedures or techniques to the aspiring practitioner. To observe the civil law in action, then, required a stay in France – hence the move of men like Julius Caesar to France to gain their experience – preferably in the household of a practising civil lawyer. We do not know the identity of the lawyer in whose care Francis was placed, but whoever he was, Bacon was undoubtedly influenced by the framework within which his new host worked. Later, he was to return compulsively to the question of the possible codification of English laws on the French model – arguing for a reduction in the number of statutes in the 1593 parliament, and elaborating his plans most comprehensively in his *Proposition Touching the Amendment of the Law* (1616).[83]

Sir Amias continued to keep his eye on Francis, even after the young man had ceased to live in his house. On 23 May 1578 he reiterated that 'although your Lordship hath often advertisements [news] from your son, yet I trust it will not offend you to know from me that he doth well, and that his good and honest doings deserve the favour of a good father.'[84]

Francis had had his own ideas about what he might do in 1578. In January that year, he implored Sir Amias to give the Lord Keeper his 'opinion touching his intended voyage into Italy'. Italy was well known as the most dangerous destination for English boys abroad: vague warnings against licentiousness were handed out, but the real reason for concern was doctrinal. In the case of Arthur Throckmorton, Paulet had specified that he might 'not go into Italy without the company of some honest and wise man'; in that of Francis Bacon, Paulet's concern was far greater and more real, for with the Bacon name, Francis carried the burden of his parents' religious convictions and a reputation for dissent which Paulet believed would place him in serious jeopardy.[85]

At this point in his period abroad the limitations of the embassy placing became obvious to Francis. He looked to his brother Edward who, having slipped from his father's grasp, was virtually a free agent, indulging in the kind of travelling and networking of which Francis, stuck with the Paulets, could only dream. Edward spent time in the reformist capital Geneva, where he made the acquaintance of important Protestant writers including Lambert Daneau and Theodore Beza, and ran into the exiled Puritan preacher Thomas Cartwright. He was the guest of Robert Sidney's landlord Jean Sturm in Strasbourg;[86] carried the post from Hubert Languet in Frankfurt to Joachim Camerarius the younger, earning Languet's approval as a 'good and pious young man'; and spent five days in Vienna ('there I saw so much as was to be seen, both persons & places'). He was planning to continue to Ratisbon when the opportunity to travel to Italy presented itself. Eight days at Venice were followed by a fortnight at Padua, whence he travelled via Zurich back to Geneva, before heading to Paris. Edward admitted that such a tour was not without its moral dangers: 'The question is how this journey will be liked by my friends. The places where I were, as there is liberty to all kind of vice, so is there no constraint to any. I fear the difference will not be great betwixt those places and Paris.'[87]

Edward's travels left their mark in print. Lambert Daneau, professor of theology at Geneva, dedicated his two volumes of commentaries on Augustine, published in 1578, to Edward, thereby apparently acknowledging the intellectual maturity of the young Englishman. But the detail of his dedicatory epistle explains the true reason for the attention to Edward Bacon. Daneau claims that he did not dare dedicate his work to the English Queen nor even to her Lord Keeper, Nicholas Bacon; so, wanting to acknowledge the protection afforded by the English government to the reformers in France, he thought of Bacon's son Edward whom he had met in Geneva.[88]

Edward was also the joint dedicatee, along with another young Englishman abroad, Francis Hastings, in an epistle added in August 1577 to the first Latin edition of the Protestant Innocent Gentillet's famous *Discours contre Machiavel*, first published in French the previous year. The anonymous dedicator exhorts these young men to follow the example of their worthy relations: in the case of Hastings, he should 'tread the steps of your uncle, the right honourable earl of Huntingdon, a man most admirable and illustrious, as well for godliness and other noble virtues, as for noble parentage and honour, that you may show yourself worthy of your place and kindred'

(Hastings' father, a Catholic, is pointedly overlooked); Edward was urged to 'imitate the wisdom, sanctimony, and integrity of your Father, the right Honourable Lord Nicholas Bacon, keeper of the broad Seal of England, a man right renowned; that you may lively express the image of your Father's virtues, in the excellent towardness, which you naturally have from your most virtuous Father'.[89]

Edward Bacon and Francis Hastings each carried his pedigree with him abroad, a pedigree that could be seen – even when viewed from across the Channel – as clearly reformist. But while family connections opened doors for Edward Bacon, allowing him access to the top layer of European Protestant society, they also closed off possibilities of movement in Catholic territories for his more carefully supervised younger brother. Now, confronted with Francis' request to travel into Italy, Paulet was forced to turn it down. In an agonisingly polite letter to Sir Nicholas he concluded, having 'conferred with some of this town who (as I thought) were able to give me good advice herein', that: 'As I am willing to your commandment, so I am no less sorry that my duty and good will towards your Lordship and the great affection which I bear to your son do force me to dissuade this voyage, being not ignorant that the same would be greatly profitable unto him in many respects.' It would simply be too dangerous. Paulet went on to explain that 'letters out of Italy' warned him that 'such of our countrymen as are known to be no papists live there in great peril.' Some, indeed, had 'been driven to depart to avoid the present and assured danger' while others were forced to 'wander secretly from place to place'. The danger, however, lay not so much in the Italians, but in 'the English malicious papists, who cannot be well affected to your Lordship's son or any that belongs unto you, and surely I have no great hope that your Lordship's son shall live safely among them'. Padua, Paulet allowed, had a good reputation 'for the exercise of learning', and the Pope had no authority to extradite men from there, as he did in Florence and elsewhere. But throughout the Signiory of Venice, 'the Inquisition is in force', and where that was the case 'it shall be easy for an bad instrument to do what mischief he can devise.' Finally, Sir Amias took a deep breath, and put the case bluntly to the Lord Keeper. The real problem was not even the manifold dangers of Italy, but the dangers of being Francis Bacon. 'To speak plainly as I think, I am of opinion that no English gentleman now being on this side the Seas should live in greater danger in Italy than your Lordship's son as the world goeth at this present. I refer this matter to your Lordship's better judgment, whereof I have considered with no less carefulness than if the same concerned my self, wishing unto the young gentleman in all things as to my own son.' Italy was not safe for Francis, and he was not allowed to leave France.[90]

Francis Bacon was given the kind of university and legal training that would enable him to become a useful intermediary in international negotiations. He was sent abroad to learn French and to see civil law procedures in practice, not to acquaint himself with the leading lights of the European Renaissance. It is ironic that this most mundane of designs inadvertently provided Francis Bacon with glimpses of the highly charged world of religious, political and courtly affairs that was later to prove so irresistible and dangerous to him.

★

Sir Amias ended his embassy as he had spent it: in a state of perpetual misery and intense disillusionment with human nature. France was a country where 'bloody and violent actions are turned into sports and pastimes', whose 'subtleties and treacheries' were 'so deep as it is very hard or rather unpossible for a stranger to find the bottom'; the reason why so few seemed actively to seek peace was that 'some do well know that these troubles and divisions are the only stay and pillar of their greatness.' As early as a year into the embassy, he was badgering his English correspondents to bring forward his recall, without which of course he was unable to return home. To his brother-in-law Sir John Clifton he wrote, only half jokingly, 'I desire much to hear from you how you profit in the French tongue, because my body is weak and may not long endure the troubles of this country, so as I shall be driven to call upon you after one year more, and indeed as this world goeth my supply cannot come too soon.' He promised him an easy life. 'You shall be happy, you shall find the country in good peace, the court at Paris, and there shall pass your two or three years in great quietness. You think I speak in sport. Well, I must now tell you that we are no changelings [we do not change] in this country, we fight and brawl after the old fashion, and have lived so long in this hell that I think we know no other heaven.'[91] By the end of 1577, too, Paulet had lost two chief members of his staff: Leicester's man Jacomo, who decided after seven years' unpaid service for the earl that enough was enough; and his own secretary Audley Dannet, who was recalled to England to work for the newly installed joint Principal Secretary of State, Thomas Wilson. Following Dannet's departure, Paulet was obliged to rely increasingly on the services of his eldest son, Hugh, who provided a nice personal touch in communications with England.[92]

In 1578, court intrigues multiplied with a series of affrays and duels between rival factions. In July of that year the duc d'Anjou entered Mons and the following month had reached an agreement with the Dutch estates whereby, in return for military support, he was given the title of 'Defender of the Liberty of the Netherlands against the tyranny of the Spaniards and their allies'. With this new advantage, he reopened marriage negotiations with Elizabeth. For Sir Amias this was yet another blow: as if being in France were not enough, he now had to take an active part, much against his conscience, in forwarding the renewed negotiations for his Queen to marry a Catholic prince.

But yet worse was to befall the unfortunate Paulet. In December 1578 Hugh was killed in a street accident, at the age of twenty. Distraught, and fearing for his sanity, Paulet stepped up his efforts to return home.[93] 'I am at the end of my Latin when I consider these French doings,' he declared in March 1579, 'which are so tickle and uncertain that nothing comes sooner to pass than what was least expected, and these things which in reason, honesty and judgement, seem to be most assured are seldom performed. Promises are made for advantage, faith and truth are esteemed according to their profit or disprofit. Inconstancy, the natural vice of those of this nation, is now encountered or rather surmounted with infidelity; no care of credit, no regard of honour, no love of virtue, no shame of vice.' His successor, Sir Henry Cobham, finally arrived on 13 November, and four days later both incoming and outgoing ambassadors were admitted to the King's presence to effect the changeover ritually.[94] Maintaining diplomatic decorum to the end, Paulet properly refused to receive the chain of gold sent from the French King until he was half a league out of Paris. As Jean Hotman reminded, 'Gifts do oblige, and those that receive them become slaves to those that give them.'[95]

The Paulet household returned to England without Francis Bacon, whose own departure had been forced some months earlier. In England, the weather had taken a turn for the worse in the new year: the chronicler John Stow recorded that on 'the 4 of February fell such abundance of snow . . . It snowed till the eight day and freezed till the tenth.' Elizabeth's Lord Keeper was one of the winter's casualties. In later years, Francis was to tell his chaplain and secretary William Rawley an anecdote concerning his father's death – an anecdote which presaged uncannily equally anecdotal accounts of his own ultimate demise: 'Old Lord Keeper Sir Nicholas Bacon had his barber rubbing and combing his head. Because it was very hot, the window was open to let in a fresh wind. The Lord Keeper fell asleep, and awaked all distempered and in great sweat. Said he to his barber, Why did you let me sleep? Why, my Lord, saith he, I durst not wake your Lordship. Why then, saith my Lord, you have killed me with kindness. So removed into his bedchamber and within a few days died.' At the moment of his father's death in London, Francis underwent an experience in Paris that was later to persuade him of the existence of 'secret passages of sympathy between persons of near blood; as parents, children, brothers, sisters, nurse-children, husbands, wives, &c.', since 'there be many reports in history, that upon the death of persons of such nearness, men have had an inward feeling of it.' He had a dream, 'which I told to divers English gentlemen, that my father's house in the country was plastered all over with black mortar'. The dream proved to be true. On 20 February 1579, Francis Walsingham added a postscript in his own hand to his despatch to William Davison: 'This morning the Lord Keeper departed this life.'[96]

Francis was back in England within a month, acting as bearer for Sir Amias' 20 March post. Sir Nicholas' death provided a suitable occasion for the return that would anyway have come about within a few months. Francis' licence would run out in June; Sir Amias' mission would be over by the year's end; and Francis himself was by no means enamoured of life in France. Three years later, when discussing his brother Anthony's extended sojourn in France, Francis 'marvelled' to Anthony's friend Nicholas Faunt how anyone staying abroad beyond a single licence – the usual limit was three years – 'could live to their contentment, seeing that himself was more than weary of his being forth, and that the home life is to be thought upon as of the end in due season'.[97]

In appointing him to carry the post again on his return journey, Sir Amias provided Francis with a further chance to place himself in the presence of the Queen, and a last testimonial to present to her. 'I know', he wrote to the monarch, 'you will take pleasure to hear of the towardness of any of your subjects, and therefore would not fail to advertise you that this bearer, Mr. Francis Bacon, is of great hope, endowed with many good and singular parts; and if God give him life will prove a very able and sufficient subject to do your Highness good and acceptable service.' The question for Francis Bacon now, fatherless at eighteen, was, what service could that be?[98]

3

Neither Well Left nor Well Friended

I desire her [my wife] to see to the well bringing up of my
two sons Anthony and Francis that are now left poor orphans
without a father.
Sir Nicholas Bacon (December 1578)

Where brethren do fall out the dislikings between them are
more hardly appeased than between strangers.
Nathaniel Bacon (June 1579)

T HE SPECTACLE OF the Bacon brothers united in their grief for
the premature death of a father did not last long and was never
to be repeated. The Lord Keeper decently laid to rest, the uneasy
truce between his two families collapsed in acrimony over his will, which
was immediately contested from both sides: by Nicholas and Nathaniel in
one camp, and by Anthony (and silently by his mother) in the other.

Sir Nicholas Bacon's will was a lengthy and, it must be said, well-
balanced document, dated 23 December 1578, containing nine pages of
bequests benefiting both families. Sir Nicholas' strategy of settling estates
on his sons during his lifetime meant that the great houses were already
assigned. Lady Bacon received her husband's interest in York House and
sizeable amounts of plate, jewels and gold. With Gorhambury, of which
Lady Bacon was a life tenant, went 'my lease of Aldenham and all copyhold
lands or tenements lying in the parishes of St. Michael or St. Stephen's
nigh St. Albans or joining to any lands of Westwick, Gorhambury or Prae'.
Sir Nicholas also left his wife £100 to keep on his household staff for a
month after his death. In return for this generous treatment of his widow,
however, Sir Nicholas made certain demands, which would in time destroy
her: 'In consideration of which legacies and in consideration of such assurances of manors, lands and tenements as I have assured unto my said wife
and for all loves that have been between us, I desire her to see to the well
bringing up of my two sons Anthony and Francis that are now left poor
orphans without a father.'

The implementation of the will set Sir Nicholas' two families at loggerheads. The brothers discovered, to their shared horror, that their father's

debts were greater than anyone suspected – and consequently focused all their energies on saving their respective legacies from being liable for these debts. Anthony wanted Nicholas to pay him rents previously raised from the leasing of the woods he inherited; Nicholas countered that the rent 'was reserved by my Lord and accounted for in his lifetime'. Anthony demanded the lease of Redbourn; Nicholas refused 'unless I may have either present money or else present assurance with the profits which are due unto it until the mortgage be redeemed'; Anthony wanted the Hertfordshire lands and leases; Nicholas suspected the generality of this request, and determined 'not to pass any assurance of lands or leases in general words but by particular names'. Nicholas argued that the lease of Redbourn and the stock of Pinner Park was 'liable to my father's will', and, that being the case, he did not mean to pass them to Anthony.[1]

Each family called on the arbitration of Lord Burghley, ostensibly in his personal capacity as the Lord Keeper's brother-in-law and overseer of the will, but inevitably as the country's highest authority in such matters. Burghley subsequently produced from their discussions, and from consultations with Anthony, a list of contested articles with his own preferred resolutions. To Burghley's intense annoyance, however, the sparring brothers refused to fall in behind his proposals, and negotiations quickly broke down. Progress was further hindered by dissension between the elder brothers as well as between the two families. As the legatees returned to their country seats, it became impossible to sort out a joint response from Nicholas and Nathaniel, as Burghley demanded. The situation deteriorated as the elder brothers made separate and contradictory replies, and letters crossed in the mail. Soon, the mood became ugly – as Nathaniel wrote, 'where brethren do fall out the dislikings between them are more hardly appeased than between strangers.' Nicholas felt 'justly grieved to see my brother Anthony to have a greater care to get what he can than to be any thing thankful for such benefits as we have promised him to have at our hands which the law hath cast upon us'.

Underlying the delays was Nicholas' claim that his stepmother was acting improperly. He alleged that she caused Burghley to be 'stirred greatly against me'. A joint answer from himself and Nathaniel, he wrote, was in any case no longer possible because Nathaniel, swayed by 'some hard speeches received at your Lordship's hands rather than upon any just cause set down in your articles', was now willing to compromise. This outcome just played into Lady Bacon's hands: 'a matter that my Lady in my father's lifetime and also since his death hath many times said should come to pass, and doth yet daily presume so greatly upon that, as if that had not been (with your Lordship's favour be it spoken) I do very [*sic*] think there had never grown any question between us.' Lady Bacon had not only broken her promise that 'no goods should be embezzled from us', but also 'hath been in offence with every man which hath informed us of them'.

Burghley took offence at the 'lack of good words or sense towards my Lady Bacon your late good father's good wife' – who was also, of course, Burghley's wife's sister – 'and also towards your natural younger brother Anthony Bacon'. Burghley expected 'a reasonable, kind and courteous regard had to the lady that hath so long time deserved well of you and yours, and hath been so good a wife to my Lord your father, and lastly who in the time of your father's death in my sight and hearing yielded so much unto you for your benefit as surely no natural mother could have yielded more to her own children'. He was anguished at the thought that the brothers meant to take Lady Bacon to court – an outcome which he thought 'unmeet [unsuitable] to be attempted by her or provoked by you or any of yours, to whom so many benefits hath come from your father and her since their intermarriage and by reason of the said marriage'.

Although matters were eventually settled, the elder and the younger brothers were never again close. The papers of Nathaniel Bacon, which survive in considerable numbers, contain no correspondence from Anthony, Francis or Lady Bacon after this date. Permanent damage had been done. Left, in the Lord Keeper's own words, 'poor orphans without a father', Anthony and Francis could not call on the good offices of their secure, landed elder brothers to establish them in life. Instead, they were entrusted to a woman, their mother, in a society where only one woman was able to make or break a young man's career.

★

Sir Nicholas Bacon's death left his widow embroiled in out-of-court legal wrangling with her stepsons, and his youngest son with severely limited options for his future. The alternatives open to Francis were to stay at home in Gorhambury with his mother, or to take up the place to which he had been admitted in June 1576 at Gray's Inn in London. He took the latter course. Within weeks of his return from Paris, Francis Bacon was established with his brother Anthony in the family chambers, opposite the gateway, next to the library.

Like a large number of Gray's Inn students, the elder Bacon brothers had no pretence to a legal vocation. Sir Nicholas had been a major figure at the Inn, serving for a time as its treasurer, and was determined that his sons should follow in his footsteps. But Nicholas, Nathaniel (admitted together on 15 December 1562), Edward (admitted in 1566) and Anthony were not inclined to take their legal studies overly seriously, regarding the family chambers at Gray's Inn rather as a convenient London base during the years before their father provided them with their own town houses.

What legal education they did glean from their years at Gray's Inn did at least prepare them appropriately for dealing with the demands of the country estate life into which a man of their class would expect to move – in the words of James Cleland, 'to defend himself from the crafty and subtle surprising of the world: and to give his friend and neighbour good counsel: to maintain a poor widow, and a little orphan from wrong and oppression'.[2]

For those seriously studying to become barristers, a strict hierarchy applied in day-to-day life, given expression in dress and position in the hall where meals were taken. At the lower end was a carved gallery; members met here for meals, 'in commons', on specific tables according to their status. Younger members would eventually be promoted to utter-barristers and sit on a table reserved for their use; another was allocated to the 'Ancients'; at the high table sat the 'Readers', who had made their public readings. The rigorously hierarchical educational progression followed by career lawyers coexisted with an alternative hierarchical arrangement which paid particular attention to social rank. While technically up to twelve years' residence were required to qualify as an 'Ancient', an honorary 'ancienty' was conferred automatically on the sons of peers and judges. These young men were at the Inn, as the fifteenth-century jurist Sir John Fortescue noted, 'not so much to make the Laws their study, much less to live by the profession, having large patrimonies of their own, but to form their manners, and to preserve them from the contagion of vice'.[3] None of the Bacon brothers before Francis progressed further than the honorary title of 'Ancient' conferred on them at their admission.

Thus it was that when Anthony and Francis Bacon, William Howes, Thomas Balgey and Roger Wilbraham were admitted at the pension of 27 June 1576, the Bacon boys and Howes were admitted *de societate magistrorum* (to the society of masters, the grand company) while Balgey and Wilbraham were admitted *de mense clericorum* (to the clerks' table). At the pension of 21 November it was clarified that all five of the Bacon sons 'shall be of the grand company and not to be bound to any vacations'. In other words, they could come and go as they liked, without regard for the Inn's formal teaching arrangements. Francis, of course, almost instantly disappeared with Sir Amias Paulet to France, and the same entry in the Pension Book, concerning the practical matter of the transfer of the Bacon chambers at the Inn (where there was a chronic shortage of rooms), significantly does not mention him at all: 'It is ordered that Mr. Edward Bacon shall be admitted in my Lord Keeper's Chamber in the absence of Mr. Nicholas Bacon his son, and that Mr. Anthony Bacon shall be admitted in the same chamber in the absence of Mr. Nathaniel Bacon.' This merely made official the loose arrangement which the brothers had been operating for some months.[4]

Anthony, even less ambitious than his older half-brothers, admitted freely to his 'want and defect' in the law.[5] The sole surviving letter written by Anthony during his time at Gray's Inn, to his brother Nathaniel, confirms this lack of interest in legal studies. Anthony's attention is taken up with some heady Puritan reading, the gossip concerning an attack on the Recorder of London, William Fleetwood, and news from the continent, presumably relayed from Francis in Paris. What Gray's Inn did, however, provide Anthony with was an immediate close social circle of friends – a group with whom he corresponded faithfully during the first lonely months in France that followed his departure from England in December 1579: Roger Wilbraham, James Altham, James Buscall, and George Chaworth.[6]

Popular opinion had the Inns of Court man down as a careless, profligate gallant. Located beyond Newgate, outside the jurisdiction of the City and suburban authorities, and within easy reach of the theatres, brothels and dicing-houses, the Inns of Court – characterised by George Whetstone as 'the first entertainers of your liberty' – offered their members an unusual freedom from surveillance, and the young men apparently behaved accordingly.[7] For Sir Nicholas, extreme religious opinions were a far graver danger than temptations to licentiousness. The Lord Keeper could not be as confident that his sons were being given a moderate, godly education at Gray's Inn as he had been when they were at Trinity. He decided not to leave his sons open to undesirable doctrinal influences, and accordingly hired a 'teacher': a young Gray's Inn lawyer, Richard Barker, who had 'grown into [his] liking', according to Burghley, 'by his toward gifts and good behaviour'. Barker's brief was to tutor Anthony and Francis, 'for good respects and commendable parts in him to be an Instructor to his two sons for the attaining of some knowledge in the study of the laws'. He was chosen not only for his prowess in the law – within five months of this appointment, Barker had been called as an utter-barrister, and went on to greater heights within the Inn and beyond – but because of his religious reliability, as a suitably Puritan-leaning anti-Catholic influence on his two young charges. When the time came to choose Ancients in 1579, Burghley specifically forwarded Barker as such a man who would not endanger the Inn's spirituality.[8]

Anthony and Francis were not long together at Gray's Inn after Sir Nicholas' death. Under the terms of his father's will, Anthony had to wait three years, until he turned twenty-four, before he could inherit. What should he do during this enforced delay? He had his sights set on continental travel, but without the constraints on his movements and conduct which had been imposed on Francis by the quasi-parental eye of an ambassador. His brother Edward was already abroad again, having departed soon after the funeral to a safe distance from the battles between his siblings over their father's legacies. Once those quarrels were settled, Anthony too had nothing to stay home for. He set off for France in December 1579 with the seal of approval not only of the French King's ambassador in London, M. de Mauvissière, but more importantly of his uncle, Lord Treasurer Burghley. As Burghley penned his letters of recommendation, he played on Anthony's family connections: 'The bearer is named Mr. Anthony Bacon son to him whom you knew here a great counsellor, the late Lord Keeper of the Great Seal of England, and to me allied in that his mother, the Lady Bacon, is my wife's sister, and since his father's death, the care of the bringing up of him and his brother, being by the testament of his honourable good father committed to me, and by his mother referred absolutely to my consideration . . .'

Here, Burghley paused, and thought better of that phrase 'the care of the bringing up of him and his brother'. A quick erasure gave him the considerably vaguer and less expensive 'the care of him and his brother'. It was the first sign of an equivocation that was to bewilder and hinder the Bacon brothers over the next nineteen years – their uncle's acknowledgement only of a non-specific 'care' for their general welfare, without the proper commitment to their 'bringing up', a phrase that had social and political ramifications beyond the immediate matter of their education. The brothers, for their part, encouraged Burghley to think of himself as their father. In a typical letter, Anthony would cite 'your Lordship's honourable and fatherly dealing with me . . . if ever poor gentleman had cause to honour and esteem so fatherly a friend I should be very unthankful if I should not judge myself to be as much bound to your Lordship as possibly I may be.'[9]

Burghley's idea was to have Anthony 'according to his honest desire to travel thither into France, to see the country there, and to learn the language'.[10] Little did he know that Anthony's travels would lead him to adopt the French language almost as his mother tongue and to develop a galloping Francophilia – for the rest of his life, he would have his papers docketed and endorsed in French, his food cooked by a French cook – and that it would take over a dozen years to entice him home. By the time Anthony Bacon returned to England he would be in his mid-thirties, his estate and his health permanently damaged by his time on the continent; Francis, on the other hand, would have sat in four parliaments, become a Reader at Gray's Inn and be profoundly implicated in the rising career of the Queen's young favourite, the earl of Essex. The trajectories of the two brothers through the 1580s appear utterly distinct. In fact, as new evidence shows, their careers were remarkably closely intertwined. We cannot begin to understand Francis Bacon's early career in England – nor, indeed, the ramifications of this period that were felt well into the next century – unless we examine that of Anthony across the Channel.

★

Anthony left England with two menservants and a sheaf of recommendations from the great and the good of English society. He quickly established himself as an 'intelligencer' – an information-gatherer working for the English government abroad, and taking instruction, at least in the earlier days, from Burghley. Nominally he was in the charge of one of Burghley's old retainers, Mr Windebank, and in April 1580 the name of Anthony Bacon headed a list of 'The English Protestants in Paris'. But being in Paris, without the restrictions imposed in the household of a zealous ambassador, Anthony – no matter how solid his Protestant credentials – was not going to restrict his social intercourse to the relatively small circle of expatriate Protestants and embattled Huguenots.[11]

From the outset, Anthony's travels were closely monitored in London by Francis, who did his best to smooth matters over when his brother began to keep what was regarded in official circles as potentially sensitive company. One of Anthony's Paris acquaintances was his brother-in-law Thomas Doyly, who was ostensibly in the service of the earl of Leicester. Somewhere along the line Anthony's dealings with Doyly were reported back to the authorities in England as cause for concern. Francis as intermediary raised the alarm, reporting to Anthony what was being said about Doyly. Alerted in turn by Anthony, Doyly wrote two letters of explanation, and sent them to Francis to be forwarded to the powers that be if he thought fit. Francis, judging that attempted explanations would do more harm than good, decided not to deliver the letters, being (as he told Doyly) 'most privy to the circumstances of the matter, and tending my brother's credit as I ought'.[12]

Doyly was a friend and executor of the exiled recusant Thomas Copley, who was also in Paris. But Copley could also claim kinship (by marriage) with Lord Burghley, to whom he offered in July 1580 'a jewel I had that I thought could not be but very welcome to your Lordship, to wit a genealogy of my lady your wife's house by the Belknap his side'. Lady Burghley shared a great-grandfather with Thomas Copley (Henry Belknap) – and therefore, perforce, so did her sister Lady Bacon. So, when pressed by post deadlines, Copley decided 'to make present to your Lordship even of my original, and for myself at leisure to take another copy out of that my cousin Bacon made to be drawn out of mine, which of late I lent him to that end'. This letter makes it clear that Anthony Bacon was also in friendly contact in Paris with Thomas Copley, a known Catholic, and moreover that he acknowledged him as a cousin.[13]

A more problematic acquaintance was the Welshman William Parry. Parry was a government spy, working for Burghley in Paris while attempting to elude creditors in England. In November 1580, returning to London, Parry broke into the Inner Temple lodgings of one such creditor, Hugh Hare, and attempted to rob and murder him. During the subsequent investigation, Parry's links with, and sympathies for, Catholic connections in Paris (including Copley) came to light. These revelations were dangerous for Anthony, who had compromised himself by becoming indebted to Parry – a note from Parry to Anthony dated 1 August 1580 records a loan of fifty crowns.

The earl of Leicester, always quick to detect weaknesses in Burghley's power base, complained to the Queen (or, in Anthony's words, 'did much stomach and impeach me to her Majesty') of Anthony's excessive intimacy with a notoriously unreliable Catholic. The matter was dropped only when Burghley vouchsafed to the Queen that his nephew was a trustworthy and utterly Protestant subject ('constituted himself surety to her Majesty for me that Parry could never shake neither my religion nor honesty') – an intervention not unrelated to the fact that Anthony, as he was later to reveal, was acting on direct orders from Burghley himself: his uncle 'advised me and persuaded me by letters to embrace the acquaintance of so dangerous and notorious a traitor'. In the long term, Leicester's fears about Parry proved well founded: he was arrested for his part in a plot to kill the Queen, and ultimately executed.[14]

Protestants abroad consorting with expatriates of known Catholic sympathies were frequently acting as part of an extensive system of espionage and counter-espionage. At this point in his life Anthony is a somewhat shadowy figure in the Elizabethan information-gathering network. What is clear, however, is that his brother Francis was in constant touch with him, monitoring his activities, receiving and transmitting his letters, and on occasion (as in the Doyly case) taking important decisions himself as to what should be shown to the authorities and how.

In late June 1580 Anthony left Paris and Mr Windebank, accompanied now by Honoré Blanchard, a fellow student at Trinity, where he had been 'an eye and earwitness of his good reputation, and report for his learning and good behaviour', considering him to have 'more understanding and judgment, than is incident commonly to the best scholars, whereof he himself notwithstanding is one, considering his grounded knowledge in Hebrew, Greek and Latin, and the travel he hath made throughout Germany and the Low Countries, and the most part of England'. During the next seven months, Anthony and Blanchard travelled together, as he later reported: 'most of which time I having travelled alone with him without any of mine own countrymen have found him by good proof so willing and serviceable, and withal so sufficient as he hath very well supplied the double room both of a friend and a servant.'[15]

At this stage, Anthony was undertaking only the most basic of tasks for Burghley, such as delivering 'this enclosed letter to Mr. Thomas Parry [perhaps the later ambassador to France; no relation to William Parry], praying him to send me his answer hereafter enclosed in some of yours'. When it came to providing a more demanding service, Anthony was at first none too adept, as his uncle complained: 'By your former letters I see you very circumspect in advertising of the affairs there whereof all the world doth take knowledge. But if you do conceal your knowledge lest you might be subject to judgments of parties you may reveal what is said on either side without revealing your own liking.'[16]

Anthony did not pin his hopes for advancement entirely on his uncle, and complemented his Burghley despatches by sending frequent newsletters to Sir Francis Walsingham, who urged him 'not to be therefore discouraged from continuing your writings, for that your letters are very welcome unto me'. Anthony confided in Walsingham his plan to visit the towns along the Loire, an idea of which Walsingham approved, provided that the young man would 'have regard not to seat yourself too much in France to the endangering of your health in this hotter season of the year'.[17]

It was also his correspondence with Walsingham which first brought Anthony into contact with a man who was to become a lasting friend – Nicholas Faunt, one of Walsingham's personal secretaries, who carried the post to Anthony from Walsingham in August 1580. On this occasion he travelled on from Paris to Germany (for three and a half months) and Geneva and the north of Italy (the next six or seven months). From his lengthy letters home, we get a detailed view of the complex and dangerous affairs in which Anthony Bacon was involved on the mainland of Europe during the 1580s and early 1590s.[18]

On 15 December 1580 Anthony arrived in Bourges in Berry, a centre of civil law learning where Beza had trained, where he met with 'especial favour and kindness at Monsieur Simier's hands'. From there, he wrote to Burghley, asking his uncle to intervene in some legal business concerning Pinner Park and complaining that his post was going astray, despite his using what he assumed was the safest means – the ambassador in Paris. He was therefore switching to two Italian merchants to deliver both 'the payment of my money and 'the conveyance of their letters'. The merchants 'may and will easily convey them unto me by their posts to any merchanded town in France, Italy or Germany, in all which countries these two have dealing'. The change of arrangements had been made particularly pressing 'seeing I mean to leave France and go to Geneva so soon as this bearer's return will give me leave', leaving behind 'this factious and divided country of Berry' for reasons he left to the bearer to explain. Abandoning the usual embassy post routes was another step for Anthony away from the control of officials, and towards a certain independence.[19]

Anthony confided to Walsingham his contempt for Bourges – he despised the corruption, he despised the religion, he despised the civil conversation. Now his only desire was to travel to Geneva. Walsingham agreed that Geneva would be 'agreeable to your natural disposition, and answerable to the good opinion, that is conceived of you'. There was a danger, he continued, in 'lying in the company of the worser sort'. Physical infection was bad enough, but mental infection worse: 'as the mind is infinite, so is the infection, that cometh from the mind, not to be limited or bounded with any certain compass of place.' Those in close proximity 'cannot but burn, unless they have some very extraordinary preservation, surpassing the nature of the salamander'. Given this natural weakness, 'they do best provide for themselves, that separate themselves, as far as they can, from the bad, and draw as nigh to the good, as by any possibility they may attain unto. And this disposition being found in you, cannot but be well liked of all, that love you, and as greatly wish'd to be continued with increase; whereof as they shall have great cause to rejoice, so it will be to me no small pleasure.'[20]

★

From the moment he left England Anthony knew that relinquishing Gorhambury to his mother was bound to cause problems. He attempted to keep tabs on life back on his estate through his servants John Stalling and Thomas Cotheram (a childhood friend), who were directed 'now and then to write me news how everything fadges'. Cotheram reassured his absent master that Lady Bacon was coping with the estate. 'The walks are kept as they were wont to be, your "desart" shall be felled the next year at felling time, and as for all the rest of your woods, shall not be felled, before you come home. My lady doth think that you will come home in debt and therefore you shall have the felling of them yourself to set you out of debt.' There were squabbles between the servants. 'Stalling is grown out of credit with my lady because he hath not nor doth do his duty at Gorhambury as it is reason he should considering how my lady and you have dealt with him, and I have said and dare be bold to say that he can scant give you a good word. My lady doth repent her of the lease she made to him and doth somewhat blame you because you did so easily grant him three years; after my lady's death I think he shall not have so much charge as he had before.' Cotheram was particularly pleased to report that the widow appeared not to have marriage on her mind. 'I hope you do not nor need fear my lady's marriage for truly she is as far off of that, as when you departed from her nor never none came to her for that as far as I can hear of. And if I do you shall hear of it by me as soon as I can send you word. But I hope to God there shall be no such occasion.'[21]

Anthony exhorted Stalling in particular to 'take the pains to write how everything goeth with Lady Bacon. The greatest pleasure you can do me is to send me word that my mother and you are of good agreement, that she continueth the good liking she had of you before my departure and you the duty and service which you were accustomed to do unto her.' Anthony reminded Stalling 'how ready and willing I have been to maintain and augment our credit with her, insomuch as my word is pledge for your honest and good behaviour towards her,' and in the same breath assured himself that Stalling would 'not forget yourself so far as any way to molest and trouble her with trifling matters or to give her any occasion of misliking with you'. Finally, he comes clean. 'I pray you good Mr. Stallinge save both our credits. It is in you to purchase me thanks at my mother's hands, if you do as you ought to do, or displeasure to me and yourself too if you do otherwise.'[22]

Anthony had left his patrimony in the hands of Hugh Mantell, a trusted family servant who had served as steward to Sir Nicholas. Mantell was engaged to collect Anthony's rents, deal with his tenants and negotiate the sales and rentals of his properties. More crucially for Anthony, he was required to transfer money to his master twice a year, at midsummer and Christmas, and to report regularly on the condition of Anthony's holdings. Anthony supplemented Mantell's information with reports from his lawyer and his brother Francis in London, especially concerning suits pending in the capital.[23]

Anthony's expenditure on the continent soon rose above the income filtered through Mantell from his estates. On one occasion, Mantell scrabbled around to raise £600 to send to Anthony, but this was not sufficient to pay his creditors: his debt to one man alone amounted to more than £300 over and above the total of his annual rents. To keep Anthony supplied, Mantell was forced to borrow money from Lady Bacon, and to delve into his own pockets – when he could; in March 1581, Mantell was unable to pay Francis £140 as Anthony directed him, and informed Anthony that he neither had it of Anthony's to pay, nor could honour it out of his own money. But it was a cycle that was not to be broken: two years later, in March 1583, the hapless steward was still covering Anthony's debts with his own money, and making it increasingly clear in his letters that he expected to be reimbursed. 'Your Worship shall so command me I will not speak to sell anything I have to raise money of and to disburse the same for your worship, so as I may have convenient time to do it,' wrote Mantell; but there were problems: 'I am verily persuaded that if you did enter into a reckoning and consideration of the great charge you have been at since your going over and the troublings of her Ladyship and other of your worship's friends, you would surely have greater desire to return to England than you hitherto seem to have.'[24]

The 1580s were a time when land was potentially profitable, and Anthony should have had no real problem subsisting on the income from his estates. However, while he continued to issue warrants that were intended to give Mantell authority to disburse money, he failed to provide proper seals and signatures, rendering these official instructions effectively worthless. Once, when two tenants paid their rent directly to Anthony in France, he neglected to inform Mantell, leading to some protracted and embarrassing negotiations for the steward. Anthony also proved a poor correspondent, failing to answer letters of account from Mantell, who was provoked into warning his master that he would not write to Anthony at all if he were not answered more promptly. In November 1581, in response to Anthony's instructions to pay all bills on sight, Mantell exploded: 'There is not one penny in my hands. Your absence is herein and in many other things here great loss unto besides that it increaseth your expences.'[25]

Apart from the incidental costs of maintaining himself, his two servants, his companion Blanchard, and his horses, Anthony was using what ready cash he had in order to further his influence, through lending money. His papers from this period, now in the library of Lambeth Palace, contain a pile of records of money lent: fifty French crowns to William Parry on 1 August 1580, 'to be paid upon request'; Maurice Fane of Stoke-upon-Trent in the country of Stafford, gent., acknowledging himself 'indebted to Mr Anthony Bacon esq. the sum of twelve crowns' on 3 August 1581; loans to George Hawys; loans to Honoré Blanchard; loans to two French brothers. Anthony Bacon used his cash to put together a team of men who were indebted to him, who owed him a favour when he needed it.[26]

Hugh Mantell's attitude towards Anthony was determined above all by a belief that his young master would – or certainly should – soon be back on English soil to repair the damage wrought by his absence. In January 1581 he wrote to Anthony saying that he would defer taking any decisions concerning the leases of or improvements to his farms until Anthony returned. But Anthony, while he had no intention of remaining where he was, equally had no plans to return home.[27]

★

Anthony followed his brother's professional progress at Gray's Inn via their mutual friends there. In January 1581 he thanked Roger Wilbraham for his mention of Francis, commenting that 'the news you write me of my brother's proceeding in the law comforteth mine own want and defect therein, thinking myself to be sufficiently furnished, if in so lewd and disorderly a country as this is I may be able to keep a good conscience.' Henry Golding evidently provided a similarly glowing report in the summer of 1581, provoking Anthony to respond that 'I hear nothing more joyfully than my brother to be well spoken of, especially by those which resembled yourself, and I doubt not but he deserveth the greatest commendation that may be given him.'[28]

In fact, Francis was very much following in his brother's footsteps. The only letter which has survived from Anthony's time at Gray's Inn notes that he is reading a controversial work by Thomas Cartwright, which he then sent on to his brother Nathaniel. It is a telling choice for a young man who had come directly from the hands-on tuition of John Whitgift. Cartwright was an old adversary of Whitgift's who had been prominent in persuading the fellows of Trinity to discard their surplices in chapel (a mark of religious radicalism).[29] When Whitgift was appointed Vice-Chancellor of the university in October 1570, he stripped Cartwright of his professorship and his college fellowship. Fleeing to sanctuary with Theodore Beza in Geneva, Cartwright played out his conflict with Whitgift in print, over a period of some four years: Anthony's reading in 1578 was the much-delayed *The rest of the second replie of Thomas Cartwright: agaynst Master Doctor Whitgifts second answer, touching the Church discipline.*[30]

Now Francis too showed signs of independent religious thinking, in his case with the explicit backing of his mother. Although he was obliged to attend the sermons of the Gray's Inn chaplain – a staunch Puritan named Thomas Crooke, who was himself a Trinity man and a Burghley protégé – Francis was observed going with his mother to the Temple chapel to hear Walter Travers preach. The Bacons were not alone in their admiration of Travers. As the seventeenth-century divine Thomas Fuller wrote, 'Mr Travers' utterance was graceful, matter profitable, method plain, and his style carried in it *indolem pietatis*, "a genius of grace" flowing from his sanctified heart.' But Francis and Lady Bacon's attraction to Travers owed more to belief than to rhetoric.[31] Travers was known for his attempts to impose a Genevan discipline on his new congregation.[32] Francis and Lady Bacon's predilection for Travers amounted to open sympathy for continental Protestantism and smacked of Nonconformity. It occasioned comment.

Francis also shared his older brother's poor health. On 13 May 1580, the Pension Book records that 'Mr. Francis Bacon in respect of his health is allowed to have the benefit of a special admittance with all benefits and privileges to a special admittance belonging for the fine of forty shillings.' In effect, barristers had very few more privileges than the students: they ate the same food (albeit at different tables) and had to pay for their wine. Francis' special admittance allowed him to have food and drink brought in from the buttery, and to consume it in his chambers, rather than in commons.[33]

Francis' uncle Lord Burghley was a Gray's Inn alumnus and took a keen interest in the institution's activities, regularly using his influence in internal appointments. He had supported the Bacons' tutor, Richard Barker, in his bid for anciency, recommending him to the readers as 'an honest and toward student in learning of your house', and desiring them 'that in your said call you will be mindful of him according to his worthiness'.[34] In 1580 Francis made his first attempt to get serious support for his own career from Burghley. Fatherless, he was badly in need of a father-substitute. On this occasion, however, his uncle behaved as he was to do many times more in the years that followed. He listened, he took a concerned interest, he offered sympathy. But he did the minimum he could respectably do under the circumstances on behalf of his struggling nephew.

Francis explained in a letter to Burghley that he intended to make the common law his profession, but was looking for some employment which would make him independent of ordinary Bar practice. He wanted Burghley's help in persuading the Queen to give him some kind of honorary legal post, so that he could spend his time in legal studies, without having to take too many cases to make ends meet. He wrote in similar terms to his mother's sister Mildred Cecil, Lady Burghley, asking her 'to vouchsafe the mention and recommendation of my suit' to her husband. To both he admitted that his request was 'rare and unaccustomed'. But he observed that it was unusual for someone from his social background to practise at the Bar at all – that there were few men 'which fall in with the study of the common laws, either being well left or friended, or at their own free election, or forsaking likely success in other studies of more delight and no less preferment, or setting hand thereunto early without waste of years'.[35] In his suit to Lord and Lady Burghley, Bacon made it clear that his legal career was an occupation in which he engaged out of necessity: becoming a lawyer was a survival strategy forced upon him by his father's death.[36]

On 18 October, Francis wrote thanking his uncle for preferring his suit to the Queen and for his 'comfortable relation of her Majesty's gracious opinion and meaning towards me'. To Francis, it was 'an exceeding comfort and encouragement to me, setting forth and putting myself in way towards her Majesty's service', to have achieved what he gratefully termed 'an example so private and domestical of her Majesty's gracious goodness and benignity'. Some modest informal arrangement had been made on his behalf. In expressing his profound gratitude to Burghley, Francis expressed the hope that the favour extended was done for his father's sake: 'made good and verified in my father so far forth as it extendeth to his posterity, accepting them as commended by his service, during the non-age, as I may term it, of their own deserts'. In inheriting his father's virtues, 'I trust my portion shall not be with the least, nor in proportion with my youngest birth.'[37]

He was probably closer to the truth than he knew. What small marks of favour the Queen showed Francis Bacon she conferred for his deceased father's sake. As far as one can see, like so many of Francis' patrons, Burghley protested commitment to his cause, but did next to nothing to further it.

★

Francis Bacon's participation in the brief parliament which sat from 16 January to 18 March 1581 was so insignificant that his name appears in no record or journal: indeed, until the researches of Sir John Neale in the mid-twentieth century, his involvement in this, his first parliament, went entirely unnoticed.

In late Elizabethan England a parliamentary seat owed nothing to the democratic process and everything to patronage in one form or another. By a bizarre twist of fate for a man constantly in poor health, Bacon owed the beginning of his parliamentary career to an epidemic. In the words of the chronicler Raphael Holinshed, there was a 'strange sickness at Oxford' during the July assizes in 1577, and some three hundred people were 'smouldered' by a 'damp', bleeding until they died.[38] Among those struck down was Sir Robert Doyly (brother to Thomas Doyly, about whom damaging reports had come from France), only thirty-five at the time of his death. Since his widow Elizabeth was Francis' elder half-sister, Francis' connections were in place to forward his election to Robert's parliamentary seat of Bossiney when the time came. Bossiney was under the complete control of the second earl of Bedford − Francis' godfather − and had multiple Bacon connections via Gray's Inn and St Albans; mutual Doyly and Bacon friends included the earls of Leicester and Bedford and Sir William Perriam (who later became Elizabeth's third husband).[39]

Events saw to it that Francis Bacon's first experience of parliamentary participation was a memorable one. When business commenced on Saturday 21 January 1581, a general fast for the Commons was agreed on and announced by Walter Travers − that Walter Travers whose Nonconformist sermons Francis and his mother attended at the Temple. The Queen countermanded, sending 'an inhibition to the House for that it pertained to her ecclesiastical power to appoint fasts, and not proper for the parliament which was only to meddle with *meum et teum*'.[40] Parliament ignored her opposition, and fasted as the radical preacher had advocated. Elizabeth did not hide her displeasure. On the Monday morning, the new Speaker rose to convey to the House 'her Majesty's great mislike of our proceeding in agreeing to the public fast, and that we contrary to her commandment had intermeddled in causes of religion'; she 'desired the House from thenceforth to forbear to enter into such actions as were not fit for them to bear and such as himself could not bear'.[41]

In a second incident, which Bacon recalled in 1601, one Arthur Hall was committed to the Tower for questioning the authority of the House of Commons. He maintained publicly that 'the Lower-House was a new person in the Trinity; which, because these words tended to the derogation of the state of this House, and giving absolute power to the other, he was committed.' Hall had recently published two tracts which contained comments about current practice in the Commons, and a historical study of the constitution, describing the Lower House (seditiously, it was suggested) as a latecomer in the Trinity of Kings, Lords and Commons. In addition to a fine and imprisonment, Hall was 'adjudged to be dismembered the House and a warrant to be made to the town of Grantham for election of a new burgess'. This was such an unprecedented act that the Speaker ordered the entire proceedings to be written and read out by the Clerk, and entered into the Journal (on 18 March).[42]

Despite the brevity of the session and the relative lack of major parliamentary activity, these two diverse displays of power – of the Queen's authority to order fasting, and of the Commons' authority to 'dismember' a member – etched themselves in Francis Bacon's mind. They were powers that were to be questioned and redefined throughout what turned out to be a lengthy and stormy parliamentary career.

★

Anthony finally reached Geneva in the summer of 1581. Now, he wrote, 'I have great cause to thank God who hath given me the grace to pass without any special inconvenience to so good a place of resting in true religion as this is: a city I assure you the best ordered the most politicly governed and the one reformed in all Christendom.' He saw Geneva as a long-awaited 'pause of my first travel', and soon 'determined here to winter'. Like his brother Edward before him, he spent time living in Theodore Beza's house, taking advantage of the teachings of the great Calvinist at the Academy. One letter to his Gray's Inn contemporary Roger Wilbraham finishes abruptly, apologising that 'I dare not now begin my long treatise, for fear I have not sufficient leisure to finish it, and the bell begins to ring to Mr. Beza his lecture.'[43] Faunt, now in Padua, approved of the arrangement: he himself had lived with the Bezas' next-door neighbour Charles Perrot.

In addition to Beza, Anthony may have benefited from the teachings of François Portus (who died in 1581) in Greek, Corneille Bertram in Hebrew, Antoine de la Faye in theology, Jules Pacius and Denis Godefroy in law, and Alexandre Brisson in philosophy. His acquaintance with Lambert Daneau may have started here, although Anthony probably left Geneva just before the great Isaac Casaubon took up his chair in Greek. Some sense of his social circle can be gleaned from a contemporary manuscript armorial book by Jean Durant now in the Bibliothèque de Genève, containing almost three hundred coats of arms of 'noble seigneurs, princes, counts, barons and gentlemen whom piety and the love of *bonnes lettres* have led to the Geneva Academy'. Among the coats of arms dating from the early 1580s are those of Georges de Sayn, count of Wittgenstein, Baron Philippe de Winnebury and Baron Charles de Zerotin, and those of Anthony Bacon, complete with his signature.[44]

Whereas Edward and Francis, in their different ways, had been helped and hindered by the shadow of their famous father, Anthony chose to exploit the reputation not of Sir Nicholas, but of Lady Bacon. While in Geneva, he persuaded Beza to dedicate his French publication of his meditations on the Penitential Psalms to his mother. In the dedicatory epistle Beza cites Lady Bacon's worthy family connections – primarily her father Sir Anthony Cooke, who had been an exile in Geneva during the reign of Queen Mary. Beza wrote of 'this constancy and Christian patience wherewith God hath so beautified you, that in you is verily acknowledged that Christianly high minded courage which I saw in these partes shining in the deceased of very happy memory, Sir Anthony Cooke Knight, during those great calamities public to the realm, and particular to him and his whole family.' The reflection of Cooke's memory is strengthened by Lady Bacon's pious learning, her 'reading of those great and holy doctors' Greek and Latin so familiar to you'; Beza writes of how he knew 'by the Latin letters wherewith it hath liked you to honour me, the great and singular, yea extraordinary graces wherewith God hath endued you'.

The question here is whether this carefully crafted picture of a pan-European learned Protestant community was Anthony's only by association, or whether it was something in which he was directly involved. Certainly, it was an impressive picture: the Nonconformist preacher Thomas Wilcox reminded Lady Bacon in 1589 of how 'you are made truly famous abroad in foreign Churches and countries, and highly reverenced of many worthy men there, endued doubtless with singular graces for God's glory, and the building up of the body of the fellowship of Saints.' Anthony Bacon, however, claimed the credit for this dedication himself: 'Going to Geneva and being lodged with late father Beza it pleased him to dedicate his meditations to my mother *for my sake*.' Beza himself states to Lady

Bacon that his manuscripts of the *Meditations* had languished forgotten in a drawer: 'I reserved them among my papers as things of no great price: where they had lien [lain] still, had not been the coming of master Anthony Bacon your son, into these parts.'[45]

Beza was a linchpin in a network which Anthony established linking funding for the activities of the Protestant community of Geneva, intelligence, and the shipping of books back to England, involving Francis' correspondent and 'cousin', Thomas Bodley. Anthony's notebooks contain accounts such as the following:

> And to Mr Bodley by one warrant by a bill of exchange to Lyons £115 4s 2d
> And to him for money by him conveyed to Mr Beza by your assignment £6 10s 2d
> And to him for money by him paid for carriage of two cases of books to Mr Francis Bacon 25s 8d
> And to Mr Bodley by your warrant more £53 12s[46]

These accounts testify to networks that were a powerful combination of religious support groups, intelligence systems, publishing distributors and intellectual circles. Sympathisers with the Genevan church criss-crossed Europe, from trusted community to trusted community, not only circulating God's word but also providing trade routes for books, a courier service for goods and money, a reliable letter-carrying facility and a conduit for intelligence. All these materials entered and left England through the ports, and thus through the English customs houses, and contacts there were a valuable part of the network for the traffic in all kinds of information in which Francis and Anthony participated. Francis developed a friendship with William Philippes (father of his old embassy friend Thomas Phelippes), who worked in London's Customs House, which provided a useful entrée into the complex world of import and export. Together on 11 August 1582 they visited the renowned scholar and book-collector John Dee, at his house at Mortlake; and the Bacon–Philippes relationship was cemented when Francis took on Philippes' son as his secretary-cum-companion.[47]

★

Leaving Geneva in late 1581, Anthony started to travel around France. On Monday 14 January 1582 he met Francis' old embassy mate, Arthur Throckmorton – who was travelling from Florence to Revanne, Orleans, Angerville and Paris – at the 'Black Angel' in Lyons, and spent three days with him. By this time Throckmorton was travelling with Robert Sidney, Henry Savile and Henry Neville, touring Europe and meeting some of the most important scientists and intellectuals of the day. They had spent some time in Breslau with the Hungarian intellectual André Dudith, and in Altdorf with the German astronomer Johannes Praetorius. Perhaps Anthony met the entire group.[48]

Nicholas Faunt was in Paris, but not enjoying it. Marginalised by Ambassador Cobham, whose anti-Walsingham stance included Faunt, he had no one with whom he could socialise; and there were only two people, he claimed, who shared his religious views. Within the year he had left for more profitable grounds – in the first instance Germany and Padua. Throughout this time, he kept Anthony supplied with a stream of lengthy, detailed letters, describing Germany and Italy and evaluating their national characters. He thought Venice safer than any part of France: the Italians were wise and discreet, avoiding religious discussion. Like Sir Amias Paulet before him, he found the French inquisitive and hot, and lacking in wisdom and courtesy. In return, he asked for Anthony's informed opinion on recent treaties, and assured Anthony that when he received letters from England, Anthony would be the first to be informed. But Faunt soon grew disillusioned with the service, 'knowing it to be unthankful and not always the most honest service'; and impending danger forced him to flee from Padua to Pisa and ultimately to Geneva, where the friends were reunited in November – a note dated Geneva, 23 November 1581, details a 20 crown loan to Faunt.[49]

From Geneva, Faunt returned to Paris, where he attempted to obtain a passport for Anthony from Cobham. Cobham received Faunt coldly, and the passport was not immediately issued; Faunt discouraged Anthony from coming to Paris during Cobham's tour of duty. In the capital, Faunt caught up on the latest intelligence, which he relayed to Anthony, including news of Amias Paulet's new life as a courtier, and of his anticipated appointment as Secretary of State. By March, this last news item was being claimed by Faunt, who had a vested interest in the matter, as 'for certain': 'It is thought, for certain, that Sir Amias Paulet is secretary, or shall be shortly; whereby I fear (under hope to prefer me in haste) some of my friends will wish me where I would not be so soon, seeing it is most likely, that my master will furnish him with some of his men.' (In fact, Paulet did not become Secretary; his next public service was not to be until 1585, when he became the guardian of Mary Queen of Scots.) By 12 March Faunt had indeed been commanded by Walsingham to return, which gave him some concern, as he was keen to 'procure some further time to spend abroad, or else some more private and solitary life'.[50]

Once back in London, Nicholas Faunt reverted from trusted confidential courier on state business to personal servant and family retainer for his master, Anthony Bacon. A series of accidents delayed his paying his respects to Lady Bacon and Francis for some weeks: Faunt's taking of physic, Lady Bacon's absence, and 'my often missing [Francis] when it was my chance to seek him'.[51] He kept Anthony informed by letter of how things were progressing at home. He had finally encountered Lady Bacon in Burghley's garden (he reported), and had a long talk, satisfying her 'in all such demands as you may imagine she did make touching your estate of health, being, motion of employing your time, charges of living in those parts, and purpose of further travel: but in such sort as I remembered to have been thoroughly acquainted withal at my being with you and as I conceived should be the very truth and according to that you would have me deliver for answer, if you had before instructed me for such a message expressly.'

Lady Bacon was particularly concerned that Anthony was 'to have respect unto your estate after your return', since travel ('which in these days is so common to all that it seemeth not a matter so respected as it hath been') had a tendency to make 'young gentleman at their return more unapt to live in their country than before they were, that they find themselves ever after much discontented'. In Lady Bacon's view, the world was 'so hard that it seemed requisite for you to have a special care in looking to your present estate and the well guiding of that your friends have provided for you, that you are not to trust overmuch to others in your absence, that you should find at your return in your possessions things much out of order, and that she wished you might take the most benefit and comfort of your best friends, whilst it pleaseth God you may enjoy them'. There were many other speeches in the same vein; Faunt soon realised that it became him 'rather to harken than to make any answer'.

After Faunt had satisfied all Lady Bacon's questions, she continued to press him 'touching all whatsoever I had heard of your resolutions or dispositions for any matter'. Faunt now told her of Anthony's 'purpose to stay a longer time abroad if you might conveniently procure the means to have a new licence' which 'at the first seemed somewhat strange unto her'. His mother was distressed at the idea that he would continue to expose himself to danger abroad. Faunt reassured her that Anthony was fully determined to return before too long, but that if by any chance family deaths occurred in the meantime, that could only mean that he stood some chance of lands coming to him, to relieve his financial difficulties. Lady Bacon pronounced herself reassured, and eventually consented to his prolonging his absence: 'Then it were good that no time were lost in procuring your new licence.' She promised to deal with Burghley herself, and ordered Faunt to put Walsingham 'in mind to get the same signed before the Queen should stir from about London'. Meanwhile, his family could take care of his interests at home until he returned.

From Lady Bacon Faunt went on to see Francis at Gray's Inn and, although they shared 'no great talk', Francis used him 'better than I deserved'. Like his mother, 'he was also desirous to be particularly informed of your being and good estate: but for other matters I cannot write you any thing of his mind; other than that he desired your return at the end of your first licence, and saith that all your friends do make account that then you will be also of the same mind.'[52] A month later, however, Faunt reported that Francis was now insisting that Anthony should return to England at the end of his licence.[53]

The friendship between Nicholas Faunt and Anthony Bacon served as a key route for information filtered back to England from the continent and for correspondence in the other direction. From Walsingham's London house, where he now resided, Faunt would send on letters from Francis Bacon to his brother, and to Theodore Beza in Geneva;[54] and by this time Anthony was already supplying information on the political situation in mainland Europe, via his correspondence with Faunt and Francis. A set of briefing notes from this period entitled 'Notes on the State of Christendom' was long attributed to Francis Bacon, until editor James Spedding noted that some of the handwriting is very like Anthony's and speculated that Faunt conveyed the material back to England. It was of the nature of such intelligence documents to be collaborative – drafted by an informant close to the English court, but supplied with detail and topical information by trusted local intelligencers abroad. In this case it looks as if the outline for these 'Notes' was devised by Francis Bacon, the detail of facts and figures supplied by his brother. One of Anthony's notebooks, now in Edinburgh University Library, includes such raw intelligences as 'The discourse concerning the greatness of the house of Austria', several 'Advertisements received from sundry parts', 'A small note touching the affairs of Poland', 'The state of the affairs in the Low Countries touching the late accident happened in Antwerp', and 'An advice touching the present state of the Low Countries'.[55] Such work demonstrates that the Bacon brothers were operating by this time as furnishers of up-to-the-minute data relevant to policy-making and international dealings on the part of the English administration. 'Notes on the State of Christendom' is a simple compilation of information concerning the ruling houses, political and religious leanings and financial situations of the protagonists on the European political stage of the moment. Each of the Italian duchies is discussed – Tuscany, Ferrara, Mantua, Urbino, Parma, Savoy – along with its duke; Lucca, Genoa and Venice are analysed, as is the Austrian empire, the princes of Germany, and the kingdoms of Poland, Denmark, Spain and France.[56]

In May 1582 a licence was sent from the Queen to enable Anthony to travel abroad for another three years. It was not a welcome move for the Bacons left at home, as Faunt reported to Anthony. 'Yet by the way, in a word or two, he [Francis] hath showed his earnest desire to have you return at your time limited by your licence, wishing me to be a persuader thereof.'[57] Faunt wrote again on 1 August: Anthony's friends, he said, wished he would return, especially since he could not now go into Italy following the outbreak of war between Savoy and Geneva in the summer, and the heightened persecution of Protestants. Acknowledging Anthony's letters and attributing his own failure to write much to his absence from city and court, Faunt also referred to the danger of correspondence in excusing the slightness of his letters: 'the time serveth not now almost to write any thing from hence into those parts' since 'such search is made of ordinary letters upon the least suspicion' and a mishap would compromise his position. He could not wait to welcome Anthony home: 'for I must needs say that this is home when all is done, I mean the place where I live and have lived before yieldeth me more experience than all my travel hath done.' Whereas abroad he 'enjoyed all outward sights and observations, here I see into the inward course of things and very cabinets of secrecies'. Faunt assured Anthony that when he was nearer, he 'would adventure more than he then could by letters'; in the meantime he was augmenting daily his store, having already recovered all his writings and books left in Italy and Frankfurt, and whatever he had collected before or since would be at Anthony's disposal.[58]

In 1582 came the first instance of what was to become a pattern during the following years. Anthony Bacon disappeared from view. In December 1582, Faunt wrote to Anthony, complaining at the poor return that was yielded from his recent deluge of letters from London – two of Anthony's in response to twelve of his, and the last from Anthony in March, from Lyons. But now he had learned from a Monsieur Mallet, newly arrived from Geneva and Lyons, that he was not alone in being thus left in the dark. Mallet 'affirmeth that neither Mr. Beza nor any your friends in those parts have of long time heard from or of you *comme estantz en grand peine pour cest affaire la, & nullement assurez quelle pourroit estre votre condition* [as being in a great deal of trouble as a result of that affair, and unable to find out what kind of state you were in]: which news hath somewhat perplexed me.' Faunt bemoaned 'the melancholy passion I am hereupon cast into, as one of your poor friends that would be loath any hard haps should befall unto you as unto myself: Howbeit I have many good grounds to conceive and hope the contrary . . . The last time I saw your brother Mr Francis here he told me that he had not heard of or from you in three months together, and that he hoped to meet you at Dover this next Spring which I leave to them can best determine.'[59]

Anthony finally made contact with Faunt when his new servant and courier Edward Selwin arrived in England in February 1583. Selwin brought news of Anthony's partial recovery from a long, severe sickness which had weakened his constitution; Faunt sent back his hopes that on Selwin's return, Anthony would be 'cured in body, mind and purse'.[60] Poor health was to dog Anthony throughout his time on the continent, just as it had done in Cambridge. There were those who thought that his hypochondria and easy recourse to medicaments exacerbated his condition. Walsingham advised him that he had been informed that Anthony too easily and often gave himself to taking physic, 'a thing', he opined, 'which as I have by experience found hurtful in myself, when I was of your years, so you shall find in time many incommodities, if you do not in time break it off. Your years will better wear out any little indisposition, by good order of exercise and abstinence, with some other little moderation in diet, than abide to be corrected by physic, the use whereof altereth nature much, yea maketh a new nature, if it be without great cause used in younger years.'[61] Here we get a glimpse of a recurrent theme in the private lives of both Anthony and Francis. Habituated to 'physic' – opiates, taken in broths, milk or wine – by recurrent bouts of childhood illness, they grew increasingly dependent on such remedies in adulthood. Walsingham's disapproval suggests that habitual 'physic taking' or mild opiate addiction was a known debilitator, hence not something to be encouraged in employees, however fragile their health.

In Faunt's reports to Anthony, there are hints of the progress of his younger brother. Writing from the court at Greenwich on 6 May 1583, Faunt mentioned to Anthony that 'your brother Mr. Francis is sometimes a courtier and whensoever we talk but three words together two and a half of them contain a most hearty wish for your speedy return.'[62] We also glimpse Francis' characteristically precipitate conduct on being called to the Bar at Gray's Inn. In August, Faunt saw Francis 'in his outward [utter] barrister's habit abroad in the city'. In spite of the custom requiring a newly qualified utter-barrister to retain his student dress for a further two years, Francis had evidently abandoned the plain, sleeveless black gown of the student, with its flap collar and round black cloth cap, in favour of the long black grogram robe with two velvet welts on its long hanging sleeves immediately after being called to the Bar on 27 June. 'He therefore must do well,' observed Faunt.[63]

The relationship between Faunt and Francis was not consistently amicable. On 30 May, Faunt visited Gray's Inn and took the opportunity 'to call in, and know whether your brother will write unto you by means of conveyance, or whether he hear more lately than myself of your being'. However, Faunt was answered by Bacon's servant, who said that Francis 'was not at leisure to speak with me, and therefore,' Faunt wrote to Anthony, 'you must excuse me if I cannot tell you how your mother and other friends do at this present; only I perceive by your brother's boy that he was but newly come from St. Albans, where I take it my Lady now is, and well.' Faunt was asked where Anthony was, and what he had lately heard from him, 'but I could say little that he knew not, neither was I so simple to say all to a boy at the door, his master being within.' This was not the first time he had been so rudely received. 'This strangeness which hath at other times been used towards me by your brother, hath made me sometimes to doubt that he greatly mistaketh me, for I do these offices both towards you and him upon no base respect or for insinuation, but only of good affection to either for the best considerations.' It was true, he admitted, that his offices towards Francis were done rather for Anthony's sake, and 'by reason of the good acceptation it hath pleased you to yield of the poor acquaintance and mutual amity that is between us, and I hope shall not be lessened hereafter'.[64]

Francis was not alone in his concern for his brother's return. Both Anthony's lawyer and his mother were tiring of his prolonged absence abroad, as the burden of his affairs fell increasingly upon them.[65] Lady Bacon eventually attempted to force Anthony's hand by refusing to disburse his summer 1583 payment of 500 crowns – vital funds which he needed in order to live in comfort. Although she eventually relented, she later refused to send Anthony's next (Christmas) payment, and converted all his revenues to her own use until she was paid back money which she had sent to him since his departure. As she grew more annoyed with Anthony, Lady Bacon became suspicious of the steward Hugh Mantell's role in the business, and she investigated Anthony's suggestion that Mantell had kept some of the money. As it turned out, Mantell *had* been creaming off some of the money, considering that he was owed it for services rendered that had remained unpaid.[66]

Anthony reported back to Faunt regularly, telling him of the events and the personalities of Marseilles, and on at least one occasion enclosing some sonnets, sadly now lost.[67] In exchange, Faunt kept him up to date with the news at court, a milieu in which he felt increasingly ill at ease. In August 1583, he reported an illness that had detained him in London for twenty days, and confided: 'to tell you the truth, I find this a more sweet life, thus in mercy to be afflicted by the Lord, where I receive other spiritual consolations, than to lead that life I have done in court, where, besides that I receive the causes of mine outward diseases and sicknesses, my mind is also most grievously wounded, with the view I am there constrained to have of all enormities, where sin reigneth in the highest degree.'[68]

★

By November 1583, Anthony was in Bordeaux, staying 'chez sire Grimalde, aupres le eglise de St. Pierre'.[69] Historically the capital of the English province of Guienne until the mid-fifteenth century, Bordeaux was now one of France's key cities, a major thoroughfare for the out-going trade – primarily wine – of south-west France. Anthony Bacon's position in the town is not clear. Although Bordeaux bordered on areas dominated by Protestant forces to the south and south-east, it was still a Catholic city, and boasted some League extremists among its inhabitants. Anthony's work was therefore now being carried out in dangerous waters.[70]

Effectively freed from exclusive links with Burghley, Anthony had built a new reputation for himself. This was firmly attested to by his winning over of the earl of Leicester, who only three years earlier had attacked Anthony's involvement with William Parry to try to damage Burghley's reputation. In November 1581, Anthony had assured Leicester from Geneva of his goodwill towards the earl.[71] Now there was a chance to serve him. Henri, duc de Montmorency, also known as d'Amville, was ostensibly a moderate Catholic, who had unexpected privy dealings with traditional enemies of Catholics. Now d'Amville wanted to contact Elizabeth and Leicester, so he gave two letters to Anthony Bacon, who also wrote to the earl and sent the letters for brother Francis to deliver, which he did on 7 October 1583.[72] Three days later, Leicester wrote to Anthony to acknowledge receipt 'by your brother Francis' and to report that the Queen was 'glad she may have so good a mean as you to send and receive letters by, and will write, to the duke again, if she may first understand that you shall still have occasion to be in place where her letters may safely both come to you and by you be delivered to the Duke'.[73]

Success with Leicester and the Queen was accompanied by trouble in Bordeaux. Anthony had planned to spend Christmas in Paris,[74] but was forced to winter in Bordeaux 'by a relapse into a quartain ague', as he put it. Anthony remained thus indisposed from August 1583 to February 1584 – indeed, so poor was his health by then that on 15 February a licence was granted him to eat meat during the weeks of Lent.[75] Writing home to one of his brothers three days earlier, he reported that he was better than he had been for a year previously, although there was still some indisposition, and his stomach remained weak.[76] In fact, news of medical ailments in Anthony's letters often signalled more complex problems. What had actually happened at Bordeaux in the intervening months, Anthony was later to confide, was that 'it appeareth by the malicious information of an old English massmonger called Wenden, penned and subscribed by two English Jesuits and presented to the Marechal Matignon against me, that my lodging was charged to be the receptacle of all rebellious Huguenots, my pen their intelligencer and director of their commotions, my personal presence and assistance at their assemblies and communions, no small countenance and encouragement unto them. In such sort as some of the court of *parlement* believing this information pronounced me worthy of the rack.'

Such a charge was extremely dangerous. Jacques de Goyon, comte de Matignon, was Henri III's lieutenant-general. His negotiations with the Protestant Navarre were tense enough to warrant the intervention of Bordeaux's then mayor, Michel de Montaigne.[77] To Anthony, however, Matignon seemed favourably disposed. 'The Marechal Matignon very honourably and kindly drew the matter into his hand and protected me in all quietness and safety: here I may not forget to refer myself to my honourable friend Mr. Edward Stafford who at the conference of la Fleche knoweth that my chief confident man was a French minister who had left late Sir Harry Cobham then Ambassador to follow my fortune.'[78]

News of this sort could not be kept secret. Faunt, who had not heard from Anthony since early April in Marseilles,[79] had despatched a barrage of increasingly angry letters, finding he could 'no longer abstain from telling you plainly, that the injury is great you do to yourself, and your best friends, in this your voluntary banishment (for so it is already termed) wherein you incur many inconveniences'.[80] Now, hearing disturbing news of Anthony's situation from a reliable source on the morning of 16 January 1584, Nicholas immediately wrote to his friend, warning him to leave Bordeaux as soon as possible.[81] In contrast, when the rumours got through to the Archbishop of Canterbury, Whitgift himself wrote to reassure Anthony that 'the reports made by those two companions are so notoriously untrue, that there needeth no confutation thereof. I am, I thank God, exercised with such like calumniators at home also, but I comfort myself in a good conscience.'[82] Anthony may not have been thrilled by the analogy.

Meanwhile, Hugh Mantell was relaying Lady Bacon's threat that 'she will from henceforth receive all your worship's revenues and convert the same to her proper use, until such time as her Ladyship shall be fully satisfied of all such money as she hath at any time, since your going over, disbursed for you.' In any case, she claimed that 'she is utterly unable to pay these great sums out of her Ladyship's so small a revenue.' These were not Mantell's own opinions, however, and he craved 'pardon of your worship for my over boldness in my rude writing to you'.[83]

And then, unaccountably, the mood at home changed. In the spring of 1584 Nicholas Faunt reported to Anthony that Walsingham and Burghley 'began to be somewhat satisfied with Mr. Bacon's longer stay abroad'.

Lady Bacon had also declared to Faunt – when they met, predictably enough, at one of Walter Travers' sermons – that she would not urge his return.[84] Anthony's time had not yet, it seemed, run out after all.

4

Strange Bedfellows:
Consorting with Catholics

Those that live single take it for a curse,
Or do things worse.
Francis Bacon, 'The World's a Bubble' (date unknown)

THE DECISION TO let Anthony Bacon stay in France in spring 1584 was taken at the very highest level – the instructions came from the Queen herself. Walsingham explained how he had shown Elizabeth a letter from Anthony, and how they had exchanged the usual pleasantries about Anthony's father and Anthony's health. The crux of the matter, however, was that Anthony, with his 'ripeness of judgment' could provide 'better intelligence in that corner than hath been received from any others in those parts; whereby it is seen that your credit is good with the evil affected of that nation remaining there.' Therefore, despite Anthony's plans to return to Paris, Walsingham urged him to stay and 'to continue your intelligence with the parties with whom it seemeth you can prevail', explicitly now – for the first time – on 'her Majesty's service'.[1]

Anthony's sudden importance was related to the new strategic significance of the 'corner' in which he now resided – Béarn, an ancient frontier province of south-west France, which at precisely that moment became the centre of French political activity. Alençon, the heir apparent to the French throne, was dying. Reports had it that King Henri's favourite, the duc d'Epernon, was travelling into Gascony to persuade Navarre to reconvert to Catholicism, in exchange for which the King would make him his heir.[2] Navarre's right-hand man Philippe Du Plessis-Mornay confirmed the rumours to Elizabeth's ambassador, Sir Edward Stafford. Stafford was concerned: 'Though the King of Navarre be taken of them to be very steadfast and constant, and his sister likewise, yet they be not without the knowledge that flesh is frail.' In a ciphered letter to Walsingham he urged the Queen to write to Navarre assuring him of English support, and strengthening his Protestant resolve.

In Stafford's opinion, if the Queen were to arrange for such letters to be carried secretly into France, a local agent could pass them to Navarre. Anthony Bacon was the obvious choice: 'Here is none properer for that purpose than Mr. Bacon [in cipher].' There were clear advantages to using Anthony Bacon: he was 'already in those quarters'; and he was free to undertake the job, 'being already with little charge or none, only of the sending of her Majesty's letters to him of direction'. That task could be undertaken via Stafford and 'a Frenchman I have here fit for that purpose that is well acquainted in these quarters'.[3] Anthony Bacon was about to become a crucial figure in Anglo-French clandestine politics.[4]

★

At home, Francis' brief taste of parliamentary life in early 1581 had whetted his appetite, and now he was becoming accustomed to voicing his opinions in public. In the run-up to selection for the next parliament Bacon finally gave up on his uncle. He rejected a seat Burghley had been instrumental in securing at Gatton, Surrey, and instead took a seat at Weymouth and Melcombe Regis, Dorset, sponsored by the earl of Bedford (to whom he was related via his aunt Elizabeth).[5]

This, Elizabeth's fifth parliament, commenced on 23 November 1584. Discussion of religion was ruled out by the Lord Chancellor. Instead, the speeches were dominated by talk of Spain and the Pope, of the dangers facing England, and of the need to protect the Queen against Jesuits and seminary priests. This time, Francis was an active member. Most of the parliamentary business was given to 'committees' (literally, 'those committed', the men appointed to what we would now term a 'committee'), who debated particular issues before reporting back to the whole House. Now Bacon was appointed to committee work, being named to a committee dealing with the redress of disorders in common informers,[6] and a legal question concerning the granting of *latitat* writs (which summoned a concealed defendant to answer in the King's Bench).[7] His real attention, however, was focused on the activities of his old tutor, John Whitgift, who had been appointed Archbishop of Canterbury in 1583. Whitgift's drive against religious Nonconformity in any guise was gaining pace. For Francis, on a personal level, this meant the end of hearing Walter Travers preach at the Temple. Whitgift suppressed and burned a new printing of Travers' *Explicatio*, intervened against him in elections for the Temple mastership in August 1584 (Elizabeth eventually chose a third party, Richard Hooker), and finally prohibited him from preaching in March 1586. Whitgift was abetted in his campaign by growing fears about rampant Catholicism, after no fewer than three plots against Elizabeth's life were discovered within twelve months, including in June 1584 the Throckmorton plot, which led to a breaking off of diplomatic relations with Spain; the following month, the news hit London that the Protestant William the Silent, Prince of Orange, had been assassinated by a fanatical Catholic.

The archbishop's current strategy, supported by the Queen, was to require all clergy to subscribe to fifteen Articles stipulating absolute submission to the discipline of the English church, or forfeit the right to preach. To the clerics patronised by Francis and his mother this was a desperate blow, and Lady Bacon petitioned her influential connections. High-level protest came from key Privy Counsellors, including Burghley and Leicester, and led to the unhelpful Lambeth Conference of December 1584, and eventually to a petition against the Articles from the Commons.

Lady Bacon was among those present in the Commons when Whitgift's unyielding response was read out on 25 February 1585, 'extraordinarily admitted' through the influence of her brother-in-law Burghley. Nicholas Faunt reported approvingly to Anthony his mother's staunch support of the Nonconformists: 'The Lord raise up such matrons for the comfort of his poor afflicted church, assuring you, Sir, that I have been a witness of her earnest care and travel for the restoring of some of them to their places, by resorting often unto this place [the court] to solicit those causes.' Court was not a place usually resorted to by Lady Bacon, who took no 'comfort or delight' there, 'except to see her Majesty and her ladyship's good friends'.[8]

Like many in the Lower House, Lady Bacon was incensed at Whitgift's response, but 'fearing to stay too long, I could not so plainly speak' to Burghley 'nor so well perceive your answer thereto as I would truly and gladly in that matter'. She therefore wrote to him at length the following day. 'The report of the late conference at Lambeth', she began, 'hath been so handled to the discrediting of those learned that labour for right reformation in the ministry of the Gospel, that it is no small grief of mind to the faithful preachers, because the matter is thus by the other side carried away as though their cause could not sufficiently be warranted by the Word of God.' Lady Bacon called for the preachers to be heard by Elizabeth herself, in preparation for which they required leave 'to assemble and to consult together purposely', which they have previously refrained from doing 'for avoiding suspicion of private conventicles'.

For her own part, she had heard the preachers 'in their public exercises as a chief duty commanded by God to widows', attending their sermons for the past seven or eight years (in fact, she had been a widow for six years) and, as 'one that hath found mercy', she had 'profited more in the inward feeling knowledge of God his holy will, though but in a small measure, by such sincere and sound opening of the Scriptures by an ordinary preaching' than 'by hearing odd sermons' at Paul's Cross for 'well nigh twenty year together'. Even if her suit could not be allowed, she urged Burghley to hear out two or three of the preachers, who would not 'come to dispute or argue to breed contention, which is the manner of the bishops' hearing'. She made it clear, however, that she was keen not to compromise either Burghley or herself: 'I am so much bound to your Lordship for your comfortable dealing towards me and mine. None is privy to this. And indeed, though I hear them, yet I see them very seldom.' Her intervention came too late to have any effect, but it serves as testimony to Lady Bacon's continued and active involvement in Puritan politics.[9]

It was during this parliament that Francis Bacon made his maiden speech in the House of Commons, on a bill concerning wards. Although only the name 'Bacon' is specified, and both Nathaniel and Edward also sat in this parliament, there are compelling reasons for believing this to be Francis Bacon's first recorded parliamentary speech. An anonymous journal records that on 25 March there was debated 'the bill of wards that none shall make lease above a hundred years'. The measure was designed to close a loophole in the feudal practice whereby the crown could claim financial restitution from any major landowner until he came of age (the practice known as wardship). This was effectively a system of irregularly imposed death duties; to avoid it, some landowners had taken to selling the land on long lease to a third party, who was not liable. The bill Francis stood up to defend retrospectively included lands held on long leases within the system of wardship. It was deeply unpopular.

After some passionate speeches against the bill, records our journalist, 'Bacon' spoke: 'Many rather mislike of jealousy and are timorous of that they conceive not. I will open plainly to you that this bill is harder in some point.' The journalist remarks tartly: 'If he had as substantially answered that as he confessed it plainly.' Bacon went on to speak 'of the Queen worthy to be respected, for his father had received by her ability to leave a fifth son, to live upon, but that is nothing to the matter'. The journalist retorts: 'Then you should have left it alone.' This tiny interchange between speaker and journalist encapsulates not only Francis' later epigrammatic style – John Neale recognised 'the authentic voice of the essayist' – but also his tendency to refer matters to his own life experience, thereby promoting himself – here as the fifth son. It also captures the annoyance that Francis Bacon was to engender in so many of his future audiences. The anonymous journal-keeper is not in the habit of commenting on what he records: clearly this interjection severely rattled him. A lengthy debate followed, with the bill being defeated: 75 for, 95 against. Francis Bacon's parliamentary career had started in earnest.[10]

On 12 March Sir Walter Mildmay had spoken out against excessively violent anti-recusant measures, on the grounds that this would 'give them cause to think that we had wholly secluded them from our society, not accounting them as natural-born Englishmen, and thereby drive a desperation into them'. Mildmay spoke for many who feared that Whitgift would enforce all the provisions of the 1559 religious settlement, at great cost to the liberty of those who were inclined towards the Puritan preachers. The Queen was bombarded by treatises and petitions pleading with her to curb Whitgift's measures, among them works by the Privy Council clerk Robert Beale, the mathematician Thomas Digges (now part of Leicester's household), and Francis Bacon. Bacon's discourse, his earliest extant work of any length, shows signs of being widely circulated, surviving in at least five manuscript copies.[11]

Bacon identifies the only dangers to the happiness of Elizabeth's estate as 'your strong factious subjects and your foreign enemies'. Domestically, the danger was posed by 'the Papists: strong I account them, because both in number they are (at the least) able to make a great army, and by their mutual confidence and intelligence may soon bring to pass an uniting; factious I call them, because they are discontented.' However, although Bacon agreed that Catholics 'must be discontented, yet I would not have them desperate: for among many desperate men, it is like some one will bring forth a desperate attempt.' The preferred method of opposing them was through judicious action at ground level: 'careful and diligent preachers in each parish' – the same men who Whitgift had claimed would 'bring the Church to an anarchy' – who, despite their 'over-squeamish and nice' opinions, did at least produce the desired result of 'the lessening and diminishing of the Papistical number'. As for Whitgift's spectre of Puritan anarchy – 'for those objections, what they would do they then gat a full and entire authority in the Church, methinks they are *inter remota et incerta mala* [remote and dubious evils]'. Overseas, Bacon advised attacks on the more vulnerable Spanish possessions, especially the Indies and the Low Countries, 'which would give themselves to you'. He also believed that English strength would derive from 'joining in good confederacy, or at least intelligence, with those that would willingly embrace the same' – specifically, and significantly, Catholic states, 'Florence, Ferrara, and especially Venice', who also 'fear and abhor the King of Spain's greatness'. Once again, it was intelligence from his brother's network on the continent that informed Francis Bacon's own policy documents.[12]

★

Francis Bacon continued to keep a steady eye on his own advancement. In August 1585 he reminded Walsingham of his 'poor suit' to the Queen for an official post, which to date had been unsuccessful, on account of his age. 'I think the objection of my years', he remarked caustically, 'will wear away with the length of my suit.' In the hope of seeing off competitors, he had approached a number of influential patrons, including the

Vice-Chamberlain, Sir Christopher Hatton, who 'promised me his further-ance'; with Walsingham's prompting (since Walsingham 'as I hear hath great interest in him'), Francis believed Hatton 'will be fast mine'. The delay, meanwhile, was hindering Francis from taking another 'course of prac-tice, which by the leave of God, if her Majesty like not of my suit, I must and will follow: not for any necessity of estate, but for my credit sake, which I know by living out of action will wear'. The alternative 'course of practice' may well have been the respectable if dull job of pleading in court, for which he would need to be promoted at Gray's Inn.[13]

Not only did Francis' suit for royal service remain unsuccessful, but soon a misunderstanding was causing him problems at Gray's Inn too. In May 1586 he approached his uncle to defuse a mischievous report which had come to Burghley's ears. Burghley, he wrote, was 'being hardly [unfairly] informed' of his nephew by 'men that did misaffect me', and who had cause 'to give colour to their own doings'. It appears that Francis was trying to accelerate his promotion to full bench status (which would allow him to plead lucrative cases). Burghley, recalling the 'favour' the Queen had earlier granted Bacon, which allowed him lighter than custom-ary legal duties, assumed that this was the cause of the problem. In fact Francis was simply seeking 'an ease in coming within Bars' – accelerated promotion without 'any extraordinary and singular note of favour'. Having been made an utter-barrister in June 1583, he should by rights have been in 'exercise of learning' another five years before being raised to the bench, and therefore permitted to plead at the courts.

It was the general rule that those raised to the bench were 'such as have before time openly read'. A reading provided the aspiring lawyer with the opportunity to demonstrate his legal expertise and rhetorical prowess by presenting the history and uses of a statute. Since there were only two readings each year and one of those (the Lent reading) was reserved for those who had already read and were benchers, technically only one reading (the August reading) was available, and therefore only one barrister a year per inn could be promoted to the bench. In practice, the rule was relaxed, and men were promoted before they had read. Sir Edward Coke, for example, was promoted to the bench of the Inner Temple in 1590, the same year that he received the recordership of Norwich; by contrast, Christopher Molineux was refused call for several years at Gray's Inn because the bench thought him 'not sufficiently learned in the laws', 'unfit to govern in the said house . . . by reason of his want of discretion', 'not sociable' and, perhaps most damningly, too poor to afford a reading.[14]

On the pension of 10 February 1586, however, it was recorded that 'Mr. Francis Bacon may have place with the Readers at the Readers' table but not to have any voice in pension nor to win anciety of any that is his ancient or shall read before him.' A marginal note indicates that this meant that Bacon had been 'Called to the Bench'. The modifying clauses specified that Francis would have no vote at the bench's meetings (the pensions), and that he would not jump the queue to becoming a Reader.

Bacon's elevation to the bench was evidently not effected without opposition. Aside from the Pension Book record, two further copies of the decision exist, which suggests that the information was circulated and discussed. The entry is copied into Burghley's papers, and followed by a note in Burghley's own impenetrable hand:

> specially admittance to be out of Commons sending for beer, victuals, wine.
> admitted of the Grand Company whereby he hath no Ancienty of 40 being but of three years' continuance.
> utter barrister upon three years' study.
> admitted to the high table where none are but readers.[15]

The note suggests that Burghley did eventually intervene to resolve a decade of his nephew's uncertain and controversial status at Gray's Inn.

Bacon conceded to Burghley that he was less likely to find his way blocked if he watched his behaviour. He would in future be

> more wary and circumspect in carriage of myself. Indeed I find in my simple observation that they which live as it were *in umbrâ* [secluded] and not in public or frequent action, how moderately and modestly soever they behave themselves, yet *laborant invidiâ* [labour under the envy of others]. I find also that such persons as are of nature bashful (as myself is), whereby they want that plausible familiarity which others have, are often mistaken for proud. But once I know well and I most humbly beseech your Lordship to believe, that arrogancy and overweening is so far from my nature, as if I think well of myself in anything it is in this that I am free from that vice. And I hope upon this your Lordship's speech I have entered into those considerations as my behaviour shall no more deliver me for other than I am.

He need not have worried, as it happened. Despite the clause that he was to have 'no voice of pension', Bacon started attending the pensions from 20 May 1586, missing only a handful over the next few years.[16]

★

Even in Bordeaux, Anthony kept in close contact with the court of Navarre. The correspondence route between him and his brother Francis was available to facilitate unofficial contacts between the courts of Elizabeth and Henri de Navarre at the highest levels, as a letter to Anthony from

Guillaume de Salluste, le sieur Du Bartas, illustrates. Du Bartas was a Gascon poet and soldier, whose devout Protestantism had led him to become a gentleman servant of Henri de Navarre, in whose service he had visited England. In April 1584 he had published the first part of his *Seconde semaine*, in which he paid tribute to Sir Nicholas Bacon, identifying him as one of the three 'firm pillars' of the English language, alongside Sir Thomas More and 'le Milor Cydné' (Philip Sidney).[17] The identification with Sir Philip Sidney was no praise from afar. Du Bartas used Sidney (who had links with the Navarre court through Du Plessis-Mornay, whose daughter was his godchild) as a means of reaching the Queen, and – through Anthony – used Francis Bacon for similar purposes. Du Bartas wrote to Anthony from Montauban on 12 September 1584, as he penned his retaliatory 'Advertisement' against readers critical of *La seconde semaine*.[18] 'I have asked Monsieur de Niort, minister at la Rochelle, to send to your brother and de Cydné [i.e. Francis Bacon and Philip Sidney] a letter I've written to the Queen . . . I thought that my letters would be more reliably delivered by yourselves, and furthermore that I should consult you as to whether they were suitable to send to her Majesty.'[19]

A postscript to a letter to Walsingham confirms the extent to which Francis Bacon was implicated in his brother's activities at this time. Anthony enclosed in his despatch 'two late discourses which forasmuch as by reason of the bearer's haste I had no leisure to copy out fair, I have given order to my brother Francis to see it done there with all speed possible'.[20] Walsingham was not the only recipient, as Anthony signalled to Francis: 'I have sent you two discourses twice doubled, the copies written in gilt papers. I have promised by letter to my Lady Burghley requesting you to cause the like copies to be made there out of hand to present to my Lord of Bedford and Mr Secretary Walsingham.'

Anthony also sent to Francis 'two books of M. la Grange, the King of Navarre's historiographer, which he himself sends to you, to the end you may aforehead know him by his style, being determined to visit our universities upon whom a few lines will be well bestowed.' And, of course, there were money matters. Francis was admonished not to dissuade Hugh Mantell from agreeing 'to come over in all speed with this bearer or the first English merchant that cometh by land', to make arrangements to lease Michenbury, one of Anthony's Hertfordshire estates, and to sell off some overgrown woods – although for form's sake he offered Francis first refusal. He asked Francis to 'open before the bearer a little walnut desk and give him the papers therein contained, closed up and sealed, as also such jewels [as] be there taking his quittance [i.e. as payment for his services]. How I mean to employ them you shall understand hereafter and neither you nor any able to dislike, no more than the rest of mine expenses if you knew as well as myself as by God his grace on day you shall the occasions the times, places, manner and end of their spending.'[21]

By 28 October 1584, Anthony Bacon was resident in Montauban, a strategic location for his new work.[22] Montauban had effectively become a Calvinist republic in 1572, one of two capitals (with La Rochelle) of the Provinces-Unies du Midi, hosting the '*politiques*' assemblies seven times between 1573 and 1581. During the early 1580s it consolidated its position as a key Protestant stronghold. By the time the League army was in the Dordogne in 1585, work on its fortifications was a round-the-clock undertaking, under the governorship of Navarre's counsellor, Philippe Du Plessis-Mornay. The Catholic churches and the château were razed, and their bricks used to build new gates and bridges; the operation cost 4,670 livres, raised from the sale of church goods. This fortification programme may have provided security (the duc de Guyenne, leading one of the Catholic armies, refused to risk attacking Montauban) but, ironically, it provoked extreme hardship (through heavy taxation) and anxiety in the Montalbanais. House searches and arbitrary arrests were commonplace. Du Plessis-Mornay lamented, 'there is no town in France where there is more disorder.'[23]

Anthony was embraced by Navarre's counsellors – he later recounted that 'at my first coming to Montauban there be witnesses enough how confidently the king's then chief counsellors as Grattens, Chancellor Clervau, Segur, Du Plessis, superintendents, Du Pin, chief Secretary did use me, vouchsafing to sit diverse times in Council in my chamber.'[24] Anthony's unusually favoured position (for him) did not, however, last for long. In 1584 Du Plessis-Mornay's wife, Charlotte Arbaleste, fell into a dispute with Michel Bérault, the minister of the Montauban church, over the application of sumptuary rules, more particularly, over the wigs, hairnets and strategic wire hair-supports she favoured. Locally, these were seen as ungodly items of vanity; the Du Plessis-Mornay household was soon refused tokens for communion, and a deputation was sent from the local senate to inform Mme Du Plessis-Mornay that she had to discard her false hair. Gossip spread that she and her husband had been excommunicated, and when Du Plessis-Mornay appeared at the King's levée on Saturday morning, his presence aroused great hilarity. In the row that followed, Anthony's support for Mme Du Plessis-Mornay was sought. Instead he made a point of telling Bérault that he supported the minister's decree.[25] Anthony had made himself a dangerous enemy.

Anthony's intentions in remaining in Montauban were not understood on the other side of the Channel. On 28 March 1585, Nicholas Faunt wrote to warn him that the mood in England was changing. Some were criticising him for his intention not to return; some were detecting too much of the 'Italian vein' in his writings. Worse still, these letters had become public knowledge, wrote Faunt, because a person to whom Anthony had written personal, confidential letters (including some which expressed his dislike of travel in the southern parts of the continent) had made them common table-talk by reading them at gatherings of his friends.[26]

Anthony had no doubt who the guilty party was. 'Truly brother,' he wrote angrily to Francis, 'it was no less troublesome than strange unto me to hear that he had so far abused your trust and familiarity as to make a plainsong of some of my letters to you to descant upon in bed and at board according to his quipping and fantastical humour.' If Francis had difficulty remembering the occasion, Anthony would help him out. 'To the end you may the better call to my mind when and where communicated unto him, the subject of his quips was the Italian proverbs which sometimes I interlace in my letters.' 'He', the guilty party, was Francis' young companion Mr Philippes, from whom he was inseparable – at board and in bed. While to Francis Philippes was a friend, to Anthony he was 'a busy body and starching head to me both unkind and unthankful'. It was Philippes who had been casting doubt on the true motives for Anthony's lengthy stay abroad. 'If he have a mind to sift and ferret any further the reason of my long abode here,' raged Anthony, 'let him obtain a commission of enquiry and come hither in post to see the cause thereof.'[27]

The culprit was the younger son of Francis' friend at the Customs House, William Philippes. In October 1586, when he was recommended by his father to the service of the new Principal Secretary, William Davison, the young Philippes was described as 'a son of mine who hath been brought up with Mr. Francis Bacon these two or three years', a man who 'besides his understanding for his time' was 'honest, virtuous and true.' Thomas Phelippes also recommended his younger brother to Davison:

> He hath the Latin tongue perfectly both to write and speak, understandeth the Italian and speaketh it somewhat, writeth a convenient speedy hand meet for dispatch of such warrants and ordinary letters as shall pass from your Honour. But being of a staid and secret nature, good judgement for his bringing up and studious will in short be as well able to serve your Honour's turn as any unexperienced man you can choose. Mr. Francis Bacon can yield some testimony of his honest discreet behaviour for some time he hath remained with him. He is but about twenty years of age and therefore the fitter for that continual attendance upon your ordinary dispatches which I wish him to be employed in to wait for bettering of his estate which in the meanwhile shall not be burdensome to your honour anyway.[28]

Four years younger than Francis, Philippes seems to have been introduced into his service to provide some support, possibly as an informal secretary.

It may be that the attraction between Bacon and the Philippes family was that William Philippes senior, with his customs post, was a source of ready cash for Francis Bacon, who, in return, provided an entrée into certain areas of society otherwise denied to him, and a smart start in life for his younger son. Certainly when William approached Burghley, asking for a suit to be granted to one of his sons, he lured the Lord Treasurer with the promise that 'if your Lordship will be so good Lord unto us as to grant the same I will most humbly present you with the discharge of the moity of the debt due to me by your lordship at this present.'[29]

But however much others might applaud the honesty and discretion of the younger Philippes, to Anthony he was dangerously free in his speech. 'I remember I have said heretofore and say once again under Mr Philippes' correction, that it is not two thousand crowns' matter that shall cast me behindhand.' He suspected that both Philippes and his father were capable of selling confidential information to anyone for a large enough sum.

Although Anthony had now been explicitly instructed to stay put, he could not reassure his family that his position had been regularised. He assumed that Walsingham would let his mother know. With the return of Navarre's man Segur from London, however, came news that this was not the case. Anthony complained bitterly to Walsingham that he found it 'no less strange than grievous unto me to understand by Monsieur Segur, that your honour and my mother likewise were ignorant of the occasion of mine abode here, and consequently begin to conceive otherwise thereof than by God his grace any one action of mine hitherto hath or ever shall deserve, not fearing the report of any whosoever be he countryman or stranger for being true it cannot turn to my prejudice, if otherwise more to his reproach than mine own blame.'[30]

There is no doubt that the secrecy of Anthony's mission was awkward for him. He explained to Julius Caesar that it was not out of simple incompetence that he was sending merely standard news reports home, 'being none of those that love to make a great matter of a little, or to write mine own conceits or common reports without ground'.[31] In the same package, however, Anthony was not only providing confidential 'advertisements' for Walsingham, but including 'such of the king's letters as I received in charge of Monsieur Du Pin by the king of Navarre's own commandments. Namely one to her Majesty, your honour, my Lord Chancellor, my Lord Treasurer, my Lord of Bedford, Leicester, Chamberlain, Sir Philip Sidney, Sir Francis Drake, Mr. Raleigh, Mr. Waad [the Privy Council clerk William Waad], all from the king.'

It would have been easier if he could have made public his role in Anglo-Navarrese relations, but he had to make do with hints. As he wrote to Francis, surely 'the present cause of my staying is manifest' – citing the occasion when Henri de Navarre, the prince de Condé and the vicomte de Turenne 'vouchsafed unto me that honour as to come and visit me'. Anthony was certainly on familiar terms with the Navarre court: 'They told me merrily that I would not return into England for fear of being married.'[32] He also assisted at (and recorded for the eyes of the English court) a carefully staged expression of the Navarre King's feelings towards Elizabeth – designed expressly to be reported home in intelligence reports.

Henri 'declared how much he was bound to her Majesty, which he would always be ready to acknowledge by any service he could do to her, or pleasure to any of her faithful servants'. To this, Segur replied 'in these terms, which, having continually in his mouth when mention is made of her Majesty, I thought good to set down as he spake them' (in French). Henri would only be doing his duty, and doing himself honour, in desiring to do Elizabeth service; for his own part, Segur continued, there was no king or queen in Christendom, whose good grace he would esteem so highly.

'Ah, my father,' replied Henry – 'for he honoureth him always with that name,' explained Anthony – 'if the queen of England could hear you talk, her Majesty would give you great thanks. But it is nothing new, because it's said that you have never been so happy as when you had occasion to praise her Majesty's counsel, her government, the order and the obedience of her subjects: in sum, everything about her.'

Anthony even made suggestions on how Elizabeth's reply might be framed, taking note of the exchange reported, and sending it by the same bearer. Henri, he suggested, 'doth look perhaps to receive her Majesty's answer by the same way', citing the fact that the King had honoured Anthony's messenger, William Fenner, 'with the state of one of his gentlemen ordinary'.[33] As he told Francis, it was this that sealed his approval by Henri: 'It pleased the king . . . to accept this gentleman into his service and to commit to my charge and his delivery letters of his to her Majesty, and the chief of her Council.'[34] As for Henri's favours towards Anthony himself, 'I am not so overweening, and unadvised as to attribute them to any other occasion than to the merit of her Majesty's perfections which are so infinite and shine so far, as I the least of her Majesty's humble servants and subjects and furthest removed am partaker of the beams, though unworthy of such an honour: which I thought it my part to advertise being assured that if your Honour think good and vouchsafe to make some particular mention of me with some word of thanks in my behalf, the King will judge them so much the better bestowed.'[35]

William Fenner arrived in England in Easter week, and promptly set about delivering Navarre's and Anthony's letters to the court at Greenwich.

He reported to Anthony 'the speeches the queen's Majesty used to me of the King my Master, also what her Majesty said of your letter'. He spoke to Hugh Mantell, and entreated him to go to Anthony, 'offering him to see him well shipped, and to bring his going, whereunto he was very willing, and would have come', if Lady Bacon had not objected. Mantell himself reported to Anthony that even if he had insisted on going to France, Lady Bacon had made it clear that she would restrain him through the Queen and the Privy Council.[36] Meeting on separate occasions with Burghley, Lady Bacon and Francis, Fenner found himself having to field some difficult questions about his master's activities. He also reported the urgent news of how Lady Bacon had successfully petitioned the Queen, 'with importunate show', to send someone over to bring Anthony back – and 'how her Majesty had granted and how there was one appointed to come for you'.[37]

The warning got lost. Fenner sent his letter to Bacon on Easter Monday, but the entire despatch had to be repeated on 22 July, when it became clear that it had gone astray en route.[38] In the meantime the mood in Montauban was worsening. During July 1585, the French King was forced to treat with the Catholic League, and signed the Treaty of Nemours. In effect, the crown was now subscribed to the Catholic League, and the Protestant Navarre barred from succession to the French throne. Inevitably, conditions for the Huguenots worsened. Protestant worship was forbidden; their ministers were outlawed and ordered to leave the country, or to convert. Anthony recorded that the town consuls had been warned that the French King was about to use force to 'restrain the use of religion in his realm'. Navarre had written to advise the consuls to hasten the harvest and complete the fortifications, 'wherein daily all kind of folks without exception of degree, sex or age, do most willingly by quarters employ their best endeavour'.[39] Financially, Anthony was suffering from the new unwillingness of merchants to exchange foreign capital because of the dangers posed by pirates and the exorbitant exchange rate.[40] By July 1585, he had received no answer to the four-month-old Fenner despatch, nor to a more recent one sent with Champernon. Another Englishman, Thomas Lawson, was therefore despatched.[41]

As 1586 dawned, Montauban saw the imposition of new taxes on grain, meat, oil, salt and candles, which lasted until 1589. Navarre's troops were overflowing the lodgings and taking much-needed food, and suspected of bringing in the plague. The breakdown in communcations hit hard at the Montauban trade in plums, wine, brandy and fabrics. In January, one of Anthony's servants (probably Edward Selwin) was sent 'in great haste' to London 'for his provision of money and other entrusted with a packet of letters to him, and other necessary business'. His friends took advantage of this bearer to send several letters to Anthony, expecting the courier to return to his master in April. Instead, reported one courtier, 'he was a long time after found to have loitered here haunting very bad company and having most lewdly consumed such money as he had to furnish his journey by way of Paris, so that being lately apprehended he remaineth presently committed to prison.' As a result, 'through this lewd part of his servant', Anthony 'received very great hindrance both in his estate and touching his more speedy return hither'.

Lady Bacon's suspicions as to what her son was up to were exacerbated when she was 'was so greatly disappointed of the extraordinary trust she reposed in this bad fellow'. In June, a concerned party appealed to the ambassador in Paris, Sir Edward Stafford, 'to devise some means for [Anthony's] speedy getting forth of the dangers wherein he now remaineth', by procuring a safe conduct from the King, or providing the money for Anthony to travel to Paris.[42] At the same time, Du Pin told Burghley that he feared that if he did not recall his nephew 'Monsieur de Bacons', and provide him with a change of air, his health would continue to deteriorate. 'He is still at Montauban, and cannot recover his strength. God has favoured him greatly, above all he has virtue and piety, and deserves his lordship's care for his preservation.'[43] These pleas seem to have been heeded: passports dated July and August show that one Peter Brown was despatched by the Queen 'to find Mr. Bacon', travelling 'upon the affairs of Mr. Bacon'; on 7 September, Anthony, 'who is going to England, with his men, servants, arms and horses', was provided with a 'pass from the king'. But still Anthony Bacon did not go to England.[44]

England's was not the only call Anthony was ignoring. Henri de Navarre wrote to him on 17 July 1586, to berate him for failing to respond to his last two letters and to express his regret that 'such a weak excuse' as ill health had kept Anthony from joining him on his travels. He would have been most welcome, Henri insisted, 'particularly since I love the Queen, your sovereign, your family and friends, and your house. I hear that you have been sent for to return. I very much want to see you, before you go to England, to speak of several matters which have arisen recently. Rest assured that I will do all within my power for you because of my friendship towards you. Your affectionate and assured friend, Henri.'[45]

The new and deafening silence from Montauban in 1586 was not only cause for concern and speculation for Anthony's friends and family at the time, but remained so for historians for the next four centuries. Something was apparently going on, above and beyond the 'secret mission' which was the ostensible reason for Anthony's continued residence outside England. Then, in 1974, a team of researchers uncovered in the Archives Départementales of Tarn-et-Garonne a set of interrogations of Anthony's servants in which he and one of his pages were accused of sodomy.[46]

Sodomy was a capital crime in France, and the punishment was burning at the stake – a sentence carried out in other contemporary cases such as those of a teacher at the Collège du Cardinal Lemoine and a Dijon *prêtre-musicien*.[47] It appears that Anthony was charged in the summer of 1586, although the original accusation cannot be found. It further appears that informal testimony was taken in August 1586 – at the time when passports were being issued for his return to England – but again there is no written record. The interrogations of three servants that do exist are dated to 16 and 17 November 1587 – over a full year after the original charge. The original testimony of two of Bacon's servants (the la Fontaines, father and son) was given before Claude de la Grange, Navarre's court historian; there is no indication that anybody else was present. A third boy-servant, David Brysson, was questioned by de la Grange in the study of Monsieur Constans, minister of Montauban (possibly consul Jacques de Constans, Navarre's chamberlain, or his brother, the pastor Léonard Constans), with Constans in attendance. When the testimonies were taken the following year, the full formal witnessing procedure was in operation: the interrogations were taken down by Montauban's royal notary, Antoine Vacquerie, and witnessed and signed (except in the case of Brysson, who was illiterate).

Paul de la Fontaine, who had been employed in Anthony's household for nine months, was examined (during the second, formal, questioning) on the afternoon of 16 November 1587. He testified that Anthony and his page Isaac Bougades were often locked away together during the day; that Anthony would kiss and fondle Bougades, and give him sweets, and money for tennis, cards and dice. Another Genevan servant of Bacon's, Michel Frutier, had told Paul that Bacon penetrated Bougades and that he had often discovered them in bed together during the day. Bougades, Paul claimed, excused their behaviour by saying that Anthony had told him that sodomy was not evil – indeed, that the Geneva minister Beza and Montauban's own minister Constans enjoyed it. Paul also told of how Bougades had penetrated another young servant, David (presumably David Brysson); he had heard this from both David and Paul's father Jean de la Fontaine (who had seen it happen). Although Jean protested to Anthony Bacon, nothing had been done to punish Isaac Bougades.[48]

The following morning, Jean de la Fontaine testified to de la Grange that when he urged Bacon to fire Bougades, whom he had found carnally violating young David, Bacon instead dismissed David from his house. He also quoted Michel Frutier's derogatory remarks about Bacon such as 'You can count on it [or a similar phrase], Mr. de la Fontaine, he's a bugger.' He reported that Anthony and Bougades were shut away together every day and most nights, and that Anthony rewarded Bougades with sweets or ordered Jean to give him money to play tennis. Jean also quoted one of Anthony's ex-servants, Barthélémy Sore, who proclaimed he would rather die than work for Bacon again, 'especially because he's a bugger'.[49]

The final witness, David Brysson, was examined during the afternoon. After he had been working as Anthony's lackey for eighteen months, he was taken by Bougades into a gallery, where Bougades took off his pants and tried to penetrate him – but David, in agony, cried out, and Michel Frutier came to help him. Bougades smoothed over the incident by bribing David to silence with a black hat, in the Spanish style, and later (when Brysson had moved on) with a few farthings.[50]

Like most young men moving around the continent, Anthony's immediate environment was almost exclusively male. In cramped lodgings, master and servants were forced into conditions of great intimacy, and shared beds. The situation was simultaneously absolutely commonplace and frighteningly vulnerable to accusations of malpractice – especially sodomy. Perhaps all we can glean from these incomplete records is that somebody accused Anthony Bacon of sodomy – possibly disgruntled servants attempting to extort money, possibly political or religious opponents attempting to disgrace a rival. The notary Vacquerie ends his report by saying that this was all that de la Grange wanted to be copied down. This raises the question: what else was there that was *not* written down? Why were Bacon and Bougades not questioned, or, if they were, why were their testimonies not recorded?

One possibility is supplied by the Montauban historian Janine Garrisson, who points out that on 22 September 1586 consul Constans was warned that tracts calling the population to revolt against the civil and religious authorities had been affixed to the main crossroads and to the door of the temple. A war council was called, houses searched and guards reinforced; as part of this action, she writes, Anthony Bacon was imprisoned.[51]

Another clue might be the intriguing invocation of Beza, the cornerstone of Genevan Calvinistic morality, as an apologist for sodomy. Catholic critics had seized on poems published in Beza's *Juvenilia*, in which he expresses love for a young man named Audebert, to blacken his name: one quipped, 'Instead of your Audebert, now you have embraced Calvin, and so have substituted a spiritual male-whore for a carnal one; thus being still what you were – a sodomist.' In the Montauban case it seems more likely that Beza, perhaps with the local minister Léonard Constans (who had himself published a book in Geneva), is being singled out for his identifiably Calvinist religious affiliation, with which Anthony seems to be aligned.[52]

Despite the absence of any records for the 1586 allegations, it would seem that Anthony was not only charged but sentenced. On 23 September

1586 Henri de Navarre wrote from La Rochelle to M. de Scorbiac, his councillor at the Château de Verlhaguet in Montauban. He had heard 'that Monsieur Bacon is appealing to my Council against a sentence given against him by the Seneschal of Quercy at the bench in Montauban' and desired de Scorbiac 'to bring his right of appeal promptly before the judge and have it granted as expeditiously as possible'.

The reason for Henri's intervention was made perfectly plain:

> The merit of those to whom he belongs is great. We owe many obligations to the Queen, his sovereign; he is also himself strongly to be recommended. He will know how to repay us in kind for mercy shown to him, and we ourselves are told by God to have care for the strangers in our midst, to safeguard their rights, and to see they win justice, and furthermore in the situation in which we find ourselves at present it is as well to show leniency, nor is it reasonable to use all the formalities and harshness of French justice towards them. I am assured of your prudence, good judgement, and fairness in these matters and that you will bring reason to bear upon them. It is not my intention to say more on the subject.[53]

Keeping Elizabeth sweet was currently a top priority for Henri. During the summer of 1586 Navarre's representatives in London had been negotiating with Elizabeth for a loan of money which would enable him to hire German mercenaries. It was in September, when Henri wrote to de Scorbiac, that the Queen finally complied.[54]

In the meantime, Buzanval, Navarre's ambassador in London, apparently took possession of 1,500 écus for Anthony – and neglected to forward them. Henri attempted to remedy the situation, directing Du Plessis-Mornay

> to gratify him [Anthony] as much for his merit and in favour of her to whom he belongs whom I esteem greatly, as being of the English nation, to pray you to help him with some sum, while he waits to receive what the said Buzanval has for him in his hands. I don't think it will be for long, but it would please me greatly, if you could lend him some 300 or 400 escus. You can request Buzanval to return to you the money he has received for this purpose by some route (he has access to many). I am confident that you will carry this out, so I will say no more, except that I will be extremely relieved when Mr Bacon shall have had satisfaction in this matter.[55]

The money, however, had still not been paid over by 7 October, when Henri despatched passports needed by Anthony 'for his return to England.'[56] Henri himself wrote to Anthony on 17 November, expressing his distress at Buzanval's withholding the money; Du Plessis-Mornay had been instructed to provide Anthony with 'four or five hundred escus'. In a handwritten postscript, Henri added: 'Mr. Bacon, please rest assured of my constant friendship, from your entire and affectionate friend, Henri.'[57] At the end of the year, the money still undelivered ('instead of relieving you, they have troubled you'), Henri directed his cousin de Tuerre to pay it promptly – 'in your case, he bears such good affection towards you, that he will be very willing to do for you all that he can.'[58]

As if he were not labouring under difficulties enough, a new obstacle now put itself in Anthony's path. Nicholas Faunt could usually be relied upon to transfer money from England, but at the end of 1586 he began to encounter trouble in persuading Lady Bacon to part with funds. In her opinion, the money-changers' prices were exorbitant, and she was boycotting them. 'I am sorry', wrote Faunt, 'that my lady, your mother, cannot be moved to bear some extraordinary charge for the exchange in respect of the hard condition I fear you are in for want of money.' He felt guilty, thinking that if he had exercised the proper amount of influence with Lady Bacon, 'she would have been content, [and] the bills should have been with you there ere this.'[59]

As a consequence of these problems, from 1586 onwards Anthony Bacon's life in Montauban became mired in an endless cycle of borrowing, debt, court cases and communication problems with England. The legal battles involved an array of Montauban residents, including the minister Michel Bérault, the merchants Jean Fournier, Pierre France and Jean Codere, the historian Claude de la Grange and his servants Jean and Paul de la Fontaine.[60] The only real chance of extricating him from this mess lay in a large injection of cash, but his mother remained unwilling to supply it.[61] To observers, however, Anthony still seemed to be remaining in France deliberately. In August 1588 Du Plessis-Mornay wrote to Buzanval: 'I do not know what pleasure he takes from pleading his case in Montauban. We've pleaded with him to get himself out; and if he doesn't, then justice will take its course.'[62]

Through some outspoken remarks of his servant Thomas Lawson, Anthony soon lost the support of two of the key Navarre councillors, Du Plessis-Mornay and Du Pin, and was subsequently forced to make some new and controversial contacts. In his own words, 'being most injuriously deprived of mine own, and unprovided', he was 'enforced to embrace and entertain a friendly correspondence with the Bishop of Cahors', who happened to be the nephew of Maréchal Biron, who thought highly of Anthony. The bishop provided 'many kind offices, as letting pass and repass freely my messengers, and advancing me the sum of a thousand crowns' – but only in return for Anthony's supplying a letter of recommendation to Burghley on behalf of two Welsh Jesuits, Powell and Meredith, whom the Lord Treasurer had imprisoned at Westminster. Anthony acquiesced, believing this to be the only way to guarantee the safe conduct of his messenger Thomas Lawson ('who has been of great service to me and others'), who was about to deliver to Burghley 'certain advertisements very important for her Majesty's service, and dangerous for myself'. To Walsingham he wrote: 'Now that I am convalescent, I hope soon to be with you. I feel sure that by your help and that of the Lord Treasurer, the King [Henri III] will make no difficulty in granting me ample passports, for the ambassador wrote to me that he would do it when asked, and I know not why the King should be offended with me.'[63]

Notwithstanding Anthony's recommendations, however, Burghley threw Lawson into prison for ten months, 'giving way', as Anthony saw it later, 'to my mother's passionate importunity grounded upon false suggestions and surmises authorised by Du Plessis and his wife; and out of mere envy against the said Lawson's merit, and credit with me'.[64]

But Anthony did not yet know of Lawson's fate. After seven months had elapsed, he sent a follow-up messenger in the form of Captain Francis Allen, who had 'kindly offered to hazard his life for the relief of my great and pressing necessity, and to prevent the dangers by which I am threatened on all sides, if I should remain longer in this uncertainty, without being able to recover my means and the passport of the King [Henri III] to enable me to leave'. Given the 'strange and sudden change' in French affairs in the months since Lawson's departure, he wrote, Burghley could 'judge by the past what may be hoped for in the future, nothing less in fact than the depth of all misfortune and misery, unless God should display his mercy by softening the heart of the King, and presenting some unexpected opening to the Assembly of the States on either side for their extrication from the present chaos of confusion'. Anthony left it to Burghley's wisdom

> to consider whether certain noble events which have occurred since my last letter have not justified a part of my statement. Messieurs Du Plessis and Du Pin have at any rate got wind of it, and are both sweating into their doublets [*l'eschauffent fort en leurs pourpoints*] to find themselves by my advertisement known, as well on that side as on this, for other than they pretend to be – as being more careful and attentive to their own welfare than well affected to the public good or to the advantage of their master Henri, who, worthy and valiant prince that he is, conducts his affairs as God's guidance wills it, without the said two gentlemen being able to take much credit for their guidance and counsel (according to informed observers, with the exception of a few of their own followers).[65]

Finally, Lady Bacon was getting her own way. Lawson was imprisoned, and she persuaded Elizabeth to take action, by instructing Walsingham to ghost an ultimatum to Anthony.

> Sir. I am commanded by her Majesty to write unto you in her name that all delays and excuses set apart you do make your repair home hither with as much expedition as you can: for which purpose this bearer is expressly sent unto you with this dispatch as well to hasten your return from there as also to bring unto you the king's general passport from Sir Edward Stafford for your safe passage by the way: So as now I am straitly to charge you in her Majesty's name so to disport your affairs as that you may use no further protestation of time in your coming home, which the sooner you do, the better you shall both satisfy her Majesty and content all your friends who will be most joyful of your safe arrival here: And so nothing doubting but you will carefully accomplish the content of this letter I commend you heartily to the Almighty.[66]

Ultimatum or not, Anthony was still without the requisite funds to extricate himself from Montauban. Ambassador Stafford was unable to suggest any better route than the Bishop of Cahors, but advised Burghley that 'if her ladyship [Lady Bacon] decides upon it, she should do so at once, for God knows when the States will end or break up without ending. *Occasio est calva* [opportunity is bald and must be seized]: if lost, knows not when any such will be recovered.'[67]

To explain his situation, Anthony once again sent Captain Francis Allen, who reported back on his meeting with Burghley. The Lord Treasurer 'demanded the cause of your not coming home and said you spent like a prince being but a squire; yet for your spending and not coming home he would not condemn you before he heard you speak.' Having made this concession, however, Burghley did not flinch from a full-on assault on his wayward nephew: 'He said you must hereafter feed men with deeds and not words. He confessed you have virtues and mettle in you. He demanded the sum of your demand, and of your health.'

On Allen's request both Burghley and Francis, whom he also visited, gave him a letter supporting Lawson in an attempt to sway his mother. But when Allen paid his respects at Gorhambury, 'my Lady used me courteously until such time I began to move her for Mr. Lawson'; and as for the letters, 'she would not once vouchsafe to look upon and was fain to deliver them where I received them.' Lawson, however, was not the principal target of her wrath.

> Being so much transported with our abode there, she let not to say you are a traitor to God and your country. You have undone her, you seek her death, and when you have that you seek for you shall have but one

hundred pounds more than you have now. She is resolute to procure her majesty's letter for to force to you to return and when that shall be if her Majesty gave you your right or desert, she should clap you up in prison. She cannot abide to hear of you; as she saith; nor of the other especially, and told me plainly she should be the worse this month for my coming without you, and asked me why you could not have come from thence as well as myself. She saith you are hated of all the chiefest in that side and cursed of God in all your actions since Mr. Lawson's being with you.

My lady said she had rather you made wars with the King of Navarre than to have stayed so long idle in Montauban and with great earnestness also tears in her eyes, she wished that when she heard of Mr. Selwin's imprisonment you had been fairly buried provided you had died in the Lord. By my simple judgement she spoke it in her passion, and repented immediately her words.

Lady Bacon also let Anthony know that it was not in his power to sell any part of his living at Gorhambury; Allen feared that 'when it shall come to that extremity for any other parcel, she will seek by all means possible to withstand the sale by intercession to her Majesty.'

Having witnessed this display, Allen counselled a pragmatic approach.

I am sorry to write it considering his deserts and your love toward him, but the truth will be known at the best and better late than never; it is in vain to look for Mr. Lawson's return, for these are her Ladyship's own words – no no saith she, I have learned not to employ ill, to do good, and if there were no more men in England, and although you should never come home, he shall be hindered from coming to you. It is to be doubted if you mention him in your letters, as I know you will, he be not clapped in prison again and so thinking to do him favour and in showing your care of him, you shall do him harm.

In conclusion, 'It is as unpossible to persuade my Lady to send him, as myself to send you Paul's steeple.'

Poor Captain Allen could not put a foot right at Gorhambury. Lady Bacon 'seemed to be angry with me because I had brought this bearer Guilliaum from you, saying you had but one honest and trusty man and I had deboshed [debauched] him from you'. Allen promptly resolved to send him back, 'not more willingly, than he is willing to return'. Ultimately, though, Allen felt sorry for Lady Bacon.

When you have received your provision make your repair here lest you be a means to shorten her days, for she told me the grief of mind received daily by reason of your stay will be her end; [she] also saith her jewels be spent for you, and that she borrowed the last money of seven several persons. Thus much I must confess unto you for a conclusion that I have never seen nor never shall see a wise lady, an honourable woman, a mother more perplexed for her son's absence, than I have seen that honourable dame for yours: Therefore lay your hand on your heart look not for Mr. Lawson, here he hath as a man may say heaven and earth against him, and his return. If you think much of my plainness take heed you give me no authority another time; for I shall do the like.

In contrast, Allen confessed that he found Francis 'most tractable and most earnest if possible it may be done, to fulfil your demand: he hath used me with great humanity for the which I humbly pray you to give him thanks.' However, he dared not help Lawson, who was now 'in great necessity' because of Lady Bacon's displeasure.[68]

★

While Anthony languished, ill and debt-ridden, in Montauban, Francis was making slow but solid progress in his chosen career. In the parliament of late 1586, sitting for Taunton,[69] he was slightly more visible than in previous sessions. On 3 November, he spoke in favour of the execution of Mary Queen of Scots, now in the custody of his old friends Sir Amias Paulet and Thomas Phelippes, and on the following day was named to a committee appointed to draw up a petition for her execution. In the new year, he was appointed to a conference on the proposed subsidy – on which he spoke – and served on three other committees: one on a bill of attainder, one concerning learned ministry, and one dealing with the continuation of statutes.[70] Bacon was speaking in support of an official line in these matters; and the fact that, as a relatively junior member, he was allowed to speak at all on such important issues suggests that he was now attracting approving notice. He was also beginning to be included in high-level legal investigation and consultation. In September 1587, the Privy Council asked the advice of Attorney-General Popham, Solicitor-General Egerton and, more surprisingly, 'Mr. Francis Bacon, Esq.' on some examination reports of two Catholic prisoners.[71]

A few of Bacon's legal writings from this period survive, but it is difficult to glean much of an insight into his thinking from what were, after all, often little more than exercises. A 'discourse' on crown prerogatives and ownership in Law French, for example, merely rehearses 'a conventional, moderate position on the constitutional doctrine', relying on yearbook precedents and statutes.[72] Others were far from indicating the direction Bacon's later legal philosophy would take. An argument on the 1557 royal commission to establish the Bridewell Hospital, which controversially conferred the power to arrest and detain vagrants, concluded that a royal grant needed to be tested by the judicial and statutory law of the land; a quarter of a century later, however, Bacon was to argue precisely the opposite case in the *Jurisdiction of the Marches* case. We might conclude from this that Bacon fundamentally changed his mind. Alternatively, and more plausibly, we might decide that what we see in these discourses is an advocate at work, arguing whatever he is engaged to argue. A more truly Baconian note is struck in the Bridewell discourse's introductory discussion of possible sources of the law, with the germ, albeit undeveloped here, of 'maxims' of the law, 'the foundations of the Law, and the full and perfect conclusions of reason'.[73]

Whatever the content of Bacon's legal arguments, his technique and practice were receiving recognition and, finally, some reward. At the pension of 3 November 1587 it was announced that the planned Reader for the following Lent, John Brograve, Attorney-General for the Duchy of Lancaster, was respited until Lent of 1589; against the tradition that Lent Readers should already be on the bench and have read previously, Bacon – who at least was physically on the bench – was elected in his place. And so, in Lent 1588, after only nine years of actual residence, Francis Bacon became a Reader of Gray's Inn, delivering his chosen lecture on the statute Westminster 2nd, Chapter 5, concerning church advowsons ('the right that a man hath to prefer his friend or some fit person presentative or donative').[74]

Quite how Bacon engineered this promotion is unclear – as indeed it was for his contemporaries. Burghley may conceivably have used his influence with his *alma mater*, but it is possible that strings were pulled at an even higher level. During a moment of annoyance with Francis years later, the Queen pointed out to him that 'she never dealt so with any as with me . . . she hath pulled me over the bar . . . she hath used me in her greatest causes.' Did Elizabeth intervene in the workings of Gray's Inn to accelerate Bacon's promotion?

Bacon returned the favour to Gray's Inn by improving its fabric. In the November following Francis' Lent reading, the bench agreed that 'the whole buildings and several rooms . . . leased and demised' to Anthony and Francis should have their grant extended to fifty years, and that the brothers should have 'liberty and power to raise and erect new buildings as well over their aforesaid lodging as also over and above the library' within the next four years, on the proviso that 'the library be left of a convenient and proportionable height' and that 'there be given into the said library a little gallery now parcel of the lodging of the said Anthony and Francis and lying on the west side of the said library so that the same may have a thorough [through] light and be enlarged'. The buildings were also restricted to be assigned only to resident Readers. This arrangement was allegedly based on a previous 'grant made about nine years since to like effect', but oddly (as the Pension Book states) this grant was 'never entered', nor was it 'now extant'. Who benefited from this expansion? Clearly it consolidated the position of Francis as a Reader, but it also provided the woefully overcrowded Gray's Inn with more rooms.[75]

In 1625, when Bacon recapitulated his lifelong commitment to the grand project of rebuilding the edifice of human knowledge from its foundations, he claimed it was 'now forty years, as I remember, since I composed a juvenile work on this subject [natural philosophy] which, with great confidence and a magnificent title, I named *Temporis partus maximus* [*The Magnificent Birth of Opportunity*]'.[76] This would mean that while Bacon was embarking on his formal career as a lawyer, he also started out on his informal scientific career. The published and similarly titled *Temporis partus masculus* [*The Masculine Birth of Time*] can be dated by internal evidence to some time after 1602, but we should probably assume that the juvenile piece to which Bacon refers is an early version.[77]

The Masculine Birth of Time (as it is somewhat misleadingly known in the Bacon literature; a better translation would be *The Bold Birth of Opportunity*) is a short declamation attacking the shortcomings of philosophy and its practitioners, from Aristotle and Plato down to 'moderns' like Paracelsus, Peter Severinus and Cornelius Agrippa, who have built scientific theories on the basis of randomly observed occurrences among natural phenomena:

> A pig might print the letter A with its snout in the mud, but you would not on that account expect it to go on to compose a tragedy. That kind of truth which is deduced from scientific analogy is very different from a mere coincidence between experience and some baseless hypothesis. Genuine truth is uniform and self-reproducing. Lucky hits are contradictory and solitary. This holds good both for truth and works. If gunpowder had been discovered, not by good luck but by good guidance, it would not have stood alone but had been accompanied by a host of noble inventions of a kindred sort.[78]

The Masculine Birth of Time bears witness to Bacon's early ambition to devise a universal system of knowledge on a very grand scale, and to promote it with those who might provide appropriately lavish sponsorship for such a project. It is also a reminder that amid the hurly-burly of Bacon's public life, jostling for advancement in the crowded chambers and galleries of the Elizabethan court, he did not lose sight of his intellectual ambitions. The treatise shows that he was reading widely – both works by classical authors and prominent contemporary European thinkers. He had a good command of current scientific, theoretical and philosophical writing.

In the long run, Bacon's scientific system was firmly grounded in evidence, practical research and empirical experiment. At this early stage the two strands – theory and practice – remained separate.[79] There was, however, already one area of his life in which applied thought prevailed. The legal work in which he was engaged on a daily basis was strenuously applied. It derived from everyday practice observed at Gray's Inn or in the courts of Westminster. Bacon's writings on political and legal subjects were also strictly case-led – produced for particular occasions, at the behest of a client, with the advice tailored to a highly specific brief, in the client's interests.

The achievement of Baconian science was, in the end, to bridge the longstanding divide between scholarly system-building and artisan-led technology. His interest in such worldly, engaged endeavours was about to be expanded by the example and encouragement of a new and charismatic patron.

PART II

THE COURTSHIP OF FAVOUR

1588–1603

5

Design Dissembled:
Brotherly Love

All which endeavours and duties for the most part were
common to myself and my brother, though by design (as
between brethren) dissembled.
Francis Bacon to King James (1603)

T HROUGHOUT THEIR EARLY public lives, both Anthony and
Francis Bacon had cannily played their potential patrons against
each other – Burghley against Leicester against Walsingham – but
from none of them had they profited long-term, in the way they both
required and expected. Now there emerged a new figure, one who was
henceforth to be identified in the public's mind with Francis Bacon, and
one who was to be dependent – although with less public awareness – on
the skills and experience of Anthony Bacon.

Robert Devereux, the second earl of Essex, had been brought up as a
ward of Lord Burghley, while his widowed mother had married the earl
of Leicester. Throughout almost two years of campaigning under Leicester
in the Low Countries, the young earl had earned himself a glittering
reputation as a military captain. When Sir Philip Sidney – the darling of
the Elizabethan court – died from wounds received at Zutphen in 1586
he bequeathed 'to my beloved and much honoured lord, the earl of Essex,
my best sword' in a codicil to his will – a symbolic act of succession.[1]

As Essex rose, so the ageing Leicester declined. When Leicester left the
Low Countries in 1587 to return to Elizabeth's side, his power was much
diminished. Essex soon seemed to take over his old position at court,
succeeding him in December that year as Master of the Horse (the first
post given to Leicester by Elizabeth), an office which gave him the right
of personal attendance on the Queen. Four months later, Essex became a
Knight of the Garter. When Leicester died in September 1588, his followers
urged Essex to take up his mantle. As Sir Francis Hastings put it: 'Now,
my lord, is the time come wherein you should put this in practice, in that
He [God] hath taken from us that honorable worthy gentleman, whom
He used many times as a notable instrument for the good both of the

church and commonwealth; and if it may please God to put into your lordship's heart not only to succeed him but to overgo him in his care in this behalf you shall be most happy.'[2]

He was certainly an imposing and charismatic figure. Fynes Moryson describes the young earl as tall, comely, fair-skinned, ruddy-cheeked, black-eyed, with distinctive black hair – 'thin on the head, where he wore it short, except a lock under the left ear, which he nourished, and being woven up, hid it in his neck under his ruff. He only used the barber for his head; for the hair on his chin, cheeks, and throat, growing slowly, he used to cut with his scissors almost daily, keeping it so low that it could scarce be discerned, keeping also the hair on his upper lip somewhat short, suffering only that under his nether lip to grow at length and full.' His physical appearance was complemented by a sartorial elegance, displayed in his customary town and court attire of 'white or black taffetas or satins; he wore two, yea, sometimes three, pair of silk stockings, with black silk grogram cloak, guarded, and ruffs of comely depth and thickness; black beaver hat, with plain black band; a taffety quilted waistcoat in summer; a scarlet waistcoat, and sometimes both, in winter'.[3]

Francis Bacon did not wait for Leicester to die before openly showing his support for Essex, and relying on Essex's patronage. This is made clear by a letter from Bacon to Leicester dated 11 June 1588 – three months *before* the elder earl's death – in which Bacon asks Leicester to support Essex in Essex's bid to advance Bacon. This letter already represents Essex as the prime mover in promoting Bacon's cause:

> My very good Lord. I am to put your Lordship in mind of my long depending suit and to pray the continuance of your good favour whereof I have already had great and assured experience. My Lord of Essex is minded to move her Majesty therein again out of hand and to govern himself in it or deferring it as he shall find her Majesty inclined. Therefore I humbly pray your good Lordship to back and assist as you have hitherto done. So wishing your Lordship all happiness and myself occasion to do you service I most humbly take my leave.[4]

Francis' devotion to the earl was passionate. Identifying Essex as 'the fittest instrument to do good to the state', he 'applied myself to him in a manner which I think happeneth rarely amongst men; for I did not only labour carefully and industriously in that he set me about, whether it were matter of advice or otherwise; but neglecting the Queen's service, mine own fortune, and in a sort my vocation, I did nothing but devise and ruminate with myself to the best of my understanding, propositions and memorials of anything that might concern his Lordship's honour, fortune, or service.'[5]

Shortly after forming this new attachment, Francis Bacon started to gain the kind of official tasks to which he had not previously been assigned. In August 1588, for example, in the aftermath of the Armada, he was among nine men ordered to commission a survey of recusants in prison.[6] In December of that year, when a concerted effort was made to identify 'unnecessary or defective' statutes that might be repealed or reformed, Francis Bacon was among four Gray's Inn men called on to lend his expertise to the project, implying that he was now thought of as a proper legal adviser to the crown.[7]

Over the next few years, as Francis gradually became more visible in parliamentary, legal and political circles, it began to look as if his assiduous courtship of favour might at last bring him significant reward. On 29 October 1589, Burghley reminded himself in his notebook to make 'a grant of the office of the Clerk of the Counsel in the Star Chamber to Francis Bacon', a promise made good by a patent of 16 November.[8] This meant that Bacon gained the right to become (or to nominate) the next occupant of that office. The clerkship was a relatively senior post requiring legal expertise. Although the councillors and Chief Justices attended the Star Chamber on Wednesday and Friday mornings, it was the clerk who saw through the business of the other days of the week.[9] The post was also worth £1,600 per annum, giving Bacon a position (or at least the promise of a position) with which he could negotiate. As it turned out, however, he did not succeed to the post for another twenty years. In Francis' words, it was no more than 'another man's ground buttailing upon his house; which might mend his prospect but did not fill his barn'.[10]

Alongside his legal work, Francis continued to produce 'advice' literature, commenting on current issues. In the midst of a print debate that blew up in 1588 between Puritans and the church establishment (known as the 'Martin Marprelate' controversy, after the pseudonym of one of the debaters), Francis penned a treatise entitled 'An Advertisement Touching the Controversies of the Church of England'. Although it was not published in print at the time, fourteen extant manuscript copies testify to its wide circulation. In a marked departure from Francis' previous public allegiance to his mother's Nonconformity, the 'Advertisement' distances itself firmly from both the established church and the Nonconformists. Bacon does, however, object to the smear tactics that the church establishment was using to link the Puritans with more extreme cults such as 'Arrians, Donatists, Anabaptists, the Family of Love, and sundry other' who advocated 'the overthrow of all government'.[11] Such comparisons were deeply resented by many, including Bacon: 'They have ever sorted and coupled them with the Family of Love, whose heresies they have laboured to descry and confuse.'

Bacon's even-handed approach, however, left his work vulnerable to appropriation from both sides. While the church's Richard Bancroft could and did quote Bacon's tract to support his own argument, a 1591 reformist tract printed in Middleburg entitled *A petition directed to her most excellent majestie* – describing the author of 'Advert. To: the Church of England, not printed' as 'a learned man, and friend to the Bishops' – also cited the tract's ideas approvingly.[12] Francis Bacon's desire to tread the *via media* in his argument may simply have been due to his customary anxiety to offend no party who might ultimately be useful to him for preferment. At any rate, this was to be only the first of many occasions on which Bacon's eagerness to take a middle path led to his work's being available for both sides to cite in their support, while pleasing neither party particularly.

The wonderful political success of the Armada's defeat had its downside in the need for a new subsidy (more taxation). Parliament therefore met again in February 1589, Bacon sitting for Liverpool (a Walsingham-sponsored seat). When a double taxation was called for, members accepted it, but made it very clear that this should not be seen as a precedent: Francis Bacon was commissioned to draft a passage to that effect, which was forwarded for inclusion in the preamble to the bill to be drafted by the Queen's Learned Counsel.[13] In this parliament Francis Bacon became more emphatically and visibly a parliamentarian, sitting on other committees throughout the session.[14]

More momentous things were happening in France. Following the assassinations in December of the duc de Guise, head of the League, and his brother the Cardinal of Lorraine, and the (natural) death of the Queen Mother, Catherine de Medici, in January 1589, the path was cleared for Henri III and Henri de Navarre to meet. It was a new era, as Burghley noted: 'The world is marvellously changed, when we true Englishmen have cause, for our own quietness, to wish good success to a French king. At this time the French King's party, by the true subjects of his crown, both Catholic and Protestant, doth prosper in every place.'[15]

It was not to last: on 1 August Henri III was stabbed to death by a Dominican monk, bequeathing France to Navarre in his last breath. As Henri de Navarre was finally crowned King of France, Bacon, apparently at Whitgift's request and with the benefit of his brother's inside familiarity with the Navarre court, prepared a letter for Walsingham to send to the new administration. The letter, addressed to M. Critoy, was effectively a justification of Elizabeth's policies on religion to the new Navarre regime – especially 'the most recent assault on the Puritan movement, a sore point with the Huguenot leadership.[16] While assuring Critoy of Elizabeth's aversion to forcing conscience, 'Walsingham' lays out clearly an establishment line on the 'Marprelate' controversialists:

Now of late years, when there issued from them a colony of those that affirmed the consent of the magistrate was not to be attended; when, under pretence of a concession to avoid slanders and imputations, they combined themselves by classes and subscriptions; when they descended into that vile and base means of defacing the government of the church by ridiculous pasquils [lampoons]; when they began to make many subjects in doubt to take an oath, which is one of the fundamental parts of justice in this land and in all places; when they began both to vaunt of the strength and number of their partisans and followers, and to use comminations that their cause would prevail though with uproar and violence; then it appeared to be no more zeal, no more conscience, but mere faction and division; and therefore, though the state were compelled to hold somewhat a harder hand to restrain them than before, yet it was with as great moderation as the peace of the church and state could permit.

Parts of the letter to Critoy turn up again in Bacon's 1592 tract, his longest to date, 'Certain Observations made upon a libel published this present year, 1592', written in response to an English translation of the Jesuit Robert Parsons' anti-government invective *Responsio ad edictum Reginae Angliae*.[17]

None of these various voices of Francis Bacon – the voice of the Commons warning that a double subsidy was a one-off occurrence, the voice of the establishment warning that Puritan threats would not be tolerated, the voice of the government berating the Jesuit threat – can be heard as in any way authentically his own. Nor can they be taken as being his 'works' in any useful sense. These are tracts written to order, their content and arguments not in his control. It was because of this that Bacon was to dismiss all affairs of state as unsuitable for systematic treatment because they are 'conversant about a subject which of all others is most immersed in matter and hardliest reduced to axiom'.[18]

★

On 6 April 1590, Sir Francis Walsingham died. After personally subsidising much of Elizabeth's intelligence operation for years, he was by this time heavily in debt, and his burial was carried out in St Paul's at night, to prevent creditors from tearing open his coffin. The repercussions of this death, more than any other single event, coloured Anthony Bacon's continued presence in France.

Shortly afterwards Anthony left Montauban for the last time, and returned (with a detour eastwards via Lisle-sur-Tarn) to Bordeaux.[19] Still he refused to go home, despite acknowledging to Burghley in January

1591 that the fleet presently assembled was the best means he could have for his return to England. He claimed that he was stayed by matters concerning Her Majesty's service: attempting to extricate English merchants from a difficult and costly predicament in which they found themselves at Blaye, a key point on the Gironde, leading from the Bay of Biscay to Bordeaux.[20]

In Bordeaux, Anthony embarked on a new friendship with an experienced intelligencer and committed English Catholic, Anthony Standen. Born a Surrey gentleman, Standen had spent the last twenty-six years abroad, in the service of Lord Darnley and Mary Queen of Scots, and later in Spain, Flanders, Constantinople and Florence. During the 1580s he had been secretly reinstated in the English service by Walsingham – indeed, Standen claimed that from Lisbon he had given Sir Francis advance warning of the Armada, supplied under various aliases including 'Pompeio Pellegrini', 'Andree Sandal' and 'La Raye'.[21] However, Standen was still working for and receiving a 40 crown monthly pension from Philip of Spain.[22] Two days after arriving in Bordeaux in August 1590 to spy on the Spanish fleet which was preparing for action against Brittany, the authorities were alerted by a former French agent in Spain, Monsieur de Langley. They assumed he was a Spanish spy – which of course he was – and promptly imprisoned him. Attempts to elicit support from his Spanish paymasters proved unsuccessful, and Standen's gloom deepened in the spring when he learned of the death of his English protector Walsingham, which meant his £100 pension from the Queen was unlikely to be paid: 'This *beau printemps* maketh me envy those that possess liberty, my prison now being loathsome'.[23]

A ray of hope of rescue seemed to gleam when Anthony Bacon arrived in Bordeaux, but it was only when Anthony recovered his health that he was able to answer Standen's pleasure and set wheels in motion to attempt his release.[24] Standen won Anthony over immediately; Anthony set about petitioning for his freedom, supplying him with cash and providing him with a route to Burghley, who now took over some of Walsingham's intelligence network.[25] Appealing to Burghley's vanity, and providing a distinctly rose-tinged autobiography, Standen urged the Lord Treasurer to effect his release, and added a plea for better treatment of all Catholics living in English dominions.[26]

Anthony's involvement with an imprisoned English recusant exile could not long escape attention at home, and particularly not the attention of his mother, who was kept well apprised by English agents in Bordeaux (whom nonetheless she dismissed as 'these lewd apprentices'). Now she seriously questioned Anthony's faith, and decided that Standen would certainly influence him to go to Rome. Hearing these rumours, Standen assured Anthony that Lady Bacon's sources, the apprentices, had convinced the prison authorities that he and Anthony were plotting – hence the delay in Standen's release. If Anthony's friends in England could not give the lie to these rumours, they would both be destroyed. Anthony promptly wrote a letter to his mother, explaining the situation, and passed it to Standen for his approval. Standen was impressed: 'You have done exceedingly well to be plain and especially with a woman, which is a vessel so frail and variable as every wind wavereth, as you know. And although I well know my lady your mother to be one of the sufficientist without comparison of that sex, yet at the end of the career *il y a toujours de la femme*, with the perfectest of them all.' To others, however, Standen was less circumspect about the mother of his new ally: 'She hath forbidden all kind of speeches of him in her presence giving him out for illegitimate and not to be born of her body,' he confided to Edward Selwin, 'that she hath enjoined all English merchants, yea, and his own brother, not to administer any support or succour unto him in sin that she doth not acknowledge him any way to appertain unto her . . . When therefore I enter into consideration of that good lady, her education, nobility of her house, her learning and good nature whereof in times past I have been better acquainted, I cannot but muse at such a change.'[27]

Lady Bacon remained obdurate, too, in respect of the unfortunate Thomas Lawson. Realising that his mother would only listen to her beloved godly preachers, Anthony called on his early idol Thomas Cartwright to intervene on Lawson's behalf, despite the slight inconvenience that Cartwright was presently incarcerated in the Fleet prison. Cartwright was granted a ninety-minute interview with Lady Bacon during which he received a pardon for another servant, George (thanks to 'his profession of repentance & sorry for his misbehaviour before me'), and even came close to negotiating an interview between Lady Bacon, Anthony and Lawson, with himself as arbitrator. This success was fleeting. Within minutes, Lady Bacon had changed her mind: 'afterwards her aggrieved mind against him [Lawson], whereby she was so impatient of hearing him, that she could not without her heart think upon him, called that back again; adding, that as thus advised he should never have her consent.'

Lawson was doomed 'in regard of his suspected condition of religion, of his swearings, of his incontinence, which she had great cause to suspect, and in regard of all things going back with you since his coming unto you, which were before his coming very acceptable to her and to all your friends, more particularly in regard of your excessive expenses after his coming, and long abode in the country, she would never condescend that by her good will you should receive him.' Lady Bacon firmly instructed Cartwright not to let Anthony know that she had almost wavered, so that it might not give him 'any hope of lingering this suit for him [Lawson]'. Like Captain Francis Allen three years earlier, Cartwright could only advise Anthony 'either [to] give over that suit, that hath so small hope of being obtained; or else if it should so greatly concern you, you might think of some stronger and more able to stand to work it, than mine is.' As he signs off his account of the interview, Cartwright reveals that he has also been in contact with Francis Bacon, thanking Anthony 'for keeping open the door of your acquaintance unto me still, and to Mr Francis for so ready an opening of it unto his.'[28]

In Bordeaux, ugly rumours were circulating that Anthony Bacon deserved to be disgraced because of the evil demons which possessed him and because of his (unspecified) vice.[29] Standen also warned that a Spanish plot was afoot to kidnap Anthony at sea, and then use him to force the release of Don Pedro de Valdés, an Armada officer imprisoned in England.[30] Standen was informed by an agent named Bringborne that Bordeaux rumour had it that Anthony was prejudicing the Spanish government against an Englishman in prison in Fontarabia, implying that Anthony was maintaining contact and influence with Spain. Standen defended his new friend, protesting that he would 'do nothing in this or any other matter without your consent as a cavalier'; Anthony was one 'whom to I am bound by liege duty'; his debt to Anthony was 'sufficient to chain me'; 'nothing [was] of too high a price for you'.[31] Anthony urged his brother not to credit 'such surmises or suspicions as malice, envy or so longe absence may have occasioned', explaining that 'it hath pleased God, partly by the troubles and indispositions of the time, partly by my bodily sickness, to arrest me perforce far longer than I meant' in 'this desolate country'.[32]

On 12 October 1591, after fourteen months of incarceration, Anthony Standen was finally released from Bordeaux prison, strings having been pulled by the Queen and Burghley. In the six-week delay while his passport was procured, Anthony Bacon took advantage of his skills in writing and deciphering, and used him as an amanuensis. It was Standen who persuaded Anthony to enter into correspondence with another Catholic intelligencer, Anthony Rolston.[33] He also negotiated with Lussan, the instigator of the merchants' controversy in Blaye. In the course of their discussions, Lussan relayed to Standen some 'dishonest and undecent speeches' made against Anthony, by none other than Bringborne. Bringborne had said to him: 'I don't know Bacon at all, nor do I know who he is. But believe me, if he is meddling in this kind of business he will certainly not be acknowledged by the counsellors, nor by the merchant community.'[34] Unsurprisingly, then, Francis asked a friend to 'take no knowledge at all' of 'intelligence standing in Spain of my brother'.[35]

Standen was also of use following an incident in which two of Anthony's servants were 'suddenly assailed and like to have been slain without the gate in the face of the corps de garde by a mutinous rout of haughty lewd youths, brokers' sons of this town'. The 'ringleaders and chief executors' of the riot – 'one Battelier son to the host of Ridley and late Peacock and one del Boq younger brother to the son-in-law of la Brosse an old broker now in England pursuing a suit against Cardinal' – 'with their complices treacherously and cowardly under favour of the corps de garde set upon William the Frenchman and Edward Yeats and wounded them both – namely the said Edward in stooping down to take up his hat which the crowd had cast down with a blow of a dagger on the bare head whereof he is in peril the skull being cut and bones to be taken out'. With Anthony once again housebound by illness, Standen solicited the Maréchal daily on his behalf: Anthony cited the incident to Burghley as 'an important occasion' in which Standen 'might make known the respect and good affection he protested to bear towards your Lordship and those which appertain to you'.[36]

More importantly, Standen appointed himself as an intermediary between Anthony and his family. He wrote to Francis, speaking of Anthony's reverence for his mother, and of his concern about the anger his family, and particularly Lady Bacon, felt towards him: 'I hope her motherly affection and wisdom will hereafter be yielded so pliable to that is just and reasonable as he shall have subject to sail homeward with a joyful spirit which as yet hangeth in suspense until he hear some good tidings from her ladyship, to which purpose arriving here yesterday three far well-appointed ships of our land, he said to me to regret deeply their departure without him. Imputing his lady mother and brother that through their defect he could not be in a readiness to voyage home with them.'[37]

At the end of November, Standen received his passport, and set about smoothing his path homewards. He wrote to Burghley and to Francis, swearing his friendship and giving them intelligence; to Francis he pledged perpetual service. 'Here I nothing of which importeth me as much as the other, for as you know, Sir, a lamp giveth no light without oil, neither can a man feed on the air.'[38] The gambit paid off. Burghley replied with a set of instructions as to what he desired to know, urging Standen to write his dispatches in 'Catholic style' for added security.[39] And so Anthony Standen finally left Bordeaux on 1 December 1591, travelling via Turkey, Italy and Spain. Using Anthony's reputation, he procured a safe passage into Spain. Gleefully, he reported how the Englishmen at Sebibure took him to be a rich French merchant disguised as a soldier.

As Anthony Standen left France, for Spain, so did Anthony Bacon – after twelve years away – for England.[40]

★

Walsingham's death left others besides Anthony Standen and Anthony Bacon dangerously exposed. Suddenly, key intelligence-gatherers were available on an open market, and Francis Bacon began to secure more key players for Essex, most notably his old colleague in the Paulet embassy, the decipherer Thomas Phelippes. An undated letter shows a quite pragmatic attitude to Francis' new young friend and patron:

> Mr. Ph. I send you the copy of my letter to the Earl touching the matter between us proposed. You may perceive what expectation and conceit I thought good to imprint into my Lord both of yourself and of this particular service. And as that which is in general touching yourself I know you are very able to make good. So in this beginning of intelligence I pray spare no care to conduct the matter to sort to good effect. The more plainly and frankly you shall deal with my Lord not only in disclosing particulars but in giving him *caveats* and admonishing him of any error which in this action he may commit (such is his Lordship's nature) the better he will take it.[41]

The Phelippes–Bacon–Essex axis soon became a well-known and acknowledged route for the pursuance of advancement and social connections. When, in September 1591, Edward Somerset, earl of Worcester, wanted to meet Francis Bacon, his servant William Sterrell approached Phelippes, saying the earl was 'desirous to be acquainted with Mr. Francis Bacon by your means'.[42]

Along with Thomas Phelippes came his own network of intelligencers, including 'Robert Robinson' (an alias for Sterrell), who was indignant at being passed on to Mr Bacon for debriefing, instead of Phelippes, as he expected: 'I was sorry to think you should send me to another to be examined, the very conceit whereof so grieved me that I have no been in quiet sithence [since]. I went as you sent me word I should, but I could hardly make him understand me. I have not communicated unto him the chief point which concerns Fitzherbert and our old service, neither shall any man know it but yourself, for I find by Mr. Bacon that there is small secrecy used.' He was later told that both Bacon's man and Francis himself had lied when they said that Phelippes had ordered the switch. Unimpressed by Bacon's abilities, Robinson concluded: 'If it so happen that by reason of your business you please to refer me over to another, let it be to such a one as knows what is what.'[43]

It seems inconceivable that, as he drew in men such as Thomas Phelippes, Francis did not introduce Anthony Bacon into the Essex intelligence network. Francis later wrote (in his revisionist account of his relationship with Essex, the *Apology* [1604]) that 'when, not long after I entered into this course, my brother, master Anthony Bacon, came from beyond the seas, being a gentleman whose ability the world taketh knowledge of for matters of state specially foreign, I did likewise knit his service to be at my Lord's disposing.'[44] Anthony recalled how he warmed to 'his rare virtue and perfections and the interest he had worthily in my Sovereign's favour, together with his special noble kindness to my germane brother; whereby he was no less bound and in deep arrearages to the Earl, than I knew myself to be free and beforehand with my Lord Treasurer'. Faced with this choice between an established loyalty and a new connection, Anthony 'did extremely long to meet with some opportunity to make the honourable earl know, how much I honoured and esteemed his excellent gifts, and how earnestly I desired to deserve his good opinion and love, and to acknowledge thankfully my brother's debt'.

The 'opportunity' to which Anthony refers came with Standen's attempted return to England from Calais – where Burghley, despite Standen's pleas, had left him '*à l'abandon* without receiving any comfort or warrant'. It was then, according to Anthony, that 'I made no scruple to address myself to the worthy earl, and to present the gentleman unto him', and Essex properly rewarded Standen with a chain.[45] In fact, this incident took place in May 1593, by which time Anthony was already an integral part of the Essex machine. His account of the relationship, in other words, cannot be taken too literally: Anthony may indeed have been involved with Essex even *before* returning to England.

Essex already had two secretaries, the Oxford scholars Thomas Smith and Edward Reynolds, and would soon supplement them with three new recruits: Henry Wotton, William Temple and Henry Cuffe. These men were in the earl's employ: Anthony and Francis, by contrast, occupied a less well-defined position, usually being described merely as 'friends'. While Francis was involved in drafting position papers, Anthony provided Essex with a rapidly growing intelligence network. His surviving papers, lodged in Lambeth Palace Library, vividly demonstrate the huge amount of paperwork flooding in from strategically placed correspondents across Europe and in Scotland. The cross-Channel news-swapping into which Anthony and Francis had fallen in the 1580s was now formalised into a first-rate intelligence clearing-house, designed to support the ever-growing political power base of the earl of Essex.[46]

Another early Essex recruit, the Oxford scholar Henry Savile, had crossed paths with Anthony during their respective travels in the early 1580s; now, in 1591, 'A.B.' (sounding suspiciously like a Bacon brother) supplied a preface to Savile's translation of Essex's favourite classical author, Tacitus:

There is no treasure so much enriches the mind of man as learning; there is no learning so proper for the direction of the life of man as

History; there is no history (I speak only of profane) so well worth the reading as Tacitus. For learning acknowledgeth reason, by leaving industry to finish her unperfect work: for without learning the conceit is like a fruitful soil without tilling, the memory like a storehouse without wares, the will like a ship without a rudder. For history, since we are easlier [more easily] taught by example than by precept, what study can profit us so much, as that which gives us patterns either to follow or to fly, of the best and worst men of all estates, countries, and times that ever were? For Tacitus I may say without probability, that he hath written the most matter with best conceit in fewest words of any historiographer ancient or modern. But he is hard. *Difficilia quae pulchra*: the second reading over will please thee more than the first, and the third than the second. And if thy stomach be so tender as thou canst not digest Tacitus in his own style, thou are beholding [beholden] to Savile, who gives thee the same food, but with a pleasant and easy taste.

The only contemporary comment we have on this preface comes from Ben Jonson, who claimed that 'Essex wrote that epistle or preface before the translation of the last part of Tacitus, which is A.B.'[47] Essex, like many great patrons, was often popularly identified with works which were produced by his immediate circle of friends, followers and servants. Much critical ink has been spilt attempting to work out which of the works that the 1590s saw as belonging to Essex were in fact the work of Francis Bacon, or Anthony Bacon, or any number of other 'Essex men'. The point is that the complex procedures of commissioning, drafting, revising, editing and publishing in this sort of situation put the 'authorship' of any given piece of writing beyond recall. Anthony and Francis Bacon understood this implicitly. The work they carried out for the earl of Essex during the 1590s was, to all extents and purposes, his. There is as little 'authentic' Francis Bacon in his Essex-commissioned work as there is in his para-governmental tracts. What he did later make his own was a true understanding of how the intricacies of this system might be exploited to his own advantage.

*

By the early 1590s Francis Bacon's prospects were looking somewhat improved. He now had an expectation of long-term financial security in the form of the Star Chamber clerkship once it reverted to him. He was securely in the employ of the earl of Essex, enjoying his backing and the increased credit rating guaranteed by association with one so close to the Queen. His parliamentary career was beginning to take off, and all the signs were that his rhetorical skills and his ability to mount a cogent argument would take him far with government business.

Around this time Francis composed a performance piece for four speakers – possibly an entertainment at Gray's Inn, where he was by now a Reader – which offers a homage or tribute to the Queen in the form of a series of orations in praise of 'the worthiest virtue', 'the worthiest affection', 'the worthiest power' and 'the worthiest person'. These turn out to be 'fortitude', 'love', 'knowledge' and 'his Sovereign'. The device is entitled 'Of Tribute, or Giving What is Due'. A prince asks each of his three companions to 'do honour to that which he esteemeth most and can most worthily praise'. Each of them in turn speaks, and then they appeal to their prince to adjudicate between the relative strengths of the cases made. He in turn praises the Queen, in such elaborate terms that there is no question as to whom tribute is due.

As an extravagant compliment to Elizabeth this piece comes appropriately from one in the service of Essex. The earl himself specialised in theatrical appearances before the Queen on public occasions, particularly when his standing was low with his temperamental monarch and some theatrical gesture was required to regain her pleasure. Nicholas Faunt, no lover of devices or of court ceremonies, reported to Anthony Bacon in 1592 that the Queen's Accession Day (17 November) 'was more solemnized than ever, and that through my Lord Essex his device: who, contrary to all the Lords' expectation, came in the morning to the presence, and so to her Majesty's presence, in his collar of Esses [a chain of office], a thing so unwonted and unlooked for, and yet hereupon suddenly taken up and used with great liking and contentment of her Highness'.[48]

'Of Tribute' is a meticulously composed, stilted piece, whose central compliment to the Queen is to attribute to her statesmanlike responsibility for the satisfactory outcomes of a carefully itemised series of European political events between the 1570s and 1590. There is no doubt that the aspiring politician who wrote it was *au fait* with the international ramifications of recent alliances, treaties, battles and dynastic settlements, both inside England and in mainland Europe.

But Francis Bacon had aspirations that went beyond the brittle court world. Some time after his thirty-first birthday in late January 1592, Bacon made one of his regular pleas to his uncle Burghley for patronage. This particular letter, however, grips the reader: Bacon's ambitions were on a new and unprecedented scale. 'I wax now somewhat ancient,' he began, 'one and thirty years is a great deal of sand in the hour-glass'. His thoughts were turning away from workaday considerations:

I confess that I have as vast contemplative ends, as I have moderate civil ends: for I have taken all knowledge to be my province; and if I could purge it of two sorts of rovers, whereof the one with frivolous disputations, confutations, and verbosities, the other with blind experiments and auricular traditions and impostures, hath committed so many spoils, I hope I should bring in industrious observations, grounded conclusions, and profitable inventions and discoveries; the best state of my province.

Whether this was 'curiosity' or '(if one take it favourably) *philanthropia*', Bacon was not sure; but, as he prophesied correctly, it was 'so fixed in my mind as it cannot be removed'.[49]

★

Anthony Bacon's return to England occurred just as France was becoming a hot topic politically at court. In August 1591 Essex had led English troops to aid Henri IV in his siege of Rouen. The siege was not a success. The duke of Parma – an ally of Spain and the League – entered France to come to Rouen's aid. When further help from England was requested, Elizabeth – already forced to supply men to the Netherlands – refused outright. Essex was ordered home; relations between Elizabeth and Henri became difficult; Elizabeth's ambassador was required to tell Henri that Elizabeth felt that he was deliberately subjecting her troops to danger before his own.

Henri knew he had to salvage the situation, and sent Du Plessis-Mornay as a special emissary to Elizabeth. Over two weeks, the Queen berated Henri and Essex, agreed to supply thousands of troops and retracted her offer two hours later, decided that Essex was 'the least suitable of men' to be employed in battle, and sent Du Plessis-Mornay back to Henri empty-handed. Bad weather at Dover held him up for three weeks, but he landed at Dieppe on 4 February 1592. On the same day, after similar delays in the opposite direction, Anthony Bacon landed back in England, after twelve years abroad, to be met by an unlikely couple – the newly freed Thomas Lawson and Nicholas Faunt.

Landing on English shores was only half the battle: Anthony now had to negotiate a return to court life, and to the presence of the Queen. Advice from friends and relatives was forthcoming. His cousin Sir Edward Hoby offered to spend a night with Anthony at Croydon, in order 'to confer with you before your repair to the court', which he advised should be his first port of call in London.[50] A few nights later, at 'much upon the stroke of eleven' on 19 February, the Queen called Sir Edward to her and asked whether he had seen Anthony since his return. 'I told her highness that I had and that I found an infirm body of you, so a much more grieved mind to have had that unhappiness as through your own infirmity not to have been able to behold her, which your heart so much coveted to serve.' He added that she would find Anthony '*un home arete* [a proper man], much more staid and admired than other of us your kinsmen'. Elizabeth concluded that 'she was sorry you were in so evil plight, earnestly affirming how that you had been greatly and from good hand recommended unto her.' Whether the good hand belonged to uncle Burghley or Essex was not specified.[51]

Francis had, on Lady Bacon's instructions, 'carefully prepared' a lodging for his brother at Gray's Inn. There Anthony was greeted by a letter from his mother, conveyed via Nicholas Faunt. It started promisingly enough. 'The grace of God be daily multiplied in you, with mercy in Christ the lord. That you are returned now at length, I am right glad. God bless it to us both.' But in the next sentence, all the maternal fears and anger came to the fore. 'But when I heard withal that Lawson, who I foresuspected, stole hence unto you, & so belike hath wrought upon you again to your hurt to serve his own turn as heretofore, how welcome that could be to your long grieved mother judge you. I can hardly say whether your gout or his company was the worse tidings.

'Let not Lawson that fox be acquainted with my letters. I disdain both it & him. He commonly opened underminingly all letters sent to you from counsel or friends. I know it & you may too much if God open your eyes as I trust he will. Send it back to be sure by Mr. Faunt sealed, but he will pry & prattle.'

Instead of Lawson, she would have Anthony fraternise with the likes of Faunt. 'He is not only an honest gentleman in civil behaviour, but one that feareth God indeed, & as wise withal, having experience of our state, and is able to advise you both very wisely and friendly. For he loveth yourself, and needeth not yours, as others have & yet dissemble with you.'

Lady Bacon, writing as 'your Christian & natural mother', also gave him one piece of advice, 'one chiefest counsel': 'That above all worldly respects you carry yourself ever at your first coming as one that doth unfeignedly profess the true religion of Christ & hath the love of the truth now by long continuance fast settled in your heart & that with judgment, wisdom, and discretion, & are not afraid or ashamed to testify the same by hearing and delighting in those religious exercises of the sincerer sort, be they French or English. *In hoc noli adhibere fratrem tuum ad consilium aut exemplum. Sed plus dehinc* [In this, don't follow the advice or example of your brother. But more hereafter].' This newly found condemnation of Francis was reiterated in her postscript: 'I trust you with your servants use prayer twice in a day having been where reformation is. Omit it not for any. It will be your best credit to serve the Lord duly & reverently. & you will be observed at the first now. Your brother is too negligent herein.'

There were 'examples and ill encouragers too many in these days' for those who wavered, and especially – and here Lady Bacon slipped into her customary secret Greek – 'that Archbishop since he was councillor, is the destruction of our church, for he loves his own glory more than the glory of Christ.' Finally, she referred him to his status. 'Remember you have no father. And you have little enough, if not too little regarded your kind and no simple mother's wholesome advice from time to time.' Only God could be 'your merciful father able to heal both mind and body'.[52]

Throughout the next few months, Anthony's ill health kept him trapped at Gray's Inn, 'feeble, through tedious travail'[53] – he had to decline an invitation to the marriage of his niece at Redgrave[54]– and Lady Bacon herself was throughout much of the spring at Gorhambury, 'but *languescens* [languishing] but in good cheer and comfort, I thank God'.[55] Lady Bacon's letters to her son, all written in her inimitable rushed stream of consciousness, describe life at Gorhambury in detail – dealings with tenants, the state of the weather – and are occasionally accompanied by gifts of strawberries ('the uppermost strawberries are good to be eaten, and were more choicely gathered for that purpose, for you or your brother') or a dozen half pigeons. But the rural scene is intermittently shattered by a harsh return to her key issues – his health and his servants.

'I pray you be careful and keep good diet and order. It is here marvellous cold and sharp: too sharp yet for you, I think ... I would gladly you had well seen her Majesty; but be in some good state of health first, and regard it carefully for any.'[56] On 24 May, 'that you increase in amending I am glad. God continue it every way. When you cease of your prescribed diet, you had need, I think, to be very wary both of your sudden change of quantity and of season of your feeding; specially suppers late or full. Procure rest in convenient time. It helpeth much to digestion.'[57] On 29 May, 'I am glad and thank God of your amendment. But my man said he heard you rose at three of the clock. I thought that was not well. So suddenly from bedding much to rise so early; newly out of your diet. Extremities be hurtful to whole, more to the sickly. Be wise and godly too, and discern what is good and what not for your health.'[58] Francis later told of how Anthony 'chid his man (Prentice) for calling him no sooner. He said it was very early day. "Nay," said Mr. Bacon, "the rooks have been up these two hours." He replied, "The rooks were but new up: It was some sick rook, that could not sleep." '[59]

Francis, too, was a constant source of worry to his mother. 'I verily think your brother's weak stomach to digest hath been much caused and confirmed by untimely going to bed, and then musing *nescio quid* [about what I don't know] when he should sleep, and then in consequent by late rising and long lying in bed: whereby his men are made slothful and himself continueth sickly. But my sons haste not to hearken to their mother's good counsel in time to prevent.'[60] Both sons were too lax with their servants, she complained. 'Look well to your servants and to your own things.'[61] 'Be not overruled still by subtle and hurtful hangers-on.'[62] 'Let not your men drink wine this hot weather; nor your brother's neither, tell him.'[63] 'I would your brother's cook were like [Peter my cook] in Christian behaviour; and yet a young man and a merry.'[64]

Lady Bacon felt that Anthony, after his long absence, was simply not equipped to deal with the rigours and duplicities of court life. 'Believe not every one that speaks fair to you at your first coming. It is to serve their turn.'[65] 'I assure you I ask not nor know not where Lawson is, but this I counsel: be very wary that his very subtle and working head work not your cumber. You have been long absent, and by your sickliness cannot be your own agent, and so, wanting right judgment of our state, may be much deceived.' His intervention in Bordeaux on behalf of the merchants had been 'scantly well taken, and fell not out as you looked.' Other occasions had provoked 'envy and dislike . . . some doubting your soundness in religion, you were so great with some such great Papists then . . . Be not overcredulous nor too open. *Sub omni lapide latet anguis* [A snake lurks under every stone].'[66]

Anthony's generosity also got him into trouble. He soon became known (to his cousin Sir Thomas Posthumous Hoby, for example) as an easy touch for the loan of a horse or his coach.[67] Lady Bacon was not impressed. 'Touching your coach, it was not wisdom to have it seen or known at the Court: you shall be so much pressed to lend, and your man for gain so ready to agree, that the discommodity thereof will be as much as the commodity.' And again a few days later: 'I like not your lending your coach yet to any Lord or Lady. If you once begin, you shall hardly end . . . It was not well it was so soon sent into the Court, to make talk and at last be procured or misliked. Tell your brother I counsel you to send it no more. What had my Lady Sheriffess to borrow your coach?'[68]

In August 1592 Anthony suddenly moved to Gorhambury: a considerable operation, which threw his servants into 'a perplexity' – they even left behind Anthony's virginals. At the same time, Francis (according to Anthony's friend George Jenkyll), 'with the company of Mr. Dunch Mr. Cecil and Mr. Gosnold abandoned Gray's Inn and went post to Twickenham where he meaneth to continue for some few days, only upon a flying report spread through the town of the sickness. Mr. Francis sent to desire Mr. Doctor Andrewes [Lancelot Andrewes, the divine] to accompany him, but I heard his man say that he thought he could hardly go, by reason that he had not preached at St. Giles the Sunday before.'[69]

Francis' out-of-town retreat on this occasion, as on many others during the 1590s, was Twickenham Park, eighty-seven acres of rough pastures and two lodges beside the Thames on the borders of the parishes of Isleworth and Twickenham, across the river from the court at Richmond.[70] The tenancy of these lands had been in the Bacon family since 1574,[71] although Thomas Bushell later maintained that it was the earl of Essex who engineered Francis' personal tenancy from 1595, as a token of his appreciation, 'upon [Bacon's] presenting him with a secret curiosity of Nature, whereby to know the season of every hour of the year by a Philosophical Glass, placed (with a small proportion of water) in his chamber)'.[72] If so, it was deeply appropriate that Bacon used this retreat from public life as a place where he could think, write, and conduct experiments.

At eight miles from London, Twickenham was 'that wholesome pleasant lodge and finely designed garden', as Anthony described it to Francis;[73] to Francis himself it was a place where 'one day draweth on another, and I am well pleased in being here; for methinks solitariness collecteth the mind, as shutting the eyes doth the sight.'[74] Twickenham Park afforded a perfect site for his experimentation – it was later to boast England's first weeping willow. In a manuscript allegedly containing 'Instructions from the Lord Chancellor Bacon to his servant Thomas Bushell' (*c*.1618–21), which outlines a project of establishing a corporation for the exploration of deserted mineral works, Bacon urged: 'Let Twickenham Park, which I sold in my younger days, be purchased, if possible, for a residence for such deserving persons to study in, since I experimentally found the situation of that place much convenient for the trial of my philosophical conclusions, expressed in a paper sealed to the trust which I myself had put in practice, and settled the same by act of parliament, if the vicissitudes of fortune had not intervened and prevented me.' (There is no record that these plans were ever put into action.)

Now Francis wrote to Thomas Phelippes, to ask him to join the group. 'You may stay as long and as little as you will; the longer the better welcome. *Otia colligunt mentem* [Leisure restores the mind]. And indeed I would be the wiser by you in many things; for that I call to confer with a man of your fullness. In sadness, come as you are an honest man.'[75] A month later, Francis wrote to Phelippes again, in a letter that hints at Phelippes' work for Essex.

I congratulate your return, hoping that all is passed on your side. Your Mercury [messenger] is returned; whose return alarmed as upon some great matter, which I fear he will not satisfy. News of his coming came before his own letter, and to other than to his proper servant, which maketh me desirous to satisfy or to salve. My Lord hath required him to repair to me; which upon his Lordship's and mine own letters received I doubt not but he will with all speed perform; where I pray you to meet him if you may, that laying our heads together we may maintain his credit, satisfy my Lord's expectation, and procure some good service. I pray the rather spare not your travail, because I think the Queen is already party to the advertisement of his coming over, and in some suspect which you may not disclose to him.[76]

It is striking that in his own memoirs Francis Bacon nowhere recalls the country house, with its coterie of writers, thinkers and experimenters, as a significant part of his own development and the evolution of his Great Instauration. The years of intimacy with the earl of Essex were in the end too painful for him to wish to recall.

★

Anthony had his own reasons for keeping a low profile in the summer of 1592. From France had come an unpleasant reminder of his vulnerability. A servant of Peter Houghton's named John Blagge had written to Anthony from Bordeaux to warn him about his 'envious adversary Ridley', the Privy Council emissary stationed in Bordeaux.[77] Anthony had once befriended Raffe Ridley, taking care of him when he was ill; indeed, at one point, Anthony had requested Francis to recommend Ridley to Walsingham. Now, Blagge reported, just after Easter Ridley had 'taken occasion to fall out with me, and so hath abused me'. Ridley had left La Rochelle for England about a week earlier, and was now probably lodging at Houghton's house in Fenchurch Street, 'but I think he plays the *vespertilio* [bat], and walks the streets in the night.' 'I have heard your worship tell me what villainies he hath offered you in calling you "bastard", which he hath been told of, and hath denied it. But I will approve I have heard him call you "sodomite". And so have others besides, as one Robert Knap of Ipswich will affirm if he hath not forgotten it.'

Not only was Ridley openly calling Anthony a sodomite, according to Blagge; he also had hold of a letter from Anthony to Francis, intercepted in Bordeaux, 'which he minds to show the Council [Privy Council]', and in so doing 'thinks to prevail against your worship there'. Blagge, who had copied the letter for Ridley, recalled that it spoke of how Anthony had not received the friendship he expected from Du Pin, and had therefore had to sell his horses. Blagge forgets the name of the bearer, but remembers that Anthony had taken care of him while he was ill, and that in the letter, Anthony 'desired Mr. Francis Bacon to prefer him to Sir Francis Walsingham. In copying it Ridley told me I should find good stuff which when I had done I said that there was no such matter as he looked for, which made him to be jealous over me at that time. It spighted him to the guts that your bills were so honourably and speedily paid, he did say that you would not go for England this year, And that your bills would be protested.' Ridley was also planning to tell the Council of Anthony's involvement with alleged Catholics, including Thomas Lawson and one Illinshawe, and to blame Anthony for nearly causing his own and Peacock's death the previous year when they were pursued by his means. For this, Ridley believed that Anthony would receive 'wonderful insupportable blame at the council's hands.'[78]

Although there is no record that Raffe Ridley ever followed through with his threat, it was enough, when combined with the plague and the presence in London of Du Plessis-Mornay's close associate Benjamin Aubery Du Maurier,[79] to keep Anthony at Gorhambury with his mother. In November, they entertained the Gray's Inn wit Henry Gosnold (a guest of Francis' at Twickenham) who assured Anthony, on his return to court, that 'Mr. Francis Bacon is, *maulgre* [in spite of] the court, your kind brother, and mine especial friend. The joy he conceived at the report of my Lady's welfare, and the sorrow of mine undersong, concerning your weak estate, called the welcomeness of my news in dispute. He offers to accommodate you at Gray's Inn, the rather because you love low and warm.'[80]

Anthony's return to Gray's Inn was required partly by the gathering of a new parliament, which was called to raise a fresh subsidy. Both Anthony and Francis held seats for this parliament (Wallingford in Berkshire, and Middlesex respectively),[81] although Anthony's poor physical condition throughout December and January made his occupancy something of a technicality.[82] On 11 January Faunt wrote of 'the hope your brother and we have of your speedy repair to Gray's Inn. He is I see careful for your lodging, and of himself to me wished you the lower lodging here both for your ease in going up and down, and especially for that you know the bedchamber is larger and warmer than that above, wherein you must abide most.'[83] By now, in fact, Anthony's health had broken down completely. He needed ground-floor accommodation and was, to all intents and purposes, bedridden.

It was not until February, perhaps encouraged by Du Maurier's return into France, that Anthony finally returned to the Bacon rooms at Gray's Inn for a five-month stay, the beginning of which was dominated by parliamentary activity. Francis was increasingly active and vocal in this parliament. Urged on by Anthony, he opposed a severe bill against recusants, of which Anthony had written to Standen: 'The rigours contained in it were of many misliked, and namely of us brothers, who will do our best against them.'[84] He also spoke at length against a bill for the better expedition of justice in the Star Chamber – since he had the reversion of that court's clerkship, he wanted no diminution in its powers (or its power to attract ready cash).

It was a superb moment for Francis to move into top gear. Shortly after parliament met on 19 February 1593, Essex was sworn into the Privy Council.[85] It was an official consolidation of what had been a maverick power base. He was now in a prime position to be of benefit to the Bacon brothers. But within days, as he was to do so many times, Francis Bacon not only destroyed that benefit, but set his own career back by several years.

Bacon's mistake centred on the subsidy, which had become an increasingly sticky issue. During the first twenty-six years of Elizabeth's reign, only six subsidies had been granted, at intervals of usually four or five years. Recently, however, the situation had changed: as Anthony observed (in a letter to Standen), parliament had already granted three subsidies to the Queen in a space of four years, a level of funding higher than had ever previously been given to her or to her predecessors.[86] The deadline for paying the 1589 double subsidy had passed on 12 February – less than a week before the commencement of the present parliament – so the issue was still fresh in the minds of the Commons.

After government heavyweights Sir Robert Cecil, Sir John Wolley and Sir John Fortescue had outlined the increased threats to the crown, and the state of the Queen's finances, a motion was made for 'a select and grave Committee to consider of the dangers of the realm and of speedy supply and aid to her Majesty'. Francis Bacon spoke in favour of the motion (although the opening lines of his speech dealt – somewhat tangentially and against the Queen's express wishes – with the need to reform English law).[87] The committee recommended a repeat performance of the previous double subsidy, with the same condition that the present necessity should be stated in the bill as the motive for this extraordinary supply. The House assented unanimously, and appointed another committee to meet to draw up the articles and preamble.

The Lords, however, were impatient: on Thursday they demanded a conference, which took place that afternoon (with Francis in attendance). It proved to be a platform for Burghley to inform them that a double subsidy was not sufficient. He warned them that the Lords would not pass any act 'of less than three entire subsidies' and indeed would not assent even 'to a treble nor a quadruple, unless the same were the better qualified, both in substance and in circumstance of time', namely to be payable in the three next years at two payments per year.[88]

This conference was reported to the Commons in a highly charged session. Francis Bacon had sat on all the committees, and knew what the reporter (his cousin Sir Robert Cecil) was going to say. How was he to respond? As a member of the Commons, he felt he had to oppose the Lords' claim to participation in what was a Commons' prerogative. And yet the measure was put forward by his uncle, the man who was still, despite all his dilatoriness, his main patron. He rose. He yielded to the subsidy, he began, but

> misliked that this House should join with the Upper House in the granting of it. For the custom and privilege of this House hath always been first to make offer of the subsidy from hence unto the Upper House. And reason it is that we should stand upon our privilege. Seeing the burden resteth upon us as the greater number, no reason the thanks should be theirs. And in joining with them in this motion we shall derogate from ourselves; for the thanks will be theirs and the blame ours, they being the first movers. Wherefore I wish that in this action we should proceed, as heretofore we have done, apart by ourselves, and not joining with their Lordships. And to satisfy them, who expect an answer from us tomorrow, some answer would be made in all obsequious and dutiful manner.

Here he produced out of his bosom an answer he had himself framed to the effect that they had considered of their Lordships' motion, and thought upon it as was fit, and in all willingness would address themselves to do as so great a cause deserved. But to join with their Lordships in this business they could not but with prejudice to this House's privileges, wherefore they desired, as they were wont, that now they might proceed therein by themselves apart from their Lordships, ending: 'Thus, I think, we may divide ourselves from their Lordships, and yet without dissension; for this is but an honourable emulation and division.'[89]

The framing of the Commons' answer was left to a rather muddled committee, which eventually returned a majority decision in favour of a further conference with the Upper House. This provoked a passionate debate in the Commons, where Francis' fellow Middlesex member Robert Wroth spoke against the conference as 'prejudicial to the ancient liberties and privileges of the house, and to the authority of the same', and Privy Council clerk Robert Beale claimed a precedent to support Wroth from the reign of Henry IV. Despite Cecil's pleading for the conference on the pragmatic grounds that the Lords, some of whom were Privy Councillors, were in a better position to understand the strength of the enemy and the resources of the kingdom, it was resolved, by a majority of 217 to 128, 'That no such conference should be had.'

When parliament met again on the morning of Monday 5 March, it was clear that the government had had an active Sabbath. The motion that the Commons should submit their precedent was silently dropped. Opening the proceedings, Robert Beale said that he had misinterpreted the precedent he had produced previously. Two Privy Councillors, Sir Thomas Heneage and Sir John Wolley, immediately moved that Saturday's resolution be reversed, having been based on this mistaken premise.

The House was not convinced. Sir Henry Unton (a friend of Essex) moved that they should agree to 'confer with the Lords about a subsidy, but not in any sort to be confirmed therein unto them.' At this point Sir Robert Cecil lost his temper. He wondered what the last speaker could be thinking of; 'his motion was that they should confer with the Lords about a subsidy, but not conclude a subsidy with them; which motion seemed contrary to his meaning, or else it was more than ever was meant; for it was never desired of them by the Lords to confer about a subsidy.' This seemed to remove lingering doubts, and a unanimous 'Aye' was raised in response to Sir Walter Ralegh's motion 'whether they would have a general conference with the Lords'.[90] It was agreed that the conference should take place on the next day, Tuesday.

After meeting the Lords, and given a deadline of Thursday to make their decisions, the committee spent Wednesday discussing the government's modified proposal to allow four years for the payment of the three subsidies (usually two years were allowed per subsidy). It was now that Francis Bacon made his error. Although agreeing to the three subsidies, Bacon maintained that these must be spread over a period of at least six years, on three grounds: impossibility or difficulty; danger and discontentment; and because there were better ways of raising the money than simple subsidy.

For impossibility, the poor men's rent is such as they are not able to yield it, and the general commonalty is not able to pay so much upon the present. The gentlemen must sell their plate and the farmers their brass pots ere this will be paid. And as for us, we are here to search the wounds of the realm and not to skin them over; wherefore we are not to persuade ourselves of their wealth more than it is.

The danger is this: we shall thus breed discontentment in the people. And in a cause of jeopardy, her Majesty's safety must consist more in the love of her people than in their wealth. And therefore we should beware not to give them cause of discontentment. In granting these subsidies thus we run into two perils. The first is that in putting two payments into one year, we make it a double subsidy; for it maketh 4s. in the pound a payment. The second is, that this being granted in this sort, other princes hereafter will look for the like; so we shall put an ill precedent upon ourselves and to our posterity; and in histories it is to be observed that of all nations the English care not to be subject, base, taxable, etc.

The manner of supply may be by levy or imposition when need shall most require. So when her Majesty's coffers are empty, they may be imbursed by these means.[91]

Bacon argued that 'whatsoever was above a double subsidy I did wish might (for precedent's sake) appear to be extraordinary, and (for discontent's sake) might not have been levied upon the poorer sort.'[92]

Ulimately it was agreed to grant three subsidies – the first payable at a single payment in the first year, the second at a single payment in the second year, the third at two payments in the third and fourth years.[93] Francis might have hoped that this outcome would negate his opposition. He may even have been encouraged when his hot-tempered cousin Sir Edward Hoby insulted Sir Thomas Heneage during a committee meeting, which ended up in his confinement and was referred to in the final speeches of both the Lord Keeper and the Queen – as Anthony Bacon noted to his mother, 'a notable public disgrace laid upon him'.[94]

But Bacon's eminently logical argument had definitely damaged his prospects. The Queen was furious at his behaviour, and sent Burghley to inform his nephew. Francis responded in a letter that sought in no way to apologise nor to mitigate his actions: it was instead a frank justification.

I was sorry to find by your Lordship's speech yesterday that my last speech in Parliament, delivered in discharge of my conscience and duty to God her Majesty and my country, was offensive. If it were misreported, I would be glad to attend your Lordship to disavow anything I said not. If it were misconstrued, I would be glad to expound my words, to exclude any sense I meant not. If my heart be misjudged by imputation of popularity or opposition by any envious or officious informer, I have great wrong; and the greater, because the manner of my speech did most evidently show that I spake simply and only to satisfy my conscience, and not with advantage or policy to sway the cause; and my terms carried all signification of duty and zeal towards her Majesty and her service.

He begged Burghley 'first to continue me in your own good opinion: and then to perform the part of an honest friend towards your poor servant and ally; in drawing her Majesty to accept of the sincerity and simplicity of my heart, and to bear with the rest, and restore me to her Majesty's favour'.[95]

The disastrous personal consequences of the parliamentary battles fought in the name of his conscience disillusioned Francis Bacon as to the possibilities of ever making his name at court. He intimated to Essex that he was thinking of abandoning the active life, as he had announced to Burghley four years previously. Essex's response was not only unenthusiastic, but conveyed to Francis the possibility that he was in danger of losing this patron as well. 'I did almost conjecture by your silence and countenance a distaste in the course I imparted to your Lordship touching mine own fortune,' Francis observed, at the same time registering the earl's care of that fortune: 'as it is no news to me, so nevertheless the main effects and demonstrations thereof past are so far from dulling in me the sense of any new, as contrariwise every new refresheth the memory of many past.' Acknowledging 'the free and loving advice' given to him by Essex, he assured him 'that I will not dispose of myself without your allowance; not only because it is the best wisdom in any man in his own matters to rest in the wisdom of a friend (for who can by often looking in the glass discern and judge so well of his own favour, as another with whom he converseth?), but also because my affection to your Lordship hath mine own contentment inseparable from your satisfaction.'[96]

It was a momentous decision. Once again, Francis Bacon snatched himself back from committing to a life of study, and decided to give his fragile political career one last chance. This time his fate lay not in the legacy of his father and the whims of his uncle, but in the wisdom of a patron become friend, the mirror that was the earl of Essex.

6

A Tired Sea-sick Suitor:
The Trials of Preferment

I thought my credit, joined with the approbation and
mediation of her greatest counsellor [Burghley], might prevail.
Essex on behalf of Bacon (March 1594)

THE TASK IN hand now was twofold: to reconcile the Queen with
the wayward Francis Bacon, and to assure Bacon of his desired
post – that of Attorney-General. Following the death in February
1593 of the Master of the Rolls Sir Gilbert Gerard, it was popularly assumed
that his place would be taken by the incumbent Attorney, Sir Thomas
Egerton. In a campaign orchestrated by Essex, Francis attempted to recap-
ture the goodwill of his uncle Burghley, engaging the services of Burghley's
secretary Michael Hickes and his cousins, Sir Thomas and Sir Robert
Cecil.

The ways in which the Cecil half-brothers dealt with this request were
markedly different. Sir Thomas promptly petitioned his father 'for one
nearly allied to your house, and whose gifts and qualities of mind I know
your Lordship will not think unfit for the place he seeketh'. Francis, he
explained, 'meaneth himself to wait upon your Lordship' but 'in the meantime forbeareth for modesty's sake to speak for himself'.[1] Sir Robert, on
the other hand, was evasive. He denied that he knew of any immediate
reshuffle plans, and advised Francis 'that if either by your own presence
or by other mediation your way be not made so that as the veil now
covering you may be uncovered, though it do but even most gingerly
hide you, according to the slender proportion of her Majesty's dislike,
whereof you have given so small cause, that surely it will be still a stumble
for any man that shall thrust resolutely to deal for that preferment'. His
real route lay with Essex: 'You must press the earl for it, who hath both
true love towards you, and the truest and greatest means to win it of her
Majesty.'[2] In reality this meant that Cecil washed his hands of the matter,
leaving it to Essex's opposed faction to sort out.

Francis continued to be baffled by the Queen's displeasure. 'It is a great
grief to me, joined with marvel,' he pondered to Essex,

that her Majesty should retain an hard conceit of my speeches in Parliament. It mought [might] please her sacred Majesty to think what my end should be in those speeches, if it were not duty, and duty alone. I am not so simple but I know the common beaten way to please. But if the not seconding of some particular person's opinion shall be presumption, and to differ upon the matter shall be to impeach the end, it shall teach my devotion not to exceed wishes, and those in silence. Yet notwithstanding (to speak vainly as in grief) it may be her Majesty hath discouraged as good a heart as ever looked towards her services, and as void of self-love.[3]

To the Queen herself he protested that he 'affected myself to no great matter, but only a place of my profession, such as I do see divers younger in proceeding to myself, and men of no great note, do without blame aspire unto'. Disingenuously, he claimed no interest in the campaign being mounted on his behalf. 'If any of my friends do press this matter more than as a simple nomination, I do assure your Majesty my spirit is not with them.' He was not interested in gain, but only to recover 'your Majesty's favour, and access to your royal person'.[4]

As the legal term finished at the beginning of June, the campaign could be put on hold for a while. Essex assured Francis that the Queen was now 'thoroughly appeased' and that the only bar to his preferment lay in 'the exception of his years' [i.e. his youth]; and he believed he would 'overcome that difficulty very soon, and that her Majesty will show it by good effects'. In the meantime, Francis could return to Twickenham, or receive Anthony Standen (newly arrived in London) into his chambers at Gray's Inn.[5]

Essex continued to assure Anthony of his concern for Francis' welfare.[6] Over the next few months, Essex engaged in some characteristic shuttle diplomacy on Francis' behalf, moving between Francis at court and Anthony at Twickenham. On 17 July 1593 the earl paid Anthony a three-hour visit at Twickenham, during which he 'most friendly and freely promised to set up, as they say, his whole rest of favour and credit for my brother's preferment before Mr. Coke', the present Solicitor-General. Essex also told Anthony that he had 'already moved the queen for my brother; and that she took no exception to him, but said, that she must first dispatch the French and Scots ambassadors, and her business abroad, before she thinketh of home matters.' Encouraged by these assurances, Anthony was eager to inform his mother that he was no longer dependent on the dilatory efforts of his uncle Burghley for his future well-being: 'Neither have I need, I thank God, to trouble my Lord Treasurer in demanding his lordship's help, by loan of any sum to satisfy my debts; the effects of whose good will towards me, according to his lordship's often protestations, and not altogether without my deserving, I would either request to some good purpose, or not at all.' This was essential, since 'the more free I keep myself, the more bold I may be with his lordship in my brother's behalf, whose benefit and advancement I have and shall always esteem as mine own'.[7]

Lady Bacon, however, was not well pleased. Her delight at Essex's support of her sons was tempered by her anxiety about the possible pernicious influence on them of Standen – 'Be not too frank with that papist; such have seducing spirits to snare the godly. Be not too open.'[8] Anthony assured that her fears were once again misplaced: his company neither had prejudiced him in mind or body, nor would in the future, 'and therefore I judge it no wise convenient, that your ladyship should show by letter or otherwise any discontentment of his abode here, so long as it shall please her Majesty to like thereof'.

Despite Essex's kind words about Francis, however, it was the new lodger in the Bacon rooms at Gray's Inn who seemed to be getting the best of the earl's attention. Standen was summoned to court, and on 1 August was introduced to the Queen by Sir Robert Cecil.[9] Anthony Bacon was almost beyond being able to take up such an invitation. A change for the worse in the weather brought on 'his familiar infirmity', according to Standen, rendering him unable even to write, 'for it hath seized his left elbow and hand likewise the right thumb in such sort as he hath not been able to write to your Lordship and that which worse is and most altereth him unapt to stir abroad to take his wonted exercises'. A month later Standen was still having to act as scribe for Anthony, whose right hand remained gripped by gout.[10]

While Anthony was indisposed, Francis, 'still at court in reasonable good health',[11] took it upon himself to take up some of the business for which his elder brother had previously been responsible. On 20 August, Standen wrote to Anthony mentioning that Francis had just written to him that, on account of Anthony's indisposition, he should commit to Francis the negotiation of an intelligence paper which, Francis informed Standen, was the concurrent opinion of Anthony and himself. As he was not now likely to deliver this paper to the Queen for some time, Standen sent it to Francis to digest the substance of it.[12] It was an early instance of the muddling of the brothers' roles that was to be of crucial importance in Francis' later career.

The next few months saw the full orchestration of Essex's campaign on behalf of Francis with the Queen. At times operating on an elevated, rational level, it just as often plumbed the depths of farce, depending on the moods and ailments of the two protagonists. On Wednesday 22 August, when Essex attempted to speak to the Queen, his timing was off and 'she cut me off short; she being come newly home and making haste to her supper'. The following day, however, Essex was granted 'a full audience but with little better success than before'. He pleaded for 'an absolute *amnestia* and an access, as in former times'. In answer to the former suit, Elizabeth argued that Francis was 'in more fault than any of the rest in parliament; and when she did forgive it, and manifest her receiving of them into favour, that offended her then, she will do it to many, that were less in fault, as well as to yourself'. Therefore, on the second point, he explained to Francis, 'Your access, she saith, is as much as you can look for. If it had been in the king her father's time, a less offence than that would have made a man be banished his presence for ever. But you did come to the court, when you would yourself; and she should precipitate too much from being highly displeased with you, to give you near access, such as she shows only to those, that she favours extraordinarily.'[13]

While Essex was appealing directly to the Queen, Lady Bacon was as usual taking the family route, intervening on her sons' behalf with her sister's husband Lord Burghley. He responded that he thought her care of her sons 'is no less than they both deserve, being so qualified in learning and virtue as if they had a supply of more health they wanted nothing. But none are, or very few,' he warned, '*ab omni parte beati* [blessed in all respects]. For such are not elect, but subject to temptation, from the highway to heaven.' Yet to the best of his ability, 'though I am of less power to do my friends good than the world thinketh, yet they shall not want the intention to do them good.'[14]

Sir Robert also advised Francis that his absence from court, which was disturbing Lady Bacon, would do him 'no good'. 'It is not likely to find the Queen apt to give you an office,' he reasoned, 'when the scruple is not removed of her forbearance to speak with you.' This trifle could be 'straight dispatched, if it were luckily handled'; or it could 'stop good when the hour comes of conclusion'.[15] Burghley wrote briefly to Francis on 27 September to assure him that 'I have attempted to place you, but her Majesty hath required the Lord Keeper to give to her the names of diverse lawyers to be preferred, wherewith he made me acquainted, and I did name you as a meet man.' Sir John Puckering, the Lord Keeper, allowed Francis' name to go forward 'in way of friendship for your father's sake, but he made scruple to equal you with certain whom he named as Brograve, and Brathwait, whom he specially commends.'[16] Puckering was clearly the next target, and Francis launched an attack via his secretary, Morgan Coleman. Puckering promised to speak to Francis on his return;[17] resigned to Francis 'the use of his chamber in the Court'; and in early November, 'kindly offered him room at his own lodging' in St Albans (allowing Francis a chance to escape his mother).[18]

At Twickenham Park, Anthony felt his intervention was needed. He was hampered in his efforts, however, by growing trouble with gout – possibly, along with 'the stone' (passing chalk stones), a side-effect of a lifetime's excessive taking of 'physic'. Although the gout had spread to the sole of his foot and his ankle, he was adamant in his plan to come to court, insisting that he could rest at the home of his friend Dr Pamant in Eton, if needed.[19] A 'long fit of ague' and a 'shrewd pang of the stone', striking during the night of 9 October, forced another postponement, which Anthony attempted to make good by writing to Essex 'a letter correspondent to the duty of a brother and of a free-devoted servant to his Lordship . . . This is the only present supply I can think on of this disastrous disappointment which I know you will accept according to the merit of my brotherly affection.'[20] Clearly, Anthony considered his own plea would carry considerably more weight with the earl than his brother's.

The court was still giving Anthony the benefit of the doubt, in spite of the ever more elaborate excuses for his absence. Standen reported that 'I have had, many and many speeches about you with personages of import of both sexes; and it should seem none of them have been thoroughly informed of your parts and quality, although they have heard something superficially. The earl hath been the author of the liking conceived, which to my power I have, following his steps, confirmed to the great satisfaction of the wiser and discreter sort.'[21]

Finally, on Saturday 13 October, Anthony set out for the court at Windsor 'with resolution to have done my most humble duty to her Majesty'. He had 'passed three parts of the way', on the road from Colbrook, when he was attacked again 'by a extreme fit of the stone', and was forced to seek sanctuary at Eton. He was now 'so weak' that to have presented himself would have shown 'a very great presumption' rather than 'a dutiful mind'. The Queen graciously accepted his excuses, proffered by Essex: as Anthony wrote to his mother, she would have seen the same in the earl's letter to him, 'but that I know your Ladyship could not read my Lord's hand it being as hard as any cipher to those that are not thoroughly acquainted therewith'.

The journey was not utterly wasted, however (at least according to Anthony). On his way back, he had the good fortune to cross paths with Lord Burghley, whom he saluted out of his coach. His uncle 'took that duty very kindly and promised to join with the Earl in the reporting to her Majesty my dutiful endeavour'. Added to this was the news from his aunt Lady Russell (as he relayed to his mother) that 'her Majesty about a sevennight ago openly in the park before diverse vouchsafed of herself without any other occasion to make mention of me and to moan much my infirmity protesting with oath that if I had been half as much for health as honesty and other sufficiency she knew not throughout her realm where to find a better servant and more to her liking.'[22] Anthony lost no time in making good his accidental meeting with Burghley, explaining to Francis that he thought it could do no harm to follow it up by writing to the Lord Treasurer, since 'for fear of troubling his Lordship by staying him too long in the highway and by reason of mine own pain I could not sufficiently perform by word of mouth to my own satisfaction.'[23]

While Anthony was afflicted on the road to Eton, Essex was keeping his word at court. That Saturday evening, he 'spake largely with the Queen', who 'kindly accepted your promise to come to her, and as she said herself, sorrowed for your sickness which arrested you by the way. She used many words which showed her opinion of your worth and desire to know you better.' While she was 'content' that he should 'plead at large' for Francis, she criticised him for advancing Francis for the attorneyship when even his own uncle placed him second; the only exception against his rival Edward Coke, she declared, 'was stronger against your brother, which was youth'. Essex replied that the comparison with Coke did not hold, 'for if they were both of one standing, yet herself knew there was such a difference in the worthiness of the persons, as if Mr. Coke's head and beard were grown grey with age it would not counterpoise the other disadvantages. And yet Mr. Bacon was the ancient [senior in rank] in standing by three or four years.' Anthony's offers – here unspecified, but perhaps to accept Francis' preferment as a reward for his own services – and Essex's 'mingling of arguments of merit with arguments of affection moved somewhat', but he still needed another audience to win his case.[24]

Despite this limited progress, general opinion seemed to assume Francis had the appointment in the bag. On 4 November Francis jokingly rebuked his cousin, the young Gray's Inn lawyer Robert Kempe, for sending his man Roger to him rather than coming himself: Roger had claimed that Kempe 'would not come except you heard I were Attorney. But I ascribe that to your man's invention, who had his reward in laughing; for I hope you are not grown so stately, but that I shall be one to you *stylo vetere* or *style novo* [old style or new style]. For my fortune (to speak court) it is very slow, if anything can be slow to him that is secure of the event.'[25]

False alarms were frequent. In late September 1593, Solicitor-General Coke's presence at court was taken as a bad omen: Cecil had to reassure Francis that this should give 'no cause of speech, for it was concerning a book to be drawn for the Bargain of Wines. If there had been you should have known, or when there shall.'[26] On Friday 18 January 1594 Francis hurried to court, following a tip-off from Puckering that Elizabeth would be appointing the next day, only to discover 'no other but the nomination of a Judge for the Common Pleas and a Baron of the Exchequer'.[27]

In such an environment even the most apparently loyal man might be an undercover spy. On 13 November 1593 Francis wrote to Essex an enigmatic, coded letter that, despite its elaborate subterfuge, he urged should be burned: 'I pray, Sir, let not my jargon privilege my letter from burning, because it is not such but the light showeth through.' The letter was delivered by Standen to Essex at Windsor, 'which he read with more length and attention than infinite others I have seen him to read before and immediately committed the same to the candle.'[28] It warned Essex of Francis' suspicion that the 'late recovered man that is so much at your Lordship's devotion' in fact 'worketh for the Huddler underhand'.[29] Conjecture as to the identities concealed here, both of the 'late recovered man' (Burghley? Cecil? Puckering? Standen?) and the 'Huddler' (Coke? Rolston? Cecil?), has been endless; perhaps all we can glean from this letter is the general atmosphere of suspicion in which Francis Bacon was working at this point in his life.[30]

On 13 November Anthony travelled back to Gorhambury, where he was joined two days later by the earl and Thomas Lawson, who had been recalled expressly from Twickenham, carrying letters from one of Anthony's Scottish correspondents, Dr Morison, 'and most earnest request to return them deciphered with all speed possible; which Phelippes could not dispatch before to-morrow.' Clearly Anthony had made himself indispensable in even the most specialised of intelligence tasks.[31]

Francis' position remained precariously balanced, its stability not enhanced by signs that the standing at court of his chosen patron might be less than entirely secure. Essex's erratic behaviour, and especially his sudden departures from court, were beginning to raise eyebrows. On 25 November Standen reported from Windsor that the earl had been 'absent these three days and returned this morning about six of the clock: which starts of his in stealing manner much trouble his followers and well-willers. He came so late to town, as he will be in bed until noon, and so no speaking to him until dinner-time.' Essex disappeared from court on the morning of Friday 7 December, and there was still no news of him by 6 p.m. on Tuesday, 'which long absence hath not been these years by past', wrote Standen, 'and is a cause, why the court doth murmur of great disgust between both parties; for that the other, ever since the earl's going, hath been in great agitation, and none can guess about what. But my thought is, that Mr. Francis' matter may be the cause.'[32] Essex's enemies took advantage of his absence to raise a 'lewd and false bruit' that he had fled to Dover, and was about to embark; at which news the Queen was 'greatly altered and resolved to have sent after him if the same night he had not come as he did at which time he was cheerfully welcomed'.[33]

The earl granted Standen an audience at Kingston on Wednesday 12

December, just before he himself waited on the Queen. Standen's pre-meeting, he told Anthony, 'was to good purpose for that I am sure he did speak with her Majesty about your brother who also had spoken to the earl before me'. Standen gave to the earl what Anthony had given him at Gorhambury 'touching your desire of effectuating that you had so long expected more wished by you for my Lord's service and good than for any interest or gain to your brother'. Standen expanded on this, stressing 'the contentment you should receive and the credit or decay thereof to my Lord by missing the mark he had so long eyed chiefly being now so familiar to the world, to all the Earl gave me grateful ear and told me what he had done in despite of contraries to stay the matter until now, which malgre [despite] them he would yet renew until Easter term'.[34]

On 20 January 1594 Edward Stanhope wrote to tell Francis that there had been 'some long arguing this afternoon betwixt the Queen and my Lord Treasurer, for your being solicitor forthwith, wherein the Queen it seemed was something stranger than she was wont'. Following this argument, the Queen ordered Burghley to send for the Master of the Rolls for his opinion (Stanhope urged Francis to petition him first). 'It pleased her to tell my Lord Treasurer that nobody else would nominate any other to the place lest they offended him, who seems only to affect you with some other like speeches of that nature.'[35] However, the question of Francis Bacon and the attorneyship was soon to become old news. On 21 January, at Essex's instigation, the Queen's physician Roderigo Lopez was arrested on suspicion of conspiracy to murder. Essex confided in Anthony, boasting that he had 'discovered a most dangerous and desperate treason. This I have so followed as I will make it appear as clear as the noonday.'[36] London had a new talking point.[37]

★

Roderigo Lopez was a familiar figure to Anthony Bacon. A Portuguese Jew who subsequently converted to Christianity, Lopez rose to become personal physician to the earl of Leicester, Sir Francis Walsingham, the earl of Essex, and, from 1586, to the Queen herself. The Cambridge scholar Gabriel Harvey dismissed Lopez as 'none of the learnedest or expertest physicians in the court', but admitted that he made 'great account of himself as the best, and by a kind of Jewish practice hath growen to much wealth, and some reputation as well with the queen herself as with some of the greatest lords and ladies'. The Lopez family expanded and prospered accordingly, with the youngest son Anthony being sent to be educated at Winchester College.

Anthony Bacon had remarked on him in a letter to Standen: 'Doctor Lopez, a physician, is lodged in a fine house in Holborn, lately built by an old gentlewoman called Mistress Allington, hard by Gray's Inn on the field side, where he is well entertained and used by her for physic as they say. There was very lately a young child laid before the door with this instruction, "Senor Lopez, here I come, Open the gate and take in thy son. Thy Spanish creed I will not disgrace. Behold the image of thy face." He is said to have denied it to be his. If truly, great is their fault that charge him therewith.'[38]

At some point Lopez contracted himself to Essex – for services beyond the medical. Skilled in five languages, Lopez was in contact with the Jewish community in Antwerp and the pretender to the Portuguese throne Don Antonio; he served in liaison with the Spanish government, via Walsingham, and with various Portuguese nationals. To complicate the picture still further, he was also – like many intelligencers – in the pay of the enemy, in this case Spain.

Along with other intelligencers, including Anthony Bacon, Standen and Rolston, Essex wanted his part of Lopez. According to Godfrey Goodman, Essex enlisted Lopez to discover designs against the Queen's life, instructing him to become friendly with any plotters. Lopez allegedly replied, 'My Lord, this is a very great business and a dangerous: you are now in favour, but how long you can continue we know not. You may die, and then the whole treason will be laid upon me.' However, the Queen agreed with Essex's proposition to Lopez, and promised him a reward for any service he might perform. Lopez accepted the challenge.

The Essex arrangement did not work out. Lopez placed the earl a clear third, and took his intelligence to either Burghley or the Queen before Essex, causing Essex to look foolish when he brought the Queen the same, now stale information. Such humiliation could be guaranteed to anger him. But the final straw came when Lopez, drunk, revealed to Don Antonio and Essex's Spanish follower Antonio Perez the nature of the venereal illness of which he had just cured the earl. The two immediately told Essex, who vowed revenge.

Now came his chance. In mid-October 1593 a Portuguese man, Ferrera de Gama, was arrested on suspicion of selling English secrets to Spain. His papers were handed over to Essex, who immediately intercepted all mail addressed to Portuguese subjects and soon concluded that some conspiracy was afoot. Ferrera sent a letter secretly to Lopez, which fell into Don Antonio's hands. This revealed that a certain messenger was expected from the continent with letters, the discovery of which would be fatal to them both. Lopez was clearly involved; Ferrara admitted that he and others had been endeavouring to make peace with Spain, and that Lopez was party to the negotiation. This declaration was written down on 11 November, but not made known to the government until 20 January 1594.

In the meantime, Essex found it easy to make the physician's dealings with Spain appear suspect. A one-time Spanish spy, Antonio da Veiga, claimed that Lopez had agreed to poison Don Antonio with Indian acacia in 1587 in return for 'good promises', and that years earlier, he had offered to poison a Portuguese pilot who helped the English in expeditions to the Indies. Armed with this back-catalogue of rumours against the doctor, Essex had no difficulty in coming up with the idea of a murder conspiracy.

On 21 January, the months of secret manoeuvring and intercepting and deciphering were over, and Roderigo Lopez was arrested. While the first examination was held at Burghley's house by a high-powered team comprising Essex, Burghley and Cecil, Lopez's house was searched for incriminating papers, and Lopez himself committed to custody at Essex House. It was a red-letter day for Essex: as Standen reported: 'The matter against Lopez hath been of long time bolted and sifted by the earl and all hath been the earl's drift.' Even now, the Cecils were not convinced; at the end of the first day of examinations, Sir Robert raced to tell the Queen that he could find 'no matter of malice, for in the poor man's house were found no kind of writings of intelligences whereof he is accused or otherwise that hold might be taken of him'. By the time Essex reached the Queen in London, 'he found his friends had marred his way, for she took him up calling him rash and temerarious youth to enter into a matter against the poor man that he could not prove, whose innocency she knew well enough, but malice against him and hatched all this matter which displeased her much.' With his usual sense of the theatrical, Essex locked himself into his chamber for two days.

Unfortunately, Lopez was not the only matter on Essex's agenda. Anthony Standen was waiting for the earl in his chamber. At length the earl appeared in a 'choler', flinging open the doors without seeing Standen and marching into his closet, where he remained alone for over an hour. Eventually emerging to find a groom and Standen still standing waiting, he noticed Standen's unhealthy pallor, and Standen admitted that 'had it not been some speeches I had to deliver to his Lordship from Mr. Bacon I would rather have been in my bed than there'. Essex made Standen sit down, and arranged for a coach to carry him to Kingston. Standen told the earl of Anthony, and answered his query as to his health, by telling him (as he later reported to Anthony) that 'the most part thereof consisted in contentment, which by some good news of your brother's matters in Court might be increased in you and consequently more health interlarding my speeches with that of Cato and Caesar, all was to good purpose and took all well and promised infallibly that night which was Saturday to move her Majesty again.'

Essex moved the Queen again on Sunday: 'Still she stood upon the wonted forms and namely upon the youth and small experience of the gentleman.' Essex urged 'the great insufficiency of his competitor', which 'she could not well answer; silently confessing my Lord's reasons good, she said she would think on it and that there was time enough for all between this and the next term; and that either the one or other place she might bestow upon Bacon.' Essex told Standen that he found the Queen 'very inconstant about this matter for sometimes she will and other times will not'; he concluded that 'all cometh from his mighty enemies.'

At noon on Tuesday 29 January, 'for all the favourers he had', Lopez was committed to the Tower, and the following morning at seven was examined before Essex and Cecil, confessing, as Anthony Standen put it, 'more than enough'. Essex and Cecil travelled back to court together in the coach, where they had the quarrel about Francis Bacon's claim to the attorneyship with which we began.

Essex lost no time in recounting his verbal triumph to Anthony Standen, who promptly relayed it to Anthony Bacon, along with his own marginal comments, and to Francis, going himself to Gray's Inn, 'much I assure you to your brother's countenance, and there was a long half hour with him, and so departed from your brother leaving him the most joyful and consolate in that his Lordship had so stoutly stuck unto him and so far declared himself for him against Monsieur de Bossu [Hunchback, i.e. Cecil]'. Standen reported to Anthony that

> after the Earl was gone he [Francis] found his heart much eased and of my Lord and his noble dealing extremely satisfied, and told me how much you both were bound to honour and serve him. Truly Sir it is so, and no other fault hath the Earl but he must continually be pulled by the ear as a boy that learneth 'Ut, re, me, fa'. This so far declaration of Sir Robert (which in my conceit was superfluous) hath made your brother to resolve to take knowledge thereof and to deal with Sir Robert, wherwith the Earl seemeth contented, and for this envy is only behoveful in that it can not long keep in the flame.[39]

Francis followed up this advantage by arguing his first case in the King's Bench, on behalf of Sir Thomas Perrot, appearing for the heir of Lord Cheyney against the purchasers of his land. Sir Thomas had only the previous year been restored to his lands (which had been forfeited after his father's execution for treason), through the efforts of his brother-in-law the earl of Essex.[40] The following day Standen attended on Essex at 9 p.m., when the earl 'told me that your brother had argued some case of importance in the King's Bench much to his commendation which was not unknown to her Majesty and to my Lord it seemed by the joy he uttered in the speech thereof that he had received thereby great content.'[41]

Following Essex's encounter with Cecil, as Anthony told his mother, 'my Lord Treasurer vouchsafed upon what motive God knoweth to a very honorable compliment towards my brother in sending Mr. Hickes his secretary to him at Gray's Inn with charge to tell him from his lordship that he did with much joy and contentment congratulate unto my brother the first fruits of his public practice and requested to send him his case and the chief points of his pleading to the end he might make report thereof there where it might do him most good.' This public practice soon increased. As Standen had reported, 'Mr. Francis hath intention to argue another case either Saturday or Monday and the earl hath given his word to be at the hearing, to all which I will lug him for it will be of great importance in this time and a choke pear to praters that say he never yet entered into the place of battle.'[42] This case — on 10 February — was 'a most famous Checker [Exchequer] Chamber case where the Lord Keeper and the Lord Treasurer (if he be able) the two Lord Chief Justices with two other judges of each bench, the Lord Chief Baron and the rest of the Barons, are to sit. I beseech God,' wrote Anthony, 'to strengthen his understanding and memory with the virtue of his holy spirit to the end that his words finding grace before so many principal magistrates he may thereby hereafter be more enabled and encouraged to employ his good gifts to the best purposes I mean to the advancement of God's glory and her Majesty and country service.'[43]

The audience included Nicholas Faunt, who reported that Francis scored a 'success the applause of which he observes to be general. I hope his Saturday's work (though half-holiday) shall weigh more than the whole week's travel employed by some; it cannot but be well in the end that is generally of all sorts so well taken.' Henry Gosnold set down his thoughts on Francis' performance:

That Mr. Francis Bacon receives his reputation gained is not strange to any that knows him. That he hath increased his, is not incredible. The absence of the Lords that were looked for was recompensed with a presence of learned judges, and seemed an assembly rather capable than honorable. The respect they have him, although it was extraordinary, was well noted but not envied. The attention of the rest springing from an experience of good and an expectation of better, could not be better. His argument contracted by the time, seemed a *bataille serrée* [in serried ranks], as hard to be discovered as conquered. The unusual words where with he had spangled his speech, were rather gracious for their propriety, than strange for their novelty, and like to serve both for occasions to report, and means to remember his argument. Certain sentences of his somewhat obscure, and as it were, presuming upon their capacities, will

I fear, make some of them rather admire than commend him. In sum, all is as well as words can make it, and if it please her Majesty to add deeds, the bacon may be too hard for the cook [Bacon may triumph over Coke].[44]

Sadly, however, Francis Bacon's newly established performance routine could not be further exploited. The legal term came to an end on 11 February, and would not recommence until mid-April; and as key players returned to their country seats, the frenzy of the last few weeks abated. However, the next weeks were to bring Francis work of equal public prominence – though perhaps not equally beneficial to himself: the Lopez trial was scheduled for 28 February and his services were to be called on by his friend and patron.

The trial of the Queen's doctor now occupied everyone's thoughts, its fascination growing as rumours of the complexity and gravity of the case, and tales of racking, leaked out.[45] The paperwork was enormous: Waad reported 'very many Spanish and other foreign letters which must be translated and abstracted'.[46] Some of these were in cipher, and Francis Bacon was among those brought in to use the skills he had acquired in diplomatic service with Sir Amias Paulet to crack the codes. Significantly, it appears that Anthony was kept at some distance from this particular Essex endeavour – at one point he had to ask Standen to obtain a cipher from Francis.[47] It was left to Faunt to fill Anthony in on the details.[48]

At the trial itself, strict security was in force, and Faunt informed Anthony that he would be better served for information 'by your brother and others that were present. What I have is but by tradition.'[49] Francis would indeed be better informed: Essex commissioned him to prepare the government's rationale for the proceedings against Lopez.[50] The trial was an irregular event, heard by fifteen persons appointed by the Queen as a special commission, and the whole of the proceedings taking place under the hand of Solicitor-General Coke, who set the tone by harping constantly on Lopez's Jewishness.[51] Ultimately, Lopez was found guilty of leaking secret intelligence to Philip and his ministers, of attempting to stir up rebellion within the realm, and of conspiring to poison the Queen; he was sentenced to be hanged, drawn and quartered at Tyburn.

Essex was a key player in this verdict. Anthony Standen reported that the earl had 'been more than ten days sequestered from all business other than those you have heard that so much purported wherein he hath won the spurs and saddle also, if right be done him'.[52] Despite the apparent victory, however, the Queen's impulse to protect Lopez had not entirely dissipated: she allowed his widow Sarah to retain the whole of her late husband's estate and to live on with her family in Mountjoy's Inn in Holborn, and delayed the execution of Lopez until early June. An account of the trial, drawn up by Bacon by the end of March, was never published.[53] The way in which Bacon's name was raised with the Queen so vehemently during this particular affair – perhaps his most visible period to date of public identification with the earl – did as much harm as good to his career hopes.

At the end of March, Attorney-General Egerton was finally appointed as Master of the Rolls. Assuming that Sir Edward Coke would gain the attorneyship, Cecil promptly wrote to Egerton 'having offered to assist Mr. Francis Bacon in his own observations with relation to the office of Solicitor-General' – not the post for which Essex had so long sued. Egerton had made Francis 'a friendly and kind offer' of the benefit of his experience: 'the better to arm him with your observations (for the exercise of the solicitorship) which otherwise may be got with time'. Cecil assured him that 'I have no kinsman living (my brother excepted) whom I hold so dear. Neither do I think, that you, or any other can confer any good turn upon any gentleman (though I say it to you in private) likelier for his own worth to deserve it.'[54]

At the same time, Essex represented to the Queen (as he reported to Francis) 'how much you were thrown down with the correction she had already given you, that she might in that point hold herself already satisfied', and went on to 'disable' the man she was currently considering as Solicitor, Tanfield. When, provoked by Elizabeth's indifference, the earl 'grew passionate' for Francis, the Queen pointed out sharply that the only people who thought Bacon fit for the place were Essex and Burghley. Essex pointed out that 'the most and wisest of her Council had delivered their opinions and preferred you before all men for that place' – presumably they must just be saying that in front of him 'for fear or for flattery'. He urged the Queen to realise that 'whatsoever they said contrary to their own words when they spake without witness might be as factiously spoken as the other way flatteringly' – then, 'she should not be deceived.'

Even if they all spoke against Francis, he continued, 'yet I thought my credit, joined with the approbation and mediation of her greatest counsellor [Burghley] might prevail in a greater matter than this.' He urged her that he might least be given 'a secret promise wherein I should receive great comfort, as in the contrary great unkindness'. The Queen replied that 'she neither was persuaded, nor would hear of it till Easter when she might advise with her Council, who were all now absent' and 'in passion bad me go to bed if I would talk of nothing else'. Not to be outdone in displays of temperament, the earl retorted that 'while I was with her I could not but solicit for the cause and the man I so much affected and therefore I would retire myself till I might be more graciously heard,' and left similarly 'in passion', planning to leave the court the following day, and then to follow up with 'an expostulating letter to her' on Thursday night or Friday morning – a plan bound to 'stir a discontentment in her'.[55]

By Friday, the tantrums were forgotten. Essex took heart from the (rather uncertain) sign that Elizabeth was not flatly contradicting him – 'which they that know the minds of women say is a sign of yielding. I will tomorrow take more time to deal with her and will sweeten her with all the art I have to make *benevolum auditorem* [solicit my listener's goodwill].'[56]

The news came as a relief to Bacon, who admitted that

this very delay hath gone so near me, and it hath almost overthrown my health. For when I revolved the good memory of my father, the near degree of alliance I stand in to my Lord Treasurer, your Lordship's so signalled and declared favor, the honorable testimony of so many counsellors, the commendation unlaboured and in sort offered by my Lords the Judges and the Master of the Rolls elect; that I was voiced with great expectation, and (though I say it myself) with the wishes of most men, to the higher plane; that I am a man that the Queen hath already done for; and princes, especially her Majesty, loveth to make an end where they begin; and then add hereunto the obscureness and many exceptions to my competitors; when (I say) I revolve all this, I cannot but conclude with myself that no man ever received a more exquisite disgrace. And therefore truly, my Lord, I was determined, and am determined, if her Majesty reject me, this to do. My nature can take no evil ply; but I will by God's assistance, with this disgrace of my fortune, and yet with that comfort of the good opinion of so many honourable and worthy persons, retire myself with a couple of men to Cambridge, and there spend my life in my studies and contemplations, without looking back.

I humbly pray your Lordship to pardon me for troubling you with my melancholy. For the matter itself, I commend it to your love. Only I pray you communicate afresh this day with my Lord Treasurer and Sir Robert Cecil; and if you esteem my fortune, remember the point of precedency. The objections to my competitors your Lordship knoweth partly. I pray spare them not, not over the Queen, but to the great ones, to show your confidence and to work their distaste.[57]

Yet again, nothing came of all their hopes. By 5 April, when Francis 'had long talk with the earl' at supper at Essex House, both Egerton and Coke had had their warrants (as Master of the Rolls and Attorney-General) signed, but there seemed to be no conclusion to Francis Bacon's case.

Essex saw his own credibility running low: as Standen pointed out, the failure to gain any post for Francis had become 'a thing as much bringing this great man's credit in question, as any other he hath managed all the time of his favours heretofore'.[58] In the same week, Burghley fell ill. Francis frantically lobbied Lord Keeper Puckering daily 'to call to remembrance my Lord Treasurer's kind course, who affirmed directly all the rest to be unfit. And because *vis unita fortior* [combined forces are stronger], I pray your Lordship to take a time with the Queen when my Lord Treasurer is present,' for fear that it might 'receive some foil before the time when it should be resolutely dealt in.'[59]

★

It was about now that Anthony Bacon finally acquired a London residence. His life had become increasingly peripatetic – Gray's Inn in July 1593, then Twickenham until November, a month at Gorhambury, Christmas at Redbourn. Now he commissioned Nicholas Faunt to look for a house to purchase in London. In March 1594 Faunt came up with one, costing £24, with all the furniture in place, with room in the upper chambers and garrets for Anthony's servants, and with an upper room that would serve as a dining room, 'and be out of the view of strangers', clearly an issue.[60] By early May, Anthony was settled in Bishopsgate Street, much to the concern of his mother, who was greatly perturbed by the reaction to this news of her friend, Mr Henshaw – to wit, 'God give him well to be there.' Bishopsgate Street and Coleman Street had both been heavily hit by the last plague; the ministry there was 'very mean', the minister was 'but ignorant and commonly withal careless'; the people were 'given to voluptuousness and the more to make them so having but mean or no edifying instruction'. The nearby Butt Inn 'with continual interludes had even infected the inhabitants there with corrupt & lewd dispositions'.

The idea of her son living 'so near a place haunted with such pernicious & obscene plays & theatre' filled Lady Bacon with anxious foreboding. 'I marvel you did not first consider of the ministry as most of all needful considerations.' Then again, there was no minister at Twickenham Park – indeed, she was 'very sorry' that he had left Gray's Inn where the company was Christian, at least in comparison to what he had now.[61]

Worse was to come: namely, the arrival in the Essex circle of a new, flamboyant and dangerous figure – Antonio Pérez. Pérez had left his homeland of Spain on the morning of 2 November 1591 disguised as a lowly shepherd but carrying a lot of baggage, metaphorical if not physical. This was the man whose recent activities had involved him in murder, a love affair with the King's mistress, imprisonment and torture, a rebellion in Aragon against the control of Spain, charges of heresy and sodomy, and a precipitate fall from power. Now he was being hunted by Philip II himself.[62]

Pérez journeyed into England twice as Henri IV's envoy, once in April and again in July 1593. By the time of the second mission, he had taken vows of the new faith. Although the July mission was unsuccessful in securing France a loan of money and troops, it proved a social success, as the leader, Vidame, became friendly with the Queen, and also with Essex. Pérez, seeing a new service opportunity, ignored Henri's orders to return in October 1593 and entered Essex's service, remaining in England until July 1595.

Pérez offered to disclose Spanish secrets to the Queen; she quite properly declined to hear them, but allowed him to tell them to Essex. She did, however, grant Pérez several audiences, include him in festivities, and give to Essex 'a hundred pounds land in fee simple and £3 in parks which for her quietness sake and in respect of his friends he was content to accept without any further contestation', to support Pérez. (Legal restrictions prevented her from giving the land directly.)[63]

Pérez, with his colourful and dangerous past – charged by the Tribunal of the Inquisition as a sodomite, the son of a clergyman with Jewish origins – was regarded by Lady Bacon as deeply unsuitable company for her sons. 'I would you were well rid of that old, dooted [doted], polling papist. He will use discourses out of season to hinder your health, the want whereof is your great hindrance.'[64] But notwithstanding such maternal anxieties, Anthony began a friendship with Pérez in the spring of 1594 which soon progressed to intimacy. Anthony became Pérez's confidant, growing closer to him than anyone else. Pérez saw Anthony as 'moderate, so self-controlled, not bibelous, not gluttonous'.[65] They worked closely together: a memorial of instructions which Pérez presented to the Queen before he left for France in July 1595 is in Anthony's own hand.[66]

Pérez came with many personal attributes which may have attracted Anthony Bacon. Serving Pérez was a way of serving Henri IV;[67] and Pérez himself was a noted humanist scholar who had translated Homer's *Odyssey* from Greek into Spanish. His Spanish letters and *Aphorisms* were in great demand in England, and copied out avidly by Anthony Bacon for the pleasure and instruction of himself and his friends. Now Anthony became personally involved in Pérez's literary activities. Arthur Atey, who had translated Pérez's *Pedaços de historia ô Relaçiones* into English, submitted his version to Anthony for editing;[68] Anthony's editing was reviewed by Henry Wotton, and circulated in manuscript form. An enlarged Spanish edition of *Relaçiones*, published in London, was dedicated to Essex, although Pérez used the pseudonym Raphael Peregrino. Richard Field published it in 1594 for sale in the Netherlands and Spain.[69] No doubt the Bacons' friend

Thomas Phelippes, now in the Customs House, cleared it for export (the English agent in Antwerp urged Phelippes to send copies of it to him immediately upon its publication).

For all his learning, however, Pérez was a dangerous man to have around. He laid bare the hitherto partially cloaked antagonism between Essex and the Council, being mockingly critical of the Cecils in public – especially of Sir Robert, whom he dubbed 'Robertus diabolus' or 'microgibbus'.[70] In his travels around Europe Pérez deliberately invited scandalous interpretations of his every action. His association with the Essex circle encouraged particular interpretations of the intense intimacy in which the young men lived, linked not by bonds of kin or employment but by an unspecified and emotionally fraught 'friendship'. Pérez and Francis appear to have had an intimate relationship: ironically, because of the very intimacy of their relationship, no letters remain to bear witness, but there are hints of its closeness. On 13 December 1594, Francis wrote from Gray's Inn to Anthony enclosing 'a few words to Senor Ant. Pérez, which, if you allow, I pray seal and deliver to my servant to bear. I did doubt I should not see him of these two or three days, which made me use *literis praecursoriis* [letters in advance]'[71] – an arrangement which suggests that Francis was not used to going two or three days without seeing Pérez. And then, in January 1595, Francis invited Pérez to dinner, an invitation which Perez discussed in a Latin letter to Anthony in striking terms:

> Your brother invited me to dinner. He has wounded me in writing – his pen being the most rabid and biting of teeth. As if he himself were above blame – some kind of chaste vestal virgin. You can tell immediately what this imagined modesty of his is all about. For I am just the same. Those who claim to love modesty are in fact the most bold of men, and submit to force, and enjoy the excuse of being taken by force, like the Roman matron in Tacitus who consented to be raped by her lover. But alas, if you do not read these letters before dinner, the provocation behind his viciousness towards me will not be clear to you.[72]

Pérez was notoriously colourful in describing his personal relations with men of importance. Nevertheless, as it stands, the insinuation in this letter is that Pérez has intimate knowledge of Francis Bacon's taste in sexual relationships.

★

For all the intimacies, of whatever nature, to be had in the circle around Essex, for so long as the earl himself was on less than intimate terms with the Queen, Francis' attempts at advancement were unlikely to flourish. On Wednesday 24 April 1594, Francis finally received a brief, hastily written note from Essex summoning him to court that afternoon, to join him and the Vice-Chamberlain, Sir Thomas Heneage, in 'a matter of access'.[73] The attempt was clearly ill-judged. A week later, Francis lamented to Cecil that 'my access at this time is grown desperate', because of the falling out of favour ('hard terms') of Essex and the Vice-Chamberlain, 'who were to have been the means thereof'.[74] Cecil agreed: 'I do think nothing cut the throat more of your present access than the earl's being somewhat troubled at this time. For the delaying, I think it not hard, neither shall there want my best endeavour to make it easy, of which I hope you shall not need to doubt by the judgment which I gather of divers circumstances confirming my opinion. I protest I suffer with you in mind, that you are thus yet gravelled; but time will founder all your competitors and set you on your feet, or else I have little understanding.'[75] At the same time, Essex urged Puckering to 'forbear pressing for a Solicitor; since now there is no cause towards the end of a term to call for it, and because the absence of Mr. Bacon's friends may be much to his disadvantage'.[76]

Within a fortnight, though, Essex was back in court and reconciled with Elizabeth. After a first audience with the Queen 'spent only in compliments', he resumed Francis' suit on the second. As he reported to Francis,

> I told her in my absence I had written to Sir Robert Cecil, to solicit her to call you to that place which all the world had named you to; and now being here, I must follow it myself; for I knew what service I should do her in procuring you the place; and she knew not what great comfort I should take in it. Her answer in playing jest was that she came not to me for that; I should talk of these things when I came to her, not when she came to me; the term was coming and she would advise. I would have replied, but she stopped my mouth.[77]

Four days later, Essex spent time with the Queen, 'through the galleries in the morning, afternoon, and at night'. He relayed to Francis that

> I had long speech with her of you; wherein I urged both the point of your extraordinary sufficiency, proved to me not only by your last argument [in the King's Bench], but by the opinion of all men I spake withal, and the point of mine own satisfaction, which I protested to her should be exceeding great, if for all her unkindnesses and discomforts past she would do this one thing for my sake.
>
> To the first she answered, that the greatness of your friends, as of my Lord Treasurer and myself, did make men give a more favourable testimony than else they would do, thinking thereby they pleased us. And that she did acknowledge you had a great wit, and an excellent gift of speech, and much other good learning. But in law she rather thought

you could make show to the uttermost of your knowledge, than that you were deep. To the second, she said she had showed her mislike of the suit as well as I had done my affection in it; and that if there were a yielding, it was fitter to be of my side. I then added that this was an answer with which she might deny me all things if she did not grant them at the first, which was not her manner to do. But her Majesty had made me suffer and give way to her in many things else, which all I should bear not only with patience but with great contentment, if she would but grant my humble suit in this one.

And for the other pretence of the approbation given you upon partiality, that all the world, lawyers, judges, and all, could not be partial to you; for some wished you were crossed for their own interest and some for their friends; but yet all did yield to your merit. She did in this as she useth in all; went from a denial to a delay, and said when the Council were all here she would think of it; and there was no haste in determining of the place. To which I answered, that my sad heart had need of hasty comfort, and therefore her Majesty must pardon me if I were hasty and importunate in it. When they come we shall see what will be done.[78]

Ten days later, the Council met at court. Essex's kinsman Sir Fulke Greville wrote to tell Francis that he had 'dealt' by letter with the earl and Sir John Fortescue, and that 'As my heart was full of your praise, so have I as freely delivered it to the Queen. Believe me her Highness was more gracious to you.'[79] But Francis' patience was running out. On 17 May, Anthony had informed their mother that 'Touching my brother, we are both resolute that in case he be not placed betwixt this and the next term, never to make any more words of it.'[80] On 9 June, however, he wrote to Lady Bacon to tell her that 'It may be I shall have occasion, because nothing is yet done in the choice of a Solicitor, to visit the Court this vacation; which I have not done this month's space: in which respect, because carriage [of] stuff to and fro spoileth it, I would be glad of that light bed of striped stuff which your Ladyship hath, if you have not otherwise disposed it.'[81]

Francis' moves towards reconciliation with the Queen, or at least renewed access to her person, were still flagging. Through the Vice-Chamberlain, he presented a jewel to Elizabeth, who returned it, but 'with exceeding praise'. Nevertheless, Francis' attempts were not going unnoticed. On 17 June Fulke Greville, waiting on the Queen at court, told her how he had met Francis on his way through London, and how Francis had lamented his misfortune, 'that remained as a withered branch of her roots, which she had cherished and made to flourish in her service'. Greville vouched for Bacon's worth, and for 'the expectation for all this the world had of her princely goodness towards you', and relayed to Francis the Queen's response: 'It pleased her Majesty to confess that indeed you began to frame very well, insomuch as she saw an amends in those little supposed errors, avowing the respect she carried to the dead, with very exceeding gracious inclination towards you.' Raising the subject of the rejected jewel, he 'marvelled that as a prince she would refuse those homages of poor subjects, because it did include a final sentence of despair; but either I deceive myself, or she was resolved to take it; and the conclusion was very kind and gracious.' Greville concluded that he would 'lay £100 to £50 that you shall be her Solicitor'.[82]

Despite her reticence towards him, Elizabeth continued to make use of Francis' legal skills, in the investigation of a further conspiracy against her life.[83] At some point in July she made him one of her Learned Counsel – a legal advisory body with no formal definition and bringing no financial reward.[84] She then appointed Francis directly on her business, instructing him to travel north to investigate the roots of the alleged conspiracy. But yet again Francis' wealth and health – or rather, his lack of both – were his undoing. Scrabbling for cash to underwrite the journey, which like so many 'official' commissions came minus official funding, he was forced to draw on Anthony's resources. Anthony offered to pledge his own estate as security for the repayment of the loan,[85] and Francis set out on 18 or 19 July. But whether because of the financial implications of continuing, or because of genuine ill health, Francis halted on his journey north at Huntingdon.[86] Anthony commiserated with his brother on 'your pain and the forced interruption of your journey'.[87] To Elizabeth, Francis sent a sadly apologetic letter, assuring her that only God could have arrested him from her service. He acknowledged 'a providence of God towards me that findeth it expedient for me *tolerare jugum in juventute meâ* [to endure the yoke during my youth]'. He did not give up hope of making 'a good ending of a hard beginning', however, since 'it hath been my hap to stumble upon somewhat unseen, which may import the same as I made my Lord Keeper acquainted before my going.'[88] What exactly he had stumbled on, however, is lost to history. He made the best of his return journey, travelling via Cambridge, where he proceeded as a Master of Arts on 27 July, and arriving in London, with his health recovered, by the end of the month.[89]

Whatever the business was that sent him on his curtailed expedition, it did not appeal to his mother, who proclaimed that 'they were not his friends that did procure him that journey, no though it were my Lord of Essex himself.'[90] But Lady Bacon's opinions were increasingly ignored by her family, who were starting to doubt her judgement on many matters. Anthony's servant Edward Spencer spent time at Gorhambury during the summer of 1594, and relayed to his master some distressing news about 'how unquiet my Lady is with all her household'. Spencer had had the misfortune to be charged with the care of a bitch at Gorhambury. As soon as Lady Bacon saw the dog, 'she sent me word she should be hanged' and sent word to her servant Crosby 'that if I did not make her away she should not sleep in her bed'. So Spencer obeyed orders: 'indeed I hung her up.' But it was the wrong move; Lady Bacon was 'very angry, and said I was fransey [frenzied], and bade me go home to my master and make him a fool, I should make none of her'. Her tirade against Spencer widened to include most of Anthony's retinue. 'There is a company of ye: I marvel where he picked ye out.' Spencer justified himself to Anthony: 'The bitch was good for nothing, else I would not a hung her. My Lady do not speak to me as yet. I will give none offence to make her angry; but nobody can please her long together.'[91]

★

Francis now wanted all to go according to plan in his suit for place. He produced unsolicited discourses ('Touching the safety of the Queen's person', 'Touching intelligence and the Queen's person');[92] he instructed Lady Bacon to refrain from writing to Burghley on his behalf.[93] Stuck in the Tower during August, involved in the Council's examination of those implicated in the most recently uncovered conspiracy,[94] he urged Lord Keeper Puckering to renew his suit to the Queen,[95] but heard 'nothing from the Court in mine own business', putting this down to news of a defeat in Ireland.[96] September came; and though the Queen late in that month 'steadfastly promised' Essex to 'dispatch my matter tomorrow',[97] nothing happened. Francis retreated to Twickenham, returning to London only to argue a case on 25 October.[98] At Twickenham, as he told Anthony, 'One day draweth on another, and I am well pleased in my being here; for methinks solitariness collecteth the mind, as shutting the eyes doth the sight.'[99]

Over Christmas he played a central part in the Gray's Inn revels, *Gesta Grayorum*, which contained an early hint of his 'Solomon's House' idea, later the cornerstone of his perennially popular utopian fiction, *New Atlantis*. Lady Bacon would not have been pleased. Only three weeks earlier, she had written to Anthony: 'I trust they will not mum nor mask nor sinfully revel at Gray's Inn. Who were sometime counted first, God grant they wane not daily and deserve to be named last.'[100] But her fears were to be realised. The 3 January performance was attended, and Bacon's words heard, by an influential array of Privy Counsellors and lords: Lord Keeper Puckering, Lord Burghley, Lord Howard of Effingham, Lord Buckhurst, the earl of Essex, Sir Thomas Heneage, Sir Robert Cecil, the earls of

Shrewsbury, Cumberland, Northumberland and Southampton, and the lords Windsor, Mountjoy, Sheffield, Compton, Rich and Monteagle.[101]

★

As 1595 dawned, Francis Bacon was once again reminding Essex of his promise to petition the Lord Keeper, although he asked the earl

> not to conceive out of this my diligence in soliciting this matter that I am either much in appetite or much in hope. For as for appetite, the waters of Parnassus are not like the waters of the Spa, that give a stomach; but rather they quench appetite and desires. And for hope, how can he hope much, that can allege no other reason than the reason of an evil debtor, who will persuade his creditor to lend him new sums and to enter further in with him to make him satisfy the old; and to her Majesty no other reason, but the reason of a waterman; I am her first man, of those who serve in Counsel of Law?[102]

Essex sued Puckering, and renewed his petition to the Queen, pleading to her 'against herself for the injury she doth Mr. Bacon in delaying him so long, and the unkindness she doth me in granting no better expedition in a suit which I have followed so long and so affectionately. And though I find that she makes some difficulty, to have the more thanks, yet I do assure myself she is resolved to make him.'[103]

Within a week of Essex's latest approach, the Queen had heard that Francis was expressing a desire to travel. She made it clear that she deemed it a particularly misguided and heavy-handed tactic. 'Why?' she demanded of her hapless counsellors. 'I have made no Solicitor. Hath anybody carried a Solicitor with him in his pocket? But he must have it in his own time' – 'as if it were but yesterday's nomination', Francis commented – 'or else I must be thought to cast him away.' If Bacon continued to behave in this way, she continued, she would 'seek all England for a Solicitor rather than take him. Yea I will send for Houghton and Coventry tomorrow next.' She never dealt so with any as she had with Francis Bacon – '*in hoc erratum non est*', he quipped – 'I have pulled him over the bar' – 'note the words, for they cannot be her own' – 'I have used him in my greatest causes.' And on she raged, Francis told his brother, with 'such-like speeches, so strange, as I should leese myself in it, but that I have cast off the care of it.'[104]

Bacon knew that the tantrum was not directed towards him, towards whom the Queen was 'never peremptory'. No – 'this is Essex,' he mused, 'and she is more angry with him than with me. I am the least part of mine own matter.' Whatever the cause, the Queen instructed Cecil to find Bacon, and he rode to London – only to find Bacon not at home; Francis responded to a written message, however, and arrived at court, where he asked Sir Robert to deliver a written reply.[105] He wrote that 'it was an exceeding grief to me that any, not motion (for there was not now a motion), but *mention* that should come from me should offend her Majesty, whom for these one-and-twenty years (for so long it is that I kissed her Majesty's hands upon my journey into France)' – it was in fact less than nineteen years – 'I have used the best of my wits to please.' As for the rumour of his intention to travel, this had arisen during a conversation 'casting the worst of my fortune with an honourable friend that had long used me privately', which friend – the earl of Essex – had 'expressly and particularly by way of caveat' been restrained by Bacon that 'he should in no wise utter or mention this matter till her Majesty had made a Solicitor,' as Essex had since confirmed. The move to travel would arise only 'upon her Majesty's rejecting me with such circumstance, though my heart might be good yet mine eyes would be sore that I should take no pleasure to look upon my friends; for that I was not an impudent man, that could face out a disgrace; that I hoped her Majesty would not be offended, if not being able to endure the sun, I fled into the shade.'[106]

It was in any case an idle threat. Unlicensed for overseas travel, Francis could in reality flee no further than Twickenham Park. Francis reported to Burghley that he had withdrawn there

> expecting that the Queen would have placed another Solicitor; and so I confess, a little to help digestion, and be out of eye, I absented myself. For I understood her Majesty not only to continue in her delay but (as I was advertised chiefly by my Lord of Essex) to be retrograde (to use the word apted to the highest powers). Since which time I have as in mine own conceit given over the suit, though I leave it to her Majesty's tenderness and the constancy of my honourable friends, so it be without pressing.[107]

With the pressures of court life removed, he seemed to regain his health, and Anthony reported to their mother that he had 'not seen him looking better'.[108]

But these idyllic Twickenham retreats were increasingly infrequent. Francis had to return each term to life and work at Gray's Inn, and inevitably to the whirlwind of rumour, suing and letter-writing that fuelled the continuing race for the post of Solicitor-General. Essex laboured to win Puckering's support, citing the 'want of assistance from them which should be Mr. Francis Bacon's friends' as the cause that 'makes me the more industrious myself, and the more earnest in soliciting mine own friends. Upon me the labour must lie of his establishment, and upon me the disgrace will light of his being refused.' He was no longer suing for a friend, but as 'a party interested [interested] in this . . . For though I know it will never be carried any other way, yet I hold both my friend and myself disgraced by this protraction.'[109]

Francis was increasingly aware that he needed this appointment. To date, after nineteen years' service to the crown, he had received precisely two benefits: the reversion of the Star Chamber clerkship from Burghley and some help from the Queen in forwarding his legal career. He hoped that Burghley, as a previous benefactor, might now benefit him: 'To speak plainly, though perhaps vainly, I do not think that the ordinary practice of the law, not serving the Queen in place, will be admitted for a good account of the poor talent which God hath given me; so as I make reckoning I shall reap no great benefit to myself in that course.'[110]

Essex's doubts about the motives of the Cecils were felt also, and keenly, by Francis and his family. Their letters refer to Robert Cecil's *outward* support – on 21 January, Francis and Robert 'parted in kindness, *secundum exterius* [outwardly at least]'; in his conversation the year before with Lady Bacon, Robert's 'speech was all kindly *outward*'. Some time in March, Francis told Cecil that he had been hearing upsetting rumours about his cousin. He had been informed by 'a wise friend of mine, and not factious toward your Honour' that Cecil had been bought by Mr Coventry for two thousand angels, and that he 'wrought in a contrary spirit' to Burghley. Further information – 'from your servants, from your Lady, from some counsellors that have deserved you in my business' – proved that Cecil 'wrought underhand against me'. He did not believe the tale to be true, he assured Cecil, but it had to be admitted that 'the strangeness of my case might make me credulous'.[111] Sir Robert's apparent betrayal hit Francis hard, coming from 'one with whom I have ever thought myself to have some sympathy of nature, though accidents have not suffered it to appear'.[112] Despite his feelings, he was forced to retract somewhat, in order to ensure his uncle's continued support, asking the elder Cecil 'that if I did show myself too credulous to idle hearsays in regard of my right honourable kinsman and good friend Sir Robert Cecil (whose good nature did well answer my honest liberty), your Lordship will impute it to the complexion of a suitor, and of a tired sea-sick suitor, and not to mine own inclination'.[113]

Bacon was now by turns intensely involved, and almost philosophical about the outcome of his suit. 'My matter is an endless question,' he told Fulke Greville.

Her Majesty had by set speech more than once assured me of her intention to call me to her service; which I could not understand but of the place I had been named to. And now whether *invidus homo hoc fecit* [some envious man has done this]; or whether my matter must be an appendix to my Lord of Essex suit; or whether her Majesty pretending to prove my ability, meaneth but to take advantage of some errors which, like enough, at one time or other I may commit; or what it is; but her Majesty is not ready to dispatch it. I have been like a piece of stuff bespoken in the shop; and if her Majesty will not take me, it may be the selling by parcels will be more gainful. For to be, as I told you, like a child following a bird, which when he is nearest flieth away and lighteth a little before, and then the child after it again, and so *in infinitum*, I am weary of it; as also of wearying my good friends.[114]

He was 'weary of asserviling myself to every man's charity' and believed that his 'fortune will set me at liberty'.[115]

Throughout the summer the bird still flew away, and the child continued to run after it. There was a moment, at the end of May, when Bacon made noises implying that he was dropping his suit, and Puckering even docketed his letter 'Mr. Fr. Bacon, his contentation to leave the Solicitorship'. He 'thought good to step aside for nine days, which is the durance of a wonder, and not for any dislike in the world; for I think her Majesty hath done me as great a favour in making an end of this matter, as if she had enlarged me from some restraint.'[116]

But Francis' detection of an end to the matter was premature. Elizabeth made it clear that until she had appointed a Solicitor, there was to be no withdrawing from the race: all competitors were required to compete. When visiting the sick Burghley after Easter Term had ended, she revealed that Francis was still 'somewhat gravelled upon the offence she took' at his subsidy speech. When Burghley passed this message on to his nephew, Francis could only reiterate his reasoning from two years previously: 'I was the first of the ordinary sort of the Lower House of Parliament that spake for the subsidy; and that which I after spake in difference was but in circumstances of time and manner, which methinks should be in no great matter, since there is variety allowed in counsel, as a discord in music, to make it more perfect.' Despite acknowledging his 'great insufficiency', Francis still thought himself an apt candidate, whose main claim was that he purposed 'not to divide myself between her Majesty and the causes of other men (as others have done) but to attend to her business only: hoping that a whole man meanly able, may do as well as half a man better able.' He considered himself a private man, apologising to Burghley, 'It is true my life hath been so private as I have had no means to do your Lordship service.' As for the fact that he was 'rather a man of study than a man of practice', he recalled that his father had been made Solicitor of the Augmentations at twenty-seven when he had not practised; and that only recently Mr Brograve had been called to be Attorney of the Duchy when he had 'practised little or nothing' and had 'discharged his place with great sufficiency'.[117]

But if the early summer brought renewed hopefulness, it rapidly dissipated, and by the end of June Francis was said to look 'very ill', a state his mother ascribed to 'inward grief'.[118] He increasingly suspected Puckering of betraying him, and at the end of July directly accused him, in writing and face to face at the Temple, of 'failing me and crossing me now in the conclusion, when friends are best tried'. Now he could do no more than hope that the right man (he named Fleming) would be chosen: if, however, 'I perceive any insufficient obscure idle man offered to her Majesty, then I thinking myself double bound to use the best means I can for myself.'[119] Puckering took offence at Bacon's tone, and Essex was forced to mediate, claiming that Francis' manner was 'only a natural freedom and plainness, which he had used with me, and in my knowledge with some other of his best friends, than any want of reverence towards your Lordship'.[120] Typically, Francis' eventual apology to Puckering read more like a reasoned defence of his actions, deeming the argument 'unpleasant though necessary', and did nothing to remedy matters: 'Good my Lord, when your Lordship favoureth others before me, do not lay the separation of your love and favour upon myself. For I will give no cause, neither can I acknowledge any where none is.'[121]

As early as December 1593, Standen had told Anthony that Essex 'liketh nothing' the distance between himself and Anthony in the Hertfordshire countryside. The earl had been at London 'to prepare some six or eight chambers in Essex House [the earl's London house], and that he will often be there to confer with friends at times for I see all matters of intelligence are wholly in his hands'.[122] Anthony's move to Bishopsgate Street was only a partial answer. Now, nearly two years later, Anthony finally took the major step of moving into Essex's own household at Essex House, occupying the apartments left vacant by the recently departed Perez, where it was reported Essex 'doth come oft unto him'.[123] In Lady Bacon's opinion, forcibly expressed as ever, 'the counsel to part with that London house so well agreed and most necessary' – the same one to which she had been so adamantly opposed – 'was more cunning than regret for your good, being gouty as you be, but you are in such things to your great hurt credulous, and suffer yourself willingly to be abused. For the other place, though honourably offered, shall find many inconveniences not light.' Besides 'your unavoidable cause of expense', 'your own stuff spoiled and lost and many incommodities', Anthony did not even benefit financially by the arrangements – he was still calling on Lady Bacon to foot his coal bill during the summer months.[124] 'The manner of your removal goes to my heart,' wrote his 'sickly and sad' mother, listing the 'inconveniences' of the new arrangement with relish.

> Envy, emulation, continual and unseasonable disquiet to increase your gout; many pains, great urging for suits, yea importune to trouble the earl and yourself. Peradventure not so well liked yourself there, as in your own house. What others already offended, not small ones, may work and lay up, I fear, having as you have, working heads about you. Some increase of suspicion and disagreement, which may hurt you privately, if not publicly, or both by all likelihood, in these so tickle times.

The essential difference, to her mind, was that this move compromised Anthony's independence: 'You have hitherto been esteemed as a worthy friend; now shall be accounted his follower . . . Before his servant did regard you. Now you must respect and be in their doing to your cumber and charge and care to please. Everything you do shall be spoken and noted abroad and yourself brought as it were into a kind of bondage where now yet free.'[125]

Lady Bacon was not the only relative of Anthony's worried about his increasingly visible dependence on Essex. Her sister Lady Russell had observed the breakdown of relations between the Cecil and Bacon cousins with similar alarm. In the first week of September 1595 she decided to be the facilitator of a reconciliation between the family's sparring branches. She quizzed Burghley on the causes of his reticence towards his nephew. He gave her a few key problems – Anthony's intimacy with Standen and the seminarian Thomas Wright; and his behaviour in France: 'for falling out with Plessy [Du Plessis-Mornay] who complained of it there, being to the king as he was, and for conversing with a bishop and other bad fellows whereof he writ unto yourself and yet notwithstanding after my Lord had not suffered one to return into France to you [Lawson], ye sent for him again as bad and lewd a fellow as could be.' Armed with this knowledge, she travelled to Essex House to confront Anthony.[126]

'Good nephew,' Lady Russell began, 'are not you much bound to your uncle that will make such a posting journey, only with one gentlewoman first in coach to Paris Garden, and then in an wherry over here to you, to visit you, and to perform a very kind office?'

Anthony answered that 'her merit, and my obligation was very great, but not greater than the thankfulness of my heart'.

'Marry nephew,' she sighed, 'it is that same heart that must ease my heart, which is almost choked with grief to hear that which I do.' She paused, 'looking wishly' at Anthony, 'belike to see whether I was dismayed, but I thank God these words served rather as a trumpet to wake cheer up and muster my spirits, and gave me occasion to reply: "Nay, good madam, go on I beseech you, and spare not to charge an innocent heart with advertisement of misreports or wrongful imputations."'

'Well nephew,' said his aunt, 'seeing you so well armed I will not flatter you a whit, but will tell you that all your bodily pains grieve me not so much, as the indisposition or alteration of your mind, which is said to be grown corrupted in religion, factious and busy, undutiful and unnatural, and all this I tell you from my Lord Treasurer who protesteth upon his salvation that he hath always loved you as a second father, and never not so much as in thought wronged you.'

'Madam,' replied Anthony, 'here are very heavy propositions, and a protestation of great price. For the first my hope and comfort is, that their proofs will be his light which I expect likewise to understand from you. For my Lord's protestation as it is comfortable to me, in that it pleaseth his Lordship to make show of kindness, by engaging a pawn inestimable to any Christian so when I call to mind the contrary effects I have felt, I apprehend the facility of his Lordship's so great an adventure.'

'For that nephew,' she retorted, 'let my Lord look to it, and bethink yourself how to answer my proofs: for the first point your familiarity with Standen a fugitive, and Wright a seminary priest.'

'Give me leave to help you (Madam),' Anthony interjected, finishing her list, 'and my Lord Harry [Howard] whom you should have done the honour to have named first.'

'Aye,' she said, 'and he too.'

At that moment Anthony's man entered and informed him hastily that his lordship was below. Lady Russell seized the opportunity. 'The daily report of these unto you makes you odious. For the second point you are too well known and beloved in Scotland to be a true Englishman, and busy yourself with matters above your reach, as foreign intelligences, and entertainment of spies. For the last, you have not only abandoned the kind old noble man, but you do ill offices, not only with the earl here, but in France, and Scotland by men of your acquaintance in one word you oppose yourself more directly, than any nobleman in England durst [dares] do how great soever.'

Here Anthony interrupted her. 'I see not why an honest poor gentleman may not apprehend as little, perhaps less my Lord Treasurer's greatness, as a rich nobleman the height of whose estate may make courage more pliable, which conceit, though at the first hearing it seem strange unto you, yet after you have heard my answer, which truth and innocency will dict unto me, I doubt not but you will find it more probable, for I confess to you freely good Madame, that being to plead for the life of my reputation at the bar of so near and dear a friend's judgement, I am resolved *de me servir de toutes mes pieces iusqu'au fonds de mon sac* [to exhaust my financial resources] to prove as clearly as daylight myself no way guilty, neither in part nor in whole.'

Anthony embarked on a lengthy vindication of his service on Burghley's behalf, beginning with his voyage into France in 1579, and running through to his decision to serve Essex – with certain omissions. 'Thus Madam,' he concluded, 'you have heard my particular confession of my faith and such circumstances as presently come to my mind.

'Touching the second point I will show your Ladyship a letter written thirteen years ago by late Sir Francis Walsingham in her Majesty's name containing her gracious acceptance of my poor endeavours and assurance of her princely favour and good opinion.'

Lady Russell read the letter. 'God's body nephew,' she exclaimed, 'thou art mightily wronged, for here is not only warrant but encouragement.'

'Yea Madam, if it had been my good hap to have found Sir Francis alive, he would have made that good and more too. Is it not a very hard case Madam that an honest loyal subject son of so faithful a servant and true patriot, having so many years sown obedience, care and expenses, should reap no other fruits than jealousy, suspicions, and misinterpretations; I deny not but that during my abode in France I rencontered [met] and knew many Scotch gentlemen both well and ill affected, but never sought unto them nor made account of their acquaintance till I had received the warrant you have seen; since when I confess to have tilled as industriously as I could so barren a soil only for her Majesty's service; which I hope his Lordship will [grant] fitter names than faction or *outrecuidance* [presumptuousness] namely seeing such poor fruits as grew in my ground have hitherto come free both to her Majesty and his Lordship.

'And now Madam to your last point which I perceive hath not moved you the least, I will first begin to excuse both Standen and myself by confessing to your Ladyship freely, that when on the one side at my first coming over I found nothing but fair words which make fools fain, and yet even in those no offer, or hopeful assurance of real kindness, which I thought I might justly expect at his Lordship's hands, who had inned my ten years' harvest into his own barn without any ha'penny charge; and on the other side understood the earl of Essex his rare virtue and perfections and the interest he had worthily in my sovereign's favour, together with his special noble kindness to my germane brother; whereby he was no less bound and in deep arrearages to the earl, than I knew myself to be free and beforehand with my Lord Treasurer, I did extremely long to be plain with your Ladyship to meet with some opportunity to make the honourable earl know, how much I honoured and esteemed his excellent gifts, and how earnestly I desired to deserve his good opinion and love, and to

acknowledge thankfully my brother's debt presuming always that my Lord
Treasurer would not only not dislike but commend and further this my
honest desire and purpose upon which confidence, when Sir Anthony
Standen having certified his Lordship of his arrival in Calais was left there
à l'abandon [bereft] without receiving any comfort or warrant from his
Lordship to his small discouragement and my discredit, upon whose
mediation to my Lord Treasurer he wholly relied, I made no scruple to
address myself to the worthy earl, and to present the gentleman unto him,
who first in respect of her Majesty's service, and then for my sake revived
his spirits utterly damped by my Lord Treasurer's carelessness and contempt
of him, with a noble welcome of a chain of a hundred marks.'

Lady Russell was incredulous. 'By my faith nephew if thy tale be true,
Topnam [Tottenham] is turned French!'

'Nay for God's sake Madam believe me now in this, whatsoever you
do hereafter in other things, for else I repent me to have spent so much
time and labour.'

'Well,' replied his aunt, 'enough for Standen.'

'As for poor Wright,' continued Anthony, 'I thought it far from humanity, much more from Christian charity to bar him my door and my board:
and as for the letter I wrote to Mr. Dean I have the copy to show
and assure your Ladyship it containeth nothing that may argue either
presumptuous or irreligious.'

This was all beside the point. 'But madam this is but a work of supererogation to pain myself to satisfy my Lord Treasurer, whom her Majesty
hath censured with admiration, what should make him so loath yea so
backward to advance his nephews, which God knoweth my brother and
I have found most true, howsoever it pleaseth his Lordship to protest the
contrary; namely after his son Mr. Secretary (whether with his Lordship's
privity God knows) had denounced a deadly feud to an ancient lady my
mother and his aunt swearing that he held me for his mortal enemy, and
would make me feel it when he could.'

'Ah vile wretched urchin!' exclaimed Lady Russell, 'is it possible?'

'Whether it be true or no madam I refer to my mother, who marvelled
when she told me of it, that I did but laugh at it alleging and expanding
to her Ladyship a gascon proverb which was *branle d'asne ne monte pas al
ciel* [an ass's bray doesn't reach heaven].'

'By God', objected his aunt, 'but he is no ass.'

'Let him go for a mule then madam,' Anthony retorted, 'the most
mischievous beast that is.'

At this, Anthony reported, his aunt 'laughed heartily and seemed to be
very glad to understand such a monstrous insolency which brought her
into a very good temper, and altered her style quite from censures and

reproofs to praise of my extemporal apology, and entreaty that I would set it down in writing.'

'God forbid madam,' said Anthony, 'that by such an arrogancy I should derogate so much from your merits: beseeching your Ladyship that if I had not conceived full assurance, that your Ladyship's credence with my Lord Treasurer and kindness towards myself would smooth the harshness and shadow the blemishes of this my free yet dutiful and true discourse in defence of innocency.'

Lady Russell returned to Burghley, who as good as admitted that Anthony would be better off with the 'friendship and kindness' of Essex, though he stressed that Sir Robert Cecil had never hindered Anthony's affairs in any way.[127]

For Anthony, this signalled the end of relations with the Cecils. 'Madam, I hope his lordship will neither find it strange nor amiss in me if with all reverent and dutiful regard to his lordship's greatness I continue my former honest course in giving no just cause of his lordship's displeasure. The heaviness whereof if it be my ill hap to have unjustly cast upon me by misinterpretations misreports and sinister impressions without mine own desert, I shall myself unfortunate, but by God's grace I shall never be proved guilty.'[128]

★

Francis made one final lacklustre attempt to promote his cause, desiring to let Puckering and the Attorney know his 'travails' on behalf of the Queen. But missed meetings, crossed wires – and on one occasion the Attorney leaving his notebook at Osterley – scuppered these plans. On 11 October Francis informed Puckering that 'I can take no further care for the matter.'[129] Elizabeth once again engaged Bacon, this time on Star Chamber business, and it was during this appointment that he learned once and for all that the bird had flown out of his hands. On 14 October he wrote to Puckering to tell him that 'I conceive the end already made'; but he saw it as 'to me a beginning of good fortune, or at least of content. Her Majesty by God's grace shall live and reign long. She is not running away, I may trust her. Or whether she look towards me or no, I remain the same, not altered in my intention. If I had been an ambitious man, it would have overthrown me. But minded as I am, *revertet benedictio mea in sinum meam* [the blessing returns to my lap].'[130]

On 5 November 1595 Sir Thomas Fleming received the patent of the office of Solicitor-General. The prize had once again eluded Francis Bacon.

7

Getting Nowhere:
The Armour of Patience Pressed

I stand indifferent whether God call me, or her Majesty.
Francis Bacon to Lord Burghley (1597)

WHEN THE NEWS broke of Francis Bacon's ultimate failure to secure the post of Solicitor-General, Essex was at the court in Richmond. He crossed the river to Twickenham Park to console his protégé. 'Master Bacon,' he opened tentatively, 'the Queen hath denied me yon place for you, and hath placed another; I know you are the least part of your own matter, but you fare ill because you have chosen me for your mean and dependance; you have spent your time and thoughts in my matter; I die if I do not somewhat towards your fortune: you shall not deny to accept a piece of land which I will bestow upon you.'

Bacon replied, 'For my fortune, it is no great matter, but your Lordship's offer made me to call to mind what was wont to be said when I was in France of the Duke of Guise, that he was the greatest usurer in France, because he had turned all his estate into obligations; meaning that he had left himself nothing, but only had bound numbers of persons to him. Now, my Lord,' he continued, 'I would not have you imitate his course, nor turn your state thus by great gifts into obligations, for you will find many bad debtors.'

'Take no care for that,' the Earl rebuked him, and pressed his gift again.

'My Lord,' said Bacon, 'I see I must be your homager, and hold land of your gift; but do you know the manner of doing homage in law? always it is with a saving of his faith to the King and his other Lords; and therefore my Lord, I can be no more yours than I was, and it must be with the ancient savings: and if I grow to be a rich man, you will give me leave to give it back to some of your unrewarded followers.'[1] He made it clear to Essex that while 'I do think myself more beholding to you than to any man,' he still reckoned himself 'as a common (not popular, but common); and as much as is lawful to be enclosed of a common, so much your Lordship shall be sure to have.'[2]

The gift of land – presumably in Twickenham Park – with which Essex 'enfeoffed' Bacon, and which he afterwards 'sold of £1,800' (though it was worth more), provided Bacon with the security to raise further money.[3] But this incident – at least as it was told by Bacon himself – makes clear that Francis Bacon was keen to be seen to distance himself politely but firmly from Essex, some years before close alliance with the earl would bring with it real dangers.

Francis now had leisure to consider his situation. The loss of the suit was, he said, 'like the pulling out of an aching tooth, which, I remember, when I was a child and had little philosophy, I was glad for when it was done'. He realised that he had 'lost some opinion, some time, and some means'. His main concern was with means: 'and the rather, because I am purposed not to follow the practice of the law . . . and my reason is only, because it drinketh too much time, which I have dedicated to better purposes.'[4]

Bacon's distancing himself from the earl's erratic fortunes seemed wise, even in the short term. November 1595 had been a difficult month for Essex: he was the dedicatee of a book published in the Netherlands dealing with the taboo subject of the succession of the crown, singled out as the one man who, because of his 'nobility, calling, favour with his prince, and high liking of the people', was likely to have some bearing on the outcome. The Queen got hold of a copy of the offending book, and confronted Essex with it in such a way that he promptly fell into a 'melancholy', looking 'wan and pale, being troubled at this villainy', and keeping to his chamber. To the general observer, it was yet another snub: according to Rowland Whyte, 'he is mightily crossed in all things; for Bacon is gone without the place of Solicitor.'[5] Once the Queen was convinced of his innocence, however, it was seen that she 'strengthens her love unto him', and, soon after, letters sent to the Queen from foreign countries were delivered 'only to my Lord of Essex, and he to answer them'.

Francis celebrated the earl's new-found position in a device prepared for the Accession Day festivities on 17 November.[6] A squire offers to the Queen his master's complaint that he is tormented by the importunities of 'a melancholy dreaming hermit, a mutinous brainsick soldier, and a busy tedious secretary', and petitions that he might be free from the trouble of them. After the hermit, the soldier and the secretary have presented their own cases, the squire reveals them to be nothing more than the messengers of Self-Love (Philautia) and proclaims that his master Erophilus, presumably Essex, will renounce Philautia and devote his life to loving the Queen with his skills 'with the Muses' and 'in the wars'.

The device was double-edged. The three messengers of Self-Love were open to identification: as Rowland Whyte noted, 'the world makes many untrue constructions of these speeches, comparing the Hermit and the Secretary to two of the Lords, and the Soldier to Sir Roger Williams' (one of Essex's military commanders).[7] White's reference to 'two of the Lords' presumably hints at the elderly, now retired Burghley and his son Cecil: such characterisations drew wittily on a Cecilian conceit developed during various shows staged for the Queen at the Cecils' country house Theobalds, when Burghley had been represented as a hermit (played by Cecil himself in May 1591 as an anchorite).[8]

On the other hand, the three messengers might be seen as possible aspects of Essex – he was known as a soldier and a politician, and occasionally presented himself as something of a hermit *manqué*, as he was later to assert to Anthony: 'My affection, in nature, it was indifferent to books and to arms, and was more inflamed with the love of knowledge, than with the love of fame: witness your rarely qualified brother, and the most learned and truly honest Master Savile [Henry Savile]; yea, my contemplative retiredness in Wales, and my bookishness from my very childhood.'[9] The device also celebrated Essex's new-found grasp of Elizabeth's foreign affairs. After the speeches, there entered 'the ordinary postboy of London, a ragged villain all bemired, upon a poor lean jade, galloping and blowing for life', who handed over a packet of letters to the earl.

The hard work of Essex's team of scholars and writers, though 'commended' elsewhere, failed to hit home at its intended audience. The Queen was unimpressed. If she had thought there had been so much said of her, she stated, deadpan, she would not have been there that night. And so she went to bed.[10]

★

In July 1593, Henri IV, once the linchpin of Protestant organisation in France, had announced his conversion to Catholicism. This development had profound implications not only for his own control of France, but for France's strategic position in European politics. The move, which secured Henri's position at home, naturally complicated relations with his Protestant neighbour. As far as old-style English politicians like Burghley were concerned, the prewar antagonisms between the nations had been restored.[11] On the other hand, in late 1595, Essex was a voluble supporter of France's bid for a formal alliance with England: he even framed a set of instructions for the ambassador Sir Henry Unton to coach the French to respond in such a way as to press the English to accept the treaty.[12]

Contradictory rumours abounded about Elizabeth's plans for her young favourite – an army command in Brittany perhaps, or a naval command off Ireland. In March 1596 a general commission was issued to Essex and the Lord High Admiral, Lord Howard of Effingham, for a voyage to the

Iberian coast.[13] The French saw the proposed mission as a waste of time and money.[14] Essex saw it as the opportunity for a fabulous English victory, with himself (and irritatingly, Howard) at the helm. He quickly reappraised his priorities and, with merciless speed, dropped his support for an Anglo-French alliance.

So it was with miserably poor timing that Antonio Pérez returned to England in April 1596, this time with the duc de Bouillon (previously known as the vicomte de Turenne), to try to effect an Anglo-French treaty and to persuade Elizabeth to send troops across the Channel. Instead, the envoys now found themselves trying to dissuade England from sending ships and soldiers to Iberia.[15] Pérez's personal position was even less comfortable than that of the mission as a whole. His continuing advocacy of an Anglo-French alliance had angered the seigneur de Sancy, the French ambassador to England; de Sancy spoke to the Queen in deprecating terms concerning Pérez, after which she denied Pérez access to her presence.[16] Perez expected to receive advice and direction from Essex, but under the circumstances the earl claimed to be too busy. Pérez turned to Anthony, whom he pestered daily to find out if Essex had asked about him, treating Anthony as 'a receptacle of friendly complaints'.[17] The receptacle eventually spilled over in complaint to Essex, whom he urged to contact Pérez himself, and to give his sanction to Pérez' return to France with Bouillon.[18] Pérez was not slow to notice Anthony's increasingly intolerant attitude towards him, and himself wrote to protest, pointedly comparing his affection to the love of a eunuch. He threatened to retaliate in kind if Anthony's indifference did not return to affection.[19]

Without access to the earl, and under constant pressure from Pérez, Anthony felt increasingly harassed. His sorry state was only exacerbated when he received a very flattering but demanding letter from Essex's sister, Penelope Rich, in the country. What she wanted, 'while I am in this solitary place, where no sound of any news can come', was to 'hear something of the world from you, especially of my brother, and then what you know of the French affairs, or whether there go any troops from hence to their aid'.[20] Answering with the proper courtesies and the barest of news about Essex and France, Anthony nonetheless took the opportunity to express his exasperation with Pérez, whom Lady Rich had dubbed 'your wandering neighbour': 'Your ladyship may well call my neighbour wandering if you knew, as I do against my will, what strange bypaths his thoughts walk in, which fester everyday and more in his mind by my lord's silence and the continual alarums that sounds in his ears of the Queen's displeasure. The duke of Bouillon presseth him to be in readiness to return with him, but he refuses to go without my lord's [Essex's] privity and consent.'[21]

Anthony protested to Essex that 'my armour of patience, as St Paul saith, which heretofore both abroad and at home hath been found to be of proof against the most violent shot of malice or misfortune, is now pressed with your lordship's absence and the apprehension of dangers daily incident to such honourable attempts; the least whereof, I take God to be recorder, is more fearful and shall be more grievous unto me than the strongest pangs of stone and gout that ever seized me.'[22] Essex's chief secretary Edward Reynolds strengthened his case: 'Mr. Bacon protesteth that he had rather be with your lordship to hear the cannons and that should not so much trouble him or hinder his rest as do the complaints, importunities, exclamations, discontentments and despairs of this man; and although he be advised by his physicians to retire himself into the country to attend his health and to take physic there without trouble, yet he is content to stay here and neglect his health to yield him some contentment and to keep him from utter desperation.'[23]

Finally, Essex responded: 'For yourself, I pray you believe that, though your mind, which so tenderly weigheth my danger, be very dear unto me, yet for my sake you must be confident; for if I be not tied by the hands, I know God hath a great work to work by me. I thank God I see my way both smooth and certain and I will make all the world see I understood myself. Farewell, worthy Mr. Bacon, and know that, though I entertain you here with short letters, yet I will send you from sea papers that shall remain as tables of my honest designs and pledges of my love to you.'[24]

Eventually the ordeal was too much and Anthony, 'constrained by extremity of both my pains, both gout and stone, and straitly enjoined by the physicians to retire myself where I might be private for three or four days',[25] travelled to Twickenham. To Francis, he was more blunt about his motives for escaping:

My patience being at the last overcharged, as I may say to you, almost turned into just anger to see that my double torment both of stone and gout could not obtain me the privilege of rest from Signior Perez's hand, but that I must daily hear my dear Lord's honour hammered upon both by him and the French and serve, as it were, hourly, in stead of a cistern, to receive his Spanish exclamations and scalding complaints. I had no other sanctuary but to retire myself here to your wholesome pleasant lodge and fine-designed garden, where with your leave and liking I would be as private as I could, namely till the duke of Bouillon and Signior Perez's departure.[26]

Finally, Anthony was safe. Once the French had obtained their treaty (with a reduced allowance of two thousand men), Pérez left London for France on or about 16 May. 'Well, at the last he is gone. God send him fair wind and weather for his passage and me but the tithe [tenth] of the thanks where I have deserved, for I dare assure you that without my watchfulness and painful patience he would have chanced upon some blot whereby to have made an after-game.'[27] Pérez and Anthony were never intimate again.

While Essex saw the Iberian expedition, now strategically centred on Cádiz, as an honourable English war, and one that would yield considerable profits and eradicate the Spanish threat to England and Ireland,[28] Francis Bacon remained unconvinced. Once it was over, he wrote to the earl: 'I am infinitely glad of this last journey, now it is past: the rather because you make so honourable a full point for a time.' The fleet sailed from Plymouth with a favourable wind on 2 June, arriving at Cádiz on the twentieth; the showdown followed almost immediately. In Bacon's words,

This journey was like lightning. For in the space of fourteen hours the King of Spain's navy was destroyed and the town of Cales [Cadiz] taken. The navy was no less than fifty tall ships, besides twenty galleys to attend them. The ships were straightways beaten, and put to flight with such terror as the Spaniards in the end were their own executioners, and fired them all with their own hands. The galleys, by the benefit of the shores and shallows, got away. The town was a fair, strong, well-built, and rich city; famous in antiquity, and now most spoken of for this disaster. It was manned with four thousand soldiers on foot, and some four hundred horse. It was sacked and burned, though great clemency was used towards the inhabitants.[29]

Despite the success at Cádiz, Essex's colleagues prevented him from going on to Terceira to intercept the Indian fleet. Instead, he set about ensuring that the version of events which was published to the English nation was written in his favour.[30] Although he returned in triumph, scandal was barely contained about what Essex had actually accomplished: at court, disputes raged about the division of the spoil, and of the credit, and of the blame. The Queen was less than impressed. A letter awaited Essex at Plymouth in which she described his mission as 'an action of honour and victory against the enemy and particular spoil to the army than any profitable to ourself'.[31] Within four hours, Essex had left Plymouth and rushed to court – where Elizabeth was 'possessed with discontented humours'.[32]

More importantly, Essex found that advantage had been taken of his absence by Cecil. After many years of deliberation, Elizabeth had finally appointed Sir Robert as her Principal Secretary; Cecil's friend Sir John Stanhope was now Treasurer of the Chamber and a Privy Counsellor. However, there was some consolation in her placing of Essex's uncle Sir William Knollys as comptroller of the household, and of both Knollys and his ally Lord North as Privy Councillors. Anthony saw these as effective counterbalances to the rise of the Cecil men.[33]

At this point Francis took it upon himself, while at Essex's Putney house, Barn Elms, to give the earl some advice, which he then consolidated in a disarmingly frank letter. He asked the earl to consider, 'before you give access to my poor advice', whence this advice came: 'to look about, even jealously a little if you will, and to consider, first, whether I have not reason to think that your fortune comprehendeth mine. Next, whether I shift my counsel, and do not *constare mihi* [remain consistent]. Thirdly, whether you have taken hurt at any time by my careful and devoted counsel' – pointing to an occasion at Nonesuch where, on Bacon's advice, he had submitted to the Queen, and thus much 'attemper[ed] a cold malignant humour then growing upon her Majesty towards your lordship', and to his recent persuasion of the earl not to estrange himself.

'Win the Queen' – this had to be the beginning of any course of action; not through 'favour or affection' but 'other correspondence and agreeableness'. But what was Essex now? 'A man of a nature not to be ruled; that hath the advantage of my affection, and knoweth it; of an estate not grounded to his greatness; of a popular reputation; of a military dependence': could there, demanded Bacon, 'be a more dangerous image than this represented to any monarch living, much more to a lady?' As long as this remained the dominant impression of Essex,

you can find no other condition than inventions to keep your estate bare and low; crossing and disgracing your actions; extenuating and blasting of your merit; carping with contempt at your nature and fashions; breeding, nourishing, and fortifying such instruments as are most factious against you; repulses and scorns of your friends and dependants that are true and steadfast; winning and inveigling away from you such as are flexible and wavering; thrusting you into odious employments and offices, to supplant your reputation; abusing you and feeding you with dalliances and demonstrations, to divert you from descending into the serious consideration of your own case; yea and percase venturing you in perilous and desperate enterprises . . .

Wheresoever the formerly-described impression is taken in any king's breast towards a subject, these other recited inconveniences must, of necessity of politic consequence, follow; in respect of such instruments as are never failing about princes: which spy into their humours and conceits, and second them; and not only second them, but in seconding increase them; yea and many times, without their knowledge, pursue them further than themselves would.

Answering the earl's (ventriloquized) question – '*Quid igitur agendum est?*

[What must then be done?]'– Bacon suggested that he must eradicate the impression of his nature being *'opiniastre* and not rulable'. Essex should credit all those matters 'which cannot be revoked' to 'insatisfaction, and not upon your nature or proper disposition. This string you cannot upon every apt occasion harp upon too much.' He advised Essex to cease 'to fly and avoid the resemblance or imitation' of Leicester and Sir Christopher Hatton, because 'it will do you much good between the Queen and you, to allege them (as oft as you find occasion) for authors and patterns.' When speaking to the Queen, Essex's expression is wrong, suggesting 'formality', 'whereas your Lordship should do it familiarly *et oratione fida* [in truthful speech]'. He should always have some 'particulars' in hand, which he should seem to pursue eagerly, and then drop them promptly when the Queen showed her opposition. The 'weightiest sort' of this genre would be 'if your Lordship offer to labour in behalf of some that you favour for some of the places now void; choosing such a subject as you think her Majesty is like to oppose unto' – Bacon reasoned that 'commendation from so good a mouth doth not hurt a man, though you prevail not'. Of less consequence would be the threat of travel, which would be promptly relinquished at a sign from the Queen – although these travel plans should not go beyond Wales. And then there are 'the lightest sort of particulars, which yet are not to be neglected, in your habits, apparel, wearings, gestures, and the like'.

The next most prejudicial impression is 'that of a military dependence'. Essex should have left that particular persona at Plymouth. Despite his gladness that the Cádiz expedition was successfully accomplished, Essex now had 'property good enough in that greatness. There is none can, of many years, ascend near you in competition. Besides, the disposing of the places and affairs both, concerning the wars, (you increasing in other greatness) will of themselves flow to you; which will preserve that dependence in full measure. It is a thing that of all things I would have you retain, the times considered, and the necessity of the service; for other reason I know none. But I say, keep it in substance, but abolish it in shows to the Queen.' The Queen loved peace, hated change, and 'that kind of dependence maketh a suspected greatness. Therefore, *quod instat agamus* [let's do what has to be done]. Let that be a sleeping honour awhile, and cure the Queen's mind in that point.'

For similar reasons, Bacon advised against pursuing the places of Earl Marshal or Master of the Ordnance, which Essex had been considering. He suggested instead the post of Lord Privy Seal, the third great office – 'a fine honour, quiet place, and worth a thousand pounds by year' – that had been held by the Lord High Admiral's father, himself 'a martial man', 'and it fits a favourite to carry her Majesty's image in seal, who beareth it best expressed in heart.' This would divert the Queen from her impression of Essex's 'martial greatness': he could also detract from that image by continuing his 'former diligence at the Star Chamber; if you shall continue such intelligences as are worth the cherishing; if you shall pretend to be as bookish and contemplative as ever you were'. And – Bacon's masterstroke – Essex should bring in 'some martial man to be of the Council; dealing directly with her Majesty in it, as for her service and your better assistance; choosing nevertheless some person that may be known not to come in against you by any former division', such as Lord Mountjoy or Lord Willoughby.

Essex's popular reputation, although a good thing in itself, needed careful treatment *vis-à-vis* the Queen.

> Take all occasions, to the Queen, to speak against popularity and popular courses vehemently; and to tax it in all others; but nevertheless to go on in your honourable commonwealth as you do. And therefore I will not advise you to cure this by dealing in monopolies, or any oppressions. Only, if in Parliament your Lordship be forward for treasure in respect of the wars, it becometh your person well. And if her Majesty object popularity to you at any time, I would say to her, a Parliament will show that; and so feed her with expectation.

The fourth impression was 'of the inequality between your estate of means and your greatness of respects'. Until Essex was seen to be 'careful of your estate', the Queen would think him 'chargeable to her' and deem 'that you have higher imaginations'. Essex should continually profess this in speaking to the Queen, to sue her in any suit 'wherein both honour, gift and profit', pleading that 'it will be this benefit to you'.

'Lastly, to be plain with your Lordship,' concluded Bacon, 'nothing can make the Queen or the world think so much that you are come to a provident care of your estate, as the altering of some of your officers,' who were suspected by many. 'But if, in respect of the bonds they be entered into for your Lordship, you cannot so well dismiss yourself of them, this cannot be done but with time.'

The fifth impression is 'of the advantage of a favourite' which was harmless itself, 'severed from the rest'. However, when 'joined with them, it maketh her Majesty more fearful and shadowy, as not knowing her own strength'. The only remedy Bacon could see was 'to give way to some other favourite', ensuring that the new favourite 'hath no ill nor dangerous aspect towards yourself'.[34]

For a while it seemed that Essex might have listened to Francis' advice. Bacon himself received 'gracious usage and speech' from the Queen during the Christmas holidays, and presented her with a sample of a work on the

Maxims of the Law, in which the rules and grounds of law were laid out, interspersed with a number of cases.[35] Circumstances were once again to overtake them, however.

The assault on Cádiz had hit hard at the Spanish King, and during the winter of 1596–7 there were rumours of naval forces being prepared against England and Ireland. As the weather cleared, it was decided that another force should be sent out against him. At the outset, Essex's participation was far from clear: the Queen raised a fleet without mentioning Essex, and eventually offered him only a coordinate command ('Lord Thomas Howard and Sir Walter Ralegh were to be joined with him in equal authority'); Essex had, it was reported, 'refused to go, and been well chidden for it', retiring to his chamber and remaining there 'for a full fortnight'. Elizabeth had apparently 'resolved to break him of his will and pull down his great heart' but 'found it a thing impossible, and says he holds it from the mother's side'.[36]

During the earl's self-imposed retirement, he was presented with a copy of Francis Bacon's first acknowledged printed book. The *Essays*, which had been circulating in manuscript form, had already been subject to pilfering a few months earlier. Now, threatened with a pirated edition, Bacon presented his own 'authorised' edition, and suppressed the pirated version. On 7 February 1597 his own version was on sale, at a price of twenty pence. The *Essays* were a succinct distillation of the kind of day-to-day counsel and self-fashioning which now occupied Bacon full-time. Perhaps modelled in form on those of Montaigne (whom Anthony had known in Bordeaux), they also proved remarkably popular. Eminently quotable, and full of 'wisdom' of the kind suitable for extemporising either in the law courts or in the Commons, they were a perfect gift from a loyal servant to his patron. Still, Bacon was too aware of Essex's precarious position to make that gift in the full public gaze.

The presentation of Bacon's *Essays* contained in miniature the complex distancing between Francis and Essex, mediated through Anthony, that was to be played out with devastating effects in the next four years. Unlike most authors of the period, who paid at least lip-service to the convention of dedicating their book to a social superior who would endorse it, Francis prefaced his book with an epistle to his 'loving and beloved brother' Anthony. After explaining that he has been forced to hurry through this printing of the essays to pre-empt a rival pirated edition, he writes that he has 'preferred them to you that are next my self, dedicating them, such as they are, to our love, in the depth whereof (I assure you) I sometimes wish your infirmities translated upon myself, that her Majesty mought have the service of so active and able and mind, and I mought be with excuse confined to these contemplations and studies for which I am fittest'. Here

Anthony is portrayed as a socially impotent figure, unable to serve the Queen; Francis as the perpetually employed man kept away from his proper studies.[37]

Such was the public image. But in private, Anthony sent a copy of the *Essays* to Essex, with a covering letter which paraphrased much of Francis' own epistle.

> I am bold, and yet out of a most entire and dutiful love wherein my german brother and myself stand infinitely bound unto your Lordship, to present unto you the first sight and taste of such fruit as my brother was constrained to gather, as he professeth himself, before they were ripe, to prevent stealing; and withal most humbly to beseech your Lordship, that as my brother in token of a mutual firm brotherly affection hath bestowed by dedication the property of them upon myself, so your Lordship, to whose disposition and commandment I have entirely and inviolably vowed my poor self, and whatever appertaineth unto me, either in possession or right, – that your Lordship, I say, in your noble and singular kindness towards us both, will vouchsafe first to give me leave to transfer my interest unto your Lordship, then humbly to crave your honourable acceptance and most worthy protection.[38]

Anthony calls on Essex's love for them both, but implicates only himself in selfless dedication to the earl. It may well be suspected that both these dedicatory epistles come from the same pen: that what we see here is Francis simultaneously exploiting Anthony's connections and obscuring his own involvement with Essex.

Essex was reconciled with the Queen by 25 February, but on 4 March he was still at loggerheads with Sir Robert Cecil (a conflict mediated by Ralegh), and on the point of storming out of the court for Wales. Two days later, the death of Lord Cobham spawned another quarrel, this time concerning his wardenship of the Cinque Ports. His eldest son was a contender for the office, but Essex wished Sir Robert Sidney to have it. When the Queen declared adamantly in favour of Cobham, the earl, 'seeing he is likely to carry it away,' declared that 'I mean resolutely to stand for it myself against him.' Essex declared that he had 'just cause to hate the Lord Cobham, for his villainous dealing and abusing of me: that he hath been my chief persecutor most injustly; that in him there is no worth: if therefore her Majesty would grace him with honour, I may have right cause to think myself little regarded by her.' When Elizabeth remained firm in her support for Cobham, Essex took umbrage, and on Thursday 10 March was ready with his followers and horses to leave the court. But after a meeting with Burghley, he was persuaded to meet the Queen at a private conference, where he was made Master of the Ordnance, 'which place he hath accepted and receives contentment by it'.

With Essex busy, Francis tried to recruit other potential patrons to his cause. Hearing from his cousin Sir Robert Cecil that he was in favour with Burghley, Francis wrote to his uncle, assuring him that 'I will use no reason to persuade your Lordship's mediation but this; that your Lordship and my other friends shall in this beg my life of the Queen; for I see well the Bar will be my bier, as I must and will use it rather than my poor estate or reputation shall decay. But I stand indifferent whether God call me, or her Majesty.' If he had come into the Star Chamber clerkship (of which he had the reversion), he claimed, 'I would never trouble her Majesty, but serve her still voluntarily without pay.'[39] But Burghley's continued ill health and the bitter weather, both of which kept him away from the court, effectively rendered such appeals worthless. Francis turned next to Sir John Stanhope – reminding him that 'your good promises sleep, which it may seem now no time to awake' – but apparently in vain.[40]

On 18 April, the patent for Essex as Master of the Ordnance was signed. Although Easter Term began the same day, Francis was eager to impress on the earl his duties towards his followers, now that his own demands had been met: 'I am glad your Lordship hath plunged out of your own business. Wherein I must commend your Lordship, as Xenophon commended the state of his country; which was thus: *that having chosen the worst form of government of all others, they governed the best in that kind.* Now, as your Lordship is my witness that I would not trouble you whilst your own cause was in hand; so, that being concluded, I presume I shall be one of your next cares.'[41]

It was a bad time to pester the earl. The period of waiting, during which (in his own words) the Queen 'had armed and victualled ten of her own ships and caused the States of the Low Countries to furnish the like number, before ever he was spoken of to go to sea,' was at an end. Now with the sole command of the mission, he urged it on, intending to destroy the fleet and the army at Ferrol, and to gain control of Spanish commerce and coasts and the Azore islands. By early June, he was on cordial working terms with Cecil, and turned a blind eye to Ralegh's new access to the Queen. Bacon later claimed that he himself was not keen on the mission: 'Nay, I remember I was thus plain with him upon his voyage to the islands, when I saw every spring put forth some actions of charge and provocation, that I said to him, "My Lord, when I came first unto you, I took you for a physician that desired to cure the diseases of the State; but now I doubt you will be like those physicians which can be content to keep their patients low because they will be always in request."' Essex took Bacon's 'plainness' 'very well, as he had an excellent ear, and was *patientissimus veri* [patience itself], and assured me the case of realm required it'. However, Bacon was sure that 'this speech of mine, and the like renewed afterwards, pricked him to write that *Apology* [Essex's defence against charges of war-mongering] which is in many men's hands.'[42]

Still, Essex found time to meet with Francis at the Tower, where he was told of Bacon's new plans. On 12 March 1597 Sir William Hatton had died, leaving a young and rich widow, who also happened to be a daughter of Sir Thomas Cecil (Burghley's eldest son) and a sister of Richard Cecil, one of Francis' Twickenham house guests. With the widow came properties including Ely House in London, Corfe Castle on the Isle of Purbeck, and Holdenby in Northamptonshire. Bacon made some suit to her – '*in genere oeconomico* [on domestic grounds]', as he put it, since '*in genere politico* [on political grounds], certain cross winds have blown contrary' – and, supported by Anthony, successfully importuned Essex, on his depar-ture, 'for your several letters to be left with me, dormant, to the gentle-woman and either of her parents; wherein I do not doubt but as the beams of your favour have often dissolved the coldness of my fortune, so is this argument your Lordship will do the like with your pen.'[43]

The letters to Lady Hatton and her parents were to no avail.[44] Francis Bacon's name was not mentioned by court gossip in connection with her remarriage (in 1597 Fulke Greville was thought likely). Ultimately, on 7 November 1598, and to general astonishment, she married Bacon's old rival for the attorneyship Sir Edward Coke: 'to the great admiration of all men that after so many large and likely offers she should decline to a man of his quality, and the world will not believe that it was without a mystery.' Once again Bacon's adversary had snatched the prize from under his nose. Had Bacon then known who his own bride would ultimately be, however, he might have taken heart from the next piece of news contained in John Chamberlain's letter: 'The day before Sir John Packington married Mistress Barnham one of our London widows.'[45]

Francis also asked Essex to petition the Lord Keeper: 'My desire is also, that your Lordship would vouchsafe unto me, as out of your care, a general letter to my Lord Keeper, for his Lordship's holding me from you recommended, both in the course of my practice and in the course of my employment in her Majesty's service. Wherein if your Lordship shall in any antithesis or relation affirm that his Lordship shall have no less fruit of me than of any other whom he may cherish, I hope your Lordship shall engage yourself for no impossibility.'[46] In asking for these favours, Francis added a note of moral exhortation to Essex:

It is true that in my well-meaning advices, out of my love to your Lordship, and perhaps out of the state of mine own mind, I have sometimes persuaded a course differing; *ac tibi pro tutis insignia facta placebunt* [and to you distinguished deeds please when they are cautious]. Be it so: yet remember, that the signing of your name is nothing, unless it be to some good patent or charter, whereby your country may be endowed with good and benefit. Which I speak, both to move you to preserve your person for further merit and service to her Majesty and your country; and likewise to refer this action to the same end.[47]

★

With Essex out of the country, and only a few letters to promote him at court, Francis turned his energies to making the most of what little he did possess: the reversion of the clerkship of the Star Chamber. The present incumbent, William Mill, was in danger of being deprived of the office, on suspicion of charging unlawful fees. The bill brought into parliament in 1593 to reform the office had been thrown out on the second reading (Bacon had spoken against it); now the new Lord Keeper, Sir Thomas Egerton, was continuing Puckering's inquiry, started two years earlier, into the matter.

William Mill, like the Bacon brothers a Grayan, was primarily known as a moneylender. Since 1591, his tenure of the clerkship had been challenged at regular intervals. The compiler of a list of 'exceptions' against Mill wrote that 'I am credibly informed that when there was a matter in question between a great personage and him, he said he had the earl of Shrewsbury as assured to him as the skin on his face, and also the earl owes him a great sum of money.' Shrewsbury was not alone: other debtors included Lord Burgh and, naturally, Francis Bacon and the earl of Essex.[48] In the summer of 1597 Egerton restrained some of the fees claimed by Mill as Clerk, prompting a petition from Mill on 3 July, and two days later one from Francis Bacon.[49]

Bacon did not leave the entire matter to chance. At the same time as he submitted his petition, he penned a lengthy and private letter to Egerton, proposing a deal. If Egerton would give him the mastership of the Rolls, an office he still held in addition to the lord keepership, Bacon would give the clerkship of the Star Chamber to Egerton's son John. This atypically frank letter was apparently known to Bacon's chaplain and editor, William Rawley – he quotes from it out of context in his *Life* of Bacon – but he evidently felt it unsuitable for publication. Bacon cited as his motives 'the consideration of mine own estate' and his thankfulness towards Egerton for his previous 'nomination and enablement of me long sithence to the

Solicitor's place'. His problems stemmed from his estate, which was 'weak and indebted, and needeth comfort; for both my father, though I think I had greatest part in his love of all his children, yet in his wisdom served me as a last comer; and myself, in mine own industry, have rather referred and aspired to virtue than to gain: whereof I am not yet wise enough to repent me.' He saw three ways to improve his estate: his practice; 'some proceeding in the Queen's service'; and the Star Chamber clerkship, which, 'as it standeth now unto me, is but like another man's ground reaching upon my house, which may mend my prospect but it doth not fill my barn'.

The problem with his practice was that 'it presupposeth my health' which, while fine at present, might well deteriorate ('I am apter to conclude in everything of change from the present tense than of a continuance'). He also realised that 'in practising the law I play not all my best game; which maketh me accept it with a *nisi quod potius* [failing anything better], as the best of my fortune, and a thing agreeable to better gifts than mine, but not to mine.' However, during 'her Majesty's strange dealing towards me', Egerton had been so good as 'to comfort and encourage me' to think that he might inherit the mastership of the Rolls from Egerton, 'signifying in your plainness that no man should better content yourself'.

Bacon went on to make three requests of Egerton. 'First, that your Lordship will hold and make good your wishes towards me in your own time; for no other I mean it. And in thankfulness thereof I will present your Lordship with the fairest flower of my estate, though it yet bear no fruit; and that is the poor reversion, which of her Majesty's gift I hold; in the which I shall be no less willing Mr. John Egerton, if it seem good to you, should succeed me in that, than I would be willing to succeed your Lordship in the other place.' Secondly, he asked Egerton to believe his 'protestation' that he, Francis, would not support 'any heaving or putting at that place' on his behalf without Egerton's 'foreknowledge and approbation'. Thirdly, he asked Egerton to 'believe an intelligence, and not take it for a fiction in court': namely, 'that there should be a plot laid of some strength between Mr. Attorney-General [Coke] and Mr. Attorney of the Wards, for the one's remove to the Rolls and the other to be drawn to his place.' Francis protested that

I do apprehend much. For first, I know Mr. Attorney-General, whatsoever he pretendeth or protesteth to your Lordship or any other, doth seek it; and I perceive well by his dealing towards his best friends to whom he oweth most, how perfectly he hath conned the adage of *proximus egomet mihi* [closer to none more than to myself]: and then I see no man ripened for the place of the Rolls in competition with Mr. Attorney-General. And lastly, Mr. Attorney of the Wards being noted for a pregnant and stirring man, the objection of any hurt her Majesty's business may receive in her causes by the drawing up of Mr. Attorney-General will wax cold.

Turning to 'my third poor help', the reversion of the clerkship, Francis wrote: 'I account [it] will do me small good, except there be a heave; and that is this place of the Star Chamber.' He argued that 'rules without examples will do little good', and that 'there is such a concordance between the time to come and the time past, as there will be no reforming the one without informing of the other.' He begged Egerton 'to conceive that it is not any money that I have borrowed of Mr. Mill, nor any gratification I receive for my aid, that makes me show myself any ways in it; but simply a desire to preserve the rights of the office, as far as it is meet and incorrupt; and secondly, his importunity; who nevertheless, as far as I see, taketh a course to bring this matter in question to his further disadvantage, and to be principal in his own harm.' If it were true as he had heard, however, that there were charges of 'deeper corruptions' against Mill,

surely, for my part, I am not so superstitious as I will take any shadow of it, nor labour to stop it, since it is a thing medicinable for the office of the realm. And then if the place by such an occasion or otherwise should come in possession, the better to testify my affection to your Lordship, I should be glad, as I offered it to your Lordship afore by way of [blank] so in this case to offer it by way of joint patency, in nature of a reversion: which, as it is now, there wanteth no goodwill in me to offer, but that both in that condition it is not worthy the offering, and besides I know not whether my necessity may enforce me to sell it away; which, if it were locked in by any reversion or joint-patentcy, I were disabled to do for my relief.

Francis concluded by remarking on 'how assured a persuasion I have of your love towards me and care of me, which hath made me as freely to communicate of my poor state with your Lordship, as I could have done to my honourable father, if he had lived', and (unsurprisingly) begging Egerton to keep the matter 'private to yourself'.[50]

The matter grew more complicated when it transpired that Mill was threatened with charges 'which in an ordinary course were intended to be proved against him', which might lead to the forfeiture of the office. That possibility meant that Francis would reap the financial benefit immediately. Unfortunately, however, Egerton was the judge in Mill's case. Since Bacon intended to sell the office to Egerton's son, Egerton's position would clearly be compromised. Bacon proposed to get round this awkwardness by inserting one more purchaser in the chain. On 12 November, he wrote to reassure Egerton that his position was unchanged, and that he had 'considered and digested with myself how I mought put in execution my purpose of good will to be carried without all note, as first to a deputation in some apt person your Lordship mought choose, and so to a passing over to such depute, and then a name in the next degree is soon changed'.[51]

The complaint, originating in the Star Chamber, was referred by the Queen to Egerton, Buckhurst, Cecil, Fortescue and Popham. When the Queen informed Francis that she had referred the hearing of Mill's case to these counsellors and judges, he had just come from speaking vehemently in parliament against depopulation and enclosures. She 'asked him how he liked of it' and he answered, ' "Oh Madam, my mind is known; I am against all enclosures, but especially against enclosed justices." '[52] In January 1598, Bacon assured Egerton that he was 'determined not to meddle' in his Star Chamber business, not least because 'looking into the matter at first, and since better informing myself, I find the ground too watery for me or any other to stand upon.'[53] Ultimately, the complaints were dismissed, the proceedings were dropped, and the commissioners settled what fees 'shall appear proper and fit to be allowed' in future and 'the same to confirm unto the said William Mill'.[54] In the end, Bacon had backed Mill in order to ensure that the perquisites of the clerkship remained intact, even though this lost him the opportunity for early enjoyment of the office. He was doubly compromised in the process: he turned a blind eye to customary malpractice, and he himself engineered the dubious means for keeping Egerton on the case.

★

Parliament sat again in October 1597, with Francis Bacon passing over a seat in Southampton in favour of one in Ipswich (both were in the gift of Essex).[55] Unlike its immediate precedessors, this Parliament was notable for its peacefulness. There was no attempt by the Lords to dictate to the Commons, no pressure on the House from the Queen to avoid ecclesiastical matters, and no heavy-handed hints that members should leave law-making alone. Indeed, Lord Keeper Egerton made a speech on 24 October that dealt with a matter close to Bacon's heart – the reduction of the huge number of English laws, 'some of them being obsolete and worn out of use, others idle and vain, serving to no purpose; some again overheavy and too severe for the offence, others too loose and slack for the faults they are to punish, and many so full of difficulty to be understood, that they cause many controversies and much difficulty to arise amongst the subjects.'[56] The relaxed mood can be ascertained from the fact that the Houses were adjourned from the day of the Speaker's presentation (27 October) for over a week.

In the meantime, the fleet arrived back, having failed to achieve any of its aims, and carrying little booty. Essex returned to court on 29 October.[57] He discovered that, once again, Cecil had taken advantage of his absence to sue for preferment (this time to the chancellorship of the Duchy of Lancaster); and only six days earlier, Elizabeth had made Lord Howard of Effingham, the Lord High Admiral, earl of Nottingham 'in an acknowledgement of his services in anno 88, and lately at Cales [Cádiz]'.[58] If these messages were not clear enough, court gossip quickly informed Essex that the Queen was not happy with him. By 5 November he was acting the injured man: 'disquieted, keeps in, and went not this day to the Parliament'.[59]

Through his non-attendance, the earl was deprived of the chance of seeing Francis Bacon play a key role in the new parliament. Once again, Bacon served extensively on committees. Among the first business, on 5 November, he introduced a motion against enclosures and depopulation of towns and houses of husbandry and tillage; its lengthy voyage through committees and reports ended only on 24 November, when Bacon joked that he was as glad to be discharged of the pains of the bill 'as an ass when he hath laid down his pack'.[60]

With memories of his disastrous 1593 subsidy speech still fresh, and its ramifications still painfully apparent in the lack of further preferment, Francis was keen to speak in support of this parliament's subsidy bill. However, on the day of the debate (15 November), he was effectively robbed of his chance. Three lengthy speeches, by Chancellor of the Exchequer Fortescue, Sir Robert Cecil and Sir Edward Hoby, had to be heard before at last Francis was allowed to speak. 'I shall speak at a great disadvantage,' he lamented, 'but because it hath been always used, and the mixture of this House doth so require it, that in causes of this nature there be some speech and opinion as well from persons of generality as by persons of authority, I will say somewhat and not much.'[61]

Essex's fit of discontent lasted nearly two months: he did not appear in parliament, at the Council table, or in court; he missed the Accession Day celebrations on 17 November, reportedly very sick.[62] Only after he had been made Earl Marshal of England, a post superior to Lord High Admiral, on 18 December,[63] did he

show himself in more public sort than he did, and he is purposed to have the patent of the late-created earl [Nottingham] altered, who absolutely refuses to consent unto it. The Queen by this long patience and suffering of my Lord Essex, is grown to consider and understand better the wrong done unto him, which she now lays upon 900 [Burghley] and 200 [Cecil]. I hear that my Lord Essex desires to have right done unto him, either by a commission to examine it, or by combat, either against the earl of Nottingham himself, or any of his sons, or of his name that will defend it. Or that her Majesty will please to see the wrong done unto him. And so will he suffer himself to be commanded by her as she please herself. Here is such ado about it, as it troubles this place and all other proceedings. Sir Walter Ralegh is employed by the Queen to end this quarrel and to make an atonement between them. But this is the resolution of Lord Essex, not to yield but with altering the patent, which cannot be done, but by persuasion to bring the earl of Nottingham unto it.[64]

As Bacon later put it in one of his *Apophthegms*: 'A great officer at Court, when my Lord of Essex was first in trouble; and that he and those that dealt for him would talk much of my Lord's friends and of his enemies; answered one of them; "I will tell you, I know but one friend and one enemy my Lord hath; and that one friend is the Queen, and that one enemy is himself." '[65]

But Essex was shortly to find his attention diverted from his local grievances by new developments. Philip II of Spain was anxious to wind up his businesses and give a settled kingdom to his son on his death, which he felt would not be far in the future. Similarly, Henri IV in France was looking for peace after twelve years of war. He had just taken Amiens, and now found Philip willing to come to terms. However, Henri's previous deals with England and the Netherlands gave them both a right to interfere. In February 1598 Sir Robert Cecil was despatched to negotiate. Elizabeth had other business for Essex. On 10 February she gave the earl a present of £7,000 worth of cochineal, part of the Azores mission booty; on the fifteenth he was 'giving very diligent attendance upon the Queen, and in some sort taking upon him the dispatching of all business, in the absence of the Secretary, that concerns her Majesty's service'. In the forefront of Elizabeth's mind was Ireland, where Hugh O'Neill, earl of Tyrone, had been in open rebellion for three years. The sudden death from typhus of the English commander Lord Thomas Burgh in October 1597 left a command vacuum.

Francis saw Essex as an obvious candidate. He took it upon himself to 'play the ignorant statesman, which I do to nobody but your Lordship; except to the Queen sometimes when she trains me on'. He told Essex that he thought such a campaign 'one of the aptest particulars, that hath come or can come upon the stage, for your Lordship to purchase honour upon', for three reasons: his father's 'noble attempts' in Ireland; 'because of all the actions of state on foot at this time, the labour resteth most in that particular'; and because the world would 'make a kind of comparison between those that have set it out of frame and those that shall bring it into frame: which kind of honour giveth the quickest kind of reflexion'. Those of the former category – Sir William Fitzwilliams, Sir John Norreys and Sir William Russell – were not associated with Essex; the latter – Sir Conyers Clifford and Thomas Butler, earl of Ormonde – were either dependent on Essex or at the least not opposed to him. Therefore, Francis reasoned, 'as all things hitherto are not only whole and entire, but of favourable aspect towards your Lordship, if hereafter you choose well', he should start by consulting Russell, Sir Richard Bingham, the earl of Toumond and Mr Wilbraham for their insider knowledge. While admitting himself 'too much a stranger to the business' to identify the most salient Irish issues, in general terms Bacon pointed to 'either of the possibility and means of accord, or of the nature of the war, or of the reformation of abuses, or of the joining of practice with force in the disunion of the rebels'. Finally, if Essex were doubtful whether he should 'put your sickle into another's harvest', Bacon urged him to think of the favourable aspects: Cecil's absence, the mission's 'matter of war', and Essex's own 'honesty and respect towards aged dignity', which would not allow him to upset Burghley.[66]

Bacon's ploy to arouse Essex's interest worked. Essex sent him the most recent intelligence from Ireland, and asked for his opinion. Tyrone was now prepared to settle for a complete pardon. Having considered his case, Ormonde had been instructed as to the terms on which his pardon would be granted. On 15 March, Tyrone was told that his submission had induced the Queen 'to receive him to mercy, and to give him and all the inhabitants of Tyrone her gracious pardon' on thirteen conditions. Tyrone took exception to five of these. He was given until 10 April to make his own submission. This was reported to the English court, and the Council in Ireland advised that the treaty should not on these conditions be proceeded with. At this point, Bacon provided his advice as requested. The letter contained the suggestion that Essex should offer to head a full-scale invasion of Ireland, should negotiations with Tyrone fail. 'And but that your Lordship is too easy to pass in such cases from dissimulation to verity, I think if your Lordship lent your reputation in this case, – that is, to pretend that if peace go not on and the Queen mean not to make a defensive war as in times past, but a full reconquest of those parts of the country, you would accept the charge; I think it would help to settle Tyrone in his seeking accord, and win you a great deal of honour gratis.'[67]

During the summer, however, the Queen proposed that Essex's uncle Sir William Knollys should be sent to Ireland; the earl insisted on Sir George Carew, whom he disliked and wanted away from court. During this quarrel, in the presence of Lord Nottingham, Cecil and Windebank,

Essex allegedly turned his back on the Queen, and she struck him. He laid his hand upon his sword, swearing that he neither could nor would swallow such an indignity, and would not have endured it from Henry VIII himself; he subsequently retired from the court, refusing to submit.[68]

In the end, Sir Henry Bagenal was sent 'with the most choice companies of foot and horse troops of the English army'; by this time, the besieged English were reportedly eating the vegetation on the walls and in the ditches. Bagenal's force became divided en route, and on 14 August 1598 Tyrone charged the foremost body, killing Bagenal and gaining a complete victory: fifteen hundred soldiers were slain and the garrison gave up the fort, supplying the rebels with arms and victuals. As Fynes Moryson reported, when the traitors celebrated and ran amok, 'the English lay in their garrisons, so far from assailing the rebels, as they rather lived in continual fear to be surprised by them.' Munster fell to Tyrone in October. Bagenal's replacement Sir Richard Bingham died on his arrival in Dublin. Factional squabbling at court had proved disastrous.

On 4 August 1598 William Cecil, Lord Burghley, died at the age of seventy-four. The Queen was overcome at the news, taking his death 'very grievously, with shedding of tears, and separating herself from all company'. The funeral, on 29 August, as reported by John Chamberlain, was performed 'with all the rites that belong to so great a personage. The number of mourners one and another were above five hundred whereof there were many noblemen and among the rest the earl of Essex, who (whether it were upon consideration of the present occasion, or for his own disfavours) methought carried the heaviest countenance of the company.'[69]

Bacon continued with his usual legal work. In September 1598, he was occupied at the Tower of London in examining one John Stanley, who was suspected of involvement in a plan to murder the Queen, masterminded by Edward Squire the previous year. Bacon was later to write a pamphlet, supposedly a letter written by a English gentleman to a friend in Padua, detailing the case – one hostile reader identified the writer as 'M. Smokey-swynes flesh, at the instance of Sir R.C.'[70] But just when the favour of the Queen was being so visibly displayed in high-level, high-profile work, Bacon was foiled again. As he left the Tower one night, he was arrested for debt.

★

In Trinity Term 1597 a goldsmith named Giles Sympson, who held a bond from Bacon for £300 principal, had sued him for restitution. Francis 'confessed the action, and by his full and direct consent respited the satisfaction' until the beginning of the following term. During the summer, the danger seemed to pass. Sympson gave no 'warning either by letter or message' that he intended action. Abruptly, two weeks before the start of Michaelmas Term, the goldsmith 'served an execution upon me, having trained me at such time as I came from the Tower'.

He was caught entirely off guard. Sympson was, he knew, 'a man noted much, as I have heard, for extremities and stoutness upon his purse: but yet I could scarcely have imagined he would have dealt so dishonestly towards myself, or so contemptuously towards her Majesty's service' – namely the Stanley investigation, which was 'a service of no mean importance'. He attempted to contact Sympson, 'this Lombard', who lived in nearby Lombard Street, but 'neither would he so much as vouchsafe to come and speak with me to take any order in it, though I sent for him divers times, and his house was just by; handling it as upon a despite', although he was 'a man I never provoked with a cross word, no nor with many delays'. Indeed, Sympson was noticeably keen to have Francis committed to gaol, 'which he had done, had not sheriff More, to whom I sent, gently recommended me to an handsome house in Coleman Street, where I am'.

Held in Coleman Street, Bacon petitioned Lord Keeper Egerton to send for Sympson and 'to bring him to some reason'. He had 'an hundred pounds lying by me, which he may have, and the rest upon some reasonable time and security; or, if need be, the whole'. Francis also pointed to 'the contempt he hath offered, in regard her Majesty's service, to my understanding, carrieth a privilege [immunity] *eundo et redeundo* [going and returning] in meaner causes, much more in matters of this nature, especially in persons known to be qualified with that place and employment, which, though unworthy, I am vouchsafed, I enforce nothing; thinking I have done my part when I have made it known; and so leave it to your Lordship's humble consideration'.[71]

The more he considered it, the more curious the incident appeared. 'Mr. Sympson might have had me every day in London,' he meditated to Sir Robert Cecil, 'and therefore to belay me, while he knew I came from the Tower about her Majesty's special service, was to my understanding very bold. And two days before he brags he forbore me, because I dined with sheriff More. So as with Mr. Sympson, examinations at the Tower are not so great a privilege, *eundo et redeundo*, as sheriff More's dinner.' If Bacon could not be arrested while dining with the sheriff, how much more so while on the Queen's business? He also complained to Essex, 'for otherwise his punishment will do me no good'.[72] Whatever the outcome, the world now knew of Bacon's debts.

Being in debt was not in itself a problem in Elizabethan England: indeed, it was the glue that bound English society in a condition of mutual indebtedness, in which everyone owed something to somebody else. The ritualistic gift-giving of each New Year was in fact the highly formalised display of demonstrating to whom one was in debt. The problem of debt lay not in the indebtedness itself but in having insufficient credit to keep creditors confident of eventual repayment.

Anthony and Francis had both been left by their father with certain amounts of property which they could use as collateral against borrowing. In Anthony's case, this comprised relatively extensive resources; in Francis' case, the legacy was far more limited. In his early career in France, Anthony made a point of lending money to his fellow expatriate travellers, and so indebted them to him, building a network of useful intelligencers who owed him money – or, failing the repayment of that money, services: repayment in kind. This strategy could, however, rebound on its practitioner, and the story of Anthony in the 1580s is the story of a man who ran out of ready cash and who was forced to become indebted to other men to the point where his freedom of movement and his physical safety were under threat.

Francis Bacon never had the advantages of his elder brothers. The second son of a second marriage – the fifth and youngest son of all – he was not, despite the claims of his first parliamentary speech, well provided for by his father. His estates were small and unlikely to yield profit: they were not the kind of property that was of any use in raising cash. Instead, he had to borrow. We have already noted the likelihood of a financial motive in Francis' close involvement with the Philippes family in the early 1580s; he was certainly borrowing by 1589, when he and his mother borrowed £200, to be repaid in six months, from a grocer-turned-moneylender named Thomas Myddleton, who had a sugar business with factors in Antwerp, Middelburg and Stade on the Elbe, but who more importantly had ready cash from his customs post. His 'Journal of all outlandish accounts' records that the Bacons repaid their loan – with 10 per cent interest – on the due date.[73]

By the time Anthony returned home at the end of 1591, the situation was beginning to turn ugly. His arrival in London provoked a blunt request from a Mr Harvy for the repayment of £32 10s that had been 'due unto me by your brother' on 31 January 1592 – that amount being just the six-monthly interest payable on the large sum borrowed by Francis, who proposed to pay it off by selling his estate, Marks. However, Marks could not be sold without his mother's consent (many such bequest agreements allowed the dowager to claim a third of the proceeds if the estate was sold). Lady Bacon had initially indicated that she might agree to part with her interest, in order to extricate him from debt, but when Anthony later wrote to remind her of her offer in April 1593,[74] she had a different memory of what she had said about 'mine own sicklings': 'I was in mind almost to make none of you both mine executors' because she was loath that 'those that greatly abused & spent you both should bear any stroke in my appointed matters & you after my death'. She had now decided that she would give her goods (money and plate) to her servants rather to her sons. 'I have been too ready for you both till nothing is left.'

She launched into an intemperate attack on the lifestyle of her younger son. She pitied Francis, she wrote, 'yet so long as he pitieth not himself but keepeth that bloody Percy I told him then, yea as a coach companion and bed companion, a proud, profane, costly fellow, whose being about him I verily fear the Lord God doth mislike and doth less bless your brother in credit and otherwise in his health.' The sharing of coach and bed suggests both a private intimacy – perhaps at Twickenham or Gray's Inn – and a public display of that intimacy in the coach, as they travelled between the various residences. Francis' followers were harming not only him, but also her: 'Surely I am utterly discouraged & make a conscience further to undo myself to maintain such wretches as he is.' She charted a history whereby 'first Enney, a filthy wasteful knave & his Welshmen one after another; for take one, & they will still swarm ill-favouredly, did so lend him as in a train. He was a toward young gentleman & a son of much good hope in godliness, but he hath nourished most sinful, proud villains wilfully.' She singled out Jones – one that 'never loved your brother indeed but for his own credit living upon your brother thankless brags, though your brother will be blind to his own hurt, and picking such vile his wicked countrymen to supply in his absence. The Lord in mercy remove them from him & evil from you both & give you a sound judgement and understanding to order yourselves in all things to please God in true knowledge & in his true fear unfeigned & to hearken to his word which only maketh wise indeed.' Francis had made it plain that he 'intended not to part with Marks' – that first he would borrow £500 from the Clerk of the Star Chamber, Mill. Lady Bacon asked him 'how he would come out of debt'. Francis replied that 'means would be made without that' and named 'Jennings & Corsellis', both known moneylenders.[75]

On a separate sheet of paper, Lady Bacon abandoned her polemic to make more practical suggestions. If Francis desired a release from Mr Harvy, she wrote, 'let him so require it himself' – in his own hand and with his own bond. Francis would also be required to 'give me a true note of all his debts and leave to me the whole order of the receipt of all his money for his bond to Harvy and the just payment of all his debts thereby'. She would then perform what was needful 'to his quiet discharge without cumbring him and to his credit. For I will not have his cormorant seducers and instruments of Satan to him committing foul sins by his countenance to the displeasing of God & his only true friends. Otherwise I will not, *pro certo.*'[76]

Francis' reply was forthcoming but unintelligible to his mother, who promptly forwarded it to Anthony for deciphering: 'I send herein your brother's letter. Construe the interpretation. I do not understand his enigmatical folded writing.' What she did understand was that he accused her of treating him like a ward:

> The scope of my so called by him circumstances, which I am sure he must understand, was not to use him as a ward, – a remote phrase to my plain motherly meaning, – and yet, I thank the Lord and the hearing of his word preached, not void of judgment and conceiving. My plain proposition was and is to do him good. But seeing so manifestly that he is robbed and spoiled wittingly by his base exalted [?] men, which with Welsh wiles prey upon him, and yet bear him in hand they have other maintenance, because their bold natures will not acknowledge, I did desire only to receive the money to discharge his debts indeed; and dare not trust such his riotous men with the dealing withal. I am sure no preacher, nor lawyer, nor friend, would have misliked this my doing for his good and my better satisfying. He perceives my good meaning by this, and before too. But Percy had winded him.

She lamented her Francis' early downfall: 'Oh that by not hearkening to wholesome and careful good counsel, and by continuing still the means of his own great hindrance, he had not procured his own early discredit; but had joined with God that hath bestowed on him good gifts of natural wit and understanding. But the same good God that hath given them to him will I trust and heartily pray to sanctify his heart by the right use of them to glorify the Giver of them to his own inward comfort.' Even in the midst of Lady Bacon's anger, however, there is a special tenderness for her youngest child: 'He was his father's first chis [choice], and God will supply if he will trust in him and call upon [him] in truth of heart; which God grant to mother and sons.'[77] Marks seems to have been redeemed from Harvy in the autumn.[78]

Throughout the 1590s, Lady Bacon alternately lavished gifts on her sons – hogsheads of beer, malt, strawberries, linen, pewter candlesticks, a dozen doves[79] – and complained about their spending. Certainly, they often seemed to be dependent on her: when he was planning a journey to Bath in the summer of 1593, Anthony asked his mother for a hogshead of beer, two geldings to draw his coach, her litter, her cook, and some wine.[80] Even when he moved into Essex House, he expected her to foot the bill for his coal supplies,[81] and his carriage.[82] For her part, Lady Bacon complied, but wanted to know why Essex House needed heating in the summer, and who was using the carriage. She even went to the lengths of sending secretly to Anthony's physician, Mr Moore, for his physick bill; she then confronted Anthony, demanding to know why it took him so long to pay it.[83] Lady Bacon constantly accused her sons of having too many horses and living beyond their income.[84] The scrupulous Lord Keeper was held up as a shining example: to Anthony, Lady Bacon pointed out, 'Your father neither in London nor here spent so many in two years and was as well cherished, son, in his gout and sickness and better in good order of expenses.'[85]

To her sons, as we have seen, Lady Bacon was just as much a cause of anxiety as they to her, berating and abusing not only them but also their servants: forcing them to go without food, as with Edward Spencer, or even inducing the Lord Treasurer to have them imprisoned, as with Thomas Lawson. All this worry on both sides stemmed from an overarching concern for the future of Anthony's estates, of which Lady Bacon was a life tenant. The causes of Lady Bacon's alleged 'unquietness' became clearer when Spencer told her that Anthony intended to buy some horses from the fair, and that the money he had sent via Spencer and Lawson was what he could spare. 'Well,' replied Lady Bacon, 'let him do as he will, he shall have none of me. He has undone me, and nobody else but he.'

Spencer, suddenly emboldened, interjected, 'Madam, I hope you hold it well bestowed; for my master hath gotten great experience and great worship both within the land and without.'

'I hold it well bestowed!' retorted Lady Bacon, 'but I know not how vainly it have been spent. But I am sure he have gotten a weak body of his own and is diseased in the meantime.'

'Now my master saith he is as well contented to be as he is in many noblemen at the Court which spend all that they can and live in discredit.'

At that Lady Bacon sighed and prayed for Anthony that the Lord's holy spirit might guide him. Spencer told her that Anthony would have written to her, 'but the Scottish gentlemen did come in the meantime'.

'No, no,' she replied, 'it is no matter. I do not care.' But when she was told that Anthony meant to buy four or five horses, she broke out again: 'My sons they be vainglorious; they will leave it one day.'[86]

There was one constituency that was protected from Lady Bacon's anger – and her thrift: 'priests, which will undo her. There is one Page which had six pound on her. Mr. Wilcox [Thomas Wilcox] had a paper with a good deal of gold in it. Wylblud [Humphrey Wylblud] had two quarterns of wheat. Dyke [William Dyke] had something the other day; what I know not.'[87] Spencer was worried about Lady Bacon's generosity (with

Anthony's estate) towards her coterie of Nonconformist ministers, which was clearly using Gorhambury as, in the words of the ecclesiastical historian William Urwick, 'the rendezvous of the silenced Puritan minsters of [the] day'. Her financial situation gradually deteriorated. In 1594, the widow of the Lord Keeper was forced to borrow £10 from neighbours.[88] The following year, she claimed to be living from hand to mouth. By 1596, she had nothing left to will.[89]

Another prominent creditor was a Yorkshireman named Nicholas Trott,[90] whose education had also taken him to Cambridge and Gray's Inn. In order to finance the Bacons, Trott had borrowed from his own mother and brother. The series of transactions before 1592 is complex. Trott reluctantly lent Francis £800, half of it due at a specified time; Francis gave Trott a New Year's gift of satin with which to make a doublet, then entered into a land-purchase bargain with him that ultimately injured Trott; Trott demanded his £400 from Francis. At this point Anthony returned.[91] Anthony borrowed £600, then, when that became due and he could not repay it, a further £1,400 from Trott. When he tried to persuade Trott to help Francis redeem some money that Francis had borrowed against his own land in Essex, Trott made it clear that he wanted nothing do with Francis financially. Anthony offered as security what he portrayed as the likelihood of Francis becoming Attorney-General. At first Trott trusted Anthony; but he suffered a temporary lapse of confidence in August 1596, which became serious the following year.[92]

Trott was also involved in lengthy and complex negotiations during 1593 to sell some of Anthony's properties in Hertfordshire to Alderman John Spencer (later the Lord Mayor of London), a process which involved circumventing Anthony's elder half-brother Sir Nicholas, who retained an interest in the sale of those lands.[93] A year later, however, Anthony seems to have learned a lesson: Spencer pressed him to see another manor; Anthony refused, and took the easy option of appealing to Thomas Phelippes for a loan of £1,000 per annum.[94]

Anthony Bacon's papers at Lambeth Palace contain several 'acknowledgments of money received from Anthony Bacon to the use of Francis Bacon by his servants', and a chart of 'Money paid by Mr. Anthony Bacon to his brother Francis and to Sir Anthony Standen':

1593.	A part ce qui a este paye a Mons. Senhouse.	
Le 21me de Septembre, a Mons. Francois Bacon		£5
11 de Septembre, 93, a Pierre pour Mr. Fr. Bacon		20
26 d'Octob. 1593, a Pierre		20
30 d'Octob. /93, a Mr. Fr. Bacon		1
31 d'Octob. /93 a Kellet pour Mons. Fr. Bacon		23

18 de Novem. /93, a Ashpoole pour Mr. Fr. Bacon	5
6 de May, /94, a Pierre pour Mr. Fr. Bacon	10
11 de Juillet, /94, a Mr. Fr. Bacon	60
31 d'Aoust, /94, a Mr. Fr. Bacon	100
9 Septemb. /94 a Mr. Fr. Bacon	50
29 Janvier, /94, a Mr. Trott pour Mr. Fr. Bacon	30
8 Mars, /94, a Rich. Gomme pour Mr. Fr. Bacon	10
14 d'April, a Kellet pour Mr. Fr. Bacon	44
14 Juin, /95, a Mons. Sugden par son homme	50

373[95]

In October 1594, Anthony made a 'Memorandum. That the fourth of October, '94, at my brother coming to me after a fit of the stone, and falling into talk of the money he ought [owed] me as principal debt, he acknowledged to be due to me £650; whereof £200 I borrowed of Mr. Mill and paid it him again; £200 of the money I had of Alderman Spencer; £100 before he went his journey into the north, £60 in money and £40 for my coach-horses; £150 after his return; besides many other payments to Mr. Senhouse and others.'[96]

By the end of 1594, Trott was beginning to grow anxious about the security of his money. Francis decided at one point that he might have to give up to Trott his sole trump card: the reversion of the clerkship of the Star Chamber, which he valued at £1,200. He proposed that Anthony and Trott should procure the reversion as joint patentees; Trott would make a down payment of £600, and – in the case of one of them dying before the present possessor died – the survivor would pay £600, in six yearly instalments, to the executors of the deceased partner. Alternatively, if Francis desired to have a yearly payment of, say, four or five hundred marks, Trott declared himself amenable, 'so that a corresponding defalkment be made out of the sum to be paid presently'.[97] Nothing came of the proposal.

In the meantime, Francis needed to raise more money, and managed to persuade Anthony to 'join with me in security for £500'.[98] On 14 January 1595, Anthony applied to his uncle Sir Henry Killigrew for a loan of £200 for six months, reiterating his request on the twenty-third and 'entreating him to believe that the circumstances of time was substantial and very important'.[99] Killigrew declined (or, as Anthony put it, 'uncled me with a frivolous excuse'), pleading that he could not help while his deputy Sugden refused. 'I am very sorry,' remarked Anthony, 'we ought [owed] him not three hundred pounds, being very well content that you should discharge yourself upon me, alleging to Sugden that if a special friend of mine, of whose kindness I made full account, had not frustrated my hope, he had ere this received satisfaction; which if you think meet I will affirm likewise unto him myself by letter, and request him to gratify me with the renewing of the bond for six months, with assurance that my uncle Killigrew will thank him in my particular behalf.'[100]

Another crisis arose in March 1596. Francis had borrowed £1,000 upon the security of 'certain marsh lands' at Woolwich worth less than £1,700. When the day to redeem the loan (24 March) came around, he did not have the money, and was forced to sell the land to save the difference. He came to an arrangement with 'a man in the City' to this end; but a few days after redemption day, the man displayed 'strange slipping and incertain or cunning dealing'. The question of assurance was raised. On 'so pressing an occasion', this time Francis turned for help to Henry Maynard and Michael Hickes – two of Burghley's secretaries – building 'somewhat upon the conceit I have of your good wills'. He offered his 'two so good friends as I esteem yourselves to be' the collateral pawn of 'the assurance of my lease at Twickenham, being a thing which will pass with easy and short assurance, and is every way clear and unsubject to incumbrance, (because it is my pleasure and my dwelling) I would not offer but to a private friend'.[101]

Over two years after helping Anthony to sell his Hertfordshire lands, Trott was still unpaid.[102] There had been attempts at payment in kind. In 1594, as we have seen, Francis suggested parting with his reversion of the clerkship of the Star Chamber to Trott. Trott's 1595 application for the post of deputy secretary of the Council in the north and his 1597 parliamentary seat at Bramber were sponsored by Essex, presumably at the instigation of one of the Bacon brothers. But it was not enough. In the spring of 1596, Trott turned angrily to the brothers' kinsman Robert Bacon, 'with more passion than reason'. Anthony and Francis determined to go to Robert personally to defend themselves – provided that Anthony was up to the demands of such a visit.[103] Three months later, Anthony warned his brother of the desperate measures Trott was about to take against Francis.[104] In December, after receiving a passionately worded letter from Trott, to which he answered, Anthony re-entered the quarrel as a mediator in the matter of Francis' overdue payments, and agreed to enter into an arrangement whereby the money lent to Francis might be repaid.[105]

But Trott eventually tired of the arrangement, presumably because he remained unpaid. In August 1597, a new plan was worked out – by Trott – whereby Francis and Anthony could both repay the money they owed to him, so that he could 'establish some more quiet course of life', because he found himself 'as much alienated from business as unfit for it'.[106] The reason soon became clear: Trott himself was in the hands of creditors. On 6 September, in a sad reversal of their previous fortunes, Nicholas Trott asked Anthony Bacon for a loan of £5 over eight days.[107]

A manuscript in the Lansdowne collection of the British Library gives some idea of the habitual borrowing in which Francis Bacon indulged during the last years of Elizabeth's reign:[108]

The state of the account between Mr. Trott and me, as far as I can collect it by such remembrances as I find; my trust in him being such as I did not carefully preserve papers; and my demands upon the same account.

The monies lent in particulars.	About 7 or 8 years passed I borrowed of him upon bonds	200 l.
	Soon I borrowed upon bond other	200 l.
	Upon my going northward I borrowed of him by my brother's means	100 l.
	But this was ever in doubt between my brother and me; and my brother's conceit was ever it was twice demanded, and that he had satisfied it upon reckonings between Mr. Trott and him.	1200 l.
	About a twelvemonth after, I borrowed of him, first upon communication of mortgage of land, and in conclusion upon bond But then upon interest and I know not what reckonings (which I ever left to his own making) and his principal sum, amounting to 1700 l. was wrapped up to 2000 l., and bond given according as I remember. And about August xlii Reginae I borrowed of him upon the mortgage of Twicknam park.	950 l.
The total of Trott's principal.	So as all the monies that Mr. Trott lent at any time amount to the total of	2650 l.
Mr. Trott's receipts at several times.	Of this sum he hath received, about 5 years since, upon the sale of certain marshes in Woolwich	300 l.
	He received about 4 years since,	450 l.

	upon sale of a lease I had of the parsonage of Redbourne	
	He received about 3 years since, upon sale of the manor of Burstone	800 l.
	He received about 2 years since, of Mr. Johnson of Gr. Inn, being my surety for 200 l. principal	233 l.
	He received of my cousin Kemp, another of my sureties, at the least	100 l.
	He hath received in divers small sums of 40, 30, 10 l., upon computation of interest trott's receits.	210 l.
	So as the sums which he hath received amount to the total of	2093 l.
	He hath now secured unto him, by mortgage of Twicknam Park	1259 l. 12 s.
	Upon my cousin Cooke's band	210 l.
	Upon Mr. Ed. Jones's band	208 l.
	Upon mine own band	220 l.
The debt depending.	Sum total	1897 l. 12 s.
His further demands of interest till November.	He demandeth furder for charges and interest until the first November 1601	138 l. 4s. 8d.
	So the total sum of the money he now demandeth is	2035. 16. 8.
The total of his demands.	So as the whole sum of principal and interest amounteth to	4128. 16. 8.
	Deduct out of this the principal viz.	2650 l.
	Remaineth in interest grown	1478. 16. 8.

By the time of his arrest in 1598, it was an habitual pattern. No matter how lofty the position he later gained, Francis Bacon's debts would always grow to meet it.

8

Losing Ground:
Matter of Charge and Accusation

Things go ill, not by accident, but by errors.
Demosthenes, quoted by Francis Bacon to the earl of Essex (1599)

AFTER STORMING OUT of court in April 1598, it was not until 12 September that Essex saw the Queen again. Although his original stance had softened, Elizabeth nevertheless took the opportunity to make it clear that she had the upper hand, claiming that the earl had 'played long enough upon her, and that she means to play awhile on him, and to stand as much upon her greatness as he had done upon his stomach'. Although Francis' Gray's Inn friend Tobie Matthew reported three days later that 'my Lord is reintegrated into the Queen's favour', the reconciliation was far from assured.[1]

Francis congratulated Essex on his rehabilitation, 'the rather, because I assure myself that of your eclipses, as this hath been the longest, it shall be the last'. This eclipse should be seen as a learning experience, since 'I believe neither your Lordship looked to have found her Majesty in all points as you have done, neither her Majesty percase looked to find your Lordship as she hath done.' From this experience 'may grow more perfect knowledge, and upon knowledge more true consent'.[2]

Whether Bacon's letter had any effect or not, it was after this date that it was detected that Essex 'became more submiss, and obtained pardon; and was received again of her into favour'.[3] Finally, the Queen and the earl had to make up, as the larger issue of agreeing upon some course for the reduction of Ireland to obedience gained urgency. From mid-October Essex's name replaced that of Lord Mountjoy as the likely leader of the Queen's campaign in Ireland. He held out for some time, in order to win for himself an unprecedented degree of control over the campaign, much to the disquiet of the court. 'In such sort did he bear himself,' recalled William Camden, 'that he seemed to his adversaries to wish nothing more than to have an army under his command and to bind martial men unto him; and that with such earnest seeking that some feared lest he entertained some monstrous design, especially seeing he showed his contumacy more and more against the Queen, that had been most bountiful to him.'[4] These fears were exacerbated by the new way in which Essex had recently 'lain so open to his enemies', according to Fynes Moryson, as if he 'had given them power to make his embracing of military courses and his popular estimation so much suspected of his sovereign, as his greatness was now judged to depend as much upon her Majesty's fear of him as her love to him'.[5] Eventually, all Essex's demands were allowed: he was supplied with the largest army ever seen in Ireland, the largest powers ever given to a deputy.

Essex was under close scrutiny from a worried court. Robert Markham advised Sir John Harington, who was to accompany Essex, to 'mark my counsel. Observe the man who commandeth, and yet is commanded himself; he goeth not forth to serve the Queen's realm, but to humour his own revenge.'[6] By 8 December, however, momentum had slackened. John Chamberlain reported that 'the earl of Essex's journey to Ireland is neither fast nor loose, but holds still in suspense by reason the proportions are daily dipt and diminished. For eight or ten days the soldiers flocked about him, and every man hoped to be a colonel at the least.' A new complication concerned the race for the lord treasurership. Lord Buckhurst was tipped for the post; some, however, said that Essex 'should have £6,000 yearly out of it; otherwhile, that he should have £20,000 toward the payment of his debts, and so to leave his hold, but we see neither come on very fast.'[7] A combination of the Queen's uneasy relationship with Essex and her reluctance fully to commit herself in Ireland stalled the situation once more. By the twentieth, 'the matters of Ireland stand at a stay, or rather go backward; for the earl of Essex's journey thither was in suspense is now they say quite dashed.' During the night of Sunday 17 December, something had happened to alter circumstances: 'some say the Queen had promised to forgive him £12,000 debt due by his father, and £20,000 he owed her himself for cochenilla since his last journey' – whatever the cause, 'all is turned upside down, and he and Mr. Secretary have so good leisure that they ply the tables hard in the presence-chamber, and play so round game as if Ireland were to be recovered at Irish.'[8]

With the New Year came new hope of action. On 3 January, Chamberlain sensed that 'The wind is come around again for Ireland, and the *disgusto* that made stay of the earl's going for a while, is sweetened and removed,' and the date set for March.[9] By the beginning of that month, however, Essex was reported to be 'crased [ill], but whether more in body or mind is doubtful': 'new difficulties arise daily about his commission, as touching the time of his abode, touching his entertainment, and touching the disposing of places and offices; he is so little satisfied, that many times he makes it a question whether he will go or not.'[10] Among the 'places and offices' on which Essex insisted were appointment of the earl of Southampton (currently out of royal favour) as General of the Horse; and of his stepfather Sir Christopher Blount, a Catholic, to a seat on the Irish Council (this was not allowed). The Queen did, however, grant him an effective release from his father's debts.[11]

A further complication came with the publication of John Hayward's book *Henry IV*, which had been dedicated to Essex. Unfortunately, it dealt with the deposition of Richard II, an episode about which Elizabeth was particularly sensitive. According to Bacon, she became 'mightily incensed . . . thinking it a seditious prelude to put into the people's heads boldness and faction'.[12] There was 'much descanting about it, why such a story should come out at this time, and many exceptions taken to the [dedicatory] epistle which was a short thing in Latin dedicated to the earl of Essex, and objected to him in good earnest, whereupon there was commandment it should be cut out of the book'. Chamberlain himself was bemused by the scandal: for his correspondent Dudley Carleton, he procured a transcript of the letter and dared him to 'pick out the offence if you can; for my part, I can pick out no such bugswords, but that every thing is as it is taken.'[13]

Elizabeth called in Bacon, as her Learned Counsel, and asked if he 'could not find any places in it that might be drawn within case of treason'. Bacon replied that 'for treason surely I found none, but for felony very many'. When the Queen asked how, Bacon quipped that 'the author had committed very apparent theft, for he had taken most of the sentences of Cornelius Tacitus, and translated them into English, and put them into his text.' But humour could not dispel the Queen's worries. On another occasion, she wondered whether Hayward was indeed the author, suspecting 'that it had some more mischievous author', and 'said with great indignation that she would have him racked to produce his author'. 'Nay, madam,' said Bacon, 'he is a Doctor, never rack his person, but rack his style; let him have pen, ink, and paper, and help of books, and be enjoined to continue the story where it breaketh off; I will undertake, by collecting [i.e. collating and comparing] the styles, to judge whether he were the author or no.'[14]

Francis Bacon was later to write that the differences between himself and the earl 'in two points so main and material, bred in process of time a discontinuance of privateness (as it is the manner of men seldom to communicate when they think their courses are not approved) between his Lordship and myself; so as I was not called nor advised with, for some year and a half before his Lordship's going into Ireland, as in former time'. It was therefore unexpected that when, 'touching his going into Ireland it pleased him expressly and in a set manner to desire mine opinion and counsel'. Bacon's views, he claimed, were quite strong:

I did not only dissuade but protest against his going; telling him with as much vehemency and asseveration as I could that absence in that kind would exulcerate the Queen's mind, whereby it would not be possible for him to carry himself so as to give her sufficient contentment, nor for her to carry herself so as to give him sufficient countenance; which will be ill for her, ill for him, and ill for the state.

And because I would omit no argument, I remember I stood also upon the difficulty of the action; setting before him out of histories that the Irish were such an enemy as the ancient Gauls or Germans or Britons were; and we saw how the Romans, who had such discipline to govern their soldiers and such donatives to encourage them and the whole world in a manner to levy them, yet when they came to deal with enemies which placed their felicity only in liberty and the sharpness of their sword, and had the natural and elemental advantages of woods, and bogs, and hardness of bodies, they ever found they had their hands full of them; and therefore concluded that going over with such expectation as he did, and through the churlishness of the enterprise not like to answer it, would mightily diminish his reputation; and many other reasons I used, so as I am sure I never in anything in my lifetime dealt with him in like earnestness, by speech, by writing, and by all the means I could devise. For I did as plainly see his overthrow chained as it were by destiny to that journey, as it is possible for a man to ground a judgement upon future contingents. But my Lord, however his ear was open, yet his heart and resolution was shut against that advice, whereby his ruin might have been prevented.[15]

Such was Bacon's version in 1604, when Essex was long dead and Bacon's political career needed to establish an honourable link between himself and the earl. But the surviving contemporary manuscripts tell a different story. Essex complained that Bacon was maintaining a strange silence during his preparations for the expedition into Ireland, and he demanded that Bacon explain himself – which he did, in a 'few wandering lines'.[16]

Essex, thought Bacon, was 'designed to a service of great merit and great peril; and as the greatness of the peril must needs include a like proportion of merit: so the greatness of the merit may include no small consequence of peril, if it be not temperately governed. For all immoderate success extinguisheth merit, and stirreth up distaste and envy; the assured forerunners of whole charges of peril.' But to say this was to leap to the end of his argument first. Bacon was assured of Essex's success, 'wherein, it is true, I am not without my oracles and divinations; none of them superstitious, and yet not all natural'. Looking at God's providence, 'I collect he hath disposed of this great defection in Ireland, thereby to give an urgent occasion to the reduction of that whole kingdom.' In going, Essex would avoid the vices of disloyalty, ingratitude and insolency – and lastly,

> he that shall have had the honour to know your lordship inwardly, as I have had, shall find *bona exta* [good entrails], whereby he may ground a better divination of good than upon the dissection of a sacrifice. But that part I leave; for it is fit for others to be confident upon you, and you to be confident upon the cause; the goodness and justice whereof is such as can hardly be matched in any example; it being no ambitious war against foreigners, but a recovery of subjects, and that after lenity of conditions often tried; and a recovery of them not only to obedience, but to humanity and policy, from more than Indian barbarism.

But there was another kind of divination, often relied on by Demosthenes,

> when he saith, *That which for the time past is worst of all, is for the time to come the best: which is, that things go ill, not by accident, but by errors.* Wherein, if your Lordship have been heretofore a waking censor, you must look for no other now, but *Medice, cura teipsum* [physician, cure thyself]. And though you should not be the blessed physician that cometh in the declination of the disease, yet you embrace that condition which many noble spirits have accepted for advantage; which is that you go upon the greater peril of your fortune, and the less of your reputation; and so the honour countervaileth the adventure. Of which honour your Lordship is in no small possession, when that her Majesty, (known to be one of the most judicious of spirits that ever governed) hath made choice of you (merely out of her royal judgement, her affection inclining rather to continue your attendance) into whose hand and trust to put the commandment and conduct of so great forces; the gathering of the fruit of so great charge; the execution of so many counsels; the redeeming of the defaults of so many former governors; and the clearing of the glory of so many and happy years' reign, only in this part eclipsed. Nay further, how far forth the peril of that State is interlaced with the peril of England, and therefore how great the honour is, to keep and defend the approaches or avenues of this kingdom, I hear many discourse; and indeed there is a great difference, whether the tortoise gather herself within her shell hurt or unhurt.

Bacon did not agree that the fact that the Irish enemy was 'but a rebel and a savage' in any way extenuated the honour of the service, any more than it compromised the greatness of the Romans when they conquered the ancient Germans and the ancient Britons, like the Irish 'people barbarous and not reduced to civility, magnifying a kind of lawless liberty, prodigal in life, hardened in body, fortified in woods and bogs, and placing such justice and felicity in the sharpness of their swords'. However, 'this nature of people doth yield a higher point of honour, considering the truth and substance, than any war can yield which should be achieved against a civil enemy, if the end may be to replant and refound the policy of that nation; to which nothing is wanting, but a just and civil government.'

Essex's own heritage led him to Ireland.

Which design as it doth descend from your noble father who lost his life in that action (though he paid tribute to nature and not to fortune), so I hope your Lordship shall be as fatal a captain to this war as Africanus was to the war of Carthage, after that both his uncle and father had lost their lives in Spain in the same war. Now although it be true that these things which I write, being but representations unto your Lordship of the honour and appearance of success of the enterprise, be not much to the purpose of any advice; yet it is that which is left to me, being no man of war, and ignorant in the particulars of State. For a man may by the eye set up the white right in the midst of the butt, though he be no archer. Therefore I will only add this wish, according to the English phrase, which terms a well-willing advice a wish; that your Lordship in this whole action, looking forward, would set down this position, That merit is worthier than fame; and looking back hither, would remember this text, That obedience is better than sacrifice. For designing to fame and glory may make your Lordship in the adventure of your person to be valiant as a private soldier, rather than as a General: it may make you in your commandments rather to be gracious than disciplinary: it may make you press action (in respect of the great expectation conceived) rather hastily than seasonably and safely; it may make you seek rather to achieve the war by fine force, than by intermixture of practice: it may make you (if God shall send prosperous beginnings) rather seek the fruition of that honour, than the perfection of the work in hand. And for the other point, that is the proceeding like a good Protestant upon express warrant, and not upon good intention, your Lordship knoweth in your wisdom that as it is most fit for you to desire convenient liberty of instructions, so it is no less fit for you to observe the due limits of them; remembering that the exceeding of them may not only procure in case of adverse accident a dangerous disavow; but also in case of prosperous success be subject to interpretation, as if all were not referred to the right end.

Essex's departure for Ireland from his London house in Seething Lane during the afternoon of 27 March 1599 was spectacular:

From thence, accompanied with divers noblemen and many others, himself very plainly attired, [he] rode through Grace Street, Cornhill, Cheapside, and other high streets, in all which places and in the fields the people pressed exceedingly to behold him, especially in the highways, for more than four miles space, crying out, saying 'God bless your Lordship!' 'God preserve your Honour!' etc.; and some followed him till the evening. When he and his company came forth of London, the sky was very clear and calm; but before he could get past Islington there arose a great black cloud in the North East, and suddenly came thunder and lightning, with a great shower of hail and rain, which some held an ominous prodigy.[17]

Thomas Churchyard wrote three poems in honour of the earl; William Shakespeare incorporated into his new play *Henry V* a vision of the reception that Essex, like Henry on his way home from Agincourt, might receive on his return from Ireland ('Bringing rebellion broached on his sword'). But they might have done better to heed the ominous prodigy. Arriving in Dublin after a slow march on 15 April, the Irish Council rejected Essex's preferred tactic of advancing on the rebels in Ulster immediately, arguing that an army could not be fed there. On 10 May, he left Dublin for the south with three thousand foot and three hundred horse, being joined by Ormonde the following day with an additional nine hundred men. While Essex was marching to Kilkenny, the lords Mountgarret and Cahir came in and made their submission. Castles surrendered en route; English garrisons were placed in them. Ignoring Council orders, Essex marched from Leinster into Munster, from Kilmallock to Dungarvan to Waterford.

Then, at Arklow on 21 June, he encountered real resistance for the first time: his newly levied soldiers did not behave well under fire, and the rebels gained the upper hand. Four days later, he sent an account of the situation to the Queen, arguing that to subdue the Irish would take time and money, and proposing instead the hunting down of the priesthood and the imposition of a strong English party among the Irish nobility.

While Essex was floundering in Ireland, his household was squabbling in London – Anthony apparently sniping at the steward Sir Gelly Merrick's relatively humble origins. Merrick complained to secretary Edward Reynolds of a letter he had received from Anthony Bacon.

The variety of Court dispositions, they never alter, but friends upon weak grounds do. I showed Mr. Bacon's letter to Mr. Crampton, Mr. Linley, Sir Anthony Standen, Mr. Foulkes, and some few others. I care not if it were in private. I am not a boy. I suffered by Mr. Anthony Bacon's censure; to whom I will, in regard of my Lord, wish well but for his taking of me of my enriching. What I have, I came by honestly.

I will bear comparisons. The ground of it all is my not giving way. I will never do it. Yet I renew and know his interest and observe his end and his brother's. Learning advanced his father; so did it mine, although not in the like measure. He hunteth after my carriage. I will not plead for myself innocency of some things of this letter, but for some other things, I am freer from it than himself.[18]

Gossip about Essex was rife. John Chamberlain wrote on 28 June that 'The Queen is given to understand that he [Essex] hath given Essex House to Anthony Bacon wherewith she is nothing pleased, but as far as I hear it is but in lieu of £2000 he meant to bestow upon him, with a clause of redemption for that sum by a day.'[19] Chamberlain's comments may help to explain a scandalous story written about Anthony after his death, by his former colleague Henry Wotton:

> The earl of Essex had accommodated Master Anthony Bacon in partition of his house, and had assigned him a noble entertainment. This was a gentleman of impotent feet, but a nimble head; and through his hand ran all the intelligences with Scotland; who being of a provident nature (contrary to his brother the Lord Viscount St Albans), and well knowing the advantage of a dangerous secret, would many times cunningly let fall some words, as if he could much amend his fortunes under the Cecilians (to whom he was near of alliance, and in blood also), and who had made (as he was not unwilling should be believed) some great proffers to win him away: which once or twice he pressed so far, and with such tokens and signs of apparent discontent, to my Lord Henry Howard that he [Howard] flies presently to my Lord of Essex (with whom he was commonly *primae admissionis*, by his bedside in the morning), and tells him that, unless that gentleman were presently satisfied with some round sum, all would be vented. This took the Earl at that time ill provided, (as indeed oftentimes his coffers were low), whereupon he was fain suddenly to give him Essex House; which the good old Lady Walsingham [Essex's mother-in-law] did afterwards disengage out of her own store with £2500: and before he had distilled £1500 at another time by the same skill. So as we may rate this one secret (as it was finely carried) at £4000 in present money, besides at the least £1000 of annual pension to a private and bedrid gentleman: What would he have gotten if he could have gone about his own business?[20]

Behind the gossip we can detect the complexity of the financial arrangements arising from the long-term mutual dependency of the earl and Anthony Bacon.

When it returned to Dublin on 11 July, Essex's army was reduced to a quarter of its original sixteen thousand men – through disease and desertion as much as battlefield death. He had appointed Southampton General of his Horse. The Queen's intense disapproval was relayed to Essex by the Council; his reply expressed disappointment with his sovereign. Elizabeth would not give way, however, and Southampton had to be given up. She then wrote attacking his entire policy, and commanded him to proceed against Ulster. Fearing that he would instead head back to England, on 30 July the Queen revoked her permission for him to return at will: 'We do charge you as you tender our pleasure that you adventure not to come out of that kingdom by virtue of any former license whatever.'

Reluctantly, Essex prepared to strike at Ulster. He sent Blount to attack the O'Connors and the O'Mearas at Leix, and Sir Conyers Clifford, governor of Connaught, to divert Tyrone's attention by attacking from the Curlew mountains. While Blount was successful, the Clifford manoeuvre failed dismally, and the Irish Council advised Essex to delay his advance. Essex angrily berated the Queen to Blount, and discussed returning home with two or three thousand soldiers. He was talked out of this plan, but still considered dark plans to return with some choice men to remove from the Council those of its members whom he blamed for his situation. The Queen continued to broadcast her displeasure, singling out for criticism the knighthoods he had thought fit to distribute at Dublin. Essex sent his secretary Henry Cuffe to reason with her, but to little avail.

Francis Bacon, meanwhile, had seen 'how true a prophet I was, in regard in the evident alteration which naturally succeeded in the Queen's mind; and thereupon I was still in watch to find the best occasion that in the weakness of my power I could either take or minister, to pull him [the earl] out of the fire if it had been possible: and not long after, methought I saw some overture thereof, which I apprehended readily; a particularity I think be known to very few.' He later revealed this to Mountjoy,

because I hear it should be talked, that while my Lord was in Ireland I revealed some matter against him, or I cannot tell what; which if it were not a mere slander as the rest is, but had any though never so little colour, was surely upon this occasion.

The Queen one day at Nonesuch, a little (I remember) before Cuffe's coming over, I attending her, showed a passionate distaste of my Lord's proceedings in Ireland, as if they were unfortunate, without judgement, contemptuous, and not without some private end of his own, and all that might be, and was pleased, as she spake of it to many that she trusted least, so to fall into the like speech with me; whereupon I, who was still awake and true to my grounds which I thought surest for my Lord's good, said to this effect:

'Madam, I know not the particulars of estate, and I know this, that Princes' actions must have no abrupt periods or conclusions, but otherwise I would think, that if you had my Lord of Essex here with a white staff in his hand, as my Lord of Leicester had, and continued him still about you for society to yourself, and for an honour and ornament to your attendance and Court in the eyes of your people, and in the eyes of foreign ambassadors, then were he in his right element: for to discontent him as you do, and yet to put arms and power into his hands, may be a kind of temptation to make him prove cumbersome and unruly. And therefore if you would *imponere bonam clausulam* [provide a good outcome], and send for him and satisfy him with honour here near you, if your affairs which (as I have said) I am not acquainted with, will permit it, I think were the best way.'

This course – as Bacon pointed out to Mountjoy – 'your Lordship knoweth, if it had been taken, then all had been well, and no contempt in my Lord's coming over, nor continuance of these jealousies, which that employment of Ireland bred, and my Lord here in his former greatness.'[21]

On 28 August, Essex left Dublin and camped five days later at Ardloff, near to Tyrone's encampment. After some minor skirmishes, the two men met – at Tyrone's request – on 6 September, for a half-hour conversation on the river Lagan (now Anagh Clint), with Tyrone on horseback in the river and Essex on the riverbank. The following day, the exercise was repeated with six companions in attendance on each side. Commissioners were appointed to negotiate a peace settlement, and a truce arranged (on a renewable six-weekly basis, with fourteen days' notice required on either side to break it) to endure until 1 May the following year; all spoil was to be restored within twenty days. The agreement was not put in writing, because Tyrone feared Spain's reaction to such a treaty; but the two men gave their word (Essex) and oath (Tyrone) on 9 September. Essex promptly retreated to Drogheda to take physic.

On 17 September a letter from Elizabeth, written after news of the first meeting with Tyrone, reached Essex. She entirely disavowed his actions, and warned him against 'making any absolute contract' with Tyrone 'till you do particularly advise us in writing'. One week later, Essex swore in Lords Justices at Dublin, appointed Ormonde commander of the army, and headed back for London.

On the road from Lambeth on Friday 28 September, the earl was overtaken by his adversary Lord Grey of Wilton. One of Essex's men, acting on his own initiative, asked Grey to allow Essex to ride ahead of him, but he replied that he had business at court, and continued on his way.[22] At that point Sir Christopher St Lawrence 'offered his services to kill both him in the way and the Secretary in the Court. But the earl, hating from his soul all impiety, would not assent to it.'[23] At ten in the morning, Essex, still covered in mud, surprised Elizabeth in her chamber at Nonesuch, before she had dressed. The Queen might have been expected to have been incandescent with rage at such a breach of decorum, but when Essex left her presence to wash and dress he was seen to be 'very pleasant – and thanked God that though he had suffered much trouble and storms abroad, he found a sweet calm at home'. A second interview also went well, and at dinner he 'discoursed merely of his travels and journeys in Ireland, of the goodness of the country, the civilities of the nobility that are true subjects, of the great entertainment he had in their houses, of the good order he found there'. The only face that did not welcome him back was that of Sir Robert Cecil.[24] But the earl's moment of glory was soon over: sometime between ten and eleven that evening, Essex was commanded to keep his chamber at Nonesuch, for leaving Ireland without the Queen's licence.

Bacon sent to Essex 'a due and joyful gratulation', admitting that

> your Lordship, in your last conference with me before your journey, spake not in vain, God making it good, That you trusted we should say *Quis putasset?* [Who would have thought?] Which as it is found true in a happy sense, so I wish you do not find another *Quis putasset* in the manner of taking this so great a service. But I hope it is, as he said, *Nubecula est, cito transibit* [It is merely a dark spot which will speedily pass]: and that your Lordship's wisdom and obsequious circumspection and patience will turn all to the best.[25]

The letter was followed by a fifteen-minute interview with the earl, who asked Bacon his opinion of the course that was being taken with him.

'My Lord,' replied Bacon, 'it is but a mist: but shall I tell your Lordship, it is as mists are, if it go upwards, it may haps cause a shower, if downwards, it will clear up. And therefore good my Lord carry it so, as you take away by all means all umbrages and distastes from the Queen.' He identified three salient points: first, Essex should present the treaty with Tyrone as a mere 'shuffling up of a prosecution which was not very fortunate'; secondly, he should leave it to the Queen to decide whether he should return to Ireland, rather than trying to force her arm; thirdly, seek access, '*importunè, opportunè* [out of season, in season], seriously, sportingly, every way'. Essex heard him out but said very little in response, occasionally shaking his head 'as if he thought I was in the wrong'. He gave as much attention to this solicited advice as he had to most of the recent verdicts delivered by Bacon: 'Sure I am, he did just contrary in every one of these three points.'[26]

On Sunday 30 September, Essex was heard, and his answers considered. The following day, he was committed to the custody of his friend Lord Keeper Egerton and removed to Francis Bacon's birthplace, York House, where, it was said, 'that he is very ill, and troubled with a flux. No man goes to him, nor he desirous to see any.'[27] His wife had given birth on 30 September, but Essex was not allowed to see her. It was generally understood that the Council were satisfied with his explanations, that the restraint was a temporary matter of form, and that 'if he would desire his liberty and go to Ireland again, he should have it; but he seems resolved never to go thither again, nor to meddle with any matter of war or state, but only lead a private country life.' Essex, 'very humble and submissive, wonderfully grieved at her Majesty's displeasure towards him,' drew up a precise account of the arrangements he had made on leaving Ireland, and delivered it to the Queen.[28] Such was the outward display; but his papers reveal that he still considered himself the only man who could deal with Ireland, and argued strongly that he should 'return with all expedition' since when the Irish 'shall hear of my present state, and shall see no new hopeful course taken, I fear that giddy people will run to all mischief'.

Cecil suspected that Essex's real objective in returning was 'to acquaint her Majesty not with the goodness of Tyrone's offers in themselves' – which included such gems as 'that the Catholic religion be openly preached' and 'that neither the Queen nor her successors shall enforce any Irishman to serve her' – 'but with the necessity of her affairs, to which the offers were suitable'.[29] But Essex held out against detailing Tyrone's offers, and in the meantime public concern about his unexplained house arrest displayed itself in the rising unpopularity of the Queen.

Elizabeth somehow got hold of a letter from Tyrone to Essex, which admitted that he 'could not draw O'Donnell and the rest of his confederates to agree' to the peace treaty. When the Council recommended the earl's release on 21 October, she would not agree. During November Essex fell seriously ill, but the Queen remained adamant. His wife was still separated from him, and not permitted to attend court. Even her godson, John Harington, who had been knighted by Essex in Ireland, was victim to her displeasure.

Some time 'about the middle of Michaelmas term', Bacon learned that the Queen 'had a purpose to dine at my lodge at Twickenham Park'. For the occasion, 'I had (though I profess not to be a poet) prepared a sonnet directly tending and alluding to draw on her Majesty's reconcilement to my Lord, which I remember also I showed to a great person, and one of my Lord's nearest friends, who commended it.' This (lost) sonnet was only 'a toy' – but, as Bacon claimed elsewhere, 'sometimes it cometh to pass, that men's inclinations are opened more in a toy, than in a serious matter'

– 'yet it showed plainly in what spirit I proceeded, and that I was ready not only to do my Lord good offices, but to publish and declare myself for him; and never was so ambitious of anything in my lifetime, as I was to have carried some token or favour from her Majesty to my Lord; using all the art I had, both to procure her Majesty to send, and myself to be the messenger.' He was not afraid to point out to the Queen that the proceedings against Essex

> was a thing towards the people very implausible; and therefore wished her Majesty, howsoever she did, yet to discharge herself of it, and to lay it upon others; and therefore that she should intermix her proceeding with some immediate graces from herself, that the world might take knowledge of her princely nature and goodness, lest it should alienate the hearts of her people from her. Which I did stand upon, knowing very well that if she once relented to send or visit, those demonstrations would prove matter of substance for my Lord's good. And to draw that employment upon myself, I advised her Majesty, that whensoever God should move her to turn the light of her favour towards my Lord, to make signification to him thereof, that her Majesty, if she did it not in person, would at the least use some such mean as might not entitle themselves to any part of the thanks, as persons that were thought mighty with her, to work her, or to bring her about; but to use some such as could not be thought but a mere conduct [conduit] of her own goodness.

But he could not prevail upon her, although he was 'persuaded she saw plainly whereat I levelled'. The reason for her holding back, Bacon thought, was that 'she had me in jealousy, that I was not hers entirely, but still had inward and deep respects towards my Lord, more than stood at that time with her will and pleasure.'[30]

Bacon later wrote that, whenever the Queen asked his opinion of Essex, he always replied 'in one tenor'. The earl's faults were 'contempts', since they 'were the transgression of her particular directions and instructions', but they might be defended on several grounds – Essex's great interest in the Queen's favour; his great place (and subsequent ample commission); the nature of the business, war not being tied to strict instructions; the distance between Queen and earl; the demands of the Council of Ireland; 'and lastly, in regard of a good intention that he would allege for himself, which I told her in some religions was held to be a sufficient dispensation for God's commandments, much more for Princes'. He consistently advised her against bringing the case 'into any public question', for Essex was 'an eloquent and well-spoken man, and besides his eloquence of nature or art, he had an eloquence of accident which passed them both, which was the pity and benevolence of his hearers; and therefore that when he should come to his answer for himself, I doubted [suspected] his words would have so unequal passage above theirs that should charge him, as would not be for her Majesty's honour.' The Queen would be better advised to 'wrap it up privately between themselves', restore Essex to his former position and throw in 'some addition of honour to take away discontent'. But, Bacon maintained, he never showed any approbation of the earl's 'being sent back again into Ireland, both because it would have carried a repugnancy with my former discourse, and because I was in mine own heart fully persuaded that it was not good, neither for the Queen, nor for the state, nor for himself: and yet I did not dissuade it neither, but left it ever as *locus lubricus* [a slippery place].'[31]

Against Bacon's advice, Elizabeth decided, 'for the satisfaction of the world', that Essex's case should be heard in the Star Chamber: the earl himself would not be present, but the occasion would dispel 'some libels then dispersed'. Bacon was predictably 'utterly against it', telling her 'plainly' that without the earl there to defend himself, 'the people would say that my Lord was wounded upon his back, and that Justice had her balance taken from her, which ever consisted of an accusation and defence.' Warming to his cause, Bacon declared that 'my Lord *in foro famae* [in public talk] was too hard for her,' advising her once again 'to wrap it up privately'. Later he was to admit that 'certainly I offended her at that time, which was rare with me: for I call to mind, that both the Christmas, Lent, and Easter term following, though I came divers times to her upon law business, yet methought her face and manner was not so clear and open to me as it was at the first.'

On 29 November, a Star Chamber hearing went ahead – without Bacon: an absence that did not go unnoticed by the Queen. 'She did directly charge me, that I was absent that day at the Star Chamber, which was very true; but I alleged some indisposition of body to excuse it: and during all the time aforesaid, there was *altum silentium* [a lofty silence] from her to me touching my Lord of Essex' causes.'[32] Bacon had left court on the previous Wednesday.[33] He urged the Queen 'not to impute my absence to any weakness of mind or unworthiness', and explained that 'I do find envy beating so strongly upon me, standing as I do (if this be to stand), as it were not strength of mind but stupidity, if I should not decline the occasions; except I could do your Majesty more service than I can any ways discern that I am able to do.' Taking his duty 'too exactly' had led to his current dilemma. 'My life hath been threatened, and my name libelled, which I count an honour. But these are the practices of those whose despairs are dangerous, but yet not so dangerous as their hopes; or else the devices of some that would put out all your Majesty's lights, and fall on reckoning how many years you have reigned; which I beseech our blessed Saviour may be doubled, and that I may never live to see any eclipse of your glory, interruption of safety, or indisposition of your person.'[34]

But attending the Queen led to other problems. 'During the while since my Lord was committed to my Lord Keeper's, I came divers times to the Queen, as I had used to do, about causes of her revenue and law business, as is well known; by reason of which accesses, according to the ordinary charities of Court, it was given out that I was one of them that incensed the Queen against my Lord of Essex. These speeches, I cannot tell, nor I will not think, that they grew any way from her Majesty's own speeches, whose memory I will ever honour.'[35] Bacon relayed the rumour to Lord Henry Howard and to Sir Robert Cecil, 'for I contemn *mendacia famae* [lying gossip], as it walks among inferiors; though I neglect it not, as it may have entrance into some ear.' 'There is shaped a tale in London's forge, that breatheth apace at this time, that I should deliver opinion to the Queen in my Lord of Essex' cause: first, that it was *praemunire*; and now last, that it was high treason; and this opinion to be in opposition and encounter of the Lord Chief Justice's opinion and the Attorney-General's.' He assured Howard that 'I thank God my wit serveth me not to deliver any opinion to the Queen, which my stomach serveth me not to maintain,' and traced the libel to 'some light-headed envy at my accesses to her Majesty; which being begun and continued since my childhood, as long as her Majesty shall think me worthy of them I scorn those that shall think the contrary'. He also cited 'the aspersion of this tale and the envy thereof upon some greater man, in regard of my nearness'. Bacon also unravelled his relationship to the earl.

> For my Lord of Essex, I am not servile to him, having regard to my superior duty. I have been much bound unto him. And on the other side, I have spent more time and more thoughts about his well doing, than ever I did about mine own. I pray God you his friends amongst you be in the right. *Nulla remedia tam faciunt dolorem quam quae sunt salutaria* [No remedies are as painful as those which are lifesaving]. For my part, I have deserved better than to have my name objected to envy, or my life to a ruffian's violence. But I have the privy coat of a good conscience. I am sure these courses and bruits hurt my Lord more than all.[36]

Howard had not, at the time of receiving Bacon's letter, heard the rumour; 'though within two days after I heard more than I would of it.' He replied, with a distinct hint of criticism at Bacon's lack of attachment to his patron, that he could not

> believe what the giddy malice of the world hath laid upon you. The travail of that worthy gentleman in your behalf, when you stood for a

place of credit, the delight he hath ever taken in your company, his grief that he could not seal up assurances of his love by fruits, effects and offices, proportionable to an infinity, his study (in my knowledge) to engage your love by the best means he could devise, are so forcible persuasions and instances to make me judge that a gentleman so well born, a wise gentleman so well levelled, and a gentleman so highly valued by a person of his virtue, worth and quality, would rather have sought after all occasions of expressing thankfulness (so far as duty doth permit) than either omit opportunity or increase indignation. No man alive, out of the strength of judgment, the grounds of knowledge and the lessons of experience, is better able to distinguish between public and private offices, and to direct a course of keeping measure in discharge of both, to which I will refer you for the finding out of the golden number, and in mine own particular opinion, esteem of you as I have ever done and your rare parts deserve, and so far as my voice hath credit, justify your carriage according to the warrant of your own profession, and the scope of my better wish in all degrees towards you.[37]

Bacon was also quizzed by his cousin Cecil, at his house in the Savoy. 'Cousin,' opened Sir Robert, 'I hear, but I believe it not, that you should do some ill office to my Lord of Essex; for my part I am merely passive and not active in this action, and I follow the Queen and that heavily, and I lead her not; my Lord of Essex is one that in nature I could consent with as well as any one living; the Queen indeed is my Sovereign, and I am her creature, I may not leese her, and the same course I would wish you to take.' Bacon satisfied him 'how far I was from any such mind'.[38]

During December, Essex's health deteriorated. On the thirteenth, his wife was finally given access, and two days later the Queen sent eight physicians to report on his illness. Their verdict was bleak: the earl was suffering from a complication of internal disorders, and seemed unlikely to live. Elizabeth was finally moved to visit York House herself, but remained firm in her anger. The earl's sister, Lady Rich, was forbidden to see him. Public sympathy was aroused, and Christmas Day saw prayers being offered in city churches for Essex's health and fortune. He began to recover.

Essex sent a New Year's gift to Elizabeth at Richmond, which was promptly returned. Francis' gift – 'one petticoat of white satin, embrothered [embroidered] all over like feathers and billets, with three broad borders, fair embrothered with snakes and fruitage' – was accepted, and in return the Queen presented him with 'in gilt plate, M. 33 oz.'[39] In the letter accompanying his offering, Bacon wrote:

Most excellent Sovereign Mistress, The only new-year's gift which I can give your Majesty is that which God hath given to me; which is a mind in all humbleness to wait upon your commandments and business: wherein I would to God that I were hooded, that I saw less, or that I could perform more: for now I am like a hawk, that bates, when I see occasion of service, but cannot fly because I am tied to another's fist. But meanwhile I continue my presumption of making to your Majesty my poor oblation of a garment, as unworthy the wearing as his service that sends it; but the approach to your excellent person may give worth to both; which is all the happiness I aspire to.[40]

Essex was spared the indignity of appearing in the Star Chamber in February – partly due to ill health, partly to the Queen's condescension. On 19 March, he returned to Essex House; but it was now empty of all his friends – and his wife – as Rowland Whyte reported: 'By her Majesty's express commandment, my Lady Leicester, Lord and Lady Southampton, Mr. Greville, Mr. Bacon [i.e. Anthony], are all removed from Essex House.' Essex was 'to remain with two keepers, Sir Dru Drury and Sir Richard Berkeley, and none to come to speak to him, but by his Majesty's leave'.[41] Appeals to the Queen on 4 April and 12 May were ignored.

On 12 March, Bacon wrote a lengthy, formal letter to the Queen, in an attempt to stabilise his financial prospects, and thus render him more useful as her servant, since 'the overthrow of my fortune includeth in it a cutting off of that thread which is so fastly wreathed with the thread of my life that I know they will end together, I meant the thread of my hopes to do your Majesty furder and better service'. The impetus for this appeal was the rapidly decreasing value of his inheritance. Anthony had started to sell off his lands: certain lands went to Robert Prentis, to raise £2,000 (8 November 1597); Redbourn rectory and tithes went for £1,800 to Edmund Bressey (28 August 1598); more lands were sold to Giles Marston (1 January 1599). On 7 October 1599, Lady Bacon 'as well for and in consideration the said Anthony is her natural son, and for the motherly care she hath for the good and preferment of the said Anthony, and for diverse and sundry other good causes', enfeoffed him of the manor of Windridge, for rent of £50 per annum, to be paid to herself. Anthony had immediately sold Windridge to John Crosby.

Francis was not asking for much: just for 'three parcels' totalling 'eighty and odd pounds, and in all respects ordinary land', which, if granted fee-simple, would make him 'a free man and a bond-man, free to all the world and only bond to yourself'. He was bound to make this suit by 'three thorns of compunction'. His first thorn was 'my love to my mother, whose health' was 'worn'. Lady Bacon's health had indeed been deteriorating for some time. She now portrayed herself as an infirm old lady with a 'slippery memory', virtually incapable; every day was a sick day, her strength failing to the extent that she could no longer on occasion receive visits from her sister or son; she had taken to signing herself, 'A. Bacon, your sickly and ancient cousin, late Lord Keeper's widow.'[42] Francis was therefore moved 'infinitely [to] desire she mought carry this comfort to the grave, not to leave my estate troubled and engaged'. With 'these perpetuities being now overthrown', Francis feared that Anthony 'will endeavour to put away Gorhambury'; the Queen's gift, however, would enable Francis 'to get into mine own hands, where I do figure to myself that one day I may have the honour and comfort to bid your Majesty welcome, and to trim and dress the grounds for your Majesty's solace'. By this 'redemption (for so I may truly call it)', Elizabeth could free him 'from the contempt of the contemptible, that measure a man by his estate, which I daily find a weakening of me both in courage and means to do your Majesty service'.[43] As far as we know, the Queen did not reply.

Towards the end of the Easter Term, the Queen finally broke her silence to Bacon concerning the Essex case. She told him 'she had found my words true'; the Star Chamber proceeding had only 'kindled factious bruits (as she termed them)'; and as a result she 'was determined now for the satisfaction of the world, to proceed against my Lord in the Star Chamber by an information *ore tenus* [orally obtained], and to have my Lord brought to his answer'. Her aim was to punish, not to destroy the earl ('*ad castigationem, et non ad destructionem* [punishing him, but not to destruction]').

Bacon attempted to divert her. 'Madam, if you will have me speak to you in this argument, I must speak to you as Friar Bacon's head spake, that said first, *Time is*, and then *Time was*, and *Time would never be*: for certainly . . . it is now far too late, the matter is cold and hath taken too much wind.' It was the wrong answer. 'She seemed again offended, and rose from me, and that resolution for a while continued.'[44]

At the beginning of the Midsummer Term, the Queen was still resolute that this was the correct course. Bacon listened impassively, but on one occasion he said 'slightly': 'Why, Madam, if you will needs have a proceeding, you were best have it in some such sort as Ovid spake of his mistress, *Est aliquid luce patente minus* [It matters less, being less publicly suffered], to make a council-table matter of it, and there an end.' Again, the wrong answer, which the Queen 'seemed to take in ill part'. But Francis was not utterly discouraged: 'I think it did good at that time, and holp [helped] to divert that course of proceeding by information in the Star Chamber.'[45]

Ultimately, Elizabeth decided upon 'a more solemn matter of the proceedings'. Order was give that the matter would be heard at York House, 'before an assembly of Councillors, Peers, and Judges, and some audience of men of quality to be admitted'. Some of the principal councillors then sent for the Learned Counsel, although it was said to Bacon 'openly by one of them, that her Majesty was not yet resolved whether she would have me forborne in the business or no'. In later years, Bacon was to identify this moment as the source of some particularly distressing gossip:

Hereupon might arise that other sinister and untrue speech that I hear is raised of me, how I was a suitor to be used against my Lord of Essex at that time: for it is very true that I, that knew well what had passed between the Queen and me, and what occasion I had given her both of distaste and distrust in crossing her disposition by standing steadfastly for my Lord of Essex, and suspecting it also to be a stratagem arising from some particular emulation, I writ to her two or three words of compliment, signifying to her Majesty, that if she would be pleased to spare me in my Lord of Essex' cause, out of the consideration she took of my obligation towards him, I should reckon it for one of her highest favours; but otherwise desiring her Majesty to think that I knew the degrees of duties, and that no particular obligation whatsoever to any subject could supplant or weaken that entireness of duty that I did owe and bear to her and her service; and this was the goodly suit I made, being a respect that no man that had his wits could have omitted: but nevertheless I had a further reach in it, for I judged that day's work would be a full period [full stop] of any bitterness or harshness between the Queen and my Lord, and therefore if I declared myself fully according to her mind at that time, which could not do my Lord any manner of prejudice, I should keep my credit with her ever after, whereby to do my Lord service.[46]

However, the next thing he heard was that 'we were all sent for again, and that her Majesty's pleasure was, we all should have parts in the business.' Bacon's chore was 'that I should set forth some undutiful carriage of my Lord, in giving occasion and countenance to a seditious pamphlet', namely Hayward's *Henry IV*. Bacon objected to the lords 'that it was an old matter, and had no manner of coherence with the rest of the charge, being matters of Ireland, and therefore that I having been wronged by bruits before, this would expose me to them more; and it would be said I gave in evidence mine own tales.' The lords answered that the allocation of the Hayward charge to Bacon was deliberate. 'Because it was considered how I stood tied to my Lord of Essex, therefore that part was thought fittest for me which did him least hurt; for that whereas all the rest was matter of charge and accusation, this only was but matter of caveat and admonition.' Bacon was 'in mine own mind little satisfied' with this reasoning, 'because I knew well a man were better to be charged with some faults, than admonished of some others: yet the conclusion binding upon the Queen's pleasure directly *volens nolens*, I could not avoid that part that was laid upon me.'[47]

On 5 June, Essex was brought before the court at York House, on the following charges: 'His making of my Lord Southampton, General of the Horse, contrary to her Majesty's pleasure. His making of knights; his going into Munster, contrary to his instructions; his return, being expressly commanded by her Majesty's own letter to stay.'[48] In Bacon's own account:

> The fifth of June in Trinity Term upon Thursday, being no Star Chamber day, at the ordinary hour when the Courts sit at Westminster, were assembled together at the Lord Keeper's house in the great chamber her Majesty's Privy Council, inlarged and assisted for the time and cause by the special call and associating of certain selected persons, viz. four Earls, two Barons, and four Judges of the law, making in the whole a council or court of eighteen persons, who were attended by four of her Majesty's Learned Counsel for charging the earl, and two Clerks of the Council, the one to read, the other as a register; and an auditory of persons to the number as I could guess of two hundred, almost all men of quality, but of every kind of profession; nobility, court, law, country, city. The upper end of the table left void for the earl's appearance, who, after the Commissioners had sat awhile, and the auditory was quiet from the first throng to get in, and the doors shut, presented himself, and kneeled down at the board's end, and so continued till he was licensed to stand up.[49]

Throughout the first part of the proceedings 'the earl himself kneeled at board's end, and had a bundle of papers in his own hand, which sometimes he laid in his hat, that was upon the ground by him.'[50] At eight in the morning, the Queen's Serjeant, Christopher Yelverton, made a short speech. Attorney-General Coke then launched an attack on the earl. According to Rowland Whyte, Coke 'would have proved wilful, and malicious contempts, to have been disloyalty in him'. The earl answered 'that he was forced to alter his purpose of coming to that place, which was not to justify himself, but to acknowledge his transgressions, being by his own opinion, and persuasion of others, misled to commit these errors. But now his honour and loyalty was called into question, he should do God great wrong, and his own conscience; and if I do not justify myself an honest man (taking his George [the jewel on the insignia of the Order of the Garter], and putting it with his hand towards his heart) this hand shall pull out this heart, when any disloyal thought shall enter into it.' The lords interrupted him, assuring him that he was not accused of disloyalty but only to answer 'those matters objected by the Queen's learned counsel against him: that he made the earl of Southampton, General of the Horse; that he made Tasborough, knight; that he went on the journey of Munster, contrary to his instructions; that he did parley very basely with Tyrone;

that he returned without leave; all these merely [completely] against her Majesty's will and pleasure'. Essex said 'something to all these, but no way to justify himself; and with all humble submissiveness, besought her Majesty's mercy. The lords did all admire at his discretion, and carriage, who never was moved at any speech spoken against him, but with patience, heard all was said; sometimes kneeling, one while standing, another while leaning at a cupboard; and at last, he had a stool given him, but never offered to leave kneeling, till the Lord Archbishop of Canterbury, desired he might stand, and then that he might lean; and lastly, that he might sit.' Coke was followed by Solicitor-General Fleming, with an account of Tyrone's increased strength in the months following the treaty.

Bacon spoke last. He insisted that Essex's letter to Egerton derogated from the Queen's reputation, and that he had allowed the dedication of Hayward's *Henry IV*. He later protested to the earl of Devonshire that 'if in the delivery I did handle not tenderly [his charge] (though no man before me did in so clear terms free my Lord from all disloyalty as I did), that, your Lordship knoweth, must be ascribed to the superior duty I did owe to the Queen's fame and honour in a public proceeding, and partly to the intention I had to uphold myself in credit and strength with the Queen, the better to be able to do my Lord good offices afterwards.'[51]

Letters to Essex from Ormonde and other associates in Ireland were read to prove that he had come to 'odious conditions' with Tyrone. Essex replied that he intended to submit himself entirely to the will of his Queen but, in a passionate speech, denied the specific charges, calling into question the genuineness of the Irish letters. Disclaiming disloyalty, he was again informed that he was not accused of disloyalty, only contempt and disobedience. Cecil admitted that Essex had not yielded to all of Tyrone's demands – 'though, by reason of Tyrone's vaunting afterwards, it might have some show of probability.' Coke made no response.

Essex's next speech was

very discreet, mild, and patient, acknowledging, that he had grievously offended her Majesty, in all these things objected against him, but with no malicious intent; and that if it would please their honours to give him leave, he would declare unto them, the blind guides, that led him to those errors, which in his opinion would have furthered her Majesty's service. But then began my Lord Keeper, upon the reasons argued by her Majesty's Learned Counsel, to deliver his opinion; that his contempts deserved to be imprisoned in the Tower, to be fined as deeply as ever subject was, to have his offices of Councillor, Earl Marshal, and Master of the Ordnance, sequestered from him. My Lord Treasurer left out the Tower; my Lord Admiral the Fine; Mr Secretary made a wise, grave speech of these contempts of his, towards her Majesty; all the rest spoke condemning him greatly, for contemptuously offending so gracious a sovereign; and it was concluded, that he should return from the place he came, till her Majesty's further pleasure were known. The poor earl then besought their honours to be a mean unto her Majesty's grace and mercy; seeing there appeared in his offences no disloyalty toward her Highness, but ignorance and indiscretion in himself. I hear it were a most pitiful and lamentable sight, to see him that was the mignon of fortune, now unworthy of the least honour, he had of many; many that were present burst out in tears at his fall to such misery.[52]

At length – at nine in the evening, after thirteen hours 'without removing'– Essex was sentenced by the Lord Keeper: he was dismissed from all his offices of state (although he did not lose the Mastership of the Horse), and was to remain a prisoner at Essex House at the Queen's pleasure.

> The Lords did in a sort give him this comfort, that her Majesty would be gracious unto him; in the meantime all his offices are sequestered from him . . . The Judges made his contempts very heinous, by the laws of the land, and by examples, and by the civil law, criminal. The poor earl continues still with a keeper at his own house, until her Majesty's pleasure be further known; who as it seems is not resolved, what she will do with him.[53]

The York House hearing contented the Queen. 'Her Majesty is very much quieted and satisfied, to see that the Lords of her Council, her Nobility, and the grave Judges of the land, do hold him worthy of far more punishment, than hath been inflicted against him. Some think his Keeper, shall be removed this week, and that he shall have the liberty of his houses in London and Barn Elms [in Putney]; and that he shall have his friends come to him; there are others that do believe, that he shall continue, as he doth, some longer time.'[54]

Although Bacon's involvement was mentioned in eyewitness accounts, the matter of the Hayward book was not. Despite Bacon's version of events, he was clearly perceived as being a prime mover against Essex. When the Queen decided to de-knight those men knighted by Essex in Ireland, Rowland Whyte recorded that 'Mr. Bacon is thought to be the man that moves her Majesty to it.'[55] None too enamoured with the Bacons already, Sir Gelly Merrick picked out Francis as being 'very idle, and I hope will have the reward of that humour in the end'. A less partisan report came from Henri IV's ambassador Boissise, who wrote an account of the hearing to the French King in which he identified 'one named Bacon, once his most intimate and familiar friend, towards whom he has been exceedingly generous, notwithstanding which he has, since the earl's disgrace, carried reports to the Queen of things he heard when the earl was in her highest favour, which offended her more than the Irish affair'.[56] Henri, replying on 2 July, was optimistic about the earl's chances, but horrified at Bacon, whom he naturally took as being his old acquaintance Anthony: 'But I am utterly scandalised by the perfidy of this Bacon, who received so many favours from him. It is true that given the way he habitually lived, the earl of Essex could hardly have expected any other recompense, for I have heard it said that he was once accused of sodomy.'[57]

On the day following the hearing, Bacon attended the Queen, 'fully resolved to try and put in ure [use] my utmost endeavour, so far as I in my weakness could give furtherance, to bring my Lord again speedily into Court and into favour; and knowing (as I supposed at least) how the Queen was to be used, I thought that to make her conceive that the matter went well then, was the way to make her leave off there.' He therefore said to her:

> You have now Madam obtained victory over two things, which the greatest princes in the world cannot at their wills subdue; the one is over fame, the other is over a great mind: for surely the world be now, I hope, reasonably well satisfied; and for my Lord, he did show that humiliation towards your Majesty, as I am persuaded he was never in his lifetime more fit for your favour than he is now; therefore if your Majesty will not mar it by lingering, but give over at the best, and now you have made so good a full point, receive him again with tenderness, I shall then think that all that is past is for the best.

The Queen 'took exceedingly great contentment, and did often iterate and put me in mind, that she had ever said that her proceedings should be *ad reparationem* and not *ad ruinam*, as who saith, that now was the time I should well perceive that that saying of hers should prove true'. She also ordered Bacon to

> set down in writing all that passed that day. I obeyed her commandment, and within some few days brought her again the narration, which I did read unto her at two several afternoons: and when I came to that part that set forth my Lord's own answer (which was my principal care), I do well bear in mind that she was extraordinarily moved with it, in kindness and relenting towards my Lord, and told me afterwards (speaking how well I had expressed my Lord's part) that she perceived old love would not easily be forgotten: whereunto I answered suddenly, that I hoped she meant that by herself.[58]

He concluded by hoping that 'now she had taken a representation of the matter to herself, that she would let it go no further: For Madam (said I) the fire blazeth well already, what should you tumble it? And besides, it may please you keep a convenience with yourself in this case; for since your express direction was, there should be no register nor clerk to take this sentence, nor no record or memorial made up of the proceeding, why should you now do that popularly, which you would not admit to be done judicially?' Elizabeth agreed that the writing should be suppressed, 'and I think there were not five persons that ever saw it.'[59] The suppression seems to have been quite thorough: sadly, only the opening portion of Bacon's narration survives – we cannot now hear Essex's speech, nor indeed Bacon's own.

Unfortunately this suppression, thorough as it was, was not enough to lay the matter of the earl's disobedience to rest.

9

Flying with Waxen Wings:
The Final Fall of Essex

I call forth Mr Bacon against Mr Bacon.
The earl of Essex (February 1601)

O NCE ESSEX HAD been freed in the summer of 1600, and allowed
to live at his uncle Sir William Knollys' Oxfordshire house,
Bacon 'might without peril of the Queen's indignation write to
him'. Throughout 'the whole latter end of that summer', therefore, he
later claimed, 'I made it my task and scope to take and give occasions for
my Lord's reintegration in his fortune.' He at once wrote to assure him
of his continued availability as an adviser . . . while at the same time making
clear on paper that his obligations to his sovereign took priority over any
commitment to his patron. 'Though I confess I love some things much
better than I love your Lordship, as the Queen's service, her quiet and
contentment, her honour, her favour, the good of my country, and the
like, yet I love few persons better than yourself, both for gratitude's sake,
and for your own virtues, which cannot hurt but by accident of abuse.'
'I am ready to yield testimony by any good offices but with such reservations as yourself cannot but allow.' Under no circumstances, he warned,
would he risk the kind of disaster that had almost befallen Essex: 'I was
ever sorry that your Lordship should fly with waxen wings, doubting
Icarus' fortune.'[1]

He received from Essex 'a courteous and loving acceptation of my good
will and endeavours', but the earl wrote that since he was 'a stranger to
all poetical conceits', he could not say anything

of your poetical example. But this I must say, that I never flew with
other wings than desire to merit, and confidence in my Sovereign's
favour; and when one of those wings failed me, I would light nowhere
but at my Sovereign's feet, though she suffered me to be bruised with my
fall. And till her Majesty, that knows I was never bird of prey, finds it to
agree with her will and her service that my wings should be imped again
[have feathers engrafted to improve flight], I have committed myself to
the mew [a pun: the cage, but also the plucking out of feathers].'[2]

Clearly, despite his disclaimer, Essex was a master of poetical conceit.

Bacon took this to mean that he was authorised to do what he could on behalf of the earl 'in all my accesses to the Queen, which were very many at that time, and purposely sought and wrought upon other variable pretences, but only and chiefly for that purpose', keeping Essex informed 'of what I found and what I wished'. To prevent the headstrong earl from further damaging himself with the Queen, it was Bacon who drafted the letters now exchanged between them. 'Though I knew well his Lordship's gift and style was far better than mine own, yet because he required it, alleging that by his long restraint he was grown almost a stranger to the Queen's present conceits, I was ready to perform it.' Bacon drafted the letters in the second person, designed for Essex to 'write' in the first person. These letters tried in vague terms to clear Essex, protesting that the world had condemned him 'out of error' and berating the Queen for being 'so perfect in the art of forgetting' and for taking 'so large a draught of poppy' after 'a quintessence of wormwood'.[3]

This campaign 'for the space of six weeks or two months prospered so well, as I expected continually his restoring to his attendance. And I was never better welcome to the Queen, nor more made of, than when I spake fullest and boldest for him: in which kind the particulars were exceeding many.' For example:

> Her Majesty was speaking of a fellow that undertook to cure, or at least to ease my brother of his gout, and asked me how it went forwards: and I told her Majesty that at the first he received good by it, but after in the course of his cure he found himself at a stay or rather worse: the Queen said again, I will tell you, Bacon, the error of it: the manner of these physicians, and especially these empirics, is to continue one kind of medicine, which at the first is proper, being to draw out the ill humour, but after they have not the discretion to change their medicine, but apply still drawing medicines, when they should rather intend to cure and corroborate the part.

'Good Lord Madam,' exclaimed Bacon,

> how wisely and aptly can you speak and discern of physic ministered to the body, and consider not that there is the like occasion of physic ministered to the mind: as now in the case of my Lord of Essex, your princely word ever was that you intended ever to reform his mind, and not ruin his fortune: I know you cannot but think that you have drawn the humour sufficiently, and therefore it were more than time, and it were but a doubt of mortifying or exulcerating, that you did apply and

minister strength and comfort unto him; for these same gradations of yours are fitter to corrupt than correct any mind of greatness.[4]

Bacon was involved in another ploy for rehabilitating his patron ('with my Lord's privity and by his appointment'). He drafted an exchange of letters ostensibly between Essex and Anthony (to whom Essex might be expected to write more candidly), designed expressly for the Queen's eyes. These were 'both to be by me in secret manner showed to the Queen; the scope of which were but to represent and picture forth unto her Majesty my Lord's mind was to be such as I knew her Majesty would fainest have had it.'[5] Bacon always maintained that these letters served no purpose beyond enhancing Essex's standing with Elizabeth, and that Essex not only commissioned them but was instrumental in circulating them. Essex may actually have had no hand in them; at his trial he claimed they had been written to discredit him.

In the first letter, 'Mr. Anthony Bacon' encourages 'Essex' to 'make your peace with God' following Leicester's example; he urges the earl to ignore those friends who would have his court career dead and buried, pointing to several factors – the Queen's deliberate avoidance of a public hearing, her deliberate omission of 'disloyalty' among the charges against him, the lack of a written record, his keeping of the Mastership of the Horse, the Queen's determination not to cause his ruin – as causes not to 'despair'. In his reply, 'Essex' thanks 'Anthony' for his kind words, but argues that the Queen's inability to forestall rumour and his ruin points to the victory of his enemies, who have gained ground in his absence.

Taken at face value, the letters provide a beautifully balanced representation of Essex's case, with an implicit call to the Queen to keep an eye on other, rival courtiers. But the letters also produce a third character – 'Francis Bacon', whom both 'Anthony' and 'Essex' discuss at some length. 'Anthony' presents 'my brother Francis Bacon, who is too wise (I think) to be abused, and too honest to abuse, though he be more reserved in all particulars than is needful'. In his parting shot, 'Anthony' presents himself as disinterested, because of his physical state, but interested, in the name of his brother:

> I know your Lordship may justly interpret that this which I persuade may have some reference to my particular, because I may truly say, *Te stante*, not *virebo* (for I am withered in myself), but *manebo*, or *tenebo*; I shall in some sort be able to hold out. But though your Lordship's years and health may expect a return of grace and fortune, yet your eclipse for a time is an *ultimum vale* to my fortune; and were it not that I desire and hope to see my brother established by her Majesty's favour (as I think him well worthy, for that he hath done and suffered), it were

time to take that course from which I dissuade your Lordship. But now in the meantime, I cannot choose but perform these honest duties to you, to whom I have been so deeply bounden.[6]

In 'Essex's' reply, also, the subject of Francis Bacon was raised:

For your brother, I hold him an honest gentleman, and wish him all good, much the rather for your sake. Yourself I know hath suffered more for me than any friend I have: but I can but lament freely, as you see I do, and advise you not to do that which I do, which is to despair. You know letters what hurt they have done me, and therefore make sure of this: and yet I could not (as having no pledge of my love) but communicate freely with you, for the ease of my heart and yours.[7]

In these letters, Anthony is produced as the hopelessly involved, suffering friend of Essex: Francis is carefully distanced, with Essex knowing him to be 'an honest gentleman', but only wishing him well for Anthony's sake.

Essex himself launched an epistolary campaign to the Queen and assorted Privy Councillors, but to no avail. His letters to Elizabeth bear all the trademarks of chivalric love-letters to the unattainable lover – for example, he urged in his 6 September letter to Elizabeth: 'Haste paper to that happy presence, whence only unhappy I am banished; kiss that fair correcting hand which now lays plasters to my lighter hurts, but to my greatest wound applieth nothing. Say thou camest from shaming, languishing, despairing Essex.'[8] It was the wrong tactic, as Bacon pointed out. The Queen, taken in by what she took to be 'the abundance of his heart', was ashamed and angry when 'she found it to be but a preparative to a suit for the renewing of his farm of sweet wines' which Essex identified as 'both my chiefest maintenance and mine only means of compounding with the merchants to whom I am indebted'. Bacon replied:

O Madam, how doth your Majesty conster [construe] of these things, as if these two could not stand well together, which indeed Nature hath planted in all creatures. For there are but two sympathies, the one towards perfection, other towards preservation. That to perfection, as the iron contendeth towards the loadstone; that to preservation, as the vine will creep towards a stake or prop that stands by it; not for any love to the stake but to uphold itself. And therefore, Madam, you must distinguish: my Lord's desire to do you service is as to his perfection, that which he thinks himself to be born for; whereas his desire to obtain this thing of you, is but for a sustentation.[9]

Even now, during Essex's disgrace, Anthony Bacon remained loyal to the earl as his primary patron. On 19 September he acquainted him with a new set of letters that had been sent from Sir Anthony Sherley, and drafted the information for a recommendation he wished Essex to provide for his friend Henry Gosnold, who had served Essex as Master of Requests, and who desired employment under the Lord Keeper. But Anthony's request contained telltale hints that Essex's recommendation might not now suffice: he also provided various considerations which might satisfy the Lord Keeper, 'if in regard of the terms wherein your Lordship presently stands with her Majesty, or he with your Lordship, he make difficulty to entertain a servant at your Lordship's hands'. If Essex still felt that his support would be counterproductive, Anthony suggested that the entire matter should be openly proposed by Lady Warwick. He signed himself, 'Your Lordship's most devoted and langourous bedesman'.[10]

On the night of 2 October, Essex finally returned to the deserted Essex House where, it was reported, 'he lives private, his gate shut day and night'. However, 'great suit is made to her Majesty, that the earl of Essex may continue the farm of the sweet wines; as yet it is not granted, but his officers continue in their places.'[11] In reality, Essex was busy communicating with King James, applying to Mountjoy for a letter of remonstrance which, should his monopoly suit fail (the lease expired at Michaelmas), he might 'by means of his friends present himself to the Queen'.[12] Some were not fooled. Sir John Harington wryly diagnosed Essex as an example of how 'ambition thwarted in his career doth speedily lead on to madness' – the earl 'shifteth from sorrow and repentance to rage and rebellion so suddenly as well proveth him devoid of good reason or of right mind'. Meeting with Harington, Essex

> uttered strange words bordering on such strange designs, that made me hasten forth and leave his presence. Thank heaven I am safe at home, and if I go in such troubles again, I deserve the gallows for a meddling fool. His speeches of the Queen become no man who hath *mens sana in corpore sano* [a healthy mind in a healthy body]. He hath ill advisers, and much evil hath sprung from this source. The Queen well knoweth how to humble the haughty spirit, the haughty spirit knoweth not how to yield, and the man's soul seemeth tossed to and fro like the waves of a troubled sea.[13]

Although Bacon did not know the cause of Essex's frustration, he saw its effects: 'The truth is that the issue of all his dealing grew to this, that the Queen, by some slackness of my Lord's, as I imagine, grew worse and worse, and grew more incensed towards him.'[14] The earl's appeal for an audience (on 18 October) and a letter of congratulation on the anniversary of Elizabeth's accession (17 November) went unanswered.[15] The last straw came when it was decided that Essex's monopoly patent should be assigned back to the Queen, relieving his suit of any double meaning: Rowland Whyte reported that 'he sues now only for grace, and that he may come to her presence, of which small hope as yet appeareth.'[16]

The breakdown in relations between the Queen and the earl was bound to affect her dealings with his primary advocate, Francis Bacon – in spite of his efforts at establishing a distance between himself and his patron. Remembering 'the continual and incessant and confident speeches and courses' that Bacon had given on Essex's behalf, she 'became utterly alienated from me, and for the space of at least three months, which was between Michaelmas and New Year's tide following, would not as much as look on me, but turned away from me with express and purposelike discountenance wheresoever she saw me; and at such time as I desired to speak with her about law-business, ever sent me forth very slight refusals.'[17]

Royal disfavour could have its positive professional side-effects, however: released from the burdens of perpetual access to a demanding sovereign, Francis concentrated on preparing his lectures for his week-long Reading on the Statute of Uses, with which he would be promoted to Double Reader at Gray's Inn the following Lent.[18]

Calculating that the immediate anger had worn off, Bacon successfully resumed his suit for access in the New Year. He 'dealt with her plainly' and spoke 'with some passion':

> Madam, I see you withdraw your favour from me, and now that I have lost many friends for your sake, I shall leese you too: you have put me like one of those that the Frenchmen call *enfans perdus* [doomed children], that serve on foot before horsemen, so have you put me into matters of envy without place, or without strength; and I know at chess a pawn before the king is ever much played upon; a great many love me not, because they think I have been against my Lord of Essex; and you love me not, because you know I have been for him: yet will I never repent me, that I have dealt in simplicity of heart towards you both, without respect of cautions to myself; and therefore *vivus vidensque pereo* [I live and see, and yet perish]. If I do break my neck, I shall do it in manner as Master Dorrington did it, which walked on the battlements of the church many days, and took a view and survey where he should fall: and so Madam, I am not so simple but that I take a prospect of mine overthrow, only I thought I would tell you so much, that you may know that it was faith and not folly that brought me into it, and so I will pray for you.

The Queen was 'exceedingly moved', and 'accumulated a number of kind and gracious words' on her Learned Counsel, willing him 'to rest upon this, *Gratia mea sufficit* [my grace suffices], and a number of other sensible and tender words and demonstrations, such as more could not be; but as touching my Lord of Essex, *ne verbum quidem* [not a single word].' Bacon left her, determining to wash his hands of the matter, which he realised would do no good to the earl and, more to the point, 'would overthrow me'. He did not see the Queen again until 8 February – 'which was the day of my Lord of Essex his misfortune'.[19]

Essex had not spent all his months of internal exile writing love-letters. He had been canvassing his allies – Mountjoy in Ireland, King James in Scotland, Sir Henry Neville in France – in connection with a new plan. Essex House was thrown open, and became a suspiciously active gathering-place for the marginal men of Elizabeth's society – unemployed soldiers, malcontents, adventurers, Puritan preachers and their audiences. A secret conclave met at Drury House, where Sir Charles Davers lodged. By the end of January 1601 plans had been laid to surprise the court, master the guard, seize the Queen's person, and force her to dismiss Cecil, Ralegh, Cobham and others, and to make changes in the state. On Saturday 7 February the stir about Essex House was such that the Council sent one of the Lord Treasurer's sons to investigate. Essex was summoned to court to be reprimanded for holding unlawful assemblies, and to be ordered back into the country; but he sent word that he was too ill to attend, and instead summoned his fellow conspirators to debate the situation. They decided to appeal to the affection in which Essex was held by the City's people, and concocted a story that there was a plot to murder him, somehow involving 'certain Jesuits to the number of four'.

Early on the morning of Sunday 8 February 'three hundred gentlemen of prime note' gathered at Essex House. While Essex briefed them, the Lord Keeper and three other lords arrived from the court, sent from the Queen to ascertain the cause of the assembly (to be communicated to them), to hear their complaint, and to order their dispersal. Essex locked them in his library and set off with his men for the City. The plan was to ride to St Paul's Cross before the end of the sermon, explain the case to the aldermen and others, and call on them for help. But now they had been rushed: the horses were not ready, and the party had to go on foot. Essex had no prepared speech, and, as he passed through Cheapside and Gracechurch Street, merely cried out that his enemies were going to murder him. He came to the house of Sheriff Thomas Smythe (who commanded the City militia); after hearing Essex out, Smythe withdrew to consult with the Lord Mayor. Essex fell back on his other story, that 'the crown of England was offered to be sold to the Infanta'. By this time he had been officially proclaimed a traitor throughout the City, and troops had been collected to oppose him.

Sir Ferdinando Gorges, a leading player in the conspiracy, advised him to stand his ground, and send someone to negotiate terms of surrender. Gorges went to Essex House with his authority, released the lords from the library, accompanied them to the court, and tried to talk up the earl's power. In the meantime, Essex set out to return to Essex House via Ludgate Hill, where he was repulsed by troops; then went round by the river, entered with some fifty followers by the watergate, burned some papers so that 'they should tell no tales' and prepared to defend himself. The news was brought to the Council and Essex House was surrounded: at 10 p.m. its inmates all surrendered and were conveyed to prison.

The government now assumed some great undiscovered treason. Early on Monday morning, the conspirators were incarcerated around London, with Essex, Southampton and some other key players committed to the Tower; their houses and papers were seized; strangers were interrogated; a watch was set on the ports and a red alert put out. Francis Bacon was summoned to the Learned Counsel, and as one of this body received on 11 February a commission from the Council 'for the perfect discovery of this wicked conspiracy'. The Council took it upon themselves to interrogate the ringleaders, while, to undertake the huge task of examining all the prisoners, which took seven days, the Learned Counsel split into small parties, Bacon working alongside Mr Wilbraham and Sir Jerome Bowes. When the preparatory consultations at Drury House came to light, the Learned Counsel were directed to re-examine their witnesses focusing on this information.[20] It was decided that Bacon would work with Sir Edward Coke in the prosecution of Southampton and Essex.

Francis Bacon's role in the proceedings was a controversial one, even at the time. He was known to have been part of the earl of Essex's inner circle. The earl's efforts to secure preferment for Francis had been public and were widely known; for Bacon to act now against Essex seemed at best ungrateful, at worst downright dishonourable. To Essex's ally Mountjoy, Bacon insisted that, after the earl's arrest, he had to perform at the bar 'in my public service . . . honestly, and without prevarication; but for any putting myself into it, I protest before God, I never moved neither the Queen, nor any person living, concerning my being used in the service, either of evidence or examination; but it was merely laid upon me with the rest of my fellows'.[21]

It has been suggested that Bacon agreed to take on his role for the prosecution in return for a guarantee of his brother's immunity: and indeed, in spite of his known closeness to the earl, there is no record that Anthony was either arrested or interrogated. Anthony, however, was ill and immobile, and he may therefore have been considered not worth bothering with as part of the 'conspiracy'. It is just as likely that Francis had already convincingly distanced himself from Essex by his involvement in the earlier

York House hearing, and had thereby already established publicly his total commitment to the Queen, with the assumption that he could be called upon to support her side of the matter. At York House he had been saddled with a red herring line of questioning and had come out of it badly, branded as 'idle'. This time he had a stronger case to press home. If he did so successfully, both he and his brother would clearly be beyond reproach in the Queen's eyes.

Essex and Southampton were arraigned at Westminster Hall on 19 February 1601 before the Lord Treasurer, Lord High Steward and twenty-five peers (nine earls and sixteen barons).[22] As he came into the court Essex's 'countenance was somewhat unsettled', according to John Chamberlain, 'but after he was once in, I assure you I never saw any go through with such boldness, and show of resolution, and contempt of death, but whether this courage were borrowed and put on for the time, or natural, it were hard to judge.' The matters objected were Essex's practice to surprise the court; his entry with arms into the City of London to raise rebellion; and defending his house against the Queen's forces. The Queen's Serjeant opened against the earl, comparing his crimes to those of Catiline. When the prayer for the Queen's safety was said, Essex said 'Amen' to it, and uttered an imprecation upon the souls of all such as wished otherwise. It was to set the tone for the proceedings. Chamberlain wrote that he delivered his answers 'with such bravery and so many words, that a man might easily perceive that as he had ever lived popularly, so his chief care was to leave a good opinion in the people's minds now at parting'.[23]

Coke, 'suddenly rising', undertook to prove that Essex's intention had been 'to take away the prince from the people', since the law stated that he who usurps the prince's authority is supposed to purpose the prince's destruction; he who assembles power and continues in arms against the prince's command usurps the prince's authority. Essex had intended to take 'not a town, but a city; not a city alone, but London the chief city; not only London, but the Tower of London; not only the Tower of London, but the royal palace and person of the prince, and to take away her life'. The earl reacted with 'wondering and passionate gestures', protesting at last that 'he never wished harm to his Sovereign more than to his own soul.' Coke then referred to 'a little black bag, wherein was contained the whole plot'; the bag's contents had been destroyed, but Coke had details of the plot: how Essex 'had plotted to surprise the Court, and had disposed of the several places thereof to be guarded by special persons about him; how the gate had been committed to Sir Christopher Blount, the hall to Sir John Davies, the presence to Sir Charles Davers; while himself was to take possession of her Majesty's sacred person', and then proceed to call a parliament. His evidence was 'for the most part examinations of such as were of the confederacy, all severed in prison, but agreeing in the chief points of their confessions'.

Despite the strength of his case, Coke's prosecution quickly went awry. The testimony of the first witness, an Essex man named Widdrington who had gone with the earl into the City, was attacked by Essex (who had been granted the right to defend each point in turn) as self-serving and uncorroborated. The evidence of the Lord Chief Justice was challenged, but it provided a chance for Essex to explain that he had detained the councillors for their own safety; that he had not dissolved his company because they believed their enemies had beset the House; that they had gone to the City rather than the Council because they feared being intercepted by their enemies. He stumbled only when pressed as to why he could not communicate his case privately to the Lord Keeper.

The examination of Sir Ferdinando Gorges, revealing 'the consultation at Drury House, where was moved the taking of the City, the Tower, and the Court', was read out: Essex counterclaimed that there had been talk, but no resolution, and that it was only to secure an audience with the Queen, in which he would urge his complaints, and seek the removal of Cobham, Cecil and Ralegh, who were responsible for them. This would have been done 'with paper', not 'with sword'.

Essex then sidetracked the process by bringing up an alleged subornation of a witness to accuse the earl of a conspiracy with the King of Scots concerning the succession, and a forgery of his handwriting by a scrivener to extort money. Cobham rose and demanded an explanation of the charges thrown out against himself. Gorges then appeared and reaffirmed his evidence, and declared that this subject had been spoken of for three months. Southampton virtually admitted such conferences had been held.

But the court wanted to hear what cause Essex had for apprehending danger to himself, 'for', as the Lord High Steward said, 'you speak things without probability.' The earl vaguely asserted that he knew of these preparations 'many ways', that he received 'intelligence upon intelligence', and finally – under pressure – said that Sir Walter Ralegh had desired to speak with Gorges, which they did on the river that Sunday morning, and Ralegh had 'wished him to come from them, or else he were a lost man and as a person entering a sinking ship: of which words, when we heard them, what other construction could we make, but that there was some imminent mischief intended towards us?' Ralegh demanded to explain, and was sworn. 'Look what book it is he swears on!' shouted the earl, pointing to a tiny decimo-sexto Bible. A folio edition being substituted and Ralegh resworn, he stated that, as a friend, he had advised Gorges to return to the country, where the Queen would want him to go. Sir Ferdinando thanked him, but answered, these were no times of going, for the earl of Essex stood upon his guard. Ralegh wondered at this news, and answered: 'If you return, then you are a lost man.' 'It was told us otherwise,' said the earl.

Coke moved on to questions concerning the speeches of the earl in the City, his lack of regard to the herald and the religious beliefs of his fellow-conspirators – providing Essex with a series of opportunities to assert his loyalty and sincerity, and to complain about the government's behaviour which 'had made an honourable, grave and wise Councillor oftentimes wish himself dead'. He then alluded to an assault on Southampton by Lord Grey, to which Grey defended himself, and a shouting match proceeded. Coke then asked the earl to justify his announcement that Cecil had sold the state to the Spaniards. Essex declared that he had heard of this 'many ways', and that he and Southampton 'had both been informed how Secretary Cecil had maintained to one of his fellow-Councillors the title of the Infanta to be the best after her Majesty's death – and in a manner before'.

Cecil appeared from behind a hanging where he had been standing, fell on his knees, and beseeched the Lord High Steward that he 'might be suffered to break course and clear himself of this slander', which he then did at some length. Finally, Sir William Knollys' name was extricated as the source of this information; when he was called for and examined, it emerged that Cecil had once mentioned to him and offered to show him a book wherein that title was preferred before any other.

Coke's haphazard questioning had exhausted him, and Bacon snatched the opportunity of rising. He passed over the chance to reiterate all the points of the case, since his audience was not 'a country jury of ignorant men', but he did crave their lordships' indulgence to make one point.

No man can be ignorant that knows matters of former ages, and all history makes it plain, that there was never any traitor heard of that durst directly attempt the seat of his liege prince, but he always coloured his practices with some plausible pretence. For God hath imprinted such a majesty in the face of a prince that no private man dare approach the person of his sovereign with a traitorous intent. And therefore they run another side course, *oblique et à latere*: some to reform corruptions of the state and religion; some to reduce the ancient liberties and customs pretended to be lost and worn out; some to remove those persons that being in high places make themselves subject to envy; but all of them aim at the overthrow of the state and destruction of the present rulers. And this likewise is the use of those that work mischief of another quality; as Cain, that first murderer, took up an excuse for his fact, shaming to outface it with impudency.

Essex had been no different. 'The earl made his colour the severing some
great men and councillors from her Majesty's favour, and the fear he stood
in of his pretended enemies lest they should murder him in his house.
Therefore he saith he was compelled to fly into the City for succour and
assistance.' Under cover of these 'pretences of dangers and assaults the earl
of Essex entered the City of London and passed through the bowels thereof,
blanching rumours that he should have been murdered and that the state
was sold; whereas he had no such enemies, no such dangers: persuading
themselves that if they could prevail, all would have done well.'

He turned to Essex. 'You, my Lord, should know that though princes
give their subjects cause of discontent, though they take away the honours
they have heaped upon them, though they bring them to a lower estate
than they raised them from, yet ought they not to be so forgetful of their
allegiance that they should enter into any undutiful act; much less upon
rebellion, as you, my Lord, have done. All whatsoever you have or can
say in answer hereof are but shadows. And therefore methinks it were best
for you to confess, not to justify.'

The earl made his reply.

> To answer Mr. Bacon's speech at once, I say thus much; and call forth
> Mr. Bacon against Mr. Bacon. You are then to know that Mr. Francis
> Bacon hath written two letters, the one of which hath been artificially
> framed in my name, after he had framed that other in Mr. Anthony
> Bacon's name to provoke me. In the latter of these two, he lays down
> the grounds of my discontentment and the reasons I pretend against
> mine enemies, pleading as orderly for me as I could do myself. Much
> such matter it contains as my sister the Lady Rich her letter, upon which
> she was called before your Honours. If those reasons were then just and
> true, not counterfeit, how can it be that now my pretences are false and
> injurious? For then Mr. Bacon joined with me in mine opinion, and
> pointed out those to be mine enemies and to hold me in disgrace with
> her Majesty, whom he seems now to clear of such mind towards me;
> and therefore I leave the truth of what I say and he opposeth unto your
> Lordships' indifferent considerations.[24]

Bacon replied, 'Those letters, if they were here, would not blush to be
seen for anything contained in them. I have spent more time in vain in
studying how to make the earl a good servant to the Queen, than I have
done in anything else.'

The confessions of Davers, Davies and Blount were read, confirming
Gorges' version of events. Essex eventually fell to protesting his nightly
practices of devotion; Coke charged him with 'hypocrisy in religion' and
'countenancing religious men of all sorts'. Further depositions were read

concerning the proceedings in the City, bringing Southampton into the spotlight. He answered that the object of the Drury House consultations was to procure the means for Essex to speak with the Queen; the action suggested there had never take place, nor been resolved upon; the action that had taken place was self-defence, not treason. He had never heard the messages of the Lord Keeper or the herald. The peers were impressed. They desired to know whether, if the coming to court were merely to present Essex's complaints with no thought of violence against the person of the Queen or any other, this was treason: to which the judges replied it was. Coke ploughed on. They must have expected resistance, he reasoned, which they would quash with violence, and therefore they had intended violence. Essex replied that the act was judged by the intent in conscience. Coke objected: 'Nay, our law judgeth the intent by the overt act.'

'Well,' smiled the earl, 'plead you law and we will plead conscience.'

The case was getting nowhere. Bacon, annoyed at Coke's apparent incompetence, rose again.

I have never yet seen in any case such favour shown to any prisoner; so many digressions, such delivering of evidence by fractions, and so silly a defence of such great and notorious treasons. May it please your Grace, you have seen how weakly he hath shadowed his purpose and how slenderly he hath answered the objection against him. But, my Lord, I doubt the variety of matters and the many digressions may minister occasion of forgetfulness, and may have severed the judgements of the Lords; and therefore I hold it necessary briefly to receite the Judges' opinions.

Now put the case that the earl of Essex's intent were, as he would have it believe, to go only as a suppliant to her Majesty. Shall their petitions be presented by armed petitioners? This must needs bring loss of liberty to the prince. Neither is it any point of law, as my Lord of Southampton would have it believed, that nothing condemns them of the treason but it is apparent in common sense to take secret counsel, to execute it, to run together in numbers armed with weapons – what can be the excuse? Warned by the Lord Keeper, by a herald, and yet persist! Will any simple man take this to be less than treason?

'If', the earl pointed out, 'I had purposed anything against others than those my private enemies, I should not have stirred with so slender a company.'

'It was not the company you carried with you,' retorted Bacon, 'but the assistance which you hoped for in the City which you trusted unto. The Duke of Guise thrust himself into the streets of Paris on the day of the Barricados in his doublet and hose, attended only with eight gentlemen, and found that help in the city which (thanks be to God) you failed of here. And what followed? The King was forced to put himself into a pilgrim's weeds and in that disguise to steal away to scape their fury. Even such was my Lord's confidence too,' he continued, turning to the lords, 'and his pretence was the same – an all-hail and a kiss to the City. But the end was treason, as hath been sufficiently proved. But when he had once delivered and engaged himself so far into that which the shallowness of his conceit could not accomplish as he expected, the Queen for her defence taking arms against him, he was glad to yield himself; and thinking to colour his practices turned his pretexts, and alleged the occasion thereof to proceed from a private quarrel.'

Where Coke had beaten about the bush and confused the issue, Bacon had put it plainly and damagingly. However the episode was construed it had, on the earl's own admission, included plans to seize the Queen. Even to make such a plan was clearly high treason. It hardly mattered what the likelihood of success had been, nor even whether Essex himself had believed it could be successful.

From the earl's lack of response it was plain that he could see himself doomed by Bacon's argument. Neither he nor Southampton said anything when it was asked if there was any reason why judgement should not be pronounced. Both were found guilty of high treason, with sentence of death. Southampton threw himself on the Queen's mercy. Essex asked pardon for his past offences, although admitting no guilt, and craved the Queen's mercy, concluding 'yet I had rather die than live in misery.' He also intimated 'that before his death he would make something known that should be acceptable to her Majesty in point of state'. According to Cecil, Essex 'then broke out to divers gentlemen that attended him in the Hall, that his confederates who had now accused him had been principal inciters of him and not he of them, ever since August last, to work his access to the Queen with force'.[25]

Overall the trial was poorly conducted. Coke's case was too weak to justify the verdicts, and Essex's protestations of faith and loyalty too compelling, as John Chamberlain recorded contemptuously: 'which no doubt caught and carried away a great part of the hearers; but I cannot be so easily led to believe protestations (though never so deep) against manifest proof.'[26] William Camden wrote that 'some called it a fear, others an error; they which censured it more hardly termed it an obstinate impatience and desire of revenge, and such as censured it most heavily called it an inconsiderate rashness; and to this day few there are who have thought it a capital crime.' Whatever the case, Francis Bacon's customarily clear powers of rational argument played the major part in the guilty verdict.

Bacon later claimed that the day after the earl's arraignment he intervened to prevent prosecution of most of the earl's followers and members of his household subsequently rounded up:

> I have many honourable witnesses that can tell . . . [that] by my diligence and information touching the quality and nature of the offenders, six of nine were stayed, which otherwise had been attainted, I bringing their Lordships' letter for their stay, after the jury was sworn to pass upon them; so near it went: and how careful I was, and made it my part, that whosoever was in trouble about that matter, as soon as ever his case was sufficiently known and defined of, might not continue in restraint, but be set at liberty; and many other parts, which I am well assured of stood with the duty of an honest man.[27]

Thus did Bacon apparently salve his conscience after the event. We do not know if one of those he 'saved' was his own brother Anthony.

Bacon admitted, though, that he had come close to allowing Sheriff Thomas Smythe to be convicted of involvement unjustly. He told the Queen that the case against him was as strong as against any of the convicted conspirators,

> because at that time I had seen only his accusation, and had never been present at any examination of his; and the matter so standing, I had been very untrue to my service, if I had not delivered that opinion. But afterwards upon a re-examination of some that charged him, who weakened their own testimony; and especially hearing himself *viva voce*, I went instantly to the Queen, out of the soundness of my conscience, and not regarding what opinion I had formerly delivered, told her Majesty, I was satisfied and resolved in my conscience, that for the reputation of the action, the plot was to countenance the action further by him in respect of his place, than they had indeed any interest or intelligence with him.[28]

In other words, although the conspirators thought Smythe would participate, there was no evidence that he himself had had any intention of joining them. The case was dropped.

Back in the Tower, Essex was visited by Dr Thomas Dove, the Dean of Norwich, who unsuccessfully angled for a confession. But then his Puritan chaplain, the Reverend Abdy Ashton, came to counsel his master. According to an account sent to Anthony Bacon, Ashton warned Essex that 'You are going out of this world but yet you know not what it is to stand before God's judgement seat, and to receive the sentence of eternal condemnation. Leave therefore all glorious pretences; free your conscience from the burden of your grievous sins.' Essex did, confessing the entire story to Ashton, who lapped it up. 'These be great matters your lordship hath opened unto me,' he said, 'and concealing them may touch my life. Also I hold myself bound in allegiance to reveal them.'[29] So Ashton, with Essex's consent, went to the Privy Council; and Essex sent for the Constable of the Tower, Lord Howard, to ask him to move the Queen to send to him the Lord Keeper, Lord Treasurer, Lord High Admiral and Secretary Cecil, 'that he might now discharge his conscience'.

When they came to him, 'he did with very great penitency confess how sorry he was for his obstinate denials at the bar: desiring he might have liberty to set down in writing his whole project of coming to the Court in that sort: which he hath done in four sheets of paper, all under his own hand.' This confession concurred in the main with those of Davers, Davies, Gorges and Littleton. The earl went on to ask forgiveness of those he had imprisoned in his house, and those he had attacked in court, 'protesting that when he had resolved of this rebellious act to come to the Court in force, he saw not what better pretext he could have than a particular quarrel to those whom he had named at the bar his adversaries'. He also sued the Queen 'that he might have the favour to die privately in the Tower; which her Majesty granted, and for which he gave her most humble thanks'.[30]

Having fully admitted his own guilt, Essex now began to implicate those around him. He alleged that Sir Henry Neville had been party to the treason; that 'no man showed himself more forward in the streets, nor readier to fight and defend the house after their return against the Queen's forces, nor more earnest that they should not have submitted themselves, than the Lord Sandys';[31] that Sheriff Smythe 'had been as far engaged in the action as any of them', but 'in that confusion he could not draw his regiment together', advising Essex 'to keep the streets';[32] that Henry Cuffe and Sir Christopher Blount had 'been his chief instigators to all those disloyal courses into which he had fallen';[33] finally saying, 'And now, I must accuse one who is most nearest unto me, my sister; who did continually urge me on with telling me how all my friends and followers thought me a coward, and that I had lost all my valour . . . She must be looked to, for she has a proud spirit.' The earl's ruthless implicating of his social inferiors and his close female kin shocked his peers. It was considered unworthy and dishonourable. The earl of Nottingham, who was present, wrote to Lord Mountjoy, 'Would your Lordship have thought this weakness and this unnaturalness in this man?'[34]

Bacon later insisted that

for the time which passed, I mean between the arraignment and my Lord's suffering, I well remember I was but once with the Queen; at what time, though I durst [dared] not deal directly for my Lord as things then stood, yet generally I did both commend her Majesty's mercy, terming it to her as an excellent balm that did continually distil from her sovereign hands, and made an excellent odour in the senses of her people; and not only so, but I took hardiness to extenuate, not the fact, for that I durst not, but the danger, telling her that if some base or cruel-minded persons had entered into such an action, it might have caused much blood and combustion; but it appeared well they were such as knew not how to play the malefactors; and some other words which I now omit.[35]

By 24 February it was reported that, despite his bravura performance, Essex 'begins to relent and among other faults to acknowledge and be sorry for his arrogant (or rather as Master Secretary well termed it to his face) his impudent behaviour at his arraignment: and which is more, to lay open the whole plot, and to appeach divers not yet called in question. His execution was expected on Saturday, then yesterday, now tomorrow or on Thursday. Most of the Council have been with him these three or four days together.'[36]

In the early morning of 25 February – Ash Wednesday – Essex, attended by three priests, sixteen guards and the Lieutenant of the Tower, walked to his execution. The Queen had granted him one final favour in conceding that this should take place inside the Tower of London, privately: but nevertheless at least one hundred people were present. Taking off his hat, he admitted all the evil he had done, but denied that he ever meant violence to the Queen's person. He approached the block and forgave the executioner: 'Thou are welcome to me, I forgive thee; thou art the minister of true justice.' Then he prayed, 'Lift my soul above all earthly cogitations, and when my soul and body shall part, send Thy blessed angels to be near unto me, which may convey it to the joys of heaven.' Sartorially elegant to the last, the earl removed his black doublet to reveal a scarlet waistcoat with scarlet sleeves. He laid his head on the block, saying 'O Lord, into thy hands I commend my spirit,' and received three strokes of the axe. The head and body were buried by the earl of Arundel and the duke of Norfolk; the Queen commanded that his banner and hatchment of the Knight of the Garter should not be removed from St George's Chapel at Windsor.

Blount, Davers, Davies, Merrick and Cuffe were brought to trial on 5 March. Coke, Fleming and Bacon were commissioned with the prosecution: Bacon spoke against Davies, who was charged with plotting at Drury House and having custody of the councillors during the insurrection at Essex House, which had a correspondence with the action outside in the street. As Coke had argued against Essex, he urged that every rebellion implied destruction of the prince, drawing on the precedents of the Spencers against Edward II and the Treasurer against Henry IV, and that therefore the act itself was treason. Unlike Coke, however, Bacon focused on the *means* used by the conspirators, means of which he knew much:

> The plot and insurrection entered into was to give laws to the Queen: the preparation was to have a choice band of men for action; men not met together by constellation; but assembled upon summons and letters sent. For I will not charge Sir John Davies, although he be a man skilful in strange arts, that he sent spirits abroad; but letters were sent about this matter. The things to be acted were the matters consulted of, and then to design fit persons for every action: and for mutual encouragement there was a list of names drawn by the earl; and these councillors out of them were to elect fit persons to every office. The second plot was in taking of the Court, and in this consultation he was *penna philosophi-scribentis*; you were clerk of that council-table and wrote all: and in the detaining of the Privy Councillors you were the man only trusted. And, as the earl of Rutland said, you held it a strategem of war to detain pledges, and [were] meant to have carried the Lord Keeper with the Great Seal to London, and to have had with you the Lord Chief Justice, a man for his integrity honoured and well beloved of the citizens. And this Achitophel plot you thought to have followed.[37]

'If with good mannners I might,' answered Sir John Davies,

> I would long since have interrupted you, and saved you a great part of labour: for my intent is not to deny anything I have said or excuse that I have done, but to confess myself guilty of all, and submit myself wholly to the Queen's mercy. But in that you call me clerk of that council, let me tell you that Sir Charles Davers was writing, but his hand being bad, I was desired to take the pen and write. But by-and-by the earl said he would speed it himself; therefore we being together so long and doing so little, the earl went to his house and set down all with his own hand, which was formerly set forth, touching the taking and possessing of the Court.[38]

Davies escaped the death penalty and a year later obtained a pardon from the Queen. The others were not so lucky. Sir Christopher Blount and Sir Charles Davers were beheaded on Tower Hill; Sir Gelly Merrick and Henry Cuffe were hanged at Tyburn.

Although most who heard the evidence were satisfied that justice had been done, there was less confidence outside Westminster. The Queen decided that an account of the proceedings needed to be published, and

Coke's conduct did not inspire her to entrust the task to him; therefore, on 16 March, Coke 'delivered to Mr. Solicitor twenty-five papers concerning the earl of Essex' treasons, etc. to be delivered to Mr. Francis Bacon for her Majesty's service'.[39] This led to his being responsible for the *Declaration of the Practices and Treasons attempted and committed by Robert late earl of Essex and his Complices*. Bacon was commanded by the Queen to write it; and he was given particular instructions as to how he should treat his subject – 'so as never secretary had more particular and express directions and instructions in every point how to guide my hand in it'. On these grounds he drafted the piece, which was then submitted 'to certain principal councillors' appointed by the Queen, 'perused, weighed, censured, altered, and made almost a new writing, according to their Lordships' better consideration'. Bacon stated that 'their Lordships and myself both were as religious and curious of truth, as desirous of satisfaction: and myself indeed gave only words and form of style in pursuing their direction.' Once allowed by the Lords, it 'was again exactly perused by the Queen herself, and some alterations made again by her appointment' in the manuscript. On 14 April 1601 it was sent to the Queen's printer, Barker.[40] But the first printed copy was not to last, as Bacon protested later to the earl of Devonshire. 'Nay, and after it was set to print, the Queen who, as your Lordship knoweth, as she was excellent in great matters so she was exquisite in small; and noted that I could not forget my ancient respect to my Lord of Essex, in terming him ever My Lord of Essex, My Lord of Essex, in almost every page of the book, which she thought not fit, but would have it made Essex, or the late earl of Essex: whereupon of force it was printed *de novo* and the first copies suppressed by her peremptory commandment.'[41]

The *Declaration* was published, according to its preamble,

> because there do pass abroad in the hands of many men divers false and corrupt collections and relations of the proceedings at the arraignment of the late earls of Essex and Southampton; and again, because it is requisite that the world do understand as well the precedent practices and inducements to the treasons, as the open and actual treasons themselves (though in a case of life it was not thought convenient to insist at the trial upon matter of inference or presumption, but chiefly upon matter of plain and direct proofs).

Appended 'for the better warranting and verifying of the narration' were 'the very confessions and testimonies themselves, word for word taken out of the originals, whereby it will be most manifest that nothing is obscured or disguised, though it do appear by divers most wicked and seditious libels thrown abroad, that the dregs of these treasons, which the late earl of Essex himself, a little before his death, did term a *Leprosy*, that had infected far and near, do yet remain in the hearts and tongues of some misaffected persons'.[42]

Bacon's prosecution of his sometime close friend and patron, and then his writing the printed version of that prosecution for posterity, have been held against him ever since. He had something of an excuse, at least so far as the written account was concerned. The Queen took 'a liking of my pen, upon that which I had done before concerning the proceeding at York House, and likewise upon some other declarations which in former times by her appointment I put in writing'. It undoubtedly suited those who wished Essex's disgrace to be as all-embracing as possible, that the published account of his culpability should come from the pen of a prominent figure who had once enjoyed the same earl's patronage.

Not only was Bacon closely involved in the guilty verdict against Essex and the disgrace of many of his circle; he also profited financially from the affair. The fines levied upon several lords and gentlemen involved were earmarked in August 1601 for deserving servants of the Queen, and Francis Bacon received a £1,200 share of Catesby's 4,000 mark fine.[43] It was less than he expected, as he reported to his long-time friend and creditor Michael Hickes: 'The Queen hath done somewhat for me, though not in the proportion I hoped.'[44]

★

One man conspicuously absent from the Essex affair was Anthony Bacon. There was no escaping the fact that Anthony had been a key player in Essex's intelligence operation. But only one person implicated him in the confessions: Essex's secretary Henry Cuffe. Cuffe wrote that Mr Anthony Bacon was one of two private gentlemen – the other being Sir Henry Bromley – for whom a Scottish cipher provided a character. He later testified that he had 'often heard that Anthony Bacon conveyed divers letters from the earl to the King of Scots' – a line that was amended in the account to the less specific 'Anthony Bacon was an agent between the earl and the King of Scots, and so he was accounted.'[45] Since Anthony's own correspondence from this period was destroyed – quite possibly by himself – we will probably remain in the dark as to the precise nature of any such exchanges.[46]

On 27 May, John Chamberlain recorded that 'Anthony Bacon died not long since but so far in debt, that I think his brother is little the better by him.'[47] He was buried on 17 May 1601 'in the chamber within the vault' in the parish church of St Olave, in Hart Street, London.[48]

Anthony's whereabouts during the final stages of the conspiracy are uncertain. He did consider leaving Essex House earlier – he had approached Sir William Cornwallis about using his Bishopsgate house in September

1598[49] – but was reported as having moved out only during Essex's disgrace of 1600. In the last days of his life, Anthony was living in a house in Crotched Friars (a continuation of Hart Street), with at least one servant – William, the brother of his old servant and friend Thomas Lawson (a letter dated 27 March 1601 from Thomas is addressed 'To Mr. William Lawson at Mr. Bacon's house in Chrocit Friers').[50]

Once dead, Anthony was an easy target for those who wished to hit at Essex and his circle. One Thomas Leitchfield, under examination by Sir John Popham, while affirming that his master Sir Robert Drewry had never used disloyal or revolutionary speeches, did confess that 'he heard Sir Robert then say that some which showed themselves the earl of Essex's friends were his enemies, meaning Mr. Bacon, the lame man.' Leitchfield denied that he carried any letter out of France to Anthony Bacon, 'but confesses that Mr. Anthony Bacon's man that was in France, who is called Parkins, wrote a letter to Anthony Bacon, but that it was so spoiled in the carriage as there was no use to be made of it, but cast it away'.[51]

On 23 June 1602, over a year after his death, the administration of Anthony's estate was granted to his brother Francis as 'the natural and legal brother of Anthony Bacon, formerly of the parish of St Olave in Hart Street in the City of London, for the good administration of the goods, rights and credits of the deceased in the person of Francis Walleys, notary public, who took oath on his behalf'.[52] On 20 November, Lady Bacon executed in favour of her 'son Francis Bacon, for and in consideration of the natural love and affection which she beareth unto the said Francis Bacon', a deed surrendering to him her life interest in the said manors.[53] In theory, Anthony's death left the way open for Francis to borrow against the Bacon estates. In practice, they were already mortgaged beyond usefulness. As those around him had already guessed, Francis found himself no better off.

★

The antagonism and resentment between Coke and Bacon, barely disguised in the Essex arraignment, was finally exposed in a case in the Exchequer in April 1601. Bacon made a motion for the confiscation of the lands of George Moore, 'a relapsed recusant, a fugitive, and a practising traitor'. Moore had previously been discharged from the penalties of recusancy upon summission, and so Bacon's motion may have been in effect a comment and attack on Coke's previous handling of his case (if he handled it). Bacon opened his case 'in as gentle and reasonable terms as might be'.

'Mr. Bacon,' interjected Coke, annoyed. 'If you have any tooth against me, pluck it out; for it will do you more hurt than all the teeth in your head will do you good.'

'Mr. Attorney,' answered Bacon coldly to these 'high words', 'I respect you: I fear you not: and the less you speak of your own greatness, the more I will think of it.' (This was one of his favourite ripostes, as he confided to William Rawley years later.)

Coke replied, 'I think scorn to stand upon terms of greatness towards you, who are less than little; less than the least,' going on, according to Bacon, to provide 'other such strange light terms . . . with that insulting which cannot be expressed'.

Bacon was stirred, but reined in his anger: 'Mr. Attorney, do not depress me so far; for I have been your better, and may be again, when it please the Queen.'

With this, Bacon told Cecil, 'he spake, neither I nor himself could tell what, as if he had been born Attorney General; and in the end bade me not meddle with the Queen's business, but with mine own; and that I was unsworn, etc.' Bacon replied that 'sworn or unsworn was all one to an honest man; and that I ever set my service first, and myself second; and wished to God, that he would do the like.'

'It were good,' said Coke, 'to clap a *cap utlegatum* upon my back,' invoking Bacon's humiliating arrest for debt in September 1598.

'To which I only said he could not; and that he was at fault, for he hunted upon an old scent.'

In answer to 'a number of disgraceful words' from Coke, Bacon remained silent, 'showing that I was not moved with them'.[54]

Generally, Bacon's annoyance with Coke was usefully sublimated in various *bons mots* for the amusement of his friends and servants. 'Sir Edward Coke, being Attorney, would seem in modesty to say, if the client kept his fee in his hand, "No, leave your fee": if he laid it down on the table; "Let your fee alone." ' 'They say Sir Edward Coke grows younger every Parliament than other. Mr. Drury said, "Two Parliaments more would make him grow a child again." '[55] But this time he was moved enough to set his annoyance down on paper in a 'letter of expostulation' to the Attorney-General. 'I thought best, once for all,' he opened,

to let you know in plainness what I find of you, and what you shall find of me. You take to yourself a liberty to disgrace and disable my law, my experience, my discretion; what it please you. I pray think of me, that I am that know both mine own wants and other men's; and it may be, perchance, that mine mend, and others stand at a stay. And surely I may not endure in public place to be wronged, without repelling the same to my best advantage to right myself. You are great, and therefore have the more enviers, which would be glad to have you paid at another's cost. Since the time I missed the Solicitor's place (the rather

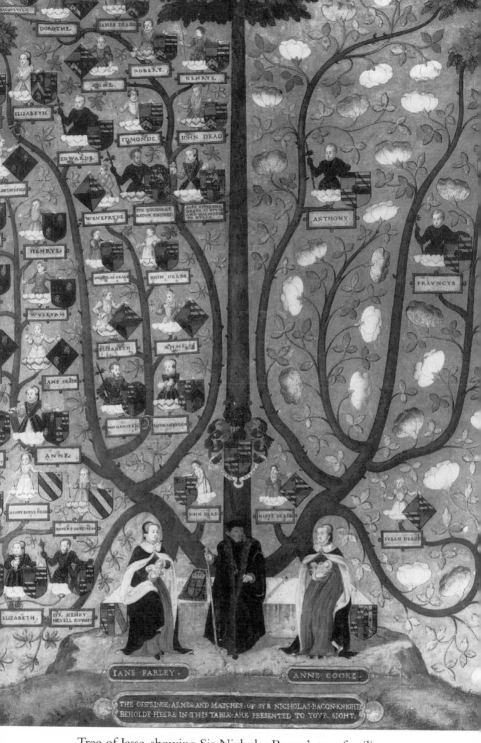

Tree of Jesse, showing Sir Nicholas Bacon's two families
(artist unknown – private collection; photograph Courtauld Institute of Art)

Terracotta bust of the young Francis Bacon, sometimes identified as Anthony Bacon
*(artist unknown – from the Gorhambury Collection and reproduced by
permission of the Earl of Verulam; photograph Courtauld Institute of Art)*

Sir Nicholas Bacon
*(artist unknown – by courtesy of the
National Portrait Gallery, London)*

Lady Bacon
*(attributed to George Gower – from the Gorhambury
Collection and reproduced by permission of the Earl of
Verulam; photograph Courtauld Institute of Art)*

After my harty commendations vnto you and to my [sister]. Sir forth
it is so that you haue promisd my Cosin Sharpe a buck agaynst the
Commencement, and the time draweth so nixe, if habe to desyre yow because he now
hath sent for it, and he must needes be at great charges if the messanger tarry there
vpon his own cost, that you will so vse the messanger that he be at
no cost eyther for lodginge or meate and drinke while he is with yon. Besides
pay the keepers no fees for the same Buck, ye shall both pleasure him and me
very much. And desiringe yow to dot this for me I leaue yon to the tuition
of God. At Cambridge the third day of July. 1574.

Your lovinge brother

Francis Bacon

My brother had written vnto yon if he by reason of sore eyes had
not taried at London.

Sir Amias Paulet
*(by George Perfect Harding – by courtesy of the
National Portrait Gallery, London)*

William Cecil, Lord Burghley
*(by M. Gheeraerts – by courtesy of the
National Portrait Gallery, London)*

Robert Devereux, earl of Essex
*(by Isaac Oliver – The Royal Collection © 1998
Her Majesty Queen Elizabeth II)*

Gentleman, presumed to be Anthony Ba
*(by Nicholas Hilliard? – from the Gorhambury Collec
and reproduced by permission of the Earl of Verulam,
photograph Courtauld Institute of Art)*

The Hilliard miniature of Francis Bacon
(by kind permission of His Grace the Duke of Rutland; photograph Arthur Pickett)

Sir Robert Cecil
*(by J. de Critz the Elder – by courtesy of the
National Portrait Gallery, London)*

Sir Tobie Matthew
*(engraved frontispiece to A Collection of Letters,
1660 – Cambridge University Library)*

James I
*(by Daniel Mytens – by courtesy of the
National Portrait Gallery, London)*

George Villiers, duke of Buckingham
*(by William Larkin – by courtesy of the
National Portrait Gallery, London)*

Sir Thomas Meautys
*(artist unknown – from the Gorhambury Collection
and reproduced by permission of the Earl of Verulam;
photograph Courtauld Institute of Art)*

Sir Edward Coke
*(artist unknown – the Earl of Leicester and the Trustees of
the Holkham Estate; photograph Courtauld Institute of Art)*

Transposita Jul. 25. 1608

To send once agayn to Stockdell.

The Argum[ent] of Elrwingstons cause
and [...] provided for [...] the
next terme.

Qu. of Robertsons Cause

M[...] the poynt of ye 4. shyres and
to think to settle a cowrse in it;
but to hold now ye K. is affected
in respect of ye promise, and to make
[...] of my [...] in it toward
the Pr.

Series Librorū cartaciorū
vt tunc vsum est; ac
~~[...]~~ secundum ordinem
in quo nunc in Theca
reponuntr.

Libri Composititorum. 6.

1 Scripta in Theologia
2 Scripta in Politicis et Moralibus
3 Scripta in Naturali et vniuersali
   philosophia
4 Scripta in Logicis Rhetoricis et
   philologicis.
5 Orationes Instrumenta, Acta
6. Litterae.

The Agas map of London, c.1562: Westminster and Charing Cross
(Guildhall Library, Corporation of London)

I think by your means) I cannot expect that you and I shall ever serve as Attorney and Solicitor together: but either to serve with another upon your remove, or to step into some other course; so as I am more free than ever I was from any occasion of unworthy conforming myself to you, more than general good manners or your particular good usage shall provoke. And if you had not been shortsighted in your own fortune (as I think) you might have had more use of me. But that tide is passed. I write not this to show my friends what a brave letter I have written to Mr. Attorney [although its survival in multiple copies might suggest otherwise!], I have none of those humours. But that I have written is to a good, that is to the more decent carriage of my mistress' service, and to our particular better understanding one of another. This letter, if it shall be answered by you in deed, and not in word, I suppose it will not be worse for us both. Else it is but a few lines lost, which for a much smaller matter I would have adventured.[56]

★

On St Matthew's Day, 23 September, Don Juan d'Aquila and four thousand men (the majority from Spain) landed on the south coast of Ireland with a mission 'to deliver Ireland from the jaws of the Devil', occupied Kinsale, and proclaimed the Queen deprived of her crown by the Pope's sentence and her subjects absolved of allegiance. The Spaniards were besieged in Kinsale by land, and ships were sent to cut off their supplies by sea; Tyrone, however, was marching from the north.

This latest news was at the forefront of the new parliament, which was opened by the Queen on 27 October.[57] Now that Francis had succeeded to Anthony's Hertfordshire estates, including Gorhambury, he was returned for St Albans; but, once again, he switched to another seat – this time, Ipswich. On 3 November, Sir Robert Cecil set out the reasons for the calling of the parliament, namely to provide means of defence against present and threatened dangers. Such a statement was bound to offend Bacon, who firmly believed that no parliament should be called merely for the raising of money. He listened, increasingly annoyed, as several bills were read and rejected, some to be redrafted, but without discussion. He therefore felt compelled to prefer a new bill (technically 'only a confirmation of the statute of the II Henry 7, with a few additions'), against abuses in weights and measures, 'for I take it to far better to scour a stream than to turn a stream', on Thursday 5 November, two days before the supply committee was due to meet. 'We have turned out divers bills without disputation,' he complained to the House, 'and for a house of wisdom and gravity, as this is, to bandy bills like balls, and to be silent, as if nobody were of Counsel with the Commonwealth, is unfitting in my understanding for the state thereof.' (The bill was subsequently rejected.)[58]

Bacon then made a motion for a committee to repeal superfluous laws, remarking to the Speaker that he did 'much wonder to see the House so continually divided, and to agree upon nothing; to see so many laws here so well framed, and offences provided against, and yet to have no better success or entertainment'. He argued that

> Laws be like pills all gilt over, which if they be easily and well swallowed down are neither bitter in digestion nor hurtful to the body. Every man knows that time is the true controller of laws, and therefore there having been a great alteration of time since the repeal of a number of laws, I know and do assure myself there are many more than I know laws both needless and dangerous. I could therefore wish that as usually every Parliament there is a committee selected for the continuance of divers statutes so the House would be pleased also that there might be a committee for the repeal of divers statutes, and of divers superfluous branches of statutes. And that every particular member of the House would give information to the committees what statues he thinketh fitting to be repealed or what branch to be superfluous, lest as he said . . . the more laws we make, the more snares we lay to entrap ourselves.[59]

As in 1597, Bacon's motion raised no discussion and was merged in an ordinary 'continuance act'.

'The Alpha and Omega' of business,[60] a grant of four subsidies, was settled with relatively little debate. The most contentious issue in which Bacon involved himself was Laurence Hyde's bill, which declared patents of monopoly illegal under common law. Since they had been granted by royal prerogative, the proposed measure effectively called that prerogative into question; the question was posed as to whether this bill meddled with prerogative.

Bacon made his own position clear.

> For the prerogative royal of the Prince, for my own part I have ever allowed of it: and it is such as I hope I shall never see discussed. The Queen, as she is our sovereign, hath both an enlarging and restraining power. For by her prerogative she may first set at liberty things restrained by statute law or otherwise; and secondly, by her prerogative, she may restrain things which be at liberty. For the first, she may grant *non obstanti* contrary to the penal laws, which truly according to my own conscience [here Bacon 'struck himself on the breast'] are as hateful to the subject as monopolies. For the second, if any man out of his wit, industry or endeavour finds out anything beneficial for the common-

wealth, or bring in any new invention, which every subject of this kingdom may use, yet in regard of his pains and travail therein, her Majesty perhaps is pleased to grant him a privilege to use the same only by himself or his deputies for a certain time. This is one kind of monopoly. Sometimes there is a glut of things when they be in excessive quality as perhaps of corn and her Majesty gives licence of transportation to one man; this is another kind of monopoly. Sometimes there is a scarcity or a small quantity and the like is granted also.

Bacon went to pinpoint the true danger of Hyde's bill, which he claimed, was

no stranger in this place but a stranger in this vestment. The use hath been ever to humble ourselves unto her Majesty and by petition to have our grievances remedied, especially when the remedy toucheth her so nigh in point of prerogative. All cannot be done at once, neither was it possible since the last Parliament to repeal all. If her Majesty make a patent (or as we term it, a monopoly) unto any of her servants, that must go, and we cry out of it; but if she grant it to a number of burgesses or a corporation, that must stand and that forsooth is no monopoly. I say and say again that we ought not to deal, to judge or meddle with her Majesty's prerogative. I wish every man therefore to be careful in this business and humbly pray this House to testify with me, that I have discharged my duty in respect for my place in speaking on her Majesty's behalf, and protest I have delivered my conscience in saying that which I have said.[61]

During a committee on the following day, Bacon interjected to dub Hyde's bill 'injurious and ridiculous': injurious to the royal prerogative and ridiculous 'in that there is a proviso that this statute shall not extend to grants made to corporations. That is a gull to sweeten the bill withal, it is only to make fools fond.'[62] The Queen defused the situation by promising to abolish some of the more contentious privileges, for which Bacon expressed his happiness and gratitude.

Bacon remained active throughout the remainder of the parliament. He spoke against the repeal of an act passed in the last session which prevented the misapplication of the revenues of colleges, hospitals and other charitable institutions. This was now thought to give bishops dangerous powers. Bacon spoke passionately: 'We should do a most uncharitable action to repeal and subvert such a mount of charity; and therefore we should rather tenderly foster it than roughly cry "away with it!" I speak out of the very strings of my heart; which doth alter my ordinary form of speech; for I speak not now out of the fervency of my brain.'

His emotionalism did not go unnoticed. The following day, during a debate on privilege, Sir Francis Hastings was about to speak when Bacon interrupted him.

'It is against the course,' Bacon objected.

'I am old enough to know when and how often to speak,' retorted Hastings.

'It is no matter,' replied Bacon, 'but you need not to be so hot in an ill cause.'

'In several matters of debate a man may speak often,' argued Sir Francis, 'so I take it is the order. He' – pointing at Bacon – 'talks of heat. If I be so hot as he was yesterday, then put me out of doors.'[63]

Bacon's passion against the appeal did not abate. That afternoon, when two bills were to be debated, Bacon 'kept such a quoil to have the bill concerning Charitable Uses put to the question' that the other 'was clean hushed up'.[64] Eventually, a new act was passed with a few provisos.

In the midst of the 1601 parliament passed a day which, although of no significance to his fellow members, was a milestone for Francis Bacon. In August 1600 he had been forced once again to borrow from Nicholas Trott; this time he had to borrow – the sum was £950 – against the mortgage of Twickenham Park. On that day, Twickenham Park, which had been mortgaged, would fall to Nicholas Trott if the debt was not paid. Anthony's death left Francis with at least some assets at his disposal, and the money from Catesby's fine provided some ready cash. He therefore called upon Henry Maynard and Michael Hickes to negotiate a settlement of Trott's claims, which was referred to Lord Treasurer Buckhurst. It appears that the Lord Treasurer's auditor awarded £1,800, to be paid by 22 December. At Hickes' intercession, Trott agreed to make some further abatement, allowing another month's delay. Presumably, by 22 January 1602, Twickenham Park was redeemed.

That pressing danger averted, Bacon started to deal once again with his debts. He successfully appealed to Michael Hickes, to whom he still owed a 'remain' of a previous loan, for £200 for six months, for which he would 'put you in good sureties', namely Francis Anger of Gray's Inn, previously executor to the late count of Lincoln, and his cousin Sir Thomas Post-humous Hoby, for £100 each.

The matter is not much to you. But the timing of it is much to me. For I am now about this term to free myself from all debts which are any ways in suit or urged, following a faster pace to free my credit than my means can follow to free my state, which yet cannot stay long after, I having resolved to spare no means I have in hand (taking other possibilities for advantage) to clear myself from the discontent speech or danger of others. And some of my debts of most clamour and importunity I have this term and some few days before ordered and in part paid.[65]

In the meantime, the situation in Ireland had moved on. On Christmas Eve 1601, Tyrone, with the largest ever rebel army in Ireland, combining with two or three thousand newly arrived Spaniards, arrived to relieve the troops in Kinsale but was defeated by Mountjoy. The Spanish general capitulated; surrendering all the places they held, they were allowed to leave with all they had brought, and help to transport it. Mountjoy pressed his advantage to establish full military control of Ireland.

Bacon volunteered to Sir Robert Cecil, probably in 'this dead vacation time' of August 1602, his own views on how to deal with the now eight-year-old rebellion. In his opinion 'the causes of Ireland, if they be taken by the right handle', could be 'the best action of importation to yourself of honour and merit of her Majesty and this crown, of ventosity or popularity, that the riches of any occasion, or the tide of any opportunity, can possibly minister or offer.' He did proceed cautiously, however: 'This I hope I may in privateness write, either as a kinsman that may be bold, or as a scholar that hath liberty of discourse, without committing any absurdity.'

Success in reducing Ireland 'as well to civility and justice as to obedience and peace' lay in four points: 'the extinguishing of the relicks of the war', 'the recovery of the hearts of the people', 'the removing of the root and occasions of new troubles', and 'plantations and buildings'. As the headings suggest, much of the tract consists of constructive, non-violent suggestions. Even in the first section, Bacon proposes moderation: 'I do think much letting of blood, *in declinatione morbi* [to alleviate the disease], is against method of cure: and that it will but induce necessity and exasperate despair, and percase discover the hollowness of that which is done already; which now blazeth to the best show.' As far as he understood 'the design of this state upon that miserable and desolate kingdom; containing the same between these two lists or boundaries; the one, that the Queen seeketh not an extirpation of that people, but a reduction; and that now she hath chastised them by her royal power and arms, according to the necessity of the occasion, her Majesty taketh no pleasure in effusion of blood, or displanting of ancient generations.'[66]

As it happened, Elizabeth did not have the time to get beyond subduing the country. Tyrone, overwhelmed by English reinforcements, submitted to Elizabeth on 22 December 1602; postal delays meant that he had received no answer by 20 March. In the meantime, the Queen's health had become a cause of serious alarm. In early March 1603 Elizabeth was suddenly overtaken by a series of maladies – 'imposthumation in her head, aches in her bones, and continual cold in her legs, besides a notable decay of judgment, insomuch as she cannot abide discourses of government and state, but delighteth to hear old Canterbury Tales to which she is very attentive'. Only Cecil dared enter her presence: all others were scared out of court by her unpredictable and now forgetful tantrums.[67] Refusing medicine throughout her illness, it was not until 22 March that the Lord Admiral finally persuaded the Queen to take to her bed, 'having lain these last days upon her cushions'.

By the evening of the twenty-third it was reported that the Queen was speechless. When the Lord High Admiral, Lord Keeper and Mr Secretary attended her, they had to ask her to signal if she still intended that James should succeed her, as she had angrily insisted the day before. 'Whereat suddenly heaving herself upwards in her bed and pulling her arms out of the bed, she held both her arms jointly together over her head in manner of a crown.' Similarly, by use of movement and 'by lifting up her eyes' she answered the archbishop's questions of her faith, and listened to him pray.

The exemplary deathbed actions of Queen Elizabeth, as relayed by a multitude of panegyrics and eyewitness accounts, belied the chaos elsewhere. With Elizabeth's life clearly in the balance, there was public unrest at the uncertain future of the country. The Venetian ambassador reported a

> great perturbation . . . lest the masterless men and malcontents may rise. In the palace the guards have been doubled and the pensioners are armed. The Queen's jewelry and silver have been sent to the Tower to be guarded with the Crown jewels; and many private persons likewise conceal their jewels, and some even themselves. Stirrings and alarms are in every house. Many of the ministers are hated of the people. In the City there is great fear of the Catholics, for there are forty thousand of them and they openly oppose themselves to the King of Scots. Moreover those Catholic lords that have been summoned to Court have not yet obeyed. Yet the Catholics have no leaders and are at variance among themselves.[68]

Some believed that the Queen's melancholy was caused because 'she hath heard some whisperings . . . that many of the nobility did by under-hand letters and messengers seek to curry favour with the King of Scots . . . This they did so openly that they quarrelled one with another about it. Hereupon she looked upon herself as a miserable forlorn woman, and her grief and indignation extorted from her such speeches as these: "They have yoked my neck: I have none whom I can trust: my condition is strangely turned upside down." '[69]

Elizabeth was right. Some of her closest ministers were busy putting in their bids with the new King.[70] Bacon's position in the new order was uncertain. He, perhaps more than any other, was a creature of Elizabeth's reign. As Thomas Dekker wrote, 'The report of her death (like a thunder-clap) was able to kill thousands, it took away hearts from millions; for having brought up (even under her wing) a nation that was almost begotten and born under her; that never shouted any other *Ave* than for her name, never saw the face of any Prince but herself, never understood what that strange outlandish word *Change* signified: how was it possible but that her sickness should throw abroad an universal fear, and her death an astonishment.'[71] But Bacon was more than a victim of *Zeitgeist*. He was Elizabeth's 'little Lord Keeper'; he was the boy who had kissed her hand before travelling into France; the man who had returned and enjoyed uncommon access to her presence. His twists of fortune had been entirely dependent on her whims. He had been for many years popularly considered and employed as one of the Learned Counsel, but this was purely on the verbal order of the Queen: he was never sworn in, nor did he possess a written warrant. Not 'in office' at the time of her death, he ran the risk of being left out of the dispositions of office thereafter.

In the days before the Queen's demise, when her end seemed inevitable, he used his friend Michael Hickes to approach Cecil: 'The apprehension of this threatened judgement of God, *percutiam pastorem et dispergentur oves gregis* [I will strike the shepherd and scatter the sheep from his flock], if it work in other as it worketh in me, knitteth every man's heart more unto his true and approving friend.' Therefore he wrote to him,

> signifying that I would be glad of the comfort of your society and familiar conference as occasion serveth. And withal, though we card-holders have nothing to do but to keep close our cards and to do as we are bidden, yet as I ever used your mean to cherish the truth of my inclination towards Mr. Secretary, so now again I pray as you find time let him know that he is the personage in this state which I love most: which containeth all that I can do, and expresseth all which I will say at this time. And this as you may easily judge proceedeth not out of any straits of my occasions, as mought be thought in times past, but merely out of the largeness and fullness of my affection.[72]

Lest Cecil prove unhelpful, Bacon covered himself by approaching Henry Percy, the earl of Northumberland, claiming a longstanding, though hidden, affection for him: 'As the time of sowing of a seed is known, but the time of coming up and disclosing is casual, or according to the season;

so I am a witness to myself, that there hath been covered in my mind a long time, a seed of affection and zeal towards your Lordship, sown by the estimation of your virtues, and your particular honours and favours to my brother deceased, and to myself, which seed still springing, now bursteth forth into this profession.' He claimed, however, that his suit derived from more elevated considerations:

> To be plain with your Lordship, it is very true, (and no winds or noises of civil matters can blow this out of my head or heart,) that your great capacity and love towards studies and contemplations of an higher and worthier nature than popular (a nature rare in this world, and in a person of your Lordship's quality almost singular,) is to me a great and chief motive to draw my affection and admiration towards you. And therefore, good my Lord, if I may be of any use to your Lordship, by my head, tongue, pen, means, or friends, I humbly pray you to hold me your own; and herewithal, not to do so much disadvantage to my good mind, nor partly to your own worth, as to conceive that this commendation of my humble service proceedeth out of any straits of my occasions, but merely out of an election, and indeed the fulness of my heart.[73]

At 2 a.m. on 24 March 1603, after all but her women had departed for the night, Elizabeth died, 'having reigned 44 years 5 months and odd days'.[74]

PART III

A PRECARIOUS POWER

1603–1621

10

Dawn of the Deserving World

*The canvassing world is gone, and the deserving world is
come. And withal I find myself as one awaked out of sleep;
which I have not been this long time.*
Francis Bacon to Tobie Matthew (April 1603)

IN THE SCRAMBLE to secure the attention of Elizabeth's successor,
making sure of the key London players was only half the battle. It
was clear that much would be swayed by the men who already swayed
the new King – his Scottish court. As the various entourages of the royal
family (King James, Queen Anne, and their eldest children Henry and
Elizabeth) made their way south they were acclaimed by Englishmen, as
James recalled, 'their eyes flaming nothing but sparkles of affection, their
mouths and tongues uttering nothing but sounds of joy, their hands, feet,
and all the rest of their members in their gestures discovering a passionate
longing, and earnestness to meet and embrace their new Sovereign'.[1]
Partly this welcome came from goodwill and a genuine joy at seeing,
as Bacon later put it, after over half a century of uncertainty, 'a king, in
the strength of his years, supported with great alliances abroad, established
with royal issue at home, at peace with all the world'. But much of the
joy was barely disguised self-interest. Once Elizabeth was dead, Bacon
recorded, there was 'continual posting by men of good quality towards
the King'. He jokingly hoped that 'as the State here hath performed the
part of good attorneys to deliver the King quiet possession of his kingdom,
so the King will redeliver them quiet possession of their places; rather
filling places void, than removing men placed.'[2]
Francis Bacon, however, had no official position of which he could
retain 'quiet possession'. His only post had been an informal understanding
that he was the Queen's 'Learned Counsel' – an appointment unsupported
by a position in the legal hierarchy, or by a single piece of paper. There
was also the problem of his reputation in Scotland, where he was known
chiefly as the notorious prosecutor of James's ally the earl of Essex, whose
popular reputation was now – with the death of the Queen – effectively
restored. Moreover, it was well known that James himself had had a soft
spot for Essex, who at one time in the late 1590s had been in sole charge

of negotiations between England and the Scottish King concerning the succession.

During the first months of James's reign Bacon penned an *Apology, in certain imputations concerning the late earl of Essex*, in which he gave his own account of their relationship, in the form of a letter written to Essex's friend and associate Mountjoy, who was now 'his very good Lord, the earl of Devonshire, Lord Lieutenant of Ireland'. Designed to repair Bacon's public reputation in the matter, the impact of the *Apology* was compromised by the strength of popular opinion against him. It was not until 8 May 1604 that the book was entered into the Stationers' Register,[3] and despite the popularity of the small volume (it was reprinted twice), it may not have been taken too seriously: the lawyer Egremont Thynne sent it to Sir John Davies, now Solicitor-General for Ireland, 'to serve you for an hour's recreation'.[4]

Bacon had one direct line to the new regime. He himself may have meant nothing positive to Scotland, but his brother Anthony had been heavily involved in Anglo-Scottish pre-succession negotiations, and had had close links with those around James. Most notable among these contacts were David Foulis, James's man in England, where he was resident ambassador from 1594 to 1596, and a key correspondent in the intelligence service Anthony provided for Essex; and Edward Bruce, Abbot of Kinloss, an ambassador extraordinary to England in April 1594 and 1600–1, who had facilitated Cecil's correspondence with James. These men were strictly Anthony's contacts, however, and if Francis was to stake his claim to them, he had to act quickly. Towards the end of March 1603 he took advantage of the Privy Council's messenger to Scotland, Mr Lake, to add to his bag a letter to Foulis in which he cited 'the remembrance of the constant and mutual good offices which passed between my good brother and yourself; whereunto (as you know) I was not altogether a stranger', albeit, as he admitted, 'the time and design (as between brethren) made me more reserved.' Now, however, he knew he wanted to cultivate 'the extraordinary sufficiency, dexterity, and temper' which Anthony had detected in Foulis. The letter was sent, but missed Foulis, arriving in Edinburgh after he had already set out southwards. Bacon wrote again. He hoped, he said, to revive 'those sparks of former acquaintance between us in my brother's time'.[5] His letter to Bruce, despatched at the same time as the first missive to Foulis, is couched in suspiciously similar terms: 'The present occasion awaketh in me a remembrance of the constant amity and mutual good offices which passed between my good brother deceased and your Lordship, whereunto I was less strange than in respect of the time I had reason to pretend.'[6]

Bacon also called on Anthony's correspondent Dr Morison, whose letters to and from Essex had, he claimed, often passed through his hands, hoping 'by this my letter to renew the ancient acquaintance which hath passed between us';[7] and on the poet John Davies who, like so many others, was making his way north, commending himself 'to your love and to the well using of my name, as well in repressing and answering for me, if there be any biting or nibbling at it in that place, as in impressing a good conceit and opinion of me, chiefly in the King (of whose favour I make myself comfortable assurance) as otherwise in that court'.[8]

Bacon backed up this epistolary bid for attention with a personal messenger, in the form of his old Gray's Inn friend Tobie Matthew, who set out for the north on 28 or 29 March bearing a letter from Bacon addressed to James and another to Sir Thomas Chaloner, asking him to present the letter to the King. Chaloner, sent to Scotland by Sir Robert Cecil while the Queen was still alive, had succeeded in capturing the trust of the Scottish King, and now accompanied him throughout his journey south; he was therefore a key target for those seeking the new monarch's favour. Luckily for Bacon, Chaloner was also yet another contact of Anthony's, having been employed as an intelligencer in Italy by Essex, upon Anthony's commendation, and his acquaintance with Francis – now described as a 'mutual friendship' – dated (at least on paper) back to 1596. This relationship, however, was tainted by financial problems. As usual, Francis owed money, and so had to start the letter on which his suit for future security depended by writing: 'For our money matters, I am assured you conceived no insatisfaction; for you know my mind, and you know my means; which now the openness of the time, caused by this blessed consent and peace, will increase; and so our agreement according to our time be observed.'[9]

Bacon's letter to James was a far more lavish composition, adorned with references judged to appeal to the King's known desire to be seen as learned. Its goal, however, was just as clear: to gain him access to James which would match that to which he had become habituated with Elizabeth.

It is observed upon a place in the Canticles by some, *Ego sum flos campi et lilium convallium* [I am the flower of the field and the lily of the valley], that, *a dispari*, it is not said, *Ego sum flos horti, et lilium montium* [I am the flower of the garden and the lily of the mountains]; because the majesty of that person is not inclosed for a few, nor appropriate to the great. And yet notwithstanding, this royal virtue of access, which nature and judgement have planted in your Majesty's mind as the portal of all the rest, could not of itself (my imperfections considered) have animated me to make oblation of myself immediately to your Majesty, had it not been joined with an habit of like liberty, which I enjoyed with my late dear Sovereign Mistress; a Prince happy in all things, but most happy in such a successor.

He was further encouraged by the thought that there might have come to James's 'sacred ears some small breath of the good memory of my father, so long a principal councillor in this your kingdom', and also 'the particular knowledge of the infinite devotion and incessant endeavours (beyond the strength of his body, and the nature of the times) which appeared in my good brother towards your Majesty's service; and were on your Majesty's part, through your singular benignity, by many most gracious and lively significations and favours accepted and acknowledged, beyond the merit of anything he could effect'. All these endeavours and duties, Bacon now claimed, 'for the most part were common to myself with him, though by design (as between brothers) dissembled.' Bacon ended his letter 'thirsting after the happiness of kissing your royal hand'.[10]

There is no record that James ever responded: John Chamberlain noted to Dudley Carleton that 'your old friend Tobie Matthew was sent with a letter from Master Bacon but I doubt neither the message nor messenger were greatly welcome.'[11] Bacon's efforts did not stop here. He took it upon himself to compose 'some gracious declaration' to take the King's attention, which might 'forerun his coming (be it never so speedy)'. It was a job, he claimed, he was used to doing, 'it being a thing familiar in my Mistress' times to have my pen used in public writings of satisfaction.' The offer contained a concealed dig at Cecil, who – before Elizabeth's death, and with James's approval – had drafted a proclamation that was issued on 24 March. In Bacon's eyes, Cecil's proclamation was inadequate: it had done little more than assert James's right to the throne, and the fact that the undersigned would uphold that succession. What was needed was an attempt at 'cherishing, entertaining and preparing men's affections'.[12] Unable to travel to attend James in person, because of 'some little physic I took', he approached Henry Percy, ninth earl of Northumberland, whom James quickly elevated to the Privy Council table, and asked him to present the draft, without using his name.[13] Bacon's proclamation had James representing himself as 'the instrument and as it were the cornerstone, to unite these two mighty and warlike nations of England and Scotland', and referred to 'this whole island of Great Brittany was ever united under one sovereign prince before this day'.[14] The proclamation was never used, but it contained in embryo the ideas on which Bacon would enlarge, and which James would pursue, over the first few years of the reign.

Between Elizabeth's death and James's arrival in London, the Queen's Privy Council continued to act, and the King released a proclamation 'to retain the Council and all other officers in their old places' until further notice.[15] Unfortunately, Bacon's 'office' was non-existent: his name appeared on no list. However, the Privy Council made sure that the King learned of the omission and confirmed, in a letter to Lord Keeper Egerton, 'that our meaning is that he [Bacon] shall continue to be of our Learned Counsel, in such manner as before he was to the Queen, during our pleasure'.[16]

After his initial botched approaches, Bacon finally 'renewed acquaintance' with Foulis, 'and it was like a bill of reviver by way of cross-suits; for he was as ready to have begun with me.' Edward Bruce arrived 'and took acquaintance of me instantly in the council-chamber, and was willing to entertain me with further demonstrations of confidence that I was willing at that time to admit'. When he wrote to Tobie Matthew to tell him of this, however, he admitted that he had had 'no serious speech with him; nor do I yet know whether any of the doubles of my letter have been delivered to the King. It may perhaps have proved your luck to be the first.'

Things were turning out reasonably well. To his cousin Robert Kempe, Bacon beamed:

> It is in vain to tell you with what wonderful still and calm this wheel is turned round; which whether it be a remnant of her felicity that is gone, or a fruit of his reputation that is coming, I will not determine: but I cannot but divide myself between her memory and his name. Yet we account it but a fair morn before sunrising, before his Majesty's presence: though for my part I see not whence any weather should arise. The Papists are contained with fear enough, and hope too much. The French is thought to turn his practice upon procuring some disturbance in Scotland, where crowns may do wonders. But this day is so welcome to the nation, and the time so short, as I do not fear the effect.

He also reported that the imprisoned earl of Southampton 'expecteth release by the next dispatch'. Realising that Southampton was likely to be a popular figure upon his release, Bacon made an attempt to win back the support of the man in whose prosecution he had been so profoundly implicated, 'assuring your Lordship (how credible soever it may seem to you at first) yet it is as true as a thing that God knoweth, that this great change hath wrought in me no other change towards your Lordship than this, that I may safely be now that which I was truly before'. There is no record of Southampton's acceptance of the suit either before or after his release on 10 April.[17] Bacon seems never to have learned that those he had badly let down politically were unlikely actively to support him thereafter.

Even though Bacon recovered his health sufficiently to travel north shortly afterwards to meet James on his way down to the capital, he failed to gain private access, as he reported to Northumberland, whose letter to James he was carrying.

I would not have lost this journey, and yet I have not that for which I went. For I have had no private conference to any purpose with the King; and no more hath almost any other English. For the speech his Majesty admitteth with some noblemen is rather matter of grace than of business. With the Attorney he spake, being urged by the Treasurer of Scotland, but yet no more than needs must. After I had received his Majesty's first welcome, I was promised private access; but yet, not knowing what matter of service your Lordship's letter might carry (for I saw it not) and well knowing that primeness in advertisement is much, I chose rather to deliver it to Sir Thomas Erskine, than to cool it in my hands, upon expectation of access.[18]

Londoners were agog for the first sight of their new King – but to those who got close enough to observe more than a fleeting image, he presented a curious picture. 'He was of middle stature,' Sir Anthony Weldon later recalled,

more corpulent through his clothes than in his body, yet fat enough, his clothes ever being made large and easy, the doublets quilted for stiletto proof, his breeches in great pleats and full stuffed. He was naturally of a timorous disposition, which was treason of his quilted doublets: his eyes large, ever rolling after any stranger that came into his presence, insomuch as many for shame have left the room, as being out of countenance; his beard was very thin: his tongue too large for his mouth, which ever made him speak full in the mouth, and made him drink very uncomely, as if eating his drink, which came out into the cup of each side of his mouth; his skin was as soft as taffeta sarsnet, which felt so, because he never washed his hands, only rubbed his fingers ends slightly with the wet end of a napkin. His legs were very weak, having had (as was thought) some foul play in his youth, or rather before he was born, that he was not able to stand at seven years of age, that weakness made him ever leaning on other men's shoulders; his walk was ever circular, his fingers ever in that walk fiddling about his cod-piece.[19]

Although England was pleased to be welcoming a royal family for the first time in over half a century, remarks like that last one of Weldon's make it clear that James was not in every respect the perfect family man. He came south with a long history of male favourites. In fact, Francis Bacon should have felt a good deal more comfortable around James's court than he had in Elizabeth's: he had, after all, operated for years within the coterie atmosphere of intimate male friendship in the service of the earl of Essex. He was used to the world of 'bed companions and coach companions'; and he knew how to indulge a passionate patron's susceptibility for the attentions of intelligent, entertaining and devoted 'friends'. But James's court proved almost as hard for Bacon to gain access to as had Elizabeth's.

James made a good first impression on Francis Bacon. To Northumberland, he praised the new King as

> a prince the farthest from the appearance of vain-glory that may be, and rather like a prince of the ancient form than of the latter time. His speech is swift and cursory, and in the full dialect of his country; and in point of business, short; in point of discourse large. He affecteth popularity by gracing such as he hath heard to be popular, and not by any fashions of his own. He is thought somewhat general in his favours, and his virtue of access is rather because he is much abroad and in press, than that he giveth easy audience about serious things.

As for Bacon himself, 'in my particular I have many comforts and assurances; but in mine own opinion the chief is, that the canvassing world is gone, and the deserving world is come. And withal I find myself as one awaked out of sleep; which I have not been this long time, nor could I think, have been now, without such a great noise as this; which yet is in *aura leni* [easy on the ear].'[20]

James's new appointments were few: Edward Bruce, Abbot of Kinloss, to the vacant mastership of the Rolls; his own Captain of the Guard, Sir Thomas Erskine, to replace Elizabeth's Captain of the Guard Sir Walter Ralegh (whom he compensated financially);[21] and two or three Scottish courtiers to key personal positions. Bacon, officially confirmed in post for the first time by the guarantee that he was to 'continue to be of our Learned Counsel, in such manner as before he was to the Queen', found that in practice he was less called upon, James leaving much of this area of business to Attorney-General Coke. For Bacon, this opened the door to a new way of life, as he confided to Sir Robert Cecil: 'For my purpose of course, I desire to meddle as little as I can in the King's causes, his Majesty now abounding in counsel; and to follow my private thrift and practice, and to marry with some convenient advancement.' His ambition, he assured Cecil, was now 'quenched'. 'In the Queen my excellent Mistress's time the quorum was small: her service was a kind of freehold, and it was a more solemn time. All those points agreed with my nature and judgment. My ambition now I shall only put upon my pen, whereby I shall be able to obtain memory and merit of the times succeeding.'[22]

★

In his comparative freedom from the demands of public business, Bacon now turned his hand to producing or revising what amounted to political advice documents: tracts designed to inform James of his new positions, responsibilities and expectations, and simultaneously to put Francis Bacon into James's line of vision. The fragment 'Of the True Greatness of Britain' may well come from this period. Addressing the King, Bacon writes 'that it may the better appear what greatness your majesty hath obtained of God, and what greatness this island hath obtained by you ... I have thought good, as far as I can comprehend, to make a true survey and representation of the greatness of this your kingdom of Britain; ... being out of doubt that none of the great monarchies which in the memory of times have risen in the habitable world, had so fair seeds and beginnings as hath this your estate and kingdom.'[23] He informs James of his newly acquired 'forces and powers', those conditions 'proper to the amplitude and growth of states'; this was his focus, not 'religion, laws, policy', which were only 'common to their [states'] preservation, happiness, and all other points of well-being.'[24]

Then, in late May or early June 1603, Bacon published *A Brief Discourse Touching the Happy Union of the Kingdoms of England and Scotland*, a short treatise that advised the King to act with prudence when pursuing his ambition to unite the two kingdoms. In Bacon's eyes, James 'hasteneth to a mixture of both kingdoms and nations, faster perhaps than policy will conveniently bear'.[25] Flattering the King's scholarly ambitions, Bacon promoted natural philosophy as the preferred medium for discussion of the issue: a wise king would appreciate 'the congruity between the principles of nature and policy'. The ancient Persian kings had been taught magic to observe 'the contemplations of nature and an application thereof to a sense politic; taking the fundamental laws of nature, with the branches and passages of them, as an original and first model, whence to take and describe and copy and imitation for government'. Nowadays, such learning had been lost 'because of the difficulty for one man to embrace both philosophies'; but to a king such as James, 'studious to conjoin contemplative virtue and active virtue together', this treatise was an ideal gift, as Bacon strove 'to revive' the ancient practice 'in the handling of one particular'.

Unions in nature are analysed. Bacon, like the 'best observers in nature', distinguishes between *compositio* (combined) – the 'putting together of bodies without a new form' – and *mistio* (mixed) – 'putting together of bodies under a new form'. In nature and in politics, *compositio* leads to strife, *mistio* to harmony; Virgil shows how, unless a new form, a *commune vinculum* (shared bond) is created, 'the old forms will be at strife and discord'. Integration requires a consideration of sovereignty, of language, of laws; *mistio* requires time, 'for the natural philosophers say well, that *compositio* is *opus hominis* [the work of man] and *mistio opus naturae* [the work of nature].' The greater element will draw the lesser: 'so we see when two lights do meet, the greater doth darken and drown the less.'[26]

Here we see Bacon arguing politics through natural philosophy, attempting to derive rules that would be applicable to all of existence.[27] In *Valerius Terminus* (1603), Bacon summoned men to commit themselves to studying nature to increase 'the power and kingdom of mankind'. The different 'sciences' can aid each other in the 'framing or correcting' of 'axioms' – a general set of axioms exists by which all sciences can be tested individually. 'There is a great affinity and consent between the rules of nature, and the true rules of policy.'[28] In the arrival of a monarch with intellectual leanings, Bacon saw real possibilities for bringing his own two spheres of interest – the laws of men and the laws of nature – together at last. Failing any official opening in respect of the former, he might at least secure backing for the latter.

Bacon also advised the new King on ecclesiastical policy. James's journey south had raised the hopes of English Puritans that further reform might finally be possible within the Anglican church, and with renewed vigour, they raised the question in the press and in their sermons. Bacon's contribution to the debate, *Certain Considerations Touching the Better Pacification and Edification of the Church of England*, penned probably in August or September 1603, placed him firmly outside the battlefield. 'Finding that it is many times seen that a man that standeth off, and somewhat removed from a plot of ground, doth better survey it and discover it than those which are upon it, I thought it not impossible but that I, as a looker on, might case mine eyes upon some things which the actors themselves . . . did not or would not see.' His *Considerations* advocated moderation – a 'golden mediocrity, in the establishment of that which is sound, and in the reparation of that which is corrupt and decayed' – and the settling of grievances that would be too expensive to suppress.

Although Bacon admits that the matters under discussion are 'things not properly appertaining to my profession', he overcomes his doubts by analysing 'the ecclesiastical state' as if it were a civil state that needed in the same time to be 'purged and restored by good and wholesome laws'. 'But if it be said to me that there is a difference between civil causes and ecclesiastical, they may as well tell me that churches and chapels need no reparations though houses and castles do: whereas commonly, to speak truth, dilapidations of the inward and spiritual edification of the Church of God are in all times as great as the outward and material.' As in civil government, where only the 'general grounds of justice and manners' are dictated by God, 'so likewise in Church matters, the substance of doctrine is immutable, and so are the general rules of government, but for rites and ceremonies, and for the particular hierarchies, policies, and disciplines of church, they be left at large.'[29]

When these matters came to a head at the Hampton Court Conference in January 1604, James started out by disputing with his own bishops, pursuing a line very similar to that outlined by Bacon in his *Certain Considerations*. On the second day, however, he became embroiled in an argument with the Puritan divines, as to what extent the church had authority to prescribe ceremonies. It was the kind of half-hearted acceptance of his advice that was to become a recurring pattern for Francis Bacon in his relations with the King over the next few years.

★

While Bacon was labouring to convince his new sovereign of his long-term loyalty and service, his past royal record came back to haunt him. On 28 December 1598, Elizabeth had declared that one Valentine Thomas, alias Thomas Anderson, 'a lewd caitiff, but born our subject, being apprehended on the borders, has delivered, without torture, menace, or persuasions, divers informations of practices contrived between the King of Scots our good brother and himself, for taking away of our life, for which he was promised great reward by the King.' Bacon had been instrumental in obtaining the confession of Thomas, and of another alleged conspirator, Robert Crawford. Although James was immediately cleared of any wrongdoing, the conspirators were imprisoned.

It was only a matter of time before Sir Edward Coke became alerted to this newly embarrassing, anti-James incident in Bacon's past. In April 1603 he gleefully informed Sir Robert Cecil that Thomas, still imprisoned at the Tower, 'with many tears hath acknowledged his former confessions, especially that concerning her Majesty's person written by Mr. Bacon, to be most false, and denieth that any person moved or incited him thereto; and yet blameth some in the course of his examination'. Crawford too 'utterly retracteth his examination written also by Mr. Bacon'. Coke felt it inappropriate 'to commit to writing what I collected upon their examinations, nor to trust any messenger with the examinations themselves', but assured Cecil that 'his Majesty is cleared of all colour or shadow of any thought of any ill or dishonourable thing'.

Luckily for Bacon, James was about to leave on a progress, and Coke 'thought it no fit time for myself to trouble him.'[30] Bacon promptly appealed to Cecil against this 'contempt' that he felt should be corrected: 'not that I would use the privilege in future time, but because I would not have the dignity of the King's service prejudiced in my instance.' Cecil presumably acquiesced in Bacon's request, because Bacon later thanked his cousin for the 'favour'.

Coke's carping was not the only problem which refused to go away: on top of this, Bacon continued to be financially distressed. A paper entitled 'A Note of my Debts', probably dating from the first two months of the new King's reign, records his woes as follows:[31]

A NOTE OF MY DEBTS.
My own proper debts.

That my L. Treasurer hath undertaken	2000 l.
That I was beholden to your Honour for procuring	500 l.
That Twicknam is mortgaged for	1200 l.
Sum. tot.	3700 l.

For my brother.

To Allen Mercer	500 l.
To Woolmer	500 l.
Other debts to the value of	300 l.
Sum. tot.	1300.

Cecil had apparently lent him money, which was due within a fortnight, a deadline that Bacon could not meet: 'Nay money I find so hard to come by at this time, as I thought to have become an humble suitor to your Honour to have sustained me with your credit for my present freeing from urgent debts, with taking up £300 more till I can put away some land. But I am so forward with some sales, as this request I hope I may forbear.'

Two weeks later, Bacon wrote again to Cecil to inform him that he could now pay up in full. He immediately resumed his customary lobbying for favour:

Your money shall be ready before your day; principal, interest, and costs of suit. So the sheriff promised, when I released errors [withdrew my appeal]; and a Jew takes no more. The rest shall not be forgotten; for I cannot forget your Lordship *dum memor ipse mei* [as long as he is mindful of me]: and if there have been *aliquid nimis* [anything inappropriate], it shall be amended. And, to be plain with your Lordship, that will quicken me now, which slackened me before. Then I thought you might have had more use of me, than now I suppose you are like to have. Not but I think the impediment will be rather in my mind than in the matter or times. But to do you service, I will come out of my religion at any time.[32]

He also called on Cecil to secure him the knighthood that had eluded him under Elizabeth. 'Lastly, for this divulged and almost prostituted title of knighthood, I could now without charge, by your Honour's mean, be content to have it, both because of this late disgrace, and because I have three new knights in my mess in Gray's Inn commons.'

Finally, Bacon broke the news to Cecil that he was embarked on an utterly new and unfamiliar course to improve his flagging finances. 'I have found out an alderman's daughter, an handsome maiden, to my liking. So as if your Honour will find the time, I will come to the court from Gorhambury upon any warning.' The alderman's daughter, one Alice Barnham, would have to wait another three years, since she was only eleven. He particularly asked that 'For my knighthood I wish the manner might be such as might grace me, since the matter will not; I mean, that I mought not be merely gregarious in a troop. The coronation is at hand.'[33] But his worst fears were realised. Francis Bacon was dubbed Sir Francis Bacon on 23 July 1603 in the Royal Garden at Whitehall, to mark James's coronation. Three hundred others received the same honour.[34]

★

By 1604 the honeymoon was over. Those at court were astounded at the King's prodigality, especially since most of it seemed to be directed at his beloved Scottish retinue.

On 11 January, it was announced by proclamation that there was to be a new parliament. Apprehensions that had been bubbling below court niceties began to surface. James's notion of parliament was, inevitably, influenced by the Scottish version, which was often in effect an advisory court which debated subjects which the King decided were fit to debate. This was not the way of the English Houses. Now, the Commons wanted to obtain certain things from the new King: for example, the redress of grievances arising from feudal tenures, from purveyance and from other antiquated crown rights such as monopolies and wardships; and they did not want to be too generous in the raising of income for government. James, for his part, was uninterested in these demands: he wanted to press on with the union between England and Scotland. It was not a recipe for success.

This first Jacobean parliament sat four times between 1604 and 1610. Sir Francis Bacon was returned as member for St Albans, but chose to leave that place for Tobie Matthew, and to sit instead once again for Ipswich.[35] For its first three sittings (March to July 1604, January to May 1606, November 1606 to July 1607), Bacon occupied an awkward and anomalous position. Lacking a named office, he was not in any real sense a crown official, and his stated opinions need not follow the royal line. On the other hand, he was a member of the King's Learned Counsel, striving for higher office, and he felt obliged – morally if not pragmatically – not to antagonise the monarch on whose favour his future depended. But he also believed in the privileges of parliament. The balancing act was going to be a difficult one.

A year on from his accession, the King's opening speech on 19 March was widely anticipated. But what he said did not please everybody. The tone was misjudged: James blithely spoke of 'the blessings which God hath in my person bestowed upon you all, wherein I protest I do more glory at the same for your weal, than for any particular respect of mine own reputation, or advantage therein'. Moreover, James's stated line on religious affairs was not calculated to appease his Puritan critics, already incensed by the events at the Hampton Court Conference. 'At my first coming,' he declared, 'although I found but one religion, and that which by myself is professed, publicly allowed, and by the law maintained, yet found I also another sort of religion, besides a private sect, lurking within the bowels of this nation.' He distinguished the Anglican 'true religion' not only from the papists, but from 'Puritans and Novelists, who do not so far differ from us in points of religion, as in their confused form of policy and parity, being ever discontented with their present government, and impatient to suffer any superiority, which maketh their sect unable to be suffered in any well-governed commonwealth.'

Worse, he acknowledged the Roman Catholic church 'to be our mother church, although defiled with some infirmities and corruptions'. He would not persecute Roman Catholics who were loyal to him, but he would not tolerate those who believed in papal authority over kings. He would be sorry, he said, 'to strait the politic government of the bodies and minds of all my subjects to my private opinions: nay, my mind was ever so free from persecution, or thralling of my subjects in matters of conscience, as I hope that those of that profession within the kingdom have a proof since my coming.' He advised parliament to be impartial as magistrates and judges, stressing that they were answerable to him, and he was answerable to God.[36]

Routine problems were blown out of all proportion. The January proclamation had included a new clause, stipulating that all parliamentary returns were to be additionally checked by the Chancery, and that if any were found to have been made contrary to the proclamation, they would be rejected 'as unlawful and insufficient'. The Buckinghamshire MP Sir Francis Goodwin fell foul of this new ruling, when it was objected that he had been outlawed for unpaid debts; the return was refused, declared void; a new writ was issued from the Chancery, and the Privy Councillor Sir John Fortescue was elected in his place. However, the House discovered that the unpaid debts had now been paid; therefore he was not an outlaw, and had been properly elected. The Clerk of the Crown was ordered to file the first return, and Goodwin took his seat.

Insignificant though this exchange might seem, it brought the Commons into direct opposition to the Court of Chancery in the matter of who should judge parliamentary returns, and thus control the composition of the House. The Lords asked to confer on the matter, but the Commons refused the request, on the grounds that 'it did not stand with the honour and order of the House to give account of any of their proceedings'. When the Lords then informed the King of the business, he claimed himself to be 'enraged and touched in honour that there might be some conference of it between the two Houses'. He supported the Chancery ruling, citing a precedent from the reign of Henry VI, and resolved that the Commons should confer with the judges who had made the ruling in Chancery, and report to the Privy Council.

Bacon had been heavily involved in this case from the beginning, heading both the list of speakers in debate on its first airing on 23 March and the committee which set down their thoughts to be delivered to the King. On the floor, he gave his opinion that 'we ought not to contest with the King', advocating instead a conference with the House of Lords, by which means 'we shall lose no privilege, but rather gain' by both satisfying the King, and 'putting in certainty our privilege. All is not said that may be said. We are not to dispute with one that is governor of thirty legions.' Instead they should 'deal plainly and freely with the Lords'. There were vested interests at stake on both sides: 'They are jealous of the honour of a Privy Councillor, we of the freedom of election. It is fit great men maintain their Prerogative, so is it fit that we maintain our privileges. This is a Court of Record, therefore ought we by all means to seek to preserve the honour and dignity of it.'

It was a neatly balanced argument, but the analogy did not convince everybody. 'They say we are but half of the body,' objected another member, 'and the Lords are the parts nearest the head.'

'Nothing ascends to the head but by the breasts,' replied Bacon. He concluded that they should 'pray, it may be explained by a law, what our privileges are; and that no man outlawed may be hereafter admitted'. There was no precedent, he continued, of any man being put out of the House for outlawry, so it had been fit that they sought to inform the King that he was misinformed.[37] Despite Bacon's rhetoric, the mood of the House was that, having already decided the matter, they could not now agree to discuss it. Despite his clearly stated views to the contrary, it fell to Bacon to deliver the Commons' objections to the Lords in the Council Chamber at Whitehall, and to ask them to cooperate.[38]

James was 'distracted in judgment' by events in parliament. By 5 April, he made it known that he no longer desired that the Commons and judges should confer, but 'desired and commanded [it] as an absolute King'.[39] The Northampton MP Henry Yelverton accurately encapsulated the Commons' feelings at this change in tone: 'The Prince's command is like a thunderbolt: his command upon our allegiance is like the roaring of a lion. To his command there is no contradiction.' A select committee was formed, as commanded, with Bacon again functioning as *rapporteur*. Reporting back on their audience with the King, he portrayed a semi-divine monarch.

> This attendance renewed the remembrance of the last, when we departed with such admiration. It was the voice of God in man, the good spirit of God in the mouth of man: I do not say the voice of God, and not of man: I am not one of Herod's flatterers: a curse fell upon him that said it, a curse on him that suffered it. We might say, as was said to Solomon, We are glad O King that we give account to you, because you discern what is spoken. We let pass no moment of time until we had resolved and set down an answer in writing, which we now had ready: That sithence we received a message from his Majesty by Mr. Speaker, of two parts. 1. The one paternal. 2. The other royal. 1. That we were as dear unto him as the safety of his person or the preservation of his posterity: 2. Royal; that we should confer with his Judges, and that in the presence of himself and his Council: That we did more now in King James than ever was done since the Conquest, in giving account of our judgements: That we had no intent in all our proceedings to encounter his Majesty, or to impeach his honour or Prerogative.

In reporting James's answer, Bacon stumbled, claiming he knew not how to report His Majesty's speeches – 'the eloquence of a King is inimitable.' The King was determined to draw to an end the difference in Goodwin's case: if required, he would be absent; he 'would not hold his Prerogative, or honour, or receive any thing of any or all his subjects – this was his magnanimity'; and he would confirm and ratify all his just privileges. 'This', Bacon proclaimed, 'was his bounty and amity; as a King, royally; as King James, sweetly and kindly, out of his good nature.'

Bacon assured the House that their privileges 'were not in question; that this was a matter merely of 'private jealousies, without any kernel or substance'. Granting that the House was indeed 'a Court of Record and a Judge of returns', Bacon nonetheless moved 'that neither Sir John Fortescue nor Sir Francis Goodwin might have place'. He likened the situation to that of a schism between a pope and an anti-pope: 'there could be no end of the difference until they were both put down.' Settled in this way, with Sir John also losing his place, Bacon concluded, 'his Majesty did meet us halfway.'[40]

The pattern was established for Bacon's behaviour in this, and the next two sittings of the parliament. Heavily involved in virtually every debate, on every committee of substance, and often acting as the voice of the House, the views he expressed were consistently his own – and were often anathema to his fellow members. His speeches are brim-full of carefully balanced analyses of the relative merits of the two sides, his advice to the Commons always tending towards compromise rather than confrontation. But this middle way was not the solid ground of Sir Nicholas' *via media*: more often, it resembled a path through quicksand. Frequently Bacon found himself almost alone in his advocacy of compromise, markedly out of step with the rest of the House; time and again he found himself having to present a case to the King, or the Lords, on behalf of the Commons only hours after he had passionately opposed that case on the floor of the Lower House.

With the Goodwin–Fortescue matter resolved, the House was able to concentrate on those issues the King wanted to discuss, of which the first to be debated was the Union.[41] Although James thought that this could be settled with little effort, in fact it was still being discussed during the 1606–7 session and even then without reaching the required conclusions. Here, Bacon's efforts were unapologetically on behalf of the King. The King believed the Union to be 'the greatest and least question that ever came in Parliament'; he merely wanted the union 'which is already in substance' to be acknowledged by an Act, with a name given to this united state ('Great Britain' being the favoured choice) and a commission appointed to settle further matters, such as laws, rites, customs and ceremonies, and to report back to parliament. This plan was supported by the Lords and by Bacon. He argued that the title 'Great Britain' was supported by the King's justice – he would not 'usurp' the title 'by any unproper style of greatness'; by his honour, since 'honour contracted was better than honour divided', like 'one fair stone in a jewel, which was more precious than a jewel compacted of many'; and by policy – the Union in name would 'draw on a unity in affection betwixt the two kingdoms'. Attempting to forestall dissent, Bacon gave voice to the possible objections 'that we should change our ancient name of England' and 'that we should prejudge the matter, and enwrap that which should be left free to the Committee', and proposed two answers: 'ever a good change for the better' and 'no danger to give by way of advance that which may be a step forward to good action'.

However, an opposition soon emerged, coalescing around the figure of Sir Edwin Sandys, which demanded that the entire issue be discussed before the name be settled. Bacon continued to express his hope that in conference the Commons 'should not be the objectors only, but to make the case indifferent betwixt the two Houses', and that the commissioners 'might treat generally with the Lords, without limitation, but conclude nothing';

and he gave answers to eight objections that had been raised. One was, as he had anticipated, that England would lose its ancient name, with all its fame and resonance of great victories. But, he argued, on the other hand 'Britain' carried with it the associations of the greatness of the Roman Empire. Names were airy and volatile. Unfortunately, Bacon's answers were none too convincing. Sir Edwin Sandys objected that, far from being airy, the cause under discussion was the most weighty that had or could come before them, and they should proceed with a leaden foot. Names involved the very nature of things. Bacon seemed, commented Carleton, 'to make answers to the objections, and did only show his good will in it: but no matter came from him worth the noting'.[42]

Once again the King raised the stakes by expressing displeasure at the length of the Commons' debate, dismissing the doubts expressed as 'curiosities of ignorant persons, such as sought to find knots in bulrushes. He desired his breast were made of crystal: and though he was unhappily embarked in former matters, in this he liked not to have his deliberations questioned.' The Commons 'thoroughly sifted' the King's words, and 'both the particularity of the King's speech and the project for the Act [were] directly oppugned . . . And now all men's opinions went this way, and nothing said by any which was not against the Union either in the name or substance.' All men but one. 'Only Sir Francis Bacon would seem to give a stop to this current.'

The business dragged on through conference between the Lords and Commons. On 25 April, an exasperated Bacon complained that they found themselves as Simonides did when Hieron asked him what he thought of God, asking for six days to think about it, then twelve, then twenty-four. 'The more we wade,' objected Bacon, 'the more we doubt'; and he listed thirteen objections that had been made. He noted the public disapproval, to which attention should be paid – 'Kings have used to do it' – but warned against inappropriate opposition, advising the House on 26 April to avoid three sorts of objections: 'light objections: lest it should be said *rebus arduis levia immiscet* [levity is mixed in with hard things]'; 'subtle and curious: lest in like manner it might be said *rerum pondera verborum frangit argutiis* [he dashes to pieces the weight of things with sharp words]'; 'high, and that we must not *scrutari arcana imperii* [examine too deeply the mysteries of empire]'. Following a speech by Sandys, adding further objections, which Bacon then incorporated into a paper, assigning 'several parts to several persons, of several qualities, as they conceived fit', Bacon himself reported on one of the two 'matters of generality or common reason', namely 'that there is no cause of change': 'That in constituting or ordaining of any innovation or change, there ought to be either urgent necessity or evident utility; but that we find no grief of our present estate, and foresee

no advancement to a better condition by this change; and therefore desire
it may be showed unto us.'

When the conference with the Lords took place, Bacon was forced to
argue against the Union. 'There was now neither necessity of change nor
evident utility,' he said. 'We were now in a good haven and loath to put
to sea: that we would not adventure upon a new condition unless there
might appear some matter of improvement.' On 1 May, the Lords' committee, although still inclined to drop the name of Britain, was happy to
proceed to confer on the same day with another committee, which was
finally formed (Bacon drafted the bill to authorise the commissioners[43]) by
a system of voting. It consisted of two Privy Councillors, two ambassadors,
four common lawyers, two civil lawyers, four merchants and sixteen
country gentlemen. Bacon's name topped the list, as he proudly recalled:
'myself was by the Commons graced with the first vote of all the Commons
selected for that cause.'[44] Throughout May, conferences between the two
Houses continued, with intense discussion: on 1 June, it was recorded in
the *Commons Journal* that the bill, like winter fruit, 'ripens slowly'. Only
on 2 June did the bill finally pass the Commons.

The parliamentary session of 1604 also dealt with wardship, purveyance
and monopolies. In each case, royal prerogative was involved, and was, in
important respects, under attack. The task facing Bacon was to find a way
of steering the House's business through without insulting the King – as,
for instance, in the matter of alleged abuses in the system of purveyance.[45]
Royalty had traditionally retained the prerogative to buy and convey provisions for the royal households, the prices for these goods and services
being decided by the King's purveyors. Complaints against purveyors were
common: they were accused of forcing people to sell goods at cripplingly
low prices, ordering more goods than they really needed and returning
the excess only after extorting a sizeable payment. In this session, on 27
April, a petition of grievances against purveyors was presented to James
by Bacon and a committee in the withdrawing chamber at Whitehall.
Before launching into a spirited account of the purveyors' abuses, Bacon
made sure to flatter the King in respect of his relations with his people:

No name is more worthy of you, nor may more truly be ascribed unto
you, than that name of *father of your people*, which you bear and express,
not in the formality of your style, but in the real course of your government. We have found in your Majesty great cause both of admiration
and commendation. For great is the admiration wherewith you have
possessed us since this Parliament began, in those two causes wherein
we have had access unto you, and heard your voice; that of the return
of Sir Francis Goodwin; and that of the Union ... God hath given

your Majesty a rare sufficiency, both to compass and fadom [embrace] the greatest matters, to discern the least we cannot but with great thankfulness profess, that your Majesty, within the circle of one year of your reign, hath endeavoured to unite your Church which was divided, to supply your nobility which was diminished, and to ease your people in cases where they were burdened and oppressed.[46]

Despite Bacon's best efforts, however, the House could not ultimately decide on how to compensate the crown for the loss in revenue that the proposed move against purveyance would entail.

On 19 June, a motion was introduced suggesting that a gratuity should be presented to the King, in the interest of national honour. Bacon supported the motion, begging his fellow members, 'Let not this Parliament end, like a Dutch feast, in salt meats; but like an English feast, in sweet meats.' But the feast ended, as most of it had been spent, in dissension and doubt. It was at this moment, arising out of a debate about wardship, that the Commons took it upon themselves to suggest to the King how to approach an English parliament, in the form of an *Apology* presented by Sandys. Bacon maintained that he was 'merely a relator' and 'no actor' in the wardship dispute, but this did not prevent some of his arguments on the abuse of purveyance being recycled in the *Apology*.[47] Unsurprisingly, the response to the gratuity motion was so lacklustre that the King forestalled further embarrassment by requesting that the House not pursue the matter further.

At the close of the parliament, the Speaker made a properly gracious and generous speech to the King; but James's own final speech was far less emollient. The King berated the Commons for their behaviour over the Union bill. In Scotland, he remarked, his counsel had been received graciously; in England, on the contrary, there was 'nothing but curiosity from morning to evening, to find fault with my propositions'. In Scotland, everything emanating from the King was warranted; here everything was suspected.

I will begin with the newest, the greatest, and the first, the Union. Look not that I will sing a palinode. Whatsoever hath been spread to distaste this Union, I set no frame to you but the matter, I avow, and more I avow the name Britanny. Else were I a rebel and a traitor to God and nature . . . He that doth not love a Scotchman as his brother, or the Scotchman that loves not an Englishman as his brother, is a traitor to God and the King . . . He merits to be buried in the bottom of the sea that shall but think of a separation, where God hath made such a Union. I am not ashamed of my project, neither have I deferred it (I'll deal plainly) out of a liking of the Judges' reasons, or yours . . . I have remitted the name till after the thing be done, lest quirks in law might take other hold than is meant.[48]

On 7 July, to the relief of all concerned, parliament was prorogued.

★

It might appear that James recognised and rewarded Bacon's parliamentary service with some alacrity, since on 18 August 1604 (the patent being signed a week later) he granted Sir Francis Bacon by patent the office of Learned Counsel ('one of the King's Council at Law'), and a pension of £60 per annum for life. But this was not so. The patent makes it clear that the pension was awarded 'on account of the good, faithful and commendable service, until recently, of our beloved servant Anthony Bacon, deceased [*in consideratione boni fidelis & acceptabilis Servitii, per nuper Dilectum nostrum* Antonium Bacon *Armigerum defunctum*]'.[49] Once again the hidden link between the two brothers had provided Bacon with a rare career break.

Finally confirmed in employment, Bacon spent much of his vacation actively preparing for the October conference of the Commissioners of the Union. He took advantage of his acquaintance with another of the committee's learned men, the antiquarian and manuscript collector Sir Robert Cotton, who had delved deep into his records to put to rest some of the debates – showing, for example, that the title 'King of Great Britain' was supported by antiquity and etymology. He was an ideal partner for Bacon, who had found in him during the parliament 'a willingness in you to confer with me in this great service concerning the Union'. In September, he played on that willingness 'to excuse my boldness to desire that now which you offered then, for both the time as to leisure is more liberal, and as to the service itself is more urgent. Whether it will like you to come to me at Gray's Inn or to appoint me where to meet with you, I am indifferent, and leave it to your choice.'[50] On the basis of his work with Cotton, Bacon drew up his 'Certain Articles or Considerations touching the Union of the Kingdoms of England and Scotland', a tract which provided support for James's policy, but in which, summarising the key issues, he emphasised the complexity of the problems to be addressed in uniting the two countries' laws, religion, courts and names, rather than supplying a pragmatic letter of advice. He claimed in this tract not 'to presume to persuade or dissuade anything', and pledged himself to follow the King's 'royal directions' however future developments fell out.[51] He also prepared a 'draught of a Proclamation touching his Majesty's style', which was ultimately not used.[52]

The Commission, consisting of forty-eight Englishmen and thirty-one

Scots, appears to have proceeded from 29 October with surprisingly little difficulty, as Bacon recalled, holding the experience up as a model for such consultation. 'The counsels at this day in most places are but familiar meetings, where matters are rather talked on than debated. And they run too swift to the order or act of counsel. It were better that in causes of weight the matter were propounded one day, and not spoken to till the next day: *In nocte consilium* [at night take counsel]. So was it done in the Commission for Union between England and Scotland; which was a grave and orderly assembly.'[53] By 24 November, it had been agreed that the Commission would recommend the naturalisation of both the *post nati* and the *ante nati* (those born after as well as those born before the accession of James to the English throne). Bacon and Sir Thomas Hamilton were directed 'to review the said articles, and to reduce and join them together in such form and method as was meet and agreeable in coherence of matter, and would be fit to be set down in the instruments themselves to be propounded to the Parliaments' by Tuesday 27 November; it seems that Bacon also took it upon himself to provide a preface (although Cecil had been asked to provide one), which was used in an altered form.[54] The articles and preface were duly written, read, agreed, and finally signed and sealed on Thursday 6 December.[55]

★

Bacon was now waging his campaign for advancement on several fronts. His parliamentary service – always hindered by the fact that he was not a crown official – spoke for itself. He was also continuing to give the King the benefits of his pen. There was plague in London, and on 24 December 1604 parliament was again prorogued until the following autumn. Bacon found himself with time on his hands. Eager as ever to alight on a project that would earn him royal favour, he spent the spring of 1605 considering a new 'History of Britain', a literary monument to complement the physical monument to Elizabeth proposed by James. He wrote to his old ally Sir Thomas Egerton, now elevated as Lord Chancellor Ellesmere, to air his thoughts on this idea, suggesting that James's reign would be seen as the natural outcome of the 'strange variety' of sovereigns since Henry's day; taking into account 'the unworthiness of the History of England (in the main continuance thereof) and the partiality and obliquity of that of Scotland, in the latest and largest author, that I have seen', Bacon concluded that 'it would be honour for his Majesty and a work very memorable, if this Island of Great Britain, as it is now joined in monarchy for the ages to come, so were joined in History for the times passed, and that our just and Complete History were compiled of both Nations.'[56]

It was now, too, that Bacon – in the spirit of 'advice to the new regime'

– set forth his first important piece of writing concerned with the growth of knowledge: *The Two Books of Francis Bacon: Of the Proficiencie and Advancement of Learning*, composed between 1603 and 1604 but published only at the end of 1605, as noted by Chamberlain in a letter of 7 November.[57] Deprived of opportunities for policy formation elsewhere, Bacon had mapped out in considerable detail a plan for the total reform and overhaul of education and research, a plan which he argued would yield dividends in terms of wealth and international importance for the Stuart monarch and his realm. A number of 'plats' (plans or projections) of this kind are to be found among the State Papers for Elizabeth's reign, in both manuscript and limited-edition printed form.[58] Bacon's more widely disseminated work both advertised his own availability to serve in the role of knowledge-developer and paid a public compliment to the new King as a monarch who could comprehend and support initiatives at the cutting edge of science.

The *Advancement of Learning* (as it came to be known) is a blueprint, a set of instructions, on how to set out to improve the current state of knowledge in King James's realm. Consciously or unconsciously, Bacon's title also indicates that advice of this kind is offered as a bid for preferment. 'Preferment' and 'advancement', in fact, are synonyms: 'the advancement of learning' is both 'how to improve the state of learning' and 'how learning can be a means to advancement'. Indeed, the letter of dedication to King James announces that the work is both a bid for favour and a personalised example of the sort of project Bacon might expertly oversee: 'There belongeth to kings from their servants both tribute of duty and presents of affection. In the former of these I hope I shall not live to be wanting, according to my most humble duty, and the good pleasure of your Majesty's employments: for the later [*sic*], I thought it more respective to make choice of some oblation which might rather refer to the propriety and excellency of your individual person, than to the business of your crown and state.'[59] Bacon was not alone in this kind of endeavour; comparable use of an educational work to bid for a prince's favour, on the open understanding that such a public (published) gesture might gain the author intellectual office in the prince's entourage, was made by Desiderius Erasmus, whose *Education of a Christian Prince* (1516), a structured treatise on raising a future monarch, was directed at the Habsburg Prince Charles, later Emperor Charles V.[60]

The *Advancement of Learning* was not only dedicated to the King; it was also presented to many of the country's leading men. Having offered it to 'the learnedst king that hath reigned', Bacon was 'desirous, in a kind of congruity, to present it to the learnedst counsellor in this kingdom' – the earl of Northampton – with the request that he present it to the King: 'to the end that so good an argument, lighting upon so bad an author, might receive some reparation by the hands into which, and by which, it should be delivered'.[61] To Robert Cecil, earl of Salisbury, now Chancellor of the University of Cambridge, Bacon noted that this 'work of my vacant time . . . appertaineth to your Lordship (besides my particular respects) in some propriety, in regard you are a great governor in a province of learning, and (that which is more) you have added to your place affection towards learning, and to your affection judgement'.[62] Another recipient was Buckhurst, 'not only as a Chancellor of an University . . .'; another was Lord Chancellor Ellesmere, 'a great planter of learning, not only in those places in the Church which have been in your own gift'.[63]

To his friend Tobie Matthew, who left England in April 1604 for Italy, Bacon wrote: 'I have now at least taught that child to go, at the swadling whereof you were. My work touching the *Proficiency* and *Advancement of Learning*, I have put into two books; whereof the former, which you saw, I count but as a page to the latter. I have now published them both; whereof I thought it a small adventure to send you a copy, who have more right to it than any man, except Bishop [Lancelot] Andrewes, who was my inquisitor.'[64] To his old correspondent Sir Thomas Bodley, Bacon confided as a fellow scholar that this book represented what he truly wanted to do:

I do confess, since I was of any understanding, my mind hath in effect been absent from that I have done; and in absence are many errors which I do willingly acknowledge; and amongst the rest this great one that led the rest; that knowing myself by inward calling to be fitter to hold a book than to play a part, I have led my life in civil causes; for which I was not very fit by nature, and more unfit by the preoccupation of my mind. Therefore calling myself home, I have now for a time enjoyed myself; whereof likewise I desire to make the world partaker. Books are the shrines where the Saint is, or is believed to be: and you having built an Ark to save learning from deluge, deserve propriety in any new instrument or engine, whereby learning should be improved or advanced.[65]

Bacon could hardly have picked a worse time to publish, particularly if the aim was to attract the attention of those prominently placed around the King: for James's administration was reeling from the Gunpowder Plot, which threatened parliament as it sat again on 5 November. The government was absorbed with the pursuit and interrogation under torture of anyone who might conceivably have been involved. It was a time of witch-hunts and score-settling.[66] Bacon himself seems to have been only peripherally concerned, examining a servant who had overheard a suspected

recusant say 'It had been brave sport if it [the Plot] had gone forwards' –
a tiny detail, but Bacon forwarded it to Cecil, thinking it 'not good to
neglect anything at such a time'.[67] Parliament was adjourned to the ninth;
on that day the King gave an account of the Plot's discovery, and adjourned
the session again until 21 January.[68]

When parliament reassembled, the first bill passed was a motion calling
for 5 November to be reserved as a day of thanksgiving – a provision
which remained in force for over 250 years. Parliament had to be seen to
be taking action against such threats, and passed new, harsher laws against
recusants, 'for the timely and severe proceeding against Jesuits, Seminaries,
and other Popish Agents and Practisers, and for the preventing and suppressing of their plots and practices'.[69] Bacon was involved in several committees on this subject; in addition, he served on committees examining
other ecclesiastical matters, and was concerned once again with various
civil causes, including the renewed discussion of purveyance (which was
effectively put off) and subsidy.

There was a single point of possible contention between King and
Commons: the petition of fourteen grievances, read to the Lower House
on 10 May 1606. It was decided that Bacon would read this to the King;
his own speech, Bacon reported back, was 'but a preamble to a preamble.
Though there were grievances, they were not meant as aspersions or
imputations to be laid to His Majesty's government, but were rather the
diseases of the time and things that had grown up and been cut down
partly by His Majesty and yet sprung again.' When the King replied that
the complaints would be favourably considered, the House was sufficiently
satisfied as to send up a grant of three subsidies – an unprecedented amount
in peacetime. 'The Commons of the Lower House', commented the earl
of Shrewsbury, 'are much more temperate than they were at the first
session; and now spend all their spirits and endeavours in devising laws
tending to his Majesty's safety, and suppressing of the dangerous members
of the state. I heard not any one transcendant speech uttered there as yet.'[70]
Parliament closed on 27 May, and was prorogued to 18 November.

★

Bacon's apparently low profile in this parliamentary session may have had
to do with the preparation and execution of another major project that
was intended to settle him in a way parliamentary service could never do.
On 27 March Bacon wrote to Salisbury: 'I cannot as I would express your
tenderness over my contentment.' The occasion of this contentment – at
the age of forty-five – was his marriage.

When Bacon had importuned the then Sir Robert Cecil for a knighthood in July 1603, he emphasised that he particularly required it because

'I have found out an alderman's daughter, an handsome maiden, to my liking.'[71] The alderman's name was Benedict Barnham; the daughter's, Alice. Alderman Barnham was the third son of the London draper Francis Barnham, an alderman of Farringdon Without, who in December 1568 became Sheriff of London. When his father died in 1575, Benedict inherited a third of his father's moveable property as well as lands in Essex, Surrey and Wales. A successful merchant, Barnham progressed through the City hierarchy (as liveryman of the Drapers' Company, Alderman of Bread Street ward and, ultimately, in 1591, Sheriff) into parliament, and even to the Privy Council table, as a trusted consultant. When on 3 April 1598 he died at the age of thirty-nine, the elaborate memorial above his grave in St Clement's, Eastcheap, earned its place in Stow's *Survey of London*, published that year.

In 1583 Benedict had married Dorothy, daughter of the Queen's silkman, Humphrey Smith. All three of their eldest children died young – an only son, Francis (March–November 1585), and two daughters: Alice (November 1588–June 1592) and Margrit (November 1589–January 1591) – but he was eventually survived by five daughters: Elizabeth, baptised in June 1591; Alice, who was baptised on the same day that her namesake elder sister was buried, 4 June 1592; Dorothy (April 1595) and Bridget (June 1596). The youngest daughter, named Benedicta in his honour, died in February 1599. At the time of their father's death, then, the girls were still all under the age of seven: the eldest, Elizabeth, six years, nine months and twenty-one days old; the youngest, Benedicta, just sixteen days.[72]

Barnham expected his widow Dorothy to remarry: in his will he entreated her to 'have good care and carriage in her marriage (as being young), and above all to choose for a husband a man wise and honest'. Sure enough, in November 1598, seven months after Benedict's death, Dorothy took as her second husband Sir John 'Lusty' Packington, a favourite of Queen Elizabeth. The marriage to Dorothy Barnham enabled Packington to emerge from an indebted retirement and build up his Worcestershire estates, to the extent that by June 1603 he was in a position to entertain the new King sumptuously at his house in Aylesbury.

By the terms of Barnham's lengthy will, his goods, which included real estate in Essex, Hampshire, Kent, Middlesex and London, were divided into three equal shares, one for his wife, one for his daughters, and one for various legatees, including the Christ's Hospital, the Bridewell and the inmates of five London prisons, and the purchase of his children's wardships. Alice received £6,000 in the form of 'my lease of certain lands at Moulsham and Chelmsford in the County of Essex. And if it happen that the same Alice do die and unmarried then I give the same lease to Elizabeth my eldest daughter, etc.'[73] The will stated that Benedict desired Alice to be brought up by his mother, during her lifetime; if his mother died, then by her own mother, with her sisters. He asked the Drapers' Company to nominate four young men of their number, and the Haberdashers' Company to choose another four young men, 'thought fittest and likest to thrive', each of these to manage £300 for each of the daughters, paying them interest at 5 per cent annually.[74] Thus the daughters became highly desirable commodities on the marriage market, independently of their personal qualities.

When Francis Bacon first wrote of Alice Barnham as a suitable wife, she was eleven years old. Little is known of Alice, and what little we do know is filtered through the unreliable eyes of Bacon's faithful and, it appears, jealous servants. His chaplain William Rawley wrote in his commonplace book: 'One asked, How my Lady Derby, came to make such good use of her time, whilst her husband [Lord Ellesmere] was chancellor; and my Lady St Albans made so little? The other answereth; Because my Lady Derby's wit lay backward, and my Lady St Albans lay forward, viz in her tongue.'[75]

Given the complexity of the Barnham estates, the marriage negotiations were prolonged. Lady Derby was involved: Bacon later remembered to the Lord Chancellor that 'my honourable Lady your wife was some mean to make me to change the name of another' [i.e. his bride], when he was himself suing Ellesmere for a further title, 'so if it please you to help me to change my own name'. Salisbury also played a part; according to Bacon, writing later, the earl told him 'that what you had done for me in my marriage, was a benefit for me, but of no use to your Lordship'.[76]

The marriage between the forty-five-year-old Sir Francis Bacon and his bride of almost fourteen took place at Marylebone Chapel on 10 May 1606. We have an eyewitness account of Bacon and 'his young wench' from Dudley Carleton. The groom, he wrote,

> was clad from top to toe in purple, and hath made himself and his wife such store of fine raiments of cloth of silver and gold that it draws deep into her portion. The dinner was kept at his father-in-law Sir John Packington's lodging over against the Savoy, where his chief guests were the three knights, Cope, Hickes, and Beeston [Sir Walter Cope, Sir Baptist (or possibly Sir Michael) Hickes, Sir Hugh Beeston]; and upon this conceit (as he said himself) that since he could not have my Lord of Salisbury in person, which he wished, he would have him at least in his representative body.[77]

Notwithstanding Carleton's quip about the dowry being spent on the wedding, Bacon's marriage was definitely of financial advantage to him. According to the marriage articles, Bacon settled upon trustees the manors of Gorhambury, Westwick and Prae, described as 'with appurtenances, and 12 messuages, 3 mills, 12 gardens, 1,200 acres of land, 100 acres of meadow, 500 acres of pasture, 400 acres of wood, £30 rents, view of frank pledge, and the advowsons of St. Michael's and Redbourn, so that the same should be for Alice for life, and of the clear value of £300 per annum'. If Francis should die before his wife, he should leave to her goods and money worth £1,000, along with her apparel, linen and personal ornaments, and such jewels as she should possess while married, but no single jewel worth over £100 in value. If he should survive her, the manors would revert to him and his issue by her, and in default for his trustees.[78]

Bacon appears to have been content with his new state, though he may have felt the difference in age between him and his spouse: he confided to Lord Ellesmere that 'a married man is seven years elder in his thoughts the first day.'[79] He wrote candidly to his cousin Sir Thomas Posthumous Hoby that the benefits were both financial and personal. 'Your loving congratulation for my doubled life, as you call it, I thank you for. No man may better conceive the joys of a good wife than yourself, with whom I dare not compare. But I thank God I have not taken a thorn out of my foot to put it into my side. For as my state is somewhat amended, so I have no other circumstance of complaint. But herein we will dilate when we meet; which meeting will be much more joyful if my Lady bear a part to mend the music.'[80]

Having married one of the Barnham girls, Bacon soon extended his hold over the others. The following year (1607), he was instrumental in marrying Alice's sister Dorothy to John Constable, 'a towardly young gentleman' and a fellow Gray's Inn man. Constable was then promptly knighted on 5 October 1607 at Royston by the King, 'most graciously at my request', as Bacon told John Murray. He was, he assured Murray, by this favour 'more bound to his Majesty, than for the benefit of ten knights'.[81] In January 1608, at Bacon's suit, Constable was one of five men granted the reversion of certain manors, lands and tenements in Hertfordshire, which had been formerly assured by Lord Keeper Bacon to his sons, and of which the entail had been conveyed to the crown.[82] It is possible that Bacon was thereby avoiding taxation himself while ensuring that the land remained in the family.

Francis' mother-in-law, Dorothy Packington, did not appreciate Bacon's efforts on behalf of his sister-in-law, perhaps because she judged that they served the interests of his towardly young friend rather than those of her daughter. The elder Dorothy was by now in difficult circumstances herself. After nine years with Sir John, during which she bore him two daughters and a son, Lady Packington – whom Chamberlain dubbed a 'violent little lady' – left her husband 'upon foul terms'.[83] She appears to have interfered in the settlement of the Constable marriage. Constable offered his wife a jointure of £400 per annum when he came into his estate, subject to certain exceptions, most notably: 'But always I understand it, that those her friends which have so intolerably slandered and wronged me, shall have no intermeddling at all either in the assurance or in the allowance of these articles.'[84] Bacon was presumably a trustee of these 'Conditions', and it would seem likely that Lady Packington was one of the 'friends' whom Constable was writing out of his marriage.

Turning to Salisbury for help, Lady Packington praised him for his 'late care had of two of my daughters in taking them from the place of danger and putting them into safe keeping'. The 'danger' which potentially threatened them was demonstrated by the fate of their sister Dorothy, who was 'by the practice of Sir Francis Bacon in marriage with one Constable cast away'. Bacon's proceedings in contracting Constable and Dorothy Barnham came, according to Lady Packington, under the scrutiny of Salisbury 'and others of the Council', since Dorothy was only twelve years old. This inquiry, 'finding her age abused, and how slenderly she was provided for without jointure or other provision, in pity of her estate took some further care for her'. Lady Packington was now demanding to know from Bacon what was to be done for her daughter, but 'instead of satisfaction', she complained, she had

> received an insolent letter of contempt, penned after his proud manner of writing. My husband nor brother knowing nothing, being thrust out from all privity of dealing therein, I am forced to beseech you to let me know what order is taken from her. Being sorry I have such cause to complain of his bad dealing whom you recommended to me, and whose folly has lately more abounded in procuring Constable to be knighted, being a man of very mean estate, whereby he has taken all ordinary means of thriving from him.[85]

Though Lady Packington found the letter from her son-in-law incomprehensible ('after his proud manner of writing'), it contains a barely disguised threat to cut off all communication between Lady Packington and her daughter Alice unless she drops her campaign against him:

> Madam,
>   You shall with right good will be made acquainted with anything which concerneth your daughters, if you bear a mind of love and concord: otherwise you must be content to be a stranger unto us. For I may not be so unwise as to suffer you to be an author or occasion of dissension between your daughters and their husbands, having seen so much misery of that kind in yourself.

And above all things I will turn back your kindness in which you say, you will receive my wife if she be cast off. For it is much more likely we have occasion to receive you being cast off, if you remember what is passed. But it is time to make an end of those follies, and you shall at this time pardon me this one fault of writing to you. For I mean to do it no more till you use me and respect me as you ought. So wishing you better than it seemeth you will draw upon yourself.[86]

Although contemporary letter-writers wrote off Lady Packington as too difficult to take seriously, it does appear that her interpretation of Bacon's motives was acute. A cryptic record in a notebook kept in July 1608 suggests that he was indeed undertaking a similar campaign for Alice's sister Bridget: 'Q[uestion] of banning and match for Bridget, therein joining with Smith, trying whether I may use his purse or credit by means of Gr. Jones.' On the following page, there is another hint that these arranged marriages were brought about for Bacon's financial advantage: 'My Lord Chancellor [Ellesmere] will not aid legacies of marriage where the woman is got away without the consent of her friends, and his by-word is, "If you provide flesh for yourself provide bread likewise." '[87] For Bacon, the bread seems to have been brought in through the trade in flesh. When he came to list his creditors on 28 October 1609, Sir John Constable headed the list at £600.[88] It would be intriguing to know if Bacon took a similar role in the marriage of Alice's remaining sister, Elizabeth, to Mervin Touchet, the young earl of Castlehaven. Elizabeth was perhaps lucky to die young; in 1631 her erstwhile husband was arraigned and executed on charges of encouraging the rape of his second wife and daughter-in-law by his male servants, and of committing sodomy with those servants.[89]

★

When parliament met again on 18 November 1606, business started with the matter of the Union. On 25 November, the question arose of how to proceed. Bacon identified the key issues as laws of hostility, commerce and naturalising. 'Of the two first, the one included in streams of water, the other of blood; and the third of both: *non in aqua tantum, sed in aqua et sanguine* [not merely in water, but in water and blood]. It was prettily and pithily said in my mind, if children, why tribute? if tribute, why are we called children?' Should the measure be carried separately in each of the two Houses of Parliament, or by conference? Bacon inclined to the latter approach, 'because it is a matter of state, a matter of future providence, and not of present feeling. Our state is good now, and therefore to see what it may be, let us take help of those who sitting upon the higher ground by such advantage have the further prospect to see more.' If by conference, where to begin? '*Dies diem docet* [the day instructs the day: i.e. tailor advice to the occasion]. Imitate yourselves in the last great bill of Recusants (providing always it be not so long). That was to make one Church, this to make one Nation. Then we made a selected Committee to prepare: so did the Lords: and our labours fell all out with that consent, that when the King's letter came from Royston, it made a unison; and therefore I wish this should have the like course.'[90]

Again, Bacon's words fell – initially, at least – on stony ground: the Commons resolved to divide the branches of the question between the two Houses, the Upper dealing with naturalization and borders, and the Lower with commerce and hostility. It was only when the Lords rejected this arrangement that they reverted to Bacon's suggestion.

The Christmas recess (from 18 December 1606 to 10 February 1607) should have provided a breathing space, but instead it proved a breeding ground for new fears. On 13 February the MP for Buckinghamshire, Sir Christopher Piggott, produced 'general amazement' with a vitriolic anti-Scottish diatribe, for which he was expelled on the following Monday. It was against this background that 'the article of the Instrument concerning Naturalization was read' on Tuesday 17 February. The debate commenced with a speech against the measure by Nicholas Fuller, who proclaimed that England had no room for Scots: the universities were overfilled, London was being destroyed by new buildings, merchants had gone three years without profit, trades were overstocked. His speech was answered by one of Bacon's greatest pieces of parliamentary rhetoric.

Once again, Bacon patiently listed and confuted the main objections. These 'inconveniences' of naturalisation had been exaggerated, he claimed; the 'inconveniences' that would occur if the policy did not go ahead were far more serious. It was objected that naturalisation would cause a 'surcharge of people'; yet, Bacon retorted, England was far from being 'peopled to the full' – an increased population could only add to the nation's stature. It was objected that naturalisation should not be invoked until a single legal system was in place. 'Naturalisation', he explained, 'is in order first and precedent to union of laws; in degree, a less matter than union of laws; and in nature, separable not inseparable, from union of laws. For naturalisation doth but take out the marks of a foreigner, but union of laws makes them entirely as ourselves. Naturalisation taketh away separation; but union of laws doth take away distinction.'[91] Union should lead to a greater, more secure England. 'I think a man may speak it soberly and without bravery, that this kingdom of England, having Scotland united, Ireland reduced, the sea provinces of the Low Countries contracted, and shipping maintained, is one of the greatest monarchies, in forces truly esteemed, that hath been in the world.'

Even in the midst of this, one of his most accomplished and eloquent speeches, on a matter of immense national significance, Bacon found it necessary to repudiate the charge that he was performing for his own benefit. 'If any man shall think that I have sung *placebo* for mine own particular, I would have him know that I am not so unseen in the world but that I discern it were much alike for my private fortune to rest a *placebo* in this business. But I have spoken out of the fountain of my heart. *Credidi, propter quod locutus sum* – I believed, therefore I spake. So as my duty is performed.'[92]

Although Bacon's speech was widely admired, and its transcript immediately became a collectable item, he was once again out of line with the House. The Commons reverted to probing the question of the *post nati* as a point of law: they determined on 23 February that the *post nati* were not naturalised *de jure*, and decided that a conference with the Lords should follow. Ironically, Bacon was once again given the task of explaining to the Lords a position with which he was deeply ill at ease; he also had to report on the conference.

If the ethical strain of this were not enough, the physical demands almost defeated Bacon. The Commons were required to stand during conference with the Lords: Fuller found this 'a great hurt and danger to the health of their bodies, and almost impossible for the strongest body to endure, considering the length of conferences and the crowding and thronging there'.[93] This particular conference lasted two days, after which Bacon was too exhausted to face his own House. When he came to report on Saturday 28 February, his account was so 'very long, consisting of many divisions and particulars, and interlaced with much variety of argument and answer on both parts, the time would not allow him to finish, and so was deferred till Monday morning'.[94]

The debates continued through February into March, with the business being referred to the Upper House judges, and then referred back down to the Commons, the main point of contention being whether the *post nati* should have equal rights in England with the English. Eventually, in the days before Easter, James spoke to the House, conveying his hope that they would still pass an act of general naturalisation, with the two kingdoms' union following on; but it became clear that the Commons would not consent to the King's proposals, and the suggestions were postponed. The only success met by the pro-Unionists was the passing, as late as 30 June, of a bill for abolishing hostile laws. Parliament was prorogued again on 4 July.

Thereafter, without parliament to take up his time, Bacon continued to pen political advice. Only two such tracts survive from this period: one relating to the jurisdiction of the Provincial Council in Wales (which had ramifications for the battle being fought between the royal prerogative and the courts of law), the other to the jury system, specifying that 'all persons which have freehold according to the law . . . shall be returned to serve upon Juries as occasion shall require.' The latter was approved, and published as a Proclamation on 5 October 1607.[95] Both of these documents were directly related to Francis Bacon's recently acquired new position – for, just before the prorogation of parliament in the summer of 1607, Bacon had finally gained the long sought-after office of Solicitor-General.

★

When Bacon's single-minded pursuit of preferment eventually paid off with the solicitorship, it was not through the legacy of his brother Anthony, nor through his published *Advancement of Learning*, but through his parliamentary endeavours on behalf of the crown. It had been a long, hard struggle over a period of two years. Opportunities for advancement appeared and vanished with startling frequency. In October 1604, during the Union Commission talks, the post of Solicitor-General became vacant for a matter of hours, before being given to the Prince of Wales's Serjeant, John Doddridge. In August 1605 Sir Edmund Anderson died; his post as Chief Justice of the Common Pleas might have been filled by Coke – and Coke's by Doddridge, leaving the solicitorship for Francis Bacon; but in the end Anderson was succeeded instead by Sir Francis Gawdy, a puisne judge of the King's Bench (buying the place 'at a dear rate').[96] As he complained to Ellesmere two years later, it seemed to Bacon that he saw 'every new man coming above me'.[97]

Gawdy, however, enjoyed his place for just four months, before dying of apoplexy in December 1605. When Coke was talked of as his replacement (and Doddridge as Coke's) the following March, Bacon solicited his cousin Salisbury (believing 'I have small store of means about the King, and to sue myself is not so fit'): 'I would be glad now at last to be Solicitor, chiefly because I think it will increase my practice, wherein God blessing me a few years, I may amend my state, and so after fall to my studies and ease, whereof one is requisite for my body, and the other sorteth with my mind.'[98] For the time being, however, neither Coke nor Doddridge moved position; and so Bacon, too, remained where he was.

Coke finally succeeded Gawdy in June 1606, and Sir Henry Hobart, the King's Serjeant, was talked of as the new Attorney. There was also talk of a plan, as Bacon later reminded the King, 'that Mr. Solicitor [Doddridge] should be made your Majesty's Serjeant, and I Solicitor; for so it was thought best to sort with both our gifts and faculties for the good of your service. And of this resolution both court and country took knowledge. Neither was this any invention or project of my own; but moved from my Lords, and I think first from the Lord Chancellor.' Indeed, Bacon charged Ellesmere as 'being the man that first devised that mean'. Again nothing happened.

Finally, after waiting for promotion for some sixteen years, Bacon decided to tackle the situation head-on, and wrote to the country's three most powerful men – the King, Lord Chancellor Ellesmere and Lord Treasurer Salisbury – to vent his frustration.

To the King he listed his recent public services: 'both in the commission of Union, (the labour whereof, for men of my profession, rested most upon my hand,) and this last Parliament, in the bill of the Subsidy (both body and preamble); in the bill of Attainders, both Tresham and the rest; in the matter of Purveyance; in the Ecclesiastical Petitions; in the Grievances, and the like; as I was ever careful (and not without good success) sometimes to put forward that which was good, sometimes to keep back that which was not so good'. His Majesty had, he reminded him, accepted his services kindly, and had been pleased 'to promise and assure me, that upon the remove of the then Attorney I should not be forgotten, but brought into ordinary place,' a promise that could be confirmed by many Lords. Since he was assured this place, he 'never opened my mouth for the greater place [the attorneyship]', although he possessed two qualities that the present incumbent could not claim: 'the one, nine years' service of the crown; the other the being cousin germain to the Lord of Salisbury, whom your Majesty esteemeth and trusteth so much. For my father's service I will not speak. But for the less place [the solicitorship], I conceived it was meant me.' But when Hobart succeeded to the attorneyship, Bacon 'heard no more of my preferment, but it seemed to be at a stop, to my great disgrace and discouragement. For (gracious Sovereign) if still, when the waters are stirred, another shall be put before me, your Majesty had need work a miracle, or else I shall be still a lame man to do your service.'[99]

To Ellesmere he urged more pressing reasons for promotion: 'Time groweth precious with me. A married man is seven years elder in his thoughts the first day. And therefore what a discomfortable thing is it for me to be unsettled still? And were it not to satisfy my wife's friends, and to get myself out of being a common gaze and a speech, I protest before God I would never speak word for it.'

To Salisbury he wrote that he wanted the post 'because I think it will increase my practice, and that it may satisfy my friends, and because I have been noised to it'. Indeed, if it were not that he was born to serve his sovereign, 'for my own comfort, it were better for me that the King did blot me out of his book, or that I should turn my course to endeavour to serve him in some other kind, than for me to stand thus at a stop, and to have that little reputation which by my industry I gather to be scattered and taken away by continual disgraces, every new man coming above me.' He also played the family card, speaking 'in the confidence of your poor kinsman, and of a man by you advanced'. He recalled the 'significant and comfortable words of hope' that Salisbury had extended to him 'during the course of my last service, that you would raise me; and that when you had resolved to raise a man, you were more careful of him than himself'. The marriage was one such way Salisbury had benefited Bacon: as he said, 'what you had done for me in my marriage, was a benefit to me, but of no use to your Lordship; and therefore I might assure myself, you would not leave me there.' He acknowledged that Salisbury was 'no dealer of holy water, but noble and real', but claimed for himself that 'I am of a sure ground that I have committed nothing that may deserve alteration.' He therefore hoped that his cousin would 'finish a good work, and consider that time groweth precious with me, and that I am now *vergentibus annis* [bowed down by years].'[100]

It was on 22 February 1607, five days after his great speech in favour of the Union, that Bacon received a distinct promise of promotion to the solicitorship when Doddridge should leave the post. Four months later, on 25 June, Doddridge was finally promoted to King's Serjeant (as the incumbent, Croke, was made a puisne judge of the King's Bench) – and so, at the age of forty-six, Sir Francis Bacon finally gained a crown office: the post of Solicitor-General, with an income he reckoned at £1,000 per annum.[101]

11

No Stage-friends:
Making Connections

*Conjunction of minds and studies has a greater part in
friendships than civil ties and offices of occasion.*
Sir Francis Bacon to Isaac Casaubon (?1608)

AT THE BEGINNING of the legal profession's long vacation in 1608,
Francis Bacon undertook an extensive review of his present state.
Over seven days from 25 July to 31 July he surveyed his life's
business, in a series of notes which bear the running title of '*transportata*'
('things carried across'), suggesting that these notes were collated and copied
from existing notebooks. He entitled this collection *Commentarius solutus*
('loose notes'): 'This book receiveth all remembrances touching my private
of what nature soever and hath two parts: *diarium* and *schedulae*. The one
being a journal of whatsoever occurreth; the other Kalendars or Titles of
things of the same nature, for better help of memory and judgment, herein
I make choice of things of present use.' He described it as 'like a merchant's
waste-book where to enter all manner of remembrance of matter, form,
business, study, touching myself, service, others, either sparsim or in sched-
ules, without any matter of restraint; only this to be divided into two
books: The one *transportata ex commentario vetere* [copied out from an old
notebook], containing all manner notes already taken in several paper
books fit to be retained (except it be such as are reduced to some more
perfect form); The other *Commentarius novus* [a new notebook].' Only the
first book survives.[1]

This major life review was occasioned by the death, on 16 July, of
William Mill, the Clerk of the Star Chamber. Finally, after nineteen years
of waiting with the reversion of the post, Bacon was sworn in as Clerk,
taking on also the post's estimated £2,000 annual income.

On Monday 25 July, Bacon set down details of his income along with
suggestions for increasing it and improving his business arrangements. Of
prime importance was financial security – or rather, cash security: 'to make
a stock of £2000 always in readiness for bargains and occasions'. Then he
must establish himself 'in credit' with wealthy individuals against the time

when he would need to borrow 'any great disbursements' – here he listed as potential sources of loans the London alderman Sir John Swinnerton; the baronet and parliamentarian Sir Richard Molineux; his half-sister Elizabeth, widow of Chief Justice Perriam; one Antropos; John Howell per Champners; and Sir Michael Hickes, a creditor of old. Sureties should be made ready from his brothers Nathaniel and Edward; his cousin Sir William Cooke; Edward Jones and Henry Fleetwood (both these names were later crossed out); Faldoe; his cousin Robert Kempe; and Hedley.

Having established a basis of financial security, his thoughts turned to ways in which he should 'set on foot and maintain access with his Majesty', through such men as the Dean of the Royal Chapel (Dr James Montague), the Groom of the Privy Chamber Humphrey May, and John Murray of the King's Bedchamber. Since Bacon was not a permanent fixture at court, this access could not always be effected in person. Therefore, he proposed 'keeping a course of access [i.e. planning to obtain access to the King's presence] in the beginning of every term and vacation with a memorial, the one being a time of execution, the other of preparation'. When possible, he would attend the King's 'repasts and fall into a course of familiar discourse'.

The aim of all this activity was 'to find means to win a conceit not open but private of being affectionate and assured to the Scots, and fit to succeed Salisbury in his management of that kind' – Scots like the King's favourite Dunbar; the dukes of Lennox and Aubigny; Sir James Elphinston and his brother Alexander; James, Lord Hay; Sir Thomas Hamilton; John Gibb of the King's Bedchamber (as well as John Murray); Ackinson; and Sir Roger Ashton – and to press forward significant projects: 'the greatness of Britain', 'union in Parliament', suits and marriages. More specifically, Bacon proposed 'setting down and finishing my argument of the *post-nati* and presenting it to the King'; 'dispersing the argument and the two speeches [on general naturalisation and on union of laws] as in one book amongst the Scotch men and namely the Lord Fivye: the Advocatus Craigius [Sir Thomas Craig]'.

Long-term planning, however, is constantly interrupted by notes of an immediate, and immediately outdated, nature – to remember to be ready for argument in Lady Arabella Stuart's cause; 'causing the walks about the wall to be sanded and made handsome against [for] Hickes' coming' to Gorhambury. We are also given intimate glimpses into Sir Francis Bacon's alimentary and purgative regimes:

> After a maceration taken in the morning and working little I took a glister about 5 o'clock to draw it down better, which in the taking found my body full and being taken but temperate and kept half an hour wrought but slowly, neither did I find that lightness and cooling

in my sides which many times I do, but soon after I found a symptom of melancholy such as long since with strangeness in beholding and darksomeness, offer to groan and sigh, whereupon finding a malign humour stirred I took three pills of aggregative corrected according to my last description, which wrought within two hours without griping or vomit and brought much of the humour sulphurous and fetid, then though my medicine was not fully settled I made a light supper without wine, and found myself light and at peace after it. I took a little of my troc[hises] of amon. [ammoniac pills] after supper and I took broth immediately after my pill.

In the margin, he noted, in explanation: 'Note, there had been extreme heats for ten days before and I had taken little or no physic.'

Notwithstanding the frequent diversions, the notes cover a great deal of ground. He plans to ensure he has ready money, and to increase his credit with James and Salisbury; he considers what subjects he should attend to, what advices he should offer, what legal cases he has to prepare for, how to increase his practice, what suits he should undertake on his own behalf, how to demonstrate his superiority to creditors, how to run his new office more effectively than his predecessor, how to prepare for the next parliament, how to improve his lands and leases, how to regulate his household, and what London house he should take. His cabinet, we learn, contains five books of compositions, four of notes on those compositions, nine on 'professional' matters, four on 'office' matters and five on personal affairs. Here, in stark quantitive terms, is a hint of how Bacon's philosophical work (amounting to nine books) is outweighed at this period by his professional and private dealings (eighteen books).

Nevertheless, his plans included the furtherance of his intellectual projects. Among his musings on the Tuesday of his stocktaking week, Bacon determined how he should obtain the help of useful people in his intellectual, and specifically experimental, work. The list of targets is an intriguing one. Closest to home was the resolution to make the 'acquaintance and privateness of my nephew Edmund Bacon', eldest son of his half-brother Sir Nicholas. He proposes also 'making much of [Thomas] Russell that depends upon Sir David Murray [Keeper of the Prince's Privy Purse] and by that means drawing Sir David and by him and Sir Thomas Chaloner in time the prince'. Thomas Russell was actively experimenting in separating silver from lead ore, with government sanction, while Chaloner had years earlier written a treatise on nitre; at the trial of Phineas Pette in 1609, for a failure in shipbuilding, he was called on to decide a geometrical question. From Russell, Bacon wrote, could be obtained 'a collection of phenomena, of surgery, distillations, mineral trials'. Other useful figures included Henry Percy, earl of Northumberland, and Sir Walter Ralegh – both currently imprisoned – 'and therefore Harriot', the mathematician Thomas Harriot, 'themselves being already inclined to experiments'.

Another potential collaborator could be Richard Bancroft, Archbishop of Canterbury and newly appointed Chancellor of the University of Oxford: 'seeing and trying whether the Bishop of Canterbury may not be affected in it, being single and glorious, and believing the sense'. Neither should he omit to draw in Bishop Lancelot Andrewes, 'being single, rich, and sickly, a professor to some experiments, this after the table of Motion or some other in part set in forwardness'. He should acquaint himself with the physician Leonard Poe, 'by him learning the experiments which he hath of physic and gaining entrance into the inner of some great persons' (and also 'for my health'). Other physicians were a possibility: 'the likest is Paddy, Dr. Hammond' – the King's physician, Sir William Paddy, and physician in ordinary, Dr John Hammond. Finally, there was the 'question of learned men beyond the seas to be made, and hearkening who they be that may be so inclined'.

These 'learned men beyond the seas' served several purposes. In 1608, Bacon penned a treatise *In felicem memoriam Reginae Elizabethae*, designed to answer the recent continental Catholic attacks on the late Queen. Latin would serve as his medium to spread across Europe his message: that Elizabeth had reigned for forty-four years without any decline in England's fortunes; that her government had given rise to various felicities; that she was of good character; and that she had proceeded against Roman Catholics fairly – this last section being at heart a recapitulation of his letter to M. Critoy of 1589 and the *Observations on a Libel* of 1592.

Aware that the French historian Jacques-Auguste De Thou was writing a history, Bacon sent a copy of his treatise to James's ambassador in Paris, Sir George Carew, via 'an old servant of my brother Anthony Bacon'. De Thou thought highly of Carew, who was well respected in intellectual circles on the continent (Scaliger wrote of him as '*vir amplissimus et sapientia et eruditione, et pietate praestantissimus*'), and had drawn on Carew's account of Polish history. Now he could provide an opening for Bacon's continental transactions. 'I would be glad the President De Thou saw it; chiefly because I know not whether it may not serve him for some use in his story. I would be glad also it were some occasion (such as absence may permit) of some acquaintance or mutual notice between us.'[2]

Carew also served to facilitate a correspondence between Bacon and the Genevan-born scholar Isaac Casaubon, who was in Paris at the time; Carew's wife stood as godmother to Casaubon's child in November 1612. Casaubon had read some of Bacon's work – indeed, his copy of *The Advancement of Learning* (now at the Henry E. Huntington Library in San

Marino, California) shows that he was using the text to learn English. He went through the text putting stress marks on the prose to aid his pronunciation; alongside learned annotations are his less impressive cribs in Latin, French and Greek to some of Bacon's English – 'neuerthelesse', 'framed', 'though neuer so excellent', 'misunderstanding', 'grounds', 'Mankind', 'youth', 'vnawares', 'ouerthrow', 'presidents', 'the old mans faggot in the bond', 'quarrell', 'insomuch', 'Barly-corne'. Casaubon's dictionaries clearly gave him most of the answers, with one exception which had him totally puzzled – Bacon's frequently used and emphatic 'Nay'.[3]

Language lesson aside, Casaubon was impressed with what he read. He wrote to Carew, and an exchange of letters was created. Bacon wrote (in Latin) to Casaubon:

> Understanding from your letter to the Lord Carew that you approve my writings, I not only took it as a matter for congratulations with myself, but thought I ought to write and tell you how much pleasure it had given me. You are right in supposing that my great desire is to draw the sciences out of their hiding-places into the light. For indeed to write at leisure that which is to be read at leisure matters little; but to bring about the better ordering of man's life and business, with all its troubles and difficulties, by the help of sound and true contemplations, – this is the thing I am at. How great an enterprise in this kind I am attempting, and with what small helps, you will learn perhaps hereafter. In the meantime you would do me a very great pleasure if you would in like manner make known to me what you are yourself revolving and endeavouring and working at. For I hold that conjunction of minds and studies has a greater part in friendships than civil ties and offices of occasion. Surely I think no man could ever more truly say of himself with the Psalm than I can, 'My soul hath been a stranger in her pilgrimage.' So I seem to have my conversation among the ancients more than among those with whom I live. And why should I not likewise converse rather with the absent than the present, and make my friendships by choice and election, rather than suffer them, as the manner is, to be settled by accident? But to return to my purpose. If in any thing my friendship can be of use or grace to you or yours, assure yourself of my good and diligent service.[4]

One of Bacon's most useful learned men overseas was in fact an Englishman, indeed a fellow Grayan with whom he had been friendly for many years – Tobie Matthew, son of the Archbishop of York. The association and friendship between the two men may have started when Tobie played the Squire in the 1595 Accession Day device; certainly it had flourished since.[5] As we have seen, it was to Matthew that Bacon entrusted his missive to James in March 1603, and to whom the following year he relinquished his parliamentary seat of St Albans. However, it was also in 1604 that the friendship became more difficult. Matthew voiced a wish to visit Italy, having 'often heard of the antiquities and other curiosities' of the country. But Tobie's mother was as afraid of the 'other curiosities' of Italy as Amias Paulet had been for Francis Bacon a quarter of a century earlier. Tobie surmounted this obstacle by agreeing to go no further than France; when he left England in early 1605, however, he immediately sailed on to Florence.

Over a period of months, Matthew was gradually drawn over to Catholicism. He was received into the Roman communion by Father Lelio Ptolomei, and remained abroad for six months more before travelling back to England via France and Flanders. Back in London, he settled initially in a French inn near the Tower, keeping his conversion secret. Then, however, he moved to Fleet Street and contacted Bacon with the news, asking him to inform the earl of Salisbury. Bacon apparently advised him to lay his case before the Archbishop of Canterbury, Richard Bancroft; Matthew did so, and was then 'committed to custody', probably at Lambeth Palace, in August 1607. Bacon remained an essential link with the outside world, and with possible rehabilitation: as Dudley Carleton wrote to Chamberlain on 27 August, 'Tobie Matthew hath leave to go as often as he will with his keeper to Sir Francis Bacon, and is put in good hope of further liberty.'[6]

Matthew's case was laid before the King, and it was decided to give him the opportunity of swearing allegiance; but he refused to take it, and was subsequently committed to the Fleet prison. He was allowed to see his friends – among them men of influence such as Thomas Morton, Sir Edwin Sandys, Sir Henry Goodyear, John Donne, Richard Martin, Bishop Lancelot Andrewes, Captain Whitelock and (through his father) Alberico Gentili – 'who sought to recover him'. Bacon wrote to Matthew asking him not to

> think me forgetful or altered towards you. But if I should say I could do you any good, I should make my power more than it is. I do hear that which I am right sorry for; that you grow more impatient and busy than at first; which maketh me exceedingly fear the issue of that which seemeth not to stand at a stay. I myself am out of doubt, that you have been miserably abused, when you were first seduced; but that which I take in compassion, others may take in severity. I pray God, that understandeth us all better than we understand one another, contain you (even as I hope he will) at the least within the bounds of loyalty to his Majesty, and natural piety towards your country. And I entreat you much, some-

times to meditate upon the extreme effects of superstition in this last Powder Treason; fit to be tabled and pictured in the chambers of meditation, as another hell above the ground: and well justifying the censure of the heathen, that superstition is far worse than atheism; by how much it is less evil to have no opinion of God at all, than such as is impious towards his divine majesty and goodness. Good Mr. Matthew, receive yourself back from these courses of perdition.[7]

Finally, events forced a resolution of Matthew's case. As the plague returned, his continued existence in the Fleet could no longer be risked and – reluctantly, in view of his own utterly opposed religious convictions – Bacon intervened on his friend's behalf. In February 1608, Matthew was called to the Council table, where Salisbury informed him that he did not approve of his imprisonment, 'foreseeing that so light a punishment would make him rather more proud and perverse'. Despite the harsh words, the hearing ended with the Council allotting him 'six weeks' space to set his affairs in order and depart the realm', and in the meantime willing him to 'make choice of some friend of good account and well affected, where he may remain'.[8] (A Mr Jones obliged.) Two months later, he received the King's leave to travel abroad. So Tobie Matthew left England once again, this time in exile – travelling first to Brussels, and then to Madrid; but he continued to correspond regularly with Bacon.

As part of this correspondence, Matthew read and commented on works by Bacon in progress, in manuscript. His instructions from Bacon were to

> take care not to leave the writing, which I left with you last, with any man, so long as that he may be able to take a copy of it; because first it must be censured by you, and then considered again by me. The thing which I expect most from you is, that you would read it carefully over by yourself; and to make some little note in writing, where you think (to speak like a critic) that I do perhaps *indormiscere* [wander from the point]; or where I do *indulgere genio* [indulge myself]; or where, in fine, I give any manner of disadvantage to myself. This, *super totam materiam* [besides all the material], you must not fail to note; besides, all such words and phrases as you cannot like; for you know in how high account I have your judgement.[9]

In early 1609, 'to show you that I have some purpose to new-mould,' Bacon sent to Matthew 'a leaf or two of the Preface, carrying some figure of the whole'. Could this have been an early draft of what was to become Bacon's major scientific work – the Great Instauration? Its burden was to be 'that the state of knowledge is not prosperous nor greatly advancing: and that a way must be opened for the human understanding entirely different from any hitherto known; and other helps provided; in order that the mind may exercise over the nature of things the authority which properly belongs to it'.[10]

Evidently Tobie Matthew shared some of these early drafts with others:

> I have sent you some copies of my book of the *Advancement*, which you desired; and a little book of my recreation, which you desired not. My *Instauration* I reserve for our conference; it sleeps not [is still in progress]. Those works of the *Alphabet* are in my opinion of less use to you where you are now, than at Paris; and therefore I conceived that you had sent me a kind of tacit countermand of your former request. But in regard that some friends of yours have still insisted here, I send them to you; and for my part, I value your own reading more than your publishing them to others.

The suggestion here is that while he was in Paris, Matthew's circle had included those sufficiently well versed in science to be interested in the more technical *Abecedarium naturae* (*Alphabet of Nature*) – in an early draft; now that he has moved on, the more general and accessible *Advancement of Learning* makes more appropriate shared reading.[11]

Later on it appears that Matthew found himself again among those equipped to understand Bacon's more technical scientific writings. These circles of scientific enthusiasts, with which Bacon engaged via his faithful friend's correspondence, included the most significant minds of his day. In 1616 Matthew wrote to Bacon with the news that he was indirectly in contact with the great Galileo himself, and relayed to him an anecdotal incident in which Galileo publicly supported Copernicus' heretical view that the earth revolved around the sun:

> I presume to send you the copy of a piece of a letter, which Galileo (of whom I am sure you have heard) wrote to a monk of my acquaintance in Italy, about the answering of that place in Josu [Joshua] which concerns the sun's standing still; and approving thereby the pretended falsehood of Copernicus' opinion. The letter was written by occasion of the opposition, which some few in Italy did make against Galileo, as if he went about to establish that by experiments, which appears to be contrary to Holy Scripture; but he makes it appear (the while) by this piece of a letter which I send you, that if that passage of scripture doth expressly favour either side, it is for the affirmative of Copernicus' opinion, and for the negative of Aristotle's. To an Attorney General in the midst of a term, and such a one as is employed in the weightiest affairs of the Kingdom, it might seem unseasonable for me to interrupt you with matter of this nature; but I know well enough in how high account

you have the truth of things, and that no day can pass wherein you give not liberty to your wise thoughts, of looking upon the works of nature.[12]

He was surely correct in thinking that Bacon would take time off from his political duties to read such news. And with Bacon's encouragement he must have pursued his Galileo contacts. In April 1619 he wrote to Bacon from Brussels to let him know (again via an intermediary) that Galileo had not only read Bacon's own draft work on the tides, but had produced a manuscript response:

> It may please your Lordship, there was with me this day one Mr Richard White, who hath spent some little time at Florence, and is now gone into England. He tells me, that Galileo had answered your discourse concerning the flux and reflux of the sea, and was sending it unto me; but that Mr White hindered him, because his answer was grounded upon a false supposition, namely, that there was in the ocean a full sea but once in twenty-four hours. But now I will call upon Galileo again. This Mr White is a discreet and understanding gentleman, though he seem a little soft, if not slow; and he hath in his hands all the works, as I take it, of Galileo, some printed, and some unprinted. He hath his discourse of the flux and reflux of the sea, which was never printed; as also a discourse of the mixture of metals. Those which are printed in his hand are these: the *Nuncius sidereus*; the *Macchie solari*, and a third *Delle Cose, che stanno su l'acqua*, by occasion of a disputation that was amongst learned men in Florence about that which Archimedes wrote *de insidentibus humido*. I have conceived that your Lordship would not be sorry to see these discourses of that man, and therefore I have thought it belonging to my service to your Lordship to give him a letter of this date.[13]

It is clear from the letter that Matthew was also acting as a book-purchasing intermediary, providing a vital conduit between continental science and Bacon.

Although he continued to assert his dislike of Matthew's Catholicism, Bacon saw in it an opportunity to further the potential of his own work. Part of Matthew's remit as reader and commentator was to assess Bacon's drafts for material which would be insulting or unacceptable to future Catholic audiences. He sent to Matthew a revised version of his eulogy of the late Queen, *In felicem memoriam Reginae Elizabethae*, 'to respite your elogy of the late duke of Florence's felicity'. This new version was 'more full, and hath more of the narrative: and further, one part that I think will not be disagreeable either to you or that place; being the true tracks of her proceedings towards the Catholics, which are infinitely mistaken [misunderstood]. And though I do not imagine they will pass allowance there, yet they will gain your excuse.'[14]

When Matthew had given his verdict, Bacon responded:

> For that of Queen Elizabeth, your judgement of the temper and truth of that part which concerns some of her foreign proceedings concurs fully with the judgement of others, to whom I have communicated part of it; and as things go, I suppose they are more likely to be more and more justified and allowed. And whereas you say, for some other part, that it moves and opens a fair occasion and broad way into some field of contradiction: on the other side it is written to me from the leiger at Paris [the ambassador, Sir George Carew], and some others also, that it carried a manifest impression of truth with it, and that it even convinces as it goes. These are their very words; which I write not for mine own glory, but to show what variety of opinion rises from the disposition of several readers.

Above all, he continued, his desire was 'that my writings should not court the present time, or some few places, in such sort as might make them either less general to persons, or less permanent in future ages'.[15]

Later on, Bacon sent Matthew his *Redargutio philosophiarum*, a dialogue (set in Paris) in which the 'Idols of the Theatre' (misleading systems of philosophical investigation) are discussed by a philosopher and an assembly of sages. Matthew objected to passages which might offend the churchmen, to which Bacon replied:

> For your caution for church-men and church-matters, as for any impediment it might be to the applause and celebrity of my work, it moveth me not; but as it may hinder the fruit and good which may come of a quiet and calm passage to the good port to which it is bound, I hold it a just respect; so as to fetch a fair wind I go not too far about. But the truth is, I shall have no occasion to meet them in my way, except it be as they will needs confederate themselves with Aristotle, who, you know, is intemperately magnified with the schoolmen; and is also allied (as I take it) to the Jesuits, by Faber, who was a companion of Loyola, and a great Aristotelian. I send you at this time the only part which hath any harshness; and yet I framed to myself an opinion, that whosoever allowed well of that preface which you so much commend, will not dislike, or at least ought not to dislike, this other speech of preparation; for it is written out of the same spirit, and out of the same necessity. Nay it doth more fully lay open that the question between me and the ancients is not of the virtue of the race, but of the rightness of the way. And to speak truth, it is to the other but as *palma* to *pugnus*, part of the

same thing more large. You conceive aright that in this and the other you have commission to impart and communicate them to others according to your discretion. Other matters I write not of. Myself am like the miller of Huntingdon, that was wont to pray for peace amongst the willows; for while the winds blew, the wind-mills wrought, and the water-mill was less customed. So I see that controversies of religion must hinder the advancement of sciences.[16]

In February 1611 Bacon sent Tobie Matthew *De sapientia veterum,*

a little work of mine that hath begun to pass the world. They tell me my Latin is turned into silver, and become current. Had you been here, you should have been my inquisitor before it came forth: but I think the greatest inquisitor in Spain [where Matthew now was] will allow it. But one thing you must pardon me if I make no haste to believe, that the world should be grown to such an ecstacy as to reject truth in philosophy, because the author dissenteth in religion; no more than they do by Aristotle or Averroes. My great work goeth forward; and after my manner, I alter ever when I add. So that nothing is finished till all be finished. This I have written in the midst of a term and parliament; thinking no time so precious, but that I should talk of these matters with so good and dear a friend.[17]

Bacon had produced, at speed, a popular little book, fashionably decoding ancient myths for their relevant contemporary significance – a much easier work to 'pass the world' than the major philosophical project, which was, as usual, on the back burner.

★

At the same time as Bacon was consulting the recusant Matthew on his work in progress, he was also seeking the opinions of old friends who stood four-square within the Anglican camp. Lancelot Andrewes, who had sixteen years earlier turned down an invitation to Twickenham in order to give a sermon, was called upon in 1608 to take part in the developing print war between the Pope and the King. James's defence of the oath of allegiance had been answered by Cardinal Bellarmin; he could not reply to a cardinal himself, and so he looked around for a lesser figure who could with propriety engage on this level. Andrewes was, at length, persuaded to oblige.[18] The book was in press by June 1609, and three months later its author was elevated to become Bishop of Ely.

It was at this time that Bacon called on him to comment on his *Cogitata et visa*, arguing that since Andrewes 'hath been so long in the church and the palace, disputing between kings and popes', he would find it pleasurable to 'look into the field, and refresh your mind with some matter of philosophy; though that science be now through age waxed a child again, and left to boys and young men'. Bolstered by Andrewes' previous approval, Bacon therefore sent him 'some of this vacation's fruits', which though 'I hasten not to publish; perishing I would prevent.' He had to respect 'as well my times as the matter. For with me it is thus, and I think with all men in my case: if I bind myself to an argument, it loadeth my mind; but if I rid my mind of the present cogitation, it is rather a recreation. This hath put me in mind of these miscellanies; which I purpose to suppress, if God give me leave to write a just and perfect volume of philosophy, which I go with though slowly.'

In his 'loose notes' of 1608 Bacon had recorded that Andrewes was 'single, rich, and sickly, a professor to some experiments'.[19] Now he asked him to 'be so good now, as when you were the good Dean of Westminster', and 'not by pricks, but by notes', to 'mark unto me whatsoever shall seem unto you either not current in the style, or harsh to credit and opinion, or inconvenient for the person of the writer; for no man can be judge and party: and when our minds judge by reflection of ourselves, they are more subject to error. And though for the matter itself my judgment be in some things fixed, and not accessible by any man's judgment that goeth not my way: yet even in those things, the admonition of a friend may make me express myself diversely.'[20]

Among the kinds of comments Bacon seems to have been soliciting from Andrewes and Matthew were some concerning the expression of ideas which might be sensitive in terms of ecclesiastical doctrine (of the various churches). As later, when Bacon came to put *The Advancement of Learning* into Latin, he suppressed all remarks which might offend a member of any contemporary congregation, so here he strives for that *via media* or middle way in matters spiritual which will allow his science and philosophy to circulate as widely as possible without giving offence.

One such set of comments from a friend with a stronger claim than Andrewes or Matthew to be able to assess the scientific content survives: Thomas Bodley's on Bacon's *Cogitata et visa*. It was Bodley who had first employed Bacon to report in meticulous detail on French affairs, during his period with the Paulet embassy. Now Bodley commented equally meticulously, responding to Bacon's argument point by point.

I think you know [Bodley wrote] that I have read your *Cogitata & visa*; which I protest I have done with great desire, reputing it a token of your singular love, that you joined me with those your chiefest friends, to whom you would commend your first perusal of your draught.

As touching the subject of your book, you have set afoot so many rare and noble speculations, as I cannot choose but wonder (and I shall wonder at it ever) that your expense of time considered in your public profession, which hath in a manner no acquaintance with any scholarship or learning, you should have culled out the quintessence, and sucked up the sap of the chiefest kinds of learning.

Because it may seem, that being willing to communicate your treatise with your friends, you are likewise willing to listen to whatsoever I, or others can except against it, I must deliver unto you for my private opinion, that I am one of that crew that say there is, and we possess a far greater holdfast of certainty in your sciences, than you by your discourse will seem to acknowledge. For whereas, first you do object the ill success and errors of practitioners in physick, you know as well they do proceed of the patient's unruliness. Not one in a hundred doth obey his physician, in observing his cautels, or by misinformation of their own indispositions.

As for Alchemy & Magick, some conclusions they have, that are worthy the preserving, but all their skill is so accompanied with subtleties and guiles, as both the crafts and craftmasters are not only despised, but named with derision, whereupon to make good your principal assertion methinks you should have drawn the most of your example from that which is taught in the Liberal Sciences. For it goeth for current amongst all men of learning, that those kinds of arts which clerks in times past did term quadrivials confirm their propositions by infallible demonstrations.

Bodley went on to express broad scepticism at the idea that this new knowledge, grounded in world-wide 'experience', or observed reality, was a substitute for (rather than a supplement to) that accumulated down through the ages. Suppose, he argued, we were 'first to condemn our present knowledge of doubts and incertitude, and disclaim all our axioms, maxims, and general assertions that are left by tradition from our elders unto us, which (as it is to be intended) have passed all probations of the sharpest wits that ever were'. Suppose we were to return, as Bacon suggested, to an alphabet of nature – an *Abecedarium*[21] – to rebuild science from first principles: a task which will take centuries. Then, Bodley concluded, we would find we had gone full circle, and arrived back with the very science passed down to us by the ancients.

We can follow Bodley's comments alongside the text of *Cogitata et visa*, and watch him entirely failing to comprehend the sweeping nature of Bacon's altered vision of the sciences. Bacon clearly ignored his friend's negative comments. It is indeed quite striking that he did not engage in the kinds of extended dialogues with fellow scientists around Europe that were fashionable among his contemporaries. Meanwhile, those he did consult (like Bodley) appear to have been utterly mystified as to what he was trying to do.

On this occasion Bodley added a charming postscript: 'Sir, one kind of boldness doth draw on another, in so much, as methinks I should offend, not to signify that before the transcript of your book be fitted for the press, it will be requisite for you to cast a censorious eye upon your style and elocution, which in the framing of some periods, and in divers words and phrases, will hardly go for current, if the copy brought to me be just the same that you would publish.'[22] Bodley might not understand the content, but he knew an infelicitous phrase when he saw one.

★

Among the plans laid during that last week of July 1608 was Bacon's vision for the development of the land at Gorhambury, most specifically his intention to build a new 'house for freshness with an upper gallery open upon the water, a terrace above that, and a supping room open under that; a dining room, a bedchamber, a cabinet [study], and a room for music, a garden.' The plans were not carried out to the letter, but in time they became the impetus for a new building, which Bacon dubbed Verulam House.[23]

The fullest account we have of Verulam House comes from John Aubrey, who visited Verulam and Gorhambury in 1656.[24] Old Verulam is the site of the Roman town of Verulamium, and some parts of the city wall were still visible in the seventeenth century (as indeed they still are). Bacon, wrote Aubrey, 'had a great mind to have made it a city again: and he had designed it, to be built with great uniformity: but fortune denied it him.'

> Within the bounds for the walls of this old city of Verulam was Verulam House; which his lordship built, the most ingeniously contrived little pile, that ever I saw. No question but that his lordship was the chiefest architect; but he had for his assistant a favourite of his, a St. Albans man, Mr. Dobson, who was his lordship's right hand, a very ingenious person (Master of the Alienation Office); but he spending his estate upon women, necessity forced his son Will Dobson to be the most excellent painter that England hath yet bred.
>
> This house did cost nine or ten thousand the building. There were good chimney pieces; the rooms were very lofty, and all were very well wainscotted. There were two bathing rooms or stuffs, whither his lordship retired afternoons as he saw cause. All the tunnels of the chimneys were carried into the middle of the house; and round about them were seats. The top of the house was very well leaded: from the leads was a

lovely prospect to the ponds, which were opposite to the east side of the house, and were on the other side of the stately walk of trees that leads to Gorhambury House: and also over that long walk of trees, whose tops afford a pleasant variegated verdure, resembling the works in an Irish stitch. In the middle of this house was a delicate staircase of wood, which was curiously carved, and on the posts of every interstice was some pretty figure, as of a grave divine with his book and spectacles, a mendicant friar, etc., not one thing twice. On the doors of the upper storey on the outside (which were painted dark umber) were the figures of the gods of the Gentiles, viz. on the south door, second storey, was Apollo; on another, Jupiter with his thunderbolt, etc., bigger than the life, and done by an excellent hand; the heightnings [elevations] were of hatchings of gold, which when the sun shone on them made a most glorious show.

The upper part of the uppermost door on the east side had inserted into it a large looking-glass, with which the stranger was very gratefully deceived, for (after he had been entertained a pretty while, with the prospects of the ponds, walks, and country, which this door faced) when you were about to return into the room, one would have sworn, *primo intuitu* [at first glance], that he had beheld another prospect through the house: for, as soon as the stranger was landed on the balcony, the concierge that showed him the house would shut the door to put this fallacy on him with the looking-glass. This was his lordship's summer house.

From hence to Gorhambury in a straight line (about a little mile, the way easily ascending, hardly so acclive as a desk) lead three parallel walks: in the middlemost three coaches may pass abreast; in the wing-walks two.

About the midway from Verulam House to Gorhambury, on the right hand, on the side of a hill which faces the passer-by, are set in artificial manner several stately trees of the like growth and height, whose diversity of greens on the side of the hill are exceeding pleasant. These delicate walks and prospects entertain the eye to Gorhambury House, which is a large well-built Gothic house. The Lord Chancellor [Bacon] made an addition of a noble portico, which fronts the garden to the south; opposite to every arch of this portico, and as big as the arch, are drawn by an excellent hand (but the mischief of it is, in water-colours) curious pictures, all emblematical, with mottos under each one. For example, one I remember is a ship tossed in a storm, the motto, *Alter erit tum Tiphys* [there will come another Tiphys].

Over this portico is a stately gallery, whose glass windows are all painted: and every pane with several figures of beast, bird, or flower: perhaps his lordship might use them as topiques for local memory. The windows look into the garden: the side opposite to them no window; but is hung all with pictures at length, as of King James, his Lordship, and several illustrious persons of his time. At the end you enter is no window, but there is a very large picture thus: In the middle of a rock in the sea stands King James in armour with his regal ornaments; on his right hand stands (but whether or no on a rock I have forgot) King Henri IV of France, in armour; and on his left hand the King of Spain in like manner. These figures are (at least) as big as the life: they are done only with umber and shell-gold; all the heightening and illuminated part being burnished gold and the shadowed umber, as in the pictures of the Gods on the doors of Verulam House. The roof of this gallery is semi-cylindrical, and painted by the same hand and same manner, with heads and busts of Greek and Roman emperors and heroes.

In the Hall (which is of the ancient building) is a large store very well painted of the feasts of the Gods, where Mars is caught in a net by Vulcan. On the wall, over the chimney, is painted an oak with acorns falling from it, the word, *Nisi quid potius* [failing some better chance] and on the wall over the table is painted Ceres teaching the sowing of corn, the word *Moniti meliora* [we now have better counsel].

The garden is large, which was rarely planted and kept in his lordship's time. Here is a handsome door, which opens into oak-wood; over this door in golden letters on blue are six verses. The oaks of this wood are very great and shady. His lordship much delighted himself here: under every tree, he planted some fine flower, or flowers, viz. peonies, tulips.

From this wood a door opens into a place as big as an ordinary park, the west part whereof is coppice-wood, where are walks cut out as straight as a line, and broad enough for a coach, a quarter of a mile long or better. Here his lordship much meditated, his servant Mr. Bushell attending him with his pen and inkhorn to set down his present notions.

The east of this parquet was a paradise. The walks, both in the coppices and other boscages, were most ingeniously designed: at several good views, were erected elegant summer houses well built of Roman architecture, well wainscotted and cieled.

The figures of the ponds were thus: they were pitched at the bottoms with pebbles of several colours, which were worked into several figures, as of fishes, etc., which were plainly to be seen through the clear water. If a poor body had brought his lordship half a dozen pebbles of a curious colour, he would give them a shilling, so curious was he in perfecting his fish-ponds, which I guess do contain four acres. In the middle of the middlemost pond, in the island, is a curious banquetting-house of Roman architecture, paved with black and white marble; covered with Cornish slat, and neatly wainscotted.

Since his earliest days at Gray's Inn, when he purchased shrubs for the grounds, Francis Bacon had taken a keen interest in gardens. He returns to this 'greatest refreshment to the spirits of man; without which, buildings and palaces are but gross handiworks', in his *Apophthegms* and *Essays*.[25] Wherever he lived, he took a keen interest in the planning of the grounds (his list of plants in the essay 'Of Gardens' is practically a gardening catalogue). Here at least he fits the conventional image of the contemplative philosopher, happiest in repose 'in a green shade'.

★

Parliament sat again in February 1610, after a gap of nearly three years. For James, the previous two sessions had been supremely unsatisfactory on the question of settling his finances: even the 1606 subsidy had been voted at the price of the petition of grievances. Now the King could no longer afford to carry out the requisite business of his government without further subsidy: Salisbury — Lord Treasurer since April 1608 — supplied figures which showed graphically that whereas Elizabeth's first two subsidies (1558 and 1562) had brought in over £190,000 each, James's subsidy in 1606 was a mere £124,000. By 1610 the national debt was running at over £1 million, with an annual deficit of some £83,000.[26]

Salisbury had to look elsewhere for revenue. He resorted to laying on 'impositions' of £60,000 per annum — customs duties on goods exported and imported, imposed by the sole authority of the crown, unsanctioned by parliament. It was a controversial move: although it had recently been verified by the Court of Exchequer, parliament had attacked that decision. In the first two years and twenty days of his treasurership, it was said, Salisbury had 'directed and signed 2,884 letters, and gotten to the King in money £37,455, and in yearly revenues £71,100'.[27] Salisbury's prodigious industry notwithstanding, the crown still stood indebted to the tune of £400,000, with a deficit each year. Eventually, Salisbury had to face parliament with a new proposal.

He realised that the crown would benefit more from a fixed revenue derived from taxation; but he had to produce a bargain with which he could effect this transformation in royal funding. Much of the crown's revenue was drawn from sources that lay outside its patrimonial property, from such tenures and privileges as wardships, knight's service, purveyance, and so on. These feudal remnants, though not in themselves disputed as crown rights, were widely experienced as burdensome. Thus emerged Salisbury's 'Great Contract', according to which James would give up his feudal rights and tenures (including wardship) in return for a fixed, steady income — 'support' rather than 'supply'.

The Lord Treasurer's first speech on the Great Contract was reported to the Commons by three men, Bacon among them. Bacon prefaced his section with a personal intervention: 'I know you will remember you are not in a theatre, but in a parliament, house of counsel, and that you will consider the most flourishing branches cannot be maintained without the root be nourished. And therefore though with less delight both to you and myself I shall, I know not *quo fato* but it falls out ever that pain is my portion, and by the grace of God whilst my breath and power will serve I will willingly undergo any labour this House shall impose upon me.'[28]

The debates about the Contract were long, involved and tedious. Much time was spent on matters that to the modern reader appear to be irrelevant distractions. To those in parliament in 1610, however, they were perceived and treated as essential matters. It was not until 19 April, after the Easter recess, that James answered the Commons' demand that tenures should be discussed.

> He would upon no terms depart with any part of his sovereign Prerogative, whereof the tenure *in capite* of his person, which is all one as of his Crown, is no small branch: But touching the dependents upon such Tenures, *videlicet* Wardships, Marriage, Primier Seizin, Relief, Respect of Homage, and the like, which be the only burdens of these Tenures (the honour and Tenures reserved) His Majesty is pleased when he shall have understood what recompense will be therefore offered unto him, with convenient speed, to give further answer for contracting for the same.

The Commons immediately offered £100,000 per annum as their recompense for relief from the tenures-related burdens. However, at a conference on 26 April, Salisbury revealed that the Contract was not all it had seemed. When he had said that the King was ready to part with his ten points of prerogative as 'retribution' for the £200,000 per annum which he demanded, and when the Commons had afterwards been told that these might also include wardships, they had mistakenly taken him to mean that the King would part with them in exchange for £200,000 per annum. Now it appeared, according to Salisbury, that this was not in fact so: the £200,000 was a condition of *negotiation*, not of relinquishment of the prerogative itself. If parliament now voted £600,000 supply and assured the King of £200,000 support per annum, James would be willing to part with the wardships, and all the rest, upon a further payment of a sum equal to what he would lose by relinquishing them. The Commons refused the King's demand.

More distractions slowed down proceedings. In May a message allegedly from the King (who was out of town) turned out to be from the Privy Council, causing a scandal. In June the Commons baulked when a message from the King was sent to them via the Lords, implying that the Lords were a body interposed between the sovereign and his subjects. Each *faux pas* had to be endlessly interrogated for its hidden meanings.

A more important diversion was the question, raised by the King in May, as to whether he had the power 'to command the House not to dispute of the King's power and prerogative in imposing upon merchandises exported or imported' – setting the King's prerogative versus the House's privilege on a matter of vital financial importance. The King was moved to speak to both Houses, warning them not to dispute his power to impose and justifying his claim to tax not only imports and exports, but all other property:

> The state of monarchy is the supremest thing upon earth; for kings are not only God's lieutenants upon earth, and sit upon God's throne, but even by God himself they are called gods. There be three principal similitudes that illustrate the state of monarchy: one taken out of the word of God, and the two other out of the grounds of policy and philosophy. In the Scriptures kings are called gods, and so their powers after a certain relation compared to the divine power. Kings are also compared to fathers of families, for the king is truly *parens patriae*, the politic father of his people. And lastly, kings are compared to the head of this microcosm of the body of man.
>
> Kings are justly called gods for that they exercise a manner or resemblance of divine power upon earth, for if you will consider the attributes of God you shall see how they agree in the person of a king. God hath power to create or destroy, make or unmake, at his pleasure; to give life or send death, to judge all and to be judged not accountable to none; to raise low things and to make high things low at his pleasure; and to God are both soul and body due. And the like power have kings: they make and unmake their subjects; they have power of raising, and casting down; of life, and of death, judges over all their subjects, and in all causes, and yet accountable to none but God only. They have power to exalt low things, and abase high things, and make of their subjects like men at the chess – a pawn to take a bishop or a knight – and cry up or down any of their subjects, as they do their money. And to the king is due both the affection of the soul and the service of the body of his subjects.
>
> But yet is all this power ordained by God, *ad aedificationem, non ad destructionem* [constructively, not destructively]. So were he a foolish father that would disinherit or destroy his children without a cause, or leave off the careful education of them; and it were an idle head that would in place of physic so poison or phlebotomise the body as might breed a dangerous distemper or destruction thereof.[29]

As Chamberlain reported to Winwood, the speech was

> so little to their satisfaction that I hear it bred generally much discomfort
> to see our monarchical power and royal prerogative strained so high,
> and made so transcendant every way, that if the practice should follow
> the positions, we are not like to leave our successors that freedom which
> we received from our forefathers, nor make account of anything we
> have longer than they list that govern. Many bold passages have been
> since [two or three days later] in the Lower House, and amongst the
> rest a wish that this speech might never come to print.[30]

Typically, James ensured that it did, placing it proudly in the 1616 edition
of his *Works*.

With this intervention, the King effectively provoked a debate on the
essential nature of Sovereignty and Liberty. In committee on the subject,
Bacon held to his usual political strategy of attending to the particular (and
if possible, ignoring the larger, more difficult) question. He cited precedents
to support the position of the King, advising the House 'to present these
matters of impositions as grievances to the Commonwealth (which the
King had given them leave to do), but not to question his power or
prerogative to impose'. He continued 'that he would rather speak therein
according to the freedom of his mind than according to the propriety of
his place'. Returning to the infancy of his parliamentary career, he spoke
of how Elizabeth had on occasion restrained the House from debating a
particular subject, an observation from which he extrapolated a rule of
thumb for procedure: 'If the matter debated concerned the right or interest
of any subject or the Commonwealth, if in that case an inhibition came,
he for his part would not advise the House to desist, but to inform the
King of the liberty of the House, and so to proceed. But if the matter in
question were an essential thing which concerned the Prerogative and the
power of the Crown, then the House did always desist from proceeding
any further upon such inhibitions received.'[31]

A petition was drafted which set out the right of parliament to debate
all matters which concerned the right and state of the subject. It claimed
it was impossible to examine the case of the new impositions without
recourse to an analysis of their legal standing, and concluded by petitioning
that they might 'according to the undoubted right and liberty of Parliament
proceed in their intended course of a full examination of these new Impositions; that so they might cheerfully pass on to his Majesty's business, from
which this stop had by diversion so long withheld them'.

James replied that they had mistaken his meaning, that he had intended
only to *suspend* discussion, 'in order that he might understand their intentions'; and that he never intended to use the legal powers of a King of

England 'for the abridgment of any of their liberties. He begged them to distinguish between his reasons and his conclusions,' granted them their petition as written, and expressed his hope that 'mistaking might no more hinder their business'.

With this distraction out of the way, the crown and the Commons had plenty of new common ground. The French King, Henri IV, had been assassinated, and the news of his death, announced to the Commons by Salisbury on 8 May, had the desired effect of reviving anti-papist feeling. Salisbury took advantage of Henri's fate to exhort members 'to be watchful for the safety and good of their prince, and assist him with those means which were requisite for it' – as John Beaulieu noted, 'seeking to insinuate unto them that this accident would put the King in need of a greater assistance from them than was before required at their hands'. Now, on the twenty-fifth, the matter of subsidy was once more brought forward. The Commons stipulated that the question of impositions should not be forgotten, but proceed *pari passu*. The following day, the Upper House sent a delegation to desire that the negotiation continue at a conference between the committees 'formerly employed in the matter of Tenures', at which it was hinted that the King was ready to lower his terms, and that this forum would be a 'free conference' (unlike the previous 'dry meeting').

After nearly two weeks during which no apparent progress was made, a message was sent from the Lords, to express the hope that 'all protraction, in this so great and necessary a business, might be avoided'. The conference replied, on Friday 8 June, 'that they were preparing for the matters in question; that therein they had slacked no time; and so soon as they were prepared the Lords should hear further from them'. The following Monday another message was sent, requesting an immediate conference that after- noon, 'touching some things which were to be imparted to them by his Majesty's late commandment'. The business of this conference – consisting solely in a speech by Salisbury – turned out to be to urge an immediate vote of 'supply by subsidies', brought about by a suspension of all other business (including, of course, 'support' and 'grievances') until parliament met again in October, a full four months away. Even Bacon, reporting this meeting, was unable to cast a positive light on it. The Commons debated a grant of two subsidies for two days – interrupted constantly by messages, amendments and propositions from the King – before postponing the whole question.

The debate about tenures and impositions took up five days between 23 June and 2 July, during which Bacon made a speech (probably on 27 June) in defence of the King's right. 'This question touching the right of Impositions is very great,' he opened, extending to the prerogative of the King on the one part, and the liberty of the subject on the other; and that in a point of profit and value, and not of conceit and fancy. And therefore, as weight in all motions increaseth force, so I do not marvel to see men gather the greatest strength of argument they can to make good their opinions. And so you will give me leave likewise, being strong in mine persuasion that it is the King's right, to show my voice as free as my thought. And for my part I mean to observe the true course to give strength to this cause, which is by yielding those things which are not tenable, and keeping the question within the true state and compass; which will discharge many popular arguments, and contract the debate into a less room.

He argued, at length, that 'the King by the fundamental laws of this kingdom hath a power to impose upon merchandise and commodities both native and foreign.'[32]

On 26 June, Salisbury had addressed a conference between the two Houses to inform them that the King would now consent to take from them £140,000 per annum, above the annual revenue which they yielded (estimated at £80,000). This worked out at a £60,000 drop in demand (or £660,000, since supply was no longer mentioned); the proposal was referred to the House, to be referred to another committee.

The Commons ultimately decided to frame in writing their 'Petitions and Grievances' to the King. This document was presented to James by Bacon, with twenty other members, on 7 July. 'Since this session of Parliament,' declared Bacon, 'we have seen your glory, in the solemnity of the creation of this most noble Prince. We have heard your wisdom, in sundry excellent speeches which you have delivered amongst us. Now we hope to find and feel the effects of your goodness, in your gracious answer to these our petitions . . . For never was there such a conservator of regality in a crown, nor ever such a protector of lawful freedom in a subject.'

He went on to urge James to not to let 'the sound of grievances (though it be sad) seem harsh to your princely ears: it is but *genitus columbae*, the mourning of a dove, with that patience and humility of heart which appertaineth to loving and loyal subjects.' Covering his own involvement, Bacon craved 'a particular pardon for myself that have used these few words, and scarcely should have been able to have used any in all, in respect of the reverence which I bear to your person and judgment, had I not been somewhat relieved and comforted by the experience which in my service and access I have had of your continual grace and favour'.[33]

James declined to give way on the matter of impositions: while promising to allow a bill to prevent any further impositions without parliamentary assent, he did not agree to revoke those recently imposed, with the result that the Commons 'went away ill satisfied'. This ill satisfaction dictated the mood of their subsidy meeting the next day, when the most they would agree was a single subsidy. 'Now we are come so near a bargain,' wrote Carleton, 'we shall be able to make judgment at our next conference with the Lords, whether this contract which hath been so long entertained, was from the beginning *de veras* [concerning truths], as the Lords would have us believe, or *de burlas* [concerning mockeries], as some of our wise men still suspect.' The memorials of the Contract were exchanged on Saturday 21 July, and parliament prorogued until 16 October.

★

The welcome break of the parliamentary vacation was marred for Bacon by the death of his mother, on or shortly after 23 August. Francis was still at Gray's Inn on that date, but was evidently called back to Gorhambury by the twenty-seventh.[34] The final years of this redoubtable woman, who had held considerable sway in the lives not only of her sons but of her husband and brother-in-law, two of the most important Elizabethan officers of state, are completely obscure. There is no mention of Lady Bacon in her younger son's letters after 12 March 1600, at which point he describes her health as being 'very worn'. The last known document bearing her signature is dated 20 November 1602, when she executed, in favour of Francis, a deed surrendering her life interest in several manors. The only account we have of Lady Bacon in later life is in Bishop Godfrey Goodman's *Court of King James the First*, where he writes of Bacon's mother that 'she was but little better than frantic in her age.'

It may well be the case that Lady Bacon's declining physical health destroyed her mental well-being. But it may also be the case that Goodman – not a Bacon supporter at the best of times – was drawing a standard picture of a powerful widow with strong, at times unorthodox, convictions. Whichever was the case, Bacon wrote to his friend Sir Michael Hickes on Monday 27 August with a request:

> It is but a wish and not any ways to desire it to your trouble. But I heartily wish I had your company here at my mother's funeral, which I purpose on Thursday next in the forenoon. I dare promise you a good sermon to be made by Mr. Fenton, the preacher of Gray's Inn; for he never maketh other. Feast I make none. But if I mought have your company for two or three days at my house I should pass over this mournful occasion with more comfort. If your son had continued at St Julian's it mought have been an adamant to have drawn you; but now if you come I must say it is only for my sake.

For a man who never missed an opportunity for ostentatious public display when occasion required, the absence of any funeral feast is significant. It is a strangely vulnerable Bacon that speaks in this letter, making a rare personal request for the company of an old friend.[35]

★

When parliament reconvened on 16 October, the matter of the King's finances was still unresolved. In November, in a message to the Commons, the regal tone changed. Now James was 'pleased to represent unto us the clear mirror of his heart, and to set before us the essential parts of the contract, lest the taking of things by parts might induce any oblivion or distraction in the contemplation of the whole'. James declared that 'it never was his intention, much less his agreement, to proceed finally with the contract, except he might have as well supply as support, to disengage himself from his debts. In reason his debts must be first paid.' He had demanded 'the supply of his wants'; the points about tenures, and the distinguishing of support and supply, 'came in by our motions'. He expected £150,000 in the way of supply, although that would prove inadequate, and that should not include the subsidy recently given, because of 'his great charges' and 'the increase of his wants'. He also wanted to know what support was to be raised: 'his purpose is that it may be certain, firm, and stable, without the meaner sort, and without diminution of his present profit,' at a rate of £200,000.[36]

The Commons resolved unanimously not to proceed with the Contract. On Wednesday 14 November, the King admitted that 'he did not see how we should go further.' It was nine months since the parliament had opened and James was no further forward, except in terms of debt. The House was adjourned on 24 November (parliament was finally dissolved on 9 February). On the previous day, Sir Francis Bacon had made a final speech. 'As things stand for the present,' he said, 'I think the point of honour and reputation is that which his Majesty standeth most upon; that our gift may at least be like those showers that may serve to lay the winds, though they do not sufficiently water the earth.' He would not labour to persuade his listeners, since he was not sure how to go about it. 'If I should enter into a laudative (though never so due and just) of the King's great merits, it may be taken for flattery: if I should speak of the strait obligations which intercede between the King and the Subject in case of the King's want, it were a kind of concluding the house: if I should speak of the dangerous consequence which Kings' want may reverberate upon subjects, it might have a show of a secret measure.'

Notwithstanding these scruples, he reminded his audience that 'there are as well benefits of the sceptre as benefits of the land; as well of government as liberality. These I am sure we will acknowledge to have come *plena manu* [generously] amongst us all, and all those whom we represent; and therefore it is every man's head in this case that must be his counsellor, and every man's heart his orator; and to those inward powers more forcible than any man's speech, I leave it.' He could not resist saying, however, that he had been 'sorry to hear such a counterpoint of the wants of the kingdom sounded, to rebound to that which is already noised of the wants of the King; for it cannot be pleasing to God above to have his blessings so extenuated. Sure I am I see feasting, rich apparel, rich portions given in marriages, fair buildings everywhere, and other magnificence; and in a word I see much excess, which though it be a cause of poverty, yet it is a sign of plenty.'[37]

★

Bacon expected some sort of payback for his performance in the 1610 parliament. Early in 1611 he wrote to the King, citing 'your great and princely favours towards me in advancing me to place' and 'your Majesty's benign and gracious acceptation from time to time of my poor services, much above the merit and value of them' as reasons which had 'almost' persuaded him 'that I may sooner perchance be wanting to myself in not asking, than find your Majesty's goodness wanting to me in any my reasonable and modest desires'.

'At this time,' he wrote, 'preferments of the law fly about mine ears, to some above me and to some below me.' Indeed, he felt James might 'think it rather a kind of dullness, or want of faith, than modesty, if I should not come with my pitcher to Jacob's well, as others do.' He was concerned now with 'that which tendeth not so much to the raising of my fortune, as to the settling of my mind: being sometimes assailed with this cogitation, that by reason of my slowness to sue and apprehend occasions upon the sudden, keeping one plain course of painful service, I may *in fine dierum* [at the end of the day], be in danger to be neglected and forgotten.' If that were the case,

> then were it much better for me, now while I stand in your Majesty's good opinion (though unworthy), and have some little reputation in the world, to give over the course I am in, and to make proof to do you some honour by my pen, either by writing some faithful narrative of your happy though not untraduced times; or by recompiling your laws, which I perceive your Majesty laboreth with and hath in your head, as Jupiter had Pallas; or some other the like work (for without some endeavour to do you honour I would not live); than to spend my wits and time in this laborious place wherein I serve, if it shall be

deprived of those outward ornaments and inward comforts which it was wont to have, in respect of an assured succession to some place of more dignity and rest; which seemeth to be an hope now altogether casual, if not wholly integrated.

His suit was that he might obtain the King's assurance 'to succeed (if I live) into the Attorney's place, whensoever it shall be void', since the attorneyship was no more than 'the nature and immediate step and rise which the place I now hold hath ever in a sort made claim to, and almost never failed of'. In this matter, he relied 'upon no other motive than your grace', and did not therefore cite friends in his suit, 'though your Majesty knoweth that I want not those which are near and assured'.

James acquiesced, and the following autumn, Coke being ill, Bacon wrote to the King, reminding him of his 'royal promise touching the Attorney's place':

> I do understand by some of my good friends, to my great comfort, that your Majesty hath in mind your Majesty's royal promise (which to me is *anchora spei* [an anchor of hope]), touching the Attorney's place. I hope Mr. Attorney shall do well. I thank God I wish no man's death ... But this I will be bold to say; if it please God that I ever serve your Majesty in the Attorney's place, I have known an Attorney Coke, and an Attorney Hobart, both worthy men and far above myself; but if I should not find a middle way between their two dispositions and carriage, I should not satisfy myself.[38]

During Coke's illness, Salisbury rallied to support his cousin, as Bacon gratefully acknowledged, writing to him at the New Year: 'I would entreat the new year to answer for the old, in my humble thanks to your Lordship, both for many your favours, and chiefly that upon the occasion of Mr. Attorney's infirmity I found your Lordship even as I would wish.'[39]

Ever the dandy, Bacon also took advantage of the Christmas break to repay Sir Michael Hickes a small but important outstanding debt – a pair of stockings. 'I do use as you know to pay my debts with time. But indeed if you will have a good and parfite [perfect] colour in a carnation stocking it must be long in the dyeing. I have some scruple of conscience whether it was my Lady's stockings or her daughter's, and I would have the restitution to be to the right person, else I shall not have absolution. Therefore I have sent to them both, desiring them to wear them for my sake, as I did wear theirs for mine own sake.'[40]

From late 1611, Bacon devoted much of his time to his legal work. That December, he advised one Mr Bernard in a case – inadvisedly, as it seems, since the Lord Mayor and his colleagues sent Bernard 'to his overthrow'. In January or February 1612 he gave the King the benefit of his advice concerning the estate of Thomas Sutton, who had left his wealth to charity.[41] In February he issued 'a certificate to Lords of the Council, upon information given touching the scarcity of silver at the Mint, and reference to the two chancellors, and the King's solicitor'.[42] He also delivered the Charge 'upon the commision of oyer and determiner for the Verge', a new court.[43] During late June and July his attention was taken up with the prosecution of Lord Sanquhar, who had procured the murder of an English fencing master, and Arabella Stuart, who had contracted a clandestine marriage to William Seymour (like herself, a claimant to the English throne) without the King's consent, and was now refusing to answer her interrogators.[44]

But there was to be a new opportunity to further his career beyond the courts. On 24 May 1612 his cousin Sir Robert Cecil, earl of Salisbury, died.

★

Bacon at last felt free to vent his frustrations with the cousin – and by extension, the uncle – who had between them thwarted his ambitions for thirty years. On 29 May 1612 he sat down to write a letter to the King. He had never before, he said, been able to show his affection to the full, 'having been as a hawk tied to another's fist, that mought sometimes bait and proffer but could never fly'.[45]

It was too harsh, too eager. He started again. In his second attempt, Salisbury was not the restraining hawker, rather 'a great subject and a great servant. But if I should praise him in propriety, I should say that he was a fit man to keep things from growing worse but no very fit man to reduce things to be much better.'

Bacon was evidently tickled by this verdict, and recast it more dramatically in later years as one of his *bon mots* provided on cue to the King. In this version, soon after the death of 'a great officer who was judged no advancer of the King's matters', James said to Bacon, 'Now tell me truly, what say you of your cousin that is gone?'

Bacon answered, 'Sir, since your Majesty doth charge me, I'll e'en deal plainly with you, and give you such a character of him as if I were to write his story. I do think he was no fit counsellor to make your affairs better; but yet he was fit to have kept them from growing worse.'

'On my soul, man,' laughed the King, 'in the first thou speakest like a true man, and in the latter like a kinsman.'[46]

Bacon continued his letter, and the character assassination of his cousin. 'He loved to have the eyes of all Israel a little too much upon himself, and to have all business still under the hammer and like clay in the hands of the potter, to mould it as he thought good; so that he was more *in operatione* than *in opere* [the operator than the workman]. And though he had fine passages of action, yet the real conclusions came slowly on.'[47]

The demolition of Salisbury went into print in the revised *Essays*, published in 1612, when, in 'Of Deformity', according to John Chamberlain, 'the world takes notice that he paints out his late little cousin to the life.'[48] (Salisbury had a crooked back.) The essay described how 'deformed persons' got even with nature, by 'being for the most part (as the Scripture saith) void of natural affection'. Deformity was not a sign, but

> a cause, which seldom faileth of the effect. Whosoever hath any thing fixed in his person, that doth induce contempt; hath also a perpetual spur in himself, to rescue and deliver himself from scorn. Therefore all deformed persons are extreme bold: first, as in their own defence, as being exposed to scorn; but in process of time, by a general habit. Also, it stirreth in them industry, and specially of this kind, to watch and observe the weakness of others, that they may have somewhat to repay. Again in their superiors, it quencheth jealousy towards them, as persons that they think they may at pleasure despise; and it layeth their competitors and emulators asleep: as never believing they should be in possibility of advancement, till they see them in possession. So that upon the whole matter, in a great wit, deformity is an advantage to rising.

He compared the state of deformed persons to that of eunuchs in ancient times, trusted to be 'good spials, and good whisperers' rather than 'good magistrates, and officers'. In conclusion, 'they will, if they be of spirit, seek to free themselves in scorn: which must be either by virtue, or malice; and therefore they prove either the best of men, or the worst, or strangely mixed.'[49]

Having vented his spleen against Salisbury to the King, Bacon offered James his 'care and observance: and as my good old mistress was wont to call me her watch-candle, because it pleased her to say I did continually burn (and yet she suffered me to waste almost to nothing), so I must much more owe the like duty to your Majesty, by whom my fortunes have been settled and raised.'[50] He even considered making a bid to become Principal Secretary of State, a post usually out of the grasp of professional lawyers.

> My life hath been conversant in things wherein I take little pleasure. Your Majesty may have heard somewhat that my father was an honest man, and somewhat you may have seen of myself, though not to make any true judgement by, because I have hitherto had only *potestatem verborum* [power of words], nor that neither. I was three of my young years bred with an ambassador in France, and since I have been an old

truant in the school-house of your council-chamber, though on the second form; yet longer than any that now sitteth hath been on the head form. If your Majesty find any aptness in me, or if you find any scarcity in others, whereby you may think it fit for your service to remove me to business of state, I will be ready as a chessman to be wherever your Majesty's royal hand shall set me.[51]

Whether or not the secretaryship was ever a possibility, it was popularly believed that Bacon was bound to profit from his cousin's death. Another title Salisbury had held was the Mastership of the Wards, a lucrative post which he had effectively inherited from his father Burghley on the latter's death. 'For the Mastership of the Wards,' reported Chamberlain on 11 June, 'the King saith he hath groped after one in the dark and will make trial if a meaner man cannot perform it as well as a great, and yet he means not to trust him too far, but will make him provisional till the end of Michaelmas term, and so longer as he shall see case, and though he saith he hath made no man privy to his resolution, yet it is thought it will light on Sir Francis Bacon.'[52] No matter that this was the most grudging and tentative of appointments: Bacon was not about to worry about niceties when the job was, as far as he could see, in the bag. He went so far as to draft some 'Notes for the Wards' for the new Master to declare at the next sitting: a set of directions for the post which the King praised as 'no tricks nor novelties, but true passages of business'.[53] But Bacon had unwittingly written the job description for another man. On 17 June Chamberlain wrote: 'On Saturday, Sir George Carew was nominated Master of the Wards, and yesterday he made his entrance there with a formal oration.' Carew had 'lighted upon it by his wife's grace with the Queen as is thought, or rather as others say by the Lord of Rochester'.[54] (Bacon was himself soon to take steps to enter the favour of Viscount Rochester, the King's new favourite.) Sir George Carew had the good fortune to find that he did not have to write his 'formal oration': he merely amended one that Sir Francis Bacon had happened to write the previous week.[55]

Despite this disappointment, Bacon soon made progress, filling some of the many spaces left by Salisbury. In May 1612 the contract was signed for the marriage of Princess Elizabeth and the Elector Palatine, who was expected to come to England to collect his wife in September. Custom dictated that the King was able to levy an 'aid' from his subjects on the marriage of his eldest daughter. Whereas two years earlier, Salisbury had called on the Attorney to make the arrangements for a similar aid when the Prince became a knight, this time Solicitor Bacon was chosen for the task.

On 8 November the earl of Northampton reported that it needed to be decided whether the aid – which had not been an issue since the reign of Henry VII – should be levied 'according to the legal form, which rifles and reveals estates without any greater benefit to the King, and so galls with acrimony, or by commission, which in some respects to be expressed at more length is better for the King and the subject, and comes with satisfaction and easiness, whereof the late experience of that for the Prince gives a precedent'. In order to bring about 'the better fitting of this service to time present', Northampton reported, the Lord Chancellor ('as a Lord paramount in his own element of law') and Mr Solicitor Bacon ('as a person very apt in that faculty both to apprehend and add') informed the Lords of the Council of the proper 'course and form'.[56] Bacon drafted 'Instructions for the better direction of the Commissioners' and forwarded them to the King, thoughtfully devising them so that 'your Majesty should not be troubled with signing every particular instruction as you were last time – that your Majesty's signature be only to this draft, and the several commissions to be signed by six of your Majesty's Privy Council, who are authorised likewise thereunto by letters under your Majesty's signature.'[57]

The £22,000 brought in by the aid to the Exchequer was only a drop in the ocean. Bacon was employed during August 1612 in an investigative subcommittee 'touching the repair and improvement' of James' means, which had as its remit 'to devise projects and means for money'. Bacon no doubt played a part in drafting the lengthy joint report,[58] and in drawing up 'a proposition concerning the augmentation of the King's yearly revenue by converting of his lands into a yearly fee farm rent multiplied in proportion to that which he now receiveth', although he concluded that he 'would be understood that I am rather provident and diligent to make the best of the proposition than confident to persuade it'.[59]

Bacon, along with the King's Serjeant Sir Henry Montagu, assisted Ellesmere and Northampton in their review of the two Great Farms, of the Customs and of the French and Rhenish Wines, and found that fraud had been rampant over a period of eight years, to the great loss of the King. The lease, they discovered, had expired, and the farmers should be called to account for their frauds. The patentees of the French and Rhenish wines had 'by cunning got a renewal' of their lease, but legal advice suggested it could be overthrown, since it was obtained fraudulently, and therefore James would be able to annul it without compromising his honour. The report, in Bacon's hand, contained a marginal postscript by Northampton: 'We may not forget to give your Majesty notice of the diligence and industry of your two faithful and painful servants, your Solicitor and Serjeant, whereby the great mass is now digested into that order that may seem to best use in your service.' Northampton valued Bacon's involvement, writing to Rochester (who had the King's ear) on 20 October:

I beseech you to move the King that in your next private letter to me you may give some touch of his Majesty's gracious acceptance of the diligence and industry of the Solicitor in this employment; for though it be true that the Recorder showed his endeavour with good will, yet to speak truly as I must ever do, yielding unto all men the fruits of their good deserts, this *mysterium iniquitatis* [mysterious practice of wickedness] was pursued extremely well by the Solicitor, that met with tricks upon the choice points of their obliquity. I am put in trust with the care of laying open of this point, and therefore for a testimony of my discharge and an argument of his Majesty's gracious acceptance of the party's endeavour, a character under your hand which I may show to himself only will be authentical.[60]

Notwithstanding his high-profile involvement in royal causes, and his top-level backers, Bacon thought it worthwhile to pursue the cause, as he informed the King in September 1612, 'by my several [separate] and private meditation. So that besides the joint account which we shall give to the Lords, I hope I shall be able to give your Majesty somewhat *ex proprio* [of my own].' Although he enjoyed and valued committee work, there were occasions 'where matter shall fall in upon the bye, perhaps of no less worth than that which is the proper subject of the consultation, or where I find things passed over too slightly, or in case where that which I should advise is of that nature as I hold it not fit to be communicated to all those with whom I am joined.' These 'parts of business', as he called them, he would 'put to my private account; not because I would be officious (though I profess I would do works of supererogation if I could), but in a true discretion and caution'. Reminding James that he 'had some taste in those notes which I gave you for the wards', it followed 'that mine own particular remembrances and observations are not like to be unprofitable. Concerning which notes for the wards,' he added ironically, 'though I might say *sic vos non vobis* [sobeit for you, though not for yours], yet let that pass.'

On the matter of the King's proposed 'conversion of your revenue of land into a multiplied present revenue of rent', he urged 'that your Majesty's recovery must be by the medicine of the Galenists and Arabians, and not of the Chemists or Paracelsians. For it will not be wrought by any one fine extract or strong water, but by a skilful compound of a number of ingredients, and those by just weight and proportion, and that of some simples which perhaps of themselves or in over-great quantity were little better than poisons, but mixed and broken and in just quantity are full of virtue.' Secondly, the recovery must be 'the work of time'; if James decided to 'do it *per saltum* [in one leap], it can hardly be without accidents of prejudice to your honour, safety, or profit.'

He concluded by praying, first, that

these cogitations of want do not any ways trouble or vex your Majesty's mind. I remember Moses saith of the land of promise, That it was not the land of Egypt that was watered with a river, but was watered with showers from heaven; whereby I gather, God preferreth sometimes uncertainties before certainties, because they teach a more immediate dependence upon his providence. Sure I am, *nil novi accidit vobis* [nothing new has happened to you]. It is no new thing for the greatest kings to be in debt; and if a man shall *parvis componere magna* [compare small things with large], I have seen an earl of Leicester, a Chancellor Hatton, an earl of Essex, and an earl of Salisbury all in debt; and yet was it no manner of diminution to their power or greatness.

He also prayed that James, in over-hasty pursuit of the 'freeing of your state would not descend to any means, or degree of means, which carrieth not a symmetry with your majesty and greatness'. There was room here, too, for another dig at Salisbury, who had made the King's needs public knowledge:

He is gone from whom those courses did wholly flow. To have your wants and necessities in particular as it were hanged up in two tablets before the eyes of your lords and commons, to be talked of for four months together: To have all your courses to help yourself in revenue or profit put into printed books, which were wont to be held *arcana imperii* [mysteries of empire]: To have such worms of aldermen to lend for ten in the hundred upon good assurance, and with such entreaty, as if it should save the bark of your fortune: To contract still where mought be had the readiest payment, and not the best bargain: To stir a number of projects for your profit, and then to blast them, and leave your Majesty nothing but the scandal of them: To pretend even carriage between your Majesty's rights and the ease of the people, and to satisfy neither: These courses and others the like I hope are gone with the deviser of them; which have turned your Majesty to inestimable prejudice.

Warming to his (albeit tangential) theme, Bacon continued: 'I protest to God, though I be not superstitious, when I saw your Majesty's book against Vorstius and Arminius, and noted your zeal to deliver the majesty of God from the vain and indign comprehensions of heresy and degenerate philosophy *perculsit illico animum* [utterly dismayed me then and there] that God would set shortly upon you some visible favour, and let me not live if I thought not of the taking away of that man.' Again, it was too much. He scored through the paragraph.

'I hope your Majesty will pardon my liberty of writing,' he concluded.

'I know these things are *majora quam pro fortuna* [more than accidents]: but they are *minora quam pro studio et voluntate* [less than by design]. I assure myself, your Majesty taketh not me for one of a busy nature; for my state being free from all difficulties, and I having such a large field for contemplations, as I have partly and shall much more make manifest to your Majesty and the world, to occupy my thoughts, nothing could make me active but love and affection.'[61]

All he could do now was wait.

12

Being Politic:
The King's Business

The King will be no merchant.
Sir Francis Bacon to the House of Commons (May 1614)

I N HIS BID for high office Bacon could not afford to rely on the King
alone. From 1608 he had begun cultivating the young Prince of Wales,
Henry, who was becoming a powerful iconic figure in his own right,
heading his own court. In Bacon's words, 'in body he was strong and
erect, of middle height, his limbs gracefully put together, his gait kinglike,
his face long and somewhat lean, his habit rather full, his countenance
composed, and the motion of his eyes rather sedate than powerful. His
forehead bore marks of severity, his mouth had a touch of pride.' But
once 'penetrated beyond those outworks', he proved 'gentle and easy to
deal with'. Like every young man, he thought of honour as virtue. 'For
both arms and military honour were in honour with him; nor was he
himself without something of a warlike spirit; he was given also to magnificence of works, though otherwise frugal enough of money; he was fond
of antiquity and arts: and a favourer of learning, though rather in the
honour he paid it than the time he spent upon it.'[1]

As Bacon had once intrigued the earl of Essex with his scientific diver-
tissements, so now he joined those bidding for the young prince's affection.
According to the metallurgist Thomas Bushell, who served as Bacon's
amanuensis in later years, Prince Henry ('the then rising sun') was the
recipient of 'an experiment of [Bacon's] second collections', namely 'to
know the heart of man by a sympathising stone, made of several mixtures'.
He sent this 'sympathising stone' with a covering letter:

Most Royal Sir, since you are by birth the prince of our country, and
your virtues the happy pledge to our posterity; and that the seigniory
of greatness is ever attended more with flatterers, than faithful friends,
and loyal subjects; and therefore needeth more helps to discern and pry
into the hearts of the people, than private persons: Give me leave noble
sir, as small rivulets run to the vast ocean to pay their tribute, so let me

have the honour to show your Highness the operative quality of these two triangular stones (as the first fruits of my philosophy) to imitate the pathetical motion of the lodestone and iron, although made up by the compounds of meteors (as starshot jelly) and other like magical ingredients, with the reflected beams of the sun, on purpose, that the warmth distilled unto them through the moist heat of the hand, might discover the affection of the heart, by a visible sign of their attraction and appetite to each other, like the hand of a watch, within ten minutes after they are laid upon a marble table, or the theatre of a great looking glass.[2]

We might prefer to believe that this flight of fancy concerning the properties of magnets was concocted to intrigue and flatter the young prince. However, Bacon's writings on natural history reveal him, like many of his contemporaries, to be persuaded of the reality of the magical sympathies of lodestones.

Another accepted way of indicating availability to a patron was publicly to dedicate a printed work, and by October 1612 the continuing revision of the *Essays* had reached a stage where they might be entered once again in the Stationers' Register. This time, the dedicatory letter (which had previously fed the triangular Essex–Anthony–Francis relationship) was addressed to Henry, appealing to the honour paid by the Prince of Wales to learning. 'Having divided my life into the contemplative and active part,' wrote Bacon,

I am desirous to give his Majesty and your Highness of the fruits of both, simple though they be. To write just treatises requireth leisure in the writer, and leisure in the reader, and therefore are not so fit, neither in regard of your Highness' princely affairs, nor in regard of my continual services; which is the cause that hath made me choose to write certain brief notes, set down rather significantly than curiously, which I have called *Essays*. The word is late, but the thing is ancient. For Seneca's epistles to Lucilius, if one mark them well, are but *Essays*, that is, dispersed meditations, though conveyed in the form of epistles. These labours of mine I know cannot be worthy of your Highness, for what can be worthy of you? But my hope is, they may be as grains of salt, that will rather give you an appetite than offend you with satiety. And although they handle those things wherein both men's lives and their pens are most conversant, yet (what I have attained I know not) but I have endeavoured to make them not vulgar, but of a nature whereof a man shall find much in experience, and little in books; so as they are neither repetitions nor fancies.[3]

Bacon's desire to 'show my most dutiful and devoted affection to your Highness in these things which proceed from myself', so that 'I shall be much more ready to do it in performance of any your princely command-ments', was typically poorly timed. On 6 November Henry died, 'in the nineteenth year of his age, of a malignant fever', as Bacon put it, 'which – springing from the great heats and droughts, greater than islanders are accustomed to, – was very general among the people during the summer, though few died of it; but became towards autumn more fatal'. Rumours suggested that poison was involved. 'But as no symptoms of such a thing appeared, especially in the stomach which is commonly most affected by poison, that report soon died away.' Denied the patronage of the future king by bad timing, Bacon had to be content to pen a eulogy of his character, *In Henricum principem Walliae elogium*, which he never saw the point of publishing.[4]

The *Essays* still had to be published, though, and Bacon hastily penned a brief dedication, again to a brother – this time his brother-in-law Sir John Constable. 'My last Essays,' he wrote,

> I dedicated to my dear brother Master Anthony Bacon, who is with God. Looking amongst my papers this vacation, I found others of the same nature: which if I myself shall not suffer to be lost, it seemeth the world will not; by the often printing of the former. [The 1597 *Essays* had been reprinted, apparently without Bacon's involvement, in 1598, 1604, and 1606.] Missing my brother, I found you next; in respect of bond both of near alliance, and of straight friendship and society, and particularly of communication in studies. Wherein I must acknowledge myself beholding to you. For as my business found rest in my contemplations; so my contem-plations ever found rest in your loving conference and judgment.[5]

The death of the Prince of Wales exacerbated what was already a very unsettled atmosphere at court. On 19 November it was reported that

> the greatest differences in court are compounded very lately, and the rumours from abroad do somewhat quicken and awake our fatal security, but specially the prince's death hath taken away the means of helping ourselves by his marriage, and stopping the gap of our wants for the present by the way, so that we must of necessity have recourse to a parliament, whereof there is speech already for February. These consider-ations put us into daily expectation of alterations and removes, and the *canditati* for every place ply their canvass and will not *demordre* [budge], specially Sir Thomas Lake and Sir Francis Bacon.[6]

There was a glimmer of hope for Bacon when the 'malignant fever' that killed Henry and blocked one route to favour opened another, as it also claimed the life on 13 November of Sir George Carew, the man who had taken the Mastership of the Wards that Bacon thought was his own. He immediately set about renewing his campaign for it, turning this time to Robert Carr, Viscount Rochester, who had previously backed Carew's successful bid for the post against Bacon. Once a page in James's household, Carr had gained the King's attention when he was thrown from his horse at a tilting match. Carr was promptly knighted and given the manor of Sherburne (which had been confiscated from Sir Walter Ralegh), and in March 1611 was created Viscount Rochester – the first Scot promoted by James to a seat in the Lords. Rochester had James's ear, and so Bacon lamented to him, with one of his favourite images, that

> This Mastership of the Wards is like a mist. Sometimes it goeth upwards, and sometimes it falleth downwards. If it go up to great Lords, then it is as it was at the first; if it fall down to mean men, then it is as it was at the last. But neither of these ways concern me in particular. But if it should in a middle region go to lawyers, then I beseech your Lordship have some care of me. The Attorney and the Solicitor are as the King's champions for civil business, and they had need have some place of rest in their eye for their encouragement. The Mastership of the Rolls, which was for the ordinary place kept for them, is gone from them. If this place should go to a lawyer, and not to them, their hopes must diminish.[7]

Despite the somewhat plaintive tone of his letter to Rochester, this time Bacon was confident, even though a clear competitor was visible in the person of Sir Walter Cope. He went so far as to 'put most of his men into new cloaks'.[8] Once again, the move was premature: by 19 November it was reported that Cope had prevailed, Chamberlain exclaiming that he should 'marvel at the luck of a thing'.[9] Bacon's overly optimistic rush to equip himself for the job did not go unnoticed, as Rawley related: 'Afterward when Sir Walter Cope carried the place, one said, merrily: That Sir Walter Cope was Master of the Wards, and Sir Francis Bacon of the Liveries.'[10]

Bacon was still in with a chance in this round of reshuffles, however, according to the news-writers. Around 20 November 'the cry', according to Chamberlain, 'was all with Sir Francis Bacon' for the post of Principal Secretary – but then it was all with Sir Fulke Greville, and then with Sir Thomas Lake; 'we are carried about with every wind, and indeed I never knew the like variety and uncertainty of report and discourse.'[11]

The death of the Prince of Wales also meant that the festivities for his sister Elizabeth's marriage had had to be postponed, even though the prospective groom, the Elector Palatine, was now in the country. After a

decent interval, the match was finally celebrated on 14 February 1613, and
Bacon was 'the chief contriver' of the masque presented by the Gray's Inn
and Inner Temple gentlemen, penned by Francis Beaumont. In recognition
of his support, when the masque was published it was dedicated to Bacon:

> Ye that spared no pain nor travail in the setting forth, ordering, and
> furnishing of this Masque, (being the first fruits of honour in this kind
> which these two societies have offered to his Majesty), will not think
> much now to look back upon the effects of your own care and work;
> for that, whereof the success was then doubtful, is now happily per-
> formed and graciously accepted; and that which you were then to think
> of in straits of time, you may now peruse at leisure; and you, Sir Francis
> Bacon, especially, as you did then by your countenance and loving
> affections advance it, so let your good word grace it and defend it,
> which is able to add value to the greatest and least matters.[12]

Gray's Inn and the Inner Temple were to provide the masque on Tuesday 16 February. The Grayans came on horseback and open chariots across
the Thames from Winchester Place in Southwark, symbolising the marriage
of the rivers of the Thames and the Rhine, a sight that was 'very gallant
by reason of infinite store of lights very curiously set and placed: and many
boats and barges with devices of light and lamps, with three peals of
ordnance, one at their taking water, another in the Temple garden, and
the last at their landing' – a display which cost upward of £300. They
were received at the privy stairs, amid general consent that they would
'every way exceed their competitors that went before them, both in device,
daintiness, of apparel, and above all in dancing (wherein they are held
excellent) and esteemed for the properer men'.

But disaster struck. 'By what ill planet it fell out I know not,' wrote
Chamberlain,

> they came home as they went without doing anything, the reason
> whereof I cannot yet learn thoroughly, but only that the hall was so
> full that it was not possible to avoid [empty] it or make room for them,
> besides that most of the ladies were in the galleries to see them land,
> and could not get in: but the worst of all was that the King was so
> wearied and sleepy with sitting up almost two whole nights before, that
> he had no edge to it, whereupon Sir Francis Bacon adventured to entreat
> his Majesty, that by this disgrace he would not as it were bury the quick:
> and I hear the King should answer, that then they must bury him quick
> for he could last no longer, but withal gave them very good words and
> appointed them to come again on Saturday: but the grace of their masque
> is quite gone when their apparel hath been already showed and their

devices vented so that how it will fall out God knows, for they are much discouraged, and out of countenance, and the world says it comes to pass after the old proverb, 'the properer men the worst luck'.[13]

On Saturday 20 February, 'nothing discouraged for all their first dodge', the two Inns tried again, 'performed their parts exceeding well and with great applause and approbation both from the King and all the company', giving 'great contentment being both dainty and curious in device and sumptuous in show'. Their two masques, he wrote, 'stood them in better than £4000 besides the gallantry and expence of private gentlemen, that were but *ante-ambulones*, and went only to accompany them'. To show his appreciation, James invited forty of the masquers and their assistants the following night 'to a solemn supper in the new marriage-room, where they were well treated and much graced with kissing his Majesty's hand, and every one having a particular *accoglienza* from him'. Cannily, James

> husbanded the matter so well that this feast was not at his own cost, but he and his company won it upon a wager of running at the ring of the Prince and his nine followers, who paid thirty pound a man: the King, Queen, Prince, Palatine and Lady Elizabeth sat at table by them-selves: and the great Lords and Ladies with the masquers (above fourscore in all) sat at another long table, so that there was no room for them that made the feast but they were fain to be lookers on, which the young Lady Rich took no great pleasure in to see her husband (who was one that paid) not so much as drink for his money.[14]

★

Bacon's life was now filled with an endless treadmill of legal work – notably the prosecution of James Whitelocke and Robert Mansell,[15] and the question of whether Irish subjects visiting England could be required to take the oath of allegiance[16] – and (often unsolicited) counsel to the King: for example, advising against taking on petitions of grievances from the newly formed Irish parliament.[17]

On 7 August 1613 Sir Thomas Fleming, Chief Justice of the King's Bench, died, and once again the key legal appointments were up for grabs. Bacon immediately appealed to the King to move Sir Henry Hobart to Fleming's vacant place, hoping to obtain Hobart's attorneyship for himself:

> Having understood of the death of the Lord Chief Justice, I do ground in all humbleness an assured hope, that your Majesty will not think of any other but your poor servants, your attorney and your solicitor, (one of them), for that place. Else we shall be like Noah's dove, not knowing where to rest our foot. For the places of rest after the extreme painful

places wherein we serve have used to be, either the Lord Chancellor's place, or the Mastership of the Rolls, or the places of the two chief justices: whereof, for the first, I would be almost loth to see this worthy counsellor fail. The Mastership of the Rolls is blocked with a reversion. My lord Coke is like to outlive us both. So as if this turn fails, I for my part know not whither to look. I have served your Majesty above a prenticehood, full seven years and more, as your solicitor, which is, I think, one of the painfulest places in your kingdom, specially as my employments have been; and God hath brought mine own years to fifty-two, which I think is older than ever any solicitor continued unpreferred. My suit is principally that you would remove Mr. Attorney to the place; if he refuse, then I hope your Majesty will seek no furder than myself, that I may at last, out of your Majesty's grace and favour, step forwards to a place either of more comfort or more ease. Besides how necessary it is for your Majesty to strengthen your service amongst the Judges by a Chief Justice which is sure to your prerogative, your Majesty knoweth.[18]

This was a scarcely veiled reference to an old enemy. As Chief Justice of the Common Pleas, Coke had become something of a popular champion. Because the Court of Common Pleas dealt with civil suits, he was constantly called upon to adjudicate in disputes between King and subject. If Coke were raised to Chief Justice of the King's Bench, technically a higher post, then his confrontations with royal prerogative could be avoided, since the King's Bench dealt with offences against the crown. Bacon formulated his argument in a paper to present to the King, urging Coke's removal to Chief Justice, 'the Attorney [Hobart] to succeed him, and' – naturally – the Solicitor, Francis Bacon, to succeed to the attorneyship.

The grounds were fourfold. First, it would strengthen James's causes among the judges. 'For both my Lord Coke will think himself near a privy councillor's place, and thereupon turn obsequious, and the attorney general, a new man and a grave person in a judge's place, will come in well to the other hold him hard to it, not without emulation between them who shall please the King best.' Second, Hobart 'sorteth not so well with his present place, being a man timid and scrupulous both in parliament and in other business, and one that in a word was made fit for the late Lord Treasurer's bent, which was to do little with much formality and protestation.' Bacon himself, on the other hand,

going more roundly to work, and being of a quicker and more earnest temper, and more effectual in that he dealeth in, is like to recover that strength to the King's prerogative which it hath had in times past, and which is due unto it. And for that purpose there must be brought in to be solicitor some man of courage and speech and a grounded lawyer; which done, his Majesty will speedily find a marvellous change in his business, for it is not to purpose for the judges to stand well disposed, except the King's Counsel, which is in the active and moving part, put the judges well to it; for in a weapon what is a back without an edge?

Thirdly,

the King shall continue and add reputation to the attorney's and solicitor's place by this orderly advancement of them, which two places are the champion's places for his rights and prerogative, and being stripped of their expectations and successions to great place will wax vile, and then his Majesty's prerogative goeth down the wind. Besides, the remove of my Lord Coke to a place of less profit [the King's Bench was less well reimbursed] (though it be with his will) yet will be thought abroad a kind of discipline to him for opposing himself in the King's causes, the example whereof will contain others in more awe.

And finally,

whereas now it is voiced abroad touching the supply of places, as if it were a matter of labour and canvass and money, and other persons are chiefly spoken to be the men, and the great suitors; this will appear to be the King's own act, and is a course so natural and regular as it is without all suspicion of those by-courses, to the King's infinite honour; for men say now, the King can make good second judges, as he hath done lately, but that is no mastery, because men sue to be kept from these places. But now is the trial in those great places how his Majesty can hold good, where there such is great suit and means.[19]

Chamberlain reported that 'The choice of a new Lord Chief Justice hath bred great variety and much canvassing, but in conclusion it was once resolved, and so stands still for ought I hear, that the Lord Coke should be Chief Justice, Master Attorney [Hobart] Chief Justice of the Common Pleas, and all to make way for Sir Francis Bacon to be attorney, whom the King hath promised to advance: these removes were looked for the first day of the term, but all things stand yet *in statu quo prius*.' The reshuffle was delayed because Coke was not keen on the proposal. 'The Lord Coke doth so stickle and fence by all the means and friends he can make, not to remove, as being loath he says to be bought out of a court of law which is his element, and out of his profit, in regard whereof he values not the dignity, that he hath written very earnestly to his Majesty about it.' Court gossip had it that James would 'not force him against his will', and had to promise that 'if he would accept it, he should do it with as much honour as ever any one went to that place,' which was understood as 'a kind of promise of a barony or a councillorship at the least'.

On Monday 25 October, 'the Lord Coke (though never so loath) was called up into the King's Bench, and there sworn Chief Justice. He parted dolefully from the Common Pleas, not only weeping himself, but followed with the tears of all that Bench, and most of the officers of that Court.' On 27 October, Coke became Chief Justice, Hobart moved to become Chief Justice of the Common Pleas, and Yelverton filled the Solicitor's place as Bacon was promoted Attorney-General – almost twenty years after he had lost the battle for the post to Coke. Coke was furious. 'This is all your doing,' he raged at Bacon, 'it is you that have made this great stir.'

'Your lordship,' replied Bacon demurely, 'all this while hath grown in breadth; you must needs now grow in height, or you will be a monster.'

Bacon won the exchange, but typically, his design was not adhered to in every point. Chamberlain commented: 'There is a strong apprehension that little good is to be expected by this change, and that Bacon may prove a dangerous instrument.' James decided not to taunt Coke with the hope of becoming a Privy Councillor, but acted immediately: on 7 November, at the ceremonials whereby Viscount Rochester was created earl of Somerset, in preparation for his marriage to the now-divorced Frances Howard, Lady Essex, 'the Lord Coke (with many good and gracious words) was sworn a Privy Councillor, which honour no man envies him if he keep in his right course, and turn not to be Attorney again.'[20]

Bacon wrote an ecstatically grateful letter to James.

A full heart is like a full pen; it can hardly make any distinguished work. The more I look into mine own weakness the more I must magnify your favours, and the more I behold your favours the more I must consider mine own weakness. This is my hope, that God who hath moved your heart to favour me will write your service in my heart. Two things I may promise; for though they be not mine own yet they are surer than mine own, because they are God's gifts; that is integrity and industry. And therefore whensoever I shall make my account to you, I shall do it in these words, *ecce tibi lucrifeci*, and not *ecce mihi lucrifeci* [I have profited for you, not for me]. And for industry, I shall take to me in this procuration not Martha's part, to be busied in many things, but Mary's part, which is to intend your service; for the less my abilities are the more they ought to be contracted *ad unum* [into one]. For the present I humbly pray your Majesty to accept my most humble thanks and vows as the forerunners of honest services which I shall always perform with a faithful heart.

He later insisted to James that 'when I moved your Majesty for the Attorney's place, it was your own sole act.' However, the direct petitioning of a monarch without high-level support was not how the court worked. The new Lord Somerset, 'when he knew your Majesty had resolved it, thrust himself into the business for a fee'.[21]

★

So at last, in 1613, two decades after the earl of Essex had first tried to get him the post, Sir Francis Bacon became Attorney-General. His first task was to put a stop to the current highly fashionable practice of duelling. As John Chamberlain put it, writing on 9 September:

> Though there be in show a settled peace in these parts of the world, yet the many private quarrels among the great ones prognosticate troubled humours, which may breed dangerous diseases, if they be not purged and prevented. I doubt not but you have heard the success of the combat betwixt Edward Sackville and the Lord Bruce (or Kinloss), 'twixt Antwerp and Lille, wherein they were both hurt, the Lord Bruce to the death, so that Sackville was driven to take sanctuary, whence by corruption or connivance I hear he is escaped. Here is speech likewise that the Lord Norris and Sir Peregrine Willoughby are gone forth for the same purpose, and that the Lord Chandos and the Lord Hay are upon the same terms. There was a quarrel kindling 'twixt the earls of Rutland and Montgomery, but it was quickly quenched by the King, being begun and ended in his presence. But there is more danger 'twixt the earl of Rutland and the Lord Davers, though I heard yesterday it was already, or upon the point of compounding. But that which most men listen after, is what will fall out 'twixt the earl of Essex and Master Henry Howard, who is challenged and called to account by the earl for certain disgraceful speeches of him. They are both gotten over, the earl from Milford Haven, the other from Harwich, with each of them two seconds . . . The last news of them was that the earl was at Calais and the other in Zealand. The King hath sent a post to Calais to the Governor, to stay them or either of them; and young Gib of the bedchamber is sent with commandment from the King to them both, if he come in time.[22]

At the end of October, the King issued a proclamation in relation to the Essex/Howard affair, consulting with his lawyers on the more general issue of how to end this new national pastime. Bacon submitted his own 'proposition for the repressing of singular combats or duels'. He hoped that the ordinance might 'not look back to any offence past' and that it would be temporary, pending a parliament, 'for that will be very acceptable to the parliament; and it is good to teach a parliament to work upon an edict or proclamation precedent.' He observed that duelling 'hath vogue only amongst noble persons, or persons of quality', and that since 'the greatest honour for subjects of quality in a lawful monarchy, is to have access and approach to their sovereign's sight and person', it would be effective if 'the principal part of the punishment be, that the offender . . . be banished perpetually from approach to the Courts of King, Queen, or Prince'. Secondly, the offender should be prosecuted 'by the King's attorney, *ore tenus*, in the Star-Chamber', no matter how great the offender, 'and that the fine set be irremissible'. The net for possible offenders was cast wide, to cover any person involved in any singular combat, whether or not death ensued; 'where any person passeth beyond the seas, with purpose to perform any singular combat, though it be never acted'; any person sending, accepting or delivering a challenge, appointing a field for combat, or agreeing to be a second.

Bacon also considered it 'fit there be published a grave and severe proclamation, induced by the overflow of the present mischief'. Accordingly, late in the year, 'His Majesty's edict and severe censure against private combats and combatants' was published – but only after the earl of Northampton had brought his own distinctive style to the piece, rendering it somewhat opaque.[23] Bacon, unsatisfied, decided to publish his own version, and engineered the hearing of an obscure duelling case which Sir Henry Hobart had had in hand, in which a challenge had been sent and refused. He promoted the case to the first sitting of the Star Chamber in Hilary Term, on 26 January 1614, and wrote up the results as *The charge of Sir Francis Bacon, knight, his Majesties Attourney generall, touching Duells, upon an information in the Star-chamber against Priest and Wright. With the Decree of the Star-Chamber in the same cause.*[24] The book was entered into the Stationers' Register by Robert Wilson on 5 March 1614.[25]

Embarrassingly enough, at the height of the debate about duels, one of Bacon's servants was implicated in one. John Chamberlain wrote to tell Sir Dudley Carleton how 'a proper young fellow that served Sir Francis Bacon was arraigned at the King's Bench for killing a Scot [in a duel]; and being found guilty of manslaughter, was burnt in the hand. The matter was eagerly pursued and brought out of the country to be tried here, for fear of partiality, and had a very sufficient and extraordinary jury. Yet all are not satisfied that they found so much, the fellow being assaulted by two, the one before and the other behind, and being dangerously hurt at least in four places.' Bacon promptly succumbed to a fortnight's fit of the stone which kept him conveniently out of the public eye until interest in the affair had ebbed away.[26]

★

Somerset's marriage on 26 December 1613, with festivities lasting until Twelfth Night, offered Bacon the opportunity to impress his new sponsor. He planned to go one better than the dual presentations of the Inns of Court at Princess Elizabeth's marriage: to present a masque by all four Inns. Unfortunately, the plan collapsed, and Bacon was forced to apologise to Somerset: 'I am sorry the joint masque from the four Inns of Court faileth; wherein I conceive there is no other ground of that event but impossibility.' However, he had another suggestion up his sleeve:

Nevertheless, because it falleth out that at this time Gray's Inn is well furnished of gallant young gentlemen, your Lordship may be pleased to know that rather than this occasion shall pass without some demonstration of affection from the Inns of Court, there are a dozen gentlemen of Gray's Inn that out of the honour which they bare to your Lordship and my Lord Chamberlain [the earl of Suffolk, father of the bride], to whom at their last masque they were so much bounden, will be ready to furnish a masque, wishing it were in their powers to perform it according to their minds.[27]

Bacon took the charges of the event upon himself. Chamberlain reported on 23 December that

Sir Francis Bacon prepares a masque to honour this marriage, which will stand him in above £2000, and though he have been offered some help by the House, and specially by Master Solicitor Sir Henry Yelverton, who would have sent him £500 yet he would not accept it, but offers them the whole charge with the honour: marry his obligations are such as well to his Majesty as to the great Lord, and to the whole house of Howards, as he can admit no partners. In the meantime his house and land at Gorhambury (by St Albans) is gone, some say to the earl of Somerset, others to the earl of Suffolk.[28]

The Maske of Flowers was performed on Twelfth Night at Whitehall. The printed version, entered into the Stationers' Register on 21 January 1614 by Robert Wilson, was dedicated by J.G., W.D. and T.B. (its authors?) to Bacon as

the principal and in effect the only person that did both encourage and warrant the gentlemen to show their good affection towards so noble a conjunction in a time of such magnificence; wherein we conceive, without giving you false attributes, which little need where so many are true, that you have graced in general the Societies of the Inns of Court, in continuing them still as third persons with the Nobility and the Court in doing the King honour; and particularly Gray's Inn, which as you have formerly brought to flourish both in the ancienter and younger sort, by countenancing virtue in every quality, so now you have made a notable demonstration thereof in the lighter and less serious kind, by this, that one Inn of Court by itself in time of a vacation, and in the space of three weeks, could perform that which hath been performed; which could not have been done but that every man's exceeding love and respect to you gave him wings to overtake Time, which is the swiftest of things.[29]

The new Attorney-General's lavishness did not stop with masquing. 'His bounty is no whit abated,' reported Chamberlain, 'for he feasts the whole University of Cambridge this Christmas, and hath sent warrants to his friends and acquaintances far and near to furnish him with venison to bestow on the colleges. He carries a great port as well in his train, as in his apparel and other ways, and lives at a great charge, and yet he pretends he will take no fees nor intermeddle in mercenary causes, but wholly applies himself to the King's affairs.'[30] At last Bacon had the kind of means to indulge his lifelong hankering after ostentatious living.

★

As early as May 1612, Bacon had been urging James to call a parliament, 'for the supply of your estate' and 'for the better knitting of the hearts of your subjects unto your Majesty, according to your infinite merit'. In this area, of course, Bacon admitted to having 'a little skill . . . as one that ever affected that your Majesty mought in all your causes not only prevail, but prevail with the satisfaction of the inner man; and though no man can say but I was a perfect and peremptory royalist, yet every man makes me believe that I was never one hour out of credit with the lower house. My desire is to know whether your Majesty will give me leave to meditate and propound unto you some preparative remembrances touching the future parliament.'[31]

The Lord Commissioners reported on 1 June 1613 on the progress made in 'bettering the King's revenue': the figures, in an account by Sir Julius Caesar, showed an increase in the ordinary revenue of £35,776, and an extraordinary collection of £309,681. While impressive in itself, however, the sum did not come close to meeting the annual deficit of £160,000 and a debt of £500,000.[32] Once again, a subsidy was needed; and therefore, once again, a parliament needed to be called.

Bacon meditated with himself on the possible reasons that could be given for calling a parliament at such a sensitive moment and concluded that 'it is fit for the King to call a Parliament, or at least not fit for any man to dissuade it.' To the King, he provided six reasons for so doing.

First, nothing done by the King since the last parliament had been 'harsh or distasteful', and so the old grievances would lie dormant. Secondly, 'the justice upon my Lord Sanquhar hath done your Majesty a great deal of right.' Thirdly, 'Let it not offend your Majesty if I say that the earls of Salisbury and Dunbar have taken a great deal of envy from you and carried it into the other world and left unto your Majesty a just diversion of many discontents.' Fourthly, the opposition evinced from the last parliament derived 'not *ex puris naturalibus* but out of party'. Now that party was 'almost dissolved': 'Yelverton is won; Sandys is fallen off; Crew and Hyde stand to be serjeants; Brock is dead; Neville hath hopes; Berkeley I think will be respective; Martin hath money in his purse; Dudley Digges and Holles are yours. Besides, they cannot but find more and more the vanity of that popular course; specially your Majesty having carried yourself in that princely temper towards them, as not to persecute or disgrace them.' Fifthly, the last parliament had been occupied with a bargain, and 'Bargain and Gift are *antitheta*, as the Apostle speaketh of Grace and Works . . . the entertaining of the thoughts of the one did cross and was a disturbance and impediment to the other.' And Bacon could not resist a final gratuitous stab at his dead cousin. 'Lastly, I cannot excuse him that is gone of an artifical animating of the Negative; which infusion or influence now ceasing I have better hope.'

He also advised James to abandon the merchant persona, and 'rest upon the person of a King'; to moderate his 'demands and expectation'; to bill this parliament in the traditional way, as being 'for some other business of estate, and not merely for money'; and counselled that it should be 'given out that there are means found in his Majesty's estate to help himself (which I partly think is true), but that, because it is not the work of a day, his Majesty must be beholding to his subjects; but as to facilitate and speed the recovery of himself rather than of an absolute necessity.'[33]

In the event, the question was put off once again. Northampton reported to Sir Thomas Lake on Sunday 4 July that the Council was fully engaged – ten or twelve hours daily – with rectifying the King's estate: 'only of the Parliament, or reasons either to move or remove the same, they had hitherto forborne to speak; because it was consequent to precedent questions or disputes which the Lords of the Commission had now in hammering'.[34]

With the new year, and from the vantage point of his new position as Attorney-General, Bacon returned to his preoccupation of the previous summer and renewed his approach to the King on the need for a new parliament. Using the occasion of the birth of a royal grandchild on 9 January – 'if your Majesty had heard and seen the thunder of the bells and the lightning of the bonfires for your grandchild, you would say there is

little cause to doubt the affections of the people of England *in puris natu-*
ralibus [utterly sincerely]' – he wrote to James to forward his opinion
about Sir Henry Neville and his party, the so-called 'undertakers' (who
'undertook' the packing and managing of the Lower House for the King).
Bacon begged James to remember the point on which they spoke, 'to put
but this case to those gentlemen which profess to do you service in Parliament, and desire (as they say) but to have some matter whereupon to
work: If your Majesty be resolved not to buy and sell this Parliament, but
to perform the part of a King, and not of a merchant or contractor, what
they can desire or propound for the satisfaction and comfort of your
people.'

Three uses might be made of this strategy. If they answered 'that the
Parliament is so now in taste with matters of substance and profit, as it is
in vain to think to draw them on but by some offer of that nature,' then
they would show themselves to be 'but brokers for bargains' whose service
was to be little esteemed. If they came up with 'anything that is fit', then
they should be allowed to pursue it, 'because they are likest to be in love
with their own child, and to nourish it'. Or thirdly, 'if they show good
will to devise some such thing, but that their intention prove barren, in
that their proposition be not such but that better may be found, then
that they may be holpen by some better proposition from your Majesty
whereupon they may work.' But this was now an urgent task, 'because
time runneth'.

Bacon also suggested that it might be 'inconvenient' to have parliaments
in England and Ireland running simultaneously, and so it might be as well
as to 'put off' the proposed Irish parliament. As he pointed out, 'the
unsettled business of the Parliament of Ireland is a just ground for the
Parliament of England to furnish your Majesty with treasure *in omnem*
eventum [whatever happens]. And on the other side the loving and frank
proceeding with you by your Parliament of England will daunt the ill
affected part of the Parliament of Ireland.'[35]

It may be that James acted upon the first part of Bacon's advice, putting
to the 'undertakers' the proposed question, and referring their answer to
his Learned Counsel. This would make sense of a letter from the Learned
Counsel – Coke, Hobart, Bacon, Montagu and Yelverton – to the King,
written on 17 February 1614, the day after the Lords decided finally to
call a parliament.[36] Citing 'our instant business of service' as the reason
that they had not been able to meet until that day, they requested James
'to give us further time of deliberation' and to allow them to give their
answer 'by word of mouth', owing to its complexity.[37]

Bacon's second speech as Attorney-General in the Star Chamber, on 31
January, the last sitting of Hilary Term, concerned the Irish Catholic

parliamentarian William Talbot, who had refused to take the oath of allegiance to James, whom he considered 'heretical'. After several months' incarceration in the Tower, he was finally to be sentenced. 'I brought before you at the last sitting of this term the cause of duels,' opened Bacon, 'but now this last sitting I shall bring before you a cause concerning the greatest duel which is in the Christian world, the duel and conflict between the lawful authority of sovereign kings, which is God's ordinance for the comfort of human society, and the swelling pride and usurpation of the See of Rome tending altogether anarchy and confusion.'

Bacon's target was not the defendant Talbot, but the Pope himself, and his power to confuse the question of allegiance of English subjects. 'The allegiance of his subjects is pinned upon the Pope's acts. And certainly, 'tis time to stop the current of this opinion of acknowledgement of the Pope's power *in temporalibus*, or else it will sap and supplant the King's seat . . . As for the point of matter of faith . . . is nothing exempt from it? If a man should ask Mr Talbot whether he do condemn murder, or adultery, or rape, or the doctrine of Mahomet . . . must the answer be . . . that therein he will submit himself to what the Church shall determine?'

Indeed, William Talbot himself was treated with some deference. 'I know my Lords out of their accustomed favour will admit you not only to your defence concerning that that hath been charged, but to extenuate your fault by any submission that now God shall put into your mind to make.' Talbot was subsequently fined £10,000 – which he probably never had to pay – and was released, returning to Ireland.[38]

By the end of February the writs had been sent out for a 5 April sitting; and March saw the usual scrabble for seats in what was clearly going to be a crucial parliament. On 3 March Chamberlain reported that 'Here is much bustling for places in Parliament, and letters fly from great persons extraordinarily: wherein methinks they do the King no great service, seeing the world is apt to conceive that it is a kind of packing.'[39] Bacon was later to comment on 'that greenness of the House' which 'leeseth the modesty and gravity by which great matters have passage, and turneth it into a kind of sport or exercise';[40] to Dudley Carleton, John Chamberlain wrote that 'Many sat there that were more fit to have been among roaring boys.'[41] Bacon had warned the King against 'brigues [intrigues] and canvasses' which 'would but increase animosities and oppositions' and make 'whatever should be done to be in evil conceit with the people in general afterwards'. Such tactics seem to have failed anyway. Two weeks later, Chamberlain was able to note that 'Letters and countenances even in meaner boroughs prove not so powerful as was imagined.'[42]

With the new parliament imminent, there was a pressing need to fill the post of Secretary of State – vacant since the death of Salisbury nearly two years previously. The Secretary was meant to be able to lead for the government within the Commons, but there was no likely candidate. In the end, Sir Ralph Winwood was appointed – a man who had conducted diplomatic business abroad admirably, but who was little versed in domestic affairs, and had never been inside the House of Commons – 'the first that ever he heard speak in that place was himself,' quipped Chamberlain.[43] Nonetheless, he was sworn in on 26 March. Such a move was bound to worry Bacon, who had been meditating on this parliament for almost a year. He now set about providing James with a 'memorial' of some points which he thought good to be touched upon during the King's speech to the two Houses. James should explain the financial needs of the crown, and pledge that he would 'not speak to them in the language of an accountant, nor of a merchant, nor of a tyrant' – indeed, that he meant 'to set down a course to myself' whereby there would be 'no more arrears but competent store for that which concerneth privy service'. It was a direct rebuttal of Salisbury's 'Great Contract' policy four years earlier.[44]

Bacon was returned for St Albans, Ipswich and Cambridge University, sitting eventually for Cambridge. The Cambridge election, on 2 April 1614, had its own share of controversy.[45] When Sir Miles Sandys was returned, the college heads promptly found him ineligible as a non-resident of Cambridge. In order to quash the suggestion that Bacon was, like Sandys, ineligible to sit for the university, the acting Vice-Chancellor, Dr John Duport, announced that he did 'choose and pronounce to be chosen by the greater part of the Regents and non Regents for the Burgesses of the University against the next Parliament the Honourable Knight Sir Francis Bacon Attorney General to his excellent Majesty and both Master of Arts and of Counsel of and to the University of Cambridge (whereby he may seem after a sort to live and breathe amongst us)'.[46] It could, of course, be pointed out that Bacon's 'Master of Arts' was a purely honorary degree, whereas Sandys held a full MA and had been a fellow of Queens' College; perhaps more important, however, was the consideration that during the previous year Bacon had been appointed Standing Counsel for Cambridge University, and had made a donation of venison to college festivities at Christmas.[47]

Bacon's problems with this parliament were not to be confined to university politics. On Friday, the question was raised as to whether, as Attorney-General, he was eligible to sit in the Commons, since an Attorney-General would inevitably be divided in his dual allegiance to the House and the King. There was no precedent immediately evident, and a committee was appointed 'to search for precedents where any Attorney-General to any King or Queen of this realm hath been chosen and served as a member of this House'; in the meantime, Bacon was sequestered from the Commons.[48] On Monday 11 April, it was reported back from the committee that the only Attorney 'appearing in the Clerk's hands' was his immediate predecessor Sir Henry Hobart, who had been 'first of this House' and only afterwards 'chosen Attorney, and by connivancy served there'. Secretary Winwood reported that the question had 'come to his Majesty's ears', and the King had asserted that he bore 'no dislike of Mr. Attorney nor unwillingness with his service', but respected 'the privileges of this House, which he will ever maintain'. He did however argue for Bacon: 'His Majesty knows no difference for the reason between the Serjeant, higher, and the Solicitor, than the Attorney. A reason of difference *ubi eadem ratio, eadem dispositio* [where by the same reason, the same arrangement].' Winwood therefore moved that because Bacon had been 'returned and sworn' he 'may be continued this parliament; for hereafter, as this House shall please'. Another committee member, Sir Roger Owen, intervened. He had received that morning 'advertisement from honourable persons' of a special cause why Bacon should serve. The information was not fit to be discovered here publicly, but he would privately inform any man why. For reasons of state, Bacon should sit in the House during this parliament – although there was an order that henceforth no Attorney-General should at any time sit in the House.[49]

Later in the parliament, a complaint was brought against Sir Thomas Parry, Chancellor of the Duchy, accusing him of rigging parliamentary elections by writing 'menacing letters' to 'a certain corporation of the Duchy' to force them to support his preferred candidate.[50] In the violent debate that this allegation provoked, Bacon begged for the House's 'carefulness and earnestness' in these 'misbegotten elections'. He did not like 'indirect elections', for 'he that enters not well is not like to sit well'. He himself 'liketh not stumbling at the threshold'. He approved the way in which the House was 'proceeding with moderation', while feeling 'their own power'; 'speaking sharply, but concluding mercifully'.[51] Despite Bacon's support, Parry was ultimately removed from the House, and a new writ issued for his replacement. The King offered to remove Parry from his seat at the Privy Council table, but his prosecutors declined any further punishment.[52] There was to be a pathetic footnote to the business: on Tuesday 17 May, Bacon delivered a paper to the Speaker which he claimed had been found upon the stairs in Parry's Duchy Court, with the superscription, 'My heart is disquieted within me because I cannot speak'.[53]

While Bacon's position was under investigation, the King made a second speech in which he anticipated the demands of the opposition by announcing the favours and graces which he meant to bestow on them – merely out of kindness, he assured them, not in the way of bargain. Despite this assurance, when Bacon returned on Tuesday 12 April, things were not going well. Secretary Winwood rose to argue the case for the state's need of money, citing the parlous state of the navy and other military defences, threatened by dissolution and mutiny; Tyrone's treating with the Pope; troubles in Germany; the imminent double marriage uniting France and Spain; and the contempt in which England's poverty was held. He concluded by comparing the King's offered graces to the Magna Carta, and asked for a cheerful and speedy contribution. Winwood was supported by Sir Julius Caesar's account of the Exchequer; and then Bacon rose, saying that 'sithence they pleased to retain him' he would do 'the best offices he can'; if they pleased to dismiss him, then he would give them 'the best wishes he could' – urging that they take into account 'what hangeth over us, viz. danger'; and 'what hangeth upon us, want'.

It was 'needless and unwise' for Bacon to persuade his fellow members. The King's speech had kindled the fire of the Commons' affection; his graces shone warmly, and they had no need of a little burning-glass. The King had made 'such a track in almost all the points of his prerogative, as the footsteps of King James will ever remain'. James, he continued, hammering home the failure of Salisbury's Great Contract strategy, had 'distinguished between laws of bargain, and mutual affection': bargain 'holdeth hard', while the other 'passeth over itself, and careth for the other'. It was clear to all that 'the King's business and the Commonwealth . . . go together.'[54]

During the debate that followed, the 'animosities and oppositions' within the House showed themselves, although the Commons seemed united in favouring a liberal supply. When the word 'undertaker' was first mentioned, the House went into uproar, with the result that it was decided to defer consideration of the subsidy until after Easter, still ten days away.[55] After the break, a vigorous attempt was made to push it through: as Thomas Lorkin wrote, despite James's advice that

> they were first to provide for the subject's ease before they entered into consideration of the King's relief, these, inverting the order, would have turned the conclusion into a beginning; and were so confident of their own strength, as they called upon Mr. Speaker to have it put to voices. But the grave speeches of Sir Edwin Sandys, Sir Dudley Digges, Sir Thomas Grantham, and some others, quieted that motion, and drew the House to a resolution to do nothing in matters of that nature till they had ordered somewhat for the good of the public.[56]

Bacon was not involved in this attempt to get the subsidy through. He thought it a mistake on the part of the undertakers which betrayed their parliamentary weakness.

When the House reassembled on Monday 2 May, Bacon brought in four Bills of Grace – 'an act for making the estates of attainted persons liable for the payment of their just and true debts'; 'an act giving authority to certain commissioners to review the state of penal laws, to the end that such as are obsolete and snaring may be repealed, and such as are fit to continue and concern one matter, may be reduced respectively into one clear form of law'; 'an act against secret offices and inquisitions to be taken on his Majesty's behalf, to the prejudice of his subjects'; and 'an act for admitting of the King's subjects to plead the general issue, and nevertheless to continue their possessions'. Bacon made no attempt to commend the bills, merely reiterating that in this parliament, 'The King will be no merchant.'[57]

The next business came from a committee concerning the undertakers that had been appointed on 13 April. Sir Roger Owen reported that undertaking was universally condemned but also disclaimed. Other members condemned it as being in violation of an order passed by the last parliament 'that no man but the Speaker might go to the King to confer with him about Parliament business', and declared that 'undertakers, if any, be worse than the Powder-traitors' because they threatened to 'blow up' the House in a subtler manner. To deal with this threat, it was proposed that the powers of the committee should be enlarged 'to examine the undertakers'. Bacon spoke against such a move;[58] but the motion was so popular that it was carried without a division, and a committee of the whole House was ordered for the following Wednesday afternoon. An agitated and unproductive period ensued: ten days after the date set for the examination, nothing had been settled. Personal quarrels had flared in physical scuffles, and the tense situation was resolved only when Sir Henry Neville volunteered his confession, and explained his own share in the 'undertaking'. This, however, turned out to be an unexceptionable share; the House decided not to pursue the matter further, and to turn to other matters.

Inevitably, the question of impositions reared its head. The King had offered to compromise by consenting to an act of parliament limiting his power in future. The Commons were not interested in this compromise, however, and ultimately decided to confer with the Lords. Sir Edwin Sandys reported the main body of the findings on impositions on 12 May, concluding that the crown had no right by law to levy impositions without parliamentary consent. It was proposed that both Houses should present James with a petition to remove impositions, with a remonstrance asserting their right, 'that so, this eased, they might with better judgement and with alacrity proceed to the King's supply, the first end of this Parliament'.[59]

The subject was divided nine ways, each division assigned to a separate speaker, or speakers. Bacon was assigned the first tranche, namely 'the introduction ... a declaration of three steps wherein his Majesty has swerved from all his ancestors': first, time – since even proclamations 'which are but one of the highest extents of prerogative' fall into abeyance at the end of a reign, impositions should not (as James claims) be 'assumed to him and his heirs forever'; second, the sheer multitude of impositions: whereas Mary added two and Elizabeth one, and between Edward III and Mary none were added, 'his Majesty lately in his time multiplied them to more than twice so many hundreds'; and third, 'his claim. Other princes have imposed but never claimed right to do it. They have laid them down upon complaint and ever excused them upon necessity and war.'[60]

Giving this speech (as Sir James Whitelocke put it, 'the introduction of the business, and to set the state of the question') to Bacon was a canny move.[61] He was Attorney-General – a post which only weeks earlier had been deemed unsuitable to be held by a member of parliament because of the postholder's bond with the King – and in April 1606 Bacon himself had spoken in defence of the imposition on currants.[62]

The startling paucity of precedents was queried, and it was moved that more men should be 'specially appointed to search' the records. Mr Hakewill moved that 'the King's learned counsel may be sent for to know whether they know of any such or not, and that they may make their protestation what they know therein'. It would indeed be 'a folly to proceed farther if they could show records that the kings of England may lawfully impose without consent of parliament'. The Attorney, Serjeant and Solicitor were sent for accordingly, and Bacon was then 'generally questioned what records he has seen'. Whereas both Serjeant Montagu and the Solicitor asserted 'that they have seen nor know no records but such as are known in this House', Bacon was less forthcoming. He replied 'that it was not fit for him to tell what records were fit and what were not for this business, but protested he knew not of any' except those which had been delivered to him.[63] Bacon's edgy response may have sent out signals that he knew more about precedents than he was prepared to admit.

When called on to speak, Bacon thanked the House for 'putting this part upon him', which he believed served as 'an argument of their good opinion' of him personally, despite their reservations about his position as Attorney: the 'trust in his person discharged the suspicion of his place'. He argued that there should be a conference between the subcommittees, followed by 'a view . . . to be taken of the records', with each man being 'bounded to his part'.[64]

While the finishing touches were being put to the submission, Bacon had little to do in the Commons. By 21 May the arrangements were complete, and the message of invitation was sent to the Lords. In the meantime, rumours spread suggesting that the Commons had been the subject of some derogatory remarks during the Lords' debate on the matter.

It was said that a bishop had urged the Lords not to give their consent to the conference, since the Lower House should not be meddling in such affairs, and that in doing so they were attacking the crown; a conference would only subject the Lords to talk of mutiny and sedition.[65] The Commons decided to take the matter directly to the King. As Sir Roger Owen defended this decision against the objections of Sir Edwin Sandys, the reply from the Lords arrived – a refusal: 'Their Lordships, having entered into a grave and serious consideration as well of the matter itself as of divers incident and necessary circumstances, did not think it convenient to enter into any conference of that cause concerning the point of Impositions at that time.' Sandys ultimately won the debate, and it was decided not to proceed in any other business until the affair was sorted. A committee was appointed, and debate continued – until another interruption arrived in the form of a letter from the King.

James wanted to know what they meant by 'forbearance of proceeding in all other business' – surely he, not they, called an end to proceedings? The Commons were alarmed by the King's knowledge of events. Somebody had misinformed the King, and a committee should be set up to clear each member in turn. Eventually, a committee was decided upon, once again, to consider how to answer the King's letter, and to survey all misinformations provided to James. The response was answered by James without further mishap.[66]

On Friday 3 June the King let it be known that unless they dealt with his supply immediately, he would dissolve parliament on the following Thursday.[67] When the Commons prevaricated, James informed the House on Monday that parliament would be dissolved on the morrow – two days short of his previous threat – 'unless they should before that time perform what was by his former letters required'. No such performance was forthcoming, and the Addled Parliament was dissolved on Tuesday.

Bacon's growing reticence speaks volumes. Virtually all of his interventions had turned sour. He had been unable to persuade the House to grant a subsidy on 12 April; his introduction of the four Bills of Grace was ignored; his defence of Sir Thomas Parry was unsuccessful. Bacon's voice, as heard in all the fragmentary evidence of this session, was still distinctive – the *Commons' Journal* introduced him before his defence of Parry as 'the heir apparent of eloquence' – but whatever power he had wielded in the Lower House was increasingly undermined by his position as Attorney-General. This was to be his final session in the House of Commons; when he next faced the Lower House it was in even less auspicious circumstances.

★

So parliament ended without a subsidy for the King, but it was not long before an ingenious scheme was devised for circumventing this setback. It was decided that various prominent men would start a subscription of their own, which would soon spread more generally, each man giving of his own free will. The impetus came from the bishops in convocation.

> The Archbishop of Canterbury began with a basin and ewer, and redeemed it with £140, the Bishop of Winchester as much, Ely £120, et *sic de caeteris*. The noblemen followed the example. The Lord Chamberlain and Lord Somerset gave each £200, the earl of Salisbury £300; the rest less but no man more. Master Secretary gave £100, and all officers toward the law or receipt according to their minds, Sir Henry Fanshaw £50, Sir Christopher Hatton as much, the Lord Coke £200 but the rest of the Judges came but slowly after, for I know where some presented but £20 which was refused. The money is paid into the Jewel House.

The next stage was the important one. 'Letters shall be sent into all the shires to see how they will follow the example.'[68]

The end of the parliament was followed, too, by a reshuffle at the top. The earl of Northampton, who had been acting Treasurer since Salisbury's death, suddenly died from a 'venomous' swelling in his thigh. James replaced him without hesitation with the earl of Suffolk, father of Somerset's bride. Somerset himself became Lord Chamberlain. But Bacon's new-found patron was not to last for long.

13

Exchanging Favours:
Somerset to Villiers

> The friendship of ill men . . . may be truly termed conspiracy
> and not friendship.
> *Sir Francis Bacon to the earl of Somerset (May 1616)*

O N 3 AUGUST 1614, a meeting took place that was to change the course of Bacon's life once again. The King's summer progress that year took him to the Northamptonshire seat of Sir Anthony Mildmay, Apethorpe, where he indulged his usual leisure activity of hunting. But his attention was diverted by a new face among the usual royal entourage, belonging to an exceptionally handsome and charming young man of twenty-one. Within a month, news of the new favourite was becoming *passé*: Lord Fenton wrote to tell his cousin but assumed 'I think your Lordship has heard before this time of a youth, his name is Villiers, a Northamptonshire man; he begins to be in favour with His Majesty.'[1]

It is not known when George Villiers first came to Bacon's attention, but given Bacon's eye for the ascendant favourite, and recalling how he had hitched himself to Essex's train even while Leicester was still alive, it is highly probable that it was only shortly after the meeting at Apethorpe. The earliest surviving letters between Villiers and Bacon, dated January 1616, bear witness to an established, familiar relationship in which favours were already expected on both sides. By then Bacon was embroiled in several important disputes concerning the King's relationship to the law; he was also firmly implicated in the spectacular deposing of the King's former favourite, Robert Carr, earl of Somerset; and he was about to achieve the kind of advancement for which he had waited so long – advancement he was to attribute explicitly to Villiers. It is our contention that all these matters – the rise of Villiers, the fall of Somerset, the fall of Coke and the establishment of the King's prerogative – are all inextricably intertwined, and that at the heart of the knot lies the figure of Sir Francis Bacon.

★

In early 1615, Attorney-General Bacon was investigating one of a spate of cases that involved slander against the King or his government.[2] Papers had been found in the course of an investigation (into an alleged libel of a bishop) against Edmund Peacham, a Somerset Puritan minister in his sixties, who held the living of Hinton St George (the Paulets' home parish). They contained a sermon which amounted to an anti-government invective, with text and prayer already prefixed – warning of judgement to come, the King's sudden death, the massacre of his officers, uprisings of the people. The discussion of state proceedings was so detailed that it was clear that Peacham had a source high up in the government apparatus. The Privy Council studied the papers, and deemed them treacherous; Peacham was committed to the Tower of London and, for the libel of the bishop, deprived of his orders.

Examined before the Archbishop of Canterbury and the other Privy Councillors, Peacham admitted that the papers were in his own handwriting. His examiners were unconvinced by his protestations that he alone was involved, certain that he was merely holding back the names of others – Winwood thought him not, 'as was related, stupid or dull, but to be full of malice and craft'. Accordingly, on 18 January, his examiners (including Bacon) issued a warrant which allowed his investigators, if they found him still 'obstinate and perverse and not otherwise willing or ready to tell the truth, then to put him to the manacles, as in your discretion you shall see occasion'.[3]

James approved the resolution of the Council, and decided to ascertain the opinions of the judges on the point of law. But, in a novel move, he wanted to take the opinions of the judges individually, 'distributing ourselves and enjoining secrecy', as Bacon put it. When the King's letter was read to the Council table on 27 January, it came up against opposition in the form of Sir Edward Coke, who claimed that 'such particular and (as he called it) *auricular* taking of opinions was not according to the custom of this realm; and seemed to divine that his brethren would never do it'. Bacon replied to Sir Edward that it was their duty to pursue the King's instructions, and so it was 'not amiss for his Lordship to leave his brethren to their own answers'.

Bacon's colleagues reported success with the judges, who were happy to be consulted individually.[4] But when Bacon attended Coke shortly after, he found that the Chief Justice continued to object to the procedure, and to insist that 'Judges were not to give opinion by fractions, but entirely according to the vote whereupon they should settle upon conference; and that this auricular taking of opinions, single and apart, was new and dangerous; and other words more vehement than I repeat.'

Faced with Bacon's attempts to sway him – citing statute precedent of

25 Edward III (*'Imaginatus est et compassavit mortem et finalem destructionem domini regis'*), which specified that the King's death could be 'compassed and imagined' 'by disabling his regiment, and making him appear to be incapable or indign to reign', which covered Peacham's treason[5] – Coke denied Bacon's premise, opining 'that no words of scandal or defamation, importing that the King was utterly unworthy to govern, were treason, except they disabled his title'.[6] Bacon was finally at a loss as to what to advise, and forwarded 'my lord Coke's answers' to the King: 'I will not call them rescripts, much less oracles.'[7]

Coke's verdict notwithstanding, the crown decided to proceed against Peacham – a lengthy process, which ended with Peacham dying in Taunton prison, maintaining that he had had no intention of publishing the writings.[8] But Coke's opposition to the prosecution would not be forgotten.

★

While Bacon argued with Coke, Sir George Villiers continued his meteoric rise at court, aided and abetted by those courtiers who had had enough of Somerset. Knowing that James had a fancy that his Queen should recommend men into his favour, the Archbishop of Canterbury, George Abbot, asked Anne for her support of Villiers. One report has it that, understandably, 'she was utterly averse from it, having before been stung with favourites; but by her observation of Villiers, she told the Archbishop, she saw that in him, that if he became a favourite, he would become more intolerable than any that were before him.' Anne informed Abbot that 'he among the rest would live to repent it. If this young man be once brought in, the first persons that he will plague must be you that labour for him; yea, I shall have my part also, the King will teach him to despise and hardly entreat us all.'[9] Eventually she relented, and on 23 April 1615 entered into her husband's bedchamber and asked that he make Villiers a Groom of the Bedchamber; the appointment duly followed.

Anne's involvement perhaps points to her understanding of the power that Villiers was likely to wield. The relationship between King, Queen and favourite was strangely intimate, with a shared language of nicknames. Anne would write to thank Villiers for his care of her husband: 'My kind dog, I have received your letter which is very welcome to me. You do very well in lugging [pulling] the sow's ear, and I thank you for it, and would have you do so still upon condition that you continue a watchful dog and be always true to him, so wishing you all happiness, Anna R.'[10]

Villiers' rise was inevitably seen as the beginning of the end for Somerset. But no one could have foreseen just how rapid the fall of the redundant favourite would be. In the late summer of 1615, word reached Secretary of State Sir Ralph Winwood that Sir Thomas Overbury, Somerset's friend who had died suddenly in the Tower on 15 September 1613, had in fact been poisoned by persons inside the Tower. The Keeper of the Tower, Sir Gervase Elwes, was summoned, and admitted that the deputy keeper Richard Weston had planned to poison Overbury but that he had been discovered and his plans scotched. On submitting a written account, however, Sir Gervase admitted that he had heard that Overbury had been victim to an arsenic-laden enema, administered by an apothecary's boy. Elwes had not spoken of this because he was afraid of impeaching 'great persons' – no less great than the earl and countess of Somerset themselves.

The King ordered a full inquiry on 13 October, to be headed by Lord Chief Justice Sir Edward Coke. James's speed in acting speaks volumes for his decaying relationship with his one-time favourite. Since Somerset's marriage at Christmas 1613 the favourite had become increasingly difficult to manage – unlike the pliable young George Villiers, who was also, despite her early reservations, now a favourite of Queen Anne, as Somerset had never been. Coke's commission of inquiry uncovered several attempts to poison Overbury before the enema, originating in the Tower's kitchens, and in particular with a woman named Mrs Turner, who had links with the countess of Somerset.

Mrs Turner, Weston and Elwes were arrested. Somerset, unnerved by the sudden interest in the case, left the King at Royston and hurried to London to clear his name, complaining to James of the composition of the commission of inquiry and threatening that the throne would lose the support of his wife's family, the Howards, if the investigation continued. James was implacable, and on 17 October the Somersets were ordered to remain in their (respective) apartments; the following day the earl was removed to the Dean of Westminster's house.

The minor players were dealt with first. Confessing, they were hanged in early November. But more revelations were to come. It was discovered that all those parties already mentioned had been placed in position only just before Overbury had been arrested. The arrest itself had been a deliberate, staged manoeuvre by some of Overbury's enemies who, incensed by his refusal to take the diplomatic post abroad they had arranged, had him imprisoned on a charge of contempt.

Overbury had been an intimate friend and counsellor of Robert Carr until 1611 or 1612. Carr, then Viscount Rochester, had fallen in love with Frances Howard, the wife of the third earl of Essex, daughter of the earl of Suffolk, and a great-niece of the earl of Northampton. The countess contrived to have her marriage with Essex annulled on the grounds that the earl was impotent, so that she might marry Rochester. Overbury disapproved of the match, which would no doubt restrict his influence over

Rochester, and informed the happy couple of his feelings. The countess retaliated, it was alleged, with the poison plot.

In the months immediately following Overbury's strange decease, all had gone according to plan for Rochester and his beloved countess. The Essex marriage was annulled in September; two months later Viscount Rochester was made earl of Somerset; and in December the couple were married – with, as we have seen, Bacon footing the bill for the celebratory *Maske of Flowers*. Somerset continued to grow in favour with James, adding to his list of honours the title of Treasurer of Scotland and succeeding Northampton in 1614 as Lord Keeper of the Privy Seal.

Now the bubble had burst. The countess quickly confessed her guilt when the murder inquiry was turned in her direction. Somerset, on the other hand, denied that he had been complicit in the affair. The crown case against him, lacking a confession, rested on interpretations of his behaviour during the inquiry – most notably, on the evening of his detention, when he burned letters he had written to Northampton at the time Overbury died. He had asked Sir Robert Cotton to alter the dates of letters received from Overbury and Northampton; he had sent officers of the law to Weston's house, to take away certain letters between Weston and Mrs Turner; and he had got a message to Turner while he was under arrest.

Somerset pleaded with James to have the investigation cancelled, but the King was adamant, saying that he could not allow such a crime 'to be suppressed and plastered over': 'In a business of this nature, I have nothing to look unto but first my conscience before God, and next my reputation in the eyes of the world. If the delation [accusation] prove false, God so deal with my soul as no man among you shall so much rejoice at it as I.'[11] The farewell scene between the King and his favourite was documented at length. 'When he came to take his leave of the King, he [James] embraced and kissed him often, wished him to make haste back, showed an extreme passion to be without him; and his back was no sooner turned, but he said with a smile, "I shall never see thy face more." '[12]

It was at this late stage that Bacon became involved. On 25 October, several friends of Somerset – including Sir Thomas Wentworth, Sir John Holles and Thomas Lumsden, 'all my particular friends', claimed Bacon – were arrested for questioning Richard Weston on the scaffold as to whether Overbury had indeed been poisoned, effectively calling into question the crown's proceedings. As Attorney-General, Bacon was called over to deliver a charge against these friends in the Star Chamber on 10 November, of 'a misdemeanour of a high nature, tending to the defacing of justice in a great cause capital'. He used the occasion to set the stage for the major trials still to come. God had 'raised an occasion' for a display of James's 'virtue of justice', by erecting 'as it were a stage or theatre, much to his honour, for him to show it and act it, in the pursuit of the violent and untimely death of Sir Thomas Overbury, and therein cleansing the land from blood'. The King's love of justice firmly established, Bacon went on to condemn poisoning as 'one of the highest offences in guiltiness' and 'the basest of all others in the mind of the offenders', being easily committed and easily concealed, an Italian crime, the arrow that flies by night and discerns not whom it hits. Poison itself, because it 'tendeth to the utter subversion and dissolution of human society, is in the nature of high treason'.

Overbury himself was not of importance. 'I knew the gentleman. It is true, his mind was great, but it moved not in any great good order; yet certainly it did commonly fly at good things. And the greatest fault that ever I heard by he was, that he made his friend his idol. But I leave him as Sir Thomas Overbury.' What aggravated the situation was Overbury's status as the King's prisoner, which made the state responsible for making good his body. Anything happening to a defenceless prisoner in the Tower, 'in custody and preservation of law', would cast 'an aspersion and a reflexion upon the State itself'. Bacon reserved his especial contempt for the manner in which Overbury was 'chased to death . . . by poison after poison, first rosaker [realgar], then arsenic, then mercury sublimate, then sublimate again; it is a thing would astonish man's nature to hear it.'

James, from the outset, he reported, 'did forerank and make it his prime direction, that it should be carried without touch to any that was innocent. Nay more, not only without impeachment, but without aspersion. Which was a most noble and a princely caution from his Majesty.' Men's reputations were to be particularly respected in this case,

> because it met with two great persons; a nobleman that his Majesty had favoured and advanced, and his Lady being of a great and honourable house (though I think it be true, that the writers say, that there is no pomegranate so fair or so sound, but may have a perished kernel). Nay, I see plainly, that in those excellent papers of his Majesty's own handwriting, being as so many beams of justice issuing from that virtue which doth so much shine in him; I say, I see it was so evenly carried without prejudice, whether it were a true accusation of the one part, or a practice of a false accusation of the other, as showed plainly that his Majesty's judgment was *tanquam tabula rasa*, as a clean pair of tables, and his ear *tanquam janua aperta*, not side open, but wide open to truth, as it should be discovered.

Indeed, the King had initially deemed the first reports not 'an information, but a rumour'.

James's conduct in the whole affair, the 'strength and resolution' of his justice in a case which did not touch him personally, had been exemplary. 'I think I may truly affirm, that there was never in this kingdom, nor in any other kingdom, the death of a private gentleman vindicated *cum tanto muto regni*, or to say better *cum tantu plausu regni*. If it had concerned the King or Prince, there could not have been better nor greater commissioners. The term hath been almost turned into a *justitium*, or vacancy; the people themselves being more willing to be lookers-on in this business, than proceeders in their own. There hath been no care of discovery omitted, nor no moment of time lost.' The fact that Somerset was involved only strengthened this appraisal of the King's behaviour: 'the King hath to his great honour showed, that were any man, in such a case of blood, as the signet of his right hand, (as the Scripture says,) he would put him off.'[13]

★

While Bacon conducted the show trial on the King's behalf, laying the groundwork for the removal of Somerset and the imposition of Villiers, Coke, still smarting from the confrontation over Peacham, found another occasion to challenge (this time indirectly) James's entitlement to grant financially lucrative favours. He annulled a patent for making writs in the Court of Common Pleas granted by James to a Groom of his Bedchamber, John Murray.[14] Three or four years earlier, Murray had procured a new patent office for John Michell, granting him the sole making of writs of *supersedeas quia improvide emanavit* in the Common Pleas. This diminished the profits taken by the Protonotary, who eventually 'brought an assize' to be restored to the possession of the ancient fees belonging to his office, thus calling the legality of Michell's patent into question. Ever vigilant on the King's behalf, Bacon thought this a question in which the King had an interest, and which according to the 'ancient and evercontinued law of the Crown' should be tried 'before the King himself as he is represented in Chancery'.[15] Therefore, when the assize was brought in Coke's King's Bench, Bacon tried to stop the proceeding by a writ *de non procedendo ad assisam Rege inconsulto* (concerning the not taking of cases to assize without consulting the King): the writ's validity was disputed, counsel heard on both sides in Trinity Term, and a further hearing was set for Monday 20 November.

Unfortunately, this landed right in the midst of the Overbury investigation, and on the Friday before the due date for the hearing Bacon asked the King for a postponement, thinking it 'not a very fit time to proceed in this business of the *Rege inconsulto* [the King not having been consulted]. I did think those greater causes would have come to period or pause sooner: but now they are in the height; and to have so great a matter as this of the *Rege inconsulto* handled when men do *aliud agere* [get immersed in other things], I think it no proper time.' He also pointed out that this affair was 'somewhat against the stream of the Judges' inclination: and it is no part of a skilful mariner to sail or row against a tide, when the tide is at strongest.' He requested James to write to Coke to say that he would postpone the hearing until Coke was '*animo sedato et libero* [calmer], and not in the midst of his assiduous and incessant cares and industries in other practices'.[16]

The hearing was therefore postponed, leaving Coke and Bacon poised against one another, respectively against and for the King. As it turned out, the prosecution against the Somersets was also postponed, partly because the countess was in the last stages of a pregnancy – which came successfully to term on 9 December.

Meanwhile, on 4 January 1616, Villiers added a new honour to his ever-growing list: the title Master of the Horse. This, perhaps more than any other, testified to his growing influence over the King. The post, which involved overseeing the King's stables and horses, came with its own staff of two hundred, and an unexceptionable cash sum per annum. But its significance went way beyond its tangible rewards. Ever since Elizabeth had appointed the young Robert Dudley to be her Master of the Horse, and to be the first to follow her on her entry into London in January 1559, the post had taken on a very particular charge. It was Essex's promotion into the mastership that had been seen to seal the switch of Elizabeth's emotions from the old incumbent Leicester to his young step-son. Moreover, Robert Carr, despite a concerted campaign in 1612, had not succeeded in gaining the place, making Villiers' acquisition of it all the more remarkable.

Finally, on 19 January 1616, the Somersets were indicted for procuring and consenting to Overbury's murder, as accessories before the fact. As Bacon informed the King, while the evidence against Somerset might be 'of a good strong thread', it was still essential that 'the thread must be well spun and woven together. For your Majesty knoweth it is one thing to deal with a jury of Middlesex and Londoners, and another to deal with the Peers; whose objects perhaps will not be so much what is before them in the present case (which I think is as odious to them as to the vulgar) but what may be hereafter.' They were also faced with the disadvantages that the evidence adduced would have lost its freshness, and heightened expectations might not be met. He asked James to 'be careful to choose a Steward of judgment, that may be able to moderate the evidence and cut off digressions; for I may interrupt, but I cannot silence.' He also asked that there be 'special care taken for the ordering of the evidence, not only for the knitting, but for the list, and (to use your Majesty's own word) the confining of it', either by James himself, or by Ellesmere, Coke and Bacon. There was time for a sideswipe at Coke – 'whose great travels as I much commend, yet that same *plerophoria*, or over-confidence, doth always subject things to a great deal of chance'.[17]

But the Somerset arraignment was again postponed: this time because Coke announced that Sir John Digby, whom James had sent to Spain to negotiate a marriage between Prince Charles and the Infanta Maria, had information suggesting that Somerset had been involved in secret dealings with the Spanish ambassador, Sarmiento. Digby was called back to explain his comments and the murder prosecution was suspended. In the lapse, the John Murray *Rege inconsulto* case was resumed on Thursday 25 January, and Bacon spoke in the King's Bench for the King's interest.[18] Subsequently he wrote modestly, 'Of myself I will say nothing, but my argument was wholly upon book law and records, and that my voice served me well for two hours and a half; and yet as they tell me I lost not one auditor that was present in the beginning, but stayed till the later end. If I should say more, there were too many witnesses (for I never saw the court more full) that mought disprove me.' Even Coke was 'pleased to say, that it was a famous argument'.

To James, Bacon announced proudly: 'Sire, I do partly perceive, that I have not only stopped, but almost turned the stream; and I see how things cool by this, that the Judges that were wont to call so hotly upon the business, when they had heard me, of themselves, took a fortnights-day to advise what they will do; by which time the term will be at an end; and I know they little expected to have the matter so beaten down with book-law, upon which my argument wholly went, so that every mean student was satisfied.' But he also begged the King, 'because the times are as they are', to renew his order given to the Lord Chief Justice in the Michaelmas Term – namely, 'that after he had heard your Attorney (which now is done,) he should forbear furder proceeding till he had spoken with your Majesty'.

Bacon spelled out why the case was important to James. It was not merely the particular case of Murray that was at stake – the ruling (which was still pending) would have consequences for fourteen separate patents dating from his own and Elizabeth's reign; but 'chiefly, because this writ is a mean provided by the ancient law of England, to bring any case that may concern your Majesty, in profit or power from the ordinary benches, to be tried and judged before your Chancellor of England, by the ordinary and legal part of his power. And your Majesty knoweth your Chancellor is ever a principal councillor and instrument of monarchy, of immediate dependence upon the King: and therefore like to be a safe and tender guardian of the regal rights.'[19]

While the Somerset prosecution and the *Rege inconsulto* case rumbled on, another front opened on which battle could be conducted – this time between Ellesmere's Court of Chancery and Coke's King's Bench. Judgement had been given in the King's Bench against a man who had been swindled by a fraudulent creditor. He appealed against the decision, only to have it upheld; he then appealed to the Court of Chancery, which reversed the decision in his favour, and imprisoned the creditor. Coke promptly issued a writ of *habeas corpus* to secure the release of the creditor, and to bring the case back into the jurisdiction of the King's Bench.[20] Bacon saw the Somerset inquiry as a useful diversion from this battle of the courts: Ellesmere and Coke's common employment in examining Somerset 'is such a *vinculum* [bond], as they will not square while those matters are in hand, so that there is *altum silentium* [a lofty silence] of that matter.'[21]

In fact, Sir Edward was still busy with the case, investigating the possible applications of the fourteenth-century law of *praemunire*, which had originally been intended to prevent appeals from English courts to Rome. Coke reinterpreted the statute, claiming that it forbade appeals to *any other court* except the High Court of Parliament. On 12 February, armed with this strategy, he secured indictments of *praemunire* against the appellant, and every Chancery officer who had been involved in the proceedings – plaintiffs, counsellors, solicitors and clerks. These indictments failed, because Coke could not satisfy the grand jury that there was a *prima facie* case to be answered, but he was not about to let the case drop. Chancery and the King's Bench were at war.

On 15 February Bacon informed the King that Ellesmere was recovering from a recent illness; but as he was 'glad to advertise your Majesty of the amendment of your Chancellor's person, so I am sorry to accompany it with an advertisement of the sickness of your Chancery court, though (by the grace of God) that cure will be much easier than the other'. He realised he had had 'too reasonable thoughts' when he thought Ellesmere and Coke's joint involvement in the Somerset case 'would so join them as they would not square at this time'. He argued now that what had happened on the last day of term 'is not so much as is voiced abroad: and therefore I beseech your Majesty not to give any believing ear to reports, but to receive the truth from me that am your Attorney-General and ought to stand indifferent for jurisdictions of all courts.' Unfortunately, since he had been absent (he does not specify where or why), he could not provide such a report immediately, and others who were 'properly and authentically to inform me touching that which passed' were also away. But he begged James not to let this 'any ways disjoint your other business, for there is a time for all things, and this very accident may be turned to good . . . some good occasion by this excess may be taken to settle that which would have been more dangerous if it had gone on by little and little.'[22]

To Villiers, Bacon wrote: 'In this difference between the two courts of Chancery and King's Bench (for so I had rather take it for this time, than between the persons of my Lord Chancellor and my Lord Chief Justice) I marvel not if rumour get way of true relation. For I know fame hath swift wings, specially that which hath black feathers.' He hoped that this affair would 'rather rouse and raise [the Lord Chancellor's] spirits, than deject him or incline him to a relapse,'[23] and was gratified to find that 'this business of the Chancery hath stirred him. He sheweth to despise it, but he is full of it, and almost like a young duellist that findeth himself behind-hand.'

Properly informed, Bacon wrote to the King to give James his verdict on the affair. He put it down to 'errors of servants', and more specifically, an error of Lord Chief Justice Coke. 'I account this a kind of sickness of my Lord Coke's, that comes almost in as ill a time as the sickness of my Lord Chancellor. And as I think it was one of the wisest parts that ever he played when he went down to your Majesty to Royston, and desired to have my Lord Chancellor joined with him; so this was one of the weakest parts that ever he played, to make all the world perceive that my Lord Chancellor is severed from him at this time.'

Bacon now had his old adversary squarely in his sights, but he nevertheless proceeded with some circumspection. 'My Lord Coke at this time is not to be disgraced,' he reasoned, 'both because he is so well habituate for that which remaineth of these capital causes, and also for that which I find is in his breast touching your finances and matters of repair of your estate. And (if I mought speak it) as I think it were good his hopes were at end in some kind, so I could wish they were raised in some other.' On the other hand, 'this great and public affront, not only to the reverend and well deserving person of your Chancellor (and at a time when he was thought to lie on dying, which was barbarous), but to your high court of Chancery, which is the court of your absolute power, may not (in my opinion) pass lightly, nor end only in some formal atonement; but use is to be made thereof for the settling of your authority and strengthening of your prerogative according to the true rules of monarchy.'

Reconciling these two opinions ('which seem almost opposite') was no easy task, but Bacon had his suggestions ready. First, James might not see Coke as in 'any way aforehand privy to that which was done, or that he did set it or animate it, but only took the matter as it came before him': in this way, 'his error was only that at such a time he did not divert it in some good manner' – although, Bacon conceded, 'I confess it to be suspicious.' Secondly, if the rumours proved true that one of the puisne judges had 'stir[red] this business' or had gone so far as to 'openly revile and menace the jury', then he should be dismissed. Indeed, 'to be plain with your Majesty, I do not think there is anything a greater *polychreston* [general benefit], *ad multa utile* to your affairs, than upon a just and fit occasion to make some example against the presumption of a judge in causes that concern your Majesty, whereby the whole body of those magistrates may be contained in better awe.' If no one person could be found at fault, then he suggested that 'the Judges should answer it upon their knees before your Majesty or your Council, and receive a sharp admonition.'

As regards 'the main point of the jurisdiction', Bacon had two suggestions for his sovereign:

> The one, that your Majesty take this occasion to redouble unto all your Judges your ancient and true charge and rule, that you will endure no innovating the point of jurisdiction, but will have every court impaled within their own precedents, and not assume to themselves new powers upon conceits and inventions of law; The other, that in these high causes that touch upon State and Monarchy, your Majesty give them strait charge, that upon any occasions intervenient hereafter, they do not make the vulgar party to their contestations by public handling them, before they have consulted with your Majesty, to whom the reglement of those things only appertaineth.

Finally, Bacon urged that there should be no thought of continuing with the arraignments until these matters 'be somewhat accommodate' and Ellesmere and Coke had been 'some outward and superficial reconciliation at least', since that 'accident is a banquet to all Somerset's friends. But this is a thing that falleth out naturally of itself, in respect of the Judges going circuit, and my Lord Chancellor's infirmity with hope of recovery. And although this protraction of time may breed some doubt of mutability, yet I have lately learned out of an excellent letter of a certain king, That the sun showeth sometimes watery to our eyes, but when the cloud is gone the sun is as before.'[24]

Capitalising on his influence with the King, he once again stepped up his bid for preferment, sending a paper to John Murray, 'a little remembrance of some things past, concerning my honest and faithful services to his Majesty; not by way of boasting (from which I am far), but as tokens of my studying his service uprightly and carefully'. Ellesmere told him on 20 February 'that if the King would ask his opinion touching the person that he would commend to succeed him upon death or disability, he would name me for the fittest man'. But the chance of becoming Lord Chancellor was fading fast as Ellesmere recovered his health.

Now might be the time, though, to set about getting himself the place at the Council table which had for so long eluded him. On the same day that he wrote to the King about Coke, 21 February, he also penned a letter to assure himself of the continuing support of Villiers, noting that with 'My Lord Chancellor's health growing with the days, and his resignation being an incertainty, I would be glad you went on with my first motion, my swearing privy councillor. This I desire not so much to make myself more sure of the other [the Lord Chancellorship] and to put it past competition (for herein I rest wholly upon the King and your excellent self), but because I find hourly that I need this strength in his Majesty's service.' He urged Villiers to make use of Ellesmere's statement of confidence in him, and to 'call for the paper, which is with Mr. John Murray, and to find a fit time that his Majesty may cast an eye upon it'. Six days later, he put further pressure on the young favourite, begging him 'not to think me over-hasty or much in appetite, if I put you in remembrance of my motion of strengthening me with the oath and trust of a privy councillor'. The timing was crucial: 'Sure I am, there were never times which did more require a King's Attorney to be well armed, and (as I said once to you) to wear a gauntlet and not a glove. The arraignments, when they proceed; the contention between the Chancery and the King's Bench; the great cause of the *Rege inconsulto*, which is so precious to the King's prerogative; divers other services which concern the King's revenue and the repair of his estate.' If the circumstances alone did not warrant it, there was also the matter of his improved position *vis-à-vis* the King. 'I see it pleaseth his Majesty to accept well of my relations touching his business, which may seem a kind of interloping (as the merchants call it) for one that is no councillor.'[25]

A month passed; then, at the end of March, during an audience, James finally expressed his favour to Bacon in promising terms, 'in favour far above that I can deserve or could expect'. Bacon's moment of glory was ruined, however, by the unexpected entry of Prince Charles, which diverted his father's attention. Bacon was forced to put in writing a 'few lines of acknowledgement' to remind the King of his hopes. 'I am afraid of nothing but that your Master of the Horse, your excellent servant, and I shall fall out about this, who shall hold your stirrup best. But were you mounted and seated without difficulties and distastes in your business, as I desire and hope to see you, I should *ex animo* desire to spend the decline of my years in my studies: wherein also I should not forget to do him honour, who besides his active and politic virtues is the best pen of kings, much more the best subject of a pen.'[26]

★

Sir John Digby arrived back in England from Spain on 21 March 1616, to be met with a barrage of questions from Coke; he soon protested to the King that the matters on which Coke 'desired to receive satisfaction' had 'no relation' to the Somerset case, and intimated his opinion

> that the coming of this letter unto my Lord Coke's hands hath been the cause of his aggravating matters very far; for he having found mention made of the discovery of your Majesty's service, of great sums of money bestowed upon your Majesty's principal ministers, of Spanish pensioners, of the selling of my despatches, etc., either conjectured these things to have been absolutely held back from your Majesty, or else, lighting upon them in the prosecution of the business concerning my Lord of Somerset, made a wrong application of them to him.

Digby had little to say of Somerset beyond 'his careless manner of keeping those papers and secrets committed unto him by your Majesty, as likewise his treating with the Spanish ambassador in the business of the marriage, both without your Majesty's privity, and clear in a contrary manner to that which your Majesty had signified unto me was your pleasure should be held'. But he did provide a new lead:

> It is likely much may be added by the light that may be gathered from Sir Robert Cotton, if he may be examined concerning all the particulars in which he was employed by my Lord of Somerset to the Spanish Ambassador; both how far he therein used your Majesty's name, as likewise what hopes and promises were given for the effecting of the said match, and especially whether by my Lord of Somerset's directions he discovered not certain propositions and demands in point of religion, which in great secrecy I had sent unto your Majesty; as likewise, what other advertisement of mine he acquainted the Spanish ambassador withal.[27]

Bacon and Ellesmere subsequently requisitioned Coke's previous examinations of Cotton, and conferred with Digby. They found Digby 'ready and willing to discover unto us what he knew', even going so far as to prepare 'some heads of examination in writing for Sir Robert Cotton'; but he remained 'somewhat reserved' on the subjects of the prince's conveyance into Spain and the Spanish pensions, since these were matters that, on the King's instruction, 'he was restrained to keep in silence, and that he conceived they could no ways be applied to Somerset.' Bacon applied to Villiers to remedy this obstacle by providing the King's warrant 'with all convenient speed', since he and Ellesmere believed that it might indeed 'have a great connexion with the examination of Somerset'. Who more likely than Somerset to be a Spanish pensioner, 'considering his mercenary nature, his great undertaking for Spain in the match, and his favour with his Majesty'?[28] Cotton was examined over two days, but found 'hitherto but empty, save only in the great point of the treaty with Spain'; nevertheless, when the King's warrant arrived on Friday morning 'for communicating to us the secrets of the pensions', there were further questions to be asked not only of Cotton, but also of Somerset and Sir William Monson, younger brother of the Keeper of the Tower, whom Digby had named as the best source of information about the Spanish ambassador Sarmiento's alleged links with the countess of Somerset.

Once again, proceedings were stalled – this time by the illness of the duke of Lennox, whose involvement, it was thought, 'should sweeten the cup of medicine, he being his [Somerset's] countryman and friend'. They also needed to know whether James wanted them to start examining Sir William Monson, and if so, 'then his Majesty may be pleased to direct his commandment and warrant to my Lord Chief Justice to deliver unto me the examinations he took of Sir William Monson, that those, joined to the information which we have received from Mr. Vice-Chamberlain [Digby], may be full instructions unto us for his examination.' The warrant was granted, and delivered on the evening of Monday 15 April; Bacon promptly wrote to Coke requesting the transcripts, praying him 'either [to] send them presently sealed up by your servant, or if you think it needful I will come to you myself and receive them with mine own hands'.[29] At a policy meeting, he taunted Coke that since the enquiries into Somerset's alleged Spanish connections had hit a brick wall, the entire case was founded on evidence which was now not going to be used. Coke denied this angrily, but the fact was that his position as chief investigator was being usurped.[30]

When Bacon, Ellesmere and Lennox examined Somerset at the Tower on 17 April, it was without Coke. They covered the articles specified by the King, and the information revealed by Cotton and Digby. They found the earl 'full of protestations, and would fain keep that quarter towards Spain: using but this for argument, that he had such fortunes from his Majesty, as he could not think of bettering his conditions from Spain, because as he said he was no military man. He cometh nothing so far on (for that which concerneth the treaty) as Cotton, which doth much aggravate suspicion against him.' At length, Ellesmere hinted at the gravity of his situation: Somerset appeared 'little moved with it, and pretended carelessness of life, since ignominy had made him unfit for his Majesty's service'. Bacon expressed to Villiers his opinion 'that the fair usage of him, as it was fit for the Spanish examinations, and for the questions touching the papers and dispatches, and all that, so it was no good preparative to make him descend into himself touching his present danger. And therefore my Lord Chancellor and myself thought not good to insist upon it at this time.'[31]

The arraignment, scheduled for 29 April, was postponed to 6 May, 'or God knows when,' as John Chamberlain remarked,

> for the world apprehends that these delays are to some such end: the rather for that there is a new commission to examine and proceed in this cause, wherein the Lord Chief Justice is omitted, and on Wednesday last and this day the Lord Chancellor, the Duke of Lennox and the Attorney General have been at the Tower to examine the Lord of Somerset, not contenting themselves with what the Lord Coke hath done before, who meddles no more since he delivered his papers and examination to the Attorney, to draw the process and inform thereupon.

At the same time, Chamberlain commented on Villiers' steady rise: 'Sir George Villiers hath been crasie [ill] of late not without suspicion of the smallpox, which if it had fallen out *actum erat de amicitia* [was caused by friendship]: but it proves otherwise and we say there is much casting about how to make him a great man, and that he shall be now made of the Garter but *non credo* [I don't believe it].' There was certainly popular sentiment against the King and his favourites:

> His great friend and favourite Sir John Grimes a known courtier died about a fortnight since, and was solemnly buried in the night at Westminster with better than 200 torches, the Duke of Lennox, the Lord Fenton, the Lord of Roxborough and all the grand Scottish men accompanying him; in apish imitation whereof (as it was suggested) certain rude knaves thereabout buried a dog with great solemnity in Tothill Field by night with good store of links which was so heinously taken that divers of them have been whipped by order from the Council, though upon examination the matter proved not so much in derogation of the Scots, seeing some of them were found to be ringleaders in that foolery.[32]

Effectively relieved of his duties in the Somerset case, Coke turned his attentions instead to a case pending in the courts which once again hinged on the King's absolute prerogative to bestow offices and favours. This time he lit upon a living which had been granted by James to one of his bishops *in commendam*, to be held alongside his existing bishopric: this living, ostensibly held only until a suitable cleric could be found to fill it permanently, was thus a sinecure that provided extra income for the recipient of this royal favour. In this case, an action had been brought against the bishop, disputing the right of presentation; this was adjourned into the Exchequer Chamber, where Bacon argued for the King's right on 20 April, the first Saturday of the new term (the case had been postponed from Hilary Term). The Bishop of Winchester (a Privy Councillor), who was present at the King's command, asserted that Serjeant Chibborne, arguing against the King's right, 'had maintained divers positions and assertions very prejudicial to his Majesty's prerogative royal', namely: 'that the translation of Bishops was against the canon law, and for authority vouched the canons of the Council of Sardis'; 'that the King had no power to grant Commendams, but in case of necessity'; 'that there could be no necessity, because there was no need of augmentation of livings, for no man was bound to keep hospitality above his means'.

Bacon wrote to the King that he had thought that 'in a cause that concerned your Majesty and your royal power', and particularly when the judges had 'heard your Attorney-General argue the Saturday before', they 'would of themselves have taken further time to be advised'. Indeed, if his memory did not fail him, had not Coke himself received from his Majesty 'a precedent commandment in Hilary term, That both in the *Rege inconsulto*, and in the Commendams, your Attorney should be heard to speak, and then stay to be made of further proceeding, till my Lord had spoken with your Majesty'?

Winchester reported to James, who, 'apprehending the matter to be of so high a nature, commanded his Attorney-General to signify his Majesty's pleasure to the Lord Chief Justice'.[33] At James's command, Bacon wrote a letter to Coke to signify the King's pleasure that the day appointed for the judges to deliver their arguments (Saturday 27 April) should be put off until he had spoken with them, and delivered the letter during the evening of Thursday 25 April.[34] On Coke's (verbal) suggestion that the other judges should hear this statement from Bacon himself, Bacon promptly wrote three letters on Friday to the Judges of the Common Pleas, the Barons of the Exchequer and the other three King's Bench judges. Having done this, he assumed that everything was in place:

> This was all I did, and thought all had been sure; in so much as the same day being appointed in Chancery for your Majesty's great cause . . . I writ two other letters to both the Chief Justices, to put them in mind of assisting my Lord Chancellor at the hearing. And when my Lord Chancellor himself took some notice upon that occasion, openly in the Chancery, that the Commendams could not hold, presently after I heard the Judges were gone about the Commendams, which I thought at first had been only to adjourn the court. But I heard after that they proceeded to argument.

Presumably, Bacon mused, 'they must either except to the nature of the commandment, or to the credence thereof':

> For if they should stand upon the general ground, *Nulli negabimus, nulli differemus justitiam* [we will neither deny nor postpone justice for any],

it receiveth two answers. The one, that reasonable and mature advice may not be confounded with delay; and that they can well allege when it pleaseth them. The other is, that there is a great difference between a case merely between subject and subject, and where the King's interest is in question directly or by consequence. As for the Attorney's place and commission, it is as proper for him to signify the King's pleasure to his Judges, as for the Secretary to signify the same to the Privy Council; and so it hath ever been.

Bacon reported back to James: 'I do think it fit to advertise your Majesty what hath passed, the rather because I suppose the Judges, since they perform not your commandment, have at least given your Majesty their reasons of their failing therein; I being to answer for the doing your Majesty's commandment, and they for the not doing.' Something was afoot: 'These things were a little strange, if there came not so many of them together, as the one maketh the other seem less strange. But your Majesty hath fair occasions to remedy all with small aid. I say no more for the present.' But he did say one thing more: 'I was a little plain with my Lord Coke in these matters, and when his answer was, that he knew all these things, I said he could never profit too much in knowing himself and his duty.'[35]

On 27 April the judges, led by Coke, replied in a letter to the King, enclosing Bacon's letter to Coke. They did not know what information had been made available to the King. As far as they were concerned, Bacon's letter proposed the hindering of the judicial system in a case between private subjects – which was 'contrary to law' (as they construed two acts of parliament, 25 Edward III and 25 Henry VIII). They had therefore proceeded with hearing the case.[36]

James noted their objections, but pointed out that he had never urged the delay of justice, and therefore 'ye may easily persuade yourselves that it was no small reason that moved us to send you that direction.' He chided them for explaining the nature of their oath, 'for although we never studied the common law of England, yet are we not ignorant of any points which belong to a King to know'. While he was 'far from crossing or delaying any thing which may belong to the interest of any private parties in this case', he could not be 'contented to suffer the prerogative royal of our crown to be wounded through the sides of a private person'. He directed them – so that his prerogative would not be wounded, 'which we account to be wounded as well if it be publicly disputed upon, as if any sentence were given against it' – 'that since the prerogative of our crown hath been more boldly dealt withal in Westminster Hall during the time of our reign, than ever it was before in the reigns of divers princes immediately preceding us, that we will no longer endure that popular and unlawful liberty': hence the letter. He commanded them to 'forbear to meddle any further in this plea till our coming to town, and that out of our own mouth you may hear our pleasure in this business'. A postscript ordered them to call Bacon, 'who will inform you of the particular points which we are unwilling shall be publicly disputed in this case'.[37]

Bacon, meanwhile, was deep in the prosecution of the Somersets. James required him to construct a case against his erstwhile favourite and his wife, but such a case that would permit him to grant them a royal pardon without being seen to compromise himself. It was a difficult brief, not least because the earl had already been announced to be complicit, although the evidence was not strong enough to make a conviction a foregone conclusion. On the other hand, public interest in the case was so strong that any failure to follow through would be seen as corrupt, since the indicted commoners had already been hanged.

On 28 April Bacon wrote to the King, surveying the situation. James responded by returning the letter with marginal notes. Bacon recommended that 'Somerset should make a clear confession of his offence, before he be produced to his trial,' which would give James three options: to 'stay the trial, and so save them both, from the stage and that public ignominy'; to 'have the trial proceed, and stay or reprieve the judgment, which save the lands from forfeiture, and the blood from corruption'; or to 'have both trial and judgment proceed, and save the blood only, not from corrupting, but from spilling'. James noted: 'I saye with Apollo, *Media tutius iter* [the middle route is safer], if it maye stande with lawe; and if it cannot, quhen I shall heare that he confessith, I ame then to make choyce of the first or the last.'

Bacon sent his letter to the King to 'the third person, whom your Majesty admitted to this secret' – Villiers.[38] Villiers was rising fast during these weeks. He was now given the Order of the Garter, which John Chamberlain thought 'a strange choice' since he was 'so lately come into the light of the world: and withal it was doubted that he had not sufficient likelihood to maintain the dignity of the place according to the express articles of the order: but to take away that scruple, the King hath bestowed on him the Lord Grey's lands, and means (they say) to mend his grant with much more not far distant in the present possesson of the earl of Somerset, if he do *cadere causa*, and sink in the business now in hand.'[39]

And it was to Villiers that Bacon confided his opinion of the case, on 2 May.

I have received my letter from his Majesty with his marginal notes, which shall be my directions, being glad to perceive I understand his

Majesty so well. That same little charm which may be secretly infused into Somerset's ear [i.e. suggestions to influence his behaviour] some few hours before his trial, was excellently well thought of by his Majesty; and I do approve it both for matter and time; only if it seem good to his Majesty, I would wish it a little enlarged. For if it be no more but to spare his blood, he hath a kind of proud humour which may overwork the medicine. Therefore I could wish it were made a little stronger, by giving him some hope that his Majesty will be good to his lady and child; and that time (when justice and his Majesty's honour is once saved and satisfied) may produce further fruit of his Majesty's compassion.

The King evidently disliked the suggestion that Somerset might recover his fortune, and Bacon later had to insist that he was 'far from opinion that the reintegration or resuscitation of Somerset's fortune can ever stand with his Majesty's honour and safety and I know well any expectation or thought abroad will do much hurt. But yet the glimmering of that which the King hath done to others by way of talk to him cannot hurt as I conceive but I would not have that part of the message as from the King, but added by the messenger as from himself.' Bacon also spent 'four or five hours with the Judges, whom his Majesty designed to take consideration with the four Judges of the King's Bench, of the evidence against Somerset. They all concur in opinion, that the questioning him, and drawing him on to trial is most honourable and just, and that the evidence is fair and good.'[40]

The trial of the countess was fixed for Wednesday 15 May 1616. Bacon suggested meticulous plans for the pre-trial hints to be given to Somerset. 'The time I wish to be the Tuesday, being the even of his Lady's arraignment. For, as his Majesty first conceived, I would not have it stay in his stomach too long, lest it sour in the digestion; and to be too near the time may be thought but to tune him for that day.' Once in the courtroom, matters had to be handled carefully.

It will be necessary, because I have distributed parts to the two serjeants . . . and they understand nothing of his Majesty's pleasure of the manner of carrying the evidence, more than they can guess by observation of my example (which they may ascribe as much to my nature as to direction), therefore that his Majesty will be pleased to write some few words to us all, signed with his own hand, that the matter itself being tragical enough, bitterness and insulting be forborne, and that we remember our part to be to make him delinquent to the peers, and not odious to the people.[41]

Bacon submitted the 'heads of the charge' against Somerset to the King, who once again commented in the margin. 'Ye will do well to remember lykeways in your preamble, that insigne, that the only zeal to justice makis me take this course. I have commandit you not to expatiate nor digresse upon any other points, that maye not serve clearlie for probation or inducement of that pointe quhairof he is accused.' On one point, James overruled Bacon's plan of action. Bacon intended to give in evidence 'the slight account of that letter which was brought to Somerset by Ashton, being found in the fields soon after the late Prince's death, and was directed to Antwerp, containing the words, "that the first branch was cut from the tree, and that he should ere long send happier and joyfuller news."' 'This evidence,' pointed out the King, 'cannot be gevin in without making me his accuser, and that upon a verrie slight ground.'

But Bacon had already covered himself. This letter, he wrote, 'is a matter I would not use, but that my Lord Coke, (who hath filled this part with many frivolous things) would think all lost except he hear somewhat of this kind. But this it is to come to the leavings of a business.' Bacon objected to each of these 'frivolous things' in turn, remarking, 'The particular reasons why I omit them I have set in the margent; but the general is partly to do a kind of right to justice, and such a solemn trial, in not giving that in evidence which touches not the delinquent or is not of weight; and partly to observe your Majesty's direction to give Somerset no just occasion of despair or flashes [outbursts].' James evidently agreed, dismissing the next page of suggestions: 'As for all the subsequent evidencis, thaye are all so litle evident as *una litura* may serve thaime all.'[42]

As it turned out the messenger was sent to speak to Somerset on the ninth: too early to be of use to Bacon, who wanted the ploy to have its effects during, rather than before, the arraignment. Now he, with the Lord Chancellor, moved to bring pressure on the countess, sending 'Mr. Whiting the preacher, a discreet man' who had been used with Elwes, to 'preach before the Lady, and teach her, and move her generally to a clear confession'.[43] On Monday 13 May, Sir George More acted as a second 'messenger' to Somerset, assuring him that 'if he would yet before his trial confess clearly unto the Commissioners his guiltiness of this fact' James would 'not only perform what he promised by his last messenger both towards him and his wife, but would enlarge it'.[44]

The commission of inquiry went to see Somerset, to persuade him that, given the legal consensus that 'the evidence was full to convict him, so as there needed neither confession nor supply of examination', he should 'lay hold upon' the King's mercy, which 'might do him good, but could do him no hurt', especially now that his wife had 'been touched with remorse and confessed'. Only when the commissioners mentioned 'the Prince or some foreign practice' did Somerset, until then 'very sober, and modest, and mild', grow 'a little stirred'; when questioned about the poisoning he was 'very cold and modest'.[45]

Bacon continued to plan the trial meticulously. There were 'questions of convenience' on which he thought the King might want 'to confer with some of his counsel': whether if Somerset confessed before the trial, James would postpone the hearing to delve further into possible treasons in Prince Henry's death or Prince Charles's conveyance into Spain, 'for till he confess the less crime, there is [no] likelihood of confessing the greater'; whether such a postponement should be discharged privately or in open court, with a declaration of the causes; whether the trials of wife and husband should be separated by a day to see if the countess, once condemned, would confess her husband's involvement; whether his trial should come first, 'because then any councils which may be wrought by her clearing of him may be prevented, and it may be he will be in the better temper, hoping of his own clearing, and of her respiting'.

Bacon also provided a series of 'memorials' to himself – to ask 'whether the axe is to be carried before the prisoner, being in the case of felony'; to ascertain 'whether, if the Lady make any digression to clear his Lordship, she is not by the Lord Steward to be interrupted and silenced'; to clarify 'whether, if there should be twelve votes to condemn, and thirteen or fourteen to acquit, if it be not a verdict for the King?'; to determine 'whether, if my Lord of Somerset should break forth into any speech of taxing the King, he be not presently by the Lord Steward to be interrupted and silenced, and if he persist he be not to be told that if he take that course he is to be withdrawn, and evidence to be given in his absence; and whether that may be; and what else to be done'. This last possibility caused Bacon considerable worry: he drafted 'a particular remembrance for his Majesty' to the effect that 'It were good that after he [Somerset] is comen into the Hall (so that he may perceive he must go to trial), and shall be retired into the place appointed till the court call for him, then the Lieutenant should tell him roundly that if in his speeches he shall tax the King, that the justice of England is that he shall be taken away, and the evidence shall go on without him, and all the people will cry *away with him*, and then it shall not be in the King's will to save his life, the people will be so set on fire.'[46]

Yet again, there was a postponement. John Chamberlain reported that 'the stage is in the midst of Westminster Hall with numbers of scaffolds roundabout was finished, the Lords assembled, and all things ready against Wednesday, when about Tuesday noon came order to put all off.' This was a grave disappointment for those who had deliberately stayed in town after the end of the legal term, and now left losing their ringside seats –

no small loss, when those seats 'were grown to so extraordinary a rate, that four or five pieces (as they call them) was an ordinary price, and I know a lawyer that had agreed to give ten pound for himself and his wife for the two days, and fifty pound was given for a corner that could hardly contain a dozen.' Speculation was rife: the countess had fallen ill; the earl was about to 'reveal secrets of great importance'.[47]

The countess made her appearance in a packed Westminster Hall at 9 a.m. on 24 May 1616, before an audience which included her ex-husband, the earl of Essex. As Bacon had hoped, she pleaded guilty. It was a good start. 'This Lady hath by her confession prevented my evidence, and your verdict,' Bacon announced to the Lords, 'and that this day's labour is eased; there resteth, in the legal proceeding, but for me to pray that her confession may be recorded, and judgement thereupon. But the occasion itself admonisheth me to give your Lordships and the hearers this contentment, as to make declaration of the proceedings of this excellent work of the King's justice, from the beginning to the end.'

Bacon then told, in detail, the story of the coming to the light of the Overbury affair, to the point where it reached the King.

> This excellent foundation of justice being laid by his Majesty's own hand, it was referred unto some counsellors to examine further; who gained some degrees of light from Weston, but yet left it unperfect. After it was referred to Sir Edward Coke, Chief Justice of the King's Bench, as a person best practised in legal examinations; who took a great deal of indefatigable pains in it without intermission, having (as I have heard him say) taken at least three hundred examinations in this business. But these things were not done in a corner, I need not speak of them. It is true that my Lord Chief Justice, in the dawning and opening of the light, finding the matter touched upon these great persons, very discreetly became suitor to the King to have greater persons than his own rank joined with him; whereupon your Lordship, my Lord Steward of England, to whom the King commonly resorteth *in arduis*, and my Lord Steward of the King's house, and my Lord Zouch, were joined with him.[48]

The Countess spoke 'humbly, fearfully, and so low that the Lord Steward could not hear it': 'I can much aggravate but nothing extenuate my fault. I desire mercy and that my Lords will intercede for me to the King.' Bacon relayed her message to the Hall: 'The Lady is so touched with remorse and sense of her fault that grief surprises her from expressing herself: but that which she hath confusedly said is to this effect, That she cannot excuse herself, but desires mercy.'[49] Thanks to the countess' confession, Chamberlain wrote, 'all was done and we at home before noon.'[50] Another onlooker, Edward Sherburn, who was later to become Bacon's secretary, opined that 'Her carriage hath much commended her: for both before and after her condemnation she behaved herself so nobly and worthily as did express to the world she was well taught and had better learned her lesson. It is conceived by many that in regard she stood not upon her justification, but confessed and submitted herself to the law and mercy of the King, that she shall not die; which they ground upon Mr. Attorney's speech, which did intimate such a kind of hope.'[51]

The earl's arraignment the following day excited even more attention than that of his wife. 'I was there at six o'clock in the morning,' wrote John Chamberlain, 'and for ten shillings had a reasonable place.' Bacon moved to his 'simple narrative of the fact', which was, in fact, far from simple.[52]

Sir Thomas Overbury for a time was known to have had great interest and great friendship with my Lord of Somerset, both in his meaner fortunes and after; insomuch as he was a kind of oracle of direction unto you; and if you will believe his own vaunts (being of an insolent Thrasonical disposition), he took upon him, that the fortune, reputation, and understanding of this gentleman (who is well known to have had a better teacher) proceeded from his company and counsel.

And this friendship rested not only in conversation and business of court, but likewise in communication of secrets of estate. For my Lord of Somerset, at that time exercising (by his Majesty's special favour and trust) the office of the Secretary provisionally, did not forbear to acquaint Overbury with the King's packets of dispatches from all parts, Spain, France, the Low Countries etc. And this not by glimpses, or now and then rounding in the ear for a favour, but in a settled manner: packets were sent, sometimes opened by my Lord, sometimes unbroken, unto Overbury, who perused them, copied, registered them, made tables of them as he thought good: so that I will undertake the time was when Overbury knew more of the secrets of state than the Council-table did.

Somerset interjected. Why, he wanted to know, did Bacon urge 'these impertinent and bye-matters, done by the King's commandment'?

'To show,' replied Bacon, 'that as there was common secrets between you, so there were common dangers.' He continued: 'Nay, they were grown to such an inwardness, as they made a play of all the world besides themselves: so as they had ciphers and jargons for the King, the Queen, and all the great men; things seldom used, but either by princes and their ambassadors and ministers, or by such as work and practice against, or at least upon princes.'

In a secret letter to More, James wrote that 'it is easy to be seen that he [Somerset] would threaten me with laying an aspersion upon me of being, in some sort, accessory to his crime.'[53] Were Bacon's insinuations pre-emptive, because he anticipated Somerset might try to implicate the King? It was rumoured that Somerset would claim that he had had sexual relations with James. Bacon, by spontaneously raising the extreme intimacy between the men in matters of service (the sharing of secrets), thereby neutralised the effect of such a claim – it had merely been intimate *political* service.

'But understand me (my Lord) I shall not charge you this day with any disloyalty; only I lay this for a foundation, that there was a great communication of secrets between you and Overbury, and that it had relation to matters of estate, and the greatest causes of this kingdom.' Turning to the lords, however, he pointed out: 'But (my Lords) as it is a principle in nature, that the best things are in their corruption the worst, and the sweetest wine makes the sharpest vinegar; so fell it out with them, that this excess (as I may term it) of friendship ended in mortal hatred on my Lord of Somerset's part. I have heard my Lord Steward say sometimes in the Chancery that fraud and frost end foul. And I may add a third, and that is the friendship of ill men; which may be truly termed conspiracy and not friendship.'

Bacon related the history of events. Overbury was opposed to his master's planned marriage, seeing that he 'was like to be dispossessed of my Lord here, whom he had possessed so long, and by whose greatness he had promised to do wonders; and being a man of an unbounded and impetuous spirit', set to dissuading Somerset from the match. Finding him determined, however, Overbury turned to 'stronger remedies, supposing that he had my Lord's head under his girdle, in respect of communication of secrets of estate (or, as he calls them himself in his letters, secrets of all natures); and therefore dealt violently with him to make him desist, with menaces of discovery of secrets, and the like.'

In the first of his conclusive 'proofs', Bacon identified Somerset's 'root of bitterness, a mortal malice or hatred, mixed with deep and bottomless fears', as proceeding from a

fear of discovering secrets: secrets (I say) of a high and dangerous nature. They were such as my Lord of Somerset for his part had made a vow, that Overbury should neither live in court nor country. That he had likewise opened himself and his own fears so far, that if Overbury ever came forth of the Tower, either Overbury or himself must die for it. And of Overbury's part, he had threatened my Lord, that whether he did live or die, my Lord's shame should never die, but he would leave him the most odious man of the world. And further that my Lord was like enough to repent it in the place where Overbury wrote, which was the Tower of London. He was a true prophet in that.

Finally, seven hours after the opening of proceedings, Bacon summed up the case for the prosecution. At 5 p.m. Somerset answered the case against him, at length but 'very confusedly, insisting most upon those particulars which were least material'. As Edward Sherburn commented: 'His answers were so poor and idle as many of the Lords his peers shook their heads and blushed to hear such slender excuses come from him, of whom much better was expected.'[54] By 8 p.m. John Chamberlain had had enough. 'The weather is so hot and I grew so faint with fasting that I could hold out no longer: especially when I heard they had sent to provide torches, so that it is verily thought he will hold them till midnight, if the Lord Chancellor, who is Lord High Steward for the time be able to continue it.'[55]

Given Somerset's ineptitude, Bacon passed over the chance to sum up.[56] After an hour's deliberation, the peers returned a unanimous guilty verdict. Now Somerset chose to speak, saying to the Lords that 'his case might be any of theirs hereafter, desired them to consider that it was but the testimony of two women of bad condition that had condemned him, protested upon his salvation that he never saw Weston's face, and that he was innocent of that he was condemned.'[57] John Chamberlain thought Somerset's response strange: the sentence 'did so little appal him that when he was asked what he could say why sentence should not be pronounced, he stood still upon his innocence, and could hardly be brought to refer himself to the King's mercy'. Somerset remained in that state, and when writing to the King merely asked that he might suffer the noble death of beheading rather than hanging, and that his daughter might have 'such of his lands as the King doth not resume and reserve in his own hands'.[58] There, for the time being, the matter rested.

★

With the Somerset trial over, Bacon was obliged to turn his energies once again to combating Coke. Although the indictment of *praemunire* against the Chancery had failed in February, Coke was now encouraging the plaintiffs to make another attempt. After a further postponement, the argument on the *commendams* case was due for Saturday 8 June. Bacon knew that if he was to triumph over Coke he needed to strengthen his own authority, and at the end of May solicited Villiers with a new sense of urgency. 'The time is as I should think now or never,' he argued,

> for his Majesty to finish his good meaning towards me, if it please him to consider what is past and what is to come. If I would tender my profit and oblige men unto me by my place and practice, I could have more profit than I can desire, and could oblige all the world and offend

none; which is a brave condition for a man's private. But my heart is not on these things. Yet on the other side, I would be sorry that worthless persons should make a note that I get nothing but pains, and enemies, and a little popular reputation which followeth me whether I will or no. If anything be to be done for yourself, I should take infinite contentment that my honour mought wait upon yours. But I would be loath it should wait upon any man's else. If you would put your strength to this business, I know it is done. And that many things more will begin.[59]

This time Villiers threw his full weight behind Bacon's suit. During the following four days, James gave Bacon a difficult choice – either to be sworn a Privy Councillor instantly, or to have the 'assurance to succeed' the Lord Chancellor. 'The King giveth me a noble choice,' Bacon reported to Villiers,

and you are the man my heart ever told me you were. Ambition would draw me to the later part of the choice. But in respect of my hearty wishes that my Lord Chancellor may live long, and the small hopes I have that I shall live long myself, and above all because I see his Majesty's service daily and instantly bleedeth, towards which I persuade myself, (vainly perhaps) but yet in mine own thoughts firmly and constantly, that I shall give when I am of the table some effectual furtherance. I do accept of the former, to be councillor for the present, and to give over pleading at the bar; let the other matter rest upon my proof, and his Majesty's pleasure, and the accidents of time. For to speak plainly I would be loth that my Lord Chancellor, to whom I owe most after the King and yourself, should be locked to his successor, for any advancement or gracing of me.[60]

Sir Francis Bacon was sworn a Privy Councillor on 9 June 1616.

 Well primed by a 'memorial for his Majesty' prepared by Bacon, James confronted his judges in front of the Privy Council at Whitehall on Thursday 6 June, taking to heart Bacon's reminder that 'though the Judges are a reverend body, yet they are (as all subjects are) corrigible'.[61] James placed the debacle of the *commendams* case in the context of a general trend: 'ever since his coming to the crown, the popular sort of lawyers have been the men that most affrontedly in all Parliaments have trodden upon his prerogative.' A king had a 'double prerogative' – the ordinary prerogative might be daily disputed in the law courts, but the other 'was of a higher nature, referring to his supreme and imperial power and sovereignty, which ought not to be disputed or handled in vulgar argument'. Recently, however, 'the courts of common law were grown so vast and transcendent, as they did both meddle with the King's prerogative, and had incroached upon all other courts of justice.' As for the form of the letter, James 'noted that it was a new thing, and very undecent and unfit, for subjects to disobey the King's commandment'.

At this point, 'all the Judges fell down upon their knees, and acknowledged their error for matter of form, humbly craving his Majesty's gracious favour and pardon for the same.' But Coke refused to submit on the point of Bacon's letter, arguing that the delay required by the King was a delay of justice, 'contrary to law and the Judges' oath'; as they intended to handle it, the case was not about the King's prerogative to grant *commendams*; if the case had been delayed, the suit would have been discontinued, 'which had been a failing in justice'; since Bacon's letter did not specify a date for an adjournment, there could not be one, since 'an adjournment must always be to a day certain.'

'Mere sophistry,' snorted the King. The judges might have decided on a day themselves. They should have consulted with him as to what involved the King's prerogative. The Lord Chancellor thought the Attorney-General should answer the King's question, 'Whether the stay that had been required by his Majesty were contrary to law, or against the Judges' oath': so it was Bacon who had the pleasure of pronouncing to Sir Edward Coke that the putting off of the day was 'without all scruple no delay of justice, nor danger of the Judges' oath'; his own letter was 'no imperious letter', but merely required them to postpone a decision until he could consult them.

Bacon's speech was endorsed by the rest of James's Learned Counsel. When Coke continued to argue, the Lord Chancellor requested that the judges' oath be read out. James then asked each judge in turn whether he would stay a case if the King believed that it concerned him 'either in power or profit, and thereupon required to consult with them'. Each one said it was his duty to do so – except Coke, who answered 'that when that case should be, he should do that should be fit for a Judge to do'. All the judges promised that they would do nothing to weaken or draw into doubt the King's prerogative for the granting of *commendams* in the hearing of the case the following Saturday; that they would 'directly and in plain terms affirm the same, and correct the erroneous and bold speeches which had been used at the bar in derogation thereof'; and that they would reprehend and silence any who spoke against the prerogative. Before the judges were dismissed, James made a final speech, admonishing them to keep within 'the bounds and limits of their several courts, and not to suffer his prerogative to be wounded by rash and unadvised pleading before them, or by new inventions of law'.

Once the judges had left the room, James checked with his Privy Council whether there was any sense in which the judges had a case against him:

'who all with one consent did give opinion, that it was far from any colour or shadow or such interpretation, and that it was against common sense to think the contrary.'[62] An account of the proceedings was drafted by Bacon, 'penned as near as I could to his Majesty's instructions, received in your [Villiers'] presence', and sent to James for approval and amendments.[63] Coke had proved himself yet again an effective thorn in James's side, even though as usual the outcome was a face-saving compromise.

Having convincingly displayed his newly acquired power as a Privy Councillor at this meeting, Bacon was starting to enjoy his new status. He promoted the disgraced Dr John Burgess – who, barred from preaching because of his Nonconformist views, had found support among the elite from the likes of Lucy, countess of Bedford (now resident in Bacon's old bolthole, Twickenham Park), Sir Ralph Winwood's wife, the Bishop of Bath and Wells, and James's physician Theodore Mayerne – and obtained his warrant to preach again.[64] But a place at the Privy Council table could be useful for less constructive campaigns. On 26 June, Coke was called before the Council to answer charges preferred against him by the Solicitor-General, including his conduct in the matter of the *praemunire*. Coke acknowledged the validity of the King's order – i.e. the authority of the King to decide the question – and 'added also further that for the time to come no man should make any opposition; for that the Judges having received your Majesty's commandment by the Attorney-General that no bill of that nature should be hereafter received, he and his brethren have caused the same to be entered as an order in the same Court; which shall be observed.'[65]

Coke's answer was relayed to the King. During that week, James dined at Wimbledon, his host the earl of Exeter. Chamberlain reported that 'The Lady Hatton [Coke's wife, who retained her first married title] was there and well graced, for the King kissed her twice, but it seems it was but a lightning.' When the King came to read Coke's answers, the graces of Lady Hatton were no defence for her husband. Called again before the Council on Sunday 30 June, Coke was informed that it was His Majesty's pleasure that he should neither sit at the Council table nor ride his summer circuit, thereby effectively obliterating his political and judicial powers. Instead, because His Majesty had heard that there were in his books of reports 'many exorbitant and extravagant opinions set down and published for positive and good law', Coke should use his new-found leisure to review and correct the said reports. 'And having corrected what in his discretion he found meet in his Reports, his Majesty's pleasure was that he should bring the same privately to himself, that he might consider thereof, as in his princely judgment should be found expedient.'[66] Coke, it seemed, was beyond rehabilitation.

The disabling of the Lord Chief Justice was the talk of the town. John Chamberlain saw it as

the sum of the censure for his corrupt dealing with Sir Robert Rich and Sir Christopher Hatton in the extent of their lands and instalment of the debt due to the King, and for words spoken touching the *praemunire* the last day of Easter term, and for his insolent behaviour when he and the Judges were before the King at Whitehall. Some that wish him well fear the matter will not end here, for he is wilful, and will take no counsel but seeking to make good his first errors (which in truth were foul) runs into worse, and entangles himself everyday more and more; and gives his enemies such advantage to work upon the King's indignation towards him that he is in great danger. The world discourses diversely how he should run so far in the King's displeasure, and will not take these alleged causes for sound payment, but stick not to say that he was too busy in the late business, and dived farther into secrets than there was need, and so perhaps might see *nudam sine veste Dianam* [Diana naked, without her clothes]. Howsoever it be he is not well advised that he doth not *cedere tempori* [give way to the times] and carry himself more dutifully and submissly to his Majesty in his actions, though his words be now humble enough. His Lady hath likewise carried herself very indiscreetly of late towards the Queen whereby she hath lost her favour and is forbidden her court, as also the King's. The story were too long to tell, but it was about braving and uncivil words to the Lady Compton [Villiers' mother] and vouching the Queen for her author.[67]

Continuing the elaborate task of simultaneously condemning and rehabilitating the Somersets, Bacon now had the task of drawing up a warrant for the countess' pardon, which gave four respects 'as motives to your Majesty's mercy': 'The respect of her father, friends, and family. Her voluntary confession both when she was prisoner and at the Bar. The promise made publicly by the Lord High Steward, and the Peers, to intercede for your Majesty's mercy'; and – Bacon's own insertion – 'that the crime was not of a principal, but of an accessory before the fact, by the instigation of base persons'. Sending the warrant to Villiers on 1 July, he noted that 'Her friends think long to have it despatched, which I marvel not at, for that in matter of life moments are numbered.'[68] Others were not so keen. Chamberlain noted with disgust how Somerset continued in some favour, thanks to the mediation of James, Lord Hay of Sawley, who made 'many allees and venues [comings and goings] betwixt the King' and the disgraced earl.

The success of these errands is already come thus far, that yesterday he [Somerset] had the liberty of the Tower granted him, and Henrickson and his wife had the fortune to see him with his Garter and George about his neck walking and talking with the earl of Northumberland [also a prisoner in the Tower] and he and his Lady saluting at the window. It is much spoken of how foreign princes of that order (to let our own pass) can digest to be coupled in society with a man lawfully and publicly convicted of so foul a fact, or how a man civilly dead, and corrupt in blood, and so no gentleman, should continue a Knight of the Garter, but this age affords things as strange and incompatible.

Evidently Chamberlain was not alone in his feelings, for the countess' pardon caused considerable outrage.

It seems the common people take not this for good payment, for on Saturday last the Queen with the Countess of Derby, the Lady Ruthin and the Lord Carew coming privately in coach to see somewhat here in town, there grew a whispering that it was the Lady Somerset and her mother, whereupon people flocked together and followed the coach in great numbers railing and reviling, and abusing the footmen, and putting them all in fear, neither would they be otherwise persuaded till they saw them enter into Whitehall, though the countess discovered herself and talked apace to them, and the Lord Carew would have gone out of the coach to satisfy them but that the Queen would not suffer him lest he could not have got in again.[69]

Bacon also conveyed to Villiers – for conveyance to the King – his views on the recent developments in Ireland. The problems of the parliament of Ireland had subsided, and the session starting on 11 October 1614 had been peaceful and virtually without incident: elections were not disputed, government measures were passed; even – after a prorogation – a subsidy bill was passed. Bacon expressed his 'contentment' in James's (and Villiers') choice of Sir Oliver St John as his deputy in Ireland,

finding upon divers conferences with him his great sufficiency; and I hope the good intelligence which he purposeth to hold with me by advertisements from time to time shall work a good effect for his Majesty's service. I am wonderful desirous to see that kingdom flourish, because it is the proper work and glory of his Majesty and his times. And his Majesty may be pleased to call to mind, that a good while since, when the great rent and divisions were in the Parliament of Ireland, I was no unfortunate remembrancer to his Majesty's princely wisdom in that business.[70]

On 2 July, Bacon wrote again to Villiers recommending for either the Attorneyship or Solicitorship of Ireland 'a gentleman of mine own breeding and framing, Mr Edward Wrytington, of Gray's Inn'.[71] He continued to advise James on policy for Ireland. He provided ideas 'for the renewing of some former commissions for Ireland, and the framing of a new commission for the Wards and the Alienations,' which would increase the year's profit from £200 to £4000; and he gave his 'advice and opinion' on three 'propositions and counsels' – that town magistrates should not be forced to take the oath of supremacy, but that a policy of slow persuasion should be followed instead; that the Council of Ireland should be reduced from its current level of nearly fifty to something nearer twenty, with a select committee of councillors to find ways to improve his revenue there; and that the army should be reinforced by 500–1,000 men by a devious scheme involving transferring some companies from one province to another.[72]

★

At the last meeting of the Star Chamber before the summer circuits, James attended in person to make a public declaration, on Bacon's advice and to Bacon's lasting approval, as he was later to declare: 'Amongst the counsels which (since the time I have the honour to be first of your learned and after of your privy council) I have given your Majesty . . . I do take comfort in none more than that I was the first that advised you to come in person into the Star Chamber.'[73] Adhering no doubt to a memorial drafted by his Attorney-General, James declared that he had come to renew the oath taken at his coronation, when he swore to do justice, to give every man his own, and to maintain the law, by which he meant 'the common law of the land, according to which the King governs, and by which the people are governed'. He had kept that oath, 'as far as human frailty might permit him or his knowledge inform him', and he intended to continue keeping it, 'especially in laws, and of laws especially the common law . . . and as to maintain it, so to purge it, for else it cannot be maintained; and especially to purge it of two corruptions, Incertainty and Novelty'. The 'Incertainty' must be removed by parliament, acting on the advice of the judges; but the judges must guard against their own 'Novelty' and act as interpreters of law, rather than makers of law. Moreover, their 'interpretations must always be subject to common sense and reason', and their opinions must be given upon conference and with deliberation.

James then defined the limits of their jurisdiction: in order not to encroach upon the crown's prerogative, they must 'keep yourselves within your own benches, not to invade other jurisdictions'. He raised the question of the *praemunire* brought against the Chancery: it was the duty of judges, he asserted, to punish those 'that seek to deprave the proceedings of any the King's Courts'. He therefore thought it 'an odious and inept speech' in Westminster Hall to say that a *praemunire* lay against the Court of Chancery and its officers: 'how can the King grant a *Praemunire* against himself?' While the Chancery should not exceed its own limits, it was the duty of the King – and the King alone – to correct it, and therefore he had been 'greatly abused in that attempt'. In conclusion, 'sitting here in a seat of judgement, I declare and command that no man hereafter presume to sue a *Praemunire* against the Chancery, which I may the more easily do, because no *Praemunire* can be sued but at my suit: and I may justly bar myself at mine own pleasure.' A decree was issued on the granting of *praemunires*.[74]

For once in his career Bacon's main patron was both heeding his advice and acting upon it.

14

Much Ado, and a Great Deal of World

You may be sure that I love the earl of Buckingham more
than anyone else.
King James to the Privy Council (September 1617)

VILLIERS' STAR HAD risen fast. In a matter of months, the Master
of the Horse had been made a Knight of the Garter, granted the
manors of Whaddon and Nash in Buckinghamshire (the former
with its own park and chase), and given the reversion of the patent for
the enrolment of pleas in the Court of King's Bench. On 7 July 1616, in
a ceremony at Windsor, he was raised into the peerage, alongside the earl
of Rutland and Lord Lisle.[1]

Sir Francis Bacon was an invisible but crucial player in these honours.
At every stage in the making of the patent of creation – from Bacon's
preliminary note, to the King's instructions, to Bacon's draft of the patent,
to the King's corrections, to the final product – Bacon, Villiers and James
worked as a team.[2] Bacon took particular care that Villiers should have
the right name in his title, proposing 'Viscount Villiers' (rather than the
alternative Bletchley or Whaddon): 'to speak truth, it is a well-sounding
and noble name, both here and abroad; and being your proper name, I
will take it for a good sign that you shall give honour to your dignity, and
not your dignity to you.' Even at this stage, Bacon was fully aware of the
importance of a name.[3]

From Gorhambury, where he had retired in early August to escape 'that
which other men hourly break my head withal, as it was in London',[4]
Bacon sent Villiers 'some of my country fruits; which with me are good
meditations; which when I am in the city are choked with business'. The
'country fruits' were an analysis of the viscount's position and prospects.
Now that his fortune was established, Villiers might well think 'your private
fortunes established'. It would then be time to 'refer your actions chiefly
to the good of your sovereign and your country'; this lack of attention to
his own fortunes would do no harm, 'for assure yourself that fortune is of
a woman's nature, that will sooner follow you by slighting than by too
much wooing'.

Bacon proposed that Villiers should 'countenance, and encourage, and advance able men and virtuous men and meriting in all kinds, degrees, and professions'. The current 'wilderness in the king's service' could be traced back to 'the time of the Cecils, the father and the son', during which 'able men were by design and of purpose suppressed'; matters had improved, but

> money, and turn-serving, and cunning canvasses, and importunity prevail too much. And in places of moment, rather make able and honest men yours, than advance those that are otherwise because they are yours. As for cunning and corrupt men, you must (I know) sometimes use them; but keep them at a distance; and let it appear that you make use of them, rather than that they lead you. Above all, depend wholly (next to God) upon the King; and be ruled (as hitherto you have been) by his instructions; for that is best for yourself.[5]

Villiers welcomed this counsel warmly, encouraging Bacon to supply a full-length 'advice' on how his new patron should deal with being the royal favourite.[6]

Bacon was not alone in identifying Villiers as the key player in James's court. 'This is now the man', wrote Edward Sherburn, 'by whom all things do and must pass; and he far exceeds the former [Somerset] in favour and affection.'[7] Queen Anne travelled to Woodstock to meet the King, raising expectations that the creation was imminent: on 24 August, Chamberlain reported that 'there they say Sir George Villiers shall be created Viscount tomorrow, once the coronet and robes are sent down for the purpose.'[8] Bacon was there on 27 August to see the man who was at once his patron and his protégé created Viscount Villiers and Baron Whaddon.

★

The King had ordered his Lord Chancellor, Attorney and Solicitor to check Coke's reports while the author was undertaking his own review. Bacon, although an admirer of the work ('Had it not been for Sir Edward Coke's Reports the law by this time had been almost like a ship without ballast'), identified 'errors, and some peremptory and extra-judicial resolutions'. Ellesmere more directly saw Coke as belittling ecclesiastical rights and attempting, 'as it were purposely', 'to disesteem and weaken the power of the King in the ancient use of his Prerogative'. Coke's evidence and court resolutions were no more than judges' opinions; he constantly took occasion '(though not offered) to range and expatiate upon bye-matters', thereby 'scattering and sowing his own conceits'.[9]

Appearing before Ellesmere, Bacon and most of the Learned Counsel on 2 October, Coke pointed out that in the five hundred cases contained in his own reports there had been found fewer errors than he could pick out of the renowned jurist Plowden's famed reports – to wit, five, which he proceeded to identify on a single sheet. Despite Coke's dismissive response (which must have made him 'an happy man'), Bacon assured the King that the work he had undertaken with the Lord Chancellor and the Solicitor 'was not altogether lost', because they had detected errors which Coke had missed.[10]

Bacon was keen to open the case before the entire Privy Council and the judges. If James was to decide the case, this would mean that the office of Lord Chief Justice would perforce remain vacant until James returned from his current progress. On the other hand, for the Privy Council to act in the absence of the King would be to 'lessen his prerogative'. More to the point, Coke was now suing for access to the King, saying he had matters of great importance to tell him, raising another dilemma: James could not give audience to the man without *de facto* pardoning him; but equally he could not afford to refuse him access if the matters were truly important.[11]

On the advice of Ellesmere and Bacon, James decided to proceed against Coke.[12] John Chamberlain saw even the choice of men to judge Coke as humiliating: Bacon, Yelverton, Montagu, Crew and Finch, 'whereof the greater part, excepting the Solicitor [Yelverton], are held no great men of law. And withal to find so coarse usage, as not to be once offered to sit down, and so unrespective and uncivil carriage from the Lord Chancellor's men, that not one of them did move a hat or make any other sign of regard towards him.' When the Queen heard of this treatment, however, James 'sent word that he would have him well used' – a sign taken by his supporters to indicate that events were going his way.

Oddly enough, Bacon was thought by some to have taken Coke's side in the proceedings. 'The Attorney', wrote Chamberlain on 26 October, 'is thought to be come about, as well for that he ever used him with more respect than the rest, as for divers speeches he gives out in his favour, as that a man of his learning and parts is not every day found nor so soon made as marred.'[13] However, while Coke was returning his 'humble and direct answer' to five selected cases on 21 October, Bacon was hard at work drafting a discussion of seventeen 'innovations introduced into the laws and governments', in which Coke's recent court behaviour was detailed and commented upon.[14] It was, indeed, Bacon's assault rather than Coke's defence that led to James's decision, on 10 November, to remove Coke from the Bench,[15] and, a few weeks later, from the Privy Council, and then from office altogether. Bacon's hand can be discovered at work throughout. It was Bacon who drafted 'remembrances of his Majesty's declarative' when he removed Coke; Bacon who drew up a warrant for certain judges to review the doubts raised by Coke's reports;[16] Bacon who drafted 'a form of discharge for my Lord Coke from his place of Chief Justice of your Bench' and the warrant for publishing a writ for for his replacement – warning that if James selected Sir Henry Montagu, he should be careful not to replace him as Recorder for London by Coventry, who was 'bred by my Lord Coke and seasoned in his ways'.[17]

James also asked Bacon to prepare an explanation of why Coke's dismissal was necessary. Bacon warmed to his task, singling out Coke's 'perpetual turbulent carriage, first towards the liberties of his [the King's] church and the state ecclesiastical; then towards his prerogative royal, and the branches thereof; and likewise towards all the settled jurisdiction of his other courts'. Coke 'had made himself popular by design only in pulling down government'. He also criticised Coke's behaviour in Peacham's case, and reminded the King that the Chief Justice had been given time to reform his reports 'wherein there be many dangerous concerts of his own uttered for law, to the prejudice of his crown, parliament, and subjects. After three months' time, he had offered his Majesty only five animadversions, being rather a scorn than a satisfaction to his Majesty.'[18]

Word was that 'Four Ps have overthrown and put him down, that is Pride, Prohibitions, *Praemunire*, and Prerogative.'[19] It was not a popular move: as Chamberlain noted, 'If Sir Edward Coke could bear this misfortune constantly it were no great disgrace to him, for he goes away with a general applause and good opinion, and the King himself when he told his resolution at the Council table to remove him, yet gave him this testimony that he thought him in no way corrupt, but a good justicer, with so many other good words as if he meant to hang him with a silken halter.'[20] Coke himself met his fate with dignity: when Montagu was indeed selected as his replacement, he sent a messenger to Coke, to offer to buy Coke's collar of esses [chain of office]: 'I will not part with it,' declared Coke, 'but leave it to my posterity, that they may one day know they had a Chief Justice to their ancestor.'[21]

Despite being reckoned 'crazie' from illness, Ellesmere revived sufficiently to swear in Montagu, welcoming him with a rapturous speech that mocked his predecessor mercilessly.[22] It was, as Whitelocke judged, 'a very bitter invective. What was the cause of Sir Edward Coke's offence is not for subjects to meddle with. But those that practised before him, or had causes before him, found him the most just, honest and incorrupt judge that ever sat on bench.'[23] For Coke, now sixty-five, it looked like the end, and he retired to Standon Lordship, the Hertfordshire house of his daughter Anne Sadleir.

Twenty-three years after Coke had stolen the attorneyship from him, Francis Bacon felt vindicated. He had effectively masterminded the official version of the fall of Coke and the rise of Villiers, as directed by the King.

# # #

Indeed, as we watch the methodical process whereby those who crossed James sooner or later fell from office, it seems remarkable that, riding high in the King's favour, Francis Bacon should not have been more alert to the possibility that it would take little for him to find himself in the same position.[24]

★

To foreign observers it seemed that James's rule had become well and truly bogged down. 'The chief causes', wrote the Venetian ambassador in cipher, 'are the daily increasing abhorrence which he feels for the toils and cares involved in government. In order to escape them he lives almost entirely in the country, accompanied by a few of his favourites whose counsels, conceived in their own interests, are very remote from decisions involving expense and trouble. Another reason is His Majesty's powerlessness to incur any considerable expense unless he receives the material from parliament . . . In proportion as his reputation continues to diminish abroad the dissatisfaction of his subjects keeps increasing.'[25]

In a move that could have been calculated precisely to make matters worse, James chose this moment to travel back into Scotland, for the first time in fourteen years. To the Privy Council he confessed that 'we are not ashamed to confess that we have had these many years a great and natural longing to see our native soil and place of our birth and breeding, and this salmonlike instinct of ours has restlessly, both when we were awake and many times in our sleep, so stirred up our thoughts and bended our desires to make a journey thither that we can never rest satisfied till it shall please God that we may accomplish it.' James may have been the only person who wanted this visit: 'I never knew a journey so generally misliked both here and there,' observed John Chamberlain.[26]

In February 1617, as James was about to set out, Bacon provided him with a set of 'remembrances'. Conceding that, since James would still be 'within your own land', his journey would be 'but as a long progress', Bacon thought it his duty nonetheless 'to put you in mind of those points of form which have relation not so much to a journey to Scotland as to an absence from your city of London for six months, or to a distance from your said city near three hundred miles; and that in an ordinary course, wherein I lead myself by calling to consideration what things there are that require your signature, and may seem not so fit to expect sending to and fro; and therefore to be supplied by some precedent warrants'.

In particular, there was the delicate matter of Chancellor Ellesmere's advanced age and fragile health: 'it doth not only admit but require the accident of his death to be thought of.' James therefore needed to consider 'whether you will not have such a commission as was prepared about this time twelvemonth in my Lord's extreme sickness for the taking of the seal into custody, and for the seal of writs and commissions for ordinary justice, till you may advise of a Chancellor or Keeper of the great seal'.

Bacon's interest in such matters clearly went beyond the strict call of duty. He admitted that his care was 'assiduous' but argued that 'it is good to err in caring even rather too much than too little. These things, for so much as concerneth forms, ought to proceed from my place as Attorney, unto which you have added some interest in matter, by making me of your Privy Council. But for the main they rest wholly in your princely judgment, being well informed; because miracles are ceased, though admiration will not cease while you live.'[27]

On 5 March, Ellesmere finally persuaded James to accept his resignation, and gave up the Seal the following day. Sir Francis Bacon at last gained the place of Lord Keeper, which his father had once held, on 7 March 1617. He attributed this latest, greatest honour to Villiers, who had himself two months earlier been made earl of Buckingham:

My dearest Lord, It is both in cares and kindness, that small ones float up to the tongue, and great ones sink down into the heart with silence. Therefore I could speak little to your Lordship today, neither had I fit time: but I must profess thus much, that in this day's work, you are the truest and perfectest mirror and example of firm and generous friendship that ever was in court. And I shall count every day lost, wherein I shall not either study your well doing in thought, or do your name honour in speech, or perform you service in deed. Good my Lord, account and accept me Your most bounden and devoted friend and servant of all men living, Fr. Bacon, C.S. [*Custos sigilli*: keeper of the seal][28]

To make the honour complete, another warrant was prepared for the King to sign before his journey north: 'a warrant for conferring a dignity upon the Lady Bacon, wife to our trusty and well-beloved Sir F.B., etc.' This declared James's will and royal pleasure that Lady Bacon 'shall be ranked in place and precedency in all places and at all meetings, as well public as private, next to the ladies or wives of the Barons of this our realm. Wherein we will command and express our royal pleasure to be, that all ladies of what estate or degree soever, under the estate and degree of a Baroness, wife or widow to a Baron of this our realm, shall hereafter at all times and in all places permit and suffer the said Lady Bacon to have, take, and enjoy the place and precedency before them and every of them.'[29] The Bacons' place in high society was assured – in writing. Since Ellesmere's widow Lady Derby could not immediately leave York House, the traditional residence of the Lord Keeper, the Bacons leased Dorset House for two terms from the earl of Dorset.[30] Bacon's concern for his wife's status gives us a rare glimpse of Francis and Alice as a couple. There are tantalisingly few indications of how the original marriage of convenience developed. The lack of epistolary evidence has traditionally been taken as a sign that they were virtually estranged; it might as readily be argued that this absence points to an intimate, domestic relationship in which letter-writing was superfluous.

James left London on 15 March, taking with him several courtiers, including Buckingham, who remained with him throughout the seven-month journey. One of James's last decisions while still in the capital was to reward the dying Ellesmere with the title of the earl of Bridgewater, making him President of the Council and giving him a pension of £3,000 per annum for life. Bacon went to inform Ellesmere of his good fortune, but discovered him '*in articulo mortis*'; according to Chamberlain, 'he was so far past that no words or worldly comforts could work with him, but only thanking his Majesty for his gracious favour, said these things were all to him but vanities.' Within half an hour, Ellesmere was dead, leaving instructions that he was to have 'no solemn funeral, no monument, but to be buried in oblivion, alleging the precedents of Seneca, Warham the Archbishop of Canterbury and chancellor, and Budaeus the learned Frenchman, who all took the like course'.

Although Ellesmere's stoicism was indulged, his heir John Egerton, Viscount Brackley, thought the proffered earldom too good a reward to pass up. Overcoming physical pain ('bound hand and foot with the gout'), Brackley embarked on a campaign to secure himself the earldom, allegedly giving £20,000 to Buckingham to encourage him to persuade the King. The bid seemed to meet with success, as James gave order for the warrant; but by the end of March, 'it sticks now I know not where, unless it be that he must give down more milk, though if it be true that is said £20,000 was a fair soup before.'[31]

In return for the money, Brackley wanted to be invested immediately, a ceremony that required the presence of the King. Bacon helped Brackley by searching out precedents that might support Buckingham's suggestion that the relevant letters patent could perhaps be delivered 'without the ordinary solemnities of a creation'.[32] However, he advised caution.

Since the King means it, I would not have your Lordship, for the satisfying a little trembling or panting of the heart in my Lord or Lady Brackley, to expose your Lordship's self, or myself (whose opinion would be thought to be relied upon), or the King our master, to envy with the nobility of this realm; as to have these ceremonies often dispensed with, which in conferring honour have used to be observed; like a kind of Doctor *Bullatus* without the ceremony of a commencement: The

King and you know I am not ceremonious in nature, and therefore you may think (if it please you) I do it in judgement.[33]

The King, it transpired, was thinking along similar lines. 'His Majesty, never having heard of any precedent in the like case, was of opinion that this would be of ill consequence in making that dignity as easy as the pulling out a sword to make a man knight, and so make it of little esteem.' Since Bacon could not supply an assured precedent, James determined 'not so to precipitate the business, as to expose that dignity to censure and contempt in omitting the solemnities required and usually belonging unto it'.[34] Ultimately, however, although Bacon played down other precedents that Brackley sent to him,[35] the King decided that it would be better 'to dispatch it rather in this time of his journey, than to stay it till his return, when he might be importuned by others for the like who cannot have the same colour to press him so long after'.[36] Lord Brackley was therefore created earl of Bridgewater on 28 May by patent, 'which now,' commented Chamberlain, 'will become as good a way to all intents and purposes as by investiture'.[37]

For a few weeks, Sir Francis Bacon effectively controlled the government of Britain. He revelled in his easy access to the royal family. 'The Queen calleth upon me for the matter of her house,' he threw into his correspondence nonchalantly. 'I made the Prince laugh, when I told him I resigned [the Prince's seal] with more comfort than I received it; he understanding me that I had changed for a better.'[38] But he was kept busy. An 'account of Council business', written on 30 March, suggests something of the range of his responsibilities: 'remedy against the infestation of pirates', including raising funds from merchants to combat the pest, and discussion on how to arm and proceed against them; 'safety and caution against tumults and disorders in and near the city', following a particularly disturbed Shrove Tuesday, in which apprentices had laid waste to a new playhouse, and thinking ahead for May Day; 'buildings in and about London', stopping all further building through a police of aldermen, justices and provosts' marshals; the case against the Witheringtons; and 'the causes of Ireland',[39] including a project for erecting staple towns in Ireland for the exportation of wool.[40] Bacon wrote to the King: 'My continual meditations upon your Majesty's service and greatness' provoked an additional 'remembrance' to be added to the instructions for Sir John Digby, now Vice-Chamberlain, which 'in my judgment, I think to be *de vero* and *ad populum* [true and popular]'.[41]

In one matter, Bacon decided to depart from instructions, namely in respect of 'the proclamation, that lieutenants (not being councillors), deputy-lieutenants, justices of the peace, and gentlemen of quality, should depart the city, and reside in their countries'. The Council declared that 'we find the city so dead of company of that kind for the present, as we account it out of season to command that which is already done. But after men have attended their business the two next terms, in the end of Trinity Term (according to their custom) when the justices attend at the Star Chamber, I shall give a charge concerning the same. And that shall be corroborated by a proclamation, if cause be.'

Secretary Winwood mentioned the Council's decision in a letter to Lake, who mentioned it to the King. 'He brake into great choler,' Lake informed Winwood, 'saying he was contemned and his commandments neglected; and whatsoever reason could be alleged, he persisted in his passion. That he would never endure that a matter so solemnly determined by him in the presence of his Council, and by them approved, should so soon as his back is turned be changed without his privity.' Lake was commanded to write immediately to Winwood and Bacon, 'and to signify his pleasure that he would have the proclamation presently to proceed, and such expedition be made in it as that without fail it be here' – at Lincoln – 'to pass his hand before his Majesty go from this town'.[42]

When nothing happened immediately, Lake was commanded to write again. 'It seemeth my Lord Keeper hath written to my Lord of Buckingham something concerning it. But his Majesty hath commanded me to let you understand that obedience is better than sacrifice, and that he knoweth he is King of England. And howsoever people be now out of town, they may return. At least the proclamation can do no hurt, but will manifest his care. I cannot well by letter tell you how much he is moved by these things, but I wish you to speak with my Lord Keeper and that it may be despatched without any more excuse.'[43]

As it happened, the Council had sent the proclamation to be signed as soon as the King's reaction became known, on 1 April. Four days later, Buckingham assured Bacon that all was in order. 'I have acquainted his Majesty with your letters, who liked all your proceedings well, saving only that point, for which you have since made amends in obeying his pleasure, touching the proclamation.'[44]

Scarcely had this panic had died down when Bacon was hit by another calamity – news of the death of Buckingham. Happily, the report was in error. 'When I heard here your Lordship was dead,' he wrote on the seventh, 'I thought I had lived too long. That was (to tell your Lordship truly) the state of my mind upon that report. Since, I hear it as an idle mistaking of my Lord Evers for my Lord Villiers. God's name be blessed, that you are alive to do infinite good, and not so much as sick or ill disposed for any thing I now hear.'[45]

On 7 May, Bacon took his seat in the Court of Chancery. The procession from Dorset House was a splendid occasion, rivalling in magnificence James's entry into Edinburgh nine days later. 'Our Lord Keeper', wrote George Gerrard, 'exceeds all his predecessors in the bravery and multitude of his servants. It amazes those that look on his beginnings, besides never so indulgent a master. On the first day of term he appeared in his greatest glory; for to the Hall, besides his own retinue, did accompany him all the Lords of his Majesty's Council and others, with all knights and gentlemen that could get horses and footcloths.' John Chamberlain was also present. 'We came to town to see the new Lord Keeper ride in pomp to Westminster accompanied by most of the Council and nobility about this town, with other gallants to the number of more than two hundred horse, besides the Judges and the Inns of Court. There was a great deal more bravery and better show of horse than was expected in the King's absence, but both Queen and Prince sent all their followers, and his other friends did their best to honour him.'[46]

In Chancery, Bacon made his first speech as Lord Keeper, setting out a manifesto for his time in office, 'whereby your Lordships and the rest of the presence shall see the whole time of my sitting in Chancery contracted into one hour'. He went on to outline plans for reformation, which would satisfy the King's four charges – to contain the Chancery's jurisdictions; to ensure that the use of the Great Seal did not become a matter of course, and that the King should be acquainted if he had any scruple concerning its use; to ensure speedy justice by getting rid of unnecessary delays; and that justice would be done 'with as easy charge as ought be; and that those same brambles that grow about justice, of needless charge and expense, and all manner of exactions, mought be rooted out so far as mought be'.[47] As John Chamberlain noted wryly, the speech's discussion of reformation was given 'not without glancing at his predecessor, whose beginnings he professed he would follow, but excepted against some of his later courses, yet would not undo anything he had done. He pleased himself much in the flourishing of the law, and that great lawyers' sons took the way to succeed their fathers' – reminding his audience that he was the son of a Lord Keeper, effectively claiming his birthright.[48]

The day's festivities did not end with the speech.

The greatest part of his train dined with him that day, which cost him the setting on, if it be as is generally reported that the charge of that dinner came to £700 wherein he followed not his pattern he seemed so much to approve, for dining the week before with the rest of the Council at Secretary Winwood's, besides all other good words and commendations of that entertainment, both he and the earl of Worcester sent to entreat to have the bill of cates, and to have the same cooks:

but sure for ought I can learn since I came, the expense of that dinner was in no sort proportionable to that sum.[49]

Bacon reported the day to Buckingham: 'Yesterday I took my place in Chancery, which I hold only from the King's grace and favour, and your friendship. There was much ado, and a great deal of world. But this matter of pomp, which is heaven to some men, is hell to me, or purgatory at least. It is true I was glad to see that the King's choice was so generally approved, and that I had so much interest in men's good wills and good opinions, because it maketh me the fitter instrument to do my master service and my friend also.'[50] Closer to home, however, there was talk that Bacon's performance had not been what it might have been. John Chamberlain put this forward as one reason why the speech, once delivered, vanished from view. He had been 'promised a copy; but as I hear himself hath hindered that none shall be dispersed: whether it be, as some think, that there is a meaning to have it printed, or rather as others to the contrary, that it was not like himself nor altogether worthy of him'.[51]

The sumptuousness of Bacon's inauguration as Lord Keeper continued to be displayed in his everyday life. John Aubrey later wrote of how, during James's Scottish progress, Bacon 'gave audiences in great state to ambassadors in the Banqueting House at Whitehall'. Even 'when his lordship was at his country house at Gorhambury, St Albans seemed as if the court were there, so nobly did he live'.[52] As he threw himself into the high life, Bacon became noticeably distanced from his legal duties. Star Chamber days, reported Chamberlain on 24 May, 'have been few or none this term, or not past once at most, by reason of the Lord Keeper's indisposition which hath greatly hindered both that court and the Chancery'. If the situation persisted, he continued, it 'would much disturb the whole course of Westminster Hall and the Council table, where matters of greatest moment are still put off and reserved till he may be present. His infirmity is given out to be the gout, and the greatest harm or sense he hath of it is in his heel; and sometimes he takes pleasure to flout and play with his disease which he says hath changed the old covetous course and is become ambitious, for never beggar had the gout but he.' Joking about his health was a dangerous strategy for the Lord Keeper, however. 'In truth the general opinion is that he hath so tender a constitution both of body and mind that he will hardly be able to undergo the burden of so much business as his place requires, and that if he do not rouse and force himself beyond his natural inclination both private subjects and the commonwealth will suffer much.'[53] It may be that Bacon realised this more than his witticisms suggested: Edward Sherburn told Carleton on 16 May that Bacon was indeed ill with the gout, although he refused to let it be so called.[54]

Bacon was well enough to deliver speeches on 19 May, when three new judicial appointments were solemnised. In his speech to Sir John Denham, being sworn in as a Baron of the Exchequer, he took the opportunity to reiterate some points 'apt for the times': 'you ought to maintain the King's prerogative, and to set down with yourself that the King's prerogative and the law are not two things; but the King's prerogative is law, and the principal part of the law; the first-born or *pars prima* of the law; and therefore in conserving and maintaining that, you conserve and maintain the law. There is not in the body of the man one law of the head, and another of the body, but all is one entire law.'[55]

His health recovered, Bacon made rapid progress through his legal business. On 8 June he could boast to Buckingham that

This day I have made even with the business of the kingdom for common justice. Not one cause unheard. The lawyers drawn dry of all the motions they were to make. Not one petition unanswered. And this I think could not be said in our age before. This I speak not out of ostentation, but out of gladness, when I have done my duty. I know men think I cannot continue, if I should thus oppress myself with business. But that account is made. The duties of life are more than life. And if I die now I shall die before the world be weary of me, which in our times is somewhat rare.

He did admit to one physical defect: 'All this while I have been a little unperfect in my foot. But I have taken pains more like the beast with four legs, than like man with scarce two legs. But if it be a gout (which I do neither acknowledge nor much disclaim) it is a good-natured gout; for I have no rage of it, and it goeth away quickly. I have hope it is but an accident of changing from a field-air to a Thames-air [from Gray's Inn to Dorset House]; or rather, I think, it is the distance of the King and your Lordship from me that doth congeal my humours and spirits.' Attempting to allay the earl's fears – which he had expressed in a letter of the third – he reinterated that 'it is true, that at this present I am very well, and my supposed gout quite vanished.'[56] Eleven days later, he was able to assure Viscount Fenton that his health, 'I thank God, is good, and I hope this supposed gout was but an incomer'.[57]

Despite Bacon's confidence, he was too far away from the King and from Buckingham to be truly secure in his place. His success in London was intensely vulnerable to jealous court gossip. In early July, while preparing for his Star Chamber speech on the last day of Trinity Term (10 July), Bacon received a letter from a friend in the court in Scotland which, while attesting to the King's 'due approbation' of the Chancery speech, hinted at an envious faction at work against him. 'I can read here whatsoever your Lordship doth act there; and your courses be such as you need not to fear to give copies of them. But the King's ears be wide and long, and he seeth with many eyes. All this works for your honour and comfort. I pray God nothing be soiled, heated or cooled in the carriage. Envy sometimes attends virtues and not for good; and these bore certain proprieties and circumstances inherent to your Lordship's mind, which men may admire.'[58] Bacon's greatest rival was about to become that envy's tool.

★

Sir Edward Coke was not the sort of man to be discouraged easily. A month after his dismissal he was seen at Newmarket, 'kissing his Majesty's hands' and receiving the royal promise 'that although his Majesty had removed him from the place of Chief Justice for some special ends, as holding him not altogether so fit a man to do his Majesty service in that office, yet his meaning was not to lose so good a servant, but that he would have him in remembrance and employ him in some other condition'. During the following week he waited on the King again, prompting speculation 'that his Majesty will create him a Baron, sometime these holidays; for either his friends (whereof the Queen and Prince are two) or else his money, or both together, hath so turned the current, as your Lordship may see which way the tide begins to turn.' But it was only in late December 1616 that the true reason for the King's favour became evident, as Chamberlain reported: 'some interpret this kindness to be but for the compassing of a match for the Lord Villiers' brother with one of his daughters.' The lucky couple were Coke's daughter Frances and Buckingham's brother Sir John Villiers; the match would alter the dynamics of the tangled relations of Bacon, Buckingham and Coke beyond recognition.[59]

On 16 June 1617 Winwood sent to Buckingham a letter expressing Coke's wish to be restored to the King's favour and to renew the marriage proposals, which had encountered some difficulties.[60] Buckingham took up the offer with alacrity, and negotiations recommenced between Coke and Sir John Villiers. However, Coke's wife – and long ago the aim of Bacon's attentions – Lady Hatton opposed the match, proclaiming that her daughter Frances was precontracted to the earl of Oxford (who was usefully absent in Italy), and, to prevent the marriage, effectively kidnapped Frances, placing her in a succession of safe houses – first with Lady Withipole, and then a house owned by Lord Argyle at Hampton Court.[61]

While these events were unfolding, Bacon quarrelled publicly with Secretary Winwood, as Bishop Goodman recounted scurrilously: 'The difference fell out upon a very small occasion, that Winwood did beat his dog from lying upon a stool, which Bacon seeing said that every gentleman did love a dog. This passed on; then at the same time having some business to sit upon, it should seem that Secretary Winwood sat too near my Lord Keeper, and his Lordship willed him either to keep or to know his distance. Whereupon he rose from table, and I think he did him no good office.' Rawley later recalled Bacon's cryptic response to Queen Anne's enquiring as to the cause of the quarrel: 'Madam, I can say no more, than he is proud, and I am proud.'[62]

In fact, there were other, more tangible causes for Bacon's conduct than pride. Since the middle of June, he had been in secret correspondence with Lady Hatton – secret because, as she put it, 'I cannot in this misinterpreting time, resort to your Lordship without injury' – and had received from her the sum of five hundred pieces. This was sent on 14 June 1617; two days later (the same day that Winwood approached Buckingham on Coke's behalf), Lady Hatton requested of Bacon that 'my Lord Coke might be summoned to attend your Lordships on Sunday', so that the Privy Council might hear the respective cases, and reach a conclusion to her advantage.[63] In other words, the Winwood–Bacon quarrel was in fact the bickering of Sir Edward Coke and Lady Hatton's respective seconds in the battle over their daughter. Bacon felt that Winwood 'hath officiously busied himself to make a match' between Villiers and Coke's daughter, and 'as we hear, he doth it,' he complained to Buckingham, rather 'to make a faction, than out of any great affection to your Lordship'.[64]

Lady Compton, mother of the Villiers brothers, applied to Bacon on Coke's behalf for a warrant to recover possession of Frances Coke. Bacon declined to grant the warrant, and wrote to Buckingham on 12 July, describing the affair as 'a business which your Lordship may think to concern myself; but I do think it concerneth your Lordship much more.' Bacon pointed out that while Winwood had Coke's consent '(as we hear) upon reasonable conditions for your brother', they were 'no better than without question may be found in some other matches'. More to the point, 'the mother's consent is not had, nor the young gentlewoman's, who expecteth a great fortune from her mother, which without her consent is endangered. This match, out of my faith and freedom towards your Lordship, I hold very inconvenient both for your brother and yourself.'

Buckingham's brother, he reasoned, would be marrying into a disgraced house, 'a troubled house of man and wife'; and Buckingham himself stood to 'lose all such your friends as are adverse to Sir Edward Coke; (myself only except, who out of a pure love and thankfulness shall ever be firm to you)'. He advised his friend to tell his mother 'that your desire is that the marriage be not pressed or proceeded in without the consent of both parents; and so either break it altogether, or defer any further [dealing] in it, till your Lordship's return'.[65]

As he wrote this letter, however, the situation was changing. Coke had located his daughter in Hampton Court: obtaining a warrant from Winwood on Saturday 12 July, he went to fetch her, 'but indeed went further than his warrant and brake open divers doors before he got her. His Lady was at his heels, and if her coach had not tired in the pursuit after him, there was like to be strange tragedies.'[66] Lady Hatton, accompanied by Sir John Holles, immediately came to seek Bacon's assistance. Their journey was aggravated by an overturn, but

> at last to my Lord Keeper's they came, but could not have instant access to him for that his people told them he was laid at rest, being not well. Then my Lady Hatton desired she might be in the next room where my Lord lay, that she might be the first that [should] speak with him after he was stirring. The door-keeper fulfilled her desire and in the meantime gave her a chair to rest herself in, and there left her alone: but not long after, she rose up and bounced against my Lord Keeper's door, and waked him and affrighted him, that he called his men to him; and they opening the door, she thrust in with them, and desired his Lordship to pardon her boldness, but she was like a cow that had lost her calf, and so justified [herself] and pacified my Lord's anger, and got his warrant and my Lord Treasurer's warrant and others of the Council to fetch her daughter from the father and bring them both to the Council.[67]

On Bacon's advice,[68] Lady Hatton appealed to the Privy Council the following day, 'complaining in somewhat a passionate and tragical manner, that while by his Majesty's grace she was settling and securing her poor fortune, she was by violence dispossessed of her child'. It was decided that Coke should deliver his daughter to the custody of Clerk of the Council Sir Clement Edmondes, and a messenger was duly despatched to Coke at Stoke Poges, in Buckinghamshire; he refused, however, given the lateness of the hour, to allow his daughter to leave. Instead, he would 'upon his peril' deliver her to Edmondes the following day.

Lady Hatton was incensed. She rushed back to the Council table to procure a warrant 'with a clause of assistance to bring her daughter to Mr. Edmondes' house accordingly'. By this time Frances Coke, accompanied by Lady Compton (Villiers' mother, her intended mother-in-law) and some horsemen, had left her father's house and was on the road. Lady Hatton set off with what she described as 'some tall fellows' – in fact, some 'three score men and pistols'. Luckily, the two parties did not meet: 'if they had,' it was reported, 'there had been a notable skirmish, for there was Clem Coke, my Lord's fighting son, and they all swore they would die in the place before they would part with her'.

Frances was delivered to Edmondes, and then moved on – when the Council became alarmed at the potential 'disorder' resulting from her numerous visitors – to the house of Lord Knyvet, near Staines, a destination mutually agreed by her parents. The Council 'likewise enjoined Sir Edward and his Lady to forbear all occasion of violence or disturbance, whatsoever, as well touching the person of their daughter as any other matters of point concerning their business'.

On Tuesday 15 July, Coke appeared before the Council to answer a charge of 'riot and force'. He claimed that he had lawfully been defending his daughter, and pressed countercharges against Lady Hatton: '(1) For conveying away her daughter *clam et secrete*. (2) For endeavouring to bind her to my Lord Oxford without her father's consent. (3) For counterfeiting a letter of my Lord of Oxford offering her marriage. (4) For plotting to surprise her daughter and take her away by force to the breach of the King's peace and for that purpose asssembling a body of desperate fellows, whereof the consequences might have been dangerous.' The Lords decided that Coke would have to answer the charges in the Star Chamber 'for the force and riot used by him upon the house of Sir Edmund Withipole, to be in that Court heard and sentenced as justice shall appertain'.

In a later sitting, the Council admonished Secretary Winwood, telling him that he was subject to a *praemunire* for giving Coke a search warrant without consulting his fellow lords. Lady Compton was then sent for and wished well by the Council, who declared that they were ready to serve her son Buckingham, 'with all true affection, whereas others did it out of faction and ambition'. At this point, Winwood produced from his sleeve a letter from the King, which gave royal support to everything Winwood had done in the affair. He asked the Lords whether they would care to reconsider whose 'faction and ambition' had inspired this trouble. 'To which', wrote Chamberlain, 'there was no reply.'

A couple of days later, the King wrote directly to Bacon. Lady Hatton had to return Frances to her father 'and not again entice her away. And the Lady Frances shall not be contracted to anyone without the assent of Sir Edward Coke.' Bacon, realising his mistake, quickly wrote to his patron. 'I do think long to hear from your Lordship touching my last letter,' he wrote from Gorhambury on 25 July, 'wherein I gave you my opinion touching your brother's match. As I then showed my dislike of the matter, so the carriage of it here in the manner I dislike as much. If your Lordship think it is humour or interest in me that leads me, God judge my sincerity.'[69]

On the same day, he also wrote to the King. He gave James the benefit of 'my honest and disinterested opinion in the business of the match of

Sir John Villiers, which I take to be *magnum in parvo* [much in miniature], preserving always the laws and duties of a firm friend to my Lord of Buckingham, whom I will never cease to love, and to whom I have written already, but have not heard yet from him'. He made 'three suits' to the King. First, that, 'if there be any merit in drawing on that match', he would thank not Coke or Winwood, but those who,

> carrying your commandments and directions with strength and justice, (in the matter of the governor of Dieppe, in the matter of Sir Robert Rich, and in the matter of protecting the Lady, according to your commandment), have so humbled Sir Edward Coke, as he seeks now that with submission, which (as your Majesty knows) before he rejected with scorn. For this is the true orator that hath persuaded this business, as I doubt not but your Majesty in your excellent wisdom doth easily discover.
>
> My second suit is, that your Majesty would not think me so pusillanimous, as that I, who when I was but Mr. Bacon, had ever through your Majesty's favour good reason at Sir Edward Coke's hands when he was at the greatest, should now that your Majesty (by your great goodness) hath placed me so near your chair, fear him or take umbrage of him in respect of mine own particular.

He also asked James to inform him directly if he did indeed wish the match to go ahead; because he believed, 'imagining with myself (though I will not wager upon women's minds) that I can prevail more with the mother than any other man. For if I should be requested in it from my Lord of Buckingham, the answer of a true friend ought to be, that I had rather go against his mind than against his good: but your Majesty I must obey; and besides I shall conceive that your Majesty out of your great wisdom and depth doth see those things which I see not.'

He asked James to take into consideration

> that your state is at this time not only in good quiet and obedience, but in good affection and disposition. Your Majesty's prerogative and authority having risen some just degrees above the horizon more than heretofore, which hath dispersed vapours. Your Judges are in good temper. Your Justices of peace, which is the body of the gentlemen of England, grow to be loving and obsequious, and to be weary of the humour of ruffling. All mutinous spirits grow to be a little poor, and to draw in their horns, and not the less for your Majesty's disauthorising the man I now speak of.

All this could be altered by the marriage: 'Now then I reasonably doubt that if there be but an opinion of his coming in with the strength of such an alliance, it will give a turn and relapse in men's minds unto the former state of things, hardly to be holpen; to the great weakening of your Majesty's service.'[70]

Days passed without word from the King, and Bacon tried to prompt a response with little upbeat notes to Buckingham: 'I am, I thank God, much relieved with my being in the country-air, and the order I keep; so that of late years I have found not my health better. Your Lordship writeth seldomer than you were wont; but when you are once gotten into England, you will be more at leisure.'[71] Finally, in early August, three weeks after his first letter, came a letter from Buckingham. But it was not the letter that Bacon had anticipated or desired. In place of the usual easy declarations of friendship and support, there was a new, unmistakable impatience in Buckingham's tone.

> My Lord,
>
> If your man had been addressed only to me, I should have been careful to have procured him a more speedy dispatch: but now you have found another way of address, I am excused; and since you are grown weary of employing me, I can be no otherwise in being employed. In this business of my brother's that you overtrouble yourself with, I understand from London by some of my friends that you have carried yourself much scorn and neglect both toward myself and my friends; which if it prove true I blame not you but myself, who was ever,
>
> Your Lordship's assured friend, G. Buckingham.[72]

The hint was enough. Bacon now had no choice but to make a complete volte-face. On the sixth he wrote to Buckingham, 'showing his acquiescence in the match'[73] – but the damage was done. Buckingham replied brusquely: 'I have received your Lordship's letter by your man; but having so lately imparted my mind to you in my former letters, I refer your Lordship to those letters, without making a needless repetition.'[74]

James also responded to Bacon; although the letter is now lost, its tenor can be inferred from Bacon's response to it. It contained 'some matter of dislike' which 'grieved me more than any event which hath fallen out in my life'. Bacon took succour, however, from the intermixed 'passages of trust and grace'. First, he acknowledged that the marriage of Sir John Villiers 'is *magnum in parvo* in both senses that your Majesty speaketh. But your Majesty perceiveth well that I took it to be in a further degree *majus in parvo*, in respect of your service. But for the second sense that your Majesty speaketh of *magnum in parvo*, in respect of the stir about it, being but a most lawful and ordinary thing,' he argued that the 'loud and vocal and as I may call it streperous carriage' proceeded from Coke's faction.

Now for the manner of my affection to my Lord of Buckingham, for whom I would spend my life, and that which is to me more, the cares of my life; I must humbly confess that it was in this a little parent-like (this being no other term than his Lordship hath heretofore vouchsafed to my counsels); but in truth (and it please your Majesty) without any grain of disesteem for his Lordship's discretion. For I know him to be naturally a wise man, of a sound and staid wit and again I know he hath the best tutor in Europe. But yet I was afraid that the height of his fortune might make him too secure, and (as the proverb is) a looker-on sometimes seeth more than a gamester.

Concerning Buckingham, whom James had claimed to have played 'the part of a true friend' toward Bacon 'in palliating some errors of mine', he acknowledged that 'it is no new thing with me to be more and more bound to his Lordship', thanking both him and James for his 'gracious construction and favour' of his many errors. 'For I am not so ignorant of mine own case but that I know I am come in with as strong an envy of some particulars, as with the love of the general.'

As for his opposition to the Coke–Villiers marriage, he could explain it. He admitted that in Council business concerning Coke, 'I was sometimes sharp (it may be too much). But it was with end to have your Majesty's will performed, or else when methought he was more peremptory than became him in respect of the honour of the table.' He also acknowleged that 'I disliked the riot or violence whereof we of your Majesty's Council gave your Majesty advertisement by our joint letter, and I disliked it the more because he justified it by law; which was his old song.' All the Council was 'as forward as myself' in granting the act. 'And all this had a fair end in a reconcilement made by Mr Attorney, whereby both husband and wife and child should have kept together; which if it had continued, I am persuaded the match had been in better and fairer forwardness than now it is.'

More important, however, was 'the times of things'. Bacon asserted emphatically that he had not 'had any word or letter from his Lordship of the business till I wrate my letter of advice; or again after my letter of advice till five weeks after,' within the past week. Therefore, 'although I did in truth presume that the earl would do nothing without your Majesty's privity, yet I was in some doubt by this his silence of his own mind, that he was not earnest in it, but only was content to embrace the officious offers and endeavours of others.' Once he was aware of Buckingham's knowledge of the affair, 'I think Sir Edward Coke himself the last time he was before the Lords mought plainly perceive an alteration in my carriage. And now that your Majesty hath been pleased to open yourself to me, I shall be willing to further the match by anything that shall be desired of me, or that is in my power.' The King had detected 'some dregs of spleen' in Bacon's using the phrase 'Mr. Bacon': 'truly it was but to express in thankfulness the comparative of my fortune unto your Majesty the author of it.'

> For the interest which I have in the mother, I do not doubt but it was increased by this, that I in judgement (as I then stood) affected that which she did in passion. But I think the chief obligation was, that I stood so firmly to her in the matter of her assurance, wherein I supposed I did your Majesty's service, and mentioned it in a memorial of council-business (as half craving thanks for it). And sure I am now, that and the like hath made Sir Edward Coke a convert, as I did write to my Majesty in my lust. For the collation of the two spirits, I shall easily subscribe to your Majesty's censure: for Solomon were no true man, if in matter of malice the woman should not be the superior.[75]

Bacon subsequently sent for the Attorney-General and let him know that 'since I heard from court I was resolved to further the match and the conditions thereof for [Sir John's] advancement the best I could.' He also let Lady Hatton and some of her friends know that he 'would in anything declare for the match; which I did to the end that if they had any apprehension of my assistance they might be discouraged in it'. He assured Buckingham that he had sent word also 'to Sir John Butler, and after by letter to your Lady your mother, to tender my performance of any good office towards the match or the advancement from the mother. This was all I could think of for the present.'

Despite this public change of heart, his doubts persisted. 'I did ever fear that this alliance would go near to leese me your Lordship that I hold so dear.' He even risked complaining to Buckingham

> that I do hear my Lady your mother and your brother Sir John do speak of me with some bitterness and neglect. I must bear with the one as a lady and the other as a lover, and with both for your Lordship's sake, whom I will make judge of anything they shall have against me. But I hope, although I be true servant to your Lordship, you will not have me vassal to their passions, especially as long as they [are] governed by Sir Edward Coke and Secretary Winwood; the latter of which I take to be the worst; for Sir Edward Coke, I think, is more modest and discreet.

He asked Buckingham to 'signify to them that you have received satisfaction from me, and would have them use me friendly and in good manner. God keep us from these long journeys and absence, which makes misunderstandings and gives advantage to untroth.'[76]

From Nantwich, James replied to Bacon's last letter, pointing out that since he was so near to London there was little need for him to write, except so that Bacon

> may not err by mistaking our meaning. The first observation we are to make is, That whereas you would invert the second sense wherein we took your *magnum in parvo*, in accounting it to be made *magnum* by their streperous carriage that were for the match, we cannot but show you your mistaking therein. For every wrong must be judged by the first violent and wrongous ground whereupon it proceeds, and was not the thefteous stealing away of the daughter from her own father the first ground whereupon all this great noise hath since proceeded? For the ground of her getting again came upon a lawful and ordinary warrant subscribed by one of our Council for redress of the former violence, and except the father of a child might be proved to be either lunatic or idiot, we never read in any law that either it could be lawful for any creature to steal his child from him or that it was matter of noise and streperous carriage for him to hunt for the recovery of his child again.

Turning to Bacon's description of his feelings for Buckingham as 'parent-like', he wrote that Bacon's alleged affection, and praise of Buckingham's natural qualities, were 'throw[n] all down by a direct imputation upon him': 'we are sure you do not deny to have had a greater jealousy of his discretion than (so far as we conceive) he ever deserved at your or any man's hands.'

The only way James could interpret Bacon's remarks is that he was 'afraid that the height of his fortune might make him misknow himself. And surely if that be your *parent-like affection* toward him he hath no obligation to you for it.' Since James could not detect a trace of that vice in Buckingham, and would be sorry if the world thought the same, 'we cannot conceal that we think it was least your part of any to enter into that jealousy of him, whom of we have heard you oft speak in a contrary style.'

Then there was 'that error of yours which he lately palliated whereof you seem to pretend ignorance'. He referred to Bacon's commendation to Buckingham of Lowden to be a Baron of the Exchequer in Ireland (at the Queen's request): how he made him undertake a long journey and supplied only 'a slight recommendation' with the result that Lowden would have been 'undone and your credit a little blasted if Buckingham had not by his importunity made us both grant your more than suit (for you had already acted a part of it), and likewise run a hazard of the hindrance of our own service, by preferring a person to so important a place whom you so slightly recommended'.

In the present business with Coke, 'you either do or at least would seem to mistake us a little.' 'For first, whereas you excuse yourself of the oppositions you made against Sir Edward Coke at the council table both for that and other causes, we never took upon us such a patrociny of Sir Edward Coke, as if he were a man not to be meddled withal in any case, for whatsoever you did against him by our employment and commandment, we ever allowed it and still do for good service on your part.' In opposition to Bacon's claim that Coke was at fault in resorting to violence, James pointed out that it was 'the riot and violence of them that stale away his daughter' which started the whole affair, and which compelled Coke 'beyond his patience'. It may have been the entire Council who opposed Coke, but the blame fell on Bacon for 'the refusal to sign a warrant for the father to the recovery of his child, clad with those circumstances (as is reported) of your slight carriage to Buckingham's mother when she repaired to you upon so reasonable an errand'.

Although Bacon claimed that he was ignorant of the King's or Buckingham's intentions when he opposed the marriage, 'that would have served for a reasonable excuse not to have furthered such a business till you had been first employed in it, but that can serve for no excuse of crossing anything that so nearly concerned one whom you profess such friendship unto.' It behoved Bacon to wait to hear what Buckingham had to say: 'for if you had willingly given your consent and hand to the recovery of the young gentlewoman, and then written both to us and to him what inconvenience appeared to you to be in such a match, that had been the part indeed of a true servant to us and a true friend to him; but first to make an opposition and then to give advice by way of friendship, is to make the plough to go before the horse.'[77]

It was a devastating attack. Bacon replied on 31 August, holding over a full answer until the King returned, but dealing with one point immediately.

There is one part of your Majesty's letter that I would be sorry to take time to answer; which is, that your Majesty conceiveth that, whereas I wrate that the height of my Lord's fortune mought make him secure, I meant that he was turned proud or unknowing of himself. Surely the opinion which I have ever had of my Lord (whereof your Majesty is best witness) is far from that. But my meaning was plain and simple. That his Lordship mought through his great fortune be the less apt to cast and foresee the unfaithfulness of friends and malignity of enviers and accidents of times. Therefore I beseech your Majesty to deliver me in this from any the least imputation upon my dear and noble Lord and friend.

He signed off, 'expecting that that sun which when it went from us left cold weather, and now it is returned towards us hath brought with it a blessed harvest, will when it cometh to us disperse all mists and mis-takings'.[78]

James reached Coventry by the end of August, and Coke went to meet him, being well received. Yelverton was hot on his heels, and reported back to Bacon miserably on 3 September that the King's face had been 'more clouded towards me than I looked for'. Coke, he reported, had 'not forborne by any engine to heave both at your Honour and at myself; and he works by the weighiest instrument, the earl of Buckingham, who as I see sets him as close to him as his shirt, the earl speaking in Sir Edward's phrase, and as it were menacing in his spirit.' Testing Buckingham's temper, Yelverton 'found it very fervent, misled by misformation which yet I find he embraced as truth, and did nobly and plainly tell me he would not secretly bite, but whosoever had had any interest or tasted of the opposition to his brother's marriage he would as openly oppose them to their faces, and they should discern what favour he had by the power he would use'. Despite Yelverton's strong protestations that he and Bacon had in no way 'opposed, but many ways had furthered the fair passage to the marriage', and that it was Coke's manner ('so transported with passion') that was the stumbling block, Yelverton left Buckingham 'leaning still to the first relation of envious and odious adversaries'.

The King gave Yelverton his hand to kiss, 'but intermixed withal that I deserved not that favour, if three or four things were true which he had to object against me.' At Yelverton's request, he agreed to reserve his judgement until he had heard his case, 'which could not be then, his other occupations pressed him so much. All this was in the hearing of the earl; and I protest I think the confidence in my innocency made me depart half justified, for I likewise kissed his Majesty's hand at his departure.'

Yelverton also intimated to Bacon that it was common knowledge that Buckingham 'professeth openly against you as forgetful of his kindness, and unfaithful to him in his love and in your actions'. Moreover, 'he returneth the shame upon himself, in not listening to counsel that dissuaded his affection from you, and not to mount you so high, not forbearing in open speech (as divers have told me, and this bearer, your gentleman, hath heard also) to tax you, as if it were an inveterate custom with you, to be unfaithful to him as you were to the earls of Essex and Somerset'. Bacon's dubious record of service to his patrons had come back to haunt him.

Rumour also had it that Bacon's 'greatness shall be abated, and as your tongue hath been as a razor to some, so shall theirs be to you', and that many petitions against Bacon had been passed to the King. All things considered, concluded Yelverton, Coke, 'as if he were already upon his wings, triumphs exceedingly; hath much private conference with his Majesty; and in public doth offer himself and thrust open the King with as great boldness of speech as heretofore. It is thought and much feared that at Woodstock he will again be recalled to the council table; for neither are the earl's eyes nor his thoughts ever off him.' Indeed, Sir Edward 'with much audacity affirmeth his daughter to be most deeply in love with Sir John Villiers, that the contract pretended with the earl [of Oxford] is counterfeit, and the letter also that is pretended to come from the earl'.

Yelverton proposed that Bacon should attend James at Woodstock ('the sight of you will fright some'); that he justify all his proceedings as 'joint acts' with the other lords; 'that you retort the clamour and noise in this business upon Sir Edward Coke, by the violence of his carriage'; and 'that you seem not dismayed, but open yourself bravely and confidently, wherein you can excel all subjects; by which means I know you shall amaze some and daunt others'.[79]

Two days later, Buckingham himself replied to Bacon, at James's request. 'I have received so many letters lately from your Lordship', he complained, 'that I cannot answer them severally.' Instead, he addressed what he identified as 'the ground of them all', namely that Bacon 'feareth I am so incensed against you that I will hearken to every information that is made unto me. As his Majesty is not apt to give ear to any idle report against men of your place; so for myself I will answer that it is far from my disposition to take any advantage of that kind.' Although Bacon was not let off the hook ('for your Lordship's unkind dealing with me in this matter of my brother's, time will try all'), Buckingham assured him 'that you know his Majesty to be so judicious that whatsoever he heareth, he will keep one ear open to you; which being indeed his own princely disposition, you may be assured of his gracious favour in that kind.'[80]

Sir Anthony Weldon supplies a characteristically broad account of Bacon's next encounter with his estranged patron. Hearing that the King was returning to London, Bacon

began to believe the play was almost at an end, he might personate a King's part no longer, and therefore did again reinvest with his old rags of baseness, which were so tattered and poor at the King's coming to Windsor; he attended two days at Buckingham's chamber, being not admitted to any better place, than the room where trencher-scrapers and lackeys attended, there sitting upon an old wooden chest, (amongst such as for his baseness, were only fit for his companions, although the honour of his place did merit far more respect) with his purse and seal lying by him on that chest; myself told a servant of my Lord of Buckingham's, it was a shame to see the purse and seal of so little value, or esteem in his chamber, though the carrier without it, merited nothing but scorn, being worst among the basest. He told me they had command it must be so; after two days he had admittance; at first entrance, fell down flat on his face at the duke's foot, kissing it, vowing never to rise till he had his pardon, then was he again reconciled, and since that time so very a slave to the duke, and all that family, that he durst not deny the command of the meanest of the kindred, nor oppose any thing; by this you see, a base spirit, is ever most concomitant with the proudest mind, and surely never so many parts, and so base and abject a spirit, tenanted together in any one earthen cottage, as in this one man.[81]

Even allowing for Weldon's talent for fiction, Bacon's first encounters with the King and the favourite must have been highly charged, edgy affairs.

James returned to London on 15 September. Bacon promptly desired to speak with him regarding a new threat against his person which had arisen at the Council, and passed a note concerning it during an interview with Buckingham on 21 or 22 September. The case concerned one Baynton or Baynham who had allegedly threatened to kill the King; he was still on the loose, 'and said by some to be mad or half mad'. Bacon counselled that James, to avoid personal contact with undesirable suitors, should 'revive the commission for suits. For it may prevent any the like wicked cogitation which the devil may put into the mind of a roarer or swaggerer upon a denial: and besides it will free his Majesty from much importunity, and save his coffers also.'[82]

James put off a decision on Bacon's suggestion until his return to Hampton Court. Reporting this verdict, Buckingham took the opportunity of appending

a discovery unto you of mine inward thoughts, proceeding upon the discourse you had with me this day. For I do freely confess that your offer of submission unto me, and in writing (if so I would have it), battered so the unkindness that I had conceived in my heart for your behaviour towards me in my absence, as out of the old sparks of my affection towards you I went to sound his Majesty's intention how he means to behave himself towards you, specially in any public meeting; where I found on the one part his Majesty so little satisfied with your late answer unto him, which he counted (for I protest I use his own terms) confused and childish, and his rigorous resolution on the other part so fixed that he would put some public exemplary mark upon you, as I protest the sight of his deep-conceived indignation quenched my passion, making me upon the instant change from the person of a party into a peace-maker; so as I was forced upon my knees to beg of his

Majesty that he would put no public act of disgrace upon you. And as I dare say no other person would have been patiently heard in this suit by his Majesty but myself, so did I (though not without difficulty) obtain thus much. That he would not so far disable you from the merit of your future service, as to put any particular mark of disgrace upon your person.

He did, however, intend to 'give a kingly reprimand' collectively to all those Privy Councillors involved in the Coke affair, without specifying individuals who had been at fault.

'Thus your Lordship seeth the fruits of my natural inclination, and I protest all this time past it was no small grief unto me to hear the mouth of so many upon this occasion open to load you with innumerable malicious and detracting speeches, as if no music were more pleasing to my ears than to rail of you: which made me rather regret the ill nature of mankind, that like dogs love to set upon him that they see once snatched at.' In a postscript, he added: 'The force of our old kindness hath made me set down this in writing unto you, which some that have deserved ill of me in this action would be glad to obtain by word of mouth, though they be far enough from it for ought I yet see. But I beseech your Lordship to reserve this secretly to yourself only, till our meeting at Hampton Court, lest his Majesty should be highly offended for a cause that I know.'[83]

Bacon replied immediately, and ecstatically:

My ever best Lord, now better than yourself, – Your Lordship's pen or rather pencil hath portrayed towards me such magnanimity and nobleness and true kindness, as methinketh I see the image of some ancient virtue, and not anything of these times. It is the line of my life, and not the lines of my letter, that must express my thankfulness: wherein if I fail, then God fail me, and make me as miserable as I think myself at this time happy by this reviver, through his Majesty's singular clemency, and your incomparable love and favour. God deserve you, prosper you, and reward you for your kindness to Your raised and infinitely obliged friend and servant, Fr. Bacon, C.S.[84]

There was a price to be paid. Once Bacon had effected a reconciliation, Buckingham started to put more and more suits before him as Lord Keeper. This is undeniably the case: Buckingham's letters were filled with suits for his followers. Two weeks taken at random – the latter half of January 1618 – will illustrate the situation. On the sixteenth the earl recommends Sir John Cotton's petition against his dismissal from the office of *Custos rotulo-rum*;[85] on the twenty-first, one of the Grooms of His Majesty's Bedchamber with a suit 'for erecting an office for the making and copying of

Commissions that go out of Chancery for examination of witnesses';[86] on the twenty-third, that Sir George Tipping might be exempted from the fear of the sale of his land.[87] On the twenty-fifth, Bacon provided Buckingham with a progress report on the cases of Buckingham's brother Christopher Villiers and Patrick Mawle, the business of Mr Leviston, of Hawkins, of Sir Rowland and Lady Egerton, of Sir Gilbert Houghton and of Mr Moor.[88] On the twenty-eighth, Buckingham recommended the suit of Mr John Huddy, who had a cause in Chancery the following Saturday;[89] on the thirty-first, he wrote concerning Houghton, and thanking Bacon for being so 'bountiful' to his sister's husband's brother Jack Butler.[90] And so on. Buckingham was seen publicly as the route to the Chancery; Bacon was seen publicly as a tool of the favourite. It was a dangerously open arrangement which was to have devastating consequences for the Lord Keeper.

While Bacon was again 'raised', Coke was reaping the harvest of the turmoil. On 28 September he was restored to his position at the Council Table. As he took his seat, James took the opportunity to apologise for his own behaviour. 'I, James, am neither a god nor an angel, but a man like any other. Therefore I act like a man, and confess to loving those dear to me more than other men. You may be sure that I love the earl of Buckingham more than anyone else, and more than you who are here assembled. I wish to speak in my own behalf, and not to have it thought to be a defect, for Jesus Christ did the same, and therefore I cannot be blamed. Christ had his John and I have my George.'[91]

On the next day Sir John Villiers married Coke's daughter, who let it be known that her consent had been obtained, and that she in fact liked Sir John 'better than any other whatsoever, yet she desired to keep a solemn promise made to her mother, not to marry any man without her consent'.[92] Not content with these results, however, Sir Edward set about prosecuting his wife, prompting a relapse in her health: by 11 October she was said to be 'crazy [ill] in body and sick in mind' at Sir William Craven's. At the same time, Bacon and some others had been commissioned 'to examine her, of conspiracy, disobedience and many other misdemeanours, and to proceed against her according as they shall find cause'. Luckily for Lady Hatton, noted Chamberlain, 'her sickness stands her in some stead for the time, and if she come again to herself, it may be that in space there will grow grace: but sure she is in a wrong way now, and so animated towards her husband, that it is verily thought that she would not care to ruin herself to overthrow him.'[93]

Lady Hatton still had to give her consent to settle her fortune on the bride. On 31 October Chamberlain wrote:

For the King coming to town yesterday, it was told me that the earl of Buckingham meant to go himself and fetch her as it were in pomp from Sir William Craven's (where she hath been so long committed) and bring her to the King, who upon a letter of her submission is graciously affected towards her. But another cause is that seeing her yielding and as it were won to give her allowance to the late marriage, he will give her all the contentment and countenance he can in hope of the great portion she may bestow upon her, for there is little or nothing more to be looked for from Sir Edward Coke, who hath redeemed the land he had allotted his daughter for £20,000, so that they have already had £30,000 of him paid down.[94]

There would be an an ironic footnote to this whole affair. John Chamberlain's July gossip that the true target of Frances Coke's affections (or at least her marital ambitions) was 'a younger son of the Lord Treasurer's' was borne out: in time, she ran away with Sir Robert Howard.[95]

15

A New Course of Thriving:
Lord Chancellor Bacon

*I see much excess, which though it be a cause of poverty, yet
it is a sign of plenty.*
Sir Francis Bacon (1610)

I N HIS DRIVE for advancement Bacon could at last relax for a while.
There were still peaks in the distance – perhaps a viscountcy, perhaps
a barony – but he had achieved the position of his dreams: his father's
place as Lord Keeper. In mid-August 1617 he left Dorset House to take
up residence in his father's house (and his own birthplace), York House
on the Strand, as ever leased by the Archbishop of York to the incumbent
Lord Keeper.[1] Using Buckingham as a broker, Bacon rejected the offer of
Tobias Matthew, Archbishop of York, to 'put it wholly into his hands, to
do with it what he pleased' for life. Instead, he asked for (and received) a
twenty-one-year lease, twenty-one 'being the number of years which my
father and my predecessors fulfilled in it. A good fine requires certainty of
term; and I am well assured, that the charge I have expended in reparations
amounting to a thousand marks at least already, is more than hath been
laid out by all the tenants that have been in it since my remembrance,
answerable to that particular circumstance which is peculiar to myself, that
I was born there, and am like to end my days there.'[2]

Bacon's *de facto* power was boosted when, on 27 October, Secretary
Ralph Winwood died, after a short illness, remaining to the end 'in his
highest favour with the King, Queen, Prince, and principal favourite'. No
successor was appointed. James decided that 'he was never so well served
as when he was his own secretary', and gave the seals to Buckingham,
'and there perhaps they shall remain till they both grow weary of the
trouble.' What this meant in effect is that between them, Bacon and
Buckingham took on many of the duties and responsibilities of a Principal
Secretary of State.[3]

To add to Bacon's general sense of well-being, Lady Hatton was discharged on 2 November and a week later was hostess to the King and
Prince Charles at a lavish dinner at Hatton House. Anyone who was anyone

was present, including the Lord Keeper, with one notable exception, as John Pory noted: 'My Lord Coke only was absent, who in all vulgar opinions was there expected. His Majesty was never merrier nor more satisfied, who had not patience to sit a quarter of an hour without drinking the health of my Lady Elizabeth Hatton, which was pledged first by my Lord Keeper and my Lord Marquis Hamilton, and then by all the lords and ladies with great gravity and respect, and then by all the gallants in the next room.'[4] Bacon's cordial links with Lady Hatton remained strong: the following summer, knowing his interest in gardens, she was to send him seeds from her own garden at Hatton House.[5]

Lavish feasts at other people's houses were a welcome commodity to the King. The Privy Council was now immersed in studying possible ways of achieving a retrenchment of superfluous expenditure in the royal household. Sir Lionel Cranfield had the requisite financial experience, but he was taken ill,[6] and the task fell to Bacon. Although Bacon had raised the issue in an earlier memorial to James,[7] the irony that a man so notoriously liberal in his own household management should be relied on to cut costs in the King's household was not lost on him: acknowledging that 'these things are out of my element' he promised to do his best, 'as ill a *mesnager* as I am'.[8]

The Venetian ambassador, in a survey of court fees, estimated that Bacon brought in the following: 23s a day as Lord Chancellor, and annual payments of £200 for attending in the Star Chamber; £300 'upon the head of annuities'; £41 for robes; 2 tuns of wine; and £72 'paid out of the wardrobe'.[9] An account of Bacon's receipts and disbursements from June to September 1618 records some sizeable amounts of money coming in: the last week of June, for example, saw £100 from Mr Champion, for the surrender of the Clerkship of the Peace of the County of Surrey; £400 from Tobie Matthew; and £22 from the Recorder of London. But the same week saw 6s go as a gift 'to one that brought your lordship cherries and other things from Gorhambury by your lordship's order'; £1 2s 'laid out for going by water to Greenwich two several [separate] times by your Lordship's order and for other expenses there'; £5 10s 'to an Italian'; £22 'to Mr. Butler by your lordship's order as a gift'; £29 8s 10d to pay 'the lining draper and sempster's bill for cloth and lace and making your lordship's ruffs, and cuffs, and shirts'.[10] Clearly Francis Bacon was a generous man.

Bacon's household was huge, and somewhat casually managed. A 'cheque' of all his servants, undertaken in 1618, reveals a vast retinue. Heading it were his chaplains, Mr Oates and Mr Lewis. Then came his serjeant-at-arms Mr Leigh, his steward Mr Sharpeigh, and his seal-bearer Mr Hatcher. His two chief secretaries, Mr John Young and Mr Thomas

Meautys, were followed by his chief gentleman usher Mr Johnson, his auditor Mr Phillips, his gentleman of the horse Mr Edmund Meautys, and two remembrancers for benefices, Mr Harris and Mr Jones. Mr Troughton and Mr Borough occupied posts now illegible, while Mr Butler and Mr Thomas Bushell – of whom we shall hear more – served as gentlemen ushers. Then there was Clerk for the Commission of the Peace Mr Alman, receiver of casual fines Mr Hunt, and the gentlemen of his chamber: Mr Lowe, Mr Edney, Mr Woder, Mr Nicholson, Mr Sherborne, Mr Goodrick and his sewer, Mr Bassano. His gentlemen waiters numbered twenty-six: Captain Garrette, Mr Kempe, Mr Faldoe, Mr Travers, Mr Wells, Mr Bowes, Mr Guilman, Mr Fletcher, Mr Anthony, Mr Percy, Mr Nicholas Bacon, Mr John Underhill, Mr Mannering, Mr Carrell, Mr Parsons, Mr Allen, Mr Portington, Mr Goodericke (or Godrick), Mr Josline, Mr Moyle, Mr Walley, Mr Hogins, Mr Ball, Mr Price, Mr Pearce and Mr Beall Saperton. Four pages (Mr Cockaine, Mr Bettenham, Mr Cooke and Mr Paddon) were followed by his doorkeeper James Edwardes, his barber Robert Durant, his messenger Stephen Read, two yeomen ushers, Humphrey Leigh and Neale, two master cooks, Henry Syll and one other (a blank in the list), three gentlemen of the wardrobe, William Ockold, John Nicolson and Christopher King, Roger Pilkington of the wine cellar, Edward Isaack and John Humphrey of the ewry and pantry, his butlers Richard Edwardes, Morrice Davies, John Oakes and one Wood, his bottleman Richard Wood, his yeoman of the horse George Prince, and a cook, presumably the master cooks' boy, John Whitney. But this is only half the list. The second column of the manuscript has been obliterated, but enough survives to show that there were another fifty names in the next column, and that the list went over the page.[11]

Not only was the staff numerous, it was also lavishly turned out. His servants all wore 'liveries with his crest (a boar)'; Aubrey tells of how 'none of his servants durst appear before him without Spanish leather boots; for he would smell the neats leather, which offended him.'[12] With this reputation, Bacon's appointment to the task of retrenchment must have raised a few ironic laughs.

The Council proposed to cut catering costs through 'the union of tables', excepting those of the Lord Chamberlain, the Lord Steward, the Groom of the Stool and, naturally, Buckingham.[13] The tables would be set a fixed budget, which would allow the costing of each table to be calculated. There would need to be added 'some large allowance for waste (because the King shall not lose his prerogative to be deceived more than other men)', and an allowance for arrears; but even so, 'no question there will be a great retrenchment.'[14]

It was a tricky business. The King declared himself offended at the tone of some of the recommendations,[15] and Bacon, via Buckingham, had to excuse himself constantly, claiming that letters had been written in his absence.[16] He arranged business so that, once again, the King could believe himself to remain in control: when Bacon drafted a letter regarding the subcommission (which he belived 'thrids [threads] all the king's business') it was 'written in wide lines, because it may be the better amended by his Majesty'.[17] As it happened, however, it was reported that James 'liketh very well of the draught your Lordship sent . . . hath signed it as it was without any alteration, and sent it to the Lords'.[18]

Most written business between Bacon and the King was usually reinforced by a more candid letter on the same subject from Bacon to Buckingham. During the retrenchment negotiations, however, there were times when the covering letter was not forthcoming. Bacon later had to admit that his attention was divided: while he should have been devoting himself to rationalising the King's household, he had in fact also been clearing a massive backlog of cases in Chancery. As a result, however, he could boast to Buckingham on 6 December: 'Now this very evening I have made even with the causes of Chancery, and comparing with the causes heard by my Lord that dead is [Lord Chancellor Ellesmere], of Michaelmas-term was twelvemonth [in Michaelmas Term a year ago], I find them to be double so many and one more; besides that the causes that I dispatch do seldom turn upon me again, as his many times did.'[19]

Cranfield's illness did not last long, and it was he who undertook much of the hard slog of the retrenchment campaign. Bacon took pleasure in pulling rank on Cranfield, summoning him to his country house for discussions.[20] He became, too, an easy target onto whom Bacon could deflect problems. On 10 October 1619 he reproved Cranfield: 'At the King's going out of town, which is now ten days since, his Majesty was offended the Commission for the debts was not dispatched. It was said it stayed upon instructions to be had from you to the learned counsel and that you were gone into the country. I pray take care with all speed to go on with it that neither you nor we be blamed.'[21] Conversely, Bacon ensured that he got the credit for the proposals generated, by making himself the conduit for progress reports. For his part, Cranfield was keen to distinguish the Lord Keeper from 'we that are the labourers in it'.[22] Labourers indeed: Bacon watched as 'the subcommissioners meet forenoon and afternoon with great diligence, and without distraction, or running several ways'; his own contribution was merely to 'speak with Sir Lionel Cranfield as cause requireth either for account or direction.'

Despite the thoroughness of the operation, Bacon's regular bulletins betray a certain impatience that he cannot be seen to deliver more the goods more promptly: 'I humbly pray his Majesty to pardon me for troubling him with these imparfite glances, which I do both because I know his Majesty thinketh long to understand somewhat, and lest his Majesty should conceive that he multiplying honours and favours upon me, I should not also increase and redouble my endeavours and cares for his service.'[23]

Bacon's involvement in the retrenchment campaign – even if it was somewhat detached – held implications for his own finances. He held a patent for the farm of the Petty Writs, from which, in return for a fixed rent paid to the King, he received the proceeds for his own use. In early December 1617 Sir George Chaworth offered a higher rent,[24] which (given that Bacon was employed in bettering the King's finances) he could not simply reject out of hand. Bacon was forced to offer a better bargain, with the result 'that now I shall retain the grace of my place, and yet he [Chaworth] rewarded. The King hath no ill bargain; for he hath four times as much as was offered by Sir George of increase, and yet I take upon me to content my servants, and to content him.'[25]

Buckingham's upward trajectory continued. In exchange for giving up his bid to become Lord Admiral,[26] he was given as a New Year's gift 'in requital' a patent to a marquisate. Bacon had made ready the letters patent, asking in return 'to be one of the witnesses at the delivery'. His own New Year's gift to the new marquis was 'a plain cup of essay [assay], in token that if your Lordship in any thing shall make me your sayman, I will be hurt before your Lordship shall be hurt. I present therewith to you my best service, which shall be my All-Year's gift.'[27]

Buckingham's promotion was celebrated by a huge feast the following Sunday afternoon, 3 January. As befitted the close relationship which the two men enjoyed, and were seen to enjoy, Buckingham's honour was accompanied by a new honour for Bacon: the Lord Keeper became Lord Chancellor Bacon. The letter-writers were quick to spot the implications of this: '(besides the title) he hath this advantage that it is for life, with £600 a year increase: the speech goes he shall be made a Baron, and hath the making of another given him to discharge his debts, which in courtesy he hath offered to his eldest brother for £1000 less than another should give, which he will not accept mindful perhaps of his father's motto or posy, *mediocria firma*: his Lordship of late is much insinuated into the King's and Lord Marquis' favour.' Bacon expressed his new position as he always did, by taking 'a new course of thriving': in Chamberlain's words, he 'at one clap cashiered [stripped of cash] sixteen of his gallants', financing his extravagance by calling in cash from his entourage.[28]

During the next month, while James was once again out of town, Bacon's public appearances started to slip again, and tongues began to wag. On 7 February 1618 Chamberlain reported that 'The Lord Chancellor hath been absent from Westminster Hall three days this week, not that he complains from any want of health, but that he doubts this cold weather should pinch him: and yet on Monday (being Candlemas Day) he dined at Gray's Inn to give countenance to their Lord or Prince of Purpoole, and see their revels.'[29] With the licence of his new honour, Bacon had started to throw his weight about, much to the dismay of some of his peers. He insisted on going everywhere 'in all the pomp of the Council', whether it was to hear the Archbishop of Spalato at the Mercers' Chapel in April in an audience that included Lady Carleton, Lucy, countess of Bedford, Lord Hamilton and Lord Lisle, or, more ridiculously, on an expedition in March to visit the shops of Sir Baptist Hickes and Edward Barnes 'to cheapen [bargain] and buy silks and velvets'.[30]

At the same time, he started to pull rank in more serious matters. In February the death of the Provost of Oriel College, Oxford, Dr Anthony Blincow, set in motion a new controversy, in which there was 'somewhat ado about the choice of a new provost'. Bacon decided that his chaplain William Lewis should have the post. George Abbot, Archbishop of Canterbury, and John King, Bishop of London, disagreed, arguing that Lewis, at twenty-six, was simply too young, and held out for other candidates 'of more years and gravity'. Bacon took King to town for daring to disagree with him, 'for crossing him in his business', but King maintained that 'he did it only in respect of the unfitness of his age which was the way to bring the university and the government of it into contempt, when such striplings should be made heads of houses.' Bacon famously retorted that 'he respected not minority of years, when there was majority of parts.' In the end, Bacon despatched his secretary Edward Sherburn to make sure of the place: after three or four days, the provostship belonged to Lewis.[31]

On 12 July 1618 Bacon was created Baron Verulam of Verulam. Once again, the honour was linked to one for Buckingham – this time conferred on the marquis' mother Mary, who became 'countess of Buckingham';[32] on 13 August, Chamberlain reported that 'the new Countess of Buckingham went on Monday to dinner with the Lord Chancellors at Gorhambury (or Verulam) to see her patent sealed and delivered.'[33] The friendship between the new countess and the 'Lord Chancellors' grew; after a strange absence from London life during the next term, it was announced in November that the Countess 'is taking a house not far from St Albans, to be as near the court and Lord Chancellor as she can'.[34]

Although Chancery was closed for the summer, Bacon's miscellaneous business continued to take up his time – whether it was steering through the prosecution of a few of the estimated 'four or five thousand' Londoners who had rioted outside the Spanish ambassador's house when one of his gentlemen ran over a child in Chancery Lane, or providing a licence to give in mortmain land worth £800 on which the retired player Edward

Alleyn might build his hospital. 'I like well that Alleyn playeth the last act of his life so well', mused Bacon; but on the other hand 'hospitals abound, and beggars abound never a whit the less.' On such reasoning, Bacon proposed that the King cut back the land to £500 and give the difference to revive the failed suits of Sir Henry Savile and Sir Edwin Sandys 'for the perpetuating of two lectures, the one in Oxford, the other in Cambridge, foundations of singular honour to his Majesty (the best learned of kings) and of which there is great want'.[35] When it came to a straight choice between the theatre and the academy, Francis Bacon's priorities were clear.

★

Throughout his chancellorship, Bacon was called upon by the King to prosecute men with whom he was familiar, even intimate: men who had, like himself, reached the pinnacle of their professional careers, only to be charged with malpractice of one type or another. Somerset had been the first example, but more were to follow. On 17 August 1618 Bacon returned from Gorhambury to London to undertake the first of many meetings to investigate the hot topic of the moment: the case of Sir Walter Ralegh.

After nearly fourteen years in the Tower, under a death sentence on charges of conspiring against James, Ralegh had received permission in August 1616 to head an expedition to a mine in Orinoco, which appeared to be far enough away from any Spanish settlement to avoid posing any threat of breach of the peace. Hearing of these plans, the Spanish ambassador Sarmiento protested, claiming that Guiana belonged to Spain; Ralegh, he claimed, planned to lie in wait for the Mexican plate fleet. Although Ralegh publicly refuted Sarmiento's claims, and was ordered not to engage in hostilities against the Spaniards, on pain of death, to Bacon he was more frank. Shortly after Bacon became Lord Keeper, the two men had a long conversation in Gray's Inn walks, which so absorbed Bacon that he kept the earl of Exeter waiting upstairs.[36] Bacon 'told him that they doubted [suspected] he would be prizing if he could do it handsomely'.

'Yea,' saith he, 'if I can light right on the Plate fleet you will think I were mad if I should refuse it.'

'Why then you will be a pirate,' replied Bacon.

'Tush,' quoth he, 'my Lord, did you ever hear of any that was counted a pirate for taking millions? They are poor mychers that are called in question for piracy, that are not able to make their peace with that they get. If I can catch the fleet, I can give this man ten thousand and that man ten thousand, and six hundred thousand to the King, and yet keep enough for myself and all my company.'[37] Many besides Bacon believed that Ralegh's motives were far from virtuous: Chamberlain wrote, as

Ralegh sailed from Dover to Plymouth on 29 March 1617, 'I fear he doth but go (as children are wont to tell their tales) to seek his fortune.'[38]

The expedition set out in August, eventually arriving, after a difficult voyage, at the Isle de Salut. When Ralegh, who was ill, remained behind to repel any hostile Spanish ships, four hundred men on five boats set off on 10 December to journey up the river. The mission failed to reach the mine, saw the loss of Ralegh's son Walter, and sacked and burned the Spanish settlement of San Tomás. Despite Ralegh's exhortations to further action, the squadron dispersed; Ralegh returned to Plymouth, via Newfoundland, arriving in mid-June 1618.

News of the San Tomás debacle preceded him. James assured Sarmiento that he would honour his promise, that if Ralegh returned to England with gold plundered from Spanish subjects, he would surrender all the gold and would give up 'the authors of the crime to be hanged in the public square of Madrid'.[39] Arrested while attempting to escape to the continent, Ralegh found himself back in the Tower.

Bacon was appointed to head the six-man commission to investigate Ralegh; on 18 October, the commission declared to James that since Ralegh had been attainted of high treason, 'he cannot be drawn in question judicially for any crime or offense since committed.' They therefore proposed two alternative courses of proceeding: either to have him executed, and 'to publish a narrative in print of his late crimes and offenses'; or to 'have such a proceeding as is nearest to legal proceeding', namely for Ralegh to be called before the Privy Council, judges and selected nobility (letting it be known 'that this form of proceeding against Sir Walter is holden for that he is civilly dead') and charged 'with his acts of hostility, depredation, abuse as well of your Majesty's commission as of your subjects under his charge, impostures, attempt of escape, and other his misdemeanours'. After Ralegh had answered, 'then he is to be withdrawn and sent back; for that of sentence is or can be given against him'. The Council and the judges would then advise James whether he 'may not with justice and honour give warrant for his execution upon his attainder'. A solemn act of Council would be made of the whole proceeding, 'with a memorial of the whole presence'.[40]

The King instead opted for 'a middle course, that he be called only before those who have been the examiners of him hitherto, and that the examinations be read, and himself heard, and others confronted with him, who were with him in this action';[41] but when Ralegh faced the commissioners for the last time, on 22 October, it was Bacon who pronounced him guilty of abusing the confidence of his sovereign, and told him he was to die. His scaffold speech, in the Old Palace Yard a week later, was the stuff of legend. As he laid his head on the block, an onlooker objected that he ought to face east. 'What matter', he quipped, 'how the head lie, so the heart be right?' As Sir Dudley Carleton commented, 'It seems that he knew better how to die than to live; and his happiest hours were those of his arraignment and execution.'[42]

Among the targets of Ralegh's scaffold speech was his cousin Sir Lewis Stucley, who had been instrumental in effecting Ralegh's arrest. Now, said Ralegh, he had forgiven Stucley, but only because 'I have received the sacrament this morning and I have forgiven all men' – he still thought Stucley 'perfidious'. Stucley's published *Apology* had little effect on his tarnished reputation, so he appealed to James in a *Petition* in which he defended his actions in the affair and asked for two favours: to receive the sacrament in His Majesty's chapel, and to have published 'a declaration from the State, for the clearing of these matters and further satisfaction of the world'. The *Petition* was published by the King's printer on 26 November, the *Declaration* on the following day – Naunton reported to Buckingham that the errors in the copies were due to the fact that the printers 'were fain to watch two nights, and set twenty presses to work at once'.[43] The *Petition*, according to Chamberlain, found 'little credit'; the *Declaration*, it was rumoured, was 'the work of the Lord Chancellor, Mr. Attorney [Yelverton], or Secretary Naunton: or rather fathered upon all three so that in all probability it must be true as well written'.[44]

Once again, Bacon had been required to put in motion the machinery by which a man with whom he might be said to be friendly would be destroyed. Essex, Somerset, Ralegh – the list was growing. There was nothing in itself odd about this: it was Bacon's job to advise the King on the most momentous matters of state. What was odd was that Bacon appeared oblivious to the fact that what he did to others could, in time, be done to him.

★

As the New Year 1619 dawned, Bacon wrote to the King. 'I do many times with gladness and for a remedy of my other labours,' he opened,

> revolve in my mind the great happiness which God (of his singular goodness) hath accumulated upon your Majesty every way; and how complete the same would be, if the state of your means were once rectified, and well ordered. Your People militar [*sic*] and obedient; fit for war, used to peace. Your Church illightened with good preachers, as an heaven of stars. Your Judges learned, and learning from you; just, and just by your example. Your Nobility in a right distance between crown and people; no oppressors of the people, no overshadowers of the crown. Your Council full of tribute of care, faith, and freedom. Your

8

gentlemen and justices of peace willing to apply your royal mandates to the nature of their several countries, but ready to obey. Your servants in awe of your wisdom, in hope of your goodness. The fields growing every day by the improvement and recovery of grounds, from the desert to the garden. The city grown from wood to brick. Your sea-walls or *pomoerium* of your island, surveyed and in edifying [*sic*]. Your merchants embracing the whole compass of the world, east, west, north, and south. The times give you peace, and yet offer you opportunities of action abroad. And lastly, your excellent royal issue entaileth these blessings and favours of God to descend to all posterity.

God, he continued, had done great things for James; James had done great things for others. It only now remained for James to 'do so much for yourself, as to go through (according to your beginnings) with the rectifying and settling of your estate of means, which only is wanting'. Bacon – 'whom only love and duty to your Majesty and royal line hath made a financier' – therefore intended to present to the King 'a perfect book of your estate, like a prospective glass, to draw your estate nearer to your sight.'[45]

On 2 March, Queen Anne died at Hampton Court, aged forty-four, after suffering from dropsy for some time. James was, as usual, absent, this time at Newmarket. The Venetian ambassador commented that Anne

breathed her last amid a few attendants in a country place, without the help of those remedies which might have lengthened her days even if they did not cure her. However, before dying, she had time to embrace the prince, her son, and had this satisfaction as mother of the succeeding king of late her Majesty had to bear a change of fortune, suffering countless bitter things and great pain. She lost her health, and fell out of favour with the king, while he following of courtiers and her royal adornments fell away from her.[46]

Bacon himself was suffering from a fit of the stone 'which held him in great pain two or three days'. But his illness was soon overtaken in importance by that of his sovereign, who had been taken ill twice with the same affliction.[47] James's slow recovery elicited great popular sympathy: Chamberlain was 'glad to see the world so tenderly affected toward him'. In early April, James was 'not so confident of himself but that he prepared to settle things as if he were to leave all; and to that end made an excellent speech to the Prince before all the Lords there present, recommending divers of them to him by name for divers good parts and services'.[48] But by 11 April the Bishop of London was able to preach a thanksgiving sermon for the King's recovery, attracting the largest audience in living memory. In fact, James was still ill, his sickness 'more than vomiting and looseness, which were accompanied with a plain fever and divers strange accidents of inequality, intermission and failing of his pulse, with vehement *singultus*, and other dangerous and deadly signs and symptoms, which you may the better conceive by his slow recovery; being yet very feeble, though he have no manner of affection either of stone or gout'.[49]

Meanwhile, it was being noticed once again that Bacon was slackening in his public duties. Even during the previous year, his health had given cause for concern: twice in late November, Star Chamber was cancelled 'by reason of the Lord Chancellor's indisposition',[50] 'either by reason of my Lord Chancellor's crasiness, or for that the weather is extraordinary cold for so early in the year'.[51] By 2 January, anxiety had increased to the point where measures were being considered to pre-empt any further costly closures of the Star Chamber – measures that could only benefit the man Bacon wanted least to benefit. Chamberlain reported that 'the tide is turned of late and runs altogether toward Sir Edward Coke', one of the main reasons being that 'there is great want of a second in the Star Chamber that may furnish the place in absence of the Lord Chancellor, who by reason of his often indispositions cannot continually attend it.' In connection with this Coke was visited by the Chancellor of the Exchequer Sir Fulke Greville, Attorney-General Sir Henry Yelverton and by Buckingham, who was seen 'with him at his house in Broad Street twice in four days'. Eventually Bacon himself had to take action, and 'went thither to him somewhat privately on Sunday last, which kind of compliment hath not been usual twixt them two of late, but seeing no mining nor counter-mining will prevail peradventure it seems best on all sides to come to parley'.[52]

Bacon made a resolution to avoid this irritating solution, but the new term did not start well. On the first Star Chamber day the Lord Chancellor 'came late to the Hall, and stayed not long'. On 11 April he was visibly absent from the Council at Paul's Cross. Five days later, Star Chamber was once again cancelled by his absence, 'which', remarked Chamberlain, 'is thought rather to proceed of tenderness than of any real indisposition or infirmity'.[53] By the twenty-fourth, Chamberlain was writing: 'The Lord Chancellor's slackness (caused by the delicacies of his constitution) hath raised a rumour as if he were like enough to have a Lord Keeper for his coadjutor, or rather to have the place executed by commission when his health will not suffer him to follow it.'

Clearly, Bacon needed to 'disperse such mists'. With a great effort, he roused himself sufficiently to go to Theobalds 'to see and congratulate his Majesty's happy recovery'. It was a clever move. The experience of shared illness somehow endeared Bacon to the King: as Bacon was later to report to Tobie Matthew, 'when once my master, and afterwards myself, were both of us in extremity of sickness (which was no time to dissemble), I never had so great pledges and certainties of his love and favour.' Confidence in the ailing Lord Chancellor was quickly restored: by 8 May it could be reported to Sir Dudley Carleton that 'Your Lordship may perhaps have heard that the Lord Chancellor was like to have some assistants put upon him, but there is no such thing: and he is now in as much favour at Court, as ever, if not more.'[54]

Restored to health, Bacon continued to give his advice on matters of policy. By the end of January, there were signs of danger from Spain.

The alarms of the Spanish preparation sounds loud here at last and ministers much matter of discourse. Most men doubt they have a mean-ing to Ireland; the rather for that they have entertained many Scottish and Irish pilots, and that the Earl of Argyle and Tyrone's son are said to be gone for Spain. We talk of order taken for twenty ships to be presently made ready, half of the King's, the rest merchants, the best that can be had. Though we cannot be persuaded that he hath any intent hitherward, yet is it not good to stand in his courtesy. For my part by all that I can gather, I should rather think he hath a mind to the Venetians; or to land his forces thereabout and go for Austria or Bohemia.[55]

Bacon's faithful correspondent Tobie Matthew wrote from the Low Countries in February 1619 with contradictory reports that in Spain there were 'very extraordinary preparations for a great Armada', yet that the local men who were intended to go to Spain had been discharged, possibly due to lack of Spanish funds.[56] It seemed on 16 March that 'all preparations for war were certainly laid aside for the year.'[57] However, when news filtered through that the Emperor Matthias had died on 10 March, the situation was changed. Towards the end of April, according to Lorkin, 'all such as had received letters out of Spain were by particular summonses commanded to bring the same to the Council table, there to be perused. I cannot understand the true cause; but I conjecture it may be to discover by the several advertisements from all parts whether the King of Spain resumes again his former designs of raising forces now upon the fresh news of the Emperor's death.'[58]

The Elector Palatine begged his father-in-law James for English support for the Bohemian revolution, with the aim of having the duke of Savoy made Emperor. Sending his councillor De Plessen to England in the hope of gaining the King's backing, the Elector also spread his campaign to those men who were of influence around the King, including the Lord Chancellor. Bacon replied in a complimentary, but utterly non-committal letter, protesting that he held it a great honour to receive a letter from the

Elector, praising his choice in councillors, and excusing 'my poor French, having been so drilled in the old forms of Normandy, but the heart will make goods the defects of the pen'.[59]

Despite the careful tone of his letter, however, privately Bacon was committed to an alliance between England and the Low Countries against Spain, and to that end drafted a tract entitled *A Short View to be taken of Great Britain and Spain*. It presents an optimistic portrait of a Jacobean Britain with huge, hitherto unrealised, international potential. Bacon argued that James was now 'of more power than any of his predecessors', now that Ireland had been 'reduced into a more absolute state of obedience and increase than heretofore', and the 'trouble' caused by the English foothold in France was no longer an issue. Instead, James had 'brought another whole kingdom to England; undivided either in amity or seat', which brought several benefits: they now controlled 'the back-door that was open in the assistance of our enemies'; they had 'another valiant nation to assist us', as witnessed by the Low Countries' action; and they were now 'an entire island, which by nature is the best fortification and the most capable of all the advantages of strength that can by art be added unto nature,' enabling them 'at one and the same time both to undertake any action abroad and defend ourselves at home without either much danger or great cost'. Also, the King 'hath the neighbourhood of the powerfullest nation at the sea that now is in world, at his devotion', linked by religious homogeneity, and with an army that was 'the best military school in the world; from whence our land-services may at least be sufficiently appointed with officers'.

Spain's empire, in comparison, was scattered, with vulnerable dominions, a shortage of seamen, and (the Indies aside) an income that made theirs 'the poorest king of Europe'. The Low Countries men, regretting their behaviour in the previous century, desired nothing more than to join with James against the bloodthirsty Spaniard. Bacon urged the 'fitness and honour' of this undertaking to James: 'He is the greatest islander of Christendom; therefore a navy is most proper to him. He is the Defender of the Faith, as well in understanding, learning, and godliness, as in title. Therefore the planting of the true Church there is a sacred work that even by office as it were belongs to him. He is of a great and liberal mind: the Indies will afford him the means to exercise it.'[60]

Bacon's advice went unheeded. As the situation in Bohemia became more difficult, the Spanish King offered James the chance to act as mediator – an honourable (and financially desirable) way out. Bacon's plans for a greater Britain would have to wait for another opportunity.

★

On 13 May 1619 the Queen was eventually buried, after her body had lain in Denmark House on the Strand for more than two months, allegedly because there were insufficient funds for a state funeral. Chamberlain claimed in March that the interment was repeatedly postponed until 'they can find out money for the master of the wardrobe is loath to wear his own credit threadbare'. Later there was 'talk of melting the Queen's golden plate and putting it into coin: besides that the commissioners for her jewels and other movables make offer to sell or pawn divers of them to good value'.[61] During those months, all the playhouses were closed and entertainments forbidden. When the funeral finally took place, with the Prince of Wales deputising for the King, the procession to Westminster Abbey was 'but a drawling, tedious sight, more remarkable for number than for any other singularity . . . and though the number of Lords and Ladies were very great, yet methought altogether they made but a poor show, which perhaps was because they were apparelled all alike, or that they came laggering all along even tired with the length of the way and weight of their clothes, every Lady having twelve yards of broad cloth about her and the countesses sixteen'.[62]

To James, who did not attend the funeral, Bacon confirmed on Friday 21 May that 'his resources and expenses were now equalled for the ordinary, and there was £120,000 now yearly for the extraordinaries; but he prayed it might be taken but as an estimate.'[63] Evidently reassured as to the state of his finances, which recently had seemed so precarious that his wife's body had lain for weeks without burial, James made another spectacular entry into London in early June 1619, resplendent in pale blue satin trimmed with silver lace and a blue and white feather. The incongruity of his widower status and his gay apparel did not pass without comment. More like a wooer than a mourner, Chamberlain whispered. Of course, one source of income had been opened up: as Thomas Lorkin relayed to a friend, 'the King is impatient to hear of the notion [his wife's testament], and means to seize upon all for himself.' According to the Venetian ambassador, Anne's death did not make 'the slightest difference in the government of these kingdoms, except the falling in of 200,000 crowns a year to the king with a quantity of rich and precious belongings and the dismissal of a countless throng of servants and officials.' But James was not that possessive: a good portion of his wife's legacy he gave to Buckingham.[64]

During the summer Bacon found himself 'pressed and distracted with infinite business that I seem hardly to breathe, or live',[65] business that included, on top of his ever-mounting Chancery work, a number of difficult Star Chamber cases, including that of Sir Thomas Lake,[66] and a long-running case concerning Dutch merchants;[67] business with the States

General;[68] and a controversy involving the Bishop of Bangor.[69] In late August he waited on the King at Windsor, to advise him of the latest turn of events in Bohemia. King Ferdinand had been deposed, and the throne offered to the Elector Palatine. The German Emperor, to whom Ferdinand was cousin and heir, declared war on the Elector, Frederick, who naturally expected aid from Great Britain. James answered that 'he would consider of it.' Bacon probably offered a written advice discourse at Windsor. On 8 September he wrote to Buckingham with 'advice touching the business of Bohemia'. As Buckingham read Bacon's letter, the King came and took the letter out of his hands, before he could read the enclosed paper, and approved of Bacon's conduct, saying that he 'had done like a wise counsellor; first setting down the state of the question, and then propounding the difficulties, the rest being to be done in its own time'. Buckingham passed on to Bacon James's 'good conceit and acceptation of your service upon your discourse with him at Windsor, which though I heard not myself, yet I heard his Majesty much commend it both for the method and the affection you showed therein to his affairs, in such earnest manner as if you made it your only study and care to advance his Majesty's service'.[70] In September the Elector Palatine, Frederick, accepted the crown of Bohemia, increasing demands for English intervention. But James was not sure, and put the matter off, stating that nothing could be decided until the validity of Frederick's accession to Bohemia could be established, a process which would take several weeks.

In October Bacon was heavily involved in another high-level prosecution, when the Star Chamber heard the case of the earl of Suffolk, his wife and the Exchequer official Sir John Bingley.[71] Bacon reported each day's events to Buckingham, who was absent in Royston with the King. The Suffolks and Bingley were found guilty of having misappropriated sums of money while the earl was Lord Treasurer. Sir Edward Coke urged a fine of £100,000 and imprisonment for both Suffolk and his wife. Lord Chief Justice Hobart and Bacon, however, argued for imprisonment with a £30,000 fine, which was the final decision. In his concluding speech, Bacon likened Suffolk to a shopkeeper: 'My Lady kept the shop, Bingley was the prentice that cried "what do you lack", but all went into my Lord's cash.' When the Suffolks argued that they might take gifts, Bacon retorted: 'new year's gifts did not last all the year.' It was a truism he should have heeded himself.

He went on to describe how these 'shopkeeper' tactics hit at the King himself:

How completely happy the King were if his Treasury and state of means were settled, what honour he had obtained above any of his predecessors as to have deserved the title of Uniter of Britain and the Planter of Ireland; how glorious the Church here was, like a firmament of stars; that the nobility were not now as in times past the shadowers and overawers of the King and Crown, nor oppressors of the subject; that the judges were never more learned, never more just, the justices of peace never more diligent and dutiful in their places. In the country the fields grew every day more and more from deserts to gardens, the city never more populous nor flourishing, the navy never in so good way for service, the merchant never farther more industriously trafficking, the king admired in his government at home and working great effects abroad by his reputation; the Prince a singular hope . . . nothing wants [is lacking] but treasure, which whosoever destroys wounds the State to death or cuts a main sinew of it and maims it.[72]

Such eulogising was becoming a habit: as one reporter put it, 'My Lord Chancellor to conclude (as his manner is,) made an eloquent speech in praise of his Majesty and the present government.'[73] The Suffolks went to the Tower in November.

In December Bacon 'left London to hide myself at Kew', explaining that 'for two months and a half together to be strong-bent is too much for my bow'. But he was not idle: he took with him Sir Giles Mompesson, another royal financial adviser, with whom he 'quietly conferred of that proposition' given to him by James and seconded by Buckingham. Bacon concluded 'that the proposition for bringing in his Majesty's revenue with small charge is no invention, but was on foot heretofore in King Philip's and Queen Mary's time, and had a grave and mighty opinion for it. I hope his Majesty will look to it, that the fines now to come in may do him most good. And if the King intend any gifts, let them stay for the second course (for all is not yet done,) but nothing out of these; except', he joked, 'the King should give me the £2000 I owe Peter Vanlore out of his fine, which is the chief debt I owe. But this I speak but merrily.' The King accepted his 'poor services', and Bacon gratefully pressed on with his labours: 'I have now other things in my mind for his Majesty's service, that no time be lost.'[74]

As another New Year came in, Bacon forwarded a list of proposals to the King. He recalled that 'I was the first that advised you to come in person into the Star Chamber; knowing very well that those virtues of your Majesty's which I saw near hand, would out of that throne, both as out of a sphere illustrate your own honour, and as out of a fountain water and refresh your whole land; and because your Majesty in that you have already done hath so well effected that which I foresaw and desired, even beyond your expectation, it is no marvel if I resort still to the branches of that counsel that hath borne so good fruit.' He argued that 'There wants a fourth part of the square to make all complete, which is, if your Majesty will be pleased to publish certain commonwealth commissions', as he had done in other areas. In so doing, James would

> do yourself an infinite honour, and win the hearts of your people to acknowledge you as well the most politic King as the most just. Secondly, it will oblige your Commissioners to a more strict account, when they shall be engaged by such a public charge and commandment. And thirdly, it will invite and direct any man that finds himself to know anything concerning those commissions to bring in their informations. So as I am persuaded it will eternise your name and merit, and that King James his commissions will be spoken [of] and put in use, as long as Britain lasts; at the least in the reign of all good Kings.

The commissions – in addition to the commissions on the navy, and on the buildings about London – would include those 'for advancing the clothing of England, as well the old drapery as the new', 'for staying treasure within the realm, and the reglement of monies', 'for the provision of the realm with corn and grain, and the government of the exportation and importation thereof; and directing of public granaries, if cause be', 'for introducing and nourishing manufactures within the realm, for the setting people a-work, and the considering of all grants and privileges of that nature', 'to prevent the depopulation of towns and houses of husbandry, and for nuisances and high-ways', 'for the recovery of drowned lands', 'for the suppressing of the grievances of informers', 'for the better proceedings in the plantations of Ireland', and 'for the provision of the realm with all kind of warlike defence'.

'Of these,' Bacon advised,

> you may take and leave, as it shall please you: and I wish the articles concerning every one of them (first allowed by your Council) to be read openly and the Commissioners' names. For the good that comes of particular and select committees and commissions, I need not commonplace; for your Majesty hath found the good of them; but nothing to that that will be when such things are published; because it will vindicate them from neglect; and make many good spirits that we little think of cooperate in them. I know very well that the world, that commonly is apt to think that the care of the commonwealth is but a pretext in matters of state, will perhaps conceive that this is but a preparative to a parliament. But let not that hinder your Majesty's magnanimity, *in opere operato* [effective in action] that is so good; and besides, that opinion, for many respects will do no hurt to your affairs.[75]

James did not read the tract until he was out of town, travelling to Royston and Newmarket. During the summer, Bacon went to Kew 'for pleasure, but I met with pain'. The pain did not, however, stop him 'from thinking of his Majesty's service' and drafting some 'papers of rules for the Star Chamber'.[76]

★

In spite of his assiduous application to the King's business, throughout these years Bacon's public image was being progressively undermined. The mockery that had always accompanied the respect for his rhetorical powers now began to take precedence. The laughter that greeted his ostentatious entrances, arrayed in all his finery and surrounded by a glittering retinue, was now interspersed with discontented whispers. Even his persistent halitosis came in for a poetic treatment, in the eloquently titled 'On the Lord Chancellor Bacons stinking breath' : 'the Muses nine upon a time / as gaping he lay winking / Shit on his tongue, when he was young, / and made his breath so stinking.'[77] Most damaging was a series of challenges, in themselves minor enough that much of the detail of them has been lost to history, but in their cumulative effect important enough to show that what was to hit the Lord Chancellor in the early months of 1621 was by no means a bolt out of the blue.

The first concerned a Norfolk gentleman named John Wraynham, who, like so many others, became aggrieved when Bacon decided a case in Chancery against him. He presented a petition to the King which effectively slandered Lord Chancellor Bacon, and then turned an account of his case and proofs into a book, complete with both a dedicatory epistle to the King and an epilogue in which he repeated 'slanders and insolencies' against both Bacon and the King. James referred the case to the Star Chamber, where it was heard on 29 April 1618. John Chamberlain reported: 'Howsoever it be, the poor gentleman is in the wrong, and suffered himself to be transported too far, for unless he can prove corruption (which were hard to do) he is like to undergo a sentence and to be censured.' Wraynham failed to justify his actions, and (in Bacon's absence) Coke led the call for a punishment which followed a precedent that he had made while Attorney-General. As Chamberlain reported, somewhat shocked, Wraynham was 'censured in the Star Chamber to imprisonment [for life], to pay £1000, to ride with his face to the horsetail and to lose his ears, which though at first sight may seem a hard sentence, yet upon the matter he deserved somewhat, and there is hope it was rather *in terrorem* than to be put in execution, for as faulty as he was, yet I hear him much pitied for his good parts, and for his free acknowledgment of his offence'. Chamberlain's prediction was correct: but it was only after fourteen months, when Bacon himself intervened in July 1619, that Wraynham was pardoned for his offence.[78]

While Bacon's eventual action in the case of John Wraynham might be interpreted as generous (albeit belated), three other incidents – concerning Lord Clifton, Lady Blount and Isaac Singleton – provoked a much more stubborn response. Some of the trouble clearly came with the territory, as in the sad story of Lord Clifton: a story which starts, oddly enough, with Clifton pursuing a bear. In February 1602, Sir Gervase Clifton attended a bear-baiting in Nottingham, during which the bear broke free and chased his son upstairs. Clifton 'opposed himself with his rapier against the fury of the beast and saved his son', but the boy soon died. Clifton was left with a single daughter – and now sole heir – whom, 'according to His Majesty's command', he bestowed in marriage on one of James's favourites, Esmé Stuart, the duke of Aubigny. In June 1611, Lord Clifton (as he had since become) accused Aubigny and his elder brother the duke of Lennox of 'fraudulent proceedings' which he feared would lead to 'his destruction'.[79] Lennox counter-charged that Clifton had procured Lennox's lands, and that he had concealed the fact that his estates were encumbered by annuities. When the matter came before the Privy Council the following year, what John Chamberlain described as 'very foul matters' were revealed, with Clifton swearing that 'he would keep half a dozen whores and, if he got any of them with child, he would marry her', thus denying his son-in-law of his inheritance.[80]

At the King's command, the case was heard in Chancery, in March 1617. Believing that if he could 'tire and weary the Lord Aubigny' his case would be enhanced, Clifton attempted to persuade Bacon to postpone the hearing. Bacon turned him down. Clifton promptly threatened to kill the Lord Keeper, claiming that 'he cared not for his own life', and 'it was but a matter of hanging' – a threat that brought him a £1,000 fine and imprisonment in the Fleet. Bacon subsequently ordered a survey of Clifton's lands, to which news Clifton, learning nothing from the results of his previous outburst, asserted that if Bacon made a 'hard decree' against him, he 'should not be Keeper long after'. This time the punishment was a downgrading in his prison accommodation to the Tower, by command of the Privy Council on 30 December 1617.[81]

At this point Bacon intervened personally with the King, via Buckingham.

If his Majesty at any time ask touching the Lord Clifton's business, I pray your Lordship represent to his Majesty thus much, That whatsoever hath passed, I thank God I neither fear him nor hate him; but I am wonderful careful of the seat of justice, that they may still be well munited, being principal sinews of his Majesty's authority. Therefore the course will be (as I am advised) that for their heinous misprision (that the party, without all colour or shadow of cause, should threaten the life of his Judge, and of the highest Judge of the kingdom next his Majesty,) he be first examined, and in he confess it, then an *ore tenus*; if he confess it not, then an information in the Star Chamber, and he to remain where he is till the hearing. But I do purposely forbear yet to have him examined, before the decree or agreement between him and my lord Aubigny (which is now ready) be perfected, lest it should seem an oppression by the terror of the one to beat him down in the other.[82]

On 16 March the King called the Chancellor of the Exchequer into his coach and told him that Clifton was to be called before Bacon to make his submission; and then to be called before the Privy Council for a 'sharp reprehension' before being enlarged. Once informed of this, Bacon immediately petitioned Buckingham again:

I pray your Lordship in humbleness to let his Majesty know that I little fear the Lord Clifton, but I much fear the example, that it will animate Ruffins and Rodomonti [bullies and boasters] extremely against the seats of justice (which are his Majesty's own seats) yea and against all authority and greatness, if this pass without public censure and example; it having gone already so far as that the person of a Baron hath been committed to the Tower. The punishment it may please his Majesty to remit, and I shall not formally but heartily intercede for him, but an example (setting myself aside) I wish, for terror of persons that may be more dangerous than he, towards the least Judge of this kingdom.[83]

James acquiesced, and delayed the examination.[84] When prosecution in the Star Chamber followed on 17 March, royal intervention ensured that Clifton was soon once again in the relative comfort of the Fleet prison, with visitors allowed.[85] Given this improvement in his conditions, and the fact that he effected a reconciliation with his relatives, it came as a shock when on 5 October 1618, Clifton decided, in Chamberlain's vivid words, to 'stab and mangle himself with a penknife in two or three places'.[86] In a final ironic twist, his lands were confiscated by the crown – on the grounds that he was a 'felon' because of the suicide – and given to Aubigny.[87]

Clifton's accusations against Bacon seem more like the desperate words of a man trapped by forces beyond his control – and indeed beyond the control of the Lord Chancellor – than true personal grievances: Bacon just got in the way. But two further cases were more strongly personalised.

On 10 June 1619 a petition containing a complaint against Lord Chancellor Bacon reached the King: the same day, the Privy Council, 'at the special request of his Lordship', called for Amy Lady Blount and anyone else involved to be examined. Lady Blount refused to identify the petition's author, but admitted 'that she gave directions for the drawing of the said petition'. While denying that anyone told her to do it, she did claim 'that some hath advised her that her cause was just against the lord chancellor but withal said it was full of danger,' although once again she refused to name names.

Although not charged, Lady Blount was imprisoned from 8 July, first in the Fleet, 'in rigorous confinement', then, from January 1620, in the Marshalsea, from where in May she petitioned the King again. Now she claimed that she had been ignorant that her punishment proceeded from him, rather than the Privy Council: she acknowledged its justice, and asked for his pardon. On 12 May the Star Chamber approved a letter 'subscribed with her hand containing an humble submission and acknowledgement of her undutiful opposition and unexcusable guiltiness, and imploring his Majesty's gracious pardon for all offences which she had committed either against his sacred Majesty or this Board'. However, the lords argued that 'forasmuch as she principally stands committed for scandalising the justice of the Court of Chancery and the honour of the Lord High Chancellor of England, whereof she had omitted to make any mention at all; offence done against the justice of that high Court and the Lord Chancellor, and not to expect any favour or liberty nor presume further to importune his Majesty or their Lordships in any kind whatsoever until she have performed the same'.[88]

Lady Blount stood firm: she demanded that either the charge against her of 'scandalising the Lord Chancellor' be withdrawn, or else the grounds of it should be stated, so that the proceedings against her 'may carry at least a show of justice'; and pleaded once again for her liberty, 'or for some course to acquit or convict her of the crime wherewith she is charged, as her health suffers by long and rigid restraint'. It was not until 8 November 1620, seventeen months after her original petition, that the Privy Council, upon receipt of a petition for her 'liberty and release out of the prison' in which Lady Blount 'promised that she will never trouble either his Majesty or this Board with that for which she standeth committed', that an end to her imprisonment was ordered.[89]

What exactly was contained in Lady Blount's complaint against Bacon is unknown, but clearly it was enough for the Lord Chancellor to feel justified in flexing muscles he was not ordinarily required to flex – presumably because her attack on him was personally demeaning. This is the lesson that we learn from perhaps the most intriguing of these attacks, which came in May 1619 from a canon of St Paul's named Isaac Singleton (or Shingleton). Once again, the origin of the conflict lay in a judgement by Bacon in Chancery. Given the opportunity of that most influential of religious soapboxes, a sermon at St Paul's, Singleton took his vengeance on the presiding judge, as Chamberlain reported: 'Shingleton an Oxford man (who preaching in Paul's on May Day and finding himself aggrieved with some decree of his wherein he thought he had hard measure) declaimed bitterly against his court [Chancery], and glanced (they say) somewhat scandalously at him and his catamites as he called them.' In Singleton's hands, a grievance against the Court of Chancery becomes an attack on the household morals of the Lord Chancellor: a wrong decision in the court somehow transmutes into scandalous charges of sodomy against that court's judge. Corruption and sodomy: these were two charges that Bacon would hear again, and that he would not be able to silence.[90]

★

On 12 October 1620 Bacon published his new system of philosophy, the *Novum Organum*. The familiar frontispiece to this printed edition carried an engraving of a ship in full sail, passing between classical pillars, with the inscription '*multi pertransibunt et augebitur scientia*' [many shall go to and fro and knowledge will increase]. Besides here alluding indirectly to the imperial motto of the Habsburg Empire ('*plus ultra*' [yet further beyond], the inscription on the pillars of Hercules), Bacon here recalled a crucial remark of his own within the text itself: 'Nor must it go for nothing that by the distant voyages and travels which have become frequent in our times, many things in nature have been laid open and discovered which may let in new light upon philosophy. And surely it would be disgraceful if, while the regions of the material globe – that is, of the earth, of the sea, and of the stars – have been in our times laid widely open and revealed, the intellectual globe should remain shut up within the narrow limits of old discoveries.'[91] The frontispiece also announces that this work is part of Bacon's *Instauratio magna*, his Great Instauration or Renewal, the comprehensive overhaul of methodical scientific investigation which was Bacon's intellectual life project.

He dedicated it to James, accomanying his 'public epistle' with some 'private lines'. 'The work,' he explained,

in what colours soever it may be set forth, is no more than a new logic, teaching to invent and judge by induction (as finding syllogism incompetent for sciences of nature), and thereby to make philosophy and sciences both more true and more active. This, tending to enlarge the bounds of Reason and to endow man's estate with new value, was no improper oblation to your Majesty, who, of men, is the greatest master of reason, and author of beneficence.

There be two of your council, and one other bishop of this land, that know I have been about some such work near thirty years; so as I made no haste. And the reason why I have published it now, specially being unperfect, is, to speak plainly, because I number my days and would have it saved. There is another reason of my so doing, which is to try whether I can get help in one intended part of this work, namely, the compiling of a natural and experimental history, which must be the main foundation of a true and active philosophy.

This work is but a new body of clay, wherein your Majesty by your countenance and protection, may breathe life. And, to tell your Majesty truly what I think, I account your favour may be to this work as much as an hundred years' time: for I am persuaded the work will gain upon men's minds in ages, but your gracing it may make it take hold more swiftly; which I would be glad of, it being a work meant not for praise or glory, but for practice, and the good of men. One thing, I confess, I am ambitious of, with hope, which is, that after these beginnings, and the wheel once set on going, men shall suck more truth out of Christian pens, than hitherto they have done out of heathen. I say with hope, because I hear my former book of the *Advancement of Learning* is well tasted in the universities here, and the English colleges abroad; and thus is the same argument sunk deeper.[92]

He supported this wish by sending copies to the Universities of Oxford and Cambridge, as well as to his old Cambridge college, Trinity.

James welcomed the letter and the book, resolving,

first, to read it through with care and attention, though I should steal some hours from my sleep; having otherwise as little spare time to read it as you had to write it. And then to use the liberty of a true friend, in not sparing to ask you the question in any point whereof I shall stand in doubt: as, on the other part, I will willingly give a due commendation to such places as in my opinion shall deserve it. In the meantime, I can with comfort assure you, that you could not have made choice of a subject more befitting your place, and your universal and methodic knowledge; and in the general, I have already observed, that you jump with me, in keeping the midway between the two extremes; as also in some particulars I have found that you agree fully with my opinion.[93]

Bacon responded enthusiastically.

I cannot express how much comfort I received by your last letter of your own royal hand. Your Majesty shall not only do to myself a singular favour, but to the business a material help, if you will be graciously pleased to open yourself to me in these those things, wherein you may be unsatisfied. For though this work, as by position and principle, doth disclaim to be tried by anything but by experience, and the resultats of experience in a true way; yet the sharpness and profoundness of your Majesty's judgment ought to be an exception to this general rule; and your questions, observations, and admonishments, may do infinite good.

This comfortable beginning makes me hope further, that your Majesty will be aiding to me, in setting men on work for the collecting of a natural and experimental history; which is *basis totius negotii* [grounds for the whole enterprise]; a thing which I assure myself will be from time to time an excellent recreation unto you; I say, to that admirable spirit of yours, that delighteth in light; and I hope well that even in your times many noble inventions may be discovered for man's use. For who can tell, now this mine of Truth is once opened, how the veins go, and what lieth higher and what lieth lower?

Elsewhere, James admitted candidly that Bacon's latest effort was beyond him: 'His last book . . . is like the peace of God, that passeth all understanding.' John Chamberlain admitted that 'I have read no more than the bare title, and am not greatly encouraged by Master [Henry] Cuffe's judgement, who having long since perused it gave this censure, that a fool could not have written such a work, and a wise man would not.'[94] New systems of knowledge were not, in truth, the kind of intellectual projects calculated to interest the dilettante reader.

★

The autumn of 1620 saw the fall of yet another prominent political player, and his committed prosecution by Lord Chancellor Bacon. Attorney-General Sir Henry Yelverton had been suspended from office after inserting some unwarranted clauses into a new charter to the City of London. Although Yelverton admitted the error, and was willing to submit by letter, and the City was willing to return the patent, James nonetheless ordered a commission to be set up to pursue the case. On 15 June, therefore, Bacon met with Naunton, Caesar, Arundel, Calvert and Coke to review the evidence, and decreed that there was sufficient cause to pursue the case in the Star Chamber against Yelverton and the Recorder of London. The hearing was set for 27 October.[95]

Bacon made notes of his position on the case. He was sorry for the person, 'being a gentleman that I lived with in Gray's Inn; served with him when I was attorney; joined with since in many services, and one that ever gave me more attributes in public than I deserved; and besides a man of very good parts; which with me is friendship at first sight; much more joined with so ancient acquaintance'. But in his capacity as Lord Chancellor he had to ignore the personal: 'as a judge, I hold the offence very great, and that without pressing measure for if it be suffered that the learned counsel shall practice the art of multiplication upon their warrants, the crown will be destroyed in small time.'[96]

It was a sorry scene. The King's Serjeant, Sir Randall Crew, opened the bill 'with tears in his eyes'; Mr Attorney stood at the bar, flanked by his counsellors, 'where with dejected looks, weeping tears, and a brief, eloquent, and humble oration, he made a submission, acknowledging his error, but denying the corruption'; against Bacon's advice – which he 'declared plain enough' – by majority vote, the case was postponed until the King might be informed of the confession. As Bacon informed Buckingham, 'I do not like of this course, in respect that it puts the King in a strait; for either the note of severity must rest upon his Majesty, if he go on; or the thanks of clemency is in some part taken away, if his Majesty go not on. I have *cor unum et via una* [a single conviction and one course of action]; and therefore did my part as a Judge and the King's Chancellor.'[97]

The case was duly referred to the King; he remitted it back to the Star Chamber, where Bacon as Lord Chancellor opened proceedings on 8 November. Yelverton's submission, on the face of it, 'sounded well', and the King had 'seemed somewhat satisfied therewith'; but when scrutinised in detail, there was found a passage which made it appear that James had made 'some covert promise' if Yelverton would submit, 'which is false'. After each lord had made his judgement, Bacon came to speak on 10 November, clearing the Recorder and commending the City's discretion. Reiterating his sympathy for Yelverton as a man, he played on 'the danger and the consequence of his offence', reiterating that if King's counsel 'be suffered to practise by multiplication on their warrant, the crown will be undone in a short time'. While he believed the City to be a 'noble body of well-deserving subjects', there had to be limits on their liberty. 'Here is a wilful excess: his authority was to be guided by precedent and anteacts: therefore erring upon a warrant, this aggravates the fault. For extenuation of the fact, I am satisfied there was no corruption of reward. But in truth that makes the offence rather divers than less: for some offences are black, some scarlet, some sordid, some presumptuous.' Following Bacon's advice 'the least fine' of £4,000 was agreed, since 'his error arose not out of money', along with imprisonment in the Tower at the King's pleasure, and discharge of his place – 'for his place I declare him unfit for it, and so leave it to his Majesty to dispose of it.'[98]

It had been a gruelling session: Bacon complained that he 'almost killed myself with sitting almost eight hours. But I was resolved to sit it through.'

He was quietly satisfied with his own performance, as he admitted to Buckingham: 'How I stirred the court, I leave it to others to speak; but things passed to his Majesty's great honour.'[99]

On 24 November came the news that the Elector Palatine had been defeated at the White Mountain, Prague, and was now on the run, the Palatinate overrun by the King of Spain and the duke of Bavaria. James made it known that he would send help to Frederick on condition that he agreed to give up his claims to Bohemia – in this way, Britain could stay on amicable terms with Spain, and the projected marriage of Charles to the Infanta could still go ahead. However, finding the £1 million and more that was needed for the continental campaign would not be easy. 'It is most certain', wrote Chamberlain, 'that England was never generally so poor since I was born as it is at this present; insomuch that all complain they cannot receive their rents. Yet is there plenty of all things but money . . . I fear when it comes to the trial, it will prove as some merchants which, having carried a great show a long time, when they are called upon too fast by their creditors, are fain to play bankrupt.'[100]

Bacon took advantage of the new intimacy in his correspondence with the King to seek a further elevation of title, namely to be made a viscount, as Doncaster was when the King went to Scotland, and as Sir William Cavendish had been on 3 November; or a baron, like Secretary Win-wood.[101] He asked Buckingham to recommend the suit, but the marquis was not sure of its appropriateness, writing to Bacon as a friend, in 'sincerity and plainness', to offer his opinion. The example of Cavendish, Buckingham argued, 'is no more than the prevention of that honour which no man knoweth how soon it may by his own right fall upon him, and only stretched a little higher at the suit of my Lord Chamberlain and my Lord Arundel. That to my Lord of Doncaster who was at his Majesty's going into Scotland and upon a consideration whereby he was no gainer, being for buying of hangings to furnish the houses.' If indeed Secretary Winwood did obtain a barony, it was 'the only gift his Majesty gave him in reward of long service, and in a time when it was not a matter of such difficulty to get as now it is'; at the moment, James 'cannot endure to hear of making any for his own benefit, notwithstanding the great necessities wherein he is'. As for rewarding Chancellors after the parliament, Buckingham only knew that 'it seems by your letter the last claimed it not. Whatsoever the use hath been after the end of the Parliament, I assure myself your Lordship will hold it very unseasonable to be done before, and likely to do more hurt than good to his Majesty's service (whereof his Majesty hath found no man more careful than your Lordship) if while he is asking with one hand he should be giving with the other.' Buckingham did not, however, categorically refuse to support Bacon's suit. 'I now leave it to your self whether I shall move his Majesty in your suit or no: wherein I will be ready so to carry myself as I shall be further directed by your Lordship.'[102] Typically, Bacon was not dissuaded, and applied to the King.

January 1621 was a cold month. Ice floes 'like rocks and mountains', with 'a strange and hideous aspect', blocked the Thames for three weeks. London was submerged by filth, while food prices soared. The parliament, originally scheduled to meet on 16 January, was twice prorogued. In stark contrast to the deprivation outside, Bacon celebrated his sixtieth birthday with a lavish banquet at York House. The great poet and playwright Ben Jonson wrote an ode entitled 'Lord Bacon's Birthday':

> Hail, happy genius of this ancient pile!
> How comes it all things so about thee smile?
> The fire, the wine, the men! And in the midst,
> Thou stand'st as if some mystery thou didst!
> Pardon, I read it in thy face, the day
> For whose returns, and many, all these pray:
> And so do I. This is the sixtieth year
> Since Bacon, and thy lord was born, and here;
> Son to the grave wise Keeper of the Seal,
> Fame, and foundation of the English weal.
> What then his father was, that since is he,
> Now with a title more to the degree;
> England's high Chancellor: the destined heir
> In his soft cradle to his father's chair,
> Whose even thread the Fates spin round and full,
> Out of their choicest, and their whitest wool.
>   'Tis a brave cause of joy, let it be known,
> For 'twere a narrow gladness, kept thine own.
> Give me a deep-crowned bowl, that I may sing
> In raising him the wisdom of my king.[103]

With the birthday celebrations came the news that Bacon's suit had been successful. A week later, on Saturday at Theobalds, Bacon was, in Chamberlain's words, 'created Viscount St. Alban's, with all the ceremonies of robes and coronet, whereas the rest were only done by patent', with the King, Prince Charles and Buckingham in attendance. It was the pinnacle of a glittering career – but Bacon's advancement, as so often, was not without detractors. The parliamentarian and diarist Simonds D'Ewes expressed surprise at the Chancellor's being raised to the title of Viscount St Alban,

all men wondering at the exceeding vanity of his pride and ambition: for his estate in land was not above four or five hundred pounds per annum at the uttermost, and his debts were generally thought to be near £30,000. Besides, he was fain to support his very household expenses, being very lavish, by taking great bribes in all causes of moment that came before him. So as men raised very bitter sarcasms or jests of him; as that he lately was *very lame*, alluding to his barony of *Verulam*, but now having fallen into a consumption of purse, without all question he was become *All-bones*, alluding to his new honour of St. *Alban*; nay, they said, *Nabal* being folly or foolishness, and the true anagram of *Alban*, might well set forth his fond and impotent ambition.[104]

St Alban penned his usual panegyric to the King who so favoured him, some of it repeated from his speech at his investiture:

I thank God that I number my days both in thankfulness to Him, and in warning to myself. I should likewise number your Majesty's benefits, which as (to take them in all kinds) they are without number; so even in this kind of steps and degrees of advancement, they are in greater number than scarcely any other of your subjects can say. For this is now the eighth time, that your Majesty hath raised me.

You found me of the Learned Counsel, Extraordinary, without patent or fee; a kind of *individuum vagum*. You established me, and brought me into Ordinary. Soon after, you placed me Solicitor, where I served seven years. Then your Majesty made me your Attorney or Procurator General. Then Privy Counsellor, while I was Attorney; a kind of miracle of your favour, that had not been in many ages. Thence Keeper of your Seal; and because that was a kind of planet and not fixed, Chancellor. And when your Majesty could raise me no higher, it was your grace to illustrate me with beams of honour; first making me Baron Verulam, and now Viscount St Alban. So this is the eighth rise or reach, a diapason in music, even a good number and accord for a close. And so I may without superstition be buried in St Alban's habit or vestment.[105]

It was a prescient sentiment. Within three months, Francis Bacon had himself become a modern St Alban, stripped of the lord chancellorship. As one wit was to put it, 'Albans much condoles the loss of this great Viscount's Charter / Who suffering for his conscience sake is turned franciscan martyr.'[106]

16

Franciscan Martyr:
Bribery, Buggery and the Fall of Francis Bacon

I know I have clean hands and a clean heart; and I hope a
clean house for friends or servants.
Francis, Viscount St Alban, to the marquis of Buckingham
(March 1621)

A s the opening procession of the 1621 parliament made its way
to Westminster on 30 January, two of the scaffolds erected to afford
spectators a better view of the royal personages and dignitaries
collapsed, causing dozens of injuries. Those of a superstitious turn of mind
might have seen this as a bad omen for what was to be the first parliament
since the troubled Addled Parliament seven years earlier – reinforced when
the King, incapacitated by arthritis, had to be carried into the House of
Lords in a chair. The gossips had a field day: James was now a cripple,
'being so weak in his legs and feet that it is doubted he will find little use
in them hereafter but be altogether *perdus* that way'.[1]

That this might be a difficult session was not in doubt. Bacon had spent
much of the latter half of 1620 investigating ways in which conflict could
be defused even before the members met. It was clear that the questions
of impositions and the monopolies held by patent were still live issues,
and the very public rise of a new young royal favourite, whose friends,
followers and family were all being pulled up on his shirt-tails, could only
exacerbate matters.

Since receiving news in autumn 1620 of the increasingly serious
threat posed by the advancing Spanish army to Prince Frederick, Elector
Palatine and King of Bohemia, James had been considering how to
raise funds to mount the requested expedition to aid his son-in-law.
Bacon had been physically prevented from being present at initial discussions with the King by a 'pain of my foot', which made walking impossible; nonetheless, James was 'pleased upon that occasion to express
before your Lords your gracious opinion and favour towards me', and to
include Bacon on a committee of judges which would draw up reasons
'which mought in true policy, without packing or degenerate arts, pre-

pare to a Parliament, in case your Majesty should resolve of one to be held'.[2]

The committee first met on 6 October 1620 to survey the grievances that would be raised in a parliament, and to decide on how best to create it – what sort of proclamation was to be issued; what persons 'were fit to be of the House' and how they were to placed – and on the drafting of 'some commonwealth bills' which might effectively demonstrate James's concern for his subjects: 'not wooing bills to make the King and his graces cheap; but good matter to set the Parliament on work, that an empty stomach do not feed upon humour'.[3]

The proclamation, drafted by Bacon, stressed peace – the 'constant purpose and provident care' of the King – which had been maintained 'in the same resolution' even after Prince Frederick's election to the Bohemian throne. It was only the invasion of the Palatinate, and the consequent consideration of the country's responsibilities and the 'balance of Christendom', that forced a change of policy: 'the uttermost of our forces and means, to recover and resettle the said Palatinate to our son and our descendants'. If war proved necessary, as seemed likely, there would be many issues 'amongst which we hold nothing more necessary than to confer and advise with the common council of our kingdom, upon this so important a subject'. Supply would also be required – James had not asked for money in ten years ('a thing unheard of in late times').

Bacon concluded that 'in respect of so long intermission of a Parliament the times may have introduced some things fit to be reformed, either by new laws or by the moderate designs of our loving subjects dutifully intimated us'. The commissioners 'do require the Lower House, at this time, if ever, to be compounded of the gravest, ablest, and worthiest members that may be found, experienced parliament-men, wise and discreet statesmen, that have been practised in public affairs, substantial citizens and burgesses, well affected in religion, without declining either on the one hand to blindness and superstition, or on the other hand to schism or turbulent disposition'.[4]

The King approved of the committee's work, but failed to follow through on its recommendations.[5] He rejected outright any discussion 'containing matters of state and the reasons of calling the parliament: whereof neither the people are capable, nor is it fit for his Majesty to open now unto them.' The King would prepare his own proclamation, that would deal solely with the 'well ordering of the election of the burgesses', incorporating 'somewhat of the latter part of the draught you have sent'.[6] James thus put paid to the Lord Chancellor's attempts to placate the country. To Buckingham, Bacon noted wryly that he of course did 'approve his Majesty's judgement and foresight above mine own. Neither would I have thought of inserting matter of state for the vulgar, but that nowadays there is no vulgar, but all statesmen. But, as his Majesty doth excellently consider, the time of it is not yet proper.'[7] When James's proclamation was published on 6 November, despite calls from Bacon and Pembroke to tone it down, it had turned Bacon's warning against 'lawyers of mean account and estimation' into a diatribe against 'curious and wrangling lawyers, who may seek reputation by stirring needless questions'.[8]

A subscription was also launched among the nobility and the Council to supply funds for immediate needs: the Prince set the tone with a £10,000 contribution; Bacon, along with most of the other principal councillors, contributed £1,000. Owing to the secrecy of the discussions, this led to speculation that there would not be a parliament at all. Bacon contributed to this rumour on the first day of the new legal term, when he addressed Sir Thomas Chamberlain, the Chief Justice of Wales and Chester, as he was sworn in as a new judge of the King's Bench, on the subject of the royal prerogative. Bacon, it was reported by John Chamberlain, 'took occasion to enlarge himself much upon the Prerogative, and how near it was akin and of blood (as he termed it) to the common law'. He continued, denying 'whatsoever some unlearned lawyers might prattle to the contrary', that the prerogative was 'the accomplishment and perfection of the Common Law: which new doctrine, but now broached, is perhaps to prepare the way to a purpose in hand that all men shall be rated and pay by way of subsidy as if it were done by Parliament; and those that refuse their names to be certified, that order may be taken with them. This hath quite put down the speech of a Parliament for the present, and perhaps the name of it for hereafter.'[9] By late October 1620, anxiety about the forthcoming parliament was tangible. Chamberlain admitted to Dudley Carleton that 'for mine own part I cannot perceive any good either way, for impositions and patents are grown so grievous that of necessity they must be spoken of, and the prerogative on the other side is become so tender that (like a *noli me tangere*) it cannot endure to be touched.'[10]

Bacon continued his own social research, perhaps on behalf of the committee. On 24 October he wrote to the late Lord Chancellor Ellesmere's son, the earl of Bridgewater, to ask for his help (from his father's collections) in tracking down various grants, 'viz. old debts, concealments of lands, customs and other duties, monopolies to sell import-export, forfeitures and penalties, dispensations with penal laws and liberties, new offices, drowned lands, and tithes out of parishes', on behalf of 'his Majesty's service'. He took care to tell Bridgewater that 'your lordship need not doubt any meaning to your prejudice: but it is for a public respect; but therein your lordship must be secret, and take no man's knowledge.'[11]

On 29 November, the committee sent a proposal to Buckingham concerning the new grievances, attempting to forestall any confrontation between King and parliament. They suggested that patents of old debts and concealments (grants permitting private individuals to search out forgotten debts to the crown and defective land titles) might be abolished by an act of parliament, proposed by a member's bill. The Privy Council should abolish those patents of monopoly that might be sacrificed: the committee included a list of selected patents. This way, the King would 'keep his greatness, and somewhat shall be done in Parliament, and somewhat out of Parliament, as the nature of the subject and business requires'.[12]

In his usual covering letter to Buckingham, Bacon was more explicit about the particular bad feeling attached to the patents of Sir Giles Mompesson and Buckingham's brother Christopher Villiers, 'your lordship's special friends, which I account as mine own friends; and so showed myself when they were in suit'. Buckingham was asked to 'put off the envy of these things (which I think in themselves bear no great fruit), and rather take the thanks for ceasing them, than the note for maintaining them . . . But howsoever, let me know your mind, and your Lordship shall find I will go your way.' The pill was sweetened by Bacon's approval of the new Lord Treasurer, Chief Justice Montagu: perhaps, he wrote, 'now a number of counsels which I have given for the establishment of his Majesty's estate, and have lien dead and buried deeper than this snow, may now spring up and bear fruit.'[13]

The committee discussed the matter of patents before the Privy Council on 14 December, at James's request. The Council rejected the recommendations. To be seen to revoke patents so near to a parliament, they argued, would lay them open to charges of 'humouring of the Parliament . . . and that after the Parliament they would come up again'. As an 'offered' grace, they would 'leese their thanks': patents should be revoked in response to 'the complaints of particular persons'. Although Bacon acquiesced at the Council table, he continued to urge Buckingham to extricate himself from the patents ('it will sort to your honour'). He expressed concern at the progress of elections: 'For if his Majesty said well, that when he knew the men and the elections he would guess at the success; the prognostics are not so good as I expected, occasioned by late occurrences abroad, and the general licentious speaking of state matters.'[14] This 'general licentious speaking' was becoming such an issue that in mid-December the Bishop of London was required to summon all his clergy 'and to charge them from the king not to meddle in their sermons with the Spanish match nor any other matter of state'.[15] At James's request, Bacon drafted a proclamation of warning, which was published on 24 December, despite Council attempts 'to have sharpened it': Buckingham told Bacon that 'his Majesty liketh [it] in every point so well, both in matter and form, that he findeth no cause to alter a word in it.'[16]

Bacon also provided for the King an analysis of the upcoming parliamentary session. 'I have broken the main of the Parliament business into questions and parts,' he reported to Buckingham.

It may be, it is an overdiligence; but still methinks there is a middle thing between art and chance: I think they call it providence, or some such thing; which good servants owe to their sovereign, specially in cases of importance and straits of occasions. And these huffing elections, and general license of speech, ought to make us the better provided. The way will be, if his Majesty will be pleased to peruse these questions advisedly, and give me leave to wait upon him; and then refer it to some few of the Council, a little to advise upon it.[17]

★

Having been carried into the Lords at the opening of the session, James launched into a lengthy speech. Asking for supplies to be granted to repay the crown's debts and to raise an army to send to Frederick's aid, he once again personalised the issues: 'I may truly say with our Saviour, I have often piped unto you and you have not danced. I have mourned and you have not lamented.' Bacon struck a more positive note:

You have heard the King speak, and it makes me call to mind what Solomon saith, who was also a king: *The words of the wise are as nails and pins driven in and fastened by the masters of assemblies.* The King is the master of this assembly, and though his words in regard of the sweetness of them do not prick, yet in regard of the weight and wisdom of them, I know they pierce through and through; that is, both into your memories and into your affections.

I would have the Parliament know itself, first in a modest carriage to so gracious a Sovereign, and secondly in valuing themselves thus far, as to know now it is in them by their cheerful dealing to procure infinite good to themselves in substance and reputation at home and abroad. As there is great expectation in the beginning of this Parliament, so I pray God it may be as good in the conclusion: that it may be generative, begetting others hereafter.[18]

Although bids for privileges and motions against papists dominated the first few days, two subsidies were agreed on 15 February, as a 'present of love' to the King. In return, the Lower House took up Coke's suggestion that such generosity entitled them 'to appoint two days every week to hear grievances'.[19] A slew of monopolies was put under scrutiny, including

London's licensing of the realm's inns and alehouses, and the gold and silver thread monopoly – with particular venom aimed at those who worked the patents, the projectors.

The question quickly arose of who was responsible for sanctioning these grievances. Sir Edward Sackville declared on 6 February that those referees should be investigated 'who misled his Majesty and are worthy to bear the shame of their own work'.[20] A fortnight later, Bacon's colleague Sir Giles Mompesson came under scrutiny, for his patent for inns. The examination discovered that the monopoly had been referred to officials who would advise the King that it was 'legal' and possessed 'conveniency'. The referees, therefore, and not the King, were to blame. 'If these did certify it,' declared Coke, 'no king in Christendom but would have granted it. Therefore his Majesty is free from all blame in it.'[21] Buckingham became nervous. Mompesson was related to him by marriage; two of his brothers (Edward and Christopher Villiers) had done very well out of patents. He begged James to dissolve parliament, a request which James, for once, denied, conscious of the financial implications of such a dissolution.

An even more exposed target than Buckingham was Bacon. He, along with Lord Treasurer Sir Henry Montagu, had been a referee, approving Mompesson's patent for inns. Sir Francis Seymour proclaimed on 27 February that the Commons were obliged to censure eminent men who failed in their duties as guardians of the commonwealth: 'And this will be for the honour of the king, the good of the subject and terror of others in time to come.'[22]

The Committee on the Courts of Justice discovered judicial abuses in Chancery. Bacon told Sir Edward Sackville, the committee's chairman, that 'any man might speak freely anything concerning his Court of Chancery.' Tobie Matthew wrote from Brussels warning him – on the tip-off of an unidentified 'nobleman', perhaps Digby – that his friends believed him to be in danger of attack, but Bacon shrugged the hint off.

> I say to you, upon the occasion which you give me in your last, *Modicae fidei quare dubitasti* [you of little faith, why do you doubt me]? I would not have my friends (though I know it to be out of love), too apprehensive either of me, or for me; for I thank God my ways are sound and good, and I hope God will bless me in them. When once my master, and afterwards myself, were both of us in extremity of sickness, (which was no time to dissemble) I never had so great pledges and certainties of his love and favour: and that which I knew then, such as took a little poor advantage of these latter times, know since.[23]

Bacon should have heeded his old friend's warnings.

With hindsight it seems remarkable that someone with Bacon's experience of the skulduggery of James's administration should not have perceived his own vulnerability. Looking particularly closely into affairs in Chancery were two men who decidedly did not have his best interests at heart – Sir Edward Coke and Sir Lionel Cranfield. It was Cranfield who was now calling for judicial reform; Coke had introduced a bill to put limits on the power of the Chancery (at a committee on 28 February).[24] By 26 February, Dr Mead was writing to a friend that 'it is said that there are many bills ready to be put up against my Lord Chancellor.'[25] On another front, the inquiry into patents now struck on the 1619 patent for gold and silver thread, for which Bacon had acted as a referee; the profits had been divided between the King, Buckingham and Buckingham's brother Sir Edward Villiers. A joint conference of the two Houses was called to discuss this and other 'matters and offences tending to the wrong of his Majesty in his justice, honour, and estate; to the disinheritance of the Commonwealth; and this by a man of quality' – the Lord Chancellor.[26] Bacon wrote calmly to Buckingham on 7 March.

> I do hear from divers of judgment, that tomorrow's conference is like to pass in a calm, as to the referees. Sir Lionel Cranfield, who hath been formerly the trumpet, said yesterday, that he did now incline to Sir John Walter's opinion and motion not to have the referees meddled with, otherwise than to discount it from the King; and so not to look back, but to the future. And I do hear almost all men of judgement in the House wish now that way. I woo no body: I do but listen, and I have doubt of Sir Edward Coke, who I wish had some round *caveat* given him from the King; for your Lordship hath no great power with him: but I think a word from the King mates him.

Once again, Bacon had misjudged Coke's relationship to popular sentiment.

> If things be carried fair by the committees of the Lower House, I am in some doubt whether there will be occasion for your Lordship to speak tomorrow; though I confess I incline to wish you did, chiefly because you are fortunate in that kind; and, to be plain, also for our better countenance; when your Lordship, according to your noble proposition, shall show more regard of the fraternity you have with great counsellors, than of the interest of your natural brother.
>
> Always, good my Lord, let us think of times out of Parliament, as well as the present time in Parliament, and let us not all be put *es pourpoint* [into doublets]. Fair and moderate courses are ever best in causes of estate; the rather, because I wish this Parliament, by the sweet and united passages thereof, may increase the King's reputation with

foreigners; who may make a far other judgment than we mean, of a beginning to question great counsellors and officers of the crown, by courts or assemblies of estates. But the reflexion upon my particular in this makes me more sparing than perhaps, as a counsellor, I ought to be.

As he wrote the date, 7 March, he noted it was the anniversary of 'the day I received the seal'.[27]

Bacon spoke in his own behalf to the conference – when he and several others were finally named explicitly – and again at further conferences on 10 and 15 March, claiming that referees could not be held responsible if those who held the grants later abused them. Then, with perfect timing, on 14 March two charges of accepting bribes directly against the Lord Chancellor were presented to the Committee on the Courts by Christopher Aubrey and Sir Edward Egerton.

Aubrey's charge was known to Bacon, who had tried to quash it earlier in the month;[28] now he tried to do the same to Egerton's.[29] But in vain: Sir George Hastings and Sir Richard Young, who had carried the bribes, were brought in to testify. From this modest beginning, the case escalated as witnesses were dragged out; the final total of charges numbered twenty-eight.

Bacon was shocked. He immediately wrote to Buckingham:

Your Lordship spake of purgatory. I am now in it, but my mind is in a calm; for my fortune is not my felicity. I know I have clean hands and a clean heart; and I hope a clean house for friends or servants. But Job himself, or whosoever was the justest judge, by such hunting for matters against him as hath been used against me, may for a time seem foul, specially in a time when greatness is the mark and accusation is the game. And if this be to be a Chancellor, I think if the great seal lay upon Hounslow Heath, nobody would take it up.

He feared for his health, 'lest continual attendance and business, together with these cares, and want of time to do my weak body right this spring by diet and physic, will cast me down,' but realised that sickness might be interpreted as 'feigning or fainting [feinting?]'. He wanted Buckingham to protect him, as he had so many times before. 'I hope the King and your Lordship will keep me from oppression,' he wrote, then thought better of such a blatant attempt to sway his patrons. More pragmatically, he substituted: 'The King and your Lordship will, I hope, put an end to these miseries, one way or another.'[30]

The Committee on the Courts reported back to parliament through Sir Robert Phelips on 15 March. Its communication fell into three parts:

'1. the person against whom it's alleged; 2. the matter alleged; 3, the opinion of the Committee wish some desire of further direction. 1, The person is no less man than the Lord Chancellor, a man so endued with all parts both of nature and art as that I will say no more of him because I am not able to say enough. 2, The matter alleged is corruption. The persons by whom this is presented to us are two, Aubrey and Egerton.' Christopher Aubrey claimed that he had been 'advised by some that are near my Lord' that the way to 'quicken' a delayed Chancery case was 'by presenting my Lord with a hundred pounds'. When Aubrey paid the amount, through two intermediaries, he was told that 'my Lord was thankful and assured him of good success in his business' – but the case remained delayed. Sir Edward Egerton gave Bacon £400 through intermediaries, money he had raised by mortgaging his estate. 'My Lord (as they say) started at it at first, saying it was too much, he would not take it but was at length persuaded because it was for favours past and took it.' Phelips requested the House attended to this matter urgently, 'because so great a man's honour is soiled with it'.[31]

The intermediaries, Sir George Hastings (who had delivered bribes in both cases) and Sir Richard Young (who had assisted Hastings in the Egerton case), were questioned by the Committee on the Courts and supported the evidence, despite John Finch's efforts to discredit Hastings' testimony.[32] It was decided by 17 March that the case of the Lord Chancellor should be presented 'single to the Lords . . . without exasperation'. The Lords were the appropriate court on two grounds, argued Phelips: precedent ('that in this course we may follow the steps of our ancestors') and necessity ('the respect of the person, being a member of the Upper House' and 'our want of that touchstone whereby truth may be bolted out'.[33]

The precedent was far from obvious to all onlookers, since the Lords had last impeached a man in 1449. William Noy, worried about the credibility of Hastings and Young, was keen that 'we should discuss the business thoroughly here before we let it fly abroad.' If Bacon were guilty, then he had offended against the King, 'forasmuch as in him lieth he hath broken the king's oath.' 'Of necessity we must go to the Lords, but there may be a question whether to them alone and without the king; in one case this was demanded but refused. In commending it to the Lords, not to deliver it as a thing certain, as we did in Sir Giles Mompesson's case but as an information.'[34]

On 19 March, Bacon wrote to the Lords, praying them 'to make a favourable and true construction of my absence. It is no feigning nor fainting, but sickness both of my heart and of my back, though joined with that comfort of mind, that persuadeth me that I am not far from heaven, whereof I feel the first fruits.' Hearing that 'some complaints of base bribery are come before your Lordships', he requested that his cause might be heard. Since he had 'sequestered my mind at this time in great part from worldly matters, thinking of my account and answer in a higher court' [i.e. he had been ill, thinking about death], he required 'some convenient time to advise with my counsel, and to make my answer'. He did not see himself using a great deal of counsel, however, because he planned not to 'trick up an innocency with cavillations; but plainly and ingenuously (as your Lordships know my manner is) declare what I know or remember'.

He requested, 'according to the course of justice', to be allowed 'to except to the witnesses brought against me, and to move questions to your Lordships for their cross-examination, and likewise to produce my own witnesses for discovery of the truth'. Finally, knowing that the petitions were likely to multiply – especially because of 'the course that have been taken for hunting out complaints against me' – he asked the Lords 'not to take any prejudice or apprehension of any number or muster of them, especially against a judge that makes two thousand decrees and orders in a year, but that I may answer them, according to the rules of justice, severally and respectively'.[35]

The letter was presented to the Lords by Buckingham, who recounted how he had seen Bacon twice (on the King's command), finding him 'very sick and heavy' on the first occasion, but better on the second, encouraged that the accusations against him were to be dealt with by a House where he might find honourable justice. The letter was read, and the Lords sent a message requesting Bacon 'to provide for his defence'.[36]

Bacon was somewhat bemused by the charges – not because they were not literally true, but because they were being used as accusations against him. Writing to James on 25 March, he claimed:

> When I enter into myself, I find not the materials of such a tempest as is comen upon me. I have been (as your Majesty knoweth best) never author of any immoderate counsel, but always desired to have things carried *suavibus modis* [smoothly]. I have been no avaricious oppressor of the people. I have been no haughty or intolerable or hateful man, in my conversation or carriage. I have inherited no hatred from my father, but am a good patriot born. Whence should this be? For these are the things that use to raise dislikers abroad. And for the briberies or gifts wherewith I am charged, when the books of hearts shall be opened, I hope I shall not be found to have the troubled fountain of a corrupt heart in a depraved habit of taking rewards to pervert justice; howsoever I may be frail, and partake of the abuse of the times.[37]

★

With the legal term over, and parliament adjourned on 27 March, Bacon had time to get his life in order. On 10 April he made a will – a fairly standard affair, except that the viscountess received noticeably short shrift: just a 'box of rings, save the great diamond I would have restored to Sir George Reynell'. Interestingly, he desired his executors 'to make the first offer of the reversion of Gorhambury and Verulam after my wife's decease, to the Prince's Highness [Prince Charles]; because they being things of pleasure and not far from Berkhampstead, it may be his Highness may take a like to deal for them.'[38]

He set about studying legal cases which might bear comparison with his own – that of Michael de la Pole in Richard II's reign; those of Thorpe, Sir John Lee, Lord Latimer and John Lord Neville in Edward III's reign – although he seems to have been looking for issues of 'deceits to the king' as much as wrongfully receiving monies.[39] More practically, he set about obtaining and preparing for an audience with the King (who assented after consulting the Lords).[40]

Two drafts of a memorandum concerning bribery – notes prepared for his interview with the King – bear witness to the Lord Chancellor's position. His impulse was to be totally open about the details of the transactions in question but to deny that there was any intent of corruption. On the one hand, he had to attempt to mount a legal defence of his actions; on the other, he had to claim that they were no more than *vitia temporis*, abuses of the times, accepted practice, rather than *vitia hominis*, culpable behaviour in the man – a distinction which he had introduced in his letter to the King of 25 March, and which he would reiterate frequently over the next few weeks, eventually pleading to the Lords: 'Neither will your Lordships forget, That there are *vitia temporis*, as well as *vitia hominis*.'[41]

Bacon's first, rough draft identifies 'three degrees or cases of bribery charged or supposed in a judge'. Of the first, 'of bargain or contract for reward to pervert justice, *pendente lite* [while the case is pending]', he takes himself 'to be as innocent as any born upon St. Innocent's day, in my heart'. He follows this with a further, perhaps compromising sentence – 'and yet perhaps in some two or three of them the proofs may stand pregnant to the contrary' – which has been erased. Second, 'where the Judge conceives the cause to be at an end by the information of the party, or otherwise, and useth not such diligence as he ought to inquire of it'; on this point, Bacon admits 'I doubt [suspect] in some particulars I may be faulty.' Third, 'when the cause is really ended, and it is *sine fraude* [without harm] without relation to any precedent promise,' he 'conceived it to be no fault, but therein I desire to be better informed, that I may be twice penitent, once for the fact, and again for the error. For I had rather be a briber, than a defender of bribes.'

He goes on to confess 'that at new-year tides and likewise at my first coming in (which was as it were my wedding), I did not so precisely as perhaps I ought examine whether those that presented me had causes before me, yea or no. And this is simply all that I can say for the present concerning my charge, until I may receive it more particularly. And all this while, I do not fly to that, as to say, that these things are *vitia temporis*, and not *vitia hominis*.'[42]

A clean but incomplete draft (evidently a planned revision), entitled 'Memoranda of what the Lord Chancellor intended to deliver to the King, April 16, 1621, upon his first access to his majesty after his troubles', elaborates on his argument, transmuting 'bribery charged or supposed in a judge' to 'gifts and rewards given to a Judge'. In the preamble, he declares that he will 'deal ingenuously with your Majesty, without seeking fig-leaves or subterfuges',[43] a striking image to which he would return compulsively over the following days.[44]

The audience with the King did indeed take place on 16 April, and was reported to the House of Lords the following day by the Lord Treasurer. Bacon, he said, had asked for 'a particular' of the charges, on the grounds that 'it was not possible for him, who passed so many orders and decrees in a year; to remember all things that fell out in them.' He also asked that, 'where his answers should be fair and clear to those things objected against him, his Lordship might stand upon his innocency, and that 'where his answer should not be so fair and clear, there his Lordship might be admitted to the extenuation of the charge; and where the proofs were full, and undeniable, his Lordship would ingenuously confess them, and put himself upon the mercy of the Lords.' The King referred his pleas back to the Lords.[45]

Another version of events is provided by Bacon's servant Thomas Bushell. In Bushell's account, the Lord Chancellor was sacrificed by the King in order to save the skin of his favourite, Buckingham:

There arose such complaints against his lordship, and the then favourite at court, that for some days put the King to this query, whether he should permit the favourite of his affection, or the oracle of his counsel to sink in his service? Whereupon his Lordship was sent for by the King, who after some discourse, gave him this positive advice: to submit himself to his House of peers, and that (upon his princely word) he would then restore him again, if they (in their honours) should not be sensible of his merits. Now though my Lord foresaw his approaching ruin, and told his Majesty there was little hopes of mercy in a multitude when his enemies were to give fire, if he did not plead for himself, yet such was his obedience to him from whom he had his being, that he resolved, his Majesty's will should be his only law, and so took leave of him, with these words: 'Those that will strike at your Chancellor, (it's much to be feared) will strike at your crown'; and wished that as he was then the first, so he might be the last of sacrifices.[46]

Although Bushell's version of events has been roundly criticised, it is at the very least an interesting retelling of the story. It would also explain why Bacon's original impulse to defend himself in specific cases with all his legal expertise so suddenly dissipated into a generalised submission. Certainly Buckingham is identified as the cause of Bacon's fall in a contemporary satire, which opens with the painfully punning line 'Great Verulam is very lame, the gout of go-out feeling'. The satirist 'cannot but marvel . . . That Bacon should neglected be when it is most in season. Perhaps the game of Buck: hath villified the Boar?' he mused.[47]

On 19 April the various committees made their reports, which included the reading of over thirty examinations; measures were taken to coordinate the information thus far gathered (and to continue with the process); the House was then adjourned until the twenty-fourth. This was perhaps the first real inkling Bacon had of the sheer weight of the accusations against him. On 20 April, he wrote again to the King:

> I think myself infinitely bounden to your Majesty, for vouchsafing me access to your Royal Person, and to touch the hem of your garment. I see your Majesty imitateth him that would not break the broken reed, nor quench the smoking flax; and as your Majesty imitateth Christ, so I hope assuredly my Lords of the Upper House will imitate you: and unto your Majesty's grace and mercy, and next to my Lords, I recommend myself. It is not possible, nor were it safe, for me to answer particulars till I have my charge; which when I shall receive, I shall without fig-leaves or disguise excuse what I can excuse, extenuate what I can extenuate, and ingenuously confess what I can neither clear nor extenuate. And if there be any thing which I mought conceive to be no offence, and yet is, I desire to be informed, that I may be twice penitent, once for my fault, and the second time for my error.[48]

By the following day, Bacon was complaining that he had spent the past three days suffering 'such extremity of headache, upon the hinder part of my head, fixed in one place, that I thought verily it had been some imposthumation. And then the little physic that I have told me, that either it must grow to a congelation, and so to a lethargy, or to break, and so to a mortal fever or sudden death. Which apprehension (and chiefly the anguish of the pain) made me unable to think of any business.' Now, however, 'the pain itself is assuaged to be tolerable', and Bacon could take up his former position, 'prostrate myself again, by my letter, at your Majesty's feet'.

This was to be the last letter, and contained another remarkable image:

Your Majesty can bear me witness, that at my last so comfortable access I did not so much as move your Majesty, by your absolute power of pardon or otherwise, to take my cause into your hands and to interpose between the sentence of the House; and according to mine own desire your Majesty left it to the sentence of the House, and so was reported by my Lord Treasurer.

But now if your Majesty will graciously save me from a sentence with the good liking of the House, and that cup may pass from me; it is the utmost of my desires.

This I move with the more belief, because I assure myself that if it be reformation that is sought, the very taking away the seal, upon my general submission, will be as much in example for these four hundred years, as any furder severity.

The means of this I most humbly leave to your Majesty. But surely I conceive, that your Majesty's opening yourself in this kind to the Lords Counsellors, and a motion from the Prince after my submission, and my Lord Marquis using his interest with his friends in the House, may effect the sparing of a sentence; I making my humble suit to the House for that purpose, joined with the delivery of the seal into your Majesty's hands.

This is the last suit I shall make to your Majesty in this business, prostrating myself at your mercy-seat, after fifteen years' service, wherein I have served your Majesty in my poor endeavours with an entire heart, and as I presumed to say unto your Majesty, am still a virgin for matters that concern your person or crown; and now only craving that after eight steps of honour I be not precipitated altogether.

Bacon, naked, 'without fig-leaves', and prostrate, protests his virginity 'for matters that concern your person or crown': an odd line which may mean that he feels his relationship with James is either unsoiled or unconsummated. Even at this critical moment, with his entire career and reputation at stake, Bacon characteristically put his faith in formal rhetoric to plead his case. He argued boldly: 'But because he that hath taken bribes is apt to give bribes, I will go furder, and present your Majesty with a bribe. For if your Majesty give me peace and leisure, and God give me life, I will present your Majesty with a good history of England, and a better digest of your laws.'[49]

On 24 April, Prince Charles rose in the House of Lords and announced that he had received Bacon's 'humble submission and supplication' in the form of a letter to the House, dated 22 April, craving that they give 'a benign interpretation' to what he wrote. The letter was read by the Clerk and the Lord Chief Justice. Bacon began with 'a very strange entrance', professing 'gladness in some things': 'that hereafter the greatness of a judge or magistrate shall be no sanctuary or protection of guiltiness; which, in few words, is the beginning of a golden world'; and 'that after this example, it is like that judges will fly from any thing that is in the likeness of corruption, as from a serpent; which tendeth to the purging of the courts of justice, and the reducing them to their true honour and splendour'.

His only justification was 'out of the justifications of Job': '*I have not hid my sin as did Adam, nor concealed my faults in my bosom.*' It only remained that he would 'ingenuously confess and acknowledge that I find matter sufficient and full, both to move me to desert the defence, and to move your Lordships to condemn and censure me'.

> Neither will I trouble your Lordships by singling those particulars, which I think may fall off.
>
> Neither will I prompt your Lordships to observe upon the proofs, where they come not home, or the scruples touching the credits of the witnesses. Neither will I represent unto your Lordships, how far a defence might in divers things extenuate the offence, in respect of the time or manner of gift, or the like circumstances, but only leave these things to spring out of your own noble thoughts, and observations of the evidence and examinations themselves.

Turning to them as 'Peers and Prelates', and hoping that they had 'a noble feeling of me, as a member of your own body', he told them a story from Livy.

> Titus Manlius took his son's life for giving battle against the prohibition of his general: not many years after, the like severity was pursued by Papirius Cursor, the Dictator, against Quintus Maximus, who being upon the point to be sentenced, by the intercession of some principal persons of the senate was spared; whereupon Livy maketh this grave and gracious observation: The discipline of war was no less established by the questioning of Quintus Maximus, than by the punishment of Titus Manlius. And the same reason is of the reformation of justice; for the questioning of men of eminent place hath the same terror, though not the same rigor, with the punishment.

His case was not in the same position, however. 'For my humble desire is, that his Majesty would take the seal into his hands, which is a great downfall, and may serve I hope in itself for an expiation of my faults.' He concluded: 'My humble suit to your Lordships is, that my penitent submission may be my sentence, and the loss of the seal my punishment; and that your Lordships will spare any further sentence, but recommend me to his Majesty's grace and pardon for all that is past.'[50]

After it was read, 'no Lord spoke to it for a long time.' Bacon's directness clearly dumbfounded its hearers. The Lord Chamberlain stated that 'the question is whether this submission be sufficient to ground your Lordships' judgment for a censure, without further examination.' A debate of the whole House in committee ensued on the status of the submission. Lord Saye argued that the submission would have been sufficient earlier, 'but coming now after the examinations and proofs it comes too late'; the earl of Suffolk declared that 'the confession is not sufficient for he desires to be a judge – to lose his seal, and that to be the sentence: wherefore it is far short of that we expect.' The Lord Chamberlain pointed out that Bacon had not actually answered any charge: 'It is not sufficient, for the confession is grounded upon a rumour . . . he neither speaks of the particular charges, nor confesseth anything particular'. Southampton was emphatic: 'He is charged by the Commons with corruption; and no word of confession of any corruption in his submission. It stands with the justice and honour of this House not to proceed without the parties' particular confession; or to have the parties to hear the charge, and we to hear the parties' answer.'[51]

It was decided that Bacon should be sent the charge, 'for three causes. 1. His Lordship confesseth not any particular bribe nor corruption. 2. Nor showeth how his Lordship heard of the charge thereof. 3. The confession, such as it is, is afterwards extenuated in the same submission: and therefore the Lords have sent him a particular of the charge, and do expect his answer to the same, with all convenient expedition.'[52] Bacon was given five days to respond.

Bacon's confession and humble submission, with detailed responses to each charge, was delivered to the Lord Chief Justice, and read to the Lords on 30 April.[53] He opened by stating clearly: 'Upon advised consideration of the charge, descending into my own conscience, and calling my memory to account so far as I am able, I do plainly and ingenuously confess that I am guilty of corruption; and do renounce all defence, and put myself upon the grace and mercy of your Lordships' and 'the judgment, grace, and mercy of the court'.

His only attempt at extenuation was appended to the response:

It may please your Lordships, out of your nobleness, to cast your eyes of compassion upon my person and estate, I was never noted for an avaricious man. And the Apostle saith, that *covetousness is the root of all evil.* I hope also that your Lordships do the rather find me in the state of grace, for that in all these particulars there are few or none that are not almost two years old; whereas those that have an habit of corruption do commonly wax worse and worse; so that it hath pleased God to prepare me, by precedent degrees of amendment, to my present penitency. And for my estate, it is so mean and poor, as my care is now chiefly to satisfy my debts.

And so, fearing I have troubled your Lordships too long, I shall conclude with an humble suit unto you, That if your Lordships proceed to sentence, your sentence may not be heavy to my ruin, but gracious, and mixt with mercy; and not only so, but that you would be noble intercessors for me to his Majesty likewise, for his grace and favour.

After hearing the submission, a committee of twelve lords was sent to ascertain, formally, that this confession was indeed in Bacon's hand. He answered, 'My Lords, it is my act, my hand, my heart. I beseech your Lordships, be merciful to a broken reed.' At the King's command, the Lord Treasurer, Lord Steward, Lord Chamberlain and the earl of Arundel went to York House on 1 May to sequester the seal. In Elsing's account, they 'wished it had been better with him', and Bacon replied, 'The worse the better. By the King's great favour I received the great seal; by my own fault I have lost it.'[54] Perhaps more likely is Tobie Matthew's version, in which Bacon merely said, with a characteristic aphorism, '*Deus dedit, culpa abstulit* [God gives, blame takes away].'[55]

On the evening of 2 May, the Lords sent the Gentleman Usher and the Serjeant-at-Arms to give notice to Bacon that he must attend them at nine the following morning to hear his sentence. The messengers reported the next day that they had found Bacon 'sick in bed. He answered that he is so sick that he is not able to repair hither; that this is no excuse, for if he had been well he would willingly have come.' The charge was read again and it was unanimously 'agreed that the Lord Chancellor is guilty of the matters wherewith he is charged, *nemine dissentiente* [with none dissenting]'.

A decision had to be taken as to Bacon's punishment. Spencer pointed out that the King had said 'he would make it a precedent to posterity.' Arundel said that although Bacon's offences were foul, his confession had been pitiful and his life should not be touched. The Lord Chamberlain's suggestion of a fine, ransom and imprisonment was agreed; Sheffield's suggestion that he should not 'be capable hereafter of any office of judicature of councillor's place' was 'well liked of'; Arundel opposed Saye's suggestion that he should be 'degraded during life, for unfit to sit here again amongst us'. It was at length agreed that while Bacon's titles would not be suspended, he would be fined £40,000, imprisoned at the King's pleasure in the Tower and held 'uncapable of any office, place, or employment in the state or commonwealth'; and he was 'never to sit in Parliament, nor to come within the verge [twelve miles] of the court'. Only Lord Admiral Buckingham dissented, commenting that Bacon was in any case 'so sick that he cannot live long'.[56]

Thomas Bushell's account of these events is somewhat different: 'Soon after (according to his Majesty's commands) he wrote a submissive letter to the House, and sent me to my Lord Windsor to know the result, which I was loath at my return to acquaint him with; for, alas! his sovereign's favour was not in so high a measure, but he (like the phoenix) must be sacrificed in flames of his own raising, and so perished (like Icarus) in that his lofty design, the great revenue of his office being lost, and his titles of honour saved but by the bishops' votes, whereto he replied, That he was only bound to thank his clergy,' punning on the 'benefit of clergy' that could save condemned men from the noose. There was a certain irony, as Bushell noted, 'to see that famous Lord, who procured his Majesty to call this Parliament, must be the first subject of their revengeful wrath; and that so unparalleled a master should be thus brought upon the public stage for the foolish miscarriages of his own servants whereof (with grief of heart) I confess my self to be one.'[57]

In the 'particular confession' on twenty-eight counts (based on twenty-one cases) which the Lords demanded from Bacon, there are three identifiable strategies by which Bacon sought to excuse himself of the charge of receiving bribes. The first was to claim that the final decree was already passed by the time he received gifts from the litigant, so the gift could not have affected his judgement; for example, £400 was 'delivered unto me in a purse . . . but, as far as I can remember, it was expressed by them that brought it, to be for favours past, and not in respect to favours to come.'[58] The second was to point out that the gift had been received on an occasion when gifts were perfectly natural – for example, at New Year: 'I confess and declare, That I received at New Year's tide, an hundred pounds from Sir John Treavor; and, because it came as a New Year's gift, I neglected to enquire whether the cause was ended or depending.'[59] The third was to assert that the transactions had somehow involved his servants – as he acknowledged in answer to the charge that he had 'given way to great exactions by his servants, both in respect of private seals, and otherwise for sealing of injunctions'. It was, he conceded, 'a great fault of neglect in me that I looked no better to my servants':

I understood that there was some money given by Holman to my servant Hatcher, with that certainly I was never made privy.

I confess and declare, That my servant Hunt did, upon his account, being my receiver of the fines of original writs, charge himself with two hundred pounds, formerly received of Smithwick, which, after that I had understood the nature of it, I ordered him to repay it, and to defaulk it of his account.[60]

What is remarkable about these accusations is not that Bacon may or may not have *taken* bribes, but that the accusers should come forward and declare that they had *given* bribes to ensure their suits' easy progress through Chancery. These men were annoyed, not that there was a Lord Chancellor who accepted bribes, but that there was a Lord Chancellor who failed to deliver the goods upon receipt of those bribes – Bacon had apparently taken the money and then ruled *against* the suits. These petitioners were not overcoming guilt in making their complaint against Bacon; they were overcoming their embarrassment at having paid out for a decision which did not go their way.

Looked at in this light, Bacon's defence makes sense in so far as he is claiming lack of knowledge that these suits were pending, and therefore lack of knowledge on how to act upon receipt of those gifts. His other major defence – that his servants accepted the gifts and that he had therefore had no knowledge of them – is however his vulnerable spot. For this shows a lack of control over his servants, an indulging of them beyond the bounds of suitable masterly behaviour. As John Chamberlain wrote at the beginning of the investigation, the Lords 'proceed very orderly and warily and will not admit any accusation of what was given to his servants and friends, but what came directly to his own hands, and was proved by oath'.[61] The Lords had wanted to hold Bacon responsible only for what was given to him directly; but this strategy was evidently dropped when it became clear that Bacon's affairs were too bound up with the activities of his servants for his 'own' acts to be extricated for inspection.

At the time, there was talk of other malpractice by his servants. Aubrey recalls how 'the East Indian merchants presented his lordship with a cabinet of jewels, which his page, Mr. Cockaine, received, and deceived his lord.' The profits were such that 'three of his lordship's servants kept their coaches, and some kept racehorses.'[62] The guilt of Bacon's servants is borne out, moreover, by the life and works of Bacon's servant Thomas Bushell. Bushell appears to have suffered a complete breakdown after Bacon's fall, a catastrophe for which he held himself partly responsible; after a period spent living in a cave on a sheer cliff on the Isle of Man, he rehabilitated himself into society, billing himself 'the superlative prodigal'. He later confessed that 'myself and others of his servants were the occasion of exhaling his virtues into a dark eclipse; which God knows would have long endured both for the honour of his King, and good of the commonalty; had not we whom his bounty nursed, laid on his guiltless shoulders our base and execrable deeds to be scanned and censured by the whole Senate of a state, where no sooner sentence was given, but most of us forsook him, which makes us bear the badge of Jews to this day.' Although there were 'some godly Daniels' among the servants, 'for myself with shame I must acquit the title, and plead guilty; which grieves my very soul, that so matchless a peer should be lost by such insinuating caterpillars, who in his own nature scorned the least thought of any base, unworthy, or ignoble act, though subject to infirmities, as ordained to the wisest.' Despite Bushell's reputation, the description he has left us of his master's attitudes and behaviour provides a rare glimpse of intimacy, and may well be a reliable account.

According to Bushell, so great was Bacon's 'hatred to bribery, corruption, or simony' that when he learned that Bushell had received the first fruits of a benefice given to him by Bacon, 'he fell into so great a passion', berating Bushell that 'I was cursed in my conception, and nursed with a tiger for deceiving the Church, threatening I should be no longer his servant; for that one scabbed sheep might infect the whole flock. Yet notwithstanding, upon my submission, the nobleness of his disposition forgave me the fact and received me into favour; but never could obtain a spiritual living afterwards.' It was therefore Bushell's opinion that 'they that ministered those hellish pills of bribery, gilded them over, not only at first with a show of gratuity, or in the love of courtesy, but waited the opportunity of his necessity: otherwise it had been impossible to have wrought an impression.' Bacon was the victim of a political campaign 'to select some man of worth for allaying clamour of the vulgar, and congratulate the giddy multitude'.[63]

Bacon's indulgence of his servants was legendary, and remained a talking point long after his death. In 1655 a bookseller's assistant overheard a conversation between two customers, one of whom had been to see Lord Chancellor Bacon at Gorhambury. While Bacon was temporarily absent from the room, he said, 'there comes into the study one of his Lordship's gentlemen, and opens my Lord's chest of drawers wherein his money was, and takes it out in handfuls and fills both his pockets, and goes away without saying any word to me. He was no sooner gone but comes a second gentleman, opens the same drawers, fills both his pockets with money, and goes away as the former did, without speaking a word to me.' When the visitor informed Bacon of what had happened, he 'shook his head; and all that he said was, "Sir, I cannot help myself".' The customer opined that Bacon 'had a fault, whatever it was he could not tell'.[64]

The contemporary parliamentarian and diarist Simonds D'Ewes commented at length on Bacon's fall. 'Never had any man in those great places of gain he had gone through so ill husbanded the time, or provided for himself; but his vast prodigality had eaten up all his gains; so as it was agreed on by all men that he owed at this present at least £20,000 more than he were worth.' Bacon might have been 'an eminent scholar, and a reasonable good lawyer', but that did not protect him from his vices, which were 'so stupendious and great, as they utterly obscured and outpoised his virtues. For he was immoderately ambitious, and excessively proud, to maintain which he was necessitated to injustice and bribery, taking some-times most basely of both sides. To this later wickedness the favour he had with the beloved marquis of Buckingham emboldened him, as I learned in discourse from a gentleman of his bedchamber, who told me he was sure his lord should never fall as long as the said marquis continued in favour.'

From this trenchant criticism D'Ewes moved on, without pausing for breath, to detail another of Bacon's failings.

His most abominable and darling sin I should rather bury in silence than mention it, were it not a most admirable instance how men are enslaved by wickedness and held captive by the devil. For whereas presently upon his censure at this time his ambition was moderated, his pride humbled, and the means of his former injustice and corruption removed, yet would he not relinquish the practice of his most horrible and secret sin of sodomy, keeping still one Godrick a very effeminate faced youth to be his catamite. After his fall men began to discourse of that his unnatural crime, which he had practised many years; deserting the bed of his lady, which he accounted as the Italians and Turks do, a poor and mean pleasure in respect of the other; and it was thought by some that he should have been tried at the bar of justice for it, and have satisfied the law most severe against that horrible villainy with the price of his blood.

Despite the gravity of his crime, however, 'he never came to any public trial for this crime; nor did ever that I could hear forbear his old custom of making his servants his bedfellows.'[65]

D'Ewes was not alone in his conviction as to Bacon's sexual tastes. In his *Brief Lives*, written with what he claimed was first-hand information from, among others, Bacon's assistant Thomas Hobbes, John Aubrey stated with some certainty that 'Bacon was a *paiderastos*' who had 'his Ganymedes and favourites'.[66] This was apparently well known at the time. A popular satirical verse on Bacon's downfall –

> Within this sty here now doth lie
> A hog well fed with bribery
> A pig, a hog, a boar, a bacon
> Whom God hath left, and the devil taken[67]

– was adapted by 'some bold and forward man', who wrote his version on a sheet of paper and 'cast it down in some part of York House in the Strand where Viscount St Alban yet lay':

> Within this sty a hog doth lie
> That must be hanged for sodomy.

(In case the hint was lost, D'Ewes provided a note to point out that 'hog' alluded 'both to his surname of Bacon and to that swinish abominable sin'.)[68] This verse was by no means unique: John Chamberlain reported on 24 March that 'Many indignities are said and done against him, and divers libels cast abroad to his disgrace not worth the repeating as savouring of too much malice and scurrility.'[69]

What is intriguing about these attacks is the easy way in which they conflate the questions of 'bribery' and 'sodomy'. Both D'Ewes and Aubrey are in fact talking of the relationship between Bacon and his servants, a relationship which they see as unhealthy. The anonymous author of the popular satirical poem 'Great Verulam is very lame' identified several Bacon servants by name:

> Young, this grief will make thee old for care with youth ill matches:
> Sorrow makes Meautys much to rust that Hatcher is under hatches.
> Bushell wants by half a peck the measure of such tears
> Because his lord's posteriors makes the buttons that he wears.
> Though Edney be cashier'd, grief moves him to compassion
> To think how suddenly is turn'd the wheel of his ambition.
> Had Butler liv'd he had vese'd and griev'd this dismal day to see
> The Hogshead that so late was broached to run so near the lee.
> Fletcher may go feather bolts for such as quickly shoot them
> Now Cockin's comb is wisely cut a man may soon non-suit him.[70]

The verse identifies Bacon's secretaries, John Young and Thomas Meautys, two of his gentleman ushers, ('buttoned') Bushell and Butler, his chamberman Francis Edney, his gentleman waiter Fletcher, and his page Cockaine.

Aubrey explains the lewd reference to Bacon's backside and buttons: ''Twas the fashion in those days for gentlemen to have their suits of clothes garnished with buttons. My Lord Bacon was then in disgrace, and his man Bushell having more buttons than usual on his cloak, they said that his Lord's breech made buttons and Bushell wore them: from whence he was called "buttoned Bushell".'[71] Aubrey can only be suggesting that it was maliciously put about that Bushell's ostentatious dress had been earned by sexual services to his master.

The nature of the intimate relationships between high-ranking men in the patronage and friendship systems that sustained Jacobean England meant that sodomy was a charge that spread out in all directions – from patron to client, from master to servant. In Bacon's case, the accusation attached itself to his ex-chaplain, William Lewis, whom he had forcibly installed as the provost of Oriel College, Oxford. Chamberlain wrote of how 'One Lewis a fine chaplain of his who he preferred to be provost of Oriel College against the hair, is run away of Paris, some say for debt, some for a fouler fault, and that he was *domini similis* [like his master].' It may be that association with Buckingham left men open to this sort of accusation. In 1624 one Anthony Robinson, who was said to be 'favoured by Buckingham', was accused of 'an unnatural offence' by his servants; it was later adjudged to be an attempt to extort money.[72] Whatever the case, it was a charge that has stuck to Francis Bacon to this day.

★

For some four weeks Bacon held the imprisonment clause of his sentence at bay by pleading illness. In the meantime parliament was kept busy with the impeachment of Sir John Bennet, Judge of the Prerogative Court of Canterbury – a man 'of so many corruptions', according to Chamberlain, 'that by his side the Chancellor seems an honest man' – and by the questioning of the suspended Attorney-General Sir Henry Yelverton, who in responding launched an offensive on Buckingham. Fearful of going this far, the Commons repudiated his testimony and returned him to the Tower, making good Buckingham's current palace boast that he was parliament-proof. In his notebook Bacon commented, in Greek characters, 'Of my offence, I will say that [which] I have good warrant for, they were not the greatest sinners in Israel upon whom the wall of Shilo fell.' In cipher he added, 'I was the justest judge that was in England these fifty years: But it was the justest censure in Parliament that was these two hundred years.' Elsewhere he declared that while he acknowledged the sentence to have been 'just, and for reformation sake fit', he still considered himself 'the justest Chancellor that hath been in the five changes since Sir Nicholas Bacon's time'.[73]

Bacon's continued presence at York House excited the animosity of those who disliked him. On 12 May, Southampton rose to point out to the Lords that the disgraced Chancellor had not yet gone to the Tower, and urged that action be taken so 'that the world may not think our sentence is in vain'. Buckingham explained that 'the King hath respited his going to the Tower in this time of his great sickness', but Sheffield moved for a warrant from the House 'to commit the late Lord Chancellor to the Tower'.[74] The renewed activity against Bacon may have been aimed as much against Buckingham as against him personally: that same day Sir Anthony Ashley wrote to Buckingham of a rumour 'lately spread touching his Majesty's untimely pardon of the late Lord Chancellor's fine and impris-

onment, with some other favours intended towards him (said to be procured by your Lordship's only intimation) hath exceedingly exasperated
the rancour of the ill-affected; which, albeit it be false, and unlikely, because
very unseasonable, it doth yet serve the present turn for the increase of
malice against you'.[75]

Sheffield's motion was not carried, but at the end of May (probably on
the twenty-seventh or twenty-eighth[76]) Bacon did make his way, via the
relative privacy of the Thames, rather than down the Strand and Fleet
Street, to the Tower, from where he demanded abruptly of Buckingham
on the thirty-first, 'Procure the warrant for my discharge this day.' It was
imprisonment that he could not face.

> Death, I thank God, is so far from being unwelcome to me, as I have
> called for it (as Christian resolution would permit) any time these two
> months. But to die before the time of his Majesty's grace, and in this
> disgraceful place, is even the worst that could be; and when I am dead,
> he is gone that was always in one tenor, a true and perfect servant to
> his master, and one that was never author of any immoderate, no, nor
> unsafe, no (I will say it) nor unfortunate counsel; and one that no
> temptation could ever make other than a trusty, and honest, and thrice
> loving friend to your Lordship.

He ended, piteously, 'God bless and prosper your Lordship, whatsoever
become of me.'[77]

The plea prevailed. As Chamberlain put it, Bacon, 'by importunity
getting the king's hand for his enlargement (with order to make no use
of it till the parliament were risen) he could defer no longer but came
away that night [Saturday 2 June] after ten o'clock to his own house.'[78]
Bacon heartily thanked Buckingham 'for getting me out of prison'. However, it was only the first step on the road to rehabilitation: 'Now my
body is out, my mind nevertheless will be still in prison, till I may be on
my feet to do his Majesty and your Lordship faithful service.'[79] He had
not lost hope of James's favour: 'For me to despair of him were a sin not
to be forgiven. I thank God I have overcome the bitterness of this cup by
Christian resolution, so that worldly matters are but mint and cumin.'[80]
His hopes seemed to be justified. Chamberlain reported on Saturday 9
June that, 'among many discourses of changes, of placing and displacing
of officers, not worth the relating (because the reports alter every day), he
[Bacon] is not forgotten, but named to be Lord President of the Council.'[81]

From the Tower Bacon was whisked away to the abode in Parsons Green
of Sir John Vaughan, one of Prince Charles's retinue; he welcomed the
house's 'sweet air and loving usage [which] much revived my languishing
spirits'. There, in an elaborately flattering letter to the Prince, he recalled

'how infinitely I am bound to your Highness, that stretched forth your arm to save me from a sentence; that took hold of me to keep me from being plunged deep in a sentence; that hath kept me alive in your gracious memory and mention since the sentence'. Now, he wrote, 'I hope by the assistance of God above (of whose grace and favour I have had extraordinary signs and effects during my afflictions) to lead such a life in the last acts thereof, as whether his Majesty employ me, or whether I live to myself, I shall make the world say that I was not unworthy such a patron.'[82]

Meanwhile a new Lord Keeper had been found – John Williams, Dean of Westminster, who was hurriedly made Bishop of Lincoln and sworn into the Privy Council. The Lords were reported to be aghast, taking 'the greatest exception that so mean a man as a dean should so suddenly leap over all their heads'. His relative youth in particular (Williams was forty years old) was held against him; but, ironically, as Chamberlain reported, 'an answer made by the late Lord Chancellor in a like case took that away, that minority of years was not to be regarded where there was majority of parts.' In any case, he was the King's choice, after he had 'resolved to have no more lawyers (as men so bred and nuzzled in corruption that they could not leave it)'.[83]

Notwithstanding his professed distaste for lawyers, James did make use of Bacon, while he was still living (illegally) within the verge – that is, within twelve miles of the King's court – in calling for his opinion on his proposed reformation of the courts of justice. Bacon, delivering his verdict on 21 June, took advantage of the opportunity to point out to the King the impossibility of his situation: 'For the particulars, your Majesty in your grace and wisdom will consider, how unproper and how unwarranted a thing it is for me, as I now stand, to send for entries of Parliament, or for searches for precedents, whereupon to ground an advice. And besides what I should now say may be thought by your Majesty (how good an opinion soever you have of me) much more by others, to be busy or officious, or relating to my present fortunes.'[84]

Bacon was keen to maintain his proximity to the court. Arguing to Buckingham that it would be unworthy of him *not* to desire to 'approach to his Majesty's person' and to Buckingham, 'my second comfort', he petitioned the King to 'give me leave to stay at London till the last of July', to enable him to settle some outstanding debts.[85] Buckingham arranged for Bacon's secretary Thomas Meautys to attend the King, and to kiss his hands; but Meautys brought back only 'his Majesty's inclination that I [Bacon] should go first to Gorhambury'; and, as Bacon noted, 'his Majesty's inclinations have ever been with me instead of directions.' Bacon claimed, however, that James was 'graciously pleased to have acquainted my Lords with my desire, if I had stood me so much upon', 'but I will accommmodate my present occasions as I may, and leave the times and seasons and ways to his Majesty's grace and choice.' He also pardoned himself if he had 'pressed unseasonably. My letters out of the Tower were *de profundis*, and the world is a prison if I may not approach his Majesty, finding in my heart as I do.'[86]

On 23 June, therefore, Bacon retired to Gorhambury, relying on Buckingham 'to maintain me in his Majesty's grace and good intention'.[87] But even out of sight, Bacon provoked bad feeling. Chamberlain reported him as 'having (as should seem) no manner of feeling of his fall, but continuing as vain and idle in all his humours as when he was at highest. His fine of £4000 to the king is so far from hurting him, that it serves for a bulwark and protection against his creditors.'[88] Buckingham was told by 'some wretched detractor' that it was strange that Bacon should be in debt, given that he could have received no less than £100,000 in gifts since being made Lord Keeper. 'Such tales as these', Bacon fulminated, 'made St James say that the tongue is a fire, and itself fired from hell, whither when these tongues shall return, they will beg a drop of cold water to cool them. I praise God for it, I never took penny for any benefice or ecclesiastical living, I never took penny for releasing anything I stopped at the seal, I never took penny for any commission or things of that nature, I never shared with any servant for any second or inferior profit.' He had declared his offences, and, 'as for my debts, I showed them your lordship, when you saw the little house and the gallery, besides a little wood or desert, which you saw not. If these things were true (although the joys of the penitent be sometimes more than the joys of the innocent) I could not be as I am.'[89]

But even in the depths of disgrace, Bacon provided a fabulous show. As he returned to his country estate Prince Charles, 'returning from hunting, espied a coach attended with a goodly troop of horsemen, who it seems were gathered together to wait upon the Chancellor to his house at Gorhambury, at the time of his declension'. The Prince commended his 'undaunted spirit and excellent parts, not without some regret that such a man should be falling off'. Looking again at the well-attended coach, however, 'The Prince smiled, "Well, do we what we can," said he. "This man scorns to go out like a snuff".'[90]

PART IV

INVENTING POSTERITY

1621–1626

17

Leisure without Loitering: Bacon's Quinquennium

For my part, I seek an *otium*, and, if it may be, a fat *otium*.
Francis, Viscount St Alban, memorandum (March 1622)

S O SEVERE A sentence as that meted out to Francis Bacon in the spring of 1621 should have been enough to crush a man in his position. A constant and notorious debtor, he faced irreparable damage from the astronomical fine. A parliamentarian of forty years, he lost his forum overnight. A man whose very political existence depended on access, he was denied the lifeline of court life. And yet Bacon turned the sentence into the cornerstone for the intellectual work he had wanted to do for the past thirty years. Forced into seclusion, he at last found time to focus his attention on the intellectual projects from which his public commitments had previously distracted him. The philosopher and scientist Francis Bacon who has come down to the twentieth century was the direct result of this infamous political disgrace.

While financial considerations meant that Bacon never ceased to bid for office, pension and access at court, alongside his long-standing pursuit of such immediate recognition he now waged a new campaign to present himself to posterity – and to a posterity that would not be circumscribed by religious, political or geographical boundaries. Thus, when he was thanking James and Buckingham for his release from the Tower, he also extended thanks – in Latin – to the Spanish ambassador Sarmiento (now the Count Gondomar), declaring: 'For myself, my age, my fortune, yea my Genius, to which I have hitherto done but scant justice, calls me now to retire from the stage of civil action and betake myself to letters, and to the instruction of the actors themselves, and the service of Posterity. In this it may be I shall find honour, and I shall pass my days as it were in the entrance halls [*in atriis*] of a better life.'[1]

Bacon's pretended 'retirement' was meticulously presented to important contemporary figures, and to his readers, in a carefully coordinated fashion. The new image he wanted to project was one that did not attempt to avoid the scandal of his fall, but instead recast it in non-parochial terms, likening Bacon to great classical authors who had also fallen from grace. He seized on his forced retirement to Gorhambury as a new strategy to serve the King:

> *Utar*, saith Seneca to his Master, *magnis exemplis; nec meae fortunae, sed tuae* [I may use great examples, not of my fortune but of yours]. Demosthenes was banished for bribery of the highest nature, yet was recalled with honour; Marcus Livius [Salinator] was condemned for exactions, yet afterwards made Consul and Censor. Seneca banished for divers corruptions; yet was afterwards restored, and an instrument of that memorable *Quinquennium Neronis*. Many more. This, if it please your Majesty, I do not say for appetite of employment, but for hope that if I do by myself as is fit, your Majesty will never suffer me to die in want or dishonour.[2]

The comparison with Demosthenes and Seneca – with the addition of Cicero – was amplified the following year in a letter to his old friend Lancelot Andrewes, now Bishop of Winchester. These men, he thought, were 'the most eminent and the most resembling' he had come across 'through the variety of my reading': all three had 'held chief place of authority in their countries'; all three were ruined 'by justice and sentence, as delinquents and criminals'; all three were 'famous writers' – the fame of their writings meaning that 'the remembrance of their calamity is now as to posterity but as a little picture of night-work, remaining amongst the fair and excellent tables of their acts and works.' Lastly, all three would 'quench any man's ambition of rising again', since their efforts in that vein led 'but to their further ruin and destruction, ending in a violent death'.

His three chosen exemplars gave Bacon a chance to compare 'how they did bear their fortunes, and principally how they did employ their times, being banished and disabled for public business'. Each took a different path: the softened, dejected Cicero wrote 'nothing but a few womanish epistles', while Demosthenes, condemned for 'bribery in the nature of treason and disloyalty', took it upon himself 'to counsel the state by letters', and Seneca took a middle path: 'though his pen did not freeze, yet he abstained from intruding into matters of business; but spent his time in writing books of excellent argument and use for all ages; though he might have made better choice (sometimes) of his dedications.' These examples persuaded Bacon to 'a resolution (whereupon I was otherwise inclined) to spend my time wholly in writing; and to put forth that poor talent, or half talent, or what it is, that God hath given me, not as heretofore to particular exchanges, but to banks or mounts of perpetuity, which will not break.'[3]

Denied the opportunity of 'particular exchanges', Bacon now saw it as imperative that 'perpetuity' should be the forum in which his ideas would be allowed their true voice. In the recently rediscovered draft of his *Abecedarium novum naturae* (1622), Bacon wrote:

> From time to time I am put in mind of the *bon mot* of the man from Greece who, when somebody had finished a great speech on behalf of a rather small town, replied, My friend, your words lack only a city big enough to match. As for me, I am pretty sure that, because I have little faith in the genius of our times, my own words (as far as the work of the Instauration goes) could be accused of lacking an age or era to match them. Nevertheless, in saying this I do not have the slightest intention of disparaging the talents of the present age in any way; rather I say it because, as one or other of the political writers has remarked, Certain things give satisfaction immediately, certain others bear fruit with the passage of time. That is why I am devoted to posterity and put forward nothing for the sake of my name or the taste of others, but, knowing well enough the nature of the things that I impart, I deal out work for ages to come.[4]

When Francis Bacon was catapulted into 'retirement' in April 1621, his published output was not the 'works' we now think of when his name is mentioned. Most were what Bacon himself referred to as 'the Recreations of my other Studies'; of the writings which later editors were to consider the 'Philosophical Works', only the *Novum Organum* was yet available to the public. It was during the next five years, the last years of his life that uncannily *became* his 'quinquennium', that Bacon wrote, revised, translated or polished most of the work for which he is generally remembered, with the project for the print rehabilitation of Verulam continuing past his death.

As he manufactured an impressive body of scientific and philosophical writings – worthy of the great man in retirement – Bacon tacitly erased all signs that his 'thought' and his 'life' (in the political arena) had hitherto been intimately linked. Instead he constructed a 'before' and an 'after': before, Francis Bacon was an active politician, caught up in the hurly-burly of court and parliamentary affairs, his outlook inevitably coloured (not to say tarnished) by the times; after, he was a patrician thinker, selflessly pursuing his scientific endeavours for posterity. It is small wonder that Bacon's biographers and scholars of Baconian science have found it hard to believe that their subject is one and the same man.

The picture bequeathed to posterity of Bacon's final years owes much to his chaplain William Rawley's version of events. 'The last five years of his life, being withdrawn from civil affairs and from an active life,' he wrote, 'he employed wholly in contemplation and studies – a thing whereof his lordship would often speak during his active life, as if he affected to die in the shadow and not in the light; which also may be found in several passages of his works.' It was during these five years, according to Rawley, that 'he composed the greatest parts of his books and writings, both in English and Latin', which he listed '(as near as I can) in the just order wherein they were written' as:

> The History of the Reign of King Henry the Seventh; Abecedarium Naturae, or a Metaphysical piece which is lost [this has now been rediscovered]; Historia ventorum; Historia vitae et mortis; Historia densi et rari, not yet printed; Historia gravis et levis, which is also lost; a Discourse of a War with Spain; a Dialogue touching an Holy War, the Fable of the New Atlantis; a Preface to a Digest of the Laws of England; the beginning of the History of the Reign of King Henry the Eighth; De Augmentis Scientiarum, or the Advancement of Learning, put into Latin, with several enrichments and enlargements; Counsels Civil and Moral, or his book of Essays, likewise enriched and enlarged; the Conversion of certain Psalms into English Verse; the Translation into Latin of the History of King Henry the Seventh, of the Counsels Civil and Moral, of the Dialogue of the Holy War, of the Fable of the New Atlantis, for the benefit of other nations; his revising of his book De sapientia veterum; Inquisitio de magnete; Topica inquisitionis de luce et lumine; both these not yet printed; lastly, Sylva sylvarum, or the Natural History.

In fact, as the editorial endeavours of Graham Rees are showing, the vast majority of these works were in progress (albeit some in extremely fragmented form) considerably before 1621.[5] Following Bacon himself, Rawley deliberately separated his master's proper intellectual work from the compromising practicalities of his civic life.

In reality, of course, it was an impossible distinction to maintain. At the most basic level, there were certain practical problems of being in 'withdrawal' – not least how to gather the archival materials needed for works such as his first task, History of the Reign of King Henry VII. But Bacon was used to having much of his work done by other men: he had always advised that the statesman–historian should make use of the initial work undertaken by scholars and antiquarians, 'industrious men'.[6] Indeed, he relied on servants in his intellectual work, just as in his professional work, throughout his career. Now he turned to John Borough, a Gray's Inn common lawyer, and John Selden – who had acted as legal consultant to Bacon earlier in the year – to search through the Westminster collection of Sir Robert Cotton, and to look further afield.[7]

Nearer at hand, his chaplain William Rawley, the infamously 'buttoned' Thomas Bushell and his secretary Thomas Meautys were his mainstays at this time. Aubrey recalls, too, how Thomas Hobbes 'was beloved by his lordship, who was wont to have him walk with him in his delicate groves where he did meditate: and when a notion darted into his mind, Mr. Hobbes was presently to write it down, and his Lordship was wont to say that he did it better than anyone else about him; for that many times, when he read their notes he scarce understood what they writ, because they understood it not clearly themselves.' (Bushell, for example, had no Latin education.) Hobbes also 'assisted his lordship in translating several of his *Essays* into Latin: one, I well remember, is that "Of the greatness of cities"'.[8]

The most pressing concern was finance, the 'means to subsist'. Having 'much fallen in love with a private life', he realised that, although he had 'lived hitherto upon the scraps of my former fortunes', he would 'not be able to hold out longer'. He therefore embarked on a campaign to restore his fortunes, calling on not only Buckingham and Prince Charles but also the bishops of Winchester, Durham and London; Lord Duke and Lord Hunsden; the Lord Chamberlain; Mr John Murray of the King's Bed-chamber; Mr Maxwell; and the Lord of Kelly (Sir Thomas Erskine).[9] On one count, he met with some partial success – 'the confinement', the repeal of which he had entrusted to Erskine. On 13 September, Bacon received a warrant 'for the space of one month or six weeks' to come to Sir John Vaughan's house at Parsons Green, 'for the settling of your estate and taking order for your debts' and because 'at this time your broken estate of health requireth that you be near help of physicians'.[10]

When James returned from his summer progress, Bacon petitioned the King directly, stressing that in the seventeen years of his service (dating from the Union commission) he had never been 'chargeable', but had paid his way 'in an honourable sweat of my labour in those places which you bestowed upon me', with the exception of the £1,200 pension given him by the King 'after my great sickness (which I wish had had his period)'. In the 'other poor prop of my estate, which is the farm of the petty writs, I improved your Majesty's revenue by four hundred pounds the year'. On becoming Lord Keeper, he had given up both the attorneyship ('a gainful place') and his Star Chamber clerkship ('which was Queen Elizabeth's favour, and was worth twelve hundred pounds by the year, which would have been a good commendam'). Precisely those honours which he had obtained at James's hands had 'put me above the means to get my living; and the misery I am fallen into hath put me below the means to subsist as I am.'[11]

James consented to reallocate Bacon's fine 'unto such persons as he himself shall nominate'. This meant not simply that James decided not to levy the fine, but that Bacon was allowed to choose to whom the fine was due. In other words, those chosen creditors took priority over all existing claimants, effectively shielding Bacon from other creditors. James also granted him a 'coronation pardon', the general pardon usually doled out only at coronations, which released Bacon from liability from all past offences 'with an exception nevertheless of the sentence given in our high Court of Parliament'.[12]

The first fruits of retirement came in October 1621. Humbly thanking him for the 'gracious remission of my fine', on 8 October Bacon sent the King a fair manuscript of his *History of the Reign of Henry VII* (the book was not printed until 1622). 'I can now (I thank God and you) die, and make a will. I desire to do, for the little time God shall send me life, like the merchants of London, which when they give over trade, lay out their money on land. So being freed from civil business, I lay forth my poor talent upon those things which may be perpetual, still having relation to do you honour with those powers I have left.' Henry VII was 'in a sort your forerunner', he explained, 'whose spirit, as well as his blood, is doubled upon your Majesty'. Hoping that the King might signal his pleasure as to any amendments, he ended his letter piteously: 'God knoweth, whether ever I shall see you again; but I will pray for you to the last gasp.'[13]

James read the *History* with interest, passing it on to Lord Brooke (Fulke Greville) to read, 'commending it much to him', according to Thomas Meautys. The King made 'very few' amendments, 'and those rather words, as *epidemic*, and *mild* instead of *debonnaire*, etc. Only that, of persons attainted, enabled to serve in Parliament, by a bare reversal of their attainder without issuing any new writs, the King by all means will have left out.' Brooke declared to Meautys that 'care should be taken by all means for good ink and paper to print it in; for that the book deserved it.'[14]

★

A second version of Bacon's pardon, signed by James on 12 October 1621 at Royston, survives, stating that the pardon should be 'either after the form of a coronation pardon, or of the pardon we lately granted to Sir Robert Cotton, Knt., at the choice of the said Viscount; with an exception nevertheless of the sentence given in our High Court of Parliament';[15] and indeed the Docquet book of the Paper Office records on 16 October a 'Grant to Visct. St Alban of a pardon to be drawn after form of the pardon lately granted to Sir R. Cotton.'[16] The preamble is suspiciously reminiscent of Bacon's own style. This pardon, however, never became effective. Word was received from the Lord Keeper that it would have to be postponed until after the dissolution of parliament. Williams argued that 'the passing of the same (the assembly in parliament so near approaching) cannot but be much prejudicial to the service of the King, to the honour of my Lord of Buckingham, to that commiseration which otherwise would be had of your Lordship's present estate, and especially to my judgment and fidelity.'[17] Bacon immediately complained to Buckingham, who pleaded ignorance; but the truth was that Williams had advised him on the change of plan before informing Bacon.[18]

During the autumn, Bacon obtained leave to return to York House 'to take physic and provide for his health'. It was not a good move. When he outstayed his welcome ('delayed the time and lingered so long') James told him to 'be gone to Gorhambury';[19] and when Buckingham asked the King if Bacon might stay in London for Christmas, he found the King, 'who hath in all other occasions, and even in that particular already, to the dislike of many of your own friends, showed with great forwardness his gracious favour towards you, very unwilling to grant you any longer liberty to abide there; which being but a small advantage to you, would be a great and general distaste, as you cannot but easily conceive, to the whole state'.[20]

At the same time, Bacon realised that his pensions were not going to be paid. His old sparring partner Sir Lionel Cranfield was appointed Lord Treasurer (among hints that his predecessor too was corrupt and unfit for office). Bacon's congratulatory note admitted that his good wishes were likely to have a hollow ring: 'If I should profess to your Lordship that I am right glad of your advancement, it may be you would not believe me. But it is true.' The effort to conciliate an old adversary was unfruitful: even if Cranfield had been willing to grant Bacon's requests for money, his hands were tied by a Privy Council order in October suspending all pensions indefinitely.[21]

A postponed pardon, a renewed banishment, unpaid pensions: it gradually dawned on Bacon that his highly theatrical withdrawal to the country was in danger of becoming a reality. The King was being strangely adamant about enforcing certain parts of his punishment – specifically, those parts which kept him out of London and useless. As usual, in seeking an explanation of James's actions, the world looked to his favourite. Suspicion rose that Buckingham was doing less than his utmost on Bacon's behalf because of his own designs on York House: in Chamberlain's words, 'it is thought some aim and look after that house: where if St Albans might continue and take his pleasure, it is like he would be loather [more loath] to leave his interest in it.'[22]

Buckingham was indeed interested in purchasing the lease on York House, and the sale of it would certainly have been a beneficial move financially for Bacon. However, York House was his birthplace, and Buckingham for once had his wishes baulked.

And I am the more sorry for this refusal of his Majesty's [to allow Bacon to stay in London over Christmas] falling in a time when I was a suitor to your Lordship in a particular concerning myself, wherein though your servant insisted farther than I am sure would ever enter into your thought, I cannot but take it as a part of a faithful servant in him. But if your Lordship or your Lady find it inconvenient for you to part with the house, I would rather provide myself otherwise than any way incommodate you.[23]

Bacon, suspicious of the turn of events, and increasingly annoyed at the inadequacies of a friendship that relied entirely on letters, appealed to Buckingham for a personal conference. Buckingham consented, and, as was his custom, Bacon set out his ideas on paper, the better to be prepared for the confrontation.

'Afflictions are truly called trials,' he began, 'trials of a man's self, and trials of friends.' He cleared himself of any unworthiness, 'except perhaps too much softness in the beginning of my troubles': now, however, 'I praise God I have not lived like a drone nor like a malcontent, nor like a man confused, but though the world hath taken her talent from me, yet God's talent I put to use.' Buckingham's friendship meant everything to him: 'He cannot have many friends that hath chosen to rely upon one.' He needed to know 'whether I stand in your favour and affection as I have done, and if there be an alteration, what is the cause, and if none, what effects I may expect for the future of your friendship and favour, my state being not unknown to you.' He suspected Buckingham's 'cooling towards me or falling from me' on several grounds: physical distance ('when a man is out of sight and out of use, it is a nobleness somewhat above this age to continue a constant friend'); the influence of others ('some that are thought to have your ear or more love me not, and may either disvalue me, or distaste your Lordship with me'); Buckingham's lack of need for him ('your Lordship hath now so many either new-purchased friends or reconciled enemies, as there is scarce room for an old friend specially set aside'); and Bacon's dated style ('that for which I was fittest, which was to carry things *suavibus modis* [smoothly], and not to bristle or undertake or give venturous counsels, is out of fashion and request').

Of the promises Buckingham had made, Bacon had received only the remission of the fine, and a (postponed) pardon. 'These I lay before you, desiring to know what I may hope for; for hopes are racks, and your Lordship that would not condemn me to the Tower I know will not condemn me to the rack.' Although the pardon was 'a thing trivial', the kind of pardon that might be got 'for five mark and after a Parliament for nothing', Bacon desired it, 'first because I have been so safted [confined], and now it is time there were an end,' and 'secondly, because I mean to live a retired life, and so cannot be at hand to shake off every clamour. I do not think any except a Turk or Tartar would wish to have another chop out of me.'[24]

Buckingham did not show, even though this time Francis had begged him. Frustrated, Bacon penned an angry letter, beginning 'I say to myself, that your Lordship hath forsaken me, and I think I am one of the last that findeth it.' If the problem was York House, he implored Buckingham to appreciate that for him to lose that house was 'a second sentence, for I conceived it sentenced me to the loss of that which I thought was saved from the former sentence, which is your love and favour'.[25]

Reading it over, Bacon decided the letter was unsuitable – he could hardly risk the only useful friendship he had left – and tried again. It took two more attempts before he settled on a longer, less abrupt message. 'The cause of change,' he concluded, 'is either in myself or your Lordship.' He found himself to be 'a true friend' to Buckingham 'in the watery trial of prosperity and the fiery trial of adversity'. Bacon needed to know whether he could continue to 'presume your Lordship's favour and help as I have done' in his requests to the King; 'for otherwise it were a kind of stupidness in me, and a trouble to your Lordship; for me, not to discern the change; for your Lordship, to have an importuner instead of a friend and a suitor.'[26]

Buckingham wrote on 14 November, from Newmarket, explaining that illness had prevented his further activity on Bacon's behalf. When he had approached the King regarding Bacon's request for access, James had replied 'that he could see no conveniency in your repair to him at this time', since he had decided to call a parliament, and Bacon could hardly 'come to kiss his hand and immediately after excuse yourself from coming to the Parliament for want of health'. But Buckingham had something else to tell his friend:

I must now upon this occasion crave your leave to deal plainly and sincerely with you according to the friendship that I truly confess toward you. When I showed his Majesty your letter, wherein you expressed your confidence in his favour in regard that he had professed unto yourself that he thought you an honest man and was fully satisfied with you, he plainly told me that both the Prince and I could bear witness that you had a little mistaken him, for albeit it be true that upon your urging him he confessed that he believed your own sincere and free declaration, and that he never suspected that you ever had any plot against his person yet the very fashion of his behaviour toward you did clearly enough demonstrate that he could not but dislike your crossing of his service at the late Parliament, and he further saith that your free and ingenuous confession of your errors moved his Majesty to deal more graciously with you than otherwise he would have done, else the fault he saith, must be laid upon him for having unjustly showed his displeasure toward you.

Moreover, James thought that Bacon's coming to London was 'in a very unseasonable time' – without warning the King, and so soon before the parliament, which undermined his excuse of ill-health and allowed Bacon's 'ill-willers' to claim his visit 'was for no good end'.

He finished by stating that Bacon would receive his pension once the 'desperate straits' of the King's finances were overcome, and James had signed the warrant to keep Bacon from the parliament. For himself, he would 'never fail to perform the part of a faithful friend towards you, wherein the best service I can do you shall be in informing you truly of his Majesty's intentions, and advising your Lordship the best way how you may fully repatriate your self in his Majesty's favour'.[27]

Clearly, Buckingham was a lost cause for the moment. Bacon attempted to appeal to the Lords, with a petition that opened: 'I am old, weak, ruined, in want, a very subject of pity.' Being exiled at Gorhambury, he claimed, was worse than the Tower. In the Tower,

> I could have company, physicians, conference with my creditors and friends about my debts and the necessities of my estate, helps for my studies and the writings I have in hand. Here I live upon the sword-point of a sharp air, endangered if I go abroad, dulled if I stay within, solitary and comfortless without company, banished from all opportunities to treat with any to do myself good, and to help out my wrecks; and that which is one of my greatest griefs, my wife that hath been no partaker of my offending, must be partaker of this misery of my restraint.[28]

The labour was in vain: parliament was prorogued on 19 December, before there was any chance to read Bacon's petition. In late December, however, a new patent for Bacon's pension was prepared, of which he would control the disbursements. On 17 January 1622 he was made a grant 'of all arrears due to him by letters patent formerly made to him, and also of an annuity of £1200 for twelve years'.[29]

Although Bacon made sporadic bids for patronage to the Spanish ambassador, Gondomar,[30] and to John Digby, now earl of Bristol,[31] it remained Buckingham on whom he pinned his hopes, and whose moods he monitored avidly. The damage wrought by Bacon's impetuous return to London needed to be repaired. However, stranded at Gorhambury, Bacon was dependent on either an epistolary correspondence – which had to be couched often in euphemistic terms, to avoid being understood by prying eyes – or a system of proxy encounters. Buckingham requested that Bacon should 'send any understanding man unto me, to whom I may in discourse open myself'.[32] Bacon agreed eagerly: if he himself might not come to London, then perhaps Buckingham would send one of his secretaries, Mr Packer or Mr Alesbury, or – if Bacon might nominate a man himself – perhaps one of the following: 'Lord Falkland, Sir Edward Sackville, Sir Robert Mansell, my brother, Mr. Solicitor General, (who though he be almost a stranger to me, yet, as my case now is, I had rather employ a man of a good nature than a friend,) and Sir Arthur Ingram, notwithstanding he be great with my Lord Treasurer'. He left the choice to Buckingham.[33] Accordingly, from New Year 1622 much of Bacon's business was conducted on his behalf in the first instance by his secretary Thomas Meautys, and then, acting on instructions, by his friend Tobie Matthew or by Sir Edward Sackville, while Buckingham was represented by the likes of Sir Arthur Ingram; on rare occasions, the Viscountess St Alban would petition Buckingham or his wife in person (since she was still resident in London). Despite (or because of) this multiplicity of conduits, the negotiations remained very much a game of 'cat-and-mouse'.[34]

The tension in Bacon's relations with Buckingham eased once the marquis took possession of a London residence, Wallingford House – part of a deal with Viscount Wallingford whereby his relatives the Somersets were released to Wallingford's country estate, well out of Buckingham's way.[35] Buckingham and Bacon discharged each other from the difficult situation over York House with elaborate courtesy: 'you may no longer hang upon the treaty which hath been between your Lordship and me touching York House; [in] which I assure your Lordship, I never desired to put you to the least inconvenience';[36] 'I was ever resolved your Lordship should have had it, or no man';[37] 'I shall be very far from taking it ill if you part with it to any else.'[38]

A selfless devotion to Buckingham served as armour against others. When the recently married duke of Lennox approached Bacon with an offer to place the viscountess in 'a very commodious and capable house', the Hertfords' old residence in Channon Row, if she would give up York House,[39] Bacon was able with a clear conscience to refuse. 'York House is the house where my father died, and where I first breathed, and there will I yield my last breath, if it so please God, and the King will give me leave. At least no money nor value shall make me part with it. Besides, as I never denied it to my Lord Marquis, so yet the difficulty I made was so like a denial, as I owe unto my great love and respect to his Lordship a denial to all my other friends.'[40]

Buckingham being partially mollified (Bacon reported 'having somewhat better signs of my Lord Marquis's good disposition towards me' by

February), the exile procured 'a temporary leave to come to London next Lent for my health, and Easter term for my business'. In March 1622 he was given leave to come as far as Highgate; Sir Edward Sackville sued Buckingham for 'the other five miles' (the distance from Highgate to Westminster), but he would not be budged: 'Let my Lord be ruled by me: it will be never the worse for him.' It seemed that Bacon was not entirely restored to his friend's favour. The marquis continued: 'Sir Edward, however you play a good friend's part for my Lord St. Alban, yet I must tell you I have not been well used by him.'[41] He told Sackville (who relayed it to Meautys, who relayed it to Bacon) 'how much he had been beholding to you, how well he loved you, how unkindly he took the denial of your house (for so he will needs understand it); but the close for all this was harmonious, since he protested he would seriously begin to study your ends, now that the world should see he had no ends on you.'

Bacon's mind now turned to ways to obtain 'a release of the confinement indefinite; for the same reasons of an infirm health and the settling the poor planks of my wracks will continue still'.[42] The only thing he had left to offer Buckingham was 'my house and lands here at Gorhambury'; the only price would be 'some satisfaction to my wife for her interest' (according to their postnuptial arrangements). Bacon asked his friend Tobie Matthew to place the matter in Gondomar's hands.[43] Buckingham refused: since he already had Bacon's future in hand, he would not hear of the viscount's offer. Sackville assured Bacon: 'The tender hath much won upon him and mellowed his heart towards you, and your genius directed you aright when you writ that letter of denial unto the Duke. The King saw it, and all the rest, which made him say unto the Marquis, you played an after-game well; that now he had no reason to be much offended.'

The key to Bacon's future life, it seemed to Sackville, lay in York House. 'My Lord Falkland by this time hath showed you London from Highgate. If York House were gone, the town were yours, and all your straitest shackles clean off, besides more comfort than the city-air only.' Sackville let Bacon know that Buckingham would be 'exceeding glad' if Cranfield were to have York House. It would be dangerous not to yield to this request. 'If you part not speedily with it, you may defer the good which is approaching near you, and disappointing other aims (which must either shortly receive content or never), perhaps anew yield matter of discontent, though you may be indeed as innocent as before.'[44]

Bacon immediately let Cranfield know that if he wanted York House, they could negotiate through Sir Arthur Ingram. He begged Cranfield to despatch the business 'touching the relief of my poor estate', and hoped to wait on Cranfield at Chiswick '(where I have taken a house) within this sevennights, and to gather some violets in your garden'.[45] The house at Chiswick was a new venture, to house the viscountess near to London – though it seems Lady St Alban had not been consulted over the move until after the decision had been taken: 'My Lady hath seen the house at Chiswick, and can make a shift to like it,' reported Meautys.[46] The viscountess' relocation established her conveniently within reach of the London and Westminster circles to which she was to make representations on her husband's behalf. However, the setting up of separate households also marked the couple's official separation.

The way now seemed clear for Bacon to be allowed back to court. Expecting an imminent audience with the King, he went to the lengths of drafting his letter of thanks to James, to be sent after such a meeting.[47]

> I may now in a manner sing *nunc dimittis*, now I have seen you. Before methought I was scant in state of grace, but in a kind of utter darkness. And therefore, amongst other your mercies and favours, I do principally thank your Majesty for this admission of me to kiss your hands. I may not forget also to thank your Majesty for your remission, for granting of my *quietus est* and general pardon; and your late recommendations of my debts; favours not small, specially to a servant out of sight, and out of use.

'I am like ground fresh,' he continued. 'If I be left to myself I will graze and bear nature philosophy: but if the King will plough me up again, and sow me with anything, I hope to give him some yield. I would live to study, and not study to live; yet I that have borne a bag can bear a wallet.'[48]

Everything was going to plan. On 20 March, Meautys reported that the printed copies of *Henry VII* were 'ready, and passing well bound up. If your Lordship's letters to the King, Prince, and my Lord Marquis be ready, I think it were good to lose no time in the delivery; for the printer's fingers itch to be selling.'[49] At Gorhambury, Bacon drew up his own warrant, as was his custom; it was taken by Meautys to Sir Edward Sackville, who took it 'as soon as I alighted from my horse'; Sackville in turn 'put it into my Lord Marquis his hands'. This haste, however, resulted in a problem: when Buckingham came to look for the warrant, he could not locate it – and Meautys had been unable, in all the rush, to make a copy, or indeed to remember exactly what Bacon had written. Meautys was forced to send a messenger to Bacon instructing him to draw up another warrant and get it back to Meautys by tomorrow at seven, so that the King might sign it at the weekend, when he visited.[50]

Bacon was not bothered about the warrant: 'It is not much material at the first.' He was more alarmed by the unexpected news that Meautys brought him – that, through some 'demur', the Bishop of London had placed a temporary injunction on the publication of Bacon's *History of*

Henry VII, the 'first fruits' of his *quinquennium* in exile. As Bacon quipped, 'there may be an error in my book; but I am sure there is none in me, since the King had it three months by him, and allowed it.'[51] Unfortunately, Bacon had tied his thank-you letters to the presenting of his new book, and so the letters no longer made sense. He advised Meautys that 'It may be signified they were sent before I knew of any stay.'[52]

Here, thanks to an unforeseen accident, we see a basic contradiction at the heart of Bacon's alleged intellectual retirement, his 'withdrawal from civic life'. The fruits of that retirement had to continue to be employed in his campaign to restore his estate – for it was only with the proper finance, which itself depended on such restoration, that the 'intellectual retirement' could be achieved.[53] In his letter to the King, he made the connection plain.

> I have raised your progenitor of famous memory (and now I hope of more famous memory than before) King Henry the 7th, to give your Majesty thanks for me; which work, most humbly kissing your Majesty's hands, I do present. And because in the beginning of my trouble, when in the midst of the tempest I had a kenning of the harbour which I hope now by your Majesty's favour I am entring into, I made a tender to your Majesty of two works *An history of England* and *A digest of your laws*; as I have (by a figure of *pars pro toto*) performed the one, so I have herewith sent your Majesty, by way of an epistle, a new offer of the other.

He asked James, in bluntly commercial terms – 'since now my study is my exchange and my pen my factor for the use of my talent' – to appoint a new 'task to write', which he might dedicate to Buckingham (the *Instauration* had been dedicated to James, and *Henry VII* to Prince Charles).[54]

Henry VII appeared on bookstalls by the end of the month, at a price of six shillings. John Chamberlain commented of Bacon's efforts: 'It is pity he should have any other employment. I have not read much of it, but if the rest of our history were answerable to it, I think we should not need to envy any other nation in that kind.'[55] Elizabeth of Bohemia, James's daughter, thought the book 'the best I ever read of the kind; I consider that worthy Prince fortunate in having found so faithful a biographer as you are'.[56]

In a letter to Elizabeth, sent with her copy of the book, Bacon reflected on his new-found 'leisure'.

> I find in books (and books I dare allege to your Majesty, in regard of your singular ability to read and judge of them even above your sex) that it is accounted a great bliss for a man to have Leisure with Honour.

That was never my fortune; nor is. For time was, I had Honour without Leisure; and now I have Leisure without Honour. And I cannot say so neither altogether; considering there remain with me the marks and stamp of the King's, your father's grace: though I go not for so much in value as I have done. But my desire is now to have Leisure without Loitering, and not to become an abbey-lubber, as the old proverb was, but to yield some fruit of my private life.[57]

★

Stuck at Gorhambury, with no source of ready income, Bacon quickly became a liability rather than an asset to both his servants and his friends. John Aubrey records that 'upon his being in disfavour his servants suddenly went away; he compared them to the flying of the vermin when the house was falling.' More damningly, men who had advanced his cause for over thirty years suddenly turned from him. 'In his lordship's prosperity', Aubrey continued, 'Sir Fulke Greville, Lord Brooke, was his great friend and acquaintance; but when he was in disgrace and want, he was so unworthy as to forbid his butler to let him have any more small beer, which he had often sent for, his stomach being nice [sensitive], and the small beer of Gray's Inn not liking his pallet.'[58]

The extent of Bacon's financial difficulties became clear for all to see when, on 28 June 1622, he and his wife exhibited a bill in the Court of Chancery against Buckingham. Earlier in the year, an agreement had been concluded in which the marquis would have the unexpired residue of the lease of York House at a price of £1,300, of which £500 was to be paid to trustees for the use of the viscountess and the remainder was to be paid to Bacon. In return, the Bacons, together with the trustees, would grant and assign the house and all their term of years therein to Buckingham, his executors and administrators. In the Chancery suit, the Bacons alleged that while they and their trustees were ready to join in the assignment of the lease, as arranged, Buckingham was delaying enactment of his side of the bargain; they asked the court to force Buckingham to show cause as to why he should not accept the assignment of the lease and pay up the £1,300. Buckingham, in making his response, confessed the bargain, but claimed that his counsel were doubting the validity of the assurance, unsure whether some question might not arise afterwards. He merely wanted these queries cleared up before he paid over the money: if he were certain that the assurance was in order then he was still ready to proceed. He now asked the court to ensure he was well secured, and then he would go ahead.

At least, that is how it looked on the surface. Many informed onlookers, including John Chamberlain, saw the situation as more complex and sinister. 'The Lord of St Albans hath put a bill into the Chancery against the Lord Marquis Buckingham which the world will not believe but to be done by consent. The substance is that having contracted for the lease of York House for the sum of £1300 whereof £500 was to be paid to the Lady of St Albans, the time of payment being past and no money appearing the poor Lady is in fear to be defrauded by her Lord for whose satisfaction he desires the Lord Marquis may show cause why he goeth not on with the contract as was agreed.'[59] In other words, Bacon and Buckingham were conniving to divert the proceeds of the lease against outstanding financial obligations, thereby cheating the viscountess of her share in the money.

When the cause was heard by the Lord Keeper on 4 July, the viscountess appeared in Chancery (since her husband was still barred from Westminster), reiterating her desire to have the bargain proceed, since both she and her friends thought it beneficial to her. The Lord Keeper decreed that Buckingham should forthwith pay the £1,300 as specified, and the deal should go ahead.[60]

Bacon himself, still desperate to get Buckingham's ear, turned to his mother, reasoning that although the marquis' friends were 'wayfarers . . . some to Waltham, some to Ware', 'he can have but one mother.' The tide was turning: 'for envy, the almanack of that year is past'; he pointed to the last parliament ('an high-coming parliament'), which saw 'not a petition, not a clamour, not a motion, not a mention of me'. He was blessed by 'visitations by all the noblemen about the town . . . The King and the Prince I hear for certain well affected . . . A little will make me happy: the debts I have paid.'[61] The connection was of limited use, however: in late September, after a relapse into embarrassingly open recusancy, the countess was sent away to her house at Dalby in Leicestershire.

As the year came to an end, Bacon and his intermediaries received a series of conflicting signals. Buckingham obtained an assurance that Bacon might kiss James's hand when the King next returned to Whitehall.[62] James issued a warrant concerning Bacon's debts, commiserating with his 'estate' on account of his efforts in 'counsel and our commission of treasure', where he was 'found faithful and very careful and diligent, running courses entire and direct for the good of our service'. However, despite being informed that Bacon was in debt, and that 'some of his servants likewise and near friends are engaged for him, of whom he hath no less care than of himself', James found that, 'the times being as they are', he could not rescue him 'by our liberality'; instead, to show his 'gracious intentions towards him, so in the mean time we have care of his subsisting and honour and quiet'. The addressees of the warrant were required 'from time to time to treat with such creditors of his as he shall desire to make some reasonable and favourable composition for him and his sureties, letting them know that what favour and case they shall do him in the composition shall be acceptable to ourselves: for which purpose we shall vouchsafe to take knowledge from you of such as shall be forward to perform our desire', to 'bring them to good terms of composition with him'.[63]

On 24 November, Bacon called on Buckingham to put an end to what he perceived to be Cranfield's stalling on Bacon's financial delivery and 'nick it with a word: for if he do me good, I doubt it may not be altogether of his own.'[64] Thomas Meautys reported 'that either my Lord Treasurer is not twice in one mind, or Sir Arthur Ingram not twice in one tale. I like my Lord Treasurer's heart to your Lordship so much every day worse than other (especially for his coarse usage of your Lordship's name in his last speech), as that I cannot imagine he means you any good.' Meautys urged that Bacon should 'surrender not your old patent, till you have the new under seal, lest my Lord Keeper should take toy, and stop it there. And I know your Lordship cannot forget they have such a savage word amongst them as fleecing. God in heaven bless your Lordship from such hands and tongues, and then things will mend of themselves.'[65]

Understandably rattled by this intelligence from London, Bacon informed Buckingham that Cranfield, despite his 'so many days and appointments, and such certain messages and promises,' meant only 'to coax me (it is his own word of old) and to saw me asunder'.[66] The threat from Cranfield was exacerbated by failing health, as the weather turned bitterly cold – one estimate had it that by early December 1622 there were 270 or 280 deaths in London per week.[67] 'This extreme winter hath turned with me weakness of body into a state that I cannot call health but rather sickness, and that more dangerous than felt.'[68]

On top of all this, Bacon's heavy scholarly workload was catching up with him. He had vowed to produce instalments of his *Natural History* on a monthly basis, starting with the History of Winds, followed by that of Density and Rarity, Heaviness and Lightness, Sympathy and Antipathy of Things, Sulphur Mercury and Salt, and then Life and Death. In the event, the output was unsurprisingly less regular. Only two instalments were published in Bacon's lifetime: the *Historia ventorum* in November 1622, followed by the *Historia vitae et mortis*. The latter was sent to Buckingham on 2 January 1623,[69] by which time Bacon was also working on an account of the reign of Henry VIII (James authorised the Paper Office Keeper, Sir Thomas Wilson, to supply Bacon with papers pertaining to the reign of Henry VIII on 10 January).[70] A month later Chamberlain reported that Bacon 'busies himself altogether about books, and hath set out two lately, *Historia Ventorum*, and *De Vita et Morte*, with promise of more. I have not seen neither of them, because I have not leisure: but if the life of Henry the eight (which they say he is about) might come out (after his own manner), I should find time and means enough to read it.'[71]

With the New Year, however, came some welcome changes. Finally, on 20 January 1623, Buckingham brought Bacon to kiss the King's hand. Bacon thought himself in a 'state of grace'. James addressed him 'not as a criminal but as a man overthrown by a tempest', acknowledging Bacon's 'constant and unfailing course of industry and integrity'.[72] More good news came with the appointment of his friend and mediator Sackville as Secretary of State. Rumours were soon rife that Bacon himself might be placed in high office once again: as Locke reported on 1 February, 'it is said that the President will be made Chancellor, and Lord Verulam President of the Council, and have his debts installed and paid from the King's coffers.'[73] On 5 February, Bacon reiterated to Buckingham that 'for my house at Gorhambury, I do infinitely desire your Lordship should have it, and howsoever I may treat, I will conclude with none, till I know your Lordship's further pleasure.'[74] Even John Williams seemed to be civil to his predecessor, writing on 7 February to thank Bacon for his copy of *Historia vitae et mortis*.[75]

But Bacon's hopes were about to be dashed again. Talk of his imminent return to prominence were soon overshadowed by the flight of Buckingham and Prince Charles, in false beards and hoods, via Dover and Boulogne to Spain to expedite negotiations for the prince's marriage.[76] Whatever the rights and wrongs of Buckingham's flight, it came at 'an ill time for myself', as he lamented to the duke, while hoping that 'this noble adventure will make your Lordship a rich return in honour abroad and at home, and chiefly in the inestimable treasure of the love and trust of that thrice-excellent Prince'. In the meantime, he was 'but a man desolate till your return, and have taken a course accordingly'.[77] The course was to return to the Bacon chambers at the Inns of Court: 'Myself for quiet and the better to hold out am retired to Gray's Inn: for when my chief friends were gone so far off, it was time for me to go to a cell.'[78]

Once the passage through France was accomplished without harm ('I think you had the ring which they write of, that when the seal was turned to the palm of the hand made men go invisible,' Bacon quipped to Buckingham), his fears began to 'vanish and diminish'. In England, a rumour circulated that Buckingham was likely 'to return and go again, before the Prince come', which did him no harm, 'for it keeps men in awe'.[79] Indeed, the security of Buckingham's position back home was proved decisively when, on 18 May, he was created a duke – as Bacon noted approvingly, 'the first English Duke that hath been created since I was born'.[80]

On 28 March Bacon entreated the aid of Gondomar, citing 'the strait alliance between our kings which is now understood to be concluded', which both rendered the count 'a more powerful intercessor, and relieves me from any scruple I might have felt in being beholden to so great a man, though a foreigner, for my whole fortunes, and accepting them as his gift'. He also pointed out that the favours Gondomar had obtained for Bacon 'when you were here . . . so far as promise went, have not as yet been either refused or carried into effect'. Therefore, 'it seems to be the intention of Providence that this work of raising me out of calamity should be altogether yours first and last.' Thirdly, 'the two stars which have always been propitious to me – the greater and the lesser – are now shining in your world; and may thereby, being reinforced by the auxiliary and benignant rays of your love towards me, gain influence enough to put me in some position not unbefitting my former fortune.' Reports from Matthew confirmed that Gondomar's 'remembrance of me is still lively and fresh, and has not been overlaid or extinguished by that great mass of arduous and high business which your Lordship has to sustain', and the Spaniard could call on his new-found favour with James. 'Meanwhile on my own part I have neither given myself up to sloth nor meddled unseasonably with business, but live in such pursuits and handle such matters as may neither misbecome the former honours which I have borne and will perhaps leave to posterity no ungrateful memory of my name. And therefore I hope that I shall be no unworthy material for you to exhibit and make known to the world the force both of your power and your friendship, – proving that you have no less a stroke in the fortunes of a private man than in your public enjoyments.'[81]

Back in England, Bacon espied a rare career opportunity when the Provost of Eton, Thomas Murray ('whom I love very well'), fell seriously ill. Eton was a pleasant prospect, which 'costs his Majesty nothing' and had incidental attractions: 'There will hardly fall (specially in the spent hourglass of such a life as mine,) any thing so fit for me, being a retreat to a place of study so near London, and where (if I sell my house at Gorhambury, as I purpose to do, to put myself into some convenient plenty) I may be accommodate of a dwelling for the summer time.'

In Buckingham's absence, Bacon successfully petitioned Secretary Conway, another Buckingham man, to present his case.[82] Conway soon discovered, however (and despite Bacon producing a discourse on usury to strengthen his suit[83]) that the provostship had been promised to another man, Sir William Becher – on Buckingham's recommendation. To Conway's proposal of Bacon's candidature, James had replied 'That he could not value you so little, or conceive you would have humbled your desires and your worth so low: That it had been a great deal of ease to him to have had such a scantling of your mind; to which he could never have laid so unequal a measure.' The King, reported Conway, went on to say that 'since your intentions moved that way, he would study your accommodation.' It was not 'out of hope', Conway assured him, that James might 'give some other contentment to Sir William Becher in due time, to accommodate your Lordship, of whom (to your comfort) it is my duty to tell you, his Majesty declared a good opinion, and princely care and respect'.[84] Bacon continued his suit until Buckingham confirmed in October that he had promised the place to Becher.[85] (Ultimately, Sir Henry Wotton took the provostship in exchange for the reversion of the mastership of the Rolls; Buckingham exchanged this reversion for another post for Becher.[86])

Bacon spent much of the summer of 1623 trying to keep his case firmly in Buckingham's mind, by sending as many letters as he thought permissible.[87] His mission was slightly eased by Tobie Matthew's travelling to Madrid at the end of April, bearing letters authorising him to discuss Bacon's affairs with Gondomar, Buckingham, the earl of Bristol, and Charles's secretary Sir Francis Cottington.[88] Buckingham was startled by the changed appearance of this new intermediary: 'Tobie Matthew is here, but what with the journey and what with the affliction he endures to find (as he says) that reason prevails nothing with these people, he is grown extreme lean and looks as sharp as an eyass.'[89] As expressed to the King, however, Buckingham's attitude toward Matthew was somewhat different: 'Sir, in the midst of serious business little pretty Tobie Matthew comes to entreat us to deliver this letter to your Majesty, which is, as he calls it, a picture of the Infanta's, drawn in black and white. We pray you, let none laugh at it but yourself and honest Kate. He thinks he has hit the nail on the head, but you will find it the foolishest thing that you ever saw.'[90]

On Sunday 20 July, Lord Andover returned from Spain, with news that 'all was in good forwardness there, that the match was to be published and she proclaimed Princess of Great Britain on their St James' day, and the contract solemnised and effected upon ours with great applause and rejoicing.'[91] However, by the time Buckingham returned in October, the marriage was off. The duke returned something of a hero, 'much applauded and commended', since the proposed match was as unpopular in England as it was popular in Spain, widely perceived as having been 'brave and resolute' in quarrelling with Gondomar and Olivares, and not carrying through the negotiations on grounds of religion – 'if it had not been for his impatience the marriage had been consummated before Christmas Day.'[92] Although the negotiations were still secret, it was popularly believed that parliament was to be summoned imminently.

On 12 October, Bacon wrote to Buckingham, rejoicing at his return: 'Myself have ridden at anchor all your Grace's absence, and my cables are now quite worn.' Sir Tobie Matthew had passed on 'a very comfortable message', namely that Buckingham had said that 'I should be the first that you would remember in any great favour after your return; and now coming from the Court, he telleth me he had commission from your Lordship to confirm it: for which I humbly kiss your hands.'[93] Buckingham replied instantly: 'The assurance of your love makes me easily believe your joy at my return; and if I may be so happy, as by the credit of my place to supply the decay of your cables, I shall account it one of the special fruits thereof. What Sir Tobie Matthew hath delivered on my behalf, I will be ready to make good, and omit no opportunity that may serve for the endeavours of, Your Lordship's faithful friend and servant.'[94]

There was nothing Bacon could do but continue to shower Buckingham with compliments and suits for favour, and hope that he would ultimately respond with the necessary strong support for his cause. Increasingly, though, he must have realised that Buckingham was making no real attempts on his behalf. Buckingham's efforts were as consistently half-hearted as those of Francis' uncle Lord Burghley had been all those years ago, at the very outset of Bacon's career. But a man in Bacon's hopelessly dependent position had no alternative: he could only live on in hope.

★

When Bacon had compiled his anticipatory 'Memorial of access' to the King in March 1622, he had noted a number of projects 'for my Pen'. These he divided according to the two possible lifestyles facing him – 'if active' and 'if contemplative'. In the former category he proposed four works: 'the recompiling of laws', 'the disposing of wards and generally education of youth', 'limiting the jurisdiction of courts, and prescribing rules for every of them' and 'reglement of trade'. The 'contemplative' options included 'going on with the story of Henry the 8th', 'General Treatise *de Legibus et Justitiâ*', and 'The Holy War'.[95]

As Bacon told Tobie Matthew, 'these modern languages will at one time or other play the bank-rowtes [bankrupts] with books: and since I have lost much time with this age, I would be glad as God shall give me leave to recover it with posterity.'[96] There was lasting profit only in Latin texts. In October 1623, 'the poor fruits of my leisure' became visible in his Latin expansion of *The Advancement of Learning, De augmentis scientiarum*. As he put it to the King, 'It is a translation, but enlarged almost to a new work. I had good helps for the language. I have been also mine own *Index Expurgatorius* [the Catholic Church's censor], that it may be read in all places. For since my end of putting it into Latin was to have it read everywhere, it had been an absurd contradiction to free it in the language and to pen it up in the matter.'[97] This book would 'live, and be a citizen of the world, as English books are not'. The trouble taken over the years by his friends, the Catholic Tobie Matthew and the Anglican Lancelot Andrewes, in commenting on his works had prepared Bacon well for producing versions which would give doctrinal offence to nobody.

As for *Henry VIII*, he told the Prince frankly that he 'did so despair of my health this summer as I was glad to choose some such work as I might compass within days; so far was I from entering into a work of length.' (To Tobie Matthew, Bacon had confided the truth – that the work had foundered on the strangely lackadaisical attitude of an old associate: 'I find Sir Robert Cotton, who poured forth what he had in my other work, somewhat dainty of his materials in this.')[98]

With Buckingham back ('with so fair a reputation of a sound Protestant, and so constant for the King's honour and errand'), Bacon tried to reopen a direct line to the King. Along with two suits – 'the one for a full pardon, that I may die out of a cloud; the other for the translation of my honours after my decease'[99]– Bacon offered his advice to the new duke.[100]But Buckingham was no longer Bacon's sole hope. When the new parliament was finally called for February 1624, he appealed to two new potential patrons, the earls of Southampton and Oxford, to help him to win the Lords' support 'to receive my writ this Parliament, that since the root of my dignity is saved to me it might also bear fruit, and that I may not die in dishonour'. As he reasoned, 'the good which the commonwealth mought reap of my suffering, is already inned. Justice is done; an example is made for reformation; the authority of the House for judicature is established. There can be no further use of my misery; perhaps some little may be of my service; for I hope I shall be found a man humbled as a Christian, though not dejected as a worldling.'[101]

Bacon's bid failed, and he did not sit in the parliament – which, among other business, saw the fall of Lord Treasurer Cranfield. He was not prevented, however, from drafting a tract entitled *Considerations Touching a War with Spain*, dedicated to Prince Charles: 'Your Highness hath an imperial name. It was a Charles that brought the empire first into France; a Charles that brought it first into Spain; why should not Great Britain have his turn?' He proposed that a committee should be appointed from the Commons 'to confer with any martial men or others, that were not of the House, for their advice and information'. This did not happen. The marriage negotiations were halted, however, and the House voted to put an end to the treaties, voting through a subsidy in late March, when, in the words of Sir Edward Conway, Jr., 'the general joy was expressed in bonfires, and Lord Verulam ran into debt to give four dozen faggots and twelve gallons of wine.'[102]

Unexpectedly, in January 1624, a potential windfall came into view, on which Bacon felt he had a symbolic (if not actual) claim. Some Exchequer officers had come across an old arrear due to the crown from Sir Nicholas, Francis' eldest half-brother. Bacon promptly informed Buckingham, pointing out that this was 'a suit whereunto I may as it were claim kindred, and may be of credit and profit unto me'. He put its potential value at £2,000; 'and yet I may deal kindly with my brother, and also reward liberally (as I mean to do) the officers of the Exchequer which brought it to light.' He petitioned Buckingham to present his case to the King: 'Good my Lord, obtain it of the King, and be earnest in it for me. It will acquit the King somewhat of his promise that he would have care of my wants. For hitherto since my misfortunes I have tasted of his Majesty's mercy, but not of his bounty.' Buckingham would also have to 'clear the coast with my Lord Treasurer; else there it will have a stop. I am almost at last cast for means.'[103] Buckingham moved Bacon's suit to the King, and found him 'very graciously inclined to grant it; but he desireth first to know from my Lord Treasurer his opinion and the value of it.'[104] Even with Cranfield involved, it seems that the suit was granted, but that it was a slow battle, still in process at the end of 1625, halted at every turn by external events – the death of Sir Nicholas, the death of the King, the end of a legal term.[105]

During the summer pause in parliamentary business – when Buckingham would have James 'private and at better leisure, the noise of soldiers, ambassadors, parliaments, a little ceasing' – Bacon once again sought his support in the presenting of yet another petition to the King. 'I am now full three years in misery,' he reasoned, 'neither hath there been any thing done for me, whereby I might die out of ignomiiny or live out of want.'[106] When no reply was forthcoming by the end of July, Bacon appealed to the King again: 'I prostrate myself at your Majesty's feet; I, your ancient servant, now sixty-four years old in age, and three years five months old in misery. I desire not from your Majesty means, nor place, nor employment, but only, after so long a time of expiation, a complete and total remission of the sentence of the Upper House, to the end that blot of ignomiiny may be removed from me, and from my memory with posterity; that I die not a condemned man, but may be to your Majesty, as I am to God, *nova creatura*.' If James granted his request, it 'may make me live a year or two happily; and denied, will kill me quickly.'[107]

While awaiting a response to this plea, Bacon was incapacitated during August and September by 'a sharp sickness of some weeks' which necessitated his putting off various business, including judging a dispute in his capacity as High Steward of Cambridge. He was not alone. By the beginning of September, London's weekly death toll had passed four hundred, with a disproportionate number of child victims, most caused by a 'spotted fever' which some traced to 'the extraordinary quantity of cucumbers this year, which the gardeners hasten and bring forward used to water out of the next ditches, which this dry time growing low, noisome, and stinking, poisoned the fruit'. Among the list of dead and ill celebrities, Chamberlain identified Bacon as 'yet in the balance to rise or fall'.[108]

Eventually, in early October, Buckingham returned the King's response to the first letter, which had been presented through Sir John Suckling. He had been long in answering, he declared, because 'the hearty affection I have borne to your person and service' had made him ambitious to be 'an eschewer' of ill news concerning Bacon. James felt able only to grant the three years' advance of the pension, ignoring.the difficulty of 'present maintenance'.[109]

However, the King did respond favourably to Bacon's request for a pardon. The *Cabala*, published in 1663, contains a warrant addressed from James to the Attorney-General with directions to prepare a full pardon: the warrant spoke of 'calling to mind his former good services, and how well and profitably he hath spent his time since his troubles', as a result of which the King (having 'formerly pardoned his fine, and released his confinement') was 'pleased to remove from him that blot of ignominy which yet remaineth upon him, of incapacity and disablement; and to remit to him all penalties whatsoever inflicted by that sentence'.[110] However, the Patent Rolls and the Signet Office Docquet books contain no trace of a pardon being issued.[111] Once again, the pardon seems to have remained unsigned.

On 17 November, Bacon acknowledged receipt of a warrant 'not for land but for the money'. Given the 'somewhat barren' state of Exchequer, he appealed for Buckingham's intervention to recommend to the Chancellor 'the speedy issuing of the money by this warrant, as a business whereof your Grace hath an especial care; The rather for that I understand from him, there be some other warrants for money to private suitors at this time on foot. But your Grace may be pleased to remember this difference: that the other are mere gifts; this of mine is a bargain, with an advance only.'[112] It was a bad time to ask for money: James had more pressing matters on his mind. In pursuit of his ambition to recover the Palatine territories (over which his daughter Elizabeth's marriage had briefly given him a claim) military disaster followed costly military disaster. The King may have got the creditors off Bacon's back, but he was not inclined to be any more generous.[113]

In December 1624, Bacon published his *Apophthegms, New and Old* and his *Translation of Certain Psalms*, in which he englished six or seven Psalms of David ('which shows he grows holy toward his end', commented Chamberlain).[114] To the reading public, the *Apophthegms* seemed shoddy, unworthy of the author's name. Chamberlain reported that the publication elicited 'so little allowance or applause that the world says his wit and judgment begins to draw near the lees',[115] and a contemporary verse (credited to 'Dr Andrews') made the same point:

> When learned Bacon wrote Essays,
> He did deserve, and had the praise:
> Learning's advancement was a book,
> With which the world was justly took;
> The Organon, and parts of it,
> Were issues of a noble wit;
> But now he writes his Apophthegms,
> Surely he either dotes, or dreams
>> One said, St Albans now is grown unable
>> And is in the highroad-way to Dunstable.[116]

The unspoken motive for publishing these rather lacklustre pieces, considerably outside the remit of his major project, may have been to help pay back debts to his printer and bookseller.[117]

Throughout 1625 Bacon continued to press Buckingham to 'be mindful of his misery'.[118] His work was constantly interrupted by business from his time as Chancellor;[119] old debtors – one dating from 1610 – surfaced to demand restitution,[120] and he was reduced to asking Sir Robert Pye 'to dispatch that warrant of a petty sum, that it may help to bear my charge of coming up to London'.[121] Yet somehow, through all this, Bacon remained focused on his intellectual and scientific work. His later editor Tenison relates how

> One day his Lordship was dictating to that Doctor [Rawley] some of the experiments in the *Sylva*. The same day he had sent a friend to Court to receive for him a final answer touching the effect of a grant which had been made him by King James. He had hitherto only hope of it, and hope deferred; and he was desirous to know the event of the matter, and to be freed, one way or other, from the suspense of his thoughts. His friend returning told him plainly that he must thenceforth despair of that grant, how much soever his fortunes needed it. 'Be it so,' said his Lordship; and then he dismissed his friend very cheerfully, with thankful acknowledgements of his service. His friend being gone, he came straightway to Dr Rawley, and said thus unto him: 'Well, Sir, yon business won't go on; let us go on with this, for this is in our power.' And then he dictated to him afresh for some hours, without the least hesitancy of speech or discernible interruption of thought.[122]

Peter Böener, who served as Bacon's apothecary and secretary until early 1623, confirmed 'that though his fortune may have changed, yet I never saw any change in his mien, his words, or his deeds towards any man: but he was always the same, both in sorrow and in joy, as a philosopher ought to be.'[123]

★

On 5 March 1625, James was taken ill while hunting. For three weeks he lay in a critical condition, unable to speak; on the twenty-seventh he died, at the age of fifty-eight. Four days later, even before the body was brought to London to be laid in state at Denmark House, and afforded a spectacular funeral, Bacon, true to form, was writing to Buckingham, 'begging his intercession with the new King'.[124]

Charles, for his part, quickly summoned a new parliament for 7 May; but in the event arrangements for his marriage to the French princess Henrietta Maria – which had taken place by proxy on 1 May – held up the meeting for six weeks. Buckingham went to fetch the bride from Paris; her arrival would open up a new opportunity for Bacon's plan for posterity, for in her retinue came the marquis d'Effiat. Voltaire recounts the anecdote telling how d'Effiat, denied access to Bacon's presence because of the latter's illness, quipped that 'his Lordship resembled the angels, of whom one hears and reads much, but whom one never sees'.[125]

Later, d'Effiat would cause *De augmentis* to be translated into French and, in 1632, published as *Neuf livres de la dignité et de l'Accroisement des Sciences*. Now, Bacon sent a copy of the new *Essays* to the marquis, whom he named 'mon filz', 'seeing how your excellency makes and treats of marriages, not only between princes of England and France, and also between languages since you had my book *The Advancement of Learning* translated into French.'[126]

In early April, Bacon was officially dismissed from the Privy Council. Chamberlain reported that 'the order was given for the earls of Suffolk, Middlesex, and Bristol, the Viscounts Wallingford and St Albans, the Lords Wotton and Baltimore not to take the oath, and so are discharged from the Council.'[127] On 23 May, Bacon revised his will, this time in great detail: the process was not finished until December of that year.[128] He followed this by composing a 'Prayer After Making His Last Will', which concluded, 'My soul has been a stranger in the course of my pilgrimage. Be merciful into [*sic*] me (O Lord).'[129]

He had already called on the Chancellor of the Duchy, Sir Humphrey May – not only an influential figure but also a private friend – once 'begging his assistance with the new King' and once 'for assistance in getting in his arrears'.[130] Now he asked May to forward his suit to Buckingham on his return from Paris, and to rebuke the Lord Treasurer, Ley, who had sent him 'a good answer touching my monies': 'A fire of old wood needeth no blowing; but old men do.' His tangible animosity towards the Lord Treasurer had been fanned by Ley's adverse comments on one of Bacon's Chancery cases. Ley would do well, he suggested, 'in this great age of yours to think of your grave as I do of mine; and to beware of hardness of heart'.[131]

Buckingham returned on 12 June 1625. When parliament finally sat on the eighteenth, Charles appealed to the Commons for means to follow through the enterprise enthusiastically promised support by the last session: 'They had drawn him into a war, and they must find means to maintain it.' This time the measure was not waved through. It was a sign of things to come for this most embattled of kings.

The summer came, and with it plague. The entire court retired first to Hampton Court, then to Windsor, and ultimately to Woodstock, near Oxford – as far as it could go. Bacon spent the summer at Gorhambury, ostensibly avoiding the city's pestilence, and in any case lying victim to a 'dangerous and tedious sickness' of his own, although by the end of October he could claim that 'by means of the sweet air of the country, I have obtained some degree of health'.[132] For all the health-giving properties of rural seclusion, his thirst for news of the world of affairs remained as keen as ever and, writing to Roger Palmer on 29 October, he asked for news of court life: 'I would be glad, in this solitary time and place, to hear a little from you how the world goeth, according to your friendly manner heretofore.'[133]

Despite ill health, and crippling financial pressures, Bacon published the third edition of the *Essays* in 1625. As he had promised when he dedicated the Instauration to James, and *Henry VII* to Charles, this volume was for Buckingham. 'Solomon says: A good name is as a precious ointment; And I assure myself, such will your Grace's name be, with posterity. For your fortune, and merit both, have been eminent . . . I do conceive, that the Latin volume of them, (being in the universal language) may last, as long as books last.'[134]

At the end of 1625, another military disaster occurred. The idea was that a new expedition – with a fleet prepared – would repeat the popular success of Essex at Cadiz almost thirty years earlier. The ships in Cadiz harbour were to be surprised and destroyed; their fleet sailing home from the Indies would be intercepted and caught. This time, however, the expedition returned after two months with one thousand men lost. The troops had landed without opposition, and re-embarked without any violence; the homeward bound fleet had sailed past unobserved during the night. The one thousand dead had all been from 'pestilence'. When Bacon wrote to Buckingham to congratulate him on a new male heir (born on 17 November 1625), he conveyed his 'rejoicing that God hath sent your Grace a son and heir, and that you are fortunate as well in your house as in the state of the kingdom'. For himself, 'I praise his divine Majesty, have gotten some step into health. My wants are great; but yet I want not a desire to do your Grace service, and', he continued, mischievously, 'I marvel that your Grace should think to pull down the monarchy of Spain without my good help. Your Grace will give me leave to be merry, however the world goeth with me.'[135] Legally constrained to the country and physically weak, Francis Bacon's contribution to Britain's political life was now no more than a joke. It is not surprising that he spent these months working on the *New Atlantis*, a work which presented an idealised picture of the intellectual's relationship with the state. Its utopian fantasy cast into stark relief the impotent isolation of its author.

★

On 19 December 1625, Bacon finally published his last will in the presence of Rawley, Robert Halpeny, Stephen Paise, William Atkins, Thomas Kent and Edward Legge, reference being made to 'my sickness'. A lengthy passage in the main body of the document dealt with bequests to his wife – but, at the end, Bacon unexpectedly added: 'Whatsoever I have given, granted, confirmed, or appointed to my wife, in the former part of this my will, I do now, for just and great causes, utterly revoke and make void, and leave her to her right only.'[136] The couple had occupied separate residences for three years. The suspicion has to be that Lady Bacon – thirty-three years old, and long neglected – had found herself someone more attentive than her elderly husband.

At the turn of the year Bacon wrote to Sir Humphrey May, Chancellor of the Duchy, exclaiming that 'I did wonder what was become of you, and was very glad to hear you were come to court; which methinks, as the times go, should miss you as well as I.' He reiterated a former request 'to sound the Duke of Buckingham's good affection towards me, before you do move him in the particular petitions.' His present motive for writing was the forthcoming parliament:

> The present occasion doth invite me to desire that his Grace would procure me a pardon of the King of the whole sentence. My writ for Parliament I have now had twice before the time, and that without any express restraint not to use it. It is true that I shall not be able, in respect of my health, to attend in Parliament; but yet I mought make a proxy. Time hath turned envy to pity; and I have had a long cleansing week of five years' expiation and more. Sir John Bennet hath his pardon; my

Lord of Somerset hath his pardon; and, they say, shall sit in Parliament. My Lord of Suffolk cometh to Parliament, though not to Council. I hope I deserve not to be the only outcast.[137]

It was perhaps in connection with this plea to be accepted back into parliament that Bacon travelled up to London at some point during January 1626. It was certainly from his chambers at Gray's Inn that he petitioned Secretary Conway on 26 January to forward a suit by his 'good friend and late servant' Mr Percy, 'for the making of a friend of his Baronet'. This is the only sure information we have of Francis Bacon's activities in early 1626. Less than three months later he was dead.[138]

18

Debt, Drugs and Bodysnatching:
Bacon's Legacy

Come, let us sit upon the grass
And tell sad tales of human ill:
How Bacon was a silly ass
Who caught a chicken and a chill.
G. K. Chesterton, 'A Ballad of Dead Men' (1938)

Children he had none; which, though they be the means to
perpetuate our names after our deaths, yet he had other issues
to perpetuate his name, the issues of his brain.
William Rawley, Life of Bacon (1657)

F RANCIS BACON DIED in the early morning of Easter Sunday, 9
April 1626, at the Highgate house of the earl of Arundel (who was
not in residence). The first printed account of his death, in 1631,
was by Pierre Amboise, French 'translator' of the *Sylva sylvarum*:

> Having thereby procured the means to extricate himself from incon-
> venience, he began to work as before researching into the most important
> secrets of nature. During the coldest months he was investigating some
> particular effects of cold, and stayed out of doors too long, without
> considering that his advanced years made him less able to suffer such
> extreme conditions. That is how this great man, whom England can
> claim as an equal to the most excellent men of all previous ages, met
> his end.[1]

In the version provided by his editor and chaplain, William Rawley, Bacon
'died on the ninth day of April in the year 1626, in the early morning of
the day then celebrated for our Saviour's resurrection, in the sixty-sixth
year of his age, at the earl of Arundel's house in Highgate, near London,
to which place he casually repaired about a week before; God so ordaining
that he should die there of a gentle fever, accidentally accompanied with
a great cold, whereby the defluxion of rheum fell so plentifully upon his
breast, that he died by suffocation.'[2]

John Aubrey later claimed that Bacon's sometime secretary Thomas Hobbes had given him another version of events:

As he was taking the air in a coach with Dr. Witherborne (a Scotchman, physician to the King) towards Highgate, snow lay on the ground, and it came into my lord's thoughts, why flesh might not be preserved in snow, as in salt. They were resolved they would try the experiment at once. They alighted out of the coach, and went into a poor woman's house at the bottom of Highgate Hill, and bought a hen, and made the woman gut it, and then stuffed the body with snow, and my lord did help to do it himself. The snow so chilled him, that he immediately fell so extremely ill, that he could not return to his lodgings (I suppose at Gray's Inn), but went to the earl of Arundel's house at Highgate, where they put him into a good bed warmed with a pan, but it was a damp bed that had not been laid-in about a year before, which gave him such a cold that in two or three days, as I remember Mr. Hobbes told me, he died of suffocation.[3]

Accounts of the circumstances surrounding a prominent death in early modern England need to be taken with more than a pinch of salt. Just like the anecdote of Sir Nicholas Bacon dispensing his last *bon mot* on the barber who thoughtfully left open a window for fresh air (that contained the 'cold' that killed him), this account of Bacon's end is carefully constructed. The composite story from Amboise, 'Hobbes' (via Aubrey) and Rawley dramatises a sequence of last actions and outcomes befitting an inveterate single-minded experimental scientist.

It is easy to see how these chroniclers seized upon the idea of an experiment concerning the 'preservation of flesh' involving cold. Bacon devotes long sections of both his compendious natural history, the *Sylva sylvarum*, and his *Historia vitae et mortis* (an appropriate text for those researching his own death to consult) to experiments concerning freezing. The *Sylva sylvarum* talks of 'salt put to ice as in the producing of artificial ice'. In 1624 Bacon declared that 'the producing of cold [by artificial means] is a thing very worthy of the inquisition.' In June 1622, in the *De augmentis*, he referred to 'the late experiment of artificial freezing' and how 'salt is discovered to have great powers of condensation'. That 'late experiment' has been tentatively identified as an attempt in 1620 by the Dutch-born inventor and demonstrator Cornelius Drebbel to provide air-conditioning on a hot summer day in Westminster's Great Hall. Its scientific success was rather undermined by its effect on the royal entourage gathered to observe: James and his attendants fled, shivering.[4]

Among the fragments of Bacon's planned specialist 'histories' are the beginnings of one entitled 'A legitimate inquiry concerning heat and cold'.[5]

It contains such observations as that 'cold in Muscovy and the like countries causes those parts which are voidest of blood, as the nose, the ears, the toes, the fingers, to mortify and rot; specially if you come suddenly to fire after you have been in the air abroad, they are sure to moulder and dissolve. They use for remedy as is said washing in snow water.'[6] It needs little imagination to picture Bacon struck down while working to complete such a fragment (even if frostbite was unlikely in Highgate in April).

The evidence to support the 'chicken' story is all anecdotal, and the suddenness of the illness it posits runs counter to the known facts of Bacon's late life. He was already unwell at the end of 1625. The codicil to his will, made on 19 December 1625 to cut out his misbehaving wife, says that it was 'made in his sickness'.[7] In a contemporary letter, James Howell informs Dr Thomas Pritchard that 'My Lord Chancellor is lately dead of a long languishing weakness.'[8] In a Latin memorial poem, George Herbert writes: 'The while thou didst groan beneath the burden of a long and lingering malady, and pining line halted with uncertain foot, what did wise fate intend? I now at last can see. Only in April, surely, couldst thou die, that here the flower with its tears, there Philomel with her laments, may follow only thy tongue's funeral-train.' An anonymous verse, 'On the long illness but unexpected death of his most noble Lord, Viscount St. Alban', tells of how 'Death first grew nigh, and then was driven hence. Methought he had repented of his errand and his crime. As the shrewd soldier deserts beleaguered towns, again to attack them when the unwary townsmen have discarded fear, Death in like manner, seeing him skilful to fend off the wound, struck cruelly when he had turned his eyes from the Muses.'[9]

As for the sudden deterioration of his condition on the road through Highgate, Bacon himself has left us a written account of the incident. Before he realised how seriously sick he was, he wrote a letter to the earl of Arundel, more or less as a courtesy, to explain why (in the earl's absence) he had had to prevail without warning upon the hospitality of his household. The letter was printed in 1660 by Tobie Matthew in his *Collection of Letters*:

My very good Lord, – I was likely to have had the fortune of Caius Plinius the elder, who lost his life by trying an experiment about the burning of the mountain Vesuvius. For I also was desirous to try an experiment or two, touching the conservation and induration [strengthening] of bodies. As for the experiment itself, it succeeded excellently well; but in the journey (between London and Highgate) I was taken with such a fit of casting [vomiting], as I knew not whether it were the stone, or some surfeit, or cold, or indeed a touch of them all three. But when I came to your Lordship's house, I was not able to go back, and therefore was forced to take up my lodging here, where your house-keeper is very careful and diligent about me; which I assure myself your Lordship will not only pardon towards him, but think the better of him for it. For indeed your Lordship's house was happy to me; and I kiss your noble hands for the welcome which I am sure you give me to it, etc.

I know how unfit it is for me to write to your Lordship with any other hand than mine own; but in troth my fingers are so disjointed with this fit of sickness, that I cannot steadily hold a pen.[10]

Read with an ear for the element of self-ironising which Bacon intended, this letter is remarkably clear and specific (it was, of course, penned before Bacon had any idea that his illness would prove fatal). Bacon had been conducting experiments concerned with the prolongation of life in living bodies somewhere in London. On the return journey he was overcome by violent vomiting and forced to break his journey at the nearby home of the earl.

The reference to the supposed cause of death of Pliny the Elder matches Aubrey's report of Hobbes's version of Bacon's death: 'As I remember Mr. Hobbes told me, he died of suffocation.' Pliny the Elder was supposed to have died as a result of inhaling sulphurous fumes from Vesuvius, while investigating the erupting volcano.[11] Bacon says that he 'also' was conducting an experiment 'touching the conservation and induration of bodies'. Pliny's 'experiment', of course, was an accidental and fatal one conducted upon his own body. Had Bacon been using himself in some way as an experimental guinea-pig, in the hope of restoring his own failing health? That would explain the presence of 'Dr. Witherborne (a Scotchman, physician to the King)' as also reported by Hobbes via Aubrey.

In the *Sylva sylvarum* Bacon describes how human life may be prolonged through various processes of 'induration' and 'conservation', and by both cold and heat:

Induration of substances more soft is a great alteration of nature. The effecting and accelerating thereof is very worthy to be inquired. It is effected by three means. The first is by cold, whose property is to condense. The second is by heat, which is not proper, but by conse-quence; for the heat doth attenuate; and by attenuation doth send forth the [vital] spirit and moister part of a body; and upon that, the more gross of the tangible parts do contract and serre [tighten] themselves together. And the third is by assimilation; when a hard body assimilateth a soft, being contiguous to it.[12]

Most of all induration by assimilation appeareth in the bodies of trees and living creatures: for no nourishment that the tree receiveth, or that the living body receiveth, is so hard as wood, bone, or horn, &c, but is indurated [hardened] after by assimilation.[13]

Like many of his contemporaries, Bacon was particularly interested in the properties of the naturally occurring chemical substance nitre for conservation and prolongation of life.[14] Nitre (or saltpetre) was widely used by apothecaries and chemists, as a fertiliser, as a crucial ingredient in explosives, and in the preparation of preserved meats. Although today nitre is identified chemically as potassium nitrate, it was rarely, if ever, found in its pure form in Bacon's day, more often as a compound of potassium nitrate and sodium nitrate (with other impurities).[15] Its chemical properties, particularly when heated, were therefore unpredictable; whereas in its pure form the vapours produced would be reviving and invigorating (in the manner of the chemically similar 'smelling salts' taken by ladies in the nineteenth century), vapours from the impure form might well be toxic.[16]

Scattered through Bacon's scientific writings are references to his first-hand experience of the supposedly beneficial properties of nitre and of opiates.[17] In particular, there are sections in both the *Sylva sylvarum* and the *Historia vitae et mortis* devoted to their use:

> A whelp that hath been fed with nitre in milk, hath become very little, but extreme lively: for the spirit of nitre is cold. Nitre [saltpetre] in milk is an excellent medicine in strength of years for prolongation of life, yet in children and young creatures an enemy to growth [stunts the growth]; for heat is requisite to growth; but after a man is come to his middle age, heat consumeth the spirits; which the coldness of the spirit of nitre doth help to condense and correct.[18]

> It appears that the human spirits can be cooled and condensed by the spirit of nitre, and made more crude and less eager. Nitre composes and restrains the spirits and tends to longevity.[19]

Specifically, in a number of places in the *Sylva sylvarum* Bacon discusses taking opiates and nitre, for prolongation of life, and by inhalation:

> Opium is by far the most powerful and effectual means for condensing the spirits by flight [so that the vital spirits may retain their youth and renew their vigour]; and next to it opiates and soporifics in general.
>
> Opium and opiates are clearly found to excite the sexual passion, which shows their power to strengthen the spirits.
>
> Distilled water of the wild poppy being doubtless a mild opiate, is successfully given in surfeit, fevers, and various diseases; and let no one wonder at the variety of its use. For this is common to opiates, as the

spirit being strengthened and condensed will fight against any disease.[20]

Opium leeseth some of his poisonous quality, if it be vapoured out, mingled with spirit of wine, or the like.[21]

There be two things which (inwardly used) do cool and condense the spirits; and I wish the same to be tried outwardly in vapours [inhaled]. The one is nitre, which I would have dissolved in Malmsey, or Greek wine, and so the smell of the wine taken; or if you would have it more forcible, pour of it upon a fire-pan, well heated, as they do rose-water and vinegar. The other is the distilled water of wild poppy [i.e. opiates], which I wish to be mingled, at half, with rose-water, and so taken with some mixture of a few cloves in a perfuming-pan.[22]

Bacon draws his discussion of opiates in the *Historia vitae et mortis* to a close with an enthusiastic endorsement of their properties for extending the life of the human body:

From these observations certain directions or advices may be drawn for the prolongation of life, according to this intention, namely, the condensing of the spirits by opiates.

From youth upwards, therefore, let there be every year a kind of opiate diet. Let it be taken at the end of May; for in summer the spirits are most wasted and weakened, and there is less fear of cold humours. Let the opiate be of a superior kind, not so strong as those in use, either as to the quantity of opium or to the proportion of very hot ingredients. Let the medicine be taken only on alternate days, and be continued for a fortnight.

Opiates may not only be taken through the mouth, but likewise inhaled in the form of smoke; but it should be such as not to excite the expulsive faculty too strongly, nor draw out the humours, but only to work upon the spirits within the brain for a short time.[23]

Bacon's precise observations of the impact of opiates on the body should not surprise us. Since the persistent illness which dogged his childhood, both he and his brother Anthony had taken 'physic' for the 'induration of the body' – graduating from nitre and poppy-water in milk to the wide range of opium compounds fashionable in high Tudor and Stuart society. We remind the reader of Walsingham's stern rebuke to Anthony Bacon, on hearing that he was a 'physic' taker:

I have been informed you too easily and too often give yourself to the taking of physic, a thing which as I have by experience found hurtful in myself, when I was of your years, so you shall find in time many incommodities, if you do not in time break it off. Your years will

better wear out any little indisposition, by good order of exercise and
abstinence, with some other little moderation in diet, than abide to be
corrected by physic, the use whereof altereth nature much, yea, maketh
a new nature, if it be without great cause used in younger years.[24]

References to Francis Bacon's own habitual recourse to remedies and
purgatives are liberally scattered through his notes and natural history. His
chaplain William Rawley explained in detail to what extent Bacon indulged
in such practices:

And for physic, he did indeed live physically, but not miserably; for he
took only a maceration of rhubarb, infused into a draught of white wine
and beer mingled together for the space of half an hour, once in six or
seven days, immediately before his meal . . . that it might dry the body
less; which (as he said) did carry away frequently the grosser humours
of the body, and not diminish or carry away any of the spirits, as sweating
doth. And this was no grievous thing to take. As for other physic, in
an ordinary way (whatsoever hath been vulgarly spoken) he took not.[25]

Rawley was evidently at pains to counter popular suggestions that Bacon's
physic-taking was in any way excessive.

In the last days of his life, we suggest, Francis Bacon tells Arundel, in a
barely veiled allusion, that he has been inhaling remedial substances in
London, in an attempt to alleviate the symptoms of ill-health and, he
hopes, help prolong his life: a course of events which 'succeeded excellently
well' – except that on the journey home he was suddenly taken violently
ill with 'a fit of casting [vomiting],' and forced to break his journey at
Arundel's house. Here he remained, dying there shortly thereafter.

If we are looking for further evidence that Bacon died from an overdose
of inhaled nitre or opiates, it is there in his final apology to Arundel for
dictating his letter rather than writing it himself: 'in troth my fingers are
so disjointed [numbed] with this fit of sickness' that he cannot hold a pen.
Both in his *Historia vitae et mortis* and in the *Novum Organum*, Bacon himself
reports that an unfortunate side-effect of opiates is that they 'mortify' the
extremities of the body: 'the spirits flee away from that part, and do not
readily flow into it again'.[26]

When he was taken ill on the road, Bacon's decision to seek refuge at
Arundel's house was probably a considered one. The earl of Arundel was
a longtime friend of his,[27] a traveller with an interest in natural science, a
collector of artworks and experimental equipment: he had purchased the
large lodestone that 'the smiths and cutlers cut and formed' for Dr William
Gilbert's experiments with magnetism undertaken in the course of
developing his general theory of the magnetic nature of the earth (a theory

in which Bacon took an interest, though he disagreed emphatically with Gilbert's own scientific system).

Shortly after James's accession in 1603, Thomas Howard was restored to the earldom of Arundel, which had been cancelled (and all lands confiscated) as punishment for the family's recusancy under Elizabeth. Only some of the family estates, however, were returned to him, the rest being given in gratitude by James to Henry Howard, earl of Northampton, Thomas Howard's great-uncle, for his services during the negotiations surrounding the succession. The earl did not, therefore, have the use of the main London seat of the Arundels – Arundel House on the Strand – until 1614, when the childless Northampton willed the Arundel lands back to him.[28] Highgate, acquired in 1610 and suitably located outside the City boundaries, was a familiar and favoured retreat: placed high above London and beautified with plants from the Low Countries and carpets and quilts bought in Italy, with a lamprey pond, canopy garden and walks, it was what John Evelyn called 'that darling villa' – the perfect place at which to distance oneself from the City and Westminster, and yet still be near at hand. As recently as June 1624, James had been Arundel's guest at Highgate to hunt the stag in nearby St John's Wood.

Bacon certainly knew the house. John Chamberlain recounted a dinner party at Highgate in June 1617, where the cream of English political society were shown up as parochial by their cosmopolitan hostess, Aletheia Howard.

> In Whitsun week the Countess of Arundel made a great feast at Highgate to the Lord Keeper, the two Lords Chief Justices, the Master of the Rolls and I know not who else. It was after the Italian manner with four courses, and four tablecloths one under another and when the first course and tablecloth were taken away the Master of the Rolls [the Arundels' neighbour at Muswell Hill, Sir Julius Caesar] thinking all had been done, said grace as his manner is when no divines are present, and was afterwards well laughed at for this labour.[29]

And among the witty sayings collected by Rawley we find the following: 'Sir Francis Bacon coming into the earl of Arundel's garden, where there were a great number of ancient statues of naked men and women, made a stand, and as astonished cried out, "The Resurrection!"'[30]

When Bacon was disgraced in 1621, he was forbidden to come within twelve miles of the court, except for designated trips 'for his health'. Although he appears to have been able to reside from time to time in his rooms at Gray's Inn (where perhaps he had repaired to 'take physic' on this occasion), the penalty was never officially rescinded. Highgate was a suitable distance from central London. Like Bacon, Arundel had enjoyed, and risen through, Buckingham's favour; like him he had recently lost the benefit of Buckingham's attentions to his career. Finally, Bacon's old and loyal friend Tobie Matthew, who shared Arundel's Catholic sympathies, was also close to the earl.[31]

Nevertheless, Arundel's house was a sensitive as well as an appropriate location: in spring 1626, at the time Bacon alighted there, Arundel himself was incarcerated. Charles had sequestered the earl from the Upper House and sent him to the Tower on 4 March, ostensibly because he had allowed his son Lord Maltravers to marry a royal ward, the daughter of the duchess of Lennox, in contradiction to the King's wishes. However, Charles had known of the marriage since at least 6 February. It was widely believed that the real reason for Arundel's imprisonment was his status as a strategic presence in the Lords. In recent weeks, he had swayed the vote on a bill to reform the House of Lords' system of proxy voting and to eliminate absenteeism – a move which threatened Buckingham's power base.

March 1626 was a crucial month. Both Bristol and Buckingham faced impeachment charges. The rivalry between Arundel and Buckingham had worsened in recent years: Arundel, made Earl Marshal in July 1621, had deeply resented Buckingham's becoming a duke in May 1623, when James refused to revive the ancient Howard dukedom for him, and it became noticeable that Arundel had 'become a stranger at the Court' in the months following. Now the Lords were furious at Arundel's banishment from the House, the first time such a move had been taken since Edward III banished the Bishop of Winchester. John Holles noted that 'Buckingham blows the coals, glad of the occasion to be rid of the Marshal, and surely this man prospers in all ways, be they never so bad, and like an Irish dog wrings our necks asunder like sheep.'[32] The Lords angrily pressed Arundel's claim to be freed in March, but the King advised them that the earl was being held on 'a personal misdemeanour to himself, and which hath no relation to the Parliament'; Buckingham declared that the release of Arundel should not be requested of the King. Perhaps to forestall an enforced release, Arundel was permitted to leave the Tower on 11 April – two days after Bacon's death – and immediately confined to another of his houses, at Horsley. In other words, then, Bacon's presence at the house of Arundel – of all people – at this time – of all times – was highly charged.[33]

So one function of the letter to Arundel (possibly delivered to him in the Tower by the faithful Tobie Matthew?) was as a kind of alibi. It explained that Bacon's stay in Arundel's house was entirely an accident, the result of a sudden catastrophe of the kind which meant that under the laws of hospitality Arundel's servants were bound to take in the sick man. As always in his political life, Bacon was covering himself, making quite sure it was understood that he hadn't *chosen* Arundel's 'side' over Buckingham's.

At the same time, the purpose of the trip is recast: from a journey to indulge in the supervised taking of more or less addictive remedies to a more respectably investigative project: 'I was desirous to try an experiment or two.' Bacon probably expected Arundel himself to read between the lines.

★

If there is a real mystery associated with Francis Bacon's death, it lies less in how he contracted his fatal illness than in some apparently premonitory actions he took some weeks earlier. The *Journal of the House of Commons* records that the first business on Thursday 16 March 1626 was 'Viscount St Albans'. The only elaboration on this comes in the journal kept by Bulstrode Whitelocke (now in the manuscripts department of Cambridge University Library), where he records a 'Bill to enable the Lord Keeper that now is, or the Chancellor or Keeper for the time being, to give power by commission for the sale of the lands, leases, and chattels of the Lord St Albans for the payment of his debts.' Such bills, allowing land to be alienated and liquidated, were generally promoted on the instruction of the owner. So, less than a month before his death, Bacon was involved in the promotion of a private bill to enable the confiscation and sale of his 'lands, leases, and chattels'.[34] This unnoticed piece of parliamentary business suggests that Bacon knew his health was deteriorating.

When Bacon added the codicil to his will in December 1625, disinheriting his wife, he made another stipulation, instructing his executors 'to have a special care to discharge a debt by bond (now made in my sickness to Mr. Thomas Meautys)'.[35] Living, as always, way beyond his means, Bacon had evidently exceeded the possibilities for credit he could rely on, and had been forced to raise a substantial loan from his personal secretary. The bill put before parliament attempted to put in place arrangements for repaying that loan after his death. Since Bacon had no direct heirs, there was no disadvantage to his alienating all his lands to raise cash to settle loans and deliver legacies to friends and servants. And, remembering that other function of the codicil to his will, he may have wished to ensure that Alice Bacon could not become the sole beneficiary of his estate by default during her lifetime by simply continuing to occupy his family home at Gorhambury. But there is no record of Bacon's bill having been passed; and after his death, his wife did indeed keep Gorhambury by the simple expedient of refusing to move out.

It seems that in the closing months of his life there were pressing matters on Bacon's mind concerning his personal finances, in the context of his declining health. In the first place, having run out of other sources of credit with Meautys, he took formal steps to guarantee that his secretary could recoup further financial outlay as first call creditor on his estate. Legally, his estranged wife stood between Meautys and the estate; Bacon therefore instigated the necessary parliamentary action to liquidate those portions of his lands which would legally pass to his widow on his death. As a further precaution, he formally disinherited his wife in the codicil to his will, at the same time specifying Meautys' official position as first claimant in settlement of his debts.

★

Bacon's fears about his wife's marital fidelity played themselves out in spectacular form. With extraordinary rapidity, the widow procured a licence and married her late husband's gentleman usher John Underhill: the wedding took place eleven days after the Easter Sunday of Francis' death, on 20 April 1626 at the parish church of St Martin-in-the-Fields, where Bacon had been baptised sixty-five years earlier.[36] John Underhill was a younger son of a minor Warwickshire gentry family, who had been in Bacon's service for at least eight years.[37] Now suddenly elevated in society by the marriage, his new position was enhanced on 12 July, when he was knighted at Oatlands.

Once remarried, the viscountess – who was to cling to her title throughout her life – returned with her new husband to Gorhambury. She chose to ignore the tiny detail that in his last will, signed four months earlier, her late husband had emphatically repudiated her claims to any of his goods and property, including Gorhambury; this problem did not have to be addressed immediately, because the executors of his will were not hurrying to deal with the impossibly debt-ridden estate. So, for six years, the Underhills made Gorhambury their home, alternating between there and Sir John's house in the Strand. According to one of John Aubrey's more scurrilous sources, the viscountess, perhaps overcompensating for twenty years of her husband's desertion of her in favour of a string of smooth-faced male servants, made Underhill 'deaf and blind with too much of Venus'. While the venereal aspect of the relationship is now beyond recall, Underhill's deafness and blindness are well attested by a number of court cases against men who had allegedly duped him, forcing him to sign documents he was unable to read. These deficiencies were to prove a real problem for Sir John Underhill and the Viscountess St Alban, since they were to spend their turbulent marriage enmeshed in almost continuous litigation.

The financial manoeuvres that were prompted by Bacon's death – and which lasted for an incredible half-century – are complex, detailed and mired in lengthy, formulaic documents. The story they tell, however, provides a fascinating insight into the financial politics of marriage and inheritance in Bacon's day. Most importantly, they show that the particular peccadillo with which Bacon was charged – neglecting his rightful spouse in favour of his servants – was one that was repeated by his widow, not only in her first marriage, but again in her second. If one were to view the early seventeenth century purely through these documents, the inevitable conclusion would be that marriage was no more than a cynical exercise in the acquisition of land, while the only true emotional bond was between master (or mistress) and servant.[38]

Bacon's codicil to his will, added in December 1625, had given Thomas Meautys priority among his many creditors. The debts of the estate amounted to £19,658 4s 4d. Meautys was joined by Sir Thomas Rich in bringing a bill in Chancery against Underhill, the viscountess, and the various trustees of the manors and lands. Its object was to implement the other stipulation of Bacon's will, namely that Meautys' claims on the estate be settled before those of his wife. The executors finally assumed their office fifteen months after Bacon's death, in July 1627. The creditors put their case that, in his will, Bacon had appointed his lands and goods to be used to pay his debts, while to Alice he left only the £500 per annum that had been settled on her at her marriage: all the proceeds from the manors and goods beyond the sum should be put towards the payment of the debts.

The viscountess, argued Meautys, had procured the deeds of Gorhambury, and persuaded Bacon to transfer the manors of Butler's and Redbourn to other trustees so that she might make use of them, to settle upon her part of the farm of the sixpenny writs, and to make to her a deed of gift of all his goods and chattels, which thus defrauded the creditors of what was rightfully theirs. 'Under colour of these fraudulent conveyances and deeds of gift,' Sir John Underhill and the viscountess had entered into the manors and received their whole rents and profits since Bacon's death. In the process they had taken as their own valuable jewels including 'a chain valued at £500, a table diamond ring worth £300, another diamond ring £300, a chain of precious stones £200, two other chains £1,500 each, besides jewels, chains, and rings of great value', as well as vast quantities of plate, pictures, sumptuous hangings and other household goods worth £5,000. They had wasted the lands, felling valuable trees for their own use. Moreover, they had persuaded the so-called heir, one Thomas Bacon, and others, not to sell the lands, and had kept hold of deeds and evidences pertaining to the property.

The viscountess, replying on her own behalf, stated that she had inherited from her father lands worth £300 per annum and goods worth £6,000. When she married, Bacon had initially settled the Gorhambury manors upon her for life, and covenanted to leave to her goods and plate worth £1,000, but the arrangements had been altered. Bacon had transferred all her lands into his own name; once this had been arranged, he cut down timber on her lands, and sold it for his own use. She also claimed that she was further entitled to lucrative legal monopolies bestowed on Bacon and herself by King James, as well as permanent rights to Redbourn, settled on her by King Charles.

When Bacon decided to return to Gray's Inn in order to pursue his studies, she continued, he granted his wife certain plate and household stuff (worth less than £400), to enable her to live suitably to her degree in his absence; her chains and jewels were in the main gifts to her by Queen Anne, King Charles and their friends. Turning to the anomaly of Bacon's last will, which first praised her, and then cut her out, she argued that Bacon had 'left her society' when she refused to join with him in the sale of lands conveyed to her in jointure. The creditors had no right to these things, she argued, and the extent of the debts had been exaggerated, largely through the efforts of his servants, 'some of whom by vicious courses did him great prejudice'.

The trustees of the manors and lands gave in their resignation to the court. Most of them disclaimed their interest in the case, and agreed to abide by whatever the court decided; but two of the trustees, Heatley and Crewe, then made a difficulty about selling the lands until the heir-at-law should be discovered and give his consent. One Thomas Bacon of Hessett, 'generally reported to be the heir', came forward, 'setting forth his pettigree' – which unfortunately the record does not contain – at which point counsel, 'finding him to have no right or title to any part of the estate', advised him to release his claim, which he did. Now it was up to the judge to find a purchaser for the land; but none was forthcoming. In the meantime the viscountess had been called before the Lord Keeper and the Lord President, along with Sir George Chaworth, to sort out a query concerning the sixpenny writs.[39]

After two or three thwarted attempts, a single offer was at last made for Gorhambury: Francis, Lord Dunsmore, would give £6,000 and a life annuity to the viscountess. The offer was accepted, and on 12 June 1632 the court made its judgement: the viscountess would retain Butler's farm, since it had been bought with her money; £600 per annum from the sixpenny writs would remain with her, since it had been given to support her as a peeress; and she should keep her jewels and household goods. Dunsmore was bound to pay her £530 per annum for the rest of her life – a sum equivalent to her jointure. Certain 'utensils which were ancient appendages to the houses' were to remain at Gorhambury:

All the tables of stone, except the black table of touch, in and about the said houses, an ancient picture hanging at the upper end of the hall, the brewing vessels, troughs, cisterns, cupboards, shelves, dressers, and together with the ancient standing tables and forms in the hall, all the images of wood and stone to adorn the workes and gardens, together with the settles and benches thereunto belonging, and the timber now lying in the yards for reparation of the houses. And as touching the Armour of about fourteen Arms of horse and foot, it is ordered that the said Defendants shall have the one half of them, and leave the other half to the house.

In return, the viscountess and Underhill would have to leave Gorhambury at Michaelmas in 1632 – which they did.

Within months, it became apparent that Lord Dunsmore's interest in Gorhambury was a front for Thomas Meautys. Dunsmore entered Gorhambury as a co-trustee with Thomas and Robert Coningsby. On 11 October 1632, the Underhills and John Hunt gave a lease of the manors to the Coningsbys and their kinsman Thomas Meautys (Meautys' mother had been a Coningsby) at a rent of £530 per annum, which Meautys bound himself to pay the viscountess during her lifetime. The men who had held Bacon's £40,000 fine since 1621 – without ever collecting a penny of it – granted it to Meautys and the Coningsbys on 20 January 1633. On 17 February, Dunsmore and the Coningsbys granted the manors to Meautys, admitting that in reality the entire process had been carried out on Meautys' behalf.

In 1634 Meautys took over the claim as Bacon's residual heir male by legal agreement with his cousin Thomas Bacon of Hessett in Norfolk. At the end of this series of byzantine legal manoeuvrings it was Thomas Meautys who finally gained legal title to Gorhambury – as, from the terms of the will, it could be argued that Bacon had always intended he would. But he could still not, apparently, afford to live in the house himself; Gorhambury was let out in the late 1630s, with Meautys receiving the rentals.

Throughout the late 1630s and early 1640s Meautys managed all the Bacon estates. In 1641 he pledged land which he had bought in 1629 as security for the raising of £1,510 as portions for his four maternal first cousins, daughters of Thomas Coningsby. Later in 1641 this and other lands were given as pledges that after his death his heirs would settle land worth £500 per annum on his new wife, his second cousin Anne Bacon, who was a daughter of the portrait painter Sir Nathaniel Bacon, a son of Francis' eldest half-brother Nicholas.

Notwithstanding the viscountess' involvement, the main battle over Gorhambury was between Bacon's male servants, who consolidated their claims – first his gentleman usher John Underhill, then his secretary Thomas Meautys – by marrying Bacon women. Soon another interest showed itself. Nicholas Bacon had also been a gentleman usher of Bacon's. The viscountess trusted him, and entrusted to him most of her legal affairs and estate business. But Nicholas was an ambitious man who saw a route to the Bacon estates through Sir John's niece Anne Underhill, who was living at Gorhambury under her uncle's supervision, having 'little means and no other friends but himself'. While her uncle bore Anne 'great affection', the viscountess apparently 'little or nothing esteemed her'.

Nicholas approached Sir John with a view to becoming a suitor to Anne, a notion that at first pleased Underhill, 'being desirous to see her well married'. However, he was swayed more 'because Nicholas Bacon had before informed him that his said Lady wife had given, or that he would undertake to gain, her consent thereto, and Sir John believed that Nicholas Bacon did really mean what he had then pretended, without any fraudulent intention.' Then, however, Nicholas became more demanding. He insisted that if he were to marry Anne he would require some portion paid down, arguing that in stipulating this 'he aimed not at any portion by her, but only for the satisfaction of the world that he did not marry and take a wife without some portion, which he pretended was the chief thing he required'. Then, 'only to gain some show of advancement to the World as he pretended by the marriage', he persuaded Sir John to make a covenant with him assuring him of £100 per annum from lands, and another £100 per annum from the sixpenny writs profits, to commence after the Underhills' death, and 'some household stuff' on the death of the viscountess. These covenants, he argued, 'would give him some credit and the world some satisfaction touching his intended marriage, and that was all the use he intended to make of them, and that he had no intention to encumber the Lady's estates without her full consent'. Nicholas Bacon added that as these propositions 'only depended on casualties, and *hopes* of my Lady's consent, that Sir John might hand him a lease of certain tithes in Lancashire which belonged to his own estate', and Sir John, 'having trust and confidence in Nicholas, allowed him to draw up some indentures, [and] signed them.' Nicholas easily persuaded Sir John that these documents could be revoked by the viscountess; and so Sir John effectively signed away his – and his wife's – property, including all the lands the pair had inherited in London, Middlesex, Essex and Hertfordshire (to pass to Bacon when the Underhills had died).

In fact, Nicholas had already secretly married Anne Underhill.

The viscountess took out her anger on her husband, while Nicholas immediately sold the Lancashire tithes for £500, making no jointure for his wife. In November 1631 the Underhills brought a bill in Chancery against the Bacons, arguing that Nicholas had induced Sir John, 'who was an almost totally deaf man, and by reason of the weakness of his eyes and the infirmity in his head could not read writings of that nature without much pain', to sign a paper without full knowledge of its content. Nicholas counter-argued that

> he did not know what to think, for the Viscountess when he saw her at Gorhambury sometimes expressed great love for her husband, and at other times quite the contrary, and sometimes after declaring she would leave everything she had to her husband, she would insist that he should have nothing from her; and at one time when her husband was quite out of favour with her, Nicholas declared she had conference with him how he, Nicholas, could have the disposing of the greatest part of her estate after her death without issue and also how he might get in the inheritance of Gorhambury at her death, protesting how glad she would be of it.

In Chancery, the Underhills claimed 'that Nicholas at one time persuaded or cheated the Viscountess into a belief that there was likely to be some question in law about certain houses which belonged to her in London, worth £50 per annum, and that it was safer for her to establish the estate thereof in him, Nicholas, than to continue it in herself, and the conveyance thereof was made to him accordingly without consideration, and in trust only for her, and to be at her disposal, and she having asked him to reconvey the same to her and her heirs, he refused and kept the deed of conveyance'. In March 1632 the suit came before Lord Keeper Coventry, who agreed to arbitrate in the case; on 11 April he pronounced a decree according to which reassurances and releases of the deeds were to be made and the plaintiffs were at the same time to pay to the defendants a specified sum of money.[40]

The viscountess spent her last years with the Anderson family (relatives of her sister Dorothy's in-laws) at Eyeworth in Bedfordshire. She died, aged fifty-eight, on 29 June 1650, and was buried in the parish church of All Saints. The parish register of burials records: 'Alice Viscountess St Alban, widow Dowager to Francis Viscount St Alban, was buried in the Chancel of Eyeworth in the south side thereof of the 9th day of July 1650.' The inscription on the chancel floor reads: 'Here lieth the body of Dame Alice, baroness Verulam, viscountess St Alban, one of the daughters of Benedict Barnham of London. She departed this life the 29th June Anno Domini 1650.' She was buried with her sister Dorothy, Lady Constable, who had died there in June of the previous year.[41]

Even with the viscountess' death, the St Alban legacy was not settled. Alice had revised her will extensively, revoking bequests to some because of 'their withdrawing themselves from me'. Noticeably absent from the beneficiaries was her husband Sir John Underhill: the viscountess bequeathed the bulk of her estate 'unto my executors hereafter named that is to say unto my nephew Stephen Soames Esq., and unto my trusty servant Robert Tyrrell, gentleman'. For those in the know, it was a particularly loaded bequest: Soames was a nephew through the Barnham family; Tyrrell was the viscountess' lover, for whose sake she had legally separated from Underhill in 1639. This was the cue for Sir John to get back into court, launching Chancery suits against both Soames and Tyrrell. Underhill was successful in his case against Tyrrell, although the income he won back returned to Tyrrell at his death. As it happened, however, Tyrrell died first (in 1672), forcing the now eighty-year-old Sir John to return to Chancery yet again to claim what was his from Tyrrell's executors.

Meanwhile Sir Thomas Meautys retired to Gorhambury in January 1642, to the general expectation that he would soon die there. He lived, however, for another seven years and more, dying in October 1649; his heir, a daughter, died a minor three years later, and her entire heritage, including the Bacon estates, passed to his brother Henry Meautys. Henry liquidated his entire interest in both the Meautys and the Bacon estates, selling to the second husband of Thomas' widow, Sir Harbottle Grimston, who went on to become Speaker of the House of Commons and Master of the Rolls, in two lots totalling £12,760.[42]

The estate soon fell into ruin. When John Aubrey visited Gorhambury in 1656 he found what had once been Bacon's 'paradise' now 'a large ploughed field', which Meautys had let as grazing land. The elegant summer-houses were 'yet standing, but defaced, so that one would have thought the barbarians had made a conquest here'. The ponds, at which visitors used to delight in the coloured-pebble figures created on the bottom, were 'now overgrown with flags and rushes'. Ten years later, Verulam House had gone, 'sold by Sir Harbottle Grimston, Baronet, to two carpenters, for £400; of which they made £800'. Aubrey regretted he had not been more meticulous in making his record of the house, 'but I little suspected it would be pulled down for the sale of the materials'.[43]

Bacon's last will had expressed his desire to be buried with his mother, in St Michael's parish church: 'For my burial, I desire it may be in St. Michael's church, near St. Alban's: there was my mother buried, and it is the parish church of my mansion house of Gorhambury, and it is the only christian church within the walls of old Verulam. I would have the charge of my funeral not to exceed three hundred pounds at the most.'[44] James Howell wrote at the time that Bacon 'died so poor that he scarce left money to bury him'.[45] But no record exists of his burial, and it has recently been revealed that Bacon is not buried under the monument in the north wall of the chancel, as had been assumed.[46]

Conspiracy theories have multiplied. In 1923, Walter A. Arensberg (founder of the Francis Bacon Library at Claremont) predicted that Bacon's body would not be found in St Michael's and argued that he was buried, as a result of a Rosicrucian conspiracy, in Lichfield. In December 1991 three members of a New Age sect, the Ministry of the Children, were forced to flee Williamsburg in Virginia, to escape charges that they had dug holes in the churchyard of Bruton parish looking for a vault containing papers by Bacon which were believed to hold his plans for a Utopian society.[47] Even the chicken that allegedly caused Bacon's death has been spotted – in its ghostly form – at Highgate.[48]

In fact, the reasons for the body's permanent disappearance were quite mundane. Grimston's destruction of Bacon's legacy reached a controversial peak in 1681, as John Aubrey noted: 'This October, 1681, it rang over all St. Albans that Sir Harbottle Grimston, Master of the Rolls, had removed the coffin of this most renowned Lord Chancellor to make room for his own to lie in the vault there at St. Michael's Church.'[49]

★

The real legacy of Francis Bacon did not lie in land or property, and its route to posterity did not lie through his blood lineage. Just as he had created the construct of the *quinquennium* in exile to place his works in a context, so Bacon reworked his idea of friendship to make it the basis for his future reputation. Tobie Matthew had importuned him to revise his essay on friendship, to make it about their own relationship. 'For the essay of friendship,' Bacon replied in June 1623, 'while I took your speech of it for a cursory request I took my promise for a compliment. But since you call for it I shall perform it.'[50] In fulfilling his promise to Matthew, Bacon stumbled on a way of preserving himself for posterity.

In his revision, Bacon trotted out the old warhorse 'that a friend is another himself', a cliché from Aristotle, Plutarch, Diogenes Laertius and Cicero. But he introduced the cliché in order to go further, to state 'that a friend is far more than himself'. He argued that 'the best way, to represent to life the manifold of friendship, is to cast and see, how many things there are, which a man cannot do himself' – particularly those things which are beyond him temporally.

Men have their time, and die many times in desire of some things, which they principally take to heart; the bestowing of a child, the finishing of a work, or the like. If a man have a true friend, he may rest almost secure, that the care of those things, will continue after him. So that a man hath as it were two lives in his desires. A man hath a body, and that body is confined to a place; but where friendship is, all offices of life, are as it were granted to him, and his deputy. For he may exercise them by his friend.[51]

Both Francis Bacon and his brother Anthony had constructed their lives around intricate networks of friendship and service. At the end of his life, in the absence of lineal heirs Francis turned to his friends and servants for continuity and posterity.

He was, in any case, by this time in real need of friends to care for him. From 1621 onwards, the limitations of his physical body were increasingly evident and Bacon was able to do less and less for himself. Buckingham had performed the usual offices of friendship, as Essex had done before him; but, as his health failed, Bacon needed friends who could do things, say things, go places that were beyond him – friends, indeed, who could continue to act for him, *as* him, once his body had given up the fight altogether. It was not Buckingham whom Bacon identified in his letters as 'another himself' – such a move would have been far too presumptuous. It was a man who was emphatically not himself: the recusant Tobie Matthew, whose activities, despite apparent official sanction, were still viewed by commentators and gossips with deep suspicion.

Matthew represented to Bacon the friend who was not of immediate use in the old, tired bids for patronage: despite his use to the crown, Matthew was not a powerful court personality. But he stood for connections across religious divides, for connections across national boundaries, and – being considerably younger than Bacon – for connections beyond Bacon's own life.

During his *quinquennium* Bacon had made detailed provisions for the handling of his written 'works and writings', which he described as 'that durable part of my memory'. His brother-in-law Sir John Constable and 'my very good friend Mr. Bosvile' [William Boswell] were requested

> to take care that of all my writings, both of English and of Latin, there may be books fair bound, and placed in the King's library, and in the library of the University of Cambridge, and in the library of Trinity College, where myself was bred, and in the library of Bene't College [Corpus Christi, Cambridge], where my father was bred, and in the library of the University of Oxford, and in the library of my Lord of Canterbury, and in the library of Eton.
>
> Also, I desire my executors, especially my brother Constable, and also Mr. Bosvile, presently after my decease, to take into their hands all my papers whatsoever, which are either in cabinets, boxes, or presses, and them to seal up until they may at their leisure peruse them.[52]

Among the bequests were two lectureships, about which Bacon corresponded with John Williams, now Lord Bishop of Lincoln. Once again he turned to his favourite classical icons. 'I find that the ancients (as Cicero, Demosthenes, Plinius Secundus, and others), have preserved both their orations and their epistles. In imitation of whom I have done the like to my own; which nevertheless I will not publish while I live. But I have been bold to bequeath them.' Bacon bequeathed his speeches and letters to Williams, and to Sir Humphrey May, Chancellor of the Duchy: 'My speeches (perhaps) you will think fit to publish.' As for the lectureships, he made arrangements for 'two lectures in perpetuity', one in Cambridge and one in Oxford, each with a £200 per annum endowment. They were designed 'for Natural Philosophy, and the sciences thereupon depending'.[53] Williams pointed out that since 'one Sidley of Kent' had already founded a similar lectureship in Oxford, this might not be the best plan. 'The universities are the two eyes of this land, and fittest to contemplate the lustre of this bounty: these two lectures are as the two apples of these eyes. An apple when it is single is an ornament, when double a pearl or a blemish in the eye ... But if Oxford in this kind be an Argus, I am sure poor Cambridge is a right Polyphemus; it hath but one eye, and that not so steadily or artificially placed; but *bonum est facile sui diffusivum* [good may easily be disseminated by its own means]: your Lordship being so full of goodness, will quickly find an object to pour it on.'[54]

It was Rawley who continued the campaign to establish Bacon's intellectual reputation. In the months following his master's death, he compiled and published a commemorative volume in his honour: *Memoriae honoratissimi Domini Francisci, Baronis de Veralumio, vice-comitis Sancti Albani sacrum*, usually known as the *Manes Verulami*.[55] This volume contained thirty-two Latin poems in praise of Bacon, the majority emanating from the universities (above all, from Cambridge): although many are anonymous, those authors that are identified include T. Vincent, I. Vincent, Thomas Rhodes, William Lee, James Duport, Henry Ferne, G. Nash, Henry Ockley, Thomas Randolph, Bacon's executor William Boswell, his household servant William Atkins, the poet George Herbert and the Middle Templar Robert Ashley. It was Rawley, too, who published the *Sylva sylvarum* in 1626, *Certaine Miscellany Works* (1629), *Operum moralium et civilium tomus* (1638), *Resuscitatio* (1657) and *Opuscula varia posthuma* (1658); who provided prefaces to *Sylva sylvarum* and *New Atlantis*, translated the *History of Life and Death* and wrote the *Life* of Bacon prefixed to the *Resuscitatio*.

When Rawley collected together four short pieces under the general title *Certaine Miscellany Works*, he confessed to the reader that he had 'thought good, as a servant, to the Labours, and Memory, of that Noble Lord, the Lord Viscount St. Alban' to gather and publish these works,

'First, to vindicate the Wrong, his Lordship suffered, by a corrupt, and surreptitious Edition, of that Discourse of his, Touching a War with Spain, lately set forth. Secondly, by way of Prevention, to exempt, from the like Injury, and Defacements, those other Discourses of his, herein contained.' While Rawley is referring to printers' piracy, the language – 'vindicate', 'Wrong', 'suffered', 'corrupt', 'surreptitious', 'exempt', 'Injury', 'Deface-ments' – is irresistibly resonant of Bacon's fall, and the need to rehabilitate his reputation.

Rawley was best employed for the task: 'Having been employed, as an amanuensis, or daily instrument, to this honourable author; and acquainted with his lordship's conceits, in the composing, of his works, for many years together; especially, in his writing time; I conceived, that no man, could pretend a better interest, or claim, to the ordering of them, after his death, than myself.'[56] Acknowledging that Bacon had intended some works to be preserved only, not published, Rawley argued that he was 'tied' to publish them. 'Through the loose keeping, of his lordship's papers, whilst he lived, divers surreptitious copies have been taken; which have since, employed the press, with sundry corrupt, and mangled, editions; whereby nothing hath been more difficult, than to find the Lord Saint Alban, in the Lord Saint Alban; And which have presented, (some of them) rather a fardle of non-sense, then any true expressions, of his lordship's happy vein.'[57] Rawley was therefore 'in a sort, tied, to vindicate these injuries, and wrongs, done to the monuments, of his lordship's pen; and at once, by setting forth, the true, and genuine, writings themselves, to prevent the like invasions, for the time to come'.[58]

Rawley also promulgated the identifications made by Bacon during his *quinquennium*. When ordering some occasional works of Bacon in his *Resuscitatio*, he 'ranked the several tractates ... according to the dignity, of the work; as Demosthenes, or Cicero's, orations, do precede Demosthenes, or Cicero's epistles'. He also took the liberty of including in Bacon's letters 'some few, which were written, by other pens, and not by his lordship's own: like as we find, in the epistolar authors; Cicero, Plinius secundus, and the rest'.[59]

Rawley's own contribution to the Bacon intellectual legacy should not be underestimated. He was responsible, for example, for putting *In felicem memoriae Reginae Elizabethae* into English: 'not, ad verbum; for that had been but flat, and injudicious; But, (as far, as my slender ability could reach,) according to the expressions, which, I conceived, his lordship would have rendered it in, if he had written the same in English: yet ever acknowl-edging, that Zeuxis, or Apelles' pencil, could not be attained, but by Zeuxis, or Apelles, himself.'[60]

Previous, unauthorised publications had come with 'scars and blemishes upon their faces'. Rawley continued, in a telling metaphor: 'they could pass, but for a spurious, and adulterine brood, and not for his lordship's legitimate issue: and the publishers, and printers, of them, deserve to have an action, of defamation, brought against them, by the state of learning, for disgracing, and personating, his lordship's works.' Rawley's collection, however, could 'verify itself, in the several parcels thereof; and manifest, to all understanding, and unpartial, readers, who is the author of it; by that spirit, of perspicuity, and aptness, and conciseness, which runs through the whole work; and is ever an annex, of his lordship's pen'. It was to this self-verifying Bacon that Rawley added his influential biography of Bacon ('wherein I have . . . endeavoured, to contribute, not my talent, but my mite, in the next following discourse; though, to give the true value, to his lordship's worth; there were more need, of another Homer, to be the trumpet, of Achilles' virtues').[61]

Servants as well as friends sustained the Bacon legacy. Thomas Bushell recalled how Bacon accepted him into his service as a fifteen-year-old boy, clearing his debts on three separate occasions to the tune of £3,000 and arranging his marriage to a rich heiress. As the marriage negotiations went ahead, he not only provided Bushell with £400 per annum,

> but to balance the consent of her father in the match, promised upon his honour to make me the heir of his knowledge in mineral philosophy, saying That if those real expressions of his love could not but find the due retaliation of my gratitude, he might then assure himself of the hoped harvest of two lives in one; inferring, that although fathers are bound to provide for their children, and worse than infidels if they do not, yet there is no such injunction upon masters, in relation to their servants; and therefore where a master's pious bounty transcends a father's natural love, there that so obliged servant must appear most prodigiously ingrateful, which shall not with much zeal and faithfulness, discharge the duty of a surviving trust.

He would use Bushell, 'my intended instrument, in the prosecution of my mineral designs, as politic princes do their nearest servants in their Cabinet-Counsels'. If they put their masters' 'conceptions into act' successfully, they own nothing more of them than 'the approbation, and the admiration of their prince's wisdom therein'; if the designs fail, 'they must sadly acknowledge the matter wholly their own; an error in their counsels, and a crime in themselves'. Therefore, he told Bushell, 'if by my theory you prosper in your practick, [you] must attribute all the honour of the whole work to me; if otherwise you must gratefully preserve my reputation, by acknowledging your own misfortune, by mistaking and misacting my directions, and so you shall be sure to gain the title and character of a grateful servant in either event.'[62]

The respective fates of Thomas Bushell and William Rawley tell us much about the legacy of Francis Bacon. Bushell was a practising mineralogist. The story of his own life is one of failure in his specialist field, and ultimately of near-insanity. Here he vividly captures the relationship between his *ad hoc* metallurgical projects ('my mineral designs') and his master's grand scientific theory. If the faithful servant's projects succeed and bear fruit, they stand as lasting testimony to the master, preserving his fame for posterity. If they fail, the blame is Bushell's alone. In other words, deprived of lineal descendants or lasting institutional monuments (because of his debts, even the university lectureships he intended to fund were never established), Bacon entrusted his reputation to his close friends and devoted servants. The scientific practitioner Bushell ultimately failed him, unlike the successful chaplain Rawley, the conscientious and pious assembler of his written memorials. Although Bushell continued assiduously to promote his old master's reputation, his own failure in smelting and refining metals (his mineral designs) meant that subsequent generations refused to take his careful assessment seriously. His Francis Bacon – the man who generously, even prodigally handed on his mineral trial secrets to his servants – is unrecognisable behind Rawley's Francis Bacon – the man who carefully arranged for the posthumous publication of his papers, and the rehabilitation of his reputation.

★

At the end of his life, Bacon himself imagined that with the help of those closest to him he could draw a veil over the frequently unsavoury career through which he had struggled in the full glare of court and parliamentary scrutiny, under two difficult monarchs. He believed that he could reinvent himself for future generations as the contemplative sage he might have been, leaving his works as his lasting legacy. He was entirely mistaken. The scandals could not be laid to rest. And the efforts his friends made to erase past dishonour as he had instructed muddied the waters of the 'Life' still further. Even without wife and children, he had left too many hostages to fortune.

Notes

The following abbreviations are used in the notes. For works other than those listed under 'Frequently cited sources', full details are given on the first citation in each chapter, with a shortened form used for subsequent citations.

PERSONAL ABBREVIATIONS

AB	Anthony Bacon	JC	John Chamberlain
ACB	Anne (Cooke) Bacon	LC	Lionel Cranfield
AP	Amias Paulet	NaB	Nathaniel Bacon
AS	Anthony Standen	NB	Nicholas Bacon (d. 1579)
DC	Dudley Carleton	NB2	Nicholas Bacon, the younger
EB	Edward Bacon	NF	Nicholas Faunt
EC	Edward Coke	RC	Robert Cecil
EH	Edward Hoby	RS	Robert Sidney
ES	Edward Sherburn	RW	Rowland Whyte
FB	Francis Bacon	TM	Tobie Matthew
FW	Francis Walsingham	TP	Thomas Phelippes
GV	George Villiers, later duke of	TPH	Thomas Posthumous Hoby
	Buckingham	WC	William Cecil, Lord Burghley

FREQUENTLY CITED SOURCES

Add. MS	Additional manuscript
APC	*Acts of the Privy Council of England*
Beal	Peter Beal, *Index of English Literary Manuscripts*, 2 vols (London: Mansell, 1980)
BL	British Library
Bodl.	Bodleian Library, Oxford
CJ	*Journal of the House of Commons*
CLSP	*Calendar of Letters and State Papers*
CPR	*Calendar of Patent Rolls*
CSP	*Calendar of State Papers*
CSPD	*Calendar of State Papers, Domestic Series*
CSPF	*Calendar of State Papers, Foreign Series*
CUL	Cambridge University Library

Devereux	Walter Bourchier Devereux, ed., *Lives and Letters of the Devereux, Earls of Essex*, 2 vols (London: John Murray, 1875)
DNB	*Dictionary of National Biography*, 63 vols (London: Smith, Elder & Co., 1885–1900)
FBL	Francis Bacon Library, Henry E. Huntington Library
FSL	Folger Shakespeare Library, Washington DC
GIPB	*Gray's Inn Pension Book*
HEH	Henry E. Huntington Library, San Marino
HMC	Historical Manuscripts Commission
HMC Hastings	*Historical Manuscripts Commission, Hastings papers*
HMCS	*Historical Manuscripts Commission, Salisbury papers*
HPT	*The House of Commons 1558–1603*, ed. P. W. Hasler, 3 vols (London: History of Parliament Trust, 1981)
L&A	*List and Analysis of State Papers, Foreign Series*
LJ	*Journal of the House of Lords*
LL	Francis Bacon, *Letters and Life*, 7 vols, ed. James Spedding (London: Longman, Green, Longman and Roberts, 1861–74)
LPL	Lambeth Palace Library
McClure	*The Letters of John Chamberlain*, 2 vols, ed. Norman Egbert McClure (Philadelphia: American Philosophical Society, 1939)
Ogle	*Copy-book of Sir Amyas Poulet's Letters, Written during his Embassy to France (AD 1577). From a MS in the Bodleian Library*, ed. Octavius Ogle (London: Roxburghe Club, 1866)
PRO	Public Record Office, London
Resuscitatio	*Resuscitatio, Or, Bringing into Publick Light Severall Pieces, of the Works, Civil, Historical, Philosophical, & Theological, Hitherto Sleeping, of the Right Honourable Francis Bacon Baron of Verulam, Viscount Saint Alban . . . Together, with his Lordships Life*, ed. William Rawley (London: William Lee, 1657)
SP	State Papers
Stiffkey	*The Papers of Nathaniel Bacon of Stiffkey*, 3 vols, ed. A. Hassell Smith, Gillian M. Baker and R.W. Kenny (Norwich: Norfolk Record Society, 1979–90)
TLS	*Times Literary Supplement*
VCH	*Victoria History of the Counties of England*
Works	Francis Bacon, *Works*, 7 vols, ed. James Spedding, Robert Leslie Ellis and Douglas Denon Heath (London: Longman et al., 1857–9)

INTRODUCTION

1 AS to AB, 3 February 1594, LPL MS 650, fo. 80^{r-v}.

2 *Advancement of Learning, Works* 3: 454.

3 ACB to AB, 24 January 1594, LPL MS 650, fo. 37.

4 FB to Henry Howard, 3 December 1599, *HMCS* 9: 405–6; *LL* 2: 161–2.

5 Howard to FB, [December 1599], *HMCS* 9: 406–7. For Howard see Linda Levy Peck, *Northampton: Patronage and Policy at the Court of James I* (London: Allen & Unwin, 1982), 13.

6 Thomas Bushell, *Mr Bushell's Abridgment of the Lord Chancellor Bacon's Philosophical Theory in Mineral Prosecutions* (London, 1659), A^r.

7 Peck, *Northampton*, 18.

8 Peck, *Northampton*, 17.

9 See Alan Stewart, *Close Readers: Humanism and Sodomy in Early Modern England* (Princeton, NJ: Princeton University Press, 1997), ch. 4.

10 FB to WC, [*c.*1592], *Resuscitatio* 95; *LL* 1: 109.

11 *Advancement of Learning*, *Works* 3: 468–9.

12 See, most recently, Nieves Mathews, *Francis Bacon: The History of a Character Assassination* (New Haven: Yale University Press, 1996).

13 FB's last will, 19 December 1625, *Opera Omnia*, ed. John Blackbourne, 4 vols (London: R. Gosling, 1730), 2: 559; *LL* 7: 539.

CHAPTER 1

1 'Of Fortune', *Essays*, *Works* 6: 472.

2 The standard accounts of Sir Nicholas Bacon are Alan Simpson, *The Wealth of the Gentry 1540–1660: East Anglian Studies* (Chicago and Cambridge: University of Chicago Press and Cambridge University Press, 1961) and Robert Tittler, *Nicholas Bacon: The Making of a Tudor Statesman* (London: Jonathan Cape, 1976). See also John Payne Collier, 'On Sir Nicholas Bacon, Lord Keeper, with Extracts from Some of his Unprinted Papers and Speeches', *Archaeologia* 36 (1859), 339–48; Gladys Scott Thomson, 'Three Suffolk Figures: Thomas Wolsey; Stephen Gardiner; Nicholas Bacon: A Study in Social History', *Proceedings of the Suffolk Institute of Archaeology and Natural History* 25 (1952), 158–63; Ernest R. Sandeen, 'Correspondence of Nicholas Bacon, Lord Keeper' (MA, University of Chicago, 1955); *Sir Nicholas Bacon's Great House Sententiae*, ed. Elizabeth McCutcheon, *English Literary Renaissance Supplements* 3 (Amherst, MA: ELR, 1977); Patrick Collinson, 'Sir Nicholas Bacon and the Elizabethan *via media*', *Historical Journal* 23 (1980), 255–73, repr. in his *Godly People: Essays on English Protestantism and Puritanism* (London: Hambledon Press, 1983), 135–54.

3 'A Book of Pedigrees of the Gentry of Suffolk entitled Drury', BL Add. MS 5523, fo. 98, quoted in Simpson, *Wealth of the Gentry*, 28 n. 3.

4 Hugh Kearney, *Scholars and Gentlemen: Universities and Society in Pre-Industrial Britain 1500–1700* (London: Faber, 1970), 27.

5 George Puttenham, *The Arte of English Poesie* (London: Richard Field, 1589), R^r.

6 Thomas Nashe, *Pierce Penilesse his Supplication to the Diuell* (London: Richard Jones, 1592), D3^v.

7 Ben Jonson, *Timber*, in *Works*, 11 vols, ed. C. H. Herford, Percy Simpson and Evelyn Simpson (Oxford: Clarendon Press, 1925–52), 8: 591.

8 Leonard Digges, *A Geometrical Practise, named Pantometria*, ed. Thomas Digges (London: Henry Bynneman, 1571), dedicatory letter to NB.

9 Thomas Fuller, *The History of the Worthies of England*, 3 vols, ed. P. Austin Nuttall (London: Thomas Tegg, 1840), 1: 509.

10 On the Cooke family see Stephen J. Barns, 'The Cookes of Gidea Hall', *The Essex Review* 21 (1912), 1–9; A. L. Rowse, 'Bisham and the Hobys', in *Times, Persons, Places: Essays in Literature* (London: Macmillan, 1965), 188–218; Marjorie Keniston McIntosh, 'The Cooke Family of Gidea Hall, Essex, 1460–1661' (PhD, Harvard University, 1967) and 'Sir Anthony Cooke: Tudor Humanist, Educator, and Religious Reformer', *Proceedings of the American Philological Society* 119 (1975), 233–50. A full-length study of Anne Cooke Bacon is still needed. The standard accounts are: *DNB* 2: 323–24; Mary Bradford Whiting, 'The Learned and Virtuous Lady Bacon', *The Hibbert Journal* 29 (1930–1), 270–83; M. St Clare Byrne, 'The Mother of Francis Bacon', *Blackwood's Magazine* 234 (1934), 758–71; Ruth Hughey, 'Lady Anne Bacon's Translations', *Review of English Studies* 10 (1934), 211; Tittler, *Nicholas Bacon*; Mary Ellen Lamb, 'The Cooke Sisters: Attitudes toward Learned Women in the Renaissance', in Margaret P. Hannay, ed., *Silent but for the Word: Tudor Women as Patrons, Translators, and Writers of Religious Works* (Kent, OH: 1985), 107–25; Elaine V. Beilin, *Redeeming Eve: Women Writers of the English Renaissance* (Princeton, NJ: Princeton University Press, 1987), 55–61; Louise Schleiner, *Tudor and Stuart Women Writers* (Bloomington, IN: Indiana University Press), 30–51.

11 John Strype, *Annals of the Reformation and Establishment of Religion . . . in the Church of England*, 4 vols (Oxford: Clarendon Press, 1874), 4: 485–9 at 489.

12 Count de Feria to Philip II, 29 December 1558, *CLSP . . . Simancas, 1558–1567*, 18. He also described Mildred as 'a much more furious heretic than her husband' (ibid., 580).

13 S. T. Bindoff, ed., *The House of Commons 1509–1558*, 3 vols (London: History of Parliament Trust, 1982), 3: 223–4; James Brabazon, fifth earl of Verulam, *The Bacon Family: Its Links with Gorhambury, St Michael's, and St Albans 1560–1880* (St Albans: St Albans City Council, 1961), 5.

14 John Aubrey, *Aubrey's Brief Lives*, ed. Oliver Lawson Dick (London: Secker & Warburg, 1960), 15; see also the discussion in Frances Yates, *The Art of Memory* (Chicago: University of Chicago Press, 1966), 370.

15 See Simpson, *Wealth of the Gentry*.

16 Ibid., 91–3.

17 On Nathaniel Bacon see *Stiffkey*.

18 Tittler, *Nicholas Bacon*, 57 and n. 3.

19 Simpson, *Wealth of the Gentry*, 96–102.

20 Thomas Twyne, *The Garlande of Godly Flowers* (London: William How, 1575?), ¶iijr.

21 Bernardino Ochino, tr. Anne Cooke, *Fouretene Sermons . . . Concernyng the Predestinacion and Eleccion of God* (London: John Day, 1550) and *Sermons . . . (to the number of 25) Concerning the Predestination and Election of God* (London: John Day, 1570); John Jewel, tr. Anne Cooke Bacon, *An Apologie or Answere in Defence of the Churche of Englande* (London: Reginald Wolfe, 1563).

22 Tittler, *Nicholas Bacon*, 212–13 nn. 22 and 23. See also William Urwick, *Nonconformity in Herts* (London: Hazell, Watson & Viney, 1884).

23 See *Correspondence of Matthew Parker*, ed. John Bruce and Thomas T. Perowne (Cambridge: Parker Society, 1853), 309–16.

24 Dedicatory verses by the Cooke sisters were appended to a manuscript copy of Bartholo Sylva of Turin's *Giardino cosmografico coltivato* (CUL MS Ii.5.37): they are discussed by Schleiner, *Tudor and Stuart Women Writers*, 39–42.

25 John Walsall, 'Epistle Dedicatorie' to *A Sermon Preached at Pauls Crosse . . . 5 October 1587* (London: George Byshop, 1578), Avi^{r–v}. See also Virgil B. Heltzel, 'Young Francis Bacon's Tutor', *Modern Language Notes* 63 (1948), 483–5; and correspondence by R. L. Eagle, S. G. Thomas and Owen Williams in *TLS*, 23 November 1946 (577), 25 January 1947 (51) and 8 February 1947 (79).

26 NaB to Anthony Stringer, n.d. [1569<>72], *Stiffkey* 1: 11.

27 NaB to Lady Anne Gresham, n.d. [1569<>72], *Stiffkey* 1: 12.

28 NaB to ACB, *c*.1572, *Stiffkey* 1: 23.

29 Anne Gresham Bacon to ACB, *c*.1572, *Stiffkey* 1: 24.

30 NaB to Lady Anne Gresham, n.d. [1569<>72], *Stiffkey* 1: 12.

31 See ACB to NaB, 6 August 1573, *Stiffkey* 1: 81–2.

32 EB to NaB, August 1575, *Stiffkey* 1: 173–4.

33 S. R. Maitland, ed., 'Archbishop Whitgift's College Pupils', *The British Magazine* 32 (1847), 361–79, 508–28, 650–6 and 33 (1848), 17–31, 185–97, 445–63. See also Lisa Jardine, *Francis Bacon: Discovery and the Art of Discourse* (Cambridge: Cambridge University Press, 1974).

34 Sir George Paul, quoted in Maitland, 'Whitgift's College Pupils', 32 (1847), 361–2.

35 Rawley, 'Life of Bacon', *Works* 1: 4.

36 This may have been one of the two sons of Sir Nicholas' sister Barbara, who married a Sharpe; Wood argues that it was fellow Trinity Member Nicholas Sharpe, who proceeded MA at this commencement in 1574, after spending eight years at the College. See E. R. Wood, 'Francis Bacon's "Cousin Sharpe"', *Notes and Queries* 196 (1951), 248–9.

37 FB to NB2, 3 July 1574. Fitzwilliam Museum, Cambridge, General Series. By permission of the Syndics of the Fitzwilliam Museum to whom rights in this publication are assigned.

38 Simpson, *Wealth of the Gentry*, 24.

CHAPTER 2

1 WC to Sir Nicholas Throckmorton, 8 May 1561, PRO SP 12/70/26, quoted in Conyers Read, *Mr. Secretary Cecil and Queen Elizabeth* (London: Jonathan Cape, 1955), 212. For Renaissance diplomacy generally see Garrett Mattingly, *Renaissance Diplomacy* (London: Jonathan Cape, 1955); Keith Hamilton and Richard Langhorne, *The Practice of Diplomacy: Its Evolution, Theory and Administration* (London: Routledge, 1995), ch. 2.

2 Languet to Sidney, 4 May 1579 and 24 September 1579, *The Correspondence of Philip Sidney and Hubert Languet*, ed. William Aspenwall Bradley (Boston: Merrymount Press, 1912), 178–82.

3 Lawrence Stone, *The Crisis of the Aristocracy 1558–1641* (Oxford: Clarendon Press, 1965), 701.

4 Valentine Dale to WC, 17 April 1576, *CSPF, 1575–1577*, 313. On the embassy see Bodl. Rawlinson MS A.331 (printed as Ogle) and Rawlinson MS vi.C.12 (not printed); F. J. Weaver, 'Anglo-French Diplomatic Relations 1558–1602 (part 3)', *Bulletin of the Institute of Historical Research* 6 (1928–9), 1–9; Gary M. Bell, *A Handlist of British Diplomatic Representatives, 1509–1688* (London: Royal Historical Society, 1990), 132.

5 On Paulet see *DNB*; *HPT*; A. C. Sarre, 'The Poulet Family: Governors etc. in Jersey 1550–1600', *Société Jersiaise Annual Bulletin* 17 (1958), 141–9; Ogle; *The Letter-Books of Sir Amias Poulet, Keeper of Mary Queen of Scots*, ed. John Morris (London: Burnes & Oates, 1874).

6 Bernardino de Mendoza to Philip II, 28 December 1579, *CLSP . . . Simancas, 1568–1579*, 709–10.

7 AP to Sir Thomas Leighton, 20 April 1578, printed in Sarre, 'The Poulet Family', 145.

8 Thomas Morgan to Mary Queen of Scots, 9 April 1585, *A Collection of State Papers Relating to Affairs in the Reign of Queen Elizabeth, from the Year 1571 to 1595*, ed. William Murdin (London: William Bowyer, 1759), 443–4. List by David Jones of London papists, October? 1578, PRO SP 15/25/118 (*CSPD, Addenda, 1566–1579*, 551).

9 J. H. M. Salmon, *Society in Crisis: France in the Sixteenth Century* (London: Ernest Benn, 1979), 199–200.

10 Jean Hotman, *The Ambassador* (London: James Shawe, 1603), B5[r-v].

11 WC to AP, quoted in Bryan Bevan, *The Real Francis Bacon* (London: Centaur Press, 1960), 36–7.

12 Patent, 30 June 1576, *CPR Elizabeth I*, vol. 7: *1575–1578*, no. 40, p. 6; Roderick Eagle, 'Bacon's Licence to Travel beyond the Seas: Letters Patent at the Record Office', *Notes and Queries* 195 (1950), 334.

13 EB to NaB, 13 August [1576], *Stiffkey* 1: 202–3.

14 FB to RC, January 1595, LPL MS 650, art. 31; *LL* 1: 350. FB to Essex, [January 1595], *Resuscitatio* 88; *LL* 1: 351.

15 AP to FW, 12 October 1576, *CSPF, 1575–1577*, 395–6.

16 Privy Council to AP, and Privy Council to George Biston, 26 August 1576, *APC, 1575–1577*, 194, 195.

17 AP to WC, 8 September 1576, *HMCS* 2: 140.

18 Patents, 1 October 1576 and 26 March 1577, *CPR Elizabeth I*, vol. 7:*1575–1578*, nos 638 and 1993, pp. 97 and 263.

19 Nicholas Gorges to FW, 17 September 1576, PRO SP 12/109/7; *CSPD, 1547–1580*, 528.

20 Hotman, *Ambassador*, B8[v], C7[r-v].

21 For the date see Burghley's diary, *HMCS* 2: 291; AP to WC, n.d., quoted in Bevan, *The Real Francis Bacon*, 37.

22 AP to FW, 12 October 1576, *CSPF, 1575–1577*, 395–6.

23 AP to John Peter, 8 September 1576, PRO E. 407/73.

24 AP to WC, 25 September 1576, *CSPD, Addenda, 1566–1579*, 504.

25 Instructions to AP, 1576, CUL MS Gg.h.36.

26 For copies see e.g. BL Cotton MS Caligula E.vii, fos 13–49; BL Sloane MS 2442, fos 59b–60; BL Harley MS 36, fo. 259; BL Lansdowne MS 155, fos 169–71; BL

Egerton MS 2790, fo. 207; *CSPF, 1575–1577*, 385–7; HMC, *Second Report of the Royal Commission on Historical Manuscripts* (London: HMSO, 1871), 97.

27 Hotman, *Ambassador*, G3[r], F8[r]–G[r]. On Walsingham, see Conyers Read, *Mr Secretary Walsingham and the Policy of Queen Elizabeth*, 3 vols (Cambridge, MA: Harvard University Press, 1925); for his intelligence network see Alan Haynes, *Invisible Power: The Elizabethan Secret Service 1570–1603* (Far Thrupp, Glos.: Alan Sutton, 1992); Alison Plowden, *The Elizabethan Secret Service* (Hemel Hempstead: Harvester Wheatsheaf, 1991).

28 AP to FW, 12 October 1576, *CSPF, 1575–1577*, 395–6.

29 Hotman, *Ambassador*, D 4[r–v].

30 Bodl. Add. MS C.82, fos 22a–29b, 36a–47b.

31 AP to FW, 22 November 1579, PRO SP 78/3/52; *CSPF, 1579–1581*, 96.

32 See e.g. Ogle 47, 60, 61–2, 123–4.

33 AP to FW, 24 September 1577, ? August 1577, n.d., 1 September, Ogle 124, 91, 50–1, 107.

34 Hotman, *Ambassador*, C7[r–v].

35 'Of Dispatch', *Essays* (1612), *Works* 6: 556. For the identification of AP with the 'wise man', see Thomas Bayly, *Witty Apophthegms delivered Severall Times, and upon Severall Occasions, by King James, King Charles, the Marquis of Worcester, Francis Lord Bacon, and Sir Thomas Moore. Collected and Revised* (London: Edward Farnham, 1658), 111 (Apophthegm no. 46): 'Sir Amice Pawlet when he saw too much hast made in any matter, was wont to say, Stay a while, that we may make an end the sooner.'

36 AP to Edward Dyer, 25 December 1577, Ogle 246; AP to Leicester, 10 January 1578, 19 July, 28 July, 24 August 1577; AP to FW, 19 November and 25 December 1577: Ogle 261, 66, 76, 102, 200–1, 242.

37 AP to Sir George Speake, [26 May 1577], Ogle 16.

38 Thomas Bodley, *The Life of Sir Thomas Bodley, the Honourable Founder of the Publique Library in the University of Oxford* (Oxford: Henry Hall, 1647), B[v]; *HPT* 1: 453–4.

39 Thomas Bodley to FB, n.d., Bodley, *Reliquiae Bodleianae: or some Genuine Remains of Sir Thomas Bodley* (London: John Hartley, 1703), 364–9. The authorship of this letter is fiercely debated. This letter was first published as from Bodley to Bacon in Richard Parr, *The Life of the Most Reverend Father in God, James Usher* (London: Nathaniel Ranew, 1686). It had been previously published as from Fulke Greville to his nephew Greville Verney, in Fulke Greville, Lord Brooke, *Certaine Learned and Elegant Workes* (London: Henry Seyle, 1633), sig. RI 4[r]: this attribution was, however, disputed at the time – see John Verney to Sir John Coke, 21 November 1632, HMC, *The Manuscripts of the Earl Cowper, Preserved at Melbourne Hall, Derbyshire*, 3 vols (London: HMSO, 1888–9), 483–4 – and is now thought erroneous. Portions of the letter also appear in a manuscript owned by Bacon, and were tentatively claimed as Bacon's work by Spedding (*LL* 2: 4, 16–19). Peter Beal concludes that the letter is 'not an original composition of Greville's but is one version of a "formula" letter perhaps originated by Bodley, and also used by Bacon or [the earl of] Essex' (Beal 1: 2: 103; for MS witnesses see Beal, GrF 16–23). We contend that this confusion (of multiple potential authors) points to the widespread nature of this kind of intelligence-gathering among young men of

Bacon's rank. For the most recent discussion see Brian Vickers, 'The Authenticity of Bacon's Earliest Writings', *Studies in Philology* 94 (1997), 248–96.

40 AP to FW, 8 December 1576, *CSPF, 1575–1577*, 441–2.

41 AP to WC, 15 November 1576, *CSPF, 1575–1577*, 420.

42 Hieronimo Lippomano to Signory of Venice, 11 July 1577, *CSP . . . Venice*, 557.

43 AP to FW, 26 May 1577, Ogle 8. See also AP to Elizabeth, 7 May 1577, Ogle 7.

44 AP to Elizabeth, 25 March 1578, BL Harley MS 1582, fo. 34a.

45 *Historia vitae et mortis, Works* 5: 319, tr. of 2: 211. Le Doeuff argues that the terms 'ingeniossimo' and 'in virum eminentissimum' suggest someone of the stature of Sully, who may well have been in Poitiers in 1577. See *La Nouvelle Atlantide*, tr. Michèle Le Doeuff and Margaret Llasera, ed. Michèle Le Doeuff (Paris: Flammarion, 1995), 168.

46 Frank Lestringant, 'La Jessée, Jean de (1551–1596)', in Jean-Pierre de Beaumarchais, Daniel Couty and Alain Rey, eds, *Dictionnaire des littératures de langue française*, 3 vols (Paris: Bordas, 1994), 2: 1277–8; La Jessée, sonnet to FB, LPL MS 653, fo. 281 (art. 154).

47 AP to Elizabeth, 22 June 1577, Ogle 35.

48 Hotman, *Ambassador*, K3^{r-v}.

49 Hotman, *Ambassador*, D6^r.

50 *Sylva sylvarum, Works* 2: 670.

51 BL Harley MS 215, fo. 2b and passim.

52 On Caesar see *DNB*; also Edmund Lodge, *Life of Sir Julius Caesar, Knt* (London: Robert Wilkinson, 1810); L. M. Hill, *Bench and Bureaucracy: The Public Career of Sir Julius Caesar, 1580–1636* (Cambridge: James Clarke, 1988).

53 AP to FW, ? August 1577, Ogle 89–90.

54 On Throckmorton see A. L. Rowse, *Ralegh and the Throckmortons* (London: Macmillan, 1962).

55 On Hilliard see Erna Auerbach, *Nicholas Hilliard* (London: Routledge & Kegan Paul, 1962); Mary Edmond, *Hilliard and Oliver: The Lives and Works of Two Great Miniaturists* (London: Robert Hale, 1983).

56 AP to FW, 19 February 1578, PRO SP 78/2 fo. 34, *CSPF, 1577–1578*, 507–8.

57 AP to Hertford, 16 June 1578, Bodl. Add. MS C.82, fo. 136; quoted in Edmond, *Hilliard and Oliver*, 65.

58 The miniature passed from the French royal collection via James Edwards to Belvoir Castle, into the hands of the duke of Rutland. Roy Strong, 'Hilliard's Miniature of Francis Bacon Rediscovered and other Minutiae', *Burlington Magazine* 106 (1964), 337.

59 PRO SP 14/99/86; *LL* 6: 330.

60 AP to NB, 30 October 1577, Ogle 165–6.

61 AP to Secretaries, 22 December 1577, Ogle 231.

62 Hotman, *Ambassador*, D5^r.

63 AP to Secretaries, 21 October 1579, quoted in David Baird Smith, 'Jean de Villiers Hotman', *Scottish Historical Review* 14 (1917), 148 n. 3. See also François Hotman to AP, 1 April 1579, François Hotman and Jean Hotman, *Epistolae . . . ex Bibliotheca Jani Gulielmi Meolii* (Amsterdam: apud Georgium Gallet, 1700), 107.

64 On Hotman, see Smith, 'Jean de Villiers Hotman'; Ernest Nys, 'Introduction' to Alberico Gentili, *De legationibus libri tres*, vol. 2, tr. Gordon J. Laing (New York: Oxford University Press, 1924), 11a–37a; Donald R. Kelley, *François Hotman: A Revolutionary's Ordeal* (Princeton, NJ: Princeton University Press, 1973), 274, 280; 'Correspondance inédite de Robert Dudley, comte de Leycester, et de François et Jean Hotman', ed. P. J. Blak, *Archives du Musée Teyler*, 2nd ser., vol. 12, pt 2 (Haarlem: Les héritiers Loosjes, 1911), 90–2.

65 Michèle Le Doeuff, 'Bacon chez les grands au siècle de Louis XIII' in Marta Fattori, ed., *Francis Bacon: terminologia e fortuna nel XVII secolo* (Rome: Ateneo, 1984).

66 FB to Isaac Wake, 1 September 1618, LPL MS 936, art. 96; LL 6: 325 ('not forgetting the knowledge I had when I was young of your good father').

67 AP to Tomson, 24 September 1577, Ogle 128–9.

68 On Thomas Phelippes, see *HPT* 3: 219–20; Haynes, *Invisible Power*.

69 AP to TP, 25 January 1586, *CSP . . . Scotland, 1585–1586*, 201.

70 See Thomas Wilson to FW, 30 June 1578, *CSPF, 1578–1579*, 37. This letter places Phelippes as Walsingham's servant, staying with Paulet in Paris.

71 *De augmentis scientarum*, *Works* 4: 445.

72 AP to NB, 28 July and 24 September 1577, Ogle 77–8, 129–30.

73 Rawley, 'Life of Bacon', *Works* 1: 4.

74 AP to FW, 22 June 1577, Ogle 48.

75 AP to FW, 30 October 1577, Ogle 159; AP to Robert Beale, 10 July 1577, Ogle 59–60; AP to FW, 10 June 1577, Ogle 23–4.

76 FB to AP, n.d., BL Add. MS 33,271, fo. 46b.

77 Ibid.

78 *Sylva sylvarum*, *Works*, 2: 427.

79 AP to NB, 24 January 1578, Bodl. Add. MS C.82, fos 7b–8a.

80 Edward Waterhouse, *Fortescutus Illustratus, or a Commentary On that Nervous Treatise De Laudibus Legum Angliae. Written by Sir John Fortescue* (London: Thomas Dicas, 1633), 539–42; see also Robert Tittler, *Nicholas Bacon: The Making of a Tudor Statesman* (London: Jonathan Cape, 1976), 32.

81 Richard Bancroft to RC, 4 April 1600, *HMCS* 10: 96–7, quoted in Brian P. Levack, *The Civil Lawyers in England 1603–1641: A Political Study* (Oxford: Clarendon Press, 1973), 26. See also Brian P. Levack, 'The English Civilians, 1500–1750', in Wilfred Prest, ed., *Lawyers in Early Modern Europe and America* (London: Croom Helm, 1981), 101–28.

82 Dr David Lewes to Julius Caesar, 18 December 1579, BL Add. MS 11406, fo. 150, quoted in Hill, *Bench and Bureaucracy*, 6–7; 'Of Travel' (1625), *Works* 6: 417; Burghley's household accounts, quoted in Conyers Read, *Lord Burghley and Queen Elizabeth* (London: Jonathan Cape, 1960), 258.

83 See J. H. Baker, *An Introduction to English Legal History*, 3rd edn (London: Butterworths, 1990), 249–50.

84 AP to NB, 23 May 1578, Bodl. Add. MS C.82, fo. 117b.

85 AP to FW, 7 August 1577, Ogle 89–90.

86 EB to ?Bacon, 1 June 1577, *Stiffkey* 2: 10–11; Thomas Cartwright to Theodore Beza, 25 July [1578], *Correspondance de Théodore de Bèze*, vol. 18 (1577), ed. Hippolyte Aubert, Alain Dufour, Béatrice Nicollier and Reinhard Bodenmann (Geneva:

Droz, 1995), 143–5 (referring to EB's stay with Beza the previous year); Jean Sturm to WC, December 1578, *CSPF, 1577–1578*, 355. See also Charles Partridge, 'Edward Bacon', *Notes and Queries* 195 (1950), 459.

87 Hubert Languet to Joachim Camerarius II, 29 March 1578, Hubert Languet, *Epistolae ad Joachimvm Camerarivm Patrem & Filium*, ed. Ludovicus Camerarius (Leipzig and Frankfurt: Mauritius Georgius Weidmann, 1685), 193–5 at 195; EB to NaB, 22 June [1578?], *Stiffkey* 2: 13.

88 Lambert Daneau, *Paratitla in D. Aurelii Augustinii tomos duos* (Geneva: Jac. Stoer, 1578), dedication. Daneau mentioned Edward in a letter to AB, 17 September 1592, BL Add. MS 4110, fo. 64; *Lambert Daneau (de Baugency-sur-Loire), Pasteur et Professeur en Théologie 1530–1595: Sa vie, ses ouvrages, ses lettres inédites*, ed. Paul de Félice (Paris: G. Fischbacher, 1881), 366–7.

89 Innocent Gentillet, *A Discourse upon the Meanes of Wel Governing and Maintaining in Good Peace, a Kingdome, or other Principalitie . . . Against Nicholas Machiavell the Florentine*, tr. Simon Patericke (London: Adam Islip, 1602), ¶iiij^v. See P. D. Stewart, *Innocent Gentillet e la sua polemica antimachiavellica* (Florence: La Nuova Italia Editrice, 1969), 41–6; Antonio d'Andrea, 'Studies on Machiavelli and his Reputation in the Sixteenth Century', *Medieval and Renaissance Studies* 5 (1961), 214–48 and 'The Political and Ideological Context of Innocent Gentillet's Anti-Machiavel', *Renaissance Quarterly* 23 (1970), 397–411; Innocent Gentillet, *Discours contre Machiavel: A New Edition . . .* , ed. A. d'Andrea and P. D. Stewart (Florence: Casalini Libri, 1974); Victoria Kahn, 'Reading Machiavelli: Innocent Gentillet's Discourse on Method', *Political Theory* 22 (1994), 539–60; C. Edward Rathé, 'Innocent Gentillet and the First "Anti-Machiavel"', *Bibliothèque d'humanisme et Renaissance* 27 (1965), 186–225; Irving Ribner, 'The Significance of Gentillet's Contre-Machiavel', *Modern Languages Quarterly* 10 (1949), 153–7.

90 AP to NB, 16 March 1578, Bodl. Add. MS C.82, fo. 52a–b. Pierre Amboise's 1631 statement that 'France, Italy and Spain as the most civilised nations of the whole world were those whither his desire for knowledge took him' is misleading.

91 AP to Horsey, December 1577; AP to Elizabeth, 26 May 1577; AP to Sir John Clifton, [26 May 1577]: Ogle 247, 5–6, 24.

92 On Jacomo, see AP to FW, June 1577, Ogle 46–7. On Dannet see *HPT*; AP to FW, 7 November 1577, Ogle 178–9; AP to Wilson, 9 December 1577, 18 December 1577, Ogle 225–6, 232; AP to FW, 18 December 1577, Ogle 233. On Hugh, see AP to FW, August 1577, Ogle 89–90; AP to FW, 27 July [1577], Ogle 73; AP to FW, 24 August 1577, Ogle 100–1; AP to Leicester, 24 August 1577, Ogle 102; AP to Warwick, 24 August 1577, Ogle 102–3; AP to FW, 1 September 1577, Ogle 106.

93 Hugh was still alive on 6 December 1578: see AP to FW, 6 December 1578, PRO SP 78/2/91. For Hugh's death see Sarre, 'The Poulet Family', 145; AP to FW, 22 January 1579, PRO SP 78/3/3; AP to WC, 29 December 1578, PRO SP 78/2/91; AP to FW, 22 January 1579, 6 February 1579, PRO SP 78/3/3 and 5; Elizabeth to AP, ? January 1579, BL Harley MS 787, fo. 17b.

94 On AP's protracted recall see AP to Secretaries, 20 March 1579, PRO SP 78/3/15; AP to Elizabeth, 4 and 31 July 1579, PRO SP 78/3/25 and 31; AP to Secretaries, 14 August 1579, PRO SP 78/3/33; AP to FW, 26 October 1579, PRO SP 78/3/40; AP to WC, 10 November 1579, PRO SP 78/3/44; Sir Henry

Cobham to WC, 22 November 1579, *HMCS* 2: 274; AP to WC, 22 November 1579, PRO SP 78/3/51; AP to FW, 22 November 1579, PRO SP 78/3/52.
95 Hotman, *Ambassador*, D7ᵛ–D8ʳ.
96 Raphael Holinshed, rev. John Stow et al., *Holinshed's Chronicles of England, Scotland and Ireland*, 6 vols (London: J. Johnson et al., 1807–8), 4: 345; *Apophthegms, Works* 7: 183; *Sylva sylvarum, Works* 2: 666; FW to William Davison, 20 February 1579, *CSPF, 1578–1579*, 424.
97 NF to AB, 8 May 1582, LPL MS 647, fo. 128 (art. 61).
98 AP to Elizabeth, 20 March 1579, PRO SP 78/3/14, *CSPF, 1578–1579*, 461–2.

CHAPTER 3

1 The debate is contained in NB2 to WC, 29 May [1579]; NaB to WC, 1 June 1579; John Baker to NaB, 23 June 1579;WC to NB2, 2 July 1579; NB2 to WC, 9 July 1579; NaB to WC, 13 July 1579; WC to NB2, 15 July 1579; NB2 to WC, 19 July 1579: *Stiffkey* 2: 77–9, 81–2, 85, 93–4, 101–7.
2 James Cleland, *HPΩ-ΠAIΔEIA, Or The Institution of a Young Noble Man* (Oxford: Joseph Barnes, 1607), M4ʳ. For Gray's Inn, see William Ralph Douthwaite, *Gray's Inn: Its History & Associations Compiled from Original and Unpublished Documents* (London: Reeves & Turner, 1886); Cecil Headlam, *The Inns of Court* (London: Adam & Charles Black, 1909); H. E. Duke and Bernard Campion, *The Story of Gray's Inn* (London: Gray's Inn, 1950); Francis Cowper, *A Prospect of Gray's Inn* (London: Stevens & Sons, 1951); D. S. Bland, *A Bibliography of the Inns of Court and Chancery* (London: Selden Society, 1965).
3 John Fortescue, *De laudibus*, quoted in Douthwaite, *Gray's Inn*, 33.
4 Pensions, 27 June 1576, 21 November 1576, 7 November 1576 and 30 January 1577; Gray's Inn, Book of Orders, 1, fos 56ʳ, 59ʳ, 57ᵛ; *GIPB* 26–7, 28. See EB to NB2, 13 August [1576]. *Stiffkey* 1: 203.
5 AB to Roger Wilbraham, 11 January 1581. EUL Laing MS La.iii.193, fo. 108a.
6 AB to NaB, [? mid-February 1578], *Stiffkey* 2: 5. For AB's correspondents, see EUL Laing MS La.iii.193, fos 108a, 115b–116a, 116a.
7 George Whetstone, *A Mirour for Magestrates of Cyties* (London: Richard Jones, 1584), [x]iᵛ – [x]iiʳ.
8 WC to Gray's Inn Masters of the Bench, 25 May 1580, Gray's Inn, Book of Orders, 1, fo. 80ᵛ; *GIPB* 37. For Barker's appointment to utter-barrister, see Pension 21 November 1576, Gray's Inn, Book of Orders, 1, fo. 59ʳ; *GIPB* 27.
9 WC to La Motte Fènelon, December 1579, PRO SP 78/3, fo. 166a–b (art. 67); AB to WC, 14 January 1581, PRO SP 12/247, fo. 13.
10 WC to La Motte Fènelon, December 1579, PRO SP 78/3, fo. 166a–b (art. 67).
11 'The English Protestants in Paris', PRO SP 78/4/63; *CSPF, 1579–1580*, 250–2.
12 *DNB*, D'Oylie, Thomas; FB to [Thomas] Doyly, 11 July 1580, LPL MS 647, fo.14; *LL* 1: 10–11; cf. also BL Add. MS 4109, fo. 122.
13 Thomas Copley to WC, 21 July 1580, PRO SP 12/140/27; *CSPD, 1547–1580*, 666; *Letters of Sir Thomas Copley*, ed. Richard Copley Christie (London: Roxburghe Club, 1897), 123.

14 William Parry, memorandum of loan, 1 August 1580, LPL MS 647, fo. 58ʳ (art. 17); AB to Essex, 1596, LPL MS 659; Thomas Birch, *Memoirs of the Reign of Queen Elizabeth, from the Year 1592 to 1617* (London: A. Millar, 1749), 1: 12; Daphne Du Maurier, *Golden Lads: Anthony Bacon, Francis, and their Friends* (London: Victor Gollancz, 1975), 47–8; Leo Hicks, 'The Strange Case of Dr William Parry: The Career of an Agent Provocateur', *Studies* 37 (1948), 343–63 at 344–6; *HPT* 3: 180–4.

15 AB to WC, 13 February 1581, PRO SP 12/147, fo. 99ᵛ (art. 51); *CSPD, 1581–1590*, 5.

16 WC to AB, 11 July and 1 August 1580, EUL Laing MS La.iii.193, fo. 139b.

17 FW to AB, 1 August 1580, 19 August 1580, LPL MS 647, fos 56ʳ, 54ʳ.

18 FW to AB, 19 August 1580, LPL MS 647, fo. 54ʳ.

19 AB to WC, 14 January, 13 February 1581, PRO SP 12/147, fos 13, 99–100 (arts 9, 51); *CSPD, 1581–1590*, 2, 5.

20 FW to AB, 25 March 1581, LPL MS 647, fos 111–12 (art. 52).

21 Thomas Cotheram to AB, 3 March 1580, LPL MS 647, fos 89–90 (art. 39).

22 AB to Thomas [Cotheram?] and AB to John Stalling, both 7 July 1581, EUL Laing MS La.iii.193, fos 118b, 119a.

23 Joyce Treskunof Freedman, 'Anthony Bacon and his World, 1558–1601' (PhD, Temple University, 1979), 37.

24 Mantell to AB, 20 March 1581, 1 March 1583, LPL MS 647, arts 30, 33; Freedman, 'Anthony Bacon', 37–8; Du Maurier, *Golden Lads*, 51.

25 Mantell to AB, 5 May 1580, 20 March 1581, 30 November 1581, LPL MS 647, arts 28, 30, 34; Freedman, 'Anthony Bacon', 40–2.

26 William Parry, memorandum of loan, 1 August 1580; Maurice Fane, memorandum of loan, 3 August 1581; George Hawys to AB, 2 July 1580; Honoré Blanchard to AB, 9 August 1581; French brothers to AB, 5 January 1582: LPL MS 647, fos 58ᵛ, 59ʳ, 60ʳ, 61ʳ , 63ʳ (arts. 17, 18, 19, 20, 22).

27 Mantell to AB, 31 January 1581, LPL MS 647, art. 29; Freedman, 'Anthony Bacon and his World', 41–2.

28 AB to Roger Wilbraham, 11 January 1581, and AB to Henry Golding, 5 July 1581, EUL Laing MS La.iii.193, fos 108a, 117b.

29 Prest, *Inns of Court*, 177; A. F. Scott Pearson, *Thomas Cartwright and Elizabethan Puritanism 1535–1603* (Cambridge: Cambridge University Press, 1925), 19.

30 AB to NaB, February 1578, *Stiffkey* 2: 5; Thomas Cartwright, *The Rest of the Second Replie of Thomas Cartwright: Agaynst Master Doctor Whitgifts Second Answer, Touching the Church Discipline* (n.p.: publisher unknown, 1577).

31 On Crooke, see WC to Gray's Inn, 30 January 1580; Douthwaite, *Gray's Inn*, 153–4; NF to AB, 20 November 1583, LPL MS 647, fo. 162 (art. 76); *LL* 1: 31 and n.1.

32 For Travers see *DNB*; Isaac Walton, 'Life of Hooker', *The Works of Mr. Richard Hooker*, 2 vols (Oxford: Clarendon Press, 1890), 1: 3–69.

33 Pension 13 May 1580, *GIPB* 43.

34 WC to Gray's Inn Masters of the Bench, 30 January 1580 and 25 May 1580, Douthwaite, *Gray's Inn*, 153–4; Gray's Inn, Book of Orders, 1, fo. 80ᵛ; *GIPB* 37.

35 FB to Lady Burghley and FB to WC, 16 September 1580, BL Lansdowne MS 31, art. 14; *LL* 1 :12, 12–13.

36 John Barksdale, reader's speech 1628, quoted in Wilfrid R. Prest, 'The English Bar, 1550–1700', in Prest, ed., *Lawyers in Early Modern England* (London: Croom Helm, 1981), 69.

37 FB to WC, 18 October 1580, BL Lansdowne MS 31, art. 16; *LL* 1: 13–15.

38 Raphael Holinshed, rev. John Stow et al., *Holinshed's Chronicles of England, Scotland, and Ireland*, 6 vols (London: J. Johnson et al., 1807–8), 4: 343–4; John Strype, *Annals of the Reformation and Establishment of Religion* . . . *in the Church of England*, 4 vols (Oxford: Clarendon Press, 1874), 2: 2: 139; WC to Shrewsbury, 4 August 1577, Edmund Lodge, *Illustrations of British History, Biography, and Manners, in the Reigns of Henry VIII, Edward VI, Mary, Elizabeth, & James I*, 2nd edn, 3 vols (London: John Chudley, 1838), 2: 86; William D'Oyly Bayley, *A Biographical, Historical, Genealogical, and Heraldic Account of the House of Doylie* (London: John Bowyer Nichols & Son, 1845), 25.

39 *HPT* 1: 123–4, 374–9; 2: 53.

40 For this parliamentary session see *CJ* 1: 115–37; T. E. Hartley, ed., *Proceedings in the Parliaments of Elizabeth*, 3 vols (Leicester: Leicester University Press, 1981–95), 1: 497–547.

41 J. E. Neale, *Elizabeth I and her Parliaments*, vol. 1: *1559–1581* (London: Jonathan Cape, 1953), 378–82.

42 FB to House of Commons, 28 November 1601, Heywood Townshend, *Historical Collections: or, An Exact Account of the Proceedings of the Four Last Parliaments of Q. Elizabeth* (London: T. Basset, W. Crooke and W. Cademan, 1680), 260; Neale, *Parliaments, 1559–1581*, 407–9.

43 AB to his aunt, [1581]; AB to Mr Parry, 5 July 1581; AB to William Waad, 5 July 1581; AB to Roger Wilbraham, [1581], EUL Laing MS iii.193, fos 116b, 118a, 116a.

44 Charles Borgeaud, *Histoire de l'Université de Genève: L'academie de Calvin 1559–1798* (Geneva: Georg, 1990), 638–9; Bibliothèque de Genève, Mhg. 151b, quoted in Borgeaud, *Histoire*, 146–8.

45 Thomas Wilcox, *A Short, Yet Sound Commentarie: Written on that Woorthie Worke Called; The Prouerbes of Salomon* (London: Thomas Man, 1589), A3^v; AB to Essex, 8 February 1597, LPL MS 659, fo. 24^r; AB to ACB, 2 June 1593, LPL MS 649, fo. 190^r (art. 123).

46 AB to FB, n.d., EUL Laing MS iii.193.

47 Bodl. Ashmole MS 487 (Dee's annotated copy of *Ephemerides* . . . *Ioannis Stadii Leonnovthensis* [1570]), Iiii^v. The entry is transcribed incorrectly in *The Private Diary of John Dee*, ed. James Orchard Halliwell (London: Camden Society, 1842), 16. On Dee see William H. Sherman, *John Dee: The Politics of Reading and Writing in the English Renaissance* (Amherst, MA: University of Massachusetts Press, 1995). On 13 April 1584, NF informed AB that 'Mr Fra: Bacon and Mr Philippes are gone into Suff:': LPL MS 647, fo. 183 (art. 90).

48 Mordechai Feingold, *The Mathematicians' Apprenticeship: Science, Universities and Society in England, 1560–1640* (Cambridge: Cambridge University Press, 1984), 125–8.

49 NF to AB, 26 May 1581, July 1581, n.d., LPL MS 647, fos 106, 108 (arts 51, 53); Freedman, 'Anthony Bacon', 57, 59, 61; AB, note of loan to NF, 23 November 1581, LPL MS 647, art. 65.

50 NF to AB, 1 and 12 March 1582, LPL 647, fos 106, 108 (arts 49, 50); Birch, *Memoirs* 1: 20–1.

51 NF to AB, 15 April 1582, LPL MS 647, fos 125–6 (art. 59).

52 Ibid.

53 NF to AB, 8 May 1582, LPL MS 647, fo. 127 (art. 60).

54 'This letter to Mr Beza was sent me even in this instant from your brother, which he would have you to convey, otherwise I would have sent it a more direct way': NF to AB, 8 May 1582, LPL MS 647, fo. 127 (art. 60).

55 EUL Laing MS La.iii.193, fos 130a–134a.

56 'Notes on the State of Christendom', BL Harley MS 7021, fos 1–11^v; *LL* 1: 18–30, discussed 1: 17–18. Printed as Bacon's in *Letters and Remains of the Lord Chancellor Bacon*, ed. Robert Stephens (London: W. Bowyer, 1734), but thought by some now to be a spurious attribution (see Beal 1: 1: 23).

57 NF to AB, LPL MS 647, fo. 128 (art. 61); *LL* 1: 31–2.

58 NF to AB, 1 August 1582, LPL MS 647, fo. 130^{r-v} (art. 62).

59 NF to AB, 1 December 1582, LPL MS 647, fo. 132^{r-v} (art. 63).

60 NF to AB, 22 February 1583, LPL MS 647, fo. 119 (art. 57); Birch, *Memoirs*, 1: 28.

61 FW to AB, 25 March 1581, LPL MS 647, fo. 111 (art. 52).

62 NF to AB, 6 May 1583, LPL MS 647, fo. 150 (art. 72).

63 Pension 27 June 1583, Gray's Inn, Book of Orders, 1, fo. 161^r; *GIPB* 55; NF to AB, 6 August 1583, LPL MS 647, fo. 74; Birch, *Memoirs*, 1: 39 On the robes see Prest, *Inns of Court*, 48.

64 NF to AB, 31 May 1583, LPL MS 647, fo. 73; Birch, *Memoirs*, 1:35; *LL* 1: 31.

65 Mantell to AB, 1 March 1583, LPL MS 647, art. 33; Freedman, 'Anthony Bacon', 42.

66 Mantell to AB, 13 December 1583, LPL MS 647, art. 80; Freedman, 'Anthony Bacon', 43.

67 Mentioned in NF to AB, 31 May 1583, LPL 647, art. 73; Birch, *Memoirs*, 1: 35.

68 NF to AB, 6 August 1583, LPL MS 647, fo. 74; Birch, *Memoirs*, 1: 39.

69 Charles Merbury to AB, 23 November 1583, LPL MS 647, fo. 164 [address] (art. 77).

70 Freedman, 'Anthony Bacon', 97–8.

71 AB to Leicester, 24 November 1581, BL Cotton MS Caligula E VII, fo. 215.

72 Birch, *Memoirs*, 1: 40. Haynes dates this exchange to 1584 in Bordeaux: Alan Haynes, *Invisible Power: The Elizabethan Secret Service 1570–1603* (Far Thrupp, Glos.: Alan Sutton, 1992).

73 Leicester to AB, 10 October 1583, LPL MS 647, fo. 160^r (art. 75).

74 In November 1583 Faunt learned from John Bodley, one of AB's correspondents, that Anthony intended to spend the winter in Paris. NF to AB, 20 November 1583, LPL MS 647, fo. 162 (art. 76).

75 Licence dated 15 February 1584 in volume owned by Thomas Birch, quoted in Birch, *Memoirs* 1: 44 n (o).

76 AB to ?, 12 February 1584, LPL MS 647, fo. 85; Birch, *Memoirs*, 1: 44–5.

77 Donald Frame, *Montaigne: A Biography* (London: Hamish Hamilton, 1965), 227.

78 AB to Essex, 12 September 1596, LPL MS 659, fo. 24^{r-v}.

79 NF to AB, 6 August 1583, LPL MS 647, art. 74.

80 NF to AB, 17 December 1583; LPL MS 647, art. 78; Birch, *Memoirs* 1: 43.

81 NF to AB, 16 January 1584, LPL MS 647, art. 67; Freedman, 'Anthony Bacon', 9.

82 Whitgift to AB, 10 May 1585, LPL MS 647, fo. 194ʳ (art. 95).

83 Mantell to AB, 23 December 1583, LPL MS 647, fo. 170 (art. 80).

84 NF to AB, 13 April 1584, LPL MS 647, fo. 183 (art. 90).

CHAPTER 4

1 FW to AB, 1 March 1584, LPL MS 647, art. 68; *LL* 3: 8.

2 Stafford to Elizabeth, 2 May 1584, PRO SP 78/11/86; *CSPF, 1583–1584*, 480.

3 Stafford to FW, 2 May 1584, PRO SP 78/11, fos 194–5 (art. 87); *CSPF, 1583–1584*, 481.

4 Stafford to FW, 30 May 1584, PRO SP 78/11, fos 257–8 (art. 118); *CSPF, 1583–1584*, 521.

5 WC to Covert, 14 and 24 November 1584, Henry Ellis, *Original Letters, Illustrative of English History, Including Numerous Royal Letters*, 3rd ser., 4 vols (London: Richard Bentley, 1846), 4: 51–2; *HPT* 1: 155–7, 252–3.

6 On this session see T. E. Hartley ed., *Proceedings in the Parliaments of Elizabeth*, 3 vols (Leicester: Leicester University Press, 1981–5), 2: 9–193.

7 Only 'Mr Bacon' is specified: Simonds D'Ewes, *The Journals of All the Parliaments during the Reign of Queen Elizabeth, both of the House of Lords and House of Commons*, rev. Paul Bowes (London: John Shirley, 1682), 363; Hartley, *Proceedings* 2: 93, 94.

8 NF to AB, 12 March 1584, LPL MS 647, art. 69.

9 ACB to WC, 26 February 1585, BL Lansdowne MS 43, fos 119–20 (art. 48); *LL* 1: 40–2; BL Lansdowne MS 115, fo. 125 (art. 55) is a copy; see also BL Lansdowne MS 68, art. 58; Patrick Collinson, 'Sir Nicholas Bacon and the Elizabethan *via media*', *Godly People: Essays on English Protestantism and Puritanism* (London: Hambledon Press, 1983), 150–1.

10 BL Lansdowne MS 43, fo. 175; Hartley, *Proceedings* 2: 126–7; J. E. Neale, *Elizabeth I and her Parliaments*, vol. 2: *1584–1601* (London: Jonathan Cape, 1957), 93. For wardship, see Christopher Hill, *Intellectual Origins of the English Revolution Revisited* (Oxford: Clarendon Press, 1997), 318–26.

11 'A Letter of Advice to Queen Elizabeth', *LL* 1: 47–56. For MS witnesses, see Beal 1: 1: 21.

12 This discussion is based on Julian Martin, *Francis Bacon, the State, and the Reform of Natural Philosophy* (Cambridge: Cambridge University Press, 1992), 31–2.

13 FB to FW, 25 August 1585, PRO SP 14/181/63; *CSPD, 1581–1590*, 262; *LL* 1: 57.

14 FB to WC, 6 May 1586, BL Lansdowne MS 51, fo. 9; *LL* 1: 59–60; Pension 10 February 1586, Gray's Inn, Book of Orders, 1. fo. 187ᵛ; *GIPB* 72; *GIPB* 123, 72, quoted in Wilfrid R. Prest, *The Inns of Court under Elizabeth and the Early Stuarts* (London: Longman, 1972), 62.

15 Note by WC, BL Lansdowne MS 51, fo. 11.

16 FB to WC, 6 May 1586, BL Lansdowne MS 51, fo. 9; *LL* 1: 59–60.

17 Du Bartas, *La seconde semaine* (1584), bk 6, ll. 611–18 in *The Works of Guillaume*

de Salluste Sieur du Bartas: A Critical Edition, 3 vols, ed. Urban Tigner Holmes, Jr, John Coriden Lyons and Robert White Linker (Chapel Hill, NC: University of North Carolina Press, 1935–40).

18 Georges Pellissier, *La vie et les oeuvres de Du Bartas* (Paris: Hachette, 1883), 17–18; H. Ashton, *Du Bartas en Angleterre* (Paris: Emile Larose, 1908), 9–32; Alan Sinfield, 'Sidney and Du Bartas', *Comparative Literature* 27 (1975), 16–18; Susan Snyder, 'Introduction' to her ed., *The Divine Weeks and Works of Guillaume de Saluste Sieur du Bartas translated by Joshua Sylvester*, 2 vols (Oxford: Clarendon Press, 1979).

19 Du Bartas to AB, 12 September 158?, BL Cotton MS Nero B.VI, fo. 288; pr. in *Works of Du Bartas*, ed. Holmes et al., 1: 201, where the recipient is misidentified as FB.

20 AB to FW, 19 March 1585, PRO SP 78/13, fo. 162 (art. 54); *CSPF, 1584–1585*, 335.

21 AB to FB, [19 March 1585], EUL Laing MS iii.143, fos 143b–144a.

22 Zacheria de Monty to AB, 18/28 October 1584, PRO SP 78/12, fos 272–3 (art. 94); *CSPF, 1584–1585*, 111.

23 On Montauban see H. Le Bret, *Histoire de Montauban*, 2nd edn, 2 vols, rev. and ed. l'abbé Marcellin and Gabriel Ruek (Montauban: Réthare, 1841), 2: 83–6; Mary Lafon, *Histoire d'une ville protestante* (Paris: Amyot, 1862), 84–93; Janine Garrisson, 'La "Genève française"', in Daniel Ligou, ed., *Histoire de Montauban* (Toulouse: Privat, 1984), ch. 6.

24 AB to Essex, 12 September 1596, LPL MS 659, fos 23a–26b.

25 For this incident, see *A Huguenot Family in the XVI Century. The Memoirs of Philippe de Mornay Sieur du Plessis Marly Written by his Wife*, tr. Lucy Crump (London: George Routledge, 1926), 71 and 198–217; Daphne Du Maurier, *Golden Lads: Anthony Bacon, Francis, and their Friends* (London: Victor Gollancz, 1976), 61–2; Alan Haynes, *Invisible Power: The Elizabethan Secret Service 1570–1603* (Far Thrupp, Glos.: Alan Sutton, 1992), 105–6.

26 NF to AB, 28 March 1584, LPL MS 647, fo. 181 (art. 69); Joyce Treskunof Freedman, 'Anthony Bacon and his World, 1558–1601' (PhD, Temple University, 1979), 69–70.

27 AB to FB, n.d., EUL Laing MS iii.143, fos 142b–144b.

28 William Philippes to Davison, 5 October 1586, PRO SP 12/194, fo. 13 (art. 8); TP to Davison, 8 October 1586, PRO SP 12/194, fo. 42 (art. 21).

29 William Philippes to WC, 25 March 1586, PRO SP 12/187, fo. 138 (art. 60).

30 AB to FW, 19 March 1585, PRO SP 78/13, fos 161–2 (art. 54); *CSPF, 1584–1585*, 334–5.

31 AB to Julius Caesar, 19 March 1585, BL Add. MS 11,403, fo. 134.

32 AB to FB, n.d., EUL Laing MS iii.143, fos 142b–144b.

33 AB to FW, 19 March 1585, PRO SP 78/13, fos 161–2 (art. 54); *CSPF, 1584–1585*, 334–5.

34 AB to FB, n.d., EUL Laing MS iii.143, fos 142b–144b. On Fenner's dual role see also Du Pin to FW, 2/12 March 1585, PRO SP 78/13/42; *CSPF, 1584–1585*, 719.

35 AB to FW, 19 March 1585, PRO SP 78/13, fos 161–2 (art. 54); *CSPF, 1584–1585*, 334–5.

36 Mantell to AB, 25 May 1585, LPL MS 647, fo. 192 (art. 94); Freedman, 'Anthony Bacon', 43.
37 NF to AB, 16 April 1585, LPL 647, fos 189–91 (art. 93).
38 Fenner to AB, 22 July 1585, LPL MS 647, fos 196–8 (art. 96).
39 See also FW to AB, 22 September 1585, LPL MS 647, fo. 199^r (art. 98); Du Pin to AB, 19 October 1585, BL Cotton MS B.VI, fo. 306; [Du Pin] to AB, 7 December 1585, BL Cotton MS Nero B.VI, fo. 302.
40 Mantell to AB, 25 May 1585, LPL MS 647, art. 94; Freedman, 'Anthony Bacon', 38.
41 AB to FW, 12/22 July 1585, PRO SP 78/14/45; *CSPF, 1584–1585*, 594.
42 ? to [Stafford] 3 June 1586, LPL MS 647, fo. 214 (art. 105).
43 Du Pin to WC, 19 June 1586, PRO SP 78/16, fo. 9 (art. 5); *CSPF, 1586–1588*, 10.
44 Passports for Peter Brown, signed by Terride (26 July 1586), the Baron of Cahors (8 August 1586) and Biron (7 September 1586), BL Add. MS 4125, fo. 4; A. Chambers Bunten, 'Notes on Anthony Bacon's Passports of 1586', *Baconiana* 18 (1925–6), 93–104.
45 Henri de Navarre to AB, 17 July [1586], LPL MS 942, art. 4; Henri IV of France, *Receuil des lettres missives de Henri IV*, 9 vols: vols 1–7 ed. M. Berger de Xivery (Paris: Imprimerie Royale, 1843–58), 2: 230.
46 We base the following account on the work of Du Maurier, *Golden Lads*, and Joyce Freedman, 'Anthony Bacon and his World, 1558–1601' (PhD, Temple University, 1979). Freedman's work has been drawn on by Haynes, *Invisible Power*.
47 Maurice Lever, *Les bûchers de Sodome: Histoire des infames* (Paris: Fayard, 1985), 89.
48 Testimony concerning sodomy charges, *La côte* 5 E 1537, pp. 1–2, 3–5, 6–8, fos 176–9, Archives Départmentales, Montauban, Préfecture de Tarn-et-Garonne, France; Freedman, 'Anthony Bacon', 104–6.
49 Freedman, 'Anthony Bacon', 106–7; Du Maurier, *Golden Lads*, 66–7.
50 Freedman, 'Anthony Bacon', 107.
51 Garrisson, 'La "Genève française"', 127.
52 On Beza, see Noel I. Garde, *The Homosexual in History* (New York: Vantage Press, 1964), 298, cited in Freedman, 'Anthony Bacon', 119; on Constans, see Eugénie Droz, *Jacques de Constans, l'ami d'Agrippa d'Aubigné: contribution à l'étude de la poésie protestante* (Geneva: Droz, 1962), 13.
53 Henri de Navarre to Scorbiac, 23 September 1586, BL Cotton MS Nero B.VI, fo. 387; Henri IV, *Missives* 2: 240; tr. Du Maurier, *Golden Lads*, 67.
54 Freedman, 'Anthony Bacon', 110.
55 Henri to Du Plessis-Mornay, 23 September 1586, BL Cotton MS Nero B.VI, fo. 387; Henri IV, *Missives* 8: 310. See also Du Pin to AB, 24 September 1586, BL Cotton MS Nero B.VI, fo. 304.
56 Du Pin to WC, 7/17 October 1586, PRO SP 78/16, fo. 124 (art. 61); *CSPF, 1586–1588*, 110.
57 Henri to AB, 17 November 1586, LPL MS 942, art. 3; Henri IV, *Missives* 8: 311. In late November, Anthony was once again forwarding letters from the Navarre court to Stafford in Paris: see Stafford to WC, 29 November 1586, PRO SP 78/16/80; *CSPF, 1586–1588*, 156.
58 On 3 January 1587 Du Pin wrote from La Rochelle to Burghley: 'M. de Bacon

is still at Montauban; we are expecting to hear from him.' *CSPF, 1586–1588,* 167.

59 NF to AB, 31 December 1586, LPL MS 647, fo. 219 (art. 108); Freedman, 'Anthony Bacon', 79–80.

60 For an account see BL Cotton MS Nero B.VI, fos 402–4, 399–401. On 5 and 7 December, de Vicose made out an order to lend Anthony 100 crowns on behalf of the King of Navarre. A receipt for payment from Codere was signed on 13 April 1589. See BL Cotton MS Nero B.VI, fo. 300.

61 At one point the widow of Lavardin became involved, offering to convey money, but ACB still refused. See La Madecayne to AB, 21 April 1588, BL Cotton MS Nero B.VI, fo. 304; also AB to WC, 8 October 1588, Salisbury MS 17/44; *HMCS* 3: 362.

62 Du Plessis-Mornay to Buzanval, August 1588; see also Du Plessis-Mornay to Buzanval, 11 October 1587, Philippe Du Plessis-Mornay, *Mémoires et correspondance de Du Plessis Mornay,* ed. A. D. de la Fontenelle de Vandoré and P. R. Auguis, 8 vols (Paris: Treuttel et Wurtz, 1824), 4: 245, 3: 536. See also NF to AB, 11/21 February 1588, LPL MS 648, fos 222–3 (art. 110); Birch, *Memoirs,* 1: 54; Du Pin to FW, 21 February 1588, BL Cotton MS Nero B. VI, fo. 240; Du Maurier, *Golden Lads,* 69.

63 AB to FW, 24 March 1588, PRO SP 15/30/92; *CSPD, Addenda 1580–1625,* 247; Du Maurier, *Golden Lads,* 69.

64 AB to Essex, 12 September 1596, LPL MS 659, fos 24^v–25^r.

65 AB to WC, 28 September [1588], Salisbury MS 17/43, *HMCS* 3: 361; Du Maurier, *Golden Lads,* 71.

66 FW to AB, 10 November 1588, LPL MS 647, fos 228–9 (art.113).

67 Stafford to WC, 23 November 1588, PRO SP 78/18/168; *CSPF, 1588,* 332–3.

68 Francis Allen to AB, 17 August 1589, LPL MS 647, fos 245–6 (art. 121).

69 *HPT* 1: 155–6, 236–7. H. J. Moule, *Descriptive Catalogue of the Charters, Minute Books and other Documents of the Borough of Weymouth and Melcombe Regis AD 1252 to 1800* (Weymouth: Sherrat & Son, 1883), 39–40; Hartley, *Proceedings,* 2: 195–400.

70 *HPT* 1: 375; D'Ewes, *Journals of all the Parliaments,* 393, 394, 410, 413, 417.

71 September 1587, PRO SP 12/203/57; *CSPD, 1581–1590,* 427. Martin suggests that FB was already working for Walsingham and other Privy Councillors in their capacity as members of the Court for Ecclesiastical Causes (the High Commission): Martin, *Francis Bacon,* 192 n. 43.

72 BL Harley MS 7017; see Roland G. Usher, 'Francis Bacon's Knowledge of Law French', *Modern Language Notes* 43 (1919), 30–1; Daniel Coquillette, *Francis Bacon* (Stanford, CA: Stanford University Press, 1992), 28.

73 'Discourse upon the Commission of Bridewell', *Works* 7: 505–16. For MS witnesses, see Beal BcF 200–1; discussed in Coquillette, *Francis Bacon,* 26–7.

74 Pension 3 November 1587, *GIPB* 77, 'Reading on the Statute of Advowsons', BL Stowe MS 424, fos 145–50. Spedding could not publish this, since the previous owner, Lord Ashburnham, would not let Heath see this MS (*Works* 7: 305.) It will be included in the forthcoming volume 1 of the new *Oxford Francis Bacon,* edited by Julian Martin (Clarendon Press).

75 FB to AB, 25 January 1594, LPL MS 650, art. 28; *LL* 2: 348. Pension 21 November 1588, Gray's Inn, Book of Orders, 1, fo. 295^{r-v}; *GIPB* 82–3.

76 FB to Fulgentio, [1625?], *Opuscula varia posthuma, philosophica, civilia, et theologica, Francisci Baconi*, ed. William Rawley (London: R. Daniel, 1658), 172; *LL* 7: 533.

77 Fulton Anderson believes this to be a juvenile work: see F. H. Anderson, *The Philosophy of Francis Bacon* (Chicago: University of Chicago Press, 1948). For the opposed view see Benjamin Farrington, *The Philosophy of Francis Bacon: An Essay on its Development from 1603 to 1609 with New Translations of Fundamental Texts* (Liverpool: Liverpool University Press, 1964), 17–18.

78 Tr. Farrington, *Philosophy of Francis Bacon*, 71.

79 Paula Findlen, *Possessing Nature: Museums, Collecting, and Scientific Culture in Early Modern Literature* (Berkeley, CA: University of California Press, 1994).

CHAPTER 5

1 On Essex see Devereux; Edwin A. Abbott, *Bacon and Essex: A Sketch of Bacon's Earlier Life* (London: Seely, Jackson, & Halliday, 1877); Robert Lacey, *Robert, Earl of Essex: An Elizabethan Icarus* (London: Weidenfeld & Nicolson, 1971); Paul E. J. Hammer, 'The Uses of Scholarship: The Secretariat of Robert Devereux, Second Earl of Essex, *c*.1585–1601', *English Historical Review* 109 (1994), 26–51.

2 Sir Francis Hastings to Essex, 9 September 1588, quoted in Julian Martin, *Francis Bacon, the State, and the Reform of Natural Philosophy* (Cambridge: Cambridge University Press, 1992), 48.

3 Fynes Moryson, quoted in Devereux 2: 215–16.

4 FB to Leicester, 11 June 1588, Longleat House, Dudley MS 2 fo. 232^r; HMC, *Calendar of the Manuscripts of the Most Honourable the Marquess of Bath, Preserved at Longleat, Wiltshire*, vol. 5: *Talbot, Dudley and Devereux Papers, 1533–1659*, ed. G. Dyfnallt Owen (London: HMSO, 1980), 210.

5 *Apology, LL* 2: 143.

6 Privy Council register, 14 August 1588, *APC, 1588*, 235–6.

7 Privy Council register, 27 December 1588, *APC, 1588*, 417.

8 BL Cotton MS Titus C.X.93; patent in PRO SO 3/1 fo. 211b.

9 Martin, *Francis Bacon*, 37.

10 Quoted in Rawley, 'Life of Bacon', *Works* 1: 7.

11 Richard Bancroft, *A Sermon Preached at Paules Crosse the 9. of Februarie, being the First Sunday in the Parleament, Anno. 1588* (London: Gregorie Seton, 1588), B2^r.

12 Bancroft, *A Survay of the Pretended Holy Discipline* (London: J. Wolfe, 1593) ★2^r. See also Thomas Nashe, *The First Parte of Pasquils Apologie* (London: J. Charlewood, 1590), A4^r.

13 Neale writes that 'The very mild, ineffective words finally incorporated into the preamble appear to have been composed by Burghley': J. E. Neale, *Elizabeth I and her Parliaments*, vol. 2: *1584–1601* (London: Jonathan Cape, 1957), 205; see Simonds D'Ewes, *The Journals of All the Parliaments during the Reign of Queen Elizabeth, both of the House of Lords and House of Commons*, rev. Paul Bowes (London: John Shirley, 1682), 431, 433–4; BL Lansdowne MS 58, fos 182–4.

14 *HPT* 1: 189–90, 374–9; D'Ewes, *Journals of All the Parliaments*, 430, 432, 433ff, 437, 438, 439–40; on this session see T. E. Hartley, ed., *Proceedings in the Parliaments of Elizabeth*, 3 vols (Leicester: Leicester University Press, 1981–95), 2: 401–97.

15 WC to Shrewsbury, Edmund Lodge, *Illustrations of British History, Biography, and Manners, in the Reigns of Henry VIII, Edward VI, Mary, Elizabeth, & James I*, 2nd edn, 3 vols (London: John Chudley, 1838), 2: 373; *LL* 1: 95; Daphne Du Maurier, *Golden Lads: Anthony Bacon, Francis, and their Friends* (London: Victor Gollancz, 1975), 71–3.

16 FB to Whitgift, n.d., *Resuscitatio*, 113; *LL* 1: 96; FW to Critoy, n.d., *Scrinia sacra: Secrets of Empire* (London: G. Bedel and T. Collins, 1654), 38; *LL* 1: 97–101. We are following Spedding's identification of FB as the author.

17 'Observations on a Libel', *LL* 1: 146–208. For MS witnesses see Beal BcF 135–52. Anthony also saw Parsons' book: see Edward Jones to AB, 8 November 1592, LPL MS 648, fo. 305 (art. 172); Thomas Birch, *Memoirs of the Reign of Queen Elizabeth, from the Year 1581 till her Death*, 2 vols (London: A. Millar, 1754), 1: 90; *LL* 1: 143.

18 *Advancement of Learning, Works* 3: 445.

19 On Lisle see Essuck [?] to AB, 22 July 1590, BL Cotton MS Nero B.VI, fo. 299.

20 AB to WC, (19) 29 January 1591, PRO SP 78/23, fo. 41; AB to WC, (31 January)/10 February 1591, PRO SP 78/23, fo. 72; Edward Grimeston to WC, 9 March 1591, PRO SP 78/23, fo. 174; *L&A, 1590–1591*, nos 488, 489 (pp. 305–6); AB to WC, [5]/15 June 1591, PRO SP 78/24 fo. 227; AB to WC, [20]/30 June 1591, PRO SP 78/24, fo. 302; *L&A, 1591–1592*, no. 521 [pp. 317–18]; *L&A, 1591–1592*, F55, F57, F100, F116. See also Maurice Wilkinson, 'The English on the Gironde in 1592–3', *English Historical Review* 31 (1916), 279–91.

21 AS to WC, 7 June 1591, LPL MS 648, fo. 37 (art. 19); Birch, *Memoirs*, 1: 67. On Standen see L. Hicks, 'The Embassy of Sir Anthony Standen in 1603, Part I', *Recusant History* 5 (1959–60), 91–127; Paul E. J. Hammer, 'An Elizabethan Spy Who Came in from the Cold: The Return of Anthony Standen to England in 1593', *Bulletin of the Institute of Historical Research* 65 (1992), 277–95.

22 LPL MS 650, fo. 65, quoted in Hammer, 'An Elizabethan Spy', 281 n. 29.

23 AS to AB, spring 1591, LPL MS 648, fo. 144 (art. 88).

24 Andree Sandal to AB, 7 April 1591, LPL MS 648, fo. 25 (art. 13); AS to AB, 8 April 1591, LPL MS 648, fo. 27 (art. 14).

25 For AS' correspondence with AB in 1591, see LPL MS 648, arts 21, 22, 24, 27, 31, 48 and 59.

26 For AS' correspondence with WC in 1591, see LPL MS 648, arts 19 and 69.

27 AS to AB, 31 August 1591, 1 May 1591, LPL MS 648, arts 45 and 58; AS to Edward Selwin, 5 September 1591, LPL MS 648 art. 51.

28 Thomas Cartwright to AB, 23 May 1591, BL Add. MS 4115, fos 2b–4, also LPL MS 653, fo. 199 (art. 108); A. F. Scott Pearson, *Thomas Cartwright and Elizabethan Puritanism 1535–1603* (Cambridge: Cambridge University Press, 1925), 464–5.

29 AS to Edward Selwin, 5 September 1591, LPL MS 648, fo. 86 (art. 51).

30 AS to AB, 31 August 1591, LPL MS 648, art. 45.

31 AS to Edward Selwin, 5 September 1591, LPL MS 648, fo. 86 (art. 51); AS to AB, 1591, LPL MS 648, fo. 80 (art. 48); LPL MS 648, fo. 27; LPL MS 648, fo. 31; LPL MS 648, fo. 139.

32 AB to EB, 10 May 1591, *Stiffkey* 3: 125.

33 AS to Rolston, November 1591, LPL MS 648, fos 118–19 (arts 71, 72).

34 AS to WC, 2/12 November 1591, PRO SP 78/26, fo. 171; *L&A, 1591–1592*, no. 613 (p. 358).

35 FB to TP, n.d., PRO SP 12/238, fo. 269^r (art. 138).

36 'Cardinalls' to WC, 30 November 1591, LPL MS 648, fo. 123 (art 73). Draft heavily corrected. This sheet is an insert in AB's hand.

37 AS to FB, November 1591, LPL MS 648, art. 79.

38 AS to WC, 30 November 1591, LPL MS 648, art. 73; AS to FB, November 1591, LPL MS 648, art. 79.

39 WC to AS, LPL MS 648, art. 86 and BL Add. MS 35841, fo. 141^v, quoted in Hammer, 'An Elizabethan Spy', 281 n. 27.

40 For a report of Standen's travels see LPL MS 648, art. 85; 'La Faye' (AS) to AB, [8 December 1591], LPL MS 648, fos 132–3 (art. 80).

41 FB to TP, n.d., PRO SP 12/238, fo. 269^r (art. 138).

42 William Sterrell to TP, [September 1591], PRO SP 12/244, fo. 235 (art. 103).

43 Robert Robinson [William Sterrell] to TP, n.d., PRO SP 12/246, fo. 167 (art. 62).

44 *Apology, LL* 3: 143.

45 AB to Essex, 12 September 1596, LPL MS 659, fo. 25^{r-v} (art. 21).

46 Hammer, 'The Uses of Scholarship'; selections from this intelligence correspondence are printed in Birch, *Memoirs*.

47 Henry Savile, tr., *The End of Nero and Beginning of Galba. Fower Bookes of the Histories of Cornelivs Tacitvs. The Life of Agricola* (Oxford: Richard Wright, 1591), ¶3^{r-v}. For the identification of 'A.B.' as Anthony Bacon, see Gustav Ungerer, *A Spaniard in Elizabethan England: The Correspondence of Antonio Peréz's Exile*, 2 vols (London: Tamesis, 1974–6), 2: 372; for the identification of Essex as author, see Ben Jonson, 'Conversations with Drummond', in *Works*, ed. C. H. Herford, Percy Simpson and Evelyn Simpson, 11 vols (Oxford: Clarendon Press, 1925–52), 1: 142.

48 'Of Tribute, or Giving What is Due', *LL* 1: 123–43; for MS witnesses see Beal BcF 319–21; NF to AB, 20 November 1592, LPL MS 648, fo. 313 (art. 176).

49 FB to WC [*c.*1592], *Resuscitatio* 95; *LL* 1: 108–9.

50 EH to AB, 6 February 1592, LPL MS 648, fo. 4^r (art. 3).

51 EH to AB, 19 February 1592, LPL MS 648, fo. 10^r (art. 6).

52 ACB to AB, 3 February 1592, LPL MS 653, fos 343–4 (art. 192); *LL* 1: 112–13.

53 Edward Standen to AS, 30 June 1592, LPL MS 648, fo. 194 (art. 119).

54 See Anne Butts Bacon to AB and FB, 16 March 1592, LPL MS 648, fo. 18^r (art. 10).

55 ACB to AB, 17 May 1592, LPL MS 648, fo. 167 (art. 103); *LL* 1: 114.

56 ACB to AB, 28 February 1592, LPL MS 648, fo. 6 (art. 4); *LL* 1: 113.

57 ACB to AB, 24 May 1592, LPL MS 648, fo. 172 (art. 106); *LL* 1: 114.

58 ACB to AB, 29 May 1592, LPL MS 648, fo. 178 (art. 110); *LL* 1: 114.

59 William Rawley's commonplace book, LPL MS 2086, p. 83.

60 ACB to AB, 24 May 1592, LPL MS 648, fo. 172 (art. 106); *LL* 1: 114.

61 ACB to AB, 28 February 1592, LPL MS 648, fo. 6 (art. 4); *LL* 1: 113.

62 ACB to AB, 17 May 1592, LPL MS 648, fo. 167 (art. 103); *LL* 1: 114.

63 ACB to AB, 29 June 1592, LPL MS 648, fo. 177 (art. 109); *LL* 1: 115.

64 ACB to AB, 24 July 1592, LPL MS 648, fo. 196 (art. 120); *LL* 1: 115.

65 ACB to AB, 2 March 1592, LPL MS 648, fo. 12 (art. 7); *LL* 1: 113–14.

66 ACB to AB, 24 July 1592, LPL MS 648, fo. 196 (art. 120); *LL* 1: 115.

67 TPH to AB, 10 July 1592, 4 August 1592, LPL MS 648, fos 205^r, 225^r (arts 12, 135).

68 ACB to AB, 24 May 1592, 29 May 1592, LPL MS 648, fos 172, 178 (arts 106, 110); *LL* 1: 114.

69 George Jenkyll to AB, 20 August 1592 (n.s. [i.e. 10 August 1592]), LPL MS 648, fo. 223^r (art. 134).

70 On Twickenham see John Norden, *Speculum Britanniae. The First Parte. An Historicall, & Chorographicall Discription of Middlesex* (1593); W. Angus, *Seats of the Nobility and Gentry in Great Britain and Wales in a Collection of Select Views* (Islington: W. Angus, 1787), commentary to plate XL; Daniel Lysons, *The Environs of London*, 4 vols (London: T. Cadell, 1792–6; Supplement, London: T. Cadell & W. Davies, 1811), 1: 446, 3: 564–6, suppl. 313; James Thorne, *Handbook to the Environs of London, 1876*, 2 vols (repr. Bath: Adams & Dart, 1970), 631–2; R. S. Cobbett, *Memorials of Twickenham: Parochial and Topographical* (London: Smith, Elder & Co, 1873), 224–36; *VCH, Middlesex*, 1: 184, 2: 230, 248, 3: 96, 141, 144, 151–3; Twickenham Corporation/Twickenham and St Margaret's Chamber of Commerce, *The Official Guide to Twickenham*, 4th edn (Cheltenham: J. Burrow, 1927), 21; Bamber Gascoigne and Jonathan Ditchburn, *Images of Twickenham with Hampton and Teddington* (Richmond-upon-Thames: Saint Helena Press, 1981), 21–2.

71 Patent, 3 March 1574, *CPR Elizabeth I*, vol. 7: *1575–1578*, no. 1320, p. 249; Patent, 10 August 1581, *CPR Elizabeth I*, vol. 9: *1580–1582*, no. 358, p. 623.

72 Thomas Bushell, *Mr Bushells Abridgment Of the Lord Chancellor Bacon's Philosophical Theory in Mineral Prosecutions* (London 1659), A^r.

73 AB to FB, 14 May 1596, LPL MS 657, art. 9; Ungerer, *Spaniard* 1: 226–7; Devereux 1: 340–1.

74 FB to AB, 15 October 1594, LPL MS 650, art. 197; *LL* 1: 321.

75 FB to TP, 14 August 1592, PRO SP 12/242/106; *CSPD, 1591–1594*, 253; *LL* 1: 117–18.

76 FB to TP, 15 September 1592, PRO SP 12/243/13; *CSPD, 1591–1594*, 271; *LL* 1: 118–19.

77 This function is revealed in a letter from Alderman Anthony Radcliffe and Essex's servant William Lucas to Ridley, Peacock and Edward Kingston in October 1590. He also named Flinshawe and Lawson as papists. Anthony Radcliffe and William Lucas to Ridley, Peacock and Edward Kingston, 6 October 1590, LPL MS 647, art. 133; Joyce Treskunof Freedman, 'Anthony Bacon and his World, 1558–1601' (PhD, Temple University, 1979), 383–4.

78 John Blagge to AB, 24 July 1592, LPL MS 648, fo. 211^{r-v} (art. 128); Freedman, 'Anthony Bacon', 380–3.

79 Du Maurier, *Golden Lads*, 77; Freedman, 'Anthony Bacon', 384–5.

80 Henry Gosnold to AB, 28 November 1592, LPL MS 653, fo. 195^r (art. 105).

81 AB to AS, February 1593, LPL MS 648, fo. 162 (art. 99); Birch, *Memoirs*, 1: 92–3.

82 For AB's health, see NF to AB, 8 December 1592, 11 January 1593, LPL MS 648, fos 331^r, 338^r (arts 186, 190).

83 NF to AB, 11 January 1593, LPL MS 648, fo. 338^r (art. 190).

84 AB to AS, 14 March 1593, LPL MS 648, fo. 161 (art. 98); *LL* 1: 226.

85 Devereux 1: 382. AB wrote to AS, 'The Earl of Essex was lately sworn of the Council', after 7 March 1593: Birch, *Memoirs*, 1: 93.

86 AB to AS before 19 February 1593, LPL MS 648, art. 99; Birch, *Memoirs*, 1: 92–3.

87 Spedding's reconstruction from BL Hargrave MS 324, fo. 10; Heywood Townshend, *Historical Collections: or, An Exact Account of the Proceedings of the Four Last Parliaments of Q. Elizabeth* (London: T. Basset, W. Crooke and W. Cademan, 1680); D'Ewes, *Journals of All the Parliaments*; *LL* 1: 213–14.

88 *LL* 1: 215–16.

89 D'Ewes, *Journal of All the Parliaments*, 483; *LL* 1: 216–17.

90 *LL* 1: 219–21.

91 D'Ewes, *Journal of All the Parliaments*, 493; *LL* 1: 223.

92 FB to WC, before 20 March 1593, BL Add. MS 5503, fo. 1; *LL* 1: 234.

93 D'Ewes, *Journal of All the Parliaments*, 495.

94 AB to ACB, 16 April 1593, LPL MS 648, fo. 109 (art. 68); Birch, *Memoirs* 1: 96.

95 FB to WC, before 20 March 1593, BL Add. MS 5503, fo.1; *LL* 1: 233–4.

96 FB to Essex, 1593, LPL MS 649, art. 74; *LL* 1: 235. This is a fragment: Francis goes on to refer to two reasons with which he will answer Essex's queries, but the copy then abruptly stops.

CHAPTER 6

1 Sir Thomas Cecil to WC, n.d., BL Lansdowne MS 89, fo. 209; *LL* 1: 236–7; FB to RC, 16 April 1593, BL Lansdowne MS 75, fo. 82; *LL* 1: 237.

2 RC to FB, 7 May 1593, LPL MS 649, fo. 57^r (art. 37); *LL* 1: 238.

3 FB to [Essex], BL Harley MS 28, fo. 232; *LL* 1: 240.

4 FB to Elizabeth, 1593, LPL MS 649, art. 315; *LL* 1: 240.

5 AB to Essex, 13 June 1593, LPL MS 649, art. 314; Thomas Birch, *Memoirs of the Reign of Queen Elizabeth, from the Year 1581 till her Death*, 2 vols (London: A. Millar, 1754), 1: 103; AB to Essex, September 1593, LPL MS 659, art. 21.

6 Essex to AB, June 1593, LPL MS 654 art. 119; Birch, *Memoirs*, 1: 103; AB to ACB, 15 June 1593, LPL MS 649, art. 121; Birch, *Memoirs*, 1: 105.

7 AB to ACB, 18 July 1593, LPL MS 649, art. 145; *LL* 1: 254; Birch, *Memoirs*, 1: 254.

8 ACB to AB, 26 June 1593, LPL MS 649, art. 100; Birch, *Memoirs*, 1: 107.

9 AS to Essex, July 1593, LPL MS 649, art. 129; Birch, *Memoirs*, 1: 108, 115; Edward Standen to AS, 4 August 1593, LPL MS 649, art. 183; Birch, *Memoirs*, 1: 11.

10 AS to Essex, 4 July 1593, LPL MS 649, fo. 200^{r-v} (art. 129); Birch, *Memoirs*, 1: 108; AS to WC, 6 August 1593, LPL MS 649, fo. 227^r (art. 148); Birch, *Memoirs*, 1: 116.

11 AB to ACB, August 1593, LPL MS 649, art. 169; Birch, *Memoirs*, 1: 117.

12 AS to AB, 20 August 1593, LPL MS 649, art. 157; Birch, *Memoirs*, 1: 117–18.

13 Essex to FB, 24 [?] August 1593, LPL MS 649, art. 168; *LL* 1: 254–5; Birch,

Memoirs, 1: 120–1. See also Essex to FB, 27 September 1593, LPL MS 649, art. 197; *LL* 1: 258; Birch, *Memoirs*, 1: 123.

14　WC to ACB, 29 August 1593, LPL MS 649, art. 168; *LL* 1: 255; Birch, *Memoirs*, 1: 120.

15　RC to FB, 27 September 1593, LPL MS 649, fo. 299^v (art. 197).

16　WC to FB, 27 September 1593, LPL MS 649, fo. 299^r (art. 197).

17　Morgan Coleman to AB, 27 September 1593, LPL MS 649, art. 195; *LL* 1: 257–8 n. 5; Birch, *Memoirs*, 1: 123.

18　AB to ACB, 2 November 1593, LPL MS 649, art. 274; *LL* 1: 262 n. 2.

19　AB to FB, 8 October 1593, LPL MS 649, fo. 334^r (art. 227).

20　AB to FB, 10 October 1593, LPL MS 649, fo. 335^r (art. 228).

21　AS to AB, 20 November 1593, LPL MS 649, art. 206; Birch, *Memoirs*, 1: 133–4.

22　AB to ACB, 19 October 1593, LPL MS 649, fo. 337^r (art. 230).

23　AB to FB, 14 October 1593, LPL MS 649, fo. 336^r (art. 229).

24　Essex to AB, 19 October 1593, LPL MS 653, art. 172; *LL* 1: 258–9; Birch, *Memoirs*, 1: 126–7.

25　FB to Robert Kemp, 4 November 1593, LPL MS 649, art. 281; Birch, *Memoirs*, 1: 127.

26　RC to FB, 27 September 1593, LPL MS 649, fo. 299^v (art. 197).

27　AS to AB, 22 January 1594, LPL MS 650, fo. 31^r (art. 20); *LL* 1: 266; Birch, *Memoirs*, 1: 147.

28　AS to AB, 11 November 1593, LPL MS 649, fo. 390^r (art. 268); Birch, *Memoirs*, 1: 130.

29　FB to Essex, 14? November 1593, LPL MS 649, art. 283.

30　For speculation see *LL* 1: 262 n. 2; Harold Hardy, 'Bacon and "The Huddler"', *Notes and Queries* 151 (1926), 39–41.

31　AB to FB, 15 November 1593, LPL MS 649, art. 273; *LL* 1: 252 n. 1; Birch, *Memoirs*, 1: 130.

32　AS to AB, 25 November 1593, 11 December 1593, LPL MS 649, arts 261, 295; Birch, *Memoirs*, 1: 134–5, 138.

33　AS to AB, 18 December 1593, LPL MS 649, fo. 425^r (art. 294); Birch, *Memoirs*, 1: 139.

34　AS to AB, 18 December 1593, LPL MS 649, fo. 425^r (art. 294); Birch, *Memoirs*, 1: 139.

35　Edward Stanhope to FB, 20 January 1594, LPL MS 650, fo. 45^r (art. 29).

36　Birch, *Memoirs*, 1: 152.

37　On the Lopez affair see Arthur Dimock, 'The Conspiracy of Dr Lopez', *English Historical Review* 9 (1894), 440–72; Martin Hume, 'The So-Called Conspiracy of Dr Ruy Lopez', *The Jewish Historical Society of England Transactions* 6 (1912), 32–5; John Gwyer, 'The Case of Lopez', *The Jewish Historical Society of England Transactions* 16 (1952), 163–84; Edgar Roy Samuel, 'Portuguese Jews in Jacobean England', *The Jewish Historical Society of England Transactions* 18 (1958), 171–230; Joyce Treskunof Freedman, 'Anthony Bacon and his World, 1558–1601' (PhD, Temple University, 1979), 344–76; James Shapiro, *Shakespeare and the Jews* (New York: Columbia University Press, 1996), 171–230.

38　AB to AS, n.d., LPL MS 648, art. 99.

39 AS to AB, 3 February 1594, LPL MS 650, fo. 80^{r-v} (art. 50).

40 *HPT* 3: 205–7.

41 AS to AB, 24 January 1594, LPL MS 650, fo. 23^r (art. 16); Birch, *Memoirs*, 1: 147–8.

42 AS to AB, 3 February 1594, LPL MS 650, fo. 80^{r-v} (art. 50).

43 AB to ACB, 9 February 1594, LPL MS 649, fo. 47^r (art. 29); *LL* 1: 267.

44 NF to AB, 11 February 1594, LPL MS 650, art. 67; *LL* 1: 168; Birch, *Memoirs*, 1: 156–7; Henry Gosnold to AB, LPL MS 653, fo.187^r (art. 101).

45 For Faunt's account of Waad's intelligence on the Lopez affair, see NF to AB, 11 February 1594, LPL MS 650, art. 67.

46 NF to AB, 25 February 1594, LPL MS 650, art. 66.

47 See AS to AB, 24 January 1594, LPL MS 650, art. 16; Freedman, 'Anthony Bacon', 314.

48 NF to AB, end January 1594, LPL MS 650, art. 34.

49 NF to AB, 28 February 1594, LPL MS 650, art. 161.

50 Freedman, 'Anthony Bacon', 374 n. 40.

51 Sidney Lee, 'Original of Shylock', *Gentleman's Magazine* 248 (1880), 185–200.

52 AS to AB, 3 March 1594, LPL MS 650, art. 81.

53 Manuscript accounts exist: three in the PRO; one in William A. Murdin, ed., *A Collection of State Papers Relating to Affairs in the Reign of Queen Elizabeth, from the Year 1571 to 1696* (London: William Bowyer, 1759), 669; another in BL Harley MS 871. See *LL* 1: 273. Spedding believes Coke drew up the *True Report of Sundry Horrible Conspiracies* printed in November 1594 (London: C. Yetsweirt); more recently, Burghley has been identified as the author.

54 RC to Egerton, 27 March 1593, LPL MS 649, art. 60; Birch, *Memoirs*, 1: 165–6.

55 Essex to FB, 28 March 1594, LPL MS 650, fo. 148^r (art. 90); Birch, *Memoirs*, 1: 166.

56 Essex to FB, 29 March 1594, LPL MS 650, fo. 147^r (art. 89); Birch, *Memoirs*, 1: 167.

57 FB to Essex, 30 March 1594, LPL MS 649, art. 62; *LL* 1: 290; Birch, *Memoirs*, 1: 167.

58 AS to AB, 5 April 1594, LPL MS 650, art. 111; Birch, *Memoirs*, 1: 168–9.

59 FB to Puckering, 7[?] and 8 April 1594, BL Harley MS 6996, arts 101, 97; *LL* 1: 292–3.

60 NF to AB, 19 March 1594, LPL MS 650, fos 171–2 (art. 105); for the date of the move, see Herbert Berry, 'Chambers, the Bull, and the Bacons', *Essays in Theatre* 7 (1988), 35–42.

61 ACB to AB, 1594, LPL MS 650, fos 187–8 (art. 114).

62 On Pérez see Gustav Ungerer, *A Spaniard in Elizabethan England: The Correspondence of Antonio Pérez's Exile*, 2 vols (London: Tamesis, 1974–6).

63 AB to FB, 25 December 1594, LPL MS 650, fo. 328 (art. 221).

64 ACB to AB, n.d. [1594?], LPL MS 653, art. 177; Ungerer, *Spaniard*, 1: 221.

65 Ungerer, *Spaniard*, 1: 215.

66 Pérez to Elizabeth, July 1595, LPL MS 653, art. 63.

67 AB to Henri IV, 1595, LPL MS 652, art. 186.

68 Atey to AB, 17 March 1594, LPL MS 653, fo. 73.

69 Gustav Ungerer, 'The Printing of Spanish Books in Elizabethan England', *Library* 10 (1965), 177–229 at 188.

70 See Pérez to Essex, 19 December 1595, AB to Dr Henry Hawkyns, 2 December 1596, Ungerer, *Spaniard*, 1: 388, 2: 191; Pérez to Essex, July 1595, Ungerer, *Spaniard*, 1: 336.

71 FB to AB, 13 December 1594, LPL MS 650, art. 225; *LL* 1: 324–5; Ungerer, *Spaniard*, 1: 221–2.

72 Pérez to AB, n.d. [January 1595?]; Pérez, *Epistolarum centuria vna* (Paris, 1601), ep. 73; Ungerer, *Spaniard*, 1: 490–1.

73 Essex to FB, 26 April 1594, LPL MS 650, fo. 178^r (art. 109); *LL* 1: 294–5; Birch, *Memoirs*, 1: 170.

74 FB to RC, 1 May 1594, LPL MS 650, art. 125; *LL* 1: 295–6.

75 RC to FB, n.d., LPL MS 650, art. 125; *LL* 1: 296.

76 Essex to Puckering, 4 May 1594, BL Harley MS 6996, art. 140; *LL* 1: 296.

77 Essex to FB, 13 May 1594, LPL MS 650, art. 122; *LL* 1: 297.

78 Essex to FB, 18 May 1594, LPL MS 650, art. 123; *LL* 1: 297–8.

79 Fulke Greville to FB, 27 May 1594, LPL MS 650, art. 131; *LL* 1: 298.

80 AB to ACB, 17 May 1594, LPL MS 650, art. 124; *LL* 1: 299.

81 FB to ACB, 9 June 1594, LPL MS 650, art. 140; *LL* 1: 300.

82 Fulke Greville to FB, 17 June 1594, LPL MS 650, art. 132; *LL* 1: 302.

83 Examinations: PRO SP 12/248/78 (27 April 1594), 91 (3 May 1594) and 112 (18 May 1594), 249/4 (4 June 1594) and 12 (13 June 1594); *CSPD, 1591–1594*, 489, 497, 509, 514, 517.

84 *LL* 1: 345 n. 1.

85 AB to Spencer, 12 July 1594, LPL MS 649, art. 138.

86 Trott to ACB, 3 August 1594, BL Harley MS 871, fo. 80; *LL* 1: 304 n. 1.

87 AB to FB, 22 July 1594, LPL MS 650, art. 148.

88 FB to Elizabeth, 20 July 1594, LPL MS 650, art. 156; *LL* 1: 304–5.

89 *Opera Omnia*, 4 vols, ed. John Blackbourne (London: R. Gosling, 1730), 1: 217, quoted in *LL* 1: 305; Edward Spencer to AB, 31 July 1594, LPL MS 650, art. 152; *LL* 1: 310–11, mentions 'the return of Mr. Francis and of his good health'.

90 Edward Spencer to AB, 31 July 1594, LPL MS 650, art. 152; *LL* 1: 310–11.

91 Edward Spencer to AB, ?late July 1594, LPL MS 650, art. 151; *LL* 1: 310.

92 *FBT* 1: 128–9.

93 ACB to FB, 20 August 1594, LPL MS 650, art. 171; *LL* 1: 312–13.

94 On these examinations see *CSPD, 1591–1594*, 544, 546–7, 548, 549, 550, 551, 555; FB to Puckering, 24 August 1594, BL Harley MS 6996, art. 196; *LL* 1: 313–14.

95 FB to Puckering, 24, 25 August 1594, BL Harley MS 6996, arts 196, 200; *LL* 1: 313–14.

96 FB to AB, 26 August 1594, LPL MS 650, art. 168; *LL* 1: 314–15.

97 FB to Puckering, 28 September 1594, BL Harley MS 6996, art. 216; *LL* 1: 320.

98 Essex to AB, 23 October 1594, LPL MS 650, art. 195; *LL* 1: 321.

99 FB to AB, 15 October 1594, LPL MS 650, art. 197; *LL* 1: 321.

100 ACB to AB, 5 December 1594, *FBT* 1: 128.

101 This list from Julian Martin, *Francis Bacon, the State, and the Reform of Natural Philosophy* (Cambridge: Cambridge University Press, 1992), 199 n. 67.

102 FB to Essex, n.d., *Resuscitatio* 85; *LL* 1: 344–5. We follow Spedding's dating here.

103 Essex to Puckering, 14 January 1595, BL Harley MS 6997, fo. 170; *LL* 1: 345.

104 FB to AB, 25 January 1595, LPL MS 650, art. 28; *LL* 1: 347–9.

105 Ibid.

106 FB to RC, ?25 January 1595, LPL MS 650, art. 31; *LL* 1: 350–1.

107 FB to WC, 21 March 1595, BL Lansdowne MS 78, fo. 74; *LL* 1: 357–8.

108 AB to ACB, 7 March 1595, *An Account of the Life and Times of Francis Bacon*, 2 vols, ed. James Spedding (Boston: Houghton, Mifflin & Co., 1880), 1: 163.

109 Essex to Puckering, n.d. [1595], BL Harley MS 6997, fo. 205; *LL* 1: 354.

110 FB to WC, 21 March 1595, BL Lansdowne MS 78, fo. 74; *LL* 1: 358.

111 FB to RC, n.d., *Resuscitatio* 87; *LL* 1: 355–6.

112 FB to RC, n.d., *Resuscitatio* 110; *LL* 1: 356–7.

113 FB to WC, 21 March 1595, BL Lansdowne MS 78, fo. 74; *LL* 1: 358.

114 FB to Fulke Greville, [?May 1595], *Resuscitatio* 89; *LL* 1: 359.

115 FB to RC, n.d., *Resuscitatio* 87; *LL* 1: 355–6.

116 FB to Puckering, 25 May 1595, BL Harley MS 6997, art. 26; *LL* 1: 360.

117 FB to WC, 7 June 1595. BL Add. MS 5503, fo. 1b; *LL* 1: 361–3.

118 ACB to AB, 30 June 1595, *LL* 1: 364 n. 1.

119 FB to Puckering, 28 July 1595, BL Harley MS 6997, fo. 72; *LL* 1: 364–5.

120 Essex to Puckering, ?August 1595, BL Harley MS 6997, fo. 92; *LL* 1: 366–7.

121 FB to Puckering, 19 August 1595, BL Harley MS 6997, fo. 86; *LL* 1: 355–6.

122 AS to AB, 20 December 1593, LPL MS 649, fo. 429^{r-v} (art. 296); Birch, *Memoirs*, 1: 144.

123 RW to RS, 27 September 1595, HMC, *Report on the Manuscripts of Lord de L'Isle & Dudley Preserved at Penshurst Place*, vol. 2, ed. C. L. Kingsford with William A. Shaw (London: HMSO, 1934), 166. See also RW to RS, 19 September 1595, HMC, *De L'Isle & Dudley* 2: 162; *Letters and Memorials of State, in the Reigns of Queen Mary, Queen Elizabeth, King James, King Charles the First, Part of the Reign of King Charles the Second, and Oliver's Usurpation*, 2 vols, ed. Arthur Collins (London: T. Osborne, 1746), 1: 347. Collins misreads 'Essex' as 'Epsom'.

124 ACB to AB, 18 March 1597, LPL MS 656, art. 29; AB to ACB, 2 October 1596, LPL MS 659, art. 142.

125 ACB to AB, August 1595, LPL MS 651, arts 212, 210; Daphne Du Maurier, *Golden Lads: Anthony Bacon, Francis, and their Friends* (London: Victor Gollancz, 1975), 138–9; Freedman, 'Anthony Bacon', 446–7.

126 AB's account of this affair is in AB to Essex, September 1595, LPL MS 659, fos 23a–26b; for its context see Jason Scott-Warren, 'The Privy Politics of Sir John Harington's *New Discourse of a Stale Subject, Called the Metamorphosis of Ajax*', *Studies in Philology* 93 (1996), 412–42 at 422–4.

127 Lady Russell to AB, 8 September [1595], LPL MS 659, fo. 104 (art. 75). Copy at LPL MS 659, fos 162–3.

128 AB to Lady Russell, Thursday 9 September 1595, LPL MS 659, fo. 187 (art. 128); draft at LPL MS 659, fo. 199 (art. 135); Lady Russell to AB, 9 September 1595, LPL MS 659, fo. 106 (art. 76).

129 FB to Puckering, 11 October 1595, BL Harley MS 6997, fo. 117; *LL* 1: 368.

See also FB to Puckering, 25 September 1595, BL Harley MS 6996, fo. 214, 6997, fo. 115; *LL* 1: 367–8.

130 FB to Puckering, 14 October 1595, BL Harley MS 6997, fo. 119; *LL* 1: 369.

CHAPTER 7

1 *Apology*; *LL* 3: 143–4.

2 FB to Essex, n.d. [?November 1595], *Resuscitatio* 111; *LL* 1: 372–3.

3 On this transaction, see William Hepworth Dixon, *Personal History of Lord Bacon from Unpublished Papers* (London: John Murray, 1861), 359; *LL* 1: 371–2.

4 FB to Essex, n.d. [?November 1595], *Resuscitatio* 111; *LL* 1: 372–3.

5 RW to RS, 5 and 7 November 1595, HMC, *Report on the Manuscripts of Lord de L'Isle & Dudley preserved at Penshurst Place* vol. 2, ed. C. L. Kingsford with William A. Shaw (London: HMSO, 1934), 182–3, 183; *Letters and Memorials of State, in the Reigns of Queen Mary, Queen Elizabeth, King James, King Charles the First, Part of the Reign of King Charles the Second, and Oliver's Usurpation*, 2 vols, ed. Arthur Collins (London: T. Osborne, 1746), 1: 357, 359.

6 'Accession Day Device', *LL* 1: 374–92; for MS witnesses, see Beal BcF 308–17.

7 RW to RS, 22 November 1595; *Letters and Memorials*, ed. Collins, 1: 362.

8 See Algernon Cecil, *A Life of Robert Cecil, Earl of Salisbury* (London: John Murray, 1915), 46–52, 94–7; P. M. Handover, *The Second Cecil: The Rise to Power 1563–1604 of Sir Robert Cecil, Later First Earl of Salisbury* (London: Eyre & Spottiswoode, 1959), 131–2; E. K. Chambers, *The Elizabethan Stage*, 4 vols (Oxford: Clarendon Press, 1923), 3: 212, 247–9; Alan Young, *Tudor and Jacobean Pageants* (London: George Philip, 1987), 174–5.

9 Robert Devereux, earl of Essex, *An Apologie of the Earle of Essex, against those which Iealovsly, and Maliciovsly, Tax him to be the Hinderer of the Peace and Qviet of his Covntry* (London: Richard Bradocke, 1603), A2ᵛ; this work was originally published in 1599, but suppressed. See also Henry Wotton, *A Parallel betweene Robert late Earle of Essex, and George late Duke of Buckingham* (London, 1641), A2ᵛ–A3ʳ; Ray Heffner, 'Essex, the Ideal Courtier', *ELH* 1 (1934), 7–36, esp. 19–21.

10 RW to RS, 22 November 1595, *Letters and Memorials*, ed. Collins, 1: 362.

11 Thomas Birch, *Memoirs of the Reign of Queen Elizabeth, from the Year 1581 till her Death*, 2 vols (London: A. Millar, 1754), 1: 465–6.

12 Ibid., 1: 353–4.

13 Wallace T. MacCaffrey, *Elizabeth I: War and Politics 1588–1603* (Princeton, NJ: Princeton University Press, 1992), 495.

14 Birch, *Memoirs*, 1: 450–2, 459–60.

15 Ibid., 466, 483.

16 Gustav Ungerer, *A Spaniard in Elizabethan England: The Correspondence of Antonio Pérez's Exile*, 2 vols (London: Tamesis, 1974–6), 1: 308–9.

17 AB to Essex 30 March 1596, LPL MS 656, art. 80.

18 AB to Essex, 28 April, 1 May, [3 May], 5 May 1596, LPL MS 656, art. 183; MS 657, arts 23, 22, 19; Ungerer, *Spaniard*, 1: 273–5.

19 Ungerer, *Spaniard*, 1: 217.

20 Penelope Rich to AB, 3 May 1596, LPL MS 657, art. 46; Ungerer, *Spaniard*, 1: 275–6.

21 AB to Penelope Rich, 5 May 1596, LPL MS 657, art. 88; Ungerer, *Spaniard*, 1: 276–7.

22 AB to Essex, 5 May 1596, LPL MS 657, art. 19; Ungerer, *Spaniard*, 1: 277–8.

23 Edward Reynolds to Essex, 6 May 1596, LPL MS 657, art. 74; Ungerer, *Spaniard*, 1: 292.

24 Essex to AB, 10 May 1596, LPL MS 657, art. 89; Devereux, 1: 348; Birch, *Memoirs*, 1: 484; Ungerer, *Spaniard*, 1: 279.

25 AB to Essex, 18 May 1596, LPL MS 657, art. 15; Ungerer, *Spaniard*, 1: 279–80.

26 AB to FB (variant to Essex), *c.*14 May 1596, LPL MS 657, art. 9; Ungerer, *Spaniard*, 1: 226–7.

27 AB to FB, *c.*17 May 1596, LPL MS 657, art. 8; Birch, *Memoirs*, 1: 486; Ungerer, *Spaniard*, 1: 228–9. See also AS to AB, 2 June 1596, n.s., LPL MS 657, art. 3; Birch, *Memoirs*, 2: 10–11.

28 MacCaffrey, *Elizabeth I*, 497–8; Devereux 2: 349–56; Birch, *Memoirs*, 2: 19–20.

29 *Considerations Touching the War with Spain*, LL 7: 469–505; for MS witnesses see Beal BcF 166–75.

30 MacCaffrey, *Elizabeth I*, 498; Birch, *Memoirs*, 2: 45, 80–2, 95.

31 BL Cotton MS Otho IX, fos 363–4, quoted in MacCaffrey, *Elizabeth I*, 498.

32 Birch, *Memoirs*, 2: 96.

33 Birch, *Memoirs*, 2: 60–1, 119–121. Essex may have had a kind of equivalent in a substantial grant of land in fee simple at the same time: MacCaffrey, *Elizabeth I*, 500 and n. 17.

34 FB to Essex, 4 October 1596, *Resuscitatio* 106; LL 2: 40–5.

35 AB to ACB, 31 December 1596, LL 2: 45.

36 RW to RS, 25 February 1597, *Letters and Memorials*, ed. Collins, 2: 19.

37 Edward Monings' *The Landrave of Hesssen his Princelie Receiuing of her Majesties Embassador* (London: R. Robinson, 1596) 'borrows' from 'Of Studies' and 'Of Followers and Friends'; see *The Essayes or Counsels, Civill and Morall*, ed. Michael Kiernan (Oxford: Clarendon Press, 1985), lxv–lxvii. For the rival edition, see the Stationers' Register entry for 24 January 1597; for FB's edition, see 5 February 1597; for suppression, see 7 February 1597; all in Edward Arber, ed., *A Transcript of the Registers of the Company of Stationers*, 5 vols (London: privately printed, 1875–94). For sale dates, see *Essayes*, ed. Kiernan, lxviii and n. 23, and *Works* 6: 522. FB to AB, 30 January 1597, *Essayes* (London: Humfrey Hooper, 1597), A3^r–A4^r.

38 AB to Essex, 8 February 1597, *Works* 6: 521–2.

39 FB to WC, n.d., *Resuscitatio* 88; LL 2: 49–50.

40 FB to Sir John Stanhope, n.d., *Resuscitatio* 87; LL 2: 50–1.

41 FB to Essex, n.d., *Resuscitatio* 86; LL 2: 51.

42 *Apology*; LL 3: 145.

43 FB to Essex, n.d., *Resuscitatio* 112; LL 2: 55–6.

44 Birch, *Memoirs* 2: 347.

45 JC to DC, 22 November 1598, McClure 1: 54.

46 FB to Essex, n.d., *Resuscitatio* 112; *LL* 2: 55–6.

47 FB to Essex, n.d., *Resuscitatio* 112; *LL* 2: 55–6.

48 *HPT* 3: 57.

49 'The humble motion and allegacions . . . concerninge certaine fees', HEH MS EL 2675; *LL* 2: 57–60.

50 FB to Egerton, n.d. [summer/autumn 1597], Queen's College, Oxford, MS Arch. D. 2; pr. in *LL* 2: 60–4. On Egerton (later Ellesmere) see Susan Cameron Miller Laffitte, 'The Literary Connections of Sir Thomas Egerton: A Study of the Influence of Thomas Egerton upon Major Writers of Renaissance Literature' (PhD, Florida State University, 1971); Louis A Knafla, *Law and Politics in Jacobean England: The Tracts of Lord Chancellor Ellesmere* (Cambridge: Cambridge University Press, 1977).

51 FB to Egerton, 12 November 1597, HEH MS EL 2681; *LL* 2: 65.

52 *Apophthegms, Works* 7: 169. See also FB to the Queen, n.d., *Resuscitatio* 93; *LL* 2: 67.

53 FB to Egerton, 22 January 1598, HEH MS EL 2684; *LL* 2: 66–7.

54 Elizabeth to Egerton, 1 February 1601, *The Egerton Papers*, ed. J. Payne Collier (London: Camden Society, 1840, vol. 12), 316–17.

55 On the 1597 parliament, see T. E. Hartley, ed., *Proceedings in the Parliaments of Elizabeth*, 3 vols (Leicester: Leicester University Press, 1981–95), 3: 177–243; *HPT* 1: 377–8; *LL* 2: 77–89; Nathaniel Bacon, *The Annals of Ipswiche. The Lawes Customes and Government of the Same*, ed. William H. Richardson (Ipswich: privately printed, 1884), 389; Simonds D'Ewes, *The Journals of All the Parliaments during the Reign of Queen Elizabeth, both of the House of Lords and House of Commons*, rev. Paul Bowes (London: John Shirley, 1682), 551–93; Heywood Townshend, *Historical Collections: or, An Exact Account of the Proceedings of the Four Last Parliaments of Q. Elizabeth* (London: T. Basset, W. Crooke and W. Cademan, 1680), 102–25; *Bulletin of the Institute for Historical Research* 12: 10–11, 13.

56 D'Ewes, *Journals of All the Parliaments*, 524.

57 RW to RS, 29 October 1597, *Letters and Memorials*, ed. Collins, 2: 74.

58 RW to RS, 23 October 1597, *Letters and Memorials*, ed. Collins, 2: 70.

59 RW to RS, 5 November 1597, *Letters and Memorials*, ed. Collins, 2: 70.

60 Committees on 5 November, 26 November, 7 February; speaking to bills and reporting on committees on 14, 18, 21 November, 5 December, 3 and 6 February.

61 *LL* 2: 84–9.

62 Devereux 1: 470.

63 Birch, *Memoirs*, 2: 365.

64 RW to RS, St Thomas Day 1597, *Letters and Memorials*, ed. Collins, 2: 77.

65 *Apophthegms, Works* 7: 167–8.

66 FB to Essex, 'to take upon him the care of Irish causes', BL Add. MS 5503, fo. 3; *LL* 2: 94–6.

67 FB to Essex, 'upon the first treaty with Tyrone, 1598, before the earl was nominated for the charge of Ireland', BL Add. MS 5503, fo. 4; *LL* 2: 98–100.

68 William Camden, *Annales rerum Anglicarum et Hibernicarum regnante Elizabetha*, 3 vols, ed. Thomas Hearne (London, 1707), 3: 771–2; John Harington, *Nugae Antiquae: Being a Miscellaneous Collection of Original Papers, in Prose and Verse*, ed. Henry Harington, new edn, 2 vols (London: J. Wright, 1824), 1: 173.

69 JC to DC, 30 August 1598, McClure 1: 41.
70 FB's text is *A Letter Written Out of England to an English Gentleman at Padua* (London: Deputies of C. Barker, 1599); the hostile response is M. A. Priest, *The Discouerie and Confutation of the Tragical Fiction Devysed by E. Squyer* (n.p.: publisher unknown, 1599), B6ᵛ, quoted in Corinne Rickert, 'An Addition to the Canon of Bacon's Writings,' *Modern Language Review* 50–1 (1955–6), 71–2.
71 FB to Egerton, 24 September 1598, *HMCS* 8: 360–1; *LL* 2: 107–8.
72 FB to RC, 24 September 1598, *HMCS* 8: 359–60; *LL* 2: 106–7.
73 A. H. Dodd, 'Mr Myddleton the Merchant of Tower Street', in S. T. Bindoff, J. Hurstfield and C. H. Williams, eds, *Elizabethan Government and Society: Essays Presented to Sir John Neale* (London: Athlone Press, 1961), 261; Evan D. Jones, 'An Account Book of Sir Thomas Myddelton for the Years 1583–1603', *National Library of Wales Journal* 1 (1939–40), facing p. 83.
74 AB to ACB, 16 April 1593, LPL MS 649, art. 67; *LL* 1: 243–4.
75 ACB to AB, 17 April [1593], LPL MS 653, fo. 318ʳ (art. 175); Ungerer, *Spaniard*, 2: 220 nn. 3–5.
76 ACB to AB, 17 April [1593], LPL MS 653, fo. 319ʳ (art. 176).
77 ACB to AB, 18 April 1593, LPL MS 653, art. 165; *LL* 1: 245–6.
78 AB to ACB, 6 September 1593, LPL MS 649, art. 210; *LL* 1: 246.
79 See Joyce Treskunof Freedman, 'Anthony Bacon and his World, 1558–1601' (PhD, Temple University, 1979), 190.
80 AB to ACB, 15 June 1593, LPL MS 649, art. 121.
81 ACB to AB, 18 March 1597, LPL MS 656, art. 29; AB to ACB, 2 October 1596, LPL MS 659, art. 142.
82 ACB to AB, 18 March 1597, LPL MS 656, art. 29.
83 ACB to AB, June 1596, LPL MS 657, art. 113.
84 ACB to AB, 7 September 1594, LPL MS 650, art. 223.
85 ACB to AB, March 1597, LPL MS 656, art. 29.
86 Edward Spencer to AB, 31 July 1594, LPL MS 650, art. 152; *LL* 1: 310–11.
87 Edward Spencer to AB, 16 August 1594, LPL MS 650, art. 169; *LL* 1: 311–12.
88 ACB to AB, March and 7 September 1594, LPL MS 650, arts 76, 223.
89 ACB to AB, n.d., LPL MS 653, art. 138.
90 On Trott see *HPT* 3: 531–2; Birch, *Memoirs*, 2: 354–7; Freedman, 'Anthony Bacon and his World, 1558–1601'; Daphne Du Maurier, *Golden Lads: Anthony Bacon, Francis and their Friends* (London: Victor Gollancz, 1975).
91 Trott to AB, 7 August 1597, LPL MS 661, art. 170; Freedman, 'Anthony Bacon', 187.
92 AB to FB, August 1596, LPL MS 658, art. 104; Trott to AB, 7 August 1597, LPL MS 661, art. 170.
93 These transactions are taken from Freedman, 'Anthony Bacon', 184–5. FB to Spencer, August 1593, LPL MS 649, art. 186; AB to Spencer, 1593, LPL MS 649, art. 104; survey of property in Barley, 1593, LPL MS 649, arts 263, 264, 265; AB to Henry Killigrew, 24 May 1593, LPL MS 649, art. 78; AB to Spencer, 6 September 1593, LPL MS 649, art. 190; AB to NB2, 17 September 1593, LPL MS 649, art. 201; AB to NB2, 28 July 1593, LPL MS 649, art. 143; *LL* 1: 247. For the final version see LPL MS 649, art. 146. For more on these negotiations see FB to Trott, LPL MS 649, fo. 283ʳ (art. 185); *LL* 1: 248; FB to Alderman

Spencer, LPL MS 649, art. 186; *LL* 1: 249; FB to Alderman Spencer, LPL MS 649, art. 282.

94 AB to TP, 23 August 1594, LPL MS 650, art. 174.

95 Birch's copy: BL Add. MS 4123, art. 28; *LL* 1: 322. The real total is in fact £428.

96 AB, memo 4 October 1594, LPL MS 661, art. 30; *LL* 1: 322.

97 Trott to FB, 2 December 1594, LPL MS 650, art. 207; Trott to AB, 1594, LPL MS 652, art. 54.

98 FB to AB, 10 December 1594, LPL MS 650 fo. 339 (art. 227); *LL* 1: 323–4.

99 AB to Killigrew, 23 January 1595, LPL MS 650 arts 3, 4. See also FB to AB, 25 January 1595, LPL MS 650, art. 28; *LL* 1: 349.

100 AB to FB, 26 January 1595, LPL MS 650, art. 27; *LL* 1: 352. See also FB to AB, [27?] January 1595, LPL MS 650, art. 237; *LL* 1: 353.

101 FB to Henry Maynard and Michael Hickes, 12 March 1596, BL Lansdowne MS 80, fo. 176; *LL* 2: 28, discussed 2: 27–8.

102 Du Maurier, *Golden Lads*, 109.

103 AB to FB, May 1596, LPL MS 657, art. 7.

104 AB to FB, August 1596, LPL MS 658, art. 104.

105 Trott to AB, August 1597, LPL MS 660, art. 82.

106 Trott to AB, 17 August 1597, LPL MS 661, art. 169.

107 Trott to AB, 6 September 1597, LPL MS 661, art. 159.

108 BL Lansdowne MS 88, fo. 50. See also Trott to Hickes, 18 December, 19 December 1601, BL Lansdowne MS 88, fos 48, 54.

CHAPTER 8

1 JC to DC, 30 August 1598, McClure 1: 41. TM to DC, 15 September 1598, *An Account of the Life and Times of Francis Bacon*, ed. James Spedding, 2 vols (Boston: Houghton, Mifflin & Co., 1880), 1: 239.

2 FB to Essex, n.d. [October 1598?], *Resuscitatio* 95; *LL* 2: 104.

3 William Camden, *Annales rerum Anglicarum et Hibernicarum regnante Elizabetha*, 3 vols, ed. Thomas Hearne (London 1707), 3: 787, tr. Spedding, *LL* 2: 127–8.

4 Camden, *Annales*, 3: 788.

5 Fynes Morison, *An Itenerary Written by Fynes Moryson, Gent. First in the Latine Tongue, and then Translated by Him into English* (London: J. Beale, 1617), 26, quoted in *LL* 2: 128 n. 1.

6 Robert Markham to Sir John Harington, [1598–9], in John Harington, *Nugae Antiquae: Being a Miscellaneous Collection of Original Papers, in Prose and Verse*, ed. Henry Harington, new edn, 2 vols (London: J. Wright, 1824), 1: 240.

7 JC to DC, 8 December 1598, McClure 1: 56.

8 JC to DC, 20 December 1598, McClure 1: 58.

9 JC to DC, 3 January 1599, McClure 1: 60.

10 JC to DC, 1 March 1599, McClure 1: 69.

11 Devereux 2: 10–11.

12 *Apology, LL* 3: 149, 150.

13 JC to DC, 1 March 1599, McClure 1: 70.

14 *Apology, LL* 3: 150.

15 *Apology, LL* 3: 145–6.

16 'A letter of advice to my Lord of Essex, immediately before his going into Ireland', BL Add. MS 5503, fo. 6; *LL* 2: 129–33.

17 John Nichols, *The Progresses and Public Processions of Queen Elizabeth*, rev. edn, 3 vols (London: John Nichols & Son, 1823).

18 Sir Gelly Merrick to Edward Reynolds, 7 May 1599, *HMCS* 9: 157–8.

19 JC to DC, 28 June 1599, McClure 1: 74.

20 Henry Wotton, *Reliquiae Wottonianae. Or, A Collection of Lives, Letters, Poems; With Characters of Sundry Personages: And other Incomparable Pieces of Language and Art* (London: R. Marriot, G. Bedel and T. Garthwait, 1651), 13.

21 *Apology, LL* 3: 146–7.

22 RW to RS, Michaelmas Day 1599, *Letters and Memorials of State, in the Reigns of Queen Mary, Queen Elizabeth, King James, King Charles the First, Part of the Reign of King Charles the Second, and Oliver's Usurpation*, 2 vols, ed. Arthur Collins (London: T. Osborne, 1746), 2: 128.

23 Camden, *Annales*, 3: 796, tr. Spedding in *LL* 2: 153 and n. 2.

24 RW to RS, Michaelmas Day 1599, *Letters and Memorials*, ed. Collins, 2: 127.

25 FB to Essex, n.d., *Resuscitatio* 86; *LL* 2: 150.

26 *Apology, LL* 3: 147–8.

27 RW to RS, 6 October 1599, *Letters and Memorials*, ed. Collins, 2: 132.

28 RW to RS, 11 October 1599, *Letters and Memorials*, ed. Collins, 2: 132.

29 RC to Sir Henry Neville, 8 October 1599, *Memorials of Affairs of State in the Reigns of Queen Elizabeth and King James I. Collected (chiefly) from the Original Papers of the Right Honourable Sir Ralph Winwood*, 3 vols, ed. Edmund Sawyer (London: T. Ward, 1725), 1: 118. For Tyrone's propositions see ibid., 1: 119.

30 *Apology, LL* 3: 148–9.

31 *Apology, LL* 3: 150–1.

32 *Apology, LL* 3: 151–2.

33 'Wednesday was sevennight' before 3 December: FB to Henry Howard, 3 December 1599, *HMCS* 9: 406.

34 FB to Elizabeth, n.d., *Resuscitatio* 99; *LL* 2: 160.

35 *Apology, LL* 3: 148.

36 FB to Lord Henry Howard, 3 December 1599, *HMCS* 9: 405–6; *LL* 2: 161–2. A very similar letter was sent to Sir Robert Cecil, [3 December 1599]; *Resuscitatio* 98; *LL* 2: 162.

37 Lord Henry Howard to FB, n.d., *HMCS* 9: 406–7.

38 *Apology, LL* 3: 148.

39 Nichols, *Progresses of Queen Elizabeth*, 3: 457, 465.

40 FB to Elizabeth, [New Year 1600?], *Resuscitatio* 3; *LL* 2: 163–4. For other New Year's letters to Elizabeth see *Resuscitatio* 3 and 99; *LL* 2: 164.

41 RW to RS, 15 March 1600, *Letters and Memorials*, ed. Collins, 2: 179.

42 ACB to AB, July 1596 and n.d., LPL MS 658, art. 20, and 653, art. 110; ACB to Dr Edward Stanhope, LPL MS 655, art. 68; cited in Joyce Treskunof Freedman, 'Anthony Bacon and his World, 1558–1601' (PhD, Temple University, 1979), 449.

43 FB to Elizabeth, 12 March 1600, BL Add. MS 12,514, fo. 97; *LL* 2: 165–6; Revd

C. Moor, 'Bacon Deeds at Gorhambury', *The Genealogists' Magazine* 7 (1937), 561–74.
44 *Apology*, *LL* 3: 152.
45 Ibid.
46 *Apology*, *LL* 3: 153.
47 *Apology*, *LL* 3: 153–4.
48 RW to RS, 7 June 1600, *Letters and Memorials*, ed. Collins, 2: 199–200.
49 'The Proceedings of the Earl of Essex', BL Harley MS 6854, fo. 177; *LL* 2: 175.
50 RW to RS, 7 June 1600, *Letters and Memorials*, ed. Collins, 2: 199.
51 *Apology*, *LL* 3: 154.
52 RW to RS, 7 June 1600, *Letters and Memorials*, ed. Collins, 2: 200.
53 RW to RS, 11 June 1600, *Letters and Memorials*, ed. Collins, 2: 200–1.
54 Ibid.
55 RW to RS, 28 June 1600, HMC, *Report on the Manuscripts of Lord de L'Isle & Dudley Preserved at Penshurst Place*, vol. 2, ed. C. L. Kingsford with William A. Shaw (London: HMSO, 1934), 471; *Letters and Memorials*, ed. Collins (with alterations and omissions), 2: 204.
56 Sir Gelly Merrick to Southampton, 11 June 1600, *HMCS* 10: 178. Boissise to Henri IV, 17 June 1600, P. Laffleur de Kermaingant, *Mission de Jean de Thumery sieur de Boissise (1598–1602)*, 2 vols (Paris: Firmin-Didot, 1886), 1: 497–8.
57 Henri IV to Boissise, 2 July 1600, Laffleur de Kermaingant, *Mission de Boissise*, 2: 158.
58 *Apology*, *LL* 3: 154–5.
59 *Apology*, *LL* 3: 155.

CHAPTER 9

1 *Apology*, *LL* 3: 155; FB to Essex, 20 July 1600, BL Lansdowne MS 87, fo. 210; see also BL Add. MS 5503 (dated 19 July 1600); *LL* 2: 190–1.
2 *Apology*, *LL* 3: 155; Essex to FB, n.d., *Resuscitatio* 10; *LL* 2: 192.
3 *Apology*, *LL* 3: 155; Essex to Elizabeth, n.d., *Resuscitatio* 94; *LL* 2: 193–4. For a draft of another letter see FB to Essex, n.d., LPL MS 941, art. 139; *LL* 2: 194–6.
4 *Apology*, *LL* 3: 155–6.
5 *Apology*, *LL* 3: 156–7.
6 'AB to Essex', [1600], BL Add. MS 5503, fos 9a–11b; *LL* 2: 197–200.
7 'Essex to AB', [1600], BL Add. MS 5503, fos 11b–12b; *LL* 2: 200–1.
8 Essex to Elizabeth, [6 September 1600], Devereux 2: 120. See also Essex to Elizabeth, 9 and 22 September 1600, Devereux 2: 120, 125–6.
9 Essex to Elizabeth, 22 September 1600, Devereux 2: 125–6. *Apology*, *LL* 3: 156.
10 AB to [Essex], 19 September 1600, *HMCS* 10: 318–19.
11 RW to RS, 3 October 1600, *Letters and Memorials of State, in the Reigns of Queen Mary, Queen Elizabeth, King James, King Charles the First, Part of the Reign of King Charles the Second, and Oliver's Usurpation*, 2 vols, ed. Arthur Collins (London: T. Osborne, 1746), 2: 216.
12 Sir Charles Davers' declaration in *A Complete Collection of State Trials, and Proceedings for High Treason and other Crimes and Misdemeanours from the Earliest Period to the*

Year 1783, 21 vols, ed. T. B. Howell (London: T. C. Hansard, 1816), 1: 1345–6.

13 Sir John Harington in his *Nugae Antiquae: Being a Miscellaneous Collection of Original Papers, in Prose and Verse*, ed. Henry Harington, new edn, 2 vols (London: J. Wright, 1824), 1: 179.

14 *Apology, LL* 3: 157.

15 Essex to Elizabeth, 18 October, 17 November 1600; Devereux 2: 126–7, 128.

16 RW to RS, 30 October 1600, *Letters and Memorials*, ed. Collins, 2: 220.

17 *Apology, LL* 3: 157.

18 'Reading on the Statute of Uses', *Works* 7: 389–450; for MS witnesses see Beal BcF 271–4. Pensions, 9 November 1599, 14 November 1599, Gray's Inn Book of Orders, 1, fos 242^v, 243^r.

19 *Apology, LL* 3: 157–8.

20 Egerton, RC and Waad to EC and FB, 19 February 1601. PRO SP 12/278/95; *CSPD, 1598–1601*, 585.

21 *Apology, LL* 3: 158.

22 On the trials of Essex and his followers, see *State Trials*, ed. Howell, 1: 1333–60, 1409–52; *Criminal Trials*, 2 vols, ed. David Jardine (London: Charles Knight, 1832–5), 1: 277–388; *LL* 2: 215–367.

23 JC to DC, 24 February 1601, McClure 1: 120.

24 Another version has Essex saying the letters were written to be shown to the Queen.

25 RC to Winwood, 7 March 1601, *Memorials of Affairs of State in the Reigns of Queen Elizabeth and King James I. Collected (chiefly) from the Original Papers of the Right Honourable Sir Ralph Winwood*, 3 vols, ed. Edmund Sawyer (London: T. Ward, 1725), 1: 300.

26 JC to DC, 24 February 1601, McClure 1: 120.

27 *Apology, LL* 3: 158–9. Chamberlain confirms the story: 'Here have yet no more been brought to trial, save nine the next day to the King's Bench bar, but six of them were carried back again without trial': JC to DC, 24 February 1601, McClure 1: 120.

28 *Apology, LL* 3: 158–9.

29 William Camden, *Annales rerum Anglicarum et Hibernicarum regnante Elizabetha*, 3 vols, ed. Thomas Hearne (London 1707), 3: 957–61.

30 RC to Winwood, 7 March 1601, *Memorials of Affairs of State*, ed. Sawyer, 1: 301.

31 Essex's confession, 23 February 1601, PRO SP 12/278/104; *CSPD, 1598–1601*, 587–8.

32 'The Proofs against Sheriff Smythe', 13 February 1601, PRO SP 12/278/58; *CSPD, 1598–1601*, 599.

33 Camden, *Annales*, 3: 834–5, tr. Spedding, *LL* 2: 236.

34 Nottingham to Montjoy, 31 May 1601, Bodl. Tanner MS 76, fo. 22; *LL* 2: 236–7 n. 5.

35 *Apology, LL* 3: 158.

36 JC to DC, 24 February 1601, McClure 1: 120.

37 *LL* 1: 237–8.

38 *State Trials*, ed. Howell, 1: 1438; *LL* 2: 238–9.

39 Memo by EC, 16 March 1601, PRO SP 12/278/28; *CSPD, 1601–1603*, 15.

40 Privy Council to Barker, 14 April 1601, *APC, 1600–1601*, 277.

41 *Apology, LL* 3: 159–60.

42 Perhaps inevitably, given Bacon's claim of verbatim reproduction of the confessions and testimonies, the *Declaration* has come under attack, by Jardine, as being a distorted record of these latter elements. Checking Bacon's version against the originals in the Public Record Office, Jardine noted that Bacon had gone through them and marked certain passages with 'om.', which he read as a signal for the printer to omit them. See Jardine, *Criminal Trials*, 1: 332–3, n.★.

43 Privy Council register, 6 August 1601, *APC, 1601–1604*, 148–9.

44 FB to Hickes, 6 or 7 August 1601, BL Lansdowne MS 107, fo. 14; *LL* 3: 14–15. For the fines see David Jardine, *A Narrative of the Gunpowder Plot* (London: John Murray, 1857), 31 n.★.

45 Cuffe to RC, Cuffe to the Council, 2 March 1601, *Correspondence of James VI with Sir Robert Cecil and others in Scotland*, ed. John Bruce (London: Camden Society, vol. 78, 1861) 88, 90.

46 The anonymous letter to AB concerning Revd Ashton (see n. 29) is dated 30 May 1601 in Camden, *Annales*, 3: 957–61; the fact that the writer did not know of Anthony's death (at least two weeks earlier) suggests that Anthony was keeping a very low profile.

47 JC to DC, 27 May 1601, McClure 1: 123.

48 Daphne Du Maurier, *Golden Lads: Anthony Bacon, Francis and their Friends* (London: Victor Gollancz, 1975), 258.

49 Sir William Cornwallis to RC, 24 September 1598, *HMCS* 8: 361.

50 Thomas Lawson to William Lawson, 27 March 1601, *HMCS* 11: 146–7.

51 Examination of Thomas Leitchfield, taken 7 May 1601, before Sir John Popham: *HMCS* 11: 201.

52 Du Maurier, *Golden Lads*, 259.

53 Revd C. Moor, 'Bacon Deeds at Gorhambury', *The Genealogists' Magazine* 7 (1937), 565.

54 FB to RC, 29 April 1601, *Letters, Speeches, Charges, Advices &c. of Francis Bacon, Lord Viscount St. Alban, Lord Chancellor of England*, ed. Thomas Birth (London: Andrew Millar, 1763), 21; *LL* 3: 2–3. See also Rawley's note of FB's riposte, LPL MS 2086, p. 86.

55 LPL MS 2086, pp. 61, 63.

56 FB to EC, n.d., BL Add. MS 5503, fo. 36; *Resuscitatio* 39; *LL* 3: 4–5. We follow Spedding in assigning this letter to an earlier period than *Resuscitatio* does.

57 On this parliament see D'Ewes, *The Journals of All the Parliaments during the Reign of Queen Elizabeth, both of the House of Lords and House of Commons*, rev. Paul Bowes (London: John Shirley, 1682), 622–84; Townshend, *Historical Collections: or, An Exact Account of the Proceedings of the Four Last Parliaments of Q. Elizabeth* (London: T. Basset, W. Crooke and W. Cademan, 1680), 189–313; *HPT* 1: 378–9.

58 D'Ewes, *Journals of All the Parliaments*, 626; Townshend, *Historical Collections*, 197; *LL* 3: 17–18, 19–20.

59 Townshend, *Historical Collections*, 194; *HPT* 1: 379; *LL* 3: 19.

60 JC to DC, 14 November 1601, McClure 1: 135.

61 *HPT* 1: 378; Townshend, *Historical Collections*, 231; D'Ewes, *Journals of All the Parliaments*, 644; *LL* 3: 26–8.

62 *HPT* 1: 378.
63 Townshend, *Historical Collections*, 297; *LL* 3: 38–9.
64 Townshend, *Historical Collections*, 298; *LL* 3: 39.
65 FB to Michael Hickes, 25 January [?] 1601, BL Lansdowne MS 78, fo. 6, 224; *LL* 2: 205, 205–6.
66 'Considerations Touching the Queen's Service in Ireland', BL Add. MS 5503, fo. 12; *LL* 3: 45–7.
67 Anthony Rivers to Giacomo Creleto, 9 March 1603, PRO SP 12/287/50; *CSPD, 1601–1603*, 298–300.
68 Giovanni Carlo Scaramelli to the Doge and Senate of Venice, 3 April 1603, *CSP . . . Venice, 1592–1603*, 562, as rendered in *A Last Elizabethan Journal: Being a Record of Those Things Most Talked of during the Years 1599–1603*, ed. G. B. Harrison (London: Constable & Co., 1933), 326. BL Cotton MS Julius C.VII, fo. 46, in John Nichols, *The Progresses and Public Processions of Queen Elizabeth*, 3 vols, rev. edn (London: John Nichols & Son, 1823), 3: 608.
69 William Camden, *The History of the Most Renowned and Victorious Princess Elizabeth, Late Queen of England* (London: M. Flesher, 1688), 659–60.
70 On these days see also *Memoirs of Robert Cary Earl of Monmouth. Written by himself*, ed. Sir Walter Scott (Edinburgh: James Ballantyne, 1808), 115–23.
71 Thomas Dekker, *The Wonderfull Yeare, 1603* (London: T. Creede, 1603), B2ʳ.
72 FB to Michael Hickes, 19 March 1603, BL Lansdowne MS 88, p. 107.
73 FB to Northumberland, [March 1603], BL Add. MS 5503, fo. 19.
74 See Nichols, *Progresses of Elizabeth*, 3: 603–13.

CHAPTER 10

1 *CJ* 1: 142; James VI and I, *The Workes of the Most High and Mightie Prince, James . . . King of Great Britaine, France and Ireland*, ed. James Montagu (London: Robert Barker and John Bill, 1616), 486.
2 *History of Great Britain, Works* 6: 276; FB to Robert Kempe, n.d., BL Add. MS 5503, fo. 22b; *LL* 3: 74.
3 Edward Arber, *Transcript of the Registers of the Company of Stationers*, 5 vols (London: privately printed, 1875–94), 3: 109ʳ.
4 Egremont Thynne to Sir John Davies, [1604], HMC, *Report on the Manuscripts of the Late Reginald Rawdon Hastings, Esq., of The Manor House, Ashby de la Zouch*, vol. 4, ed. Francis Buckley (London: HMSO, 1947), 2.
5 FB to David Foulis, 25 March, 28 March 1603, BL Add. MS 5503, fos 20b, 22b; *LL* 3: 59, 64–5.
6 FB to Edward Bruce, 25 March 1603, LPL MS 936, art. 3; *LL* 3: 60–1. This letter may not have been sent. Bacon also wrote a letter to the new King, a copy of which he asked Bruce to present to James – but this request to Bruce is deleted.
7 FB to Dr Morison, [March 1603], *The Remaines of the Right Honorable Francis Lord Verulam . . .* (London: Lawrence Chapman, 1648), 63; *LL* 3: 66.
8 FB to [John] Davies, 28 March 1603, LPL MS 936, art. 4; *LL* 1: 65. This is the letter which concludes, 'So desiring you to be good to concealed poets', much

beloved by Baconians; Spedding supposes that Bacon may have written verses for Essex, of which Davies was aware.

9 FB to Thomas Chaloner, [March 1603], BL Add. MS 5503, fo. 21a; *LL* 3: 63–4. See Thomas Chaloner to AB, 27 October 1596, LPL MS 659, art. 222, when he asks AB 'most heartily to salute your brother'.

10 FB to James, [March 1603], BL Add. MS 5503, fo. 19b; *LL* 3: 62–3.

11 JC to DC, 12 April 1603, McClure 1: 192.

12 FB to Northumberland, [March? 1603], BL Add. MS 5503, fo. 23a; *LL* 3: 67.

13 Ibid.

14 'A Proclamation drawn for his Majesty's first coming in, prepared but not used', BL Harley MS 6797, fo. 13; *LL* 3: 67–71.

15 JC to DC, 12 April 1603, McClure 1: 192.

16 James to Egerton, 21 April 1603, *The Egerton Papers*, ed. J. Payne Collier (London: Camden Society, 1840, vol. 12), 368.

17 FB to TM, [?April 1603], Tobie Matthew, *A Collection of Letters* (London: Henry Herringman, 1660), 18–20; *LL* 3: 73–4; FB to Robert Kempe, n.d., FB to Southampton, n.d., BL Add. MS 5503, fos 22b, 23b; *LL* 3: 74, 75–6.

18 FB to Northumberland, n.d., BL Add. MS 5503, fo. 24; *LL* 3: 76–7.

19 Anthony Weldon, *Character of King James*, in W. Scott, ed., *Secret History of the Court of James the First*, 2 vols (Edinburgh: James Ballantyne, 1811), 2: 1–12.

20 FB to Northumberland, [?April 1603], BL Add. MS 5503, fo. 24; *LL* 3: 76–7; FB to TM, [?April 1603], Matthew, *Collection*, 18–20; *LL* 3: 73–4.

21 Samuel R. Gardiner, *History of England from the Accession of James I to the Outbreak of the Civil War 1603–1642*, 10 vols (London: Longmans, Green, and Co., 1899–1900), 1: 94.

22 FB to RC, 3 July 1603, Salisbury MS 100/155; *HMCS* 15: 166–7; *LL* 3: 79–81.

23 'Of the True Greatness of Britain', *Works* 7: 47. We are following Jonathan Marwil's dating: *The Trials of Counsel: Francis Bacon in 1621* (Detroit, Michigan: Wayne State University Press, 1976), 214–15 n. 5.

24 'Of the True Greatness of Britain', *Works* 7: 49.

25 FB to Northumberland, [1603], BL Add. MS 5503, fo. 24; *LL* 3: 77.

26 *A Brief Discourse Touching the Happy Union of the Kingdoms of England and Scotland*, BL Harley MS 532, fo. 61ff; *LL* 3: 90–8.

27 *Advancement of Learning*, *Works* 3: 346–9.

28 *Valerius Terminus*, *Works* 3: 215–52; *A Brief Discourse*, BL Harley MS 532, fo. 61; *LL* 3: 90.

29 *Certain Considerations Touching the Better Pacification and Edification of the Church of England*, PRO SP 14/5/51; *LL* 3: 103–27.

30 Declaration by Elizabeth, 20 December 1598, PRO SP 12/269/20; *CSPD, 1598–1601*, 134–5; EC to RC, 6 April 1603, Salisbury MS 99/95; *HMCS* 15: 34.

31 'A Note of my Debts', *LL* 3: 82. Spedding cites his source as the 1603 papers in the Public Record Office, but this document appears not be listed in *CSPD, 1603–1610*. It seems likely that the note dates from before Cecil's creation as Baron Cecil of Essenden on 16 May 1603.

32 FB to RC, 3, 16 July 1603, Salisbury MS 100/155 and 101/55, *HMCS* 15: 166–7, 193–4; *LL* 3: 79–81, 81.

33 FB to RC, 3 July, 16 July 1603, Salisbury MS 100/155 and 101/55, *HMCS* 15: 166–7, 193–4; *LL* 3: 79–81.

34 *The Progresses, Processions, and Magnificent Festivities of King James the First, his Royal Consort and Family*, 4 vols, ed. John Nichols (London: J. B. Nichols, 1828), 1: 208. See also *The Knights of England*, 2 vols, ed. William A. Shaw (London: Sherratt & Hughes, 1906), 2: 114.

35 For the 1604 session see *CJ* 1: 139–256; *LL* 3: 162–215; Wallace Notestein, *The House of Commons 1604–1610* (New Haven: Yale University Press, 1971); Joel J. Epstein, *Francis Bacon: A Political Biography* (Athens, OH: Ohio University Press, 1977), 75–81.

36 James, *Workes*, 486, 490–1.

37 *CJ* 1: 159; and cf. 939.

38 *CJ* 1: 165.

39 *CJ* 1: 166, 943.

40 *CJ* 1: 168.

41 This account of the Union debates draws on *CJ*; *LL* 3: 190–207; Notestein, *House of Commons*, 78–85.

42 Dudley Carleton, 'The Several Conferences with the Lords and Debates in the Lower House Touching the Union', *LL* 3: 191–2.

43 'An Act for the Better Grounding of a Further Union', PRO SP 14/8/5; *LL* 3: 204–6.

44 'Certain Articles or Considerations Touching the Union of the Kingdoms of England and Scotland', *Resuscitatio* 206; *LL* 3: 218.

45 On purveyors, see *CJ*; *LL* 3: 181–90; Notestein, *House of Commons*, 96–106.

46 BL Harley MS 6797, fo. 170; *LL* 3: 181–7.

47 *CJ* 1: 153–5, 935, 937.

48 Notestein, *House of Commons*, 84–5.

49 Grant of pension to FB, 18 August 1604. *Foedera, conventiones, literae, Et cujuscunque generis Acta Publica, inter regis Angliae*, ed. Thomas Rymer, 3rd edn, 10 vols (The Hague: John Neaulme, 1739–45), 7: 2: 121; *CSPD, 1603–1610*, 144.

50 FB to RC, 8 September 1604, BL Cotton MS Julius C.iii, fo. 30; *LL* 3: 217; Kevin Sharpe, *Sir Robert Cotton 1586–1631: History and Politics in Early Modern England* (Oxford: Oxford University Press, 1979), 152.

51 'Certain Articles or Considerations Touching the Union', *LL* 3: 234.

52 'A Draught of a Proclamation', BL Harley MS 6767, fo. 17b ff; *LL* 3: 325–9.

53 'On Counsel', *Essays* (1625), *Works* 6: 426.

54 'The Most Humble Certificate or Return of the Commissioners', *Letters and Remains of the Lord Chancellor Bacon*, ed. Robert Stephens (London: W. Bowyer, 1734); *LL* 3: 242–5.

55 Lincoln's Inn MS 83, quoted in *LL* 3: 240–2.

56 FB to Ellesmere, 2 April 1605, HEH EL MS 128; *LL* 3: 249–52.

57 JC to DC, 7 November 1605, McClure 1: 214.

58 See William H. Sherman, *John Dee: The Politics of Reading and Writing in the English Renaissance* (Amherst, MA: University of Massachusetts Press, 1995), ch. 7.

59 *Advancement of Learning, Works* 3: 261.
60 Lisa Jardine, 'Introduction' to Desiderius Erasmus of Rotterdam, *Education of a Christian Prince*, ed. Lisa Jardine (Cambridge: Cambridge University Press, 1997).
61 FB to Northampton, n.d., BL Add. MS 5503, fo. 29; *LL* 3: 252–3.
62 FB to RC, n.d., BL Add. MS 5503, fo. 28; *LL* 3: 253–4.
63 FB to Buckhurst, and to Ellesmere; n.d., BL Add. MS 5503, fos 28b, 29a; *LL* 3: 254–5.
64 FB to TM, n.d., Matthew, *Collection*, 11; *LL* 3: 255–6.
65 FB to Sir Thomas Bodley, n.d., BL Add. MS 5503, fo. 31; *LL* 3: 253.
66 Antonia Fraser, *The Gunpowder Plot: Terror and Faith in 1605* (London: Weidenfeld & Nicolson, 1996).
67 FB to RC, [8 November 1605?], with enclosure, examination of John Drake, PRO SP 14/16/29; *CSPD, 1603–1610*, 245.
68 Bacon had to put off a meeting with Sir Michael Hickes because he was 'commanded to attend the indictments at Westminster': FB to Hickes, 17 [or 27?] January 1606, BL Lansdowne MS 89, fo. 76; *LL* 3: 259.
69 Gardiner, *History of England*, 1: 287–9.
70 Shrewsbury to Edmunds, 12 February 1606, *The Court and Times of James the First; Illustrated by Authentic and Confidential Letters, from Various Public and Private Collections*, 2 vols, ed. Thomas Birch, rev. Robert Folkestone Williams (London: Henry Colburn, 1848), 1: 52.
71 FB to RC, 3 July 1603, Salisbury MS 100/155; *HMCS* 15: 166–7; *LL* 3: 80.
72 A. W. Hughes Clarke, ed., *The Register of St Clement, Eastcheap and St Martin Ongar* part 1 (London: Harleian Society, 1937, vol. 67), 12, 13, 14, 80, 165, 166, 167, 170; Inquisition Post Mortem, PRO, Chancery Series II, vol. 258, no. 78, quoted in A. Chambers Bunten, *Life of Alice Barnham (1592–1650)* (London: Page & Thomas, 1919), 8.
73 Ibid. The will was dated 24 March 1597, proved 29 May 1598 and upheld by sentence 2 December 1598.
74 Revd C. Moor, 'Bacon Deeds at Gorhambury', *The Genealogists' Magazine* 7 (1937), 565–6.
75 LPL MS 2086, p. 32.
76 FB to Ellesmere, n.d., FB to RC, n.d., BL Add. MS 5503, fos 37, 36; *LL* 3: 295–6, 296–7.
77 DC to JC, 11 May 1606, PRO SP 14/21/22; *CSPD, 1603–1610*, 317.
78 Moor, 'Bacon Deeds at Gorhambury'.
79 FB to Ellesmere, n.d., BL Add. MS 5503, fo. 37; *LL* 3: 295.
80 FB to TPH, 4 August 1606, whereabouts unknown; *LL* 3: 298–9.
81 FB to Murray, n.d., Bodl. Tanner MS 82, p. 241; *LL* 4: 2. He also retracted his support for a Mr Temple, whose suit had accidentally been put forward in his name.
82 Docquet, 31 January 1608, *CSPD, 1603–1610*, 400.
83 JC to DC, 13 February 1607, McClure 1: 243.
84 John Constable, 'Conditions to which I may content to yield unto, and did from the beginning intend and offer, for the jointure and advancement of Dorothy

Barnham, my spouse', January 1608, PRO SP 14/31/17; *CSPD, 1603–1610*, 400.

85 Lady Packington to RC, 28 November 1607, *HMCS* 19: 346.

86 FB to Lady Packington, n.d., FSL MS V.a.239, pp. 357–8; *LL* 4: 14 (corrected from MS).

87 *Commentarius solutus*, BL Add. MS 27,278, fos 9b, 10a; *LL* 4: 57.

88 *Commentarius solutus*, BL Add. MS 27,278, fos 34, 42; *LL* 4: 95.

89 On Castlehaven, see Cynthia Herrup, 'The Patriarch at Home: The Trial of the Second Earl of Castlehaven for Rape and Sodomy', *History Workshop Journal* 41 (1996), 1–18.

90 BL Harley MSS 6842, fo. 5, 6850 fo. 55; *LL* 3: 303–4.

91 *LL* 3: 313–14.

92 BL Harley MS 6797, fos 93, 182; *LL* 3: 307–25.

93 *CJ* 352; *LL* 3: 326.

94 *CJ* 345; *LL* 3: 326.

95 'A Proclamation for Jurors', PRO SP 14/28/67; *LL* 3: 389–92.

96 FB to TM, n.d., Matthew, *Collection*, 11; *LL* 3: 256; *HPT* 2: 178.

97 FB to Ellesmere, n.d., BL Add. MS 5503, fo. 37; *LL* 3: 296.

98 Sir Henry Neville to Winwood, 11 March 1606, *Memorials of Affairs of State in the Reigns of Queen Elizabeth and King James I. Collected (chiefly) from the Original Papers of the Right Honourable Sir Ralph Winwood*, 3 vols, ed. Edmund Sawyer (London: T. Ward, 1725), 2: 198. FB to RC, [March 1607], BL Add. MS 5503, fo. 102; *LL* 3: 288–9.

99 FB to James, n.d., BL Add. MS 5503, fo. 38; *LL* 3: 293–5; FB to Ellesmere, n.d., BL Add. MS 5503, fo. 37; *LL* 3: 295.

100 FB to RC, n.d., BL Add. MS 5503, fo. 36b; *LL* 3: 296–7.

101 Thomas Forster to TM, 16 February 1607, PRO SP 14/26/51; *CSPD, 1603–1610*, 348. *Commentarius solutus*, BL Add. MS 27, 278; *LL* 4: 86.

CHAPTER 11

1 *Commentarius solutus*, BL Add. MS 27,278; *LL* 4: 39–45.

2 FB to Sir George Carew, n.d. [1608], BL Add. MS 5503, fo. 41b; *LL* 4: 109–10.

3 *Advancement of Learning* (1605 edn), Isaac Casaubon's copy, HEH shelfmark 56251.

4 FB to Isaac Casaubon, n.d., LPL MS 654, art. 272; *LL* 4: 146–7. On Carew see *DNB*.

5 For Tobie Matthew, see Revd Alban Butler, *The Life of Sir Tobie Matthews* (London: J. P. Coghlan, 1795); *A Brief Description of a Curious Manuscript in the collection of the Rev. Dr. Neligan, Entitled A True Historicall Relation of the Conversion of Sir Tobie Matthew, to the Holie Catholic Family, with the Antecedents & Consequents Thereof* (n.p.: privately printed, n.d.); A. H. Matthew, ed., *A True Historical Relation of the Conversion of Sir Tobie Matthew to the Holy Catholic Faith: With the Antecedents and Consequences Thereof* (London: Burns & Oates, 1904); Arnold Harris Matthew and Annette Calthrop, *The Life of Sir Tobie Matthew: Bacon's alter ego* (London: Elkin Matthews, 1907); David Mathew, *Sir Tobie Mathew* (London: Max Parrish, 1950).

See also Tobie Matthew, *A Collection of Letters* (London: Henry Herringman, 1660); John P. Feil, 'Sir Tobie Matthew and his *Collection of Letters*' (PhD, University of Chicago, 1962).

6 DC to JC, 27 August 1607, *Dudley Carleton to John Chamberlain 1603–1624: Jacobean Letters*, ed. Maurice Lee Jr (New Brunswick, NJ: Rutgers University Press, 1972), 98–9.

7 FB to TM, n.d., *Resuscitatio* 38; *LL* 4: 10.

8 JC to DC, 11 February 1608, McClure 1: 255.

9 FB to TM, n.d., Matthew, *Collection*, 22; *LL* 4: 9.

10 FB to TM, early 1609, BL Add. MS 5503, fo. 33b; *LL* 4: 132–3.

11 FB to TM, n.d., Matthew, *Collection*, 14; *LL* 4: 134. If this is the *Abecedarium* it is very early. Bodley's letter (see n. 22), which also refers to it, confirms that this is a scientific work. This would match Graham Rees' suggestion: see Rees, 'Bacon's Philosophy: Some New Sources with Special Reference to the *Abecedarium novum naturae*', in Marta Fattori, ed., *Francis Bacon: Terminologia e fortuna nel XVII secolo* (Rome: Ateneo, 1984), 223–44 at 227.

12 TM to FB, 21 April 1616, LPL MS 936, art. 30.

13 TM to FB, 4 April 1619, LPL MS 936, art. 103; *LL* 7: 36–7.

14 FB to TM, n.d., BL Add. MS 5503, fo. 33b; *LL* 4: 132–3.

15 FB to TM, n.d., Matthew, *Collection*, 12; *LL* 4: 135–6.

16 FB to TM, 10 October 1609, BL Add. MS 5503, fo. 33; *LL* 4: 137–8.

17 FB to TM, 17 [27?] February 1610[–11?], BL Add. MS 5503, fo. 34b; *LL* 4: 144–5.

18 See JC to DC, 21 October 1608, 11 November 1608, McClure 1: 264, 270.

19 *Commentarius solutus*, BL Add. MS 27,278; *LL* 4: 63.

20 FB to Lancelot Andrewes, n.d. [September 1609?], BL Add. MS 5503, fo. 31b; *LL* 4: 141.

21 See Rees, 'Bacon's Philosophy', *passim*.

22 Bodley to FB, 19 February 1608, collated from *The Remaines of the Right Honourable Francis Lord Verulam* (London: Lawrence Chapman, 1648), L4ᵛ–M4ʳ; Bodley, *Reliquiae Bodleianae: Or, some Genuine Remains of Sir Thomas Bodley* (London: John Hartley, 1703), 369–81; *Trecentale Bodleianum: A Memorial Volume for the Three Hundreth Anniversary of the Public Funeral of Sir Thomas Bodley, March 29, 1613* (Oxford: Clarendon Press, 1913), 145–63.

23 *Commentarius solutus*, BL Add. MS 27,278; *LL* 4: 76–7.

24 John Aubrey, *Aubrey's Brief Lives*, ed. Oliver Lawson Dick (London: Secker & Warburg, 1960), 12–15. See also A. Hassell Smith, 'The Gardens of Sir Nicholas and Sir Francis Bacon: An Enigma Resolved and a Mind Explored', in Anthony Fletcher and Peter Roberts, eds, *Religion, Culture and Society in Early Modern England: Essays in Honour of Patrick Collinson* (Cambridge: Cambridge University Press, 1994), 125–60.

25 'Of Gardens', *Essays* (1625), *Works* 6: 485.

26 Sir Vincent Skinner to RC, 'Comparison of the Amounts of Subsidies and Fifteenths since I Eliz.', 10 February 1610, PRO SP 14/52/58; CSPD, *1603–1610*, 587. On the 1610 parliament see Samuel Rawson Gardiner, ed., *Parliamentary Debates in 1610* (London: Camden Society, 1862); Elizabeth R. Foster, ed., *Proceedings in Parliament 1610*, 2 vols. (New Haven: Yale University Press, 1966).

27 BL Lansdowne MS 168, fo. 306; *LL* 4: 150.

28 Foster, ed., *Proceedings in Parliament 1610*, 2: 29.

29 James VI and I, *The Workes of the Most High and Mightie Prince, James . . . King of Great Britaine, France and Ireland*, ed. James Montagu (London: Robert Barker and John Bill, 1616), 529–31.

30 JC to Winwood, 24 May 1610, *Memorials of Affairs of State in the Reigns of Queen Elizabeth and King James I. Collected (chiefly) from the Original Papers of the Right Honourable Sir Ralph Winwood*, 3 vols, ed. Edmund Sawyer (London: T. Ward, 1725), 3: 174.

31 Gardiner, ed., *Parliamentary Debates in 1610*, 38; *LL* 4: 182–3.

32 BL Harley MS 6797, fo. 147; *LL* 4: 191–8. See also BL Add. MS 4210, fo. 56b; Gardiner, ed., *Parliamentary Debates in 1610*, 69; *LL* 4: 198–201.

33 BL Harley MS 6797, fo. 135; *LL* 4: 202–3.

34 See FB to Caesar, 23 August 1610, PRO SP 14/57/26; *LL* 4: 215–16. There is no mention of ACB's death in this letter.

35 Revd C. Moor, 'Bacon Deeds at Gorhambury', *The Genealogists' Magazine* 7 (1937), 565; FB to Hickes, 27 August 1610, BL Lansdowne MS 91, fo. 183; *LL* 4: 217–18.

36 Gardiner, ed., *Parliamentary Debates in 1610*, 126–8; *LL* 4: 225–6.

37 BL Harley MS 6797; *LL* 4: 234–5.

38 FB to James, [autumn 1611], BL Add. MS 5503, fo. 40; *LL* 4: 243.

39 FB to RC, [1 January 1612], BL Add. MS 5503, fo. 43b; *LL* 4: 246.

40 FB to Hickes, 8 January 1612, BL Lansdowne MS 92, fo. 139; *LL* 4: 246–7.

41 FB to Lord Mayor Pemberton, 27 December 1611, Guildhall MS, pr. in B. Brogden Orridge, *Illustrations of Jack Cade's Rebellion, from Researches in the Guildhall Records, Together with Some Newly-found Letters of Lord Bacon, &c.* (London: John Camde Hotten, 1869), 83–4. Spedding, who had access only to a copy in BL Add. MS 5503, fo. 42, tentatively dates this to early 1612. For Sutton, see BL Harley MS 6797, fo. 155; *LL* 4: 249–54. The case was ultimately argued in 1613.

42 BL Harley MS 7020, fo. 164; *LL* 4: 255–9.

43 BL Harley MS 6797, fo. 161; *LL* 4: 265–75.

44 *Scrinia Ceciliana: Mysteries of State & Government: in Letters of the Most Famous Lord Burghley, And other Grand Ministers of State: In the Reigns of Queen Elizabeth, and King James. Being a further Additional Supplement of the Cabala* (London: G. Bedel & T. Collins, 1663), 368, 369; *LL* 4: 291–3, 297–300.

45 FB to James, 29 May 1612, abandoned, LPL MS 936, art. 6; *LL* 4: 279.

46 *Apophthegms, Works* 7: 175.

47 FB to James, 31 May 1612, LPL MS 936, art. 7; *LL* 4: 279–80.

48 JC to DC, 17 December 1612, McClure 1: 397. Carleton begged Chamberlain for a copy: DC to JC, 9 July 1613, *Dudley Carleton to John Chamberlain 1603–1624*, ed. Lee, 145.

49 'Of Deformity', *Essays* (1612), *Works* 6: 570–1.

50 FB to James, 31 May 1612, LPL MS 936, art. 7; *LL* 4: 279–80.

51 FB to James, n.d. [May/June 1612?], LPL MS 936, art. 224; *LL* 4: 281–2.

52 JC to DC, 11 June 1612, McClure 1: 354–5.

53 'Notes for the Wards', BL Harley MS 7020, fos 161ff; *LL* 4: 284–8; FB to James, 18 September 1612, LPL MS 936, arts 9, 242; *LL* 4: 311.

54 JC to DC, 17 June 1612, McClure 1: 357–8.

55 Sir George Carew, discourse to the Court of Wards, [16 June 1612], PRO SP 12/69/69; *CSPD, 1611–1618*, 135.

56 Northampton to Rochester, 8 August 1612, PRO SP 14/70/30; *CSPD, 1611–1618*, 141. FB originally planned to present his case on 3 August: see Northampton to Rochester, [3 August 1612], PRO SP 14/70/25; *CSPD, 1611–1618*, 140. See also BL Harley MS 354, art. 9, quoted in *LL* 4: 304.

57 FB to James, [August 1612], BL Harley MS 298, fo. 13b; *LL* 4: 305. 'Instructions to the Commissioners for collecting the Aid on the marriage of the Princess Elizabeth', BL Harley MS 298, fo. 10; *LL* 4: 305–10.

58 'Account of the Committees for repair of the King's estate and raising of monies', BL Cotton MS Cleopatra F.vi, fo. 82; *LL* 4: 314–27.

59 'A proposition concerning the augmentation of the King's revenue by converting of his lands into a yearly fee farm rent multiplied in proportion to that which he now receiveth', BL Cotton MS Cleopatra F.vi, fo. 119; *LL* 4: 327–37.

60 Northampton and Ellesmere to James, 11 October 1612, PRO SP 14/71/18; *CSPD, 1611–1618*, 152; Northampton to Rochester, 20 October 1612; PRO SP 14/71/16; *CSPD, 1611–1618*, 151–2.

61 FB to James, 18 September 1612, LPL MS 936, arts 9, 242; *LL* 4: 311–14.

CHAPTER 12

1 'In Henricum principem Walliae elogium', *Works* 6: 323–5, tr. Spedding, 6: 327–9. For the planned *Essays*: Stationers' Register entry, 12 October 1612, *A Transcript of the Registers of the Company of Stationers*, ed. Edward Arber, 5 vols (London: privately printed, 1875–94).

2 FB to Henry, n.d., Thomas Bushell, *Mr Bushells Abridgment of the Lord Chancellor Bacon's Philosophical Theory in Mineral Prosecutions* (London, 1659), A^{r–v}.

3 FB, proposed dedicatory epistle to Prince Henry [October 1612], BL Add. MS 4259, fo. 155; *LL* 4: 340–1.

4 BL Add. MS 4259, fo. 155; *LL* 4: 340–1; BL Harley MS 1893, fo. 75; *Works* 6: 327–9.

5 'Epistle dedicatory', *Essays* (1612), *Works* 6: 539.

6 JC to DC, 19 November 1612, McClure 1: 391.

7 FB to Rochester, [November 1612], PRO SP 14/71/34; *LL* 4: 342.

8 LPL MS 2086, p. 12.

9 JC to DC, 19 November 1612, McClure 1: 392.

10 LPL MS 2086, p. 12.

11 JC to DC, 26 November 1612, McClure 1: 393.

12 *The Maske of Flowers. Presented by the Gentlemen of Graies-Inne* (London: R. Wilson, 1614), dedicatory epistle.

13 JC to Alice Carleton, 18 February 1613, McClure 1: 425–6.

14 JC to DC, 25 February 1613, McClure 1: 430–1.

15 'The Charge of Whitelocke', LPL MS 936, art. 249; *LL* 4: 353–6; see also Sir Julius Caesar's notes, *LL* 4: 356; Act of Council, 12 June 1613, BL Add. MS 4149, fo. 173; *LL* 4: 348–53, discussed 4: 345–8.

16 FB and Henry Hobart, 'Opinion of the law officers upon the legality of exacting the oath of allegiance from Irish subjects', *CSP* . . . *Ireland, 1611–1614*, 424; *LL* 4: 388.

17 FB to James, 13 August 1613, BL Add. MS 19,402, fo. 77; *LL* 4: 386–7.

18 FB to James, [7 August 1613], LPL MS 936, art. 276; *LL* 4: 378–9.

19 'Reasons for the Remove of Coke', LPL MS 936, art. 257; *LL* 4: 381–2.

20 JC to DC, 14 October, 27 October, 11 November 1613, McClure 1: 479, 481–2, 485.

21 FB to James, [October 1613?], LPL MS 936, art. 277; *LL* 4: 391.

22 JC to DC, 9 September 1613, McClure 1: 474–5.

23 See Northampton to Lake, 18 November 1613, PRO SP 14/75/13; *CSPD, 1611–1618*, 208.

24 *Charge of Sir Francis Bacon . . . touching Duells*, LL 4: 399–416.

25 Arber, *Stationers' Register*, 3: 542.

26 JC to DC, 25 November 1613, McClure 1: 488.

27 FB to Somerset, BL Lansdowne MS 107, fo. 13; *LL* 4: 394.

28 JC to DC, 23 December 1613, McClure 1: 493.

29 *Stationers' Register*, ed. Arber, 3: 540; *Maske of Flowers*, dedicatory epistle.

30 JC to DC, 23 December 1613, McClure 1: 493.

31 FB to James, 31 May 1612, LPL MS 936, art. 7; *LL* 4: 279–80.

32 'Memorial of the Lords Commissioners their employments for bettering the King's revenue', 1 June 1613, BL Lansdowne MS 165, fo. 223; *LL* 4: 358–62.

33 FB to James, n.d. [?June 1613], BL Cotton MS Titus F.iv, fo. 332; *LL* 4: 368–73. For earlier notes on this, see 'Reasons for calling a Parliament', BL Cotton MS Titus F.iv, fo. 334; *LL* 4: 365–6. Bacon also penned twenty 'Incidents of a Parliament': BL Cotton MS Titus F.iv, fo. 335; *LL* 4: 366–8.

34 Northampton to Sir Thomas Lake, 4 July 1613, PRO SP 14/74/23; *CSPD, 1611–1618*, 189.

35 FB to James, [January 1614], BL Cotton MS Titus F.iv, fo. 333; *LL* 5: 1–3.

36 Privy Council to James, 16 February 1614, PRO SP 14/76/22; *CSPD, 1611–1618*, 223.

37 Coke, Hobart, Bacon, Montagu and Yelverton to James, 17 February 1614, PRO SP 14/76/26; *LL* 5: 13.

38 Daphne Du Maurier, *The Winding Stair: Francis Bacon, His Rise and Fall* (London: Victor Gollancz, 1976), 90–1.

39 JC to DC, 3 March 1614, McClure 1: 515.

40 FB to James, advising him to call a parliament, n.d., Inner Temple MS vol. 37, no. 538, pr. in *LL* 5: 176–91 at 181.

41 JC to DC, 9 June 1614, McClure 1: 538.

42 JC to DC, 17 March 1614, McClure 1: 518.

43 JC to DC, 7 April 1614, McClure 1: 523.

44 'Memorial of some points', privately owned MS, pr. in *LL* 5: 24–30.

45 On the election see T. Bass Mullinger, 'The Relations of Francis Bacon, Lord Verulam, with the University of Cambridge', *Proceedings of the Cambridge Antiquarian Society* 38 (1897), 227–37; John William Cooper, ed., *The Annals of Cambridge*, vol. 5 (Cambridge: Cambridge University Press, 1908), 348–51; Millicent Barton Rex, *University Representation in England 1604–1690* (London: George Allen &

Unwin, 1954), 63–5, 66–7; *CJ* 1: 456, 459–60. For the 1614 parliament see *CJ* 1: 455–506; Maija Jansson, ed., *Proceedings in Parliament 1614 (House of Commons)* (Philadelphia: American Philosophical Society, 1988); Thomas L. Moir, *The Addled Parliament of 1614* (Oxford: Clarendon Press, 1964).

46 Mullinger, 'Relations of Bacon with Cambridge', 229.

47 JC to DC, 23 December 1613, McClure 1: 493. For the aftermath (Sandys eventually sat) see JC to DC, 14 April 1614, McClure 1: 525; Rex, *University Representation*, 63–4.

48 *CJ* 1: 456.

49 See *CJ* 1: 458; Jansson, ed., *Proceedings in Parliament 1614*, 52–3.

50 Thomas Lorkin, quoted in *LL* 5: 51.

51 *CJ* 1: 478; Jansson, ed., *Proceedings in Parliament 1614*, 189, 196; *LL* 5: 52.

52 *CJ* 1: 480–1.

53 Jansson, ed., *Proceedings in Parliament 1614*, 267, 278.

54 *CJ* 1: 462; Jansson, ed., *Proceedings in Parliament 1614*, 63–4; *LL* 5: 36–7 n. 1. For a speculative reconstruction of this speech by Spedding, see *LL* 5: 36–8.

55 *CJ* 1: 464.

56 Revd Thomas Lorkin to Sir Thomas Puckering, 28 May 1614, *The Court and Times of James the First; Illustrated by Authentic and Confidential Letters, from Various Public and Private Collections*, 2 vols, ed. Thomas Birch, rev. Robert Folkestone Williams (London: Henry Colburn, 1848).

57 *CJ* 1: 470, quoted in *LL* 5: 40–1.

58 *Resuscitatio* 48–53; *LL* 5: 42–8.

59 *CJ* 1: 481.

60 *CJ* 1: 481; Jansson, ed., *Proceedings in Parliament 1614*, 213, 222, 225; *LL* 5: 53–4.

61 Sir James Whitelocke, *Liber Famelicus* (London: Camden Society, 1858, vol. 70), 42.

62 Jansson, ed., *Proceedings in Parliament 1614*, 259 n. 12.

63 Ibid., 259, 260, 264, 266.

64 *CJ* 1: 486; Jansson, ed., *Proceedings in Parliament 1614*, 261; *LL* 5: 56–7.

65 *CJ* 1: 496.

66 Jansson, ed., *Proceedings in Parliament 1614*, 375.

67 *CJ* 1: 505; *LJ* 1: 716.

68 JC to DC, 30 June 1614, McClure 1: 542.

CHAPTER 13

1 Quoted in Roger Lockyer, *Buckingham: The Life and Political Career of George Villiers, First Duke of Buckingham 1592–1628* (London: Longman, 1981), 12.

2 For Oliver St John and John Owen see *LL* 5: 130–68.

3 On Peacham see *LL* 5: 90–7, 98–110, 120–8; Privy Council to Winwood et al., 18 January 1615, PRO SP 14/80/6; *LL* 5: 92. See also FB to James, 21 January 1615, LPL MS 936, art. 11; *LL* 5: 96.

4 FB to James, 27 January 1615, BL Add. MS 5503, fo. 53; *LL* 5: 100–2.

5 FB to James, 31 January 1615, LPL MS 936, art. 12; *LL* 5: 107–11.

6 EC, quoted in *LL* 5: 120.

7 FB to James, 14 February 1615, Balfour MSS, pr. in *LL* 5: 121.

8 For Peacham, see FB to James, 28 February 1615, BL Add. MS 5503, fo. 78b; *LL* 5: 123–4; examination of Peacham, 10 March 1615, Sir David Dalrymple, Lord Hailes, *Memorials and Letters Relating to the History of Britain in the Reign of James the First* (Glasgow: Robert & Andrew Foulis, 1762), 59; FB to James, 12 March 1615, LPL MS 936, art. 17; *LL* 5: 125–6.

9 Roger Coke, *A Detection of the Court and State of England during the Four Last Reigns, and the Inter-Regnum*, 2nd edn, 2 vols (London: Andrew Bell, 1694), 1: 83, 84, 146.

10 David Bergeron, *Royal Family, Royal Lovers: King James of England and Scotland* (Columbia: University of Missouri Press, 1991), 138–9.

11 *Letters of King James VI and I*, ed. G. P. V. Akrigg (Berkeley, CA: University of California Press, 1984), 343–5. On the Somerset affair, see Anne Somerset, *Unnatural Murder: Poison at the Court of James I* (London: Weidenfeld & Nicolson, 1997).

12 Bergeron, *Royal Family*, 132.

13 'Charge against Wentworth, Hollys and Lumsden', 10 November 1615, PRO SP 14/83/15; *LL* 5: 213–23.

14 *LL* 5: 96–98, 125, 169–70.

15 'Innovations introduced into the laws and government', cit. *LL* 5: 221.

16 FB to James, 17 November 1615, Balfour MSS, pr. in *LL* 5: 224–5.

17 FB to James, 22 January 1616. BL Add. MS 5503, fo. 80; *LL* 5: 231–2. For a result of Coke's *plerophoria*, see the case of Sir Thomas Monson: FB and Yelverton to James, 7 December 1616, PRO SP 14/89/65; *LL* 6: 120 and, more generally, *LL* 6: 118–21.

18 'Argument on the writ *de non procendo rege inconsulto*', *Works* 7: 681–725.

19 FB to James, 27 January 1616, Balfour MSS and draft BL Add. MS 5503, fo. 81b; *LL* 5: 233–6.

20 For an account of this case, see *LL* 5: 246.

21 FB to James, 27 January 1616, Balfour MSS, pr. in *LL* 5: 236.

22 FB to James, 15 February 1616, LPL MS 936, art. 25; *LL* 5: 246–8.

23 FB to GV, 19 February 1616, LPL MS 936, art. 27; *LL* 5: 248–9.

24 FB to James, 21 February 1616, LPL MS 936, art. 28; *LL* 5: 249–54.

25 FB to GV, 21, 27 February 1616, BL Add. MS 5503, fos 45, 46; *LL* 5: 255, 260.

26 FB to James, 1 April 1616, LPL MS 936, art. 30; *LL* 5: 260–1.

27 Sir John Digby to James, 3 April 1616, quoted in *LL* 5: 262–3.

28 FB to GV, [9] April 1616, BL Add. MS 5503, fo. 91; *LL* 5: 263–5.

29 FB to GV, 13 April 1616, BL Add. MS 5503, fo. 89; *LL* 5: 265–8; FB to Coke, 16 April 1616, PRO SP 14/86/135; *LL* 5: 269–70.

30 FB to GV, 13 April 1616, BL Add. MS 5503, fo. 89; *LL* 5: 265–8.

31 FB to GV, 18 April 1616, BL Add. MS 5503, fo. 87b; *LL* 5: 270–1.

32 JC to DC, 20 April 1616, McClure 1: 623.

33 Act of Council, 6 June 1616, BL Lansdowne MS 174, fo. 217; *LL* 5: 358.

34 FB to EC, 25 April 1616, quoted in Act of Council, 6 June 1616, BL Lansdowne MS 174, fo. 217; *LL* 5: 359.

35 FB to James, on or before 27 April 1616, BL Add. MS 5503, fo. 92b; *LL* 5: 273–5.

36 Coke and the judges to James, 27 April 1616, quoted in Act of Council, 6 June
   1616, BL Lansdowne MS 174, fo. 217; *LL* 5: 359–60.
37 James to the judges, after 27 April 1616, quoted in Act of Council, 6 June 1616,
   BL Lansdowne MS 174, fo. 217; *LL* 5: 361–3.
38 FB to James, 28 April 1616, CUL MS Dd.3.63; *LL* 5: 275–80.
39 JC to DC, 30 April 1616, McClure 1: 625.
40 FB to GV, 2, 5 May 1616, BL Add. MS 5503, fos 83b, 82; *LL* 5: 281–3, 285.
41 FB to GV, 5 May 1616, BL Add. MS 5503, fo. 82; *LL* 5: 285–6.
42 'Somerset's business and charge, with the King's postilles', LPL MS 933, fo. 125;
   LL 5: 286–9.
43 FB to GV, 10 May 1616, LPL MS 936, art. 32; *LL* 5: 290–2.
44 Sir George More, quoted in *LL* 5: 292.
45 FB and 'some great Lords Commissioners' to James, [May 1616], BL Add. MS
   5503, fo. 94b; *LL* 5: 292–4.
46 'Memorial touching the course to be held in my Lord of Somerset's arraignment',
   [May 1616], LPL MS 941, fo. 113; *LL* 5: 295–6.
47 JC to DC, 18 May 1616, McClure 2: 1.
48 'Charge against Frances Countess of Somerset', *Baconiana: Or Certain Genuine
   Remains of Sir Francis Bacon*, ed. Thomas Tenison (London: Richard Chiswell,
   1679), 3; *LL* 5: 297–304.
49 *A Complete Collection of State Trials, and Proceedings for High Treason and other Crimes
   and Misdemeanours from the Earliest Period to the Year 1783*, 21 vols, ed. T. B. Howell
   (London: T. C. Hansard, 1816), 2: 957.
50 JC to DC, 25 May 1616, McClure 2: 5.
51 ES to DC, 25 May 1616, PRO SP 14/87/29; *CSPD, 1611–18*, 368.
52 For FB's charge see *LL* 5: 307–20, based primarily on *Baconiana*, 14ff, with
   occasional collation with BL Harley MS 2194, BL Add. MS 1002, and CUL MS
   Ee.IV.12.
53 *Letters of James VI and I*, ed. Akrigg, 353; G. P. V. Akrigg, *Jacobean Pageant, or,
   The Court of King James I* (London: Hamish Hamilton, 1962), 204.
54 ES to DC, 25 May 1616, PRO SP 14/87/29; *LL* 5: 336.
55 JC to DC, 25 May 1616, McClure 2: 4–5.
56 *State Trials*, ed. Howell, 2: 996.
57 *LL* 5: 334.
58 JC to DC, 8 June 1616, McClure 2: 6.
59 FB to GV, 30 May 1616, LPL MS 936, art. 33; *LL* 5: 347–8.
60 FB to GV, 3 June 1616, LPL MS 936, art. 34; *LL* 5: 348.
61 *Letters of Sir Francis Bacon, Baron of Verulam, Viscount St. Alban, and Lord High
   Chancellor of England. Written during the Reign of King James the First*, ed. Robert
   Stephens (London: Benjamin Tooke, 1702), 140 ff; *LL* 5: 349–54.
62 Act of Council, 6 June 1616, BL Lansdowne MS 174, fo. 217; *LL* 5: 357–9.
63 FB to GV, 12 June 1616, LPL MS 936, art. 36; *LL* 5: 356.
64 JC to DC, 1 August 1613 and 3 March 1614, McClure 1: 470 and 517; FB to
   GV, 13 June 1616, *Letters of Sir Francis Bacon* (1702), ed. Stephens, 167; *LL* 5:
   373; FB to GV, 12 June 1616, LPL MS 936, art. 35; *LL* 5: 372. Spedding believes
   that only the later letter was sent: *LL* 5: 373.
65 *Biographia Britannica: or, the Lives of the Most Eminent Persons who have Flourished in*

Great Britain and Ireland, from the Earliest Ages, Down to the Present Times: Collected from the Best Authorities, both Printed and Manuscript, and Digested in the Manner of Mr. Bayle's Historical and Critical Dictionary, 6 vols (London: W. Innys, 1747–66), 1390.

66 JC to DC, 6 July 1616, McClure 2: 14.

67 Ibid.

68 FB to GV, 1 July 1616, Bodl. Add. MS D.112, fo. 17; *LL* 5: 375. Pardon for the countess of Somerset, *State Trials*, ed. Howell, 2: 1002; *LL* 5: 375–6.

69 JC to DC, 20 July 1616, McClure 2: 17.

70 FB to GV, 1 July 1616, Bodl. Add. MS D.112, fo. 17; *LL* 5: 375.

71 FB to GV, 2 July 1616, Bodl. Add. MS D.112, fo. 20; *LL* 5: 377.

72 FB to GV, 5 July 1616, *Letters of Sir Francis Bacon* (1702), ed. Stephens, 169; *LL* 5: 378–80.

73 FB to James, n.d. [1 January 1620?], LPL MS 936, art. 227; *LL* 7: 70–2.

74 James VI and I, *The Workes of the Most High and Mightie Prince, James . . . King of Great Britaine, France and Ireland*, ed. James Montagu (London: Robert Barker and John Bill, 1616), 556–60; 'King's decree touching the granting of praemunires', BL Lansdowne MS 174, fo. 119; *LL* 5: 385–95.

CHAPTER 14

1 JC to DC, 20 July 1616; McClure 2: 16–17.

2 FB to James, 28 July 1616, Bodl. Add. MS D.112, fo. 23; *LL* 6: 4.

3 FB to GV, 5 August 1616, LPL MS 936, art. 40; *LL* 6: 4–5; FB to GV, 12 August 1616, LPL MS 936, art. 41; *LL* 6: 6–7. See also FB to James, 12 August 1616, LPL MS 936, art. 42; *LL* 6: 7. Also, on the creation, see FB to GV, 20 August 1616, LPL MS 936, art. 44; *LL* 6: 8–9.

4 FB to GV, 5 August 1616, LPL MS 936, art. 40; *LL* 6: 4–5.

5 FB to GV, 12 August 1616, LPL MS 936, art. 41; *LL* 6: 6–7.

6 FB to GV, 20 August 1616, LPL MS 936, art. 44; *LL* 6: 8–9. See also FB to James, 12 August 1616, LPL MS 936, art. 42; *LL* 6: 7–8. For the advice (in two versions) see FB to GV, n.d., *Scrinia Ceciliana: Mysteries of State & Government: in Letters of the Most Famous Lord Burghley, And other Grand Ministers of State: In the Reigns of Queen Elizabeth, and King James. Being a further Additional Supplement of the Cabala* (London: G. Bedel & T. Collins, 1663), 43–66; *LL* 6: 13–26, 27–56.

7 ES to DC, 20 August 1616, PRO SP 14/88/57; *CSPD, 1611–1618*, 391.

8 JC to DC, 24 August 1616, McClure 2: 19.

9 'The Lord Chancellor Egerton's observations on the Lord Coke's Reports', privately owned MS, quoted in *LL* 6: 87–8.

10 Ellesmere and FB to James, [2 October 1616], LPL MS 936, art. 50; *LL* 6: 76–7.

11 *LL* 6: 78; GV to FB, 3 October 1616, LPL MS 936, art. 51; *LL* 6: 79.

12 Ellesmere and FB to James, 6 October 1616, LPL MS 936, art. 52; *LL* 6: 79–82.

13 JC to DC, 26 October 1616, McClure 2: 229.

14 Ellesmere to James, 22 October 1616, *LL* 6: 88 (no source given). 'Innovations introduced into the laws and government', LPL MS 936, art. 243; *LL* 6: 90–3.

15 William Camden, *V. cl. Gulielmi Camdeni et illustrium virorum ad G. Camdenum Epistolae. Cum appendice varii argumenti. Accesserunt Annalium Regni Regis Jacobi I. Apparatus, et Commentarius de antiquitate, dignitate, & officio*, 2 vols (London: Richard Chiswell, 1691), Hhh^r.

16 FB to James, 17 November 1616, LPL MS 936, art. 280; *LL* 6: 105.

17 FB to James, 13 November [1616], LPL MS 936, art. 279; *LL* 6: 97.

18 *LL* 6: 95–6.

19 JC to DC, 14 November 1616, McClure 2: 34.

20 JC to DC, 23 November 1616, McClure 2: 37.

21 Catherine Drinker Bowen, *The Lion and the Throne: The Life and Times of Sir Edward Coke (1552–1634)* (Boston: Little, Brown & Co., 1956), 388.

22 Ibid. See JC to DC, 23 November 1616, McClure 2: 381.

23 Sir James Whitelocke, *Liber Famelicus* (London: Camden Society, 1858, vol. 70), 51.

24 For FB's advice to GV after EC's fall, see FB to GV, 29 November 1616, *Letters of Sir Francis Bacon, Baron of Verulam, Viscount St. Alban, and Lord High Chancellor of England. Written during the Reign of King James the First*, ed. Robert Stephens (London: Benjamin Tooke, 1702), 188–92; *LL* 6: 115–18.

25 Giovanni Battista Lionello to the Doge and Senate of Venice, 7 October 1616, *CSP . . . Venice, 1615–1617*, 315.

26 *The Progresses, Processions, and Magnificent Festivities of King James the First, his royal Consort and family*, 4 vols, ed. John Nichols (London: J. B. Nichols, 1828), 3: 309; JC to DC, 15 March 1617, McClure 2: 63.

27 FB to James, [21 February 1617], LPL MS 936, art. 56; *LL* 6: 139–40.

28 FB to GV, 7 March 1617, LPL MS 936, art. 58; *LL* 6: 152.

29 Warrant to Sir Henry Yelverton, – March [1617], BL Add. MS 4259 (John Locker's copy); *LL* 6: 153–4.

30 '[My] Lord [Richard Sackville, 3rd earl of Dorset] had . . . lent out his house [Dorset House] to my Lord Keeper for two terms till my Lady Derby was gone out of York House': Anne Clifford, *The Diary of Anne Clifford 1616–1619: A Critical Edition*, ed. Katherine O. Acheson (New York: Garland, 1995), 77, entry for 22 March 1617.

31 JC to DC, 29 March 1617, McClure 2: 65.

32 FB to GV, 13 April 1617, *Letters of Sir Francis Bacon*, ed. Stephens (1702), 196–7; *LL* 6: 167–8; FB to [Brackley?], 13 April 1617, HEH EL MS 6460; *LL* 6: 166–7.

33 FB to GV, 13 April 1617, *Letters of Sir Francis Bacon*, ed. Stephens (1702), 196–7; *LL* 6: 167–8.

34 GV to FB, 18 April 1617, BL Harley MS 7006, fo. 11; *LL* 6: 168–9.

35 See FB to GV, 8 May 1617 [LPL MS 936, art. 63; *LL* 6: 194] and the enclosed 'Precedents that come near the Lord Brackley's case' (Bridgewater House MS 47/624, pr. in *LL* 6: 195–6); see also FB's rejection of a precedent provided in the form of a private letter: FB to Mr B, 28 April 1617, Bridgewater House MS 76/72, pr. in *LL* 6: 175.

36 GV to FB, 18 May 1617, BL Harley MS 7006, fo. 67; *LL* 6: 199.

37 JC to DC, 4 June 1617, McClure 2: 79.

38 FB to GV, 7 April 1617, Bodl. Add. MS D.112, fo. 29; *LL* 6: 163. For other

business involving the Queen, see FB to GV, 25 May 1617, Bodl. Add. MS D.112, fo. 35; *LL* 6: 207–8.

39 Account of Council business, 30 March 1617, LPL MS 936, art. 60b; *LL* 6: 159–61.

40 See Privy Council to the Lord Deputy of Ireland, 16 March 1617, pr. in *LL* 6: 154–6.

41 FB to James, 23 March 1617, LPL MS 936, art. 60; *LL* 6: 157; instructions to Digby, 23 March 1617, LPL MS 936, art. 59; *LL* 6: 158–9.

42 Lake to Winwood, [?30 March 1617], PRO SP 14/90/150; *CSPD, 1611–1618*, 455.

43 Lake to Winwood, 3 April 1617, PRO SP 14/91/10; *CSPD, 1611–1618*, 457.

44 Winwood to Lake, 1 April 1617, PRO SP 14/91/2, *CSPD, 1611–1618*, 456; GV to FB, [5?] April 1617, BL Harley MS 7006; *LL* 6: 163.

45 FB to GV, 7 April 1617, *Letters and Remains of the Lord Chancellor Bacon*, ed. Robert Stephens (London: W. Bowyer, 1734), 33–5; *LL* 6: 163–4.

46 George Gerrard to DC, 9 May 1617, PRO SP 14/92/15; *CSPD, 1611–1618*, 464–5; JC to DC, 10 May 1617, McClure 2: 72–3. See also Winwood to Lake, 8 May 1617, PRO SP 14/92/14; *CSPD, 1611–1618*, 464; Clifford, *Diary*, 82: 'the 7th [May 1617] my Lord Keeper rode from Dorset House to Westminster in great pomp & state amongst by wish my Lord was one.'

47 Speech in Chancery, 7 May 1617, PRO SP 14/92/13; PRO SP 14/92/26.1; *Resuscitatio*, 79; *LL* 6: 182–93.

48 JC to DC, 10 May 1617, McClure 2: 73.

49 Ibid.

50 FB to GV, 8 May 1617, LPL MS 936, art. 63; *LL* 6: 194–5.

51 JC to DC, 10 May 1617, McClure 2: 73.

52 John Aubrey, *Aubrey's Brief Lives*, ed. Oliver Lawson Dick (London: Secker & Warburg, 1960), 9.

53 JC to DC, 24 May 1617, McClure 2: 76.

54 ES to DC, 16 May 1617, PRO SP 14/92/26; *CSPD, 1611–1618*, 466.

55 Speech in Common Pleas to Justice Hutton, PRO SP 14/92/7 (*Resuscitatio* 93; *LL* 6: 201–2); speech in Exchequer to Sir John Denham (PRO SP 14/92/6; *Resuscitatio* 91; *LL* 6: 203–4); speech to Sir William Jones (*Resuscitatio* 89; *LL* 6: 205–7; see also BL Harley MS 1576, fo. 151; FSL MS V.a.206); dating deduced from JC to DC, 24 May 1617, McClure 2: 76.

56 FB to GV, 7 June 1617, LPL MS 936, art. 65; *LL* 6: 208–9.

57 FB to Lord Viscount Fenton, 18 June 1617, LPL MS 936, art. 66; *LL* 6: 209.

58 ? to FB, 28 June 1618, PRO SP 14/92/75; *CSPD, 1611–1618*, 473. For the Star Chamber speech, 10 July 1617, see *Resuscitatio* 87; *LL* 6: 211–14; there is a report in BL Harley MS 1576.

59 ES to DC, 7 and 14 December 1616, PRO SP 14/89/68 and 80; *CSPD, 1611–1618*, 412 and 413; JC to DC, [21] December 1616, McClure 2: 45.

60 *LL* 6: 221.

61 JC to DC, 19 July 1617, McClure 2: 88–9.

62 Godfrey Goodman, *The Court of King James the First*, 2 vols, ed. John S. Brewer (London: Richard Bentley, 1839), 1: 283; *Apophthegms*, *Works* 7: 184.

63 See Lady Hatton to FB, 12, 14, 16, 18 and 20 June 1617, *Letters of John Holles 1587–1637*, 3 vols, ed. P. R. Seddon (Nottingham: Thornton Society, 1975, vols 31, 35 and 36), 1: 165–6, 2: 168–9, 170.

64 FB to GV, 12 July 1617, *Letters of Sir Francis Bacon*, ed. Stephens (1702), 207–9; *LL* 6: 223–4.

65 Ibid.

66 JC to DC, 19 July 1617, McClure 2: 89.

67 ? to Ann Sadler, 26 July [1617], Trinity College, Cambridge MSS R.v.3, quoted in *LL* 6: 225. For an alternative account see George Gerrard to DC, 22 July 1617, PRO SP 14/92/101; *CSPD, 1611–1618*, 477.

68 For this affair see *LL* 6: 220–31; Bowen, *Lion*.

69 FB to GV, 25 July 1617, *Letters of Sir Francis Bacon*, ed. Stephens (1702), 213–14; *LL* 6: 235.

70 FB to James, 25 July 1617, LPL MS 936, art. 71; *LL* 6: 232–4.

71 FB to GV, LPL MS 936, art. 67; *LL* 6: 235–6.

72 GV to FB, [early August? 1617], *LL* 6: 237. Spedding gives as his source BL Add. MS 4260, but the letter is no longer in that volume.

73 Letter not extant but listed in BL Add. MS 4259, fo. 60b; *LL* 7: 590–3.

74 GV to FB, 12 August 1617, LPL MS 936, art. 72; *LL* 6: 243.

75 FB to James, [*c*.12 August 1617], LPL MS 936, art. 69(a); *LL* 6: 238–42.

76 FB to GV, 23 August 1617, LPL MS 936, art. 73; *LL* 6: 242–3.

77 James to FB, [25 or 26 August 1617], LPL MS 936, art. 69b; *LL* 6: 243–5.

78 FB to James, 31 August 1617, BL Lansdowne MS 90, fo. 42; *LL* 6: 245–6.

79 Yelverton to FB, 3 September 1617, LPL MS 936, art. 74; *LL* 6: 247–9.

80 GV to FB, 5 September 1617, LPL MS 936, art. 230; *LL* 6: 249.

81 Sir A[nthony] W[eldon], *The Court and Character of King James* (London: John Wright, 1650), 131–4.

82 Note for James, September 1617, LPL MS 936, art. 75; *LL* 6: 250–1.

83 GV to FB, [22 September 1617], LPL MS 936, art. 265; *LL* 6: 251–2.

84 FB to GV, 22 September 1617, HEH FBL MS 4; LPL MS 936, art. 76; *LL* 6: 252–3.

85 GV to FB, 16 January 1618, BL Harley MS 7006, fo. 62; *LL* 6: 290; FB to GV, 20 January 1618, LPL MS 936, art. 91; *LL* 7: 292; GV to FB, 24 January 1618, BL Harley MS 7006, fo. 66; *LL* 6: 293.

86 GV to FB, 21 January 1618, Bodl. Tanner MS 74, fo. 104; *LL* 6: 292.

87 GV to FB, 23 January 1618, BL Harley MS 7006, fo. 64; *LL* 6: 293.

88 FB to GV, 25 January 1618, *Letters of Sir Francis Bacon*, ed. Stephens (1702), 224–7; *LL* 6: 294–5.

89 GV to FB, 28 January 1618, BL Harley MS 7006, fo. 70; *LL* 6: 296–7.

90 GV to FB, 31 January 1618, BL Harley MS 7006, fo. 72a; *LL* 6: 297.

91 James to the Privy Council, quoted in Hugh Ross Williamson, *George Villiers, First Duke of Buckingham: Study for a Biography* (London: Duckworth, 1940), 68.

92 Adam Newton to Sir Thomas Puckering, 30 September 1617, *The Court and Times of James the First; Illustrated by Authentic and Confidential Letters, from Various Public and Private Collections*, 2 vols, ed. Thomas Birch, rev. Robert Folkestone Williams (London: Henry Colburn, 1848), 2: 34.

93 JC to DC, 11 October 1617, McClure 2: 100–1.

94 JC to DC, 31 October 1617, McClure 2: 110.

95 JC to DC, 19 July 1617, McClure 2: 89–90.

CHAPTER 15

1 Anne Clifford, *The Diary of Anne Clifford 1616–1619: A Critical Edition*, ed. Katherine O. Acheson (New York: Garland, 1995), 88: 'About this time my Lord Keeper & all his Company went away from Dorset House' (marginal note *c.*16 August 1617).

2 FB to Archbishop of York, n.d., LPL MS 936, art. 245; *LL* 6: 270–1.

3 JC to DC, 31 October, 8 November 1617, McClure 2: 109, 113.

4 John Pory to DC, 8 November 1617, PRO SP 14/94/15, *CSPD, 1611–1618*, 495.

5 Daphne Du Maurier, *The Winding Stair: Francis Bacon, His Rise and Fall* (London: Victor Gollancz, 1976), 143.

6 'Sir Lionel Cranfield is now reasonably well recovered': FB to GV, 27 November 1617, LPL MS 936, art. 84; *LL* 6: 279–80. On Cranfield, see Menna Prestwich, *Cranfield: Politics and Profits under the Early Stuarts: The Career of Lionel Cranfield, Earl of Manchester* (Oxford: Clarendon Press, 1966).

7 'Memorial to James' [September 1617], *Letters and Remains of the Lord Chancellor Bacon*, ed. Robert Stephens (London: W. Bowyer, 1734), 58–61; *LL* 6: 254–6.

8 FB to GV, 22 November 1617, LPL MS 936 art. 82; *LL* 6: 276–7; FB to GV, 19 November 1617, *Letters of Sir Francis Bacon, Baron of Verulam, Viscount St Alban, and Lord High Chancellor of England. Written during the Reign of King James the First*, ed. Robert Stephens (London: Benjamin Tooke, 1702), 245–6; *LL* 6: 275.

9 Piero Contarini [?], 'True Collection of the Fees and Offices of his Majesty in all the Courts of Westminster', early 1618 [?], *CSP . . . Venice, 1617–1619*, 600.

10 'Receipts and Disbursements', 1618, PRO SP 14/99/86; *LL* 6: 327–36.

11 PRO SP 14/95/64; *LL* 6: 327–36.

12 John Aubrey, *Aubrey's Brief Lives*, ed. Oliver Lawson Dick (London: Secker & Warburg, 1960), 9, 10.

13 FB to GV, 19 November 1617, *Letters of Sir Francis Bacon*, ed. Stephens (1702), 245–6; *LL* 6: 275.

14 FB to GV, 22 November 1617, LPL MS 936, art. 82; *LL* 6: 276–7.

15 For James's complaints see GV to FB, 19 November 1617, BL Harley MS 7006; *LL* 6: 275–6.

16 FB to GV, 20 November 1617, LPL MS 936, art. 81; *LL* 6: 276.

17 FB to GV, 27 November 1617, *Letters of Sir Francis Bacon*, ed. Stephens (1702), 222; *LL* 6: 279–80; a copy is in LPL MS 936, art. 84. For the letter regarding the subcommission, see Spedding's collation of LPL MS 936, art. 85, and *Letters of Sir Francis Bacon*, ed. Stephens (1702), 222–3: *LL* 6: 280–1.

18 GV to FB, 2 December 1617, BL Harley MS 7006, fo. 50; *LL* 6: 281. For further retrenchment business see FB to GV, 6 December 1617, LPL MS 936, fo. 83; *LL* 6: 283–5; Council to James, 5 December 1617, *Letters and Remains*, ed.

Stephens, 69–71; *LL* 6: 281–3. For James's positive response see GV to FB, 9 December 1617, BL Harley MS 7006, fo. 56; *LL* 6: 285.

19 FB to GV, 6 December 1617, LPL MS 936, art. 83; *LL* 6: 283–5.

20 See ES to LC, 23 August 1617, Sackville MS 1527 (M873), quoted in Robert C. Johnson, 'Francis Bacon and Lionel Cranfield', *Huntington Library Quarterly* 23 (1960), 306 n. 11.

21 FB to LC, 10 October 1619, Sackville MS 144, quoted in Johnson, 'Bacon and Cranfield', 306.

22 LC to GV, 14 January 1618, pr. in *LL* 6: 289.

23 FB to GV, 16 January 1618, Bodl. Add. MS D.112, fo. 43; *LL* 6: 289–90.

24 FB to GV, 10 December 1617, concerning 'the farming of the small writs', beginning 'I find Sir Geo. Chaworth'; see catalogue of letters now lost: BL Add. MS 4259, fo. 61b; *LL* 7: 590–3.

25 FB to GV, 31 December 1617, LPL MS 936, art. 87; *LL* 6: 286. For a later complication see Williams to GV, 23 August 1622, *Scrinia Ceciliana: Mysteries of State & Government: in Letters of the Most Famous Lord Burghley, And other Grand Ministers of State: In the Reigns of Queen Elizabeth, and King James. Being a further Additional Supplement of the Cabala* (London: G. Bedel & T. Collins, 1663), 291; *LL* 7: 389–90.

26 See JC to DC, 15 November 1617, McClure 2: 118; Sir Edward Harwood to DC, 7 January 1618, PRO SP 14/95/8; *CSPD, 1611–1618*, 511.

27 FB to GV, 31 December 1617, LPL MS 936, art. 86; *LL* 6: 287–8. See also, for his gift to Charles, FB to Sir James Fullerton, 31 December 1617, LPL MS 936, art. 88; *LL* 6: 288.

28 JC to DC, 10 January 1618, McClure 2: 127.

29 JC to DC, 7 February 1618, McClure 2: 136.

30 JC to DC, 20 April 1618, McClure 2: 157.

31 JC to DC, 14 February 1618, McClure 2: 139–40.

32 FB to GV, 5 August 1618, *Letters of Sir Francis Bacon*, ed. Stephens (1702), 231–2; *LL* 6: 321–2.

33 JC to DC, 13 August 1618, McClure 2: 165–6.

34 JC to DC, 7 November 1618, McClure 2: 181.

35 On the Spanish ambassador incident, see Lorkin to Puckering, *The Court and Times of James the First; Illustrated by Authentic and Confidential Letters, from Various Public and Private Collections*, 2 vols, ed. Thomas Birch, rev. Robert Folkestone Williams (London: Henry Colburn, 1848), 2: 81; FB to Julius Caesar, 6 August 1618, BL Add. MS 12,607, fo. 40, *LL* 6: 323; JC to DC, 13 August 1618, McClure 2: 165. On the Alleyn money, see FB to GV, 18 August 1618, *Letters of Sir Francis Bacon*, ed. Stephens (1702), 233–4; *LL* 6: 234.

36 *Apophthegms, Works* 7: 168.

37 Notes by Thomas Wilson, 28 September 1618, PRO SP 14/99/77; *CSPD, 1611–1618*, 577.

38 JC to DC, 29 March 1617, McClure 2: 67.

39 Samuel R. Gardiner, *History of England from the Accession of James I to the Outbreak of the Civil War 1603–1642*, 10 vols (London: Longmans, Green, and Co., 1899–1900), 3: 132.

40 Commissioners to James, 18 October 1618, LPL MS 936, art. 21; *LL* 6: 361–2.

41 James to commissioners, [October 1618], pr. in *LL* 6: 363–4.

42 DC to JC, *Court and Times of James the First*, ed. Birch, 2: 106.

43 Naunton to GV, 27 November 1618, pr. in *LL* 6: 382.

44 JC to DC, 28 November 1618, McClure 2: 188.

45 FB to James, 2 January 1619, Bodl. Tanner MS 74, fo. 176; *LL* 6: 452–3.

46 Antonio Donato to the Doge and Senate of Venice, 14 March 1619, *CSP . . . Venice, 1617–1619*, 494–5.

47 JC to DC, 6 March 1619, McClure 2: 220.

48 JC to DC, 27 March and 10 April 1619, McClure 2: 225, 227

49 JC to DC, 24 April 1619, McClure 2: 232.

50 JC to DC, 21 November 1618, McClure 2: 185.

51 JC to DC, 28 November 1618, McClure 2: 188.

52 JC to DC, 2 January 1619, McClure 2: 197.

53 JC to DC, 17 April 1619, McClure 2: 230.

54 JC to DC, 24 April 1619, McClure 2: 233; FB to TM, n.d., Tobie Matthew, *A Collection of Letters* (London: Henry Herringman, 1660), 32; *LL* 7: 201; Brent to DC, 8 May 1619, PRO SP 14/109/19; *CSPD, 1619–1623*, 44.

55 JC to DC, 30 January 1619, McClure 2: 208.

56 TM to FB, 4/14 Feb 1619, LPL MS 936, art. 123; *LL* 7: 20; John P. Feil, 'Sir Tobie Matthew and his *Collection of Letters*' (PhD, University of Chicago, 1962), 136.

57 Lorkin to Puckering, 16 March 1619, *Court and Times of James I*, ed. Birch, 2: 146.

58 Lorkin to Puckering, 26 April 1619, *Court and Times of James I*, ed. Birch, 2: 155.

59 FB to the Count Palatine, [13 May 1619], LPL MS 936, art. 107; *LL* 7: 21–2.

60 'A Short View to be Taken of Great Britain and Spain', *LL* 7: 22–8; for MS witnesses see Beal BcF 281–2.

61 JC to DC, 27 March and 24 April 1619, McClure 2: 224, 232.

62 JC to DC, 14 May 1619, McClure 2: 237.

63 Note by Sir Julius Caesar, BL Lansdowne MS 165, fo. 288b; *LL* 7: 33.

64 JC to DC, 5 June 1619, McClure 2: 242; Donato to the Doge and Senate of Venice, 14 March 1619, *CSP . . . Venice, 1617–1619*, 495.

65 FB to Christian IV, 16 June 1619, pr. in Samuel Rawson Gardiner, 'On Four Letters from Lord Bacon to Christian IV, King of Denmark', *Archaeologia* 41 (1867) 219–69 at 266–7; *LL* 7: 82–3; tr. Spedding, *LL* 7: 83 n. 1.

66 See FB to GV, 29 June 1619, LPL MS 936, art. 108; *LL* 7: 34–5.

67 FB to Lord Warden of the Cinque Ports, 3 August 1619, PRO SP 14/110/10; *LL* 7: 40; FB to GV, 9 October 1619, *Letters of Sir Francis Bacon*, ed. Stephens (1702), 241–3; *LL* 7: 47–8; GV to FB, 10 October 1619, BL Harley MS 7000, fo. 144; GV to FB, 14 October [1619], BL Harley MS 7006, fo. 142a; *LL* 7: 49.

68 FB to the States General, 20 July 1619, BL Add. MS 17,667, fo. 433 (art. 143); *LL* 7: 38.

69 FB to GV, 31 July 1619, *Letters of Sir Francis Bacon*, ed. Stephens (1702), 240–1;

LL 7: 39. For other correspondence this summer, see FB to GV, 19 July, 28 August 1619, LPL MS 936, arts 109, 100; *LL* 7: 37, 40–1. GV to FB, 29 August 1619, BL Harley MS 7006, fo. 136a; *LL* 7: 41.

70 GV to FB, 9 September 1619, BL Harley MS 7006, fo. 138a; *LL* 7: 43–4.

71 See FB to GV, 14 October 1619, LPL MS 936, art. 111; *LL* 7: 50; FB to GV, 21 October 1619, LPL MS 936, art. 112; *LL* 7: 50–1; FB to GV, 22 October 1619, *Letters of Sir Francis Bacon*, ed. Stephens (1702), 243–4; LPL MS 936, art. 241; *LL* 7: 51–2; GV to FB, 23 October 1619, BL Harley MS 7006, fo. 146a; *LL* 7: 53; FB to GV, 27 October 1619, LPL MS 936, art. 113; *LL* 7: 53–4; FB to GV, 13 November 1619, *Letters and Remains*, ed. Stephens (1734), 102; *LL* 7: 55.

72 Sir John Finet to the earl of Salisbury, 14 November 1619, *HMCS* 22: 113.

73 Proceedings against Suffolk et al., 13 November 1619, PRO SP 14/111/18; *CSPD, 1619–1623*, 94.

74 FB to GV, 12 December 1619, LPL MS 936, art. 119; *LL* 7: 68–9. For the King's acceptance, see GV to FB, 10 December 1619, BL Harley MS 7006; *LL* 7: 68.

75 FB to James, [January 1620], LPL MS 936, art. 227; *LL* 7: 70–2.

76 FB to GV, 9 June 1620, LPL MS 936, art. 126; *LL* 7: 95–6. The rules are lost.

77 Quoted in Thomas Cogswell, 'Underground Verse and the Transformation of Early Stuart Political Culture', in Susan D. Amussen and Mark A. Kishlansky, eds, *Political Culture and Cultural Politics in Early Modern England* (Manchester: Manchester University Press, 1995), 282.

78 JC to DC, 29 April, 5 May 1618, McClure 2: 159–60, 161; grant of pardon to Wraynham, 16 July 1619, *CSPD, 1619–1623*, 63.

79 Clifton to James, 12 June 1611, PRO SP 14/64/27; *CSPD, 1611–1618*, 42.

80 JC to DC, 29 April 1612, McClure 1: 346.

81 Clifton is mentioned in JC to DC, 3 January 1618, McClure 2: 126. Sir Gerard Herbert to DC, 30 December 1617, PRO SP 14/94/83; *CSPD, 1611–1618*, 505. George Lord Carew to Sir Thomas Roe, 18 January 1618, PRO SP 14/95/22; *CSPD, 1611–1618*, 517.

82 FB to GV, 25 January 1618, *Letters of Sir Francis Bacon*, ed. Stephens (1702), 224–7; *LL* 6: 295–6.

83 FB to GV, 17 March 1618, *Letters of Sir Francis Bacon*, ed. Stephens (1702), 228–9; *LL* 6: 307–8.

84 GV to FB, 18 March 1618, BL Harley MS 7006, fo. 83; *LL* 6: 308.

85 See *APC, 1617–1619*, 86, 87.

86 JC to DC, 14 October 1618, McClure 2: 170. See also Sir Henry Carey to DC, 16 October 1618, PRO SP 14/103/39; *CSPD, 1611–1618*, 585: 'Lord Clifton has killed himself with two knives.' See also Sir Thomas Lake to Sir Thomas Puckering, 5 October 1618, *Court and Times of James I*, ed. Birch, 2: 91. 'This day was fatal to my lord Clifton, who in his lodgings in Holborn stabbed and murdered himself.'

87 Grant to Aubigny, 18 November 1618, *CSPD, 1611–1618*, 596. On Clifton see *HPT* 1: 618.

88 *APC, 1617–1619*, 468; *APC 1619–1621*, 8, 102, 192; PRO SP 14/109/162–3, 14/115/24–5 (*CSPD, 1619–1623*, 68, 144).

89 *APC, 1619– 1621,* 299; PRO SP 14/115/26– 7, 14/117/66 (*CSPD,1619– 1623,* 144, 190).

90 JC to DC, 5 June 1619, McClure 2: 243. In *CSPD, 1619– 1623,* 51, the editor reads 'Latinities' for 'catamites'. On Singleton, see Joseph Foster, ed., *Alumni Oxonienses: The Members of the University of Oxford, 1500– 1714,* vol. 3 (S–Z) (Oxford: Parker & Co., n.d.), 1359.

91 *Novum Organum, Works* 4: 82.

92 FB to James, 12 October 1620, LPL MS 936, art. 129; *LL* 7: 119– 20.

93 James to FB, 16 October 1620, *Resuscitatio* 83; *LL* 7: 122.

94 FB to James, 20 October 1620, LPL MS 936, art. 130; *LL* 7: 130– 1; JC to DC, 3 February 1621 and 28 October 1620, McClure 2: 339 and 329.

95 FB et al. to James, 16 June 1620, *Letters of Sir Francis Bacon,* ed. Stephens (1702), 248– 9; *LL* 7: 98– 9.

96 'Notes upon Mr. Attorney's cause', 24 October 1620, LPL MS 936, fo. 133; *LL* 7: 133– 4.

97 BL Harley MS 6055; *LL* 7: 134; FB to GV, 28 October 1620, LPL MS 936, fo. 134; *LL* 7: 135.

98 BL Harley MS 6055, with amendments by Spedding; *LL* 7: 138– 9.

99 FB to GV, 11 November 1620, *LL* 7: 140 (location unknown).

100 JC to DC, 10 February 1621, McClure 2: 342.

101 Spedding assumed the suit was for some friend, but it must be about Bacon himself, with its references to 'rewarding Chancellors before the Parliament': *LL* 7: 157– 9.

102 GV to FB, n.d. [November 1620 to January 1621], *The Fortescue Papers,* ed. Samuel Rawson Gardiner (London: Camden Society, 1871, n.s., vol. 1), 149– 50; *LL* 7: 158.

103 Ben Jonson, 'Lord Bacon's Birthday', *Works,* 11 vols, ed. C. H. Herford, Percy Simpson and Evelyn Simpson (Oxford: Clarendon Press, 1925– 52), 8: 435– 8.

104 Simonds D'Ewes, *Extracts from the MS Journal of Sir Simonds D'Ewes, with Several Letters to and from Sir Simonds and his Friends* (London: J. Nichols, 1783), 18.

105 FB to James, n.d., LPL MS 936 fo. 225; *LL* 7: 168– 9. On the investiture see Camden's note, *LL* 7: 168 n. 2.

106 BL Harley MS 7009, fo. 325a– b.

CHAPTER 16

1 JC to DC, 3 February 1621, McClure 2: 338. On the 1621 parliament and Bacon's fall, see *LJ* 3; Edward Nicholas, *Proceedings and Debates in the House of Commons in 1620 and 1621,* 2 vols (Oxford: Clarendon Press, 1766); Wallace Notestein, Frances Helen Relf and Hartley Simpson, eds, *Commons Debates 1621,* 7 vols (New Haven: Yale University Press, 1935); Robert Zaller, *The Parliament of 1621: A Study in Constitutional Conflict* (Berkeley, CA: University of California Press, 1971); John T. Noonan, Jr, *Bribes* (Berkeley, CA: University of California Press, 1984), 334– 65.

2 FB to James, 2 October 1620, *Letters and Remains of the Lord Chancellor Bacon,* ed. Robert Stephens (London: W. Bowyer, 1734), 114– 15; *LL* 7: 114– 15. See also

FB to GV, 2 October 1620, *Letters and Remains*, ed. Stephens (1734), 113; *LL* 7: 113–14.

3 FB to GV, 7 October 1620, LPL MS 936, art. 128; *LL* 7: 115–17. On a later meeting, see FB et al. to GV, 29 November 1620, Bodl. Tanner MS 290, fo. 33; *LL* 7: 145–8.

4 Proclamation for a parliament, 18 October 1620, *Letters of Sir Francis Bacon*, ed. Robert Stephens (London: Benjamin Tooke, 1702), 257–63; *LL* 7: 124–8; Daphne Du Maurier, *The Winding Stair: Francis Bacon, His Rise and Fall* (London: Victor Gollancz, 1976), 161–2.

5 GV to FB, 9 October 1620, BL Harley MS 7000, fo. 20; *LL* 7: 117–18.

6 GV to FB, 19 October 1620, BL Harley MS 7000, fo. 26; *LL* 7: 128.

7 FB to GV, 19 October 1620, LPL MS 936, art. 132; *LL* 7: 129.

8 *Stuart Royal Proclamations*, vol. 1, ed. J. F. Larkin and P. L. Hughes (Oxford: Clarendon Press, 1973), 493–4.

9 JC to DC, 14 October 1620, McClure 2: 321.

10 JC to DC, 28 October 1620, McClure 2: 323.

11 FB to Bridgewater, 24 October 1620, HEH EL MS 6471 (not published in *LL*).

12 FB et al. to GV, 29 November 1620, Bodl. Tanner MS 290, fo. 33; *LL* 7: 145–8.

13 FB to GV, 29 November 1620, LPL MS 936, art. 135; *LL* 7: 148–9.

14 FB to GV, 16 December 1620, LPL MS 936, art. 137; *LL* 7: 151–2.

15 JC to DC, 22 December 1620, McClure 2: 331.

16 FB to GV, 23 December 1620, LPL MS 936, art. 138; *LL* 7: 155; GV to FB, 21 December 1620, BL Harley MS 7000, fo. 37; *LL* 7: 154–5.

17 FB to GV, 23 December 1620, LPL MS 936, art. 138; *LL* 7: 155.

18 Notestein et al., eds, *Commons Debates 1621*, 6: 374; 'Beginning of a speech intended to be spoken after the King's speech to the two houses', LPL MS 936, fo. 239; *LL* 7: 171–2. 'Cancellarius', PRO SP 14/119/48; *LL* 7: 172–3.

19 Notestein et al., *Commons Debates 1621*, 2: 92–3.

20 Ibid., 4: 20.

21 Ibid., 4: 108.

22 Ibid., 2: 147.

23 FB to TM, n.d., Tobie Matthew, *A Collection of Letters* (London: Henry Herringman, 1660), 32; *LL* 7: 201. See also Digby to Fermat, n.d., in *The Works of Francis Bacon, Lord Chancellor of England. A New Edition*, ed. Basil Montagu, vol. 16 (London: William Pickering, 1834), pt 2 n. GGG.

24 Notestein et al., *Commons Debates 1621*, 6: 272–5, 292–5; Nicholas, *Proceedings and Debates*, 1: 109–12.

25 Mead to Sir Martin Stuteville, 25 February 1621, *The Court and Times of James the First; Illustrated by Authentic and Confidential Letters, from Various Public and Private Collections*, ed. Thomas Birch, rev. Robert Folkestone Williams, 2 vols (London: Henry Colburn, 1848), 2: 232.

26 Nicholas, *Proceedings and Debates*, 1: 114.

27 FB to GV, 7 March 1621, LPL MS 936, art. 139; *LL* 7: 191–2.

28 Samuel R. Gardiner, *History of England from the Accession of James I to the Outbreak of the Civil War 1603–1642*, 10 vols (London: Longmans, Green, and Co., 1899–1900), 1: 432.

29 LL 7: 213–14; Nicholas, *Proceedings and Debates*, 1: 162.
30 FB to GV, 14 March 1621, LPL MS 936, art. 220; *LL* 7: 213.
31 Notestein et al., *Commons Debates 1621*, 2: 224–6.
32 Ibid., 4: 160–1, 5: 44–5, 301–2; 6: 66–8; Nicholas, *Proceedings and Debates*, 1: 183–5.
33 Notestein et al., *Commons Debates 1621*, 2: 237–9, 4: 166–7, 5: 306; Nicholas, *Proceedings and Debates*, 1: 183–5.
34 Notestein et al., *Commons Debates 1621*, 4: 167–8.
35 FB to the Lords, 19 March 1621. *LJ* 3: 54; *LL* 7: 215–16.
36 *LJ* 3: 55.
37 FB to James, 25 March 1621, Bodl. Tanner MS 72, fo. 105; *LL* 7: 225–6.
38 Will, 10 April 1621, BL Add. MS 4259, fos 111a–112b; *LL* 7: 228–9.
39 LPL MS 936, art. 259; *LL* 7: 232–4.
40 *LJ* 3: 75.
41 Drafts of memorandum, LPL MS 936, art. 146; *LL* 6: 235–6, 237–8. FB to the Lords, 22 April 1621, *LJ* 3: 84; *LL* 7: 242–5 at 244.
42 LPL MS 936, art. 146; *LL* 7: 235–6.
43 LPL MS 936, art. 146; *LL* 7: 237–8.
44 See FB to James, 20 April 1621: 'I shall without fig-leaves or disguise excuse what I can excuse'. *Letters and Remains*, ed. Stephens (1734), 138; *LL* 7: 240; and FB to the Lords, 22 April 1621, which claims to tell all 'without fig-leaves', *LJ* 3: 84; *LL* 7: 242–5 at 243.
45 *LJ* 3: 75.
46 Thomas Bushell, *Mr Bushell's Abridgment of the Lord Chancellor Bacon's Philosophical Theory in Mineral Prosecutions* (London, 1659), A3^r.
47 BL Harley MS 7009, fo. 325a–b; see also Bodl. Rawlinson MS B.151, fo. 108^v.
48 FB to James, 20 April 1621, *Letters and Remains*, ed. Stephens (1734), 138; *LL* 7: 240.
49 FB to James, 21 April 1621, Bodl. Tanner MS 73(i), fo. 3; *LL* 7: 240–2 at 241–2.
50 FB's submission to the Lords, 22 April 1621, *LJ* 3: 84; *LL* 7: 242–5.
51 *LL* 7: 248–9.
52 *LJ* 3: 85.
53 FB's submission to the Lords, 30 April 1621, *LJ* 3: 85; *LL* 7: 252–62.
54 *LL* 7: 262.
55 Matthew, *Collection*, 69, 70; John P. Feil, 'Sir Tobie Matthew and his *Collection of Letters*' (PhD, University of Chicago, 1962), 160 n. 2.
56 *LL* 7: 267–70.
57 Bushell, *Abridgement*, A3^r.
58 Edward Egerton's and Aubrey's were for past favours; those of Barker, Dunch, Fisher, Lentall, Ruswell, Scott, Wroth and Young taken after the case was over; those of Rowland, Egerton, Hansby and Montagu after all the legal issues were decided. See Noonan, *Bribes*, 357.
59 Reynell's ring also fitted into this category. See Noonan, *Bribes*, 357.
60 FB's confession, *LJ* 3: 98–101; *LL* 7: 252–62.
61 JC to DC, 24 March 1621, McClure 2: 355.
62 John Aubrey, *Aubrey's Brief Lives*, ed. Oliver Lawson Dick (London: Secker & Warburg, 1960), 10.

63 Thomas Bushell, *The First Part of Youths Errors* (London, 1628), 16^v–18^v.

64 Preface to Moses Pitt, *The Crisis of the Oppressed* (London: M. Pitt, 1691); quoted in *LL* 7: 563–4.

65 BL Harley MS 646, fos 58b–59b; pr. Simonds D'Ewes, *Extracts from the MS Journal of Sir Simonds D'Ewes, with Several Letters to and from Sir Simonds and his Friends* (London: J. Nichols, 1783), 25–6.

66 Aubrey, *Brief Lives*, 11.

67 'Vpon S'F Ba', FSL MS V.a.345, p. 25; see also Arthur Marotti, *Manuscript, Print, and the English Renaissance Lyric* (Ithaca, NY: Cornell University Press, 1995), 105 n. 66.

68 BL Harley MS 646, fos 58b–59b; pr. D'Ewes, *Extracts*, 25–6.

69 JC to DC, 24 March 1621, McClure 2: 356.

70 BL Harley MS 7009, fos 324a–325b.

71 Aubrey, *Brief Lives*, 42.

72 See *CSPD, 1623–1625*, 246, 262, 264, 273, 279, 340, 487.

73 FB to GV, 31 May 1621, LPL MS 936, art. 147; *LL* 7: 280.

74 *LL* 7: 279.

75 Ashley to ?GV, 12 May 1621, *Scrinia Ceciliana: Mysteries of State & Government: in Letters of the Most Famous Lord Burghley, And other Grand Ministers of State: In the Reigns of Queen Elizabeth, and King James. Being a further Additional Supplement of the Cabala* (London: G. Bedel & T. Collins, 1663), 2; *LL* 7: 279.

76 JC wrote on Saturday 2 June that FB went to the Tower 'at the beginning of the week': JC to DC, 2 June 1621, McClure 2: 377.

77 FB to GV, 31 May 1621, LPL MS 936, art. 147; *LL* 7: 280.

78 JC to DC, 9 June 1621, McClure 2: 381.

79 FB to GV, 4 June 1621, *Letters and Remains*, ed. Stephens (1734), 147; *LL* 7: 281. See also FB to James, 4 June 1621, *Letters and Remains*, ed. Stephens (1734), 146–7; *LL* 7: 281.

80 FB to GV, [5 June 1621], LPL MS 936, art. 219; *LL* 7: 282–3.

81 JC to DC, 9 June 1621, McClure 2: 381.

82 FB to Charles, [7] June 1621, *Letters and Remains*, ed. Stephens (1734), 145–6; *LL* 7: 287–8.

83 JC to DC, 23 June 1621, McClure 2: 383.

84 FB to James, [21 June 1621], LPL MS 936, art. 251; *LL* 7: 291.

85 FB to GV, 20 June 1621, *Letters and Remains*, ed. Stephens (1734), 150; *LL* 7: 291–2.

86 FB to GV, 22 June 1621, *Letters and Remains*, ed. Stephens (1734), 151; *LL* 7: 292–3 and draft of the same, LPL MS 936, art. 287; *LL* 292 n. 8.

87 FB to GV, [on or after 23 June 1621], *Letters and Remains*, ed. Stephens (1734), 152; *LL* 7: 293. For the date see JC to DC, 23 June 1621, McClure 2: 385.

88 JC to DC, 23 June 1621, McClure 2: 385.

89 FB to GV, n.d., LPL MS 936, art. 270; *LL* 7: 296.

90 Sir A[nthony] W[eldon], *Aulicus Coquinariae*, in *Secret History of the Court of James the First*, 2 vols (Edinburgh: James Ballantyne, 1811), 2: 99–298 at 267–8. There seems no need to date this incident to early April, as Spedding suggests (*LL* 7: 227).

CHAPTER 17

1 FB to Gondomar, 6 June 1621, LPL MS 936, art. 168; *LL* 7: 285.
2 FB to James, 16 July 1621, *Letters and Remains of the Lord Chancellor Bacon*, ed. Robert Stephens (London: W. Bowyer, 1734), 152–3; *LL* 7: 296–7.
3 FB to Andrewes, [1622?], *Certain Miscellany Works of the Right Honourable, Francis Lo. Verulam, Viscount S. Alban*, ed. William Rawley (London: Humphrey Robinson, 1629), 79; HEH EL MS 1594a; *LL* 7: 371–4.
4 *Abecedarium novum naturae* (1622), Paris, Bibliothèque Nationale MS Coll. Dupuy no. 5, tr. Graham Rees. This text will be published in its entirety in the new *Works*, vol. XIII, ed. Rees (Clarendon Press, forthcoming). We are extremely grateful to Graham Rees for drawing our attention to this passage, and for permission to quote from his unpublished translation.
5 Rawley, 'Life of Bacon', *Works* 1: 9–10; Rees, 'Introduction' to *The Oxford Francis Bacon*, vol. 6: *Philosophical Writings 1611–1618* (Oxford: Clarendon Press, 1996).
6 *De augmentis scientiarum* (1623), *Works* 4: 303–4.
7 Selden to FB, 20 August 1621; pr. Daniel R. Woolf, 'John Selden, John Borough and Francis Bacon's *History of Henry VII*', *Huntington Library Quarterly* 47 (1984), 47–53.
8 John Aubrey, *Aubrey's Brief Lives*, ed. Oliver Lawson Dick (London: Secker & Warburg, 1960), 9, 150.
9 FB to GV, n.d., FB to Charles, n.d., Note by Meautys, 1621, LPL MS 936, arts 236, 237, 237ᵛ; *LL* 7: 297–8, 299, 299 n. 2.
10 Licence to FB, 13 September 1621, BL Add. MS 4259; *LL* 7: 300, 300–1.
11 FB to James, 5 September 1621, LPL MS 936, arts 155, 235, 242; *LL* 7: 298–9.
12 James to Coventry, 12 October 1621, BL Add. MS 4259, fo. 109b; *LL* 7: 301.
13 FB to James, 8 October 1621, LPL MS 936, art. 150; *LL* 7: 303. The last sentence is deleted.
14 Meautys to FB, 7 January 1622, LPL MS 936, art. 157; *LL* 7: 325–6.
15 James to Coventry, 12 October 1621, BL Add. MS 4259, fo. 109b; *LL* 7: 306.
16 Grant of pardon to FB, 16 October 1621, *CSPD, 1619–1623*, 299; *LL* 7: 307–8. For the pardon see BL Cotton MS Titus B.vii, fo. 144; *LL* 7: 307.
17 Williams to FB, 18 October 1621, LPL MS 936, art. 153; *LL* 7: 308.
18 FB to GV, 18 October 1621, pr. in *LL* 7: 309. For draft, see LPL MS 936, art. 151; *LL* 7: 309 n. 1. See also FB to Williams, 18 October 1621, LPL MS 936, art. 152; *LL* 7: 308–9. GV to FB, 20 October 1621, BL Harley MS 7000, fo. 75; *LL* 7: 310; Williams to GV, 27 October 1621, *Scrinia Ceciliana: Mysteries of State & Government: in Letters of the Most Famous Lord Burghley, And other Grand Ministers of State: In the Reigns of Queen Elizabeth, and King James. Being a further Additional Supplement of the Cabala* (London: G. Bedel & T. Collins, 1663), 287; *LL* 7: 310–11.
19 JC to DC, 20 October 1621, McClure 2: 402.
20 GV to FB, [pre 8 October 1621], BL Harley MS 7000, fo. 69; *LL* 7: 305.

21 JC to DC, 13 October 1621, McClure 2: 399. FB to Cranfield, 7 October 1621, Sackville MS 2416; Robert C. Johnson, 'Francis Bacon and Lionel Cranfield', *Huntington Library Quarterly* 23 (1960), 314–16.

22 JC to DC, 20 October 1621, McClure 2: 402.

23 GV to FB, [pre 8 October 1621], BL Harley MS 7000, fo. 69; *LL* 7: 305.

24 'A Memorial of Conference when I expected my Lord Marquis at York House', n.d., LPL MS 936, art. 244; *LL* 7: 312–14.

25 FB to GV, n.d., LPL MS 936, art. 253; *LL* 7: 314–15.

26 FB to GV, n.d., LPL MS 936, art. 196; *LL* 7: 316–17. For the second draft see FB to GV, n.d., LPL MS 936, art. 197; *LL* 7: 315.

27 GV to FB, 14 November 1621, HEH FBL MS 29^{r-v} (not published in *LL*). It is not altogether clear that it was Buckingham who obtained the pardon.

28 Petition to the House of Lords, n.d., LPL MS 936, art. 261; *LL* 7: 321–2.

29 'Warrant to Mr. Attorney', 26 December 1621, Sackville MS 2464, quoted in Johnson, 'Bacon and Cranfield', 316; Thomas Locke to DC, 4 February 1622, in *The Court and Times of James the First; Illustrated by Authentic and Confidential Letters, from Various Public and Private Collections*, 2 vols, ed. Thomas Birch, rev. Robert Folkestone Williams (London: Henry Colburn, 1848), 2: 290. For grant of 17 January 1622, see *CSPD, 1619–1623*, 337; Spedding assumes that this 'was only an authority to the Lord Treasurer to pay him what was overdue upon the patents which belonged to him', *LL* 7: 330.

30 See FB to TM, 28 February 1622, LPL MS 936, art. 161; *LL* 7: 335–6. See alternate version in Matthew, *Collection*; *LL* 7: 337–8.

31 FB to Digby, 31 December 1621, LPL MS 936, art. 154; *LL* 7: 322–3.

32 GV to FB, 16 December 1621, BL Harley MS 7000, fo. 79; *LL* 7: 319.

33 FB to GV, answer to letter of 16 December 1621, LPL MS 936, art. 199; *LL* 7: 320. Bacon had already written to Sackville on 3 December about petitioning the parliament: see BL Add. MS 4259, fos. 27b–28a; *LL* 7: 590–3.

34 See e.g. Meautys to FB, 3, 7 January 1622, LPL MS 936, arts 156, 157; *LL* 7: 323–4, 324–5; FB to GV, 30 January, 3 February 1622, LPL MS 936, arts 149, 172; *LL* 7: 328, 329; Meautys to FB, 3 March 1622, LPL MS 936, art. 163; *LL* 7: 339; FB to GV, n.d., unsent, LPL MS 936, art. 162; *LL* 7: 340–1 (an earlier draft, also unsent: LPL MS 936, art. 223; *LL* 7: 340). FB to GV, 5 March 1622, BL Add. MS 5503, fo. 105; *LL* 7: 341.

35 Roger Lockyer, *Buckingham: The Life and Political Career of George Villiers, First Duke of Buckingham 1592–1628* (London: Longman, 1981), 119.

36 GV to FB, n.d., BL Harley MS 7000, fo. 65; *LL* 7: 328.

37 FB to GV, 3 February 1622, LPL MS 936, art. 172; *LL* 7: 329.

38 GV to FB, answer to letter of 3 February 1622, BL Harley MS 7000, fo. 7; *LL* 7: 329.

39 Lennox to FB, 29 January 1622, LPL MS 936, art. 158; *LL* 7: 326–7.

40 FB to Lennox, answer to letter of 29 January 1622, LPL MS 936, art. 159; *LL* 7: 327.

41 Meautys to FB, 10? March 1622, LPL MS 936, art. 266; *LL* 7: 342.

42 FB to TM, 15 February 1622, BL Add. MS 5503, fo. 103; *LL* 7: 335.

43 FB to TM, 28 February 1622, LPL MS 936, art. 161; *LL* 7: 335–6. See alternative version in Matthew, *Collection*; *LL* 7: 337–8. See also FB, [Notes for someone

who was to deal with Buckingham on Bacon's behalf], LPL MS 936, art. 246; *LL* 7: 338–9.

44 Sackville to FB, received 11 March 1622, LPL MS 936, art. 177; *LL* 7: 342–4.
45 FB to LC, [endorsed 12 March 1622], LPL MS 936, art. 260; *LL* 7: 346. FB to LC, n.d., LPL MS 936, art. 247; *LL* 7: 346–7.
46 Meautys to FB, 20? March 1622, LPL MS 936, art. 234; *LL* 7: 354–5.
47 Spedding fixes it to the third week of March 1622 – after the 'recommendation of his debts' by the King, but before the restoration of his liberty: *LL* 7: 348.
48 FB, 'Memorial of access', March 1622, LPL MS 936, art. 273; *LL* 7: 349–52.
49 Meautys to FB, 20? March 1622, LPL MS 936, art. 234; *LL* 7: 354–5.
50 Ibid.
51 FB to Meautys, 21 March 1622, LPL MS 936, art. 164; *LL* 7: 355.
52 FB to Meautys, 21 March 1622, LPL MS 936, art. 164; *LL* 7: 355–6.
53 For acknowledgement of receipts of the warrant, see FB to LC, 31 March 1622, Sackville MS 146, quoted in Johnson, 'Bacon and Cranfield', 317.
54 FB to James, 20 March 1622, Bodl. Tanner MS 63(I), fo. 109; drafts, LPL MS 936, art. 142; *LL* 7: 357–8. See also FB to GV, 20 March 1622, Bodl. Tanner MS 73(I), fo. 111; draft, LPL MS 936, art. 141; *LL* 7: 356–7. For 'An Offer to the King of a Digest to be made of the Laws of England', see *Certaine Miscellany Works*, ed. Rawley, 135; *LL* 7: 358–64.
55 JC to DC, 30 March 1622, McClure 2: 430.
56 Elizabeth of Bohemia to FB, 11 June 1622, quoted in Peter Boëner, dedicatory epistle in his translation of the *Essays: De Proef-Stucken (beschreven in 't Engelsch) van den Wel-Edelen, en Hoogh-Geleerden Heer Franciscus Bacon, in sÿn leven Baron van Verulam, Grave van St. Alban, en Opperste Cancelier van Engelandt, Midtsgaders, sÿn Heylige Meditatien, en de Wÿsheyt der Oude* (Leiden: Willem Christiaens van der Boxe, 1646). Boëner's epistle was printed in English in A. C. Loffelt, 'A Notice of Bacon', *The Athenaeum*, pt 522, no. 2276 (10 June 1871), 720–1; *LL* 7: 366.
57 FB to Elizabeth of Bohemia, 20 April 1622, LPL MS 936, art. 166; *LL* 7: 364–5.
58 Aubrey, *Brief Lives*, 12, 8.
59 JC to DC, 1 July 1622, McClure 2: 443–4.
60 John Ritchie, ed., *Reports of Cases Decided by Francis Bacon, Baron Verulam, Viscount St Albans, Lord Chancellor of England, in the High Court of Chancery (1617–1621)* (London: Sweet & Maxwell, 1932), xxiv–xxv.
61 Memoranda to countess of Buckingham [September 1622?], LPL MS 936, art. 273; *LL* 7: 391–2. FB to the countess of Buckingham, 29 October 1622, LPL MS 936, art. 170; *LL* 7: 392–3.
62 GV to FB, 13 November 1622, BL Harley MS 7000, fo. 105; *LL* 7: 393. FB docketed the letter as 'touching my warrant and access'.
63 James, warrant, 14 November 1622, BL Add. MS 12, 496, fo. 23^r; *LL* 7: 393–4.
64 FB to GV, 22 November 1622, LPL MS 936, art. 171; *LL* 7: 395. See also 'Rembr. upon my going to Treasurer', LPL MS 936, art. 273; *LL* 7: 396.
65 Thomas Meautys to FB, ?25 November 1622, LPL MS 936, art. 269; *LL* 7: 396–7.

66 FB to GV, n.d., LPL MS 936, art. 262; *LL* 7: 397.

67 JC to DC, 7 December 1622, McClure 2: 466.

68 FB to GV, n.d., LPL MS 936, art. 221; *LL* 7: 398.

69 Letter not extant: BL Add. MS 4259, fos 70b–71a; *LL* 7: 590–3.

70 Thomas Wilson to James, 10 January 1623, PRO SP 14/137/13.

71 JC to DC, 10 February 1623, McClure 2: 476.

72 FB to Gondomar, 28 March 1623, LPL MS 936, art. 282; *LL* 7: 411–12; tr. Spedding, *LL* 7: 412 n. 1. FB to Conway, 21 January 1623, PRO SP 14/137/23; *LL* 7: 402.

73 Locke to DC, 1 February 1623, PRO SP 14/138/3; *CSPD, 1619–1623*, 486.

74 FB to GV, 5 February 1623, LPL MS 936, art. 173; *LL* 7: 402–3.

75 Williams to FB, 7 February 1623, LPL MS 936, art. 174; *LL* 7: 404.

76 Lockyer, *Buckingham*, 135–6.

77 FB to GV, 21 February, 10 March 1623, LPL MS 936, arts 175, 176; *LL* 7: 404–5, 405.

78 FB to Cottington, 22 March 1623, LPL MS 936, art. 178; *LL* 7: 405–6.

79 FB to GV, 30 March 1623, LPL MS 936, art. 182; *LL* 7: 412–13.

80 FB to GV, 18 May 1623 or soon after, LPL MS 936, art. 250; *LL* 7: 426.

81 FB to Gondomar, 28 March 1623, LPL MS 936, art. 282; *LL* 7: 411–12; tr. Spedding, *LL* 7: 412 n. 1.

82 FB to Conway, 25 March 1623, PRO SP 14/140/33; *LL* 7: 407–8; FB to James, 25 March 1623, PRO SP 14/140/32; *LL* 7: 408. FB to GV, 30 March 1623, LPL MS 936, art. 182; *LL* 7: 412–13; FB to Conway, 29 March 1623, PRO SP 14/140/59; *LL* 7: 409–10.

83 FB to Conway, 29 March, 2 April 1623, PRO SP 14/140/59, 14/142/12; *LL* 7: 409–10, 414.

84 Conway to FB, 27 March 1623, pr. in *LL* 7: 409.

85 FB to Conway, 4 September 1623, PRO SP 14/152/12; *LL* 7: 433; GV to FB, 27 October 1623, BL Harley MS 7000, fo. 120; *LL* 7: 437–8.

86 *LL* 7: 451. See also JC to DC, 5 April 1623, McClure 2: 489; FB to Conway, 7 April 1623, PRO SP 14/142/40; *LL* 7: 421; JC to DC, 19 April 1623, McClure 2: 489–90; Conway to FB, 27 October 1623, *CSPD 1623–1625*, 104.

87 FB to GV, 22 July 1623, LPL MS 936, art. 189; *LL* 7: 430–1; see FB to GV in Spain, 2 May 1623, 'congratulating his good success', beginning 'The very face of Mr Clarke' (BL Add. MS 4259 fos 70b–71a; *LL* 7: 591); and FB to Cottington, 10 May 1622 [i.e. 1623], beginning 'In the small time' and described as 'Begging his good offices' (BL Add. MS 4259 fos 80b–81a; *LL* 7: 591).

88 FB to Bristol, [18 April 1623], LPL MS 936, art. 184(e); *LL* 7: 424–5; FB to Cottington, [18 April 1623], LPL MS 936, art. 184(e); *LL* 7: 425; FB to Gondomar [c.18 April 1623], LPL MS 936, art. 184(a); *LL* 7: 422–3; Latin version:, LPL MS 936, art. 184(c); *LL* 7: 421–2.

89 GV to FB, 29 May 1623, LPL MS 936, art. 186; *LL* 7: 426. See FB to GV, 18 April 1623, Bodl. Tanner MS 73(2), fo. 313; *LL* 7: 423–4. An early draft is in LPL MS 936, art. 184(b); *LL* 7: 424 n. 1. FB to GV, [June 1623], LPL MS 936, art. 214; *LL* 7: 427–8. FB to TM, n.d. [1623], LPL MS 936, art. 188; *LL* 7: 429–30.

90 GV to James, 26 June 1623, BL Harley MS 6987, fo. 107; Williamson, *George Villiers*, 314.

91 JC to DC, 26 July 1623, McClure 2: 510.

92 JC to DC, 11 October 1623, McClure 2: 516.

93 FB to GV, 12 October 1623, Bodl. Add. MS D.112, fo. 84; *LL* 7: 482–3. FB mentions this promise in his letter of 29 August 1623 to GV, and his undated letter to TM (LPL MS 936, art. 191; *LL* 7: 431).

94 GV to FB, 14 October 1623, BL Harley MS 7004, fo. 118; *LL* 7: 433. Docketed 'D. Buc. 12 Oct. 1623': *LL* 7: 433 n. 1.

95 'Memorial of access', March 1622, LPL MS 936, art. 273; *LL* 7: 349–52.

96 FB to TM, 26 June 1623, LPL MS 936, art. 232; *LL* 7: 428–9.

97 FB to James, n.d. [22 October 1623], LPL MS 936, art. 271ᵛ; *LL* 7: 436. For passages excised in this self-censorship, see *Works* 3: 277, 282, 287, 288, 300, 307, 321, 323, 337, 414, 477, 483, 488; Spedding, *LL* 7: 436 n. 2.

98 FB to TM, 26 June 1623, LPL MS 936, art. 232; *LL* 7: 428–9. FB to Prince Charles, n.d. [22 October 1623], LPL MS 936, art. 271ᵛ; *LL* 7: 346–7. Further copies went to Buckingham and the universities: FB to GV, 22 October 1623, Bodl. Add. MS D.112, fo. 84ʳ; *LL* 7: 437; GV to FB, 27, 29 October 1623, BL Harley MS 7000, fos 120, 122; *LL* 7: 437–8, 438; FB to the University of Cambridge, the University of Oxford, and to Trinity College, Cambridge [all 1623], *Baconiana. Or Certain Genuine Remains of Sir Francis Bacon*, ed. Thomas Tenison (London: Richard Chiswell, 1679), 189, 193; *Opera omnia*, 4 vols, ed. John Blackbourne (London: R. Gosling, 1730), 2: 405; *LL* 7: 438–9, 439, 439–40.

99 FB, minute for an advice to GV, LPL MS 936, art. 271; *LL* 7: 441; FB to GV, 25 November 1623, Bodl. Add. MS D.112, fo. 87ʳ; *LL* 7: 442.

100 'Notes for conferences with Buckingham', LPL MS 936, art. 192; *LL* 7: 442–7; FB to GV, n.d., BL Harley MS 1581, fo. 391; LPL MS 936, art. 233; *LL* 7: 447–51.

101 FB to Southampton, 31 January 1624, Latimer MSS, pr. in *LL* 7: 454. FB to Oxford, 2 February 1624, LPL MS 936, art. 194; *LL* 7: 454–5.

102 Sir Edward Conway, Jr, to [DC], 23 March 1624, PRO SP 14/161/30; *CSPD, 1623–1625*, 197.

103 FB to GV, 23 January 1624, LPL MS 936, art. 193; *LL* 7: 451–2.

104 GV to FB, 28 January 1624, BL Harley MS 7000, fo. 74; *LL* 7: 452.

105 Coventry to FB, 29 October 1625, LPL MS 936, art. 212; *LL* 7: 534–5.

106 FB to GV, [June 1624], LPL MS 936, art. 200; *LL* 7: 516. See also FB to GV, 30 June 1624, LPL MS 936, art. 201; *LL* 7: 516–17. FB to James, [1624], BL Add. MS 5504, fo. 109; *LL* 7: 517; FB to GV, [August 1624], LPL MS 936, art. 203; *LL* 7: 518.

107 FB to James, n.d., *Letters of Sir Francis Bacon, Baron of Verulam, Viscount St. Alban, and Lord High Chancellor of England*, ed. Robert Stephens (London: Benjamin Tooke, 1702); *LL* 7: 518–19.

108 FB to the Mayor &c. of Cambridge, 8 September 1624, BL Cole MS 20, fo. 229; *LL* 7: 520; JC to DC, 4 September 1624, McClure 2: 578–9. On Bacon's health during 1623 see FB to TM, 2 May 1623 ('My health, I thank God, is better than when you left me, and to my thinking better than before my

last sickness'), LPL MS 936, art. 185; *LL* 7: 425–6; see FB to GV, 29 August 1623, ('prettily recovered; for I have lain at two wards, the one against my disease, the other against my physicians, who are strange creatures'), LPL MS 936, art. 191^v; *LL* 7: 431–2.

109 GV to FB, [early October 1624], BL Harley MS 7000, fo. 73; *LL* 7: 521.

110 James to Thomas Coventry, n.d., *Scrinia Ceciliana*, 270; *LL* 7: 519–20.

111 *LL* 7: 519 n. 2.

112 FB to GV, 17 November 1624, Bodl. Add. MS D.112, fo. 90; *LL* 7: 522.

113 FB to GV, 9 October 1624, LPL MS 936, art. 204; *LL* 7: 521–2.

114 JC to [DC], 18 December 1624, McClure 2: 592.

115 Ibid.

116 BL Harley MS 4955, fo. 70a. We are grateful to James Knowles for this reference.

117 The suggestion is Spedding's: *LL* 7: 523. For a counter-argument, see *The Poems of Francis Bacon*, ed. Alexander B. Grosart (London: privately pr. [Miscellanies of The Fullers Worthies' Library], 1870), 7.

118 Letter not extant. BL Add. MS 4259; *LL* 7: 590–3.

119 For Privy Seal, see FB to Sir Francis Barnham, 14 March 1624, LPL MS 936, art. 195; *LL* 7: 513–14; for apothecaries' patent, see FB to Sir Humphrey May, [March/April 1624], LPL MS 936, art. 231; *LL* 7: 514–15.

120 See case of Harris: FB to Williams, 30 May 1622, LPL MS 936, art. 167; *LL* 7: 366–7; Ritchie, *Reports of Cases*, xxiii–xxiv.

121 FB to Sir Robert Pye, May, June 1625, LPL MS 936 art. 148; *LL* 7: 527. See also FB to GV, 3 July 1625, letter listed in BL Add. MS 4259, fos 91b–92a (*LL* 7: 590–3), on the same subject. FB to Ley, 20 June 1625, BL Add. MS 5503, fo. 109b; *LL* 7: 528; FB to Sir Robert Pye, [July?] 1625, LPL MS 936, art. 206; *LL* 7: 528–9.

122 *Baconiana. Or Certain Genuine Remains of Sir Francis Bacon*, ed. Thomas Tenison (London: Richard Chiswell, 1679), 45; *LL* 7: 525.

123 Loffelt, 'A Notice of Bacon'.

124 FB to GV, 31 March 1625. Letter not extant. See BL Add. MS 4259, fos 91b–92a; *LL* 7: 590–3.

125 François Marie Arouet de Voltaire, *Lettres philosophiques. Edition critique avec une introduction et un commentaire*, 3 vols, ed. Gustave Lanson (Paris, 1909), 1: 153.

126 FB to d'Effiat, 1625, *Baconiana* 201; *LL* 7: 536. See also FB to d'Effiat, 18 June 1625, LPL MS 936, art. 148; *LL* 7: 527–8.

127 JC to DC, 9 April 1625, McClure 2: 609.

128 FB's last will, 19 December 1625. *Opera Omnia*, 4 vols, ed. John Blackbourne (London: R. Gosling, 1730), 2: 559; *LL* 7: 539–45.

129 'Prayer After Making His Last Will', *LL* 7: 230–1.

130 FB to May, 1625 (twice), BL Add. MS 4259, fos 79b–80a; *LL* 7: 590–3.

131 FB to Ley, 20 June 1625, BL Add. MS 5503, fo. 109b; *LL* 7: 528.

132 FB to Roger Palmer, 29 October 1625, LPL MS 936, art. 211; *LL* 7: 534. On 30 September 1625 he writes to Dorset (Sackville) 'An account of his country life', now lost: BL Add. MS 4259, fos 78b–79a; *LL* 7: 590–3.

133 FB to Roger Palmer, 29 October 1625, LPL MS 936, art. 211; *LL* 7: 534.

134 *The Essayes or Counsels, Civill and Morall* (London: Hanna Barret, 1625), A3^r–A4^r.

135 FB to GV, 17 November 1625<>1 January 1626, LPL MS 936, art. 208; *LL* 7: 538.

136 Will, *LL* 7: 545.

137 FB to Sir Humphrey May, [December 1625/January 1626], LPL MS 936, art. 209; *LL* 7: 548–9.

138 FB to Conway, 26 January 1626, PRO SP 16/19/49; *LL* 7: 549. Bacon had previously recommended men to Conway: see FB to Conway, 3 June 1624, PRO SP 14/167/11; *LL* 7: 515–16.

CHAPTER 18

1 Pierre Amboise, 'Discours svr la vie de Mre Francois Bacon', in *Histoire natvrelle de Mre Francois Bacon, Baron de Verulan, Vicomte de sainct Alban, & Chancelier d'Angleterre* (Paris: Antoine de Sommaville et André Sovbron, 1631), 1–26 at 24–6. The 'translation' may be for the most part spurious.

2 Rawley, 'Life of Bacon', *Works* 1: 17–18.

3 John Aubrey, *Aubrey's Brief Lives*, ed. Oliver Lawson Dick (London: Secker & Warburg, 1960), 16.

4 Elizabeth David, *Harvest of the Cold Months: The Social History of Ice and Ices*, ed. Jill Norman (London: Michael Joseph, 1994).

5 'Calor et frigus', *Works* 3: 644–52.

6 Ibid., 650.

7 FB's last will, 19 December 1625, *Opera Omnia*, 4 vols, ed. John Blackbourne (London: R. Gosling, 1730), 2: 559; *LL* 7: 545.

8 J[ames] H[owell], *Epistolae Ho-Elianae. Familiar Letters Domestic and Forren* (London: Humphrey Moseley, 1645), Aaa 4^v.

9 William Rawley, ed., *Memoriae honoratissimi Domini Francisci, Baronis de Verulamio, vice-comitis Sancti Albani sacrum* (London: John Haviland, 1626), tr. as *A Translation of Thirty-two Latin Poems in Honor of Francis Bacon Published by Rawley in 1626* (Boston: privately printed, 1904). We quote from this translation: 19, 81.

10 FB to Arundel, n.d., Tobie Matthew, *A Collection of Letters* (London: Henry Herringman, 1660), 57–8; *LL* 7: 550.

11 For Pliny's death see Pliny the Younger to Cornelius Tacitus in Pliny the Younger, *Letters and Panegyrics*, 2 vols, tr. Betty Radice (London: Heinemann [Loeb Classical Library], 1969), 1: 424–35, and Suetonius, *Vita Plinii Secundi*, in *Suetonius*, 2 vols, tr. J. C. Rolfe (London: Heinemann [Loeb Classical Library], 1914), 1: 504–5.

12 *Sylva sylvarum*, Century I, *Works* 2: 374.

13 *Sylva sylvarum*, Century I, *Works* 2: 377.

14 On the widespread interest in nitre on the part of seventeenth-century scientists see Robert G. Frank, Jr, *Harvey and the Oxford Physiologists* (Berkeley: University of California Press, 1980), ch. 9, 'Niter, niter everywhere'.

15 See ibid., 117–18.

16 We were greatly assisted in understanding the chemical properties of Renaissance nitre by the alchemist at the Kentwell Hall Tudor Recreation (personal communication, July 1997).

17 For Bacon's list of 'opiates' see *Historia vitae et mortis*, *Works* 5: 271.

18 *Sylva sylvarum*, Century IV, *Works* 2: 459.

19 *Historia vitae et mortis*, *Works* 5: 274.

20 *Historia vitae et mortis, Works* 5: 270–1.

21 *Sylva sylvarum,* Century I, *Works* 2: 346.

22 *Sylva sylvarum,* Century X, *Works* 2: 650.

23 *Historia vitae et mortis, Works* 5: 271–2.

24 See above, chapter 3 and n. 61.

25 Rawley, 'Life of Bacon', *Works* 1: 17.

26 *Historia vitae et mortis, Works* 5: 270; *Novum Organum, Works* 4: 238.

27 On Arundel see Mary F. S. Hervey, *The Life, Correspondence and Collections of Thomas Howard, Earl of Arundel* (Cambridge: Cambridge University Press, 1921); David Howarth, *Lord Arundel and his Circle* (New Haven: Yale University Press, 1985). For the loadstone, see Mark Ridley, *Magneticall Animadversions . . . Upon Certain Magneticall Advertisements, Lately Published. From Maister William Barlow* (London: Nicholas Oakes, 1617), A3ᵛ.

28 Kevin Sharpe, 'The Earl of Arundel, his Circle and the Opposition to the Duke of Buckingham', in Kevin Sharpe, ed., *Faction and Parliament* (Oxford: Clarendon Press, 1978), 209–44.

29 JC to DC, 21 June 1617, McClure 2: 83.

30 *Apophthegms, Works* 7: 177.

31 Sharpe, 'The Earl of Arundel'.

32 *Letters of John Holles 1587–1637,* 3 vols, ed. P. R. Seddon (Nottingham: Thornton Society, 1975, vols 31, 35 and 36), 2: 324.

33 V. F. Snow, 'The Arundel Case 1626', *The Historian* 26 (1964), 323–49; Roger Lockyer, *Buckingham: The Life and Political Career of George Villiers, First Duke of Buckingham 1592–1628* (London: Longman, 1981), 319; *LJ* 3: 526.

34 *CJ* 837; CUL MS Dd.12.20, fo. 51; *Proceedings in Parliament 1626,* ed. William B. Bidwell and Maija Jansson, 4 vols (New Haven: Yale University Press, 1992), 2: 295, 297.

35 FB's last will, 19 December 1625, *Opera Omnia,* ed. Blackbourne, 2: 559; *LL* 7: 545.

36 J. V. Kitto, ed., *The Register of St Martin-in-the-Fields London 1619–1636* (London: Harleian Society, 1936, vol. 66), 138.

37 J. H. Morrison, *The Underhills of Warwickshire: An Essay in Family History* (Cambridge: privately printed at the University Press, 1932), 141, 143.

38 See A. Chambers Bunten, *Life of Alice Barnham (1592–1650)* (London: Page & Thomas, 1919); Morrison, *Underhills of Warwickshire;* Revd C. Moor, 'Bacon Deeds at Gorhambury', *The Genealogists' Magazine* 7 (1937), 561–74.

39 Coventry and James earl of Marlborough, Lord President, to Charles, 27 July 1628, PRO 16/111/14; *CSPD, 1628–1629,* 234.

40 John Ritchie, ed., *Reports of Cases Decided by Francis Bacon, Baron Verulam, Viscount St. Albans, Lord Chancellor of England, in the High Court of Chancery (1617–1621)* (London: Sweet & Maxwell, 1932), xxvi; Bunten, *Alice Barnham.*

41 Revd Daniel Lysons and Samuel Lysons, *Magna Britannia; being a Concise Topographical Account of the Several Counties of Great Britain, Vol 1 – Part 1 Containing Bedfordshire* (London: T. Cadell and W. Davies, 1813), 82, 83; F. G. Emmison, ed., *Bedfordshire Parish Registers,* vol. 2 (Bedford: County Record Office, 1931), D21.

42 G. E. Aylmer, *The King's Servants: The Civil Servants of Charles I 1625–1642,* rev. edn (London: Routledge & Kegan Paul, 1974), 292–4; Daphne Du Maurier, *The*

Winding Stair: Francis Bacon, His Rise and Fall (London: Victor Gollancz, 1976), 226–7; Maurice W. Brockwell, 'Bacon and Meautys', *Notes and Queries* 181 (1941), 77; Lionel M. Munby, ed., *Early Stuart Household Accounts* (Hertford: Hertfordshire Record Society, 1986, vol. 2).

43 Aubrey, *Brief Lives*, 15, 13.

44 FB's last will, 19 December 1625, *Opera Omnia*, ed. Blackbourne, 2: 559; *LL* 7: 539.

45 Howell, *Epistolae Ho-Elianae*, Aaa 4^v.

46 Daniel Coquillette, *Francis Bacon* (Stanford, CA: University of California Press, 1992), p. x n. 1.

47 Walter A. Arensberg, *The Secret Grave of Francis Bacon at Lichfield* (San Francisco, 1923); *The Burial of Francis Bacon and his Mother in the Lichfield Chapter House* (Pittsburgh, 1924); Coquillette, *Francis Bacon*, p. x n. 1.

48 Coquillette, *Francis Bacon*, 298 n. 8.

49 Aubrey, *Brief Lives*, 16.

50 FB to TM, 26 June 1623, LPL MS 936, art. 232; *LL* 7: 428–9.

51 'Of Friendship', *Essays* (1625), *Works* 6: 442.

52 FB's last will, 19 December 1625, *Opera Omnia*, ed. Blackbourne, 2: 559; *LL* 7: 539–40. For an earlier draft see *Baconiana. Or Certain Genuine Remains of Sir Francis Bacon*, ed. Thomas Tenison (London: Richard Chiswell, 1679), 203.

53 Bacon to Williams, [December 1625], *Baconiana* 195; *LL* 7: 546.

54 Williams to FB, 31 December 1625, *Letters and Remains of the Lord Chancellor Bacon*, ed. Robert Stephens (London: W. Bowyer, 1734), 190; *LL* 7: 547–8.

55 *Memoriae*, ed. Rawley; tr. as *A Translation*.

56 *Resuscitatio* (a)2^r.

57 Ibid., (a)2^v.

58 Ibid.

59 Ibid.

60 Ibid.

61 Ibid.

62 Thomas Bushell, *Mr. Bushell's Mineral Overtures* (London, 1659), A^v–A2^r.

Bibliography

The bibliography is divided into the following sections:

I   Manuscripts, subdivided in alphabetical order by location of collection:

   Cambridge: Cambridge University Library
   Cambridge: Fitzwilliam Museum
   Edinburgh: Edinburgh University Library
   Hatfield: Hatfield House
   London: British Library
   London: Gray's Inn Library
   London: Lambeth Palace Library
   London: Public Record Office
   Oxford: Bodleian Library
   San Marino, CA: Henry E. Huntington Library
   Warminster: Longleat
   Washington DC: Folger Shakespeare Library

II   Calendars and transcripts of manuscript sources
III Editions of Bacon's works
IV   Early printed sources (to 1700) and later editions
V   Later printed sources (after 1700)
VI   Unpublished dissertations

I   MANUSCRIPTS

Cambridge: Cambridge University Library

Dd.3.63
Ee.IV.12
Gg.h.36
Hh.ii.2
Ii.5.37

Cambridge: Fitzwilliam Museum

General series

Edinburgh: Edinburgh University Library

Laing manuscripts, iii.193

Hatfield: Hatfield House

Salisbury manuscripts

London: British Library

Additional manuscripts
Cole manuscripts
Cotton manuscripts
Hargrave manuscripts
Harley manuscripts
Lansdowne manuscripts
Sloane manuscripts
Stowe manuscripts

London: Gray's Inn Library

Book of Orders 1
Ledger Book I

London: Lambeth Palace Library

647–62 (Anthony Bacon Papers, vols 1–16)
933 (Gibson Papers, vol. 5)
936 (Gibson Papers, vol. 8)
941 (Gibson Papers, vol. 13)
942 (Gibson Papers, vol. 14)

London: Public Record Office

E.407
State Papers 12 Domestic – Elizabeth I
State Papers 14 Domestic – James I
State Papers 15 Domestic – Addenda
State Papers 78 Foreign – France

Oxford: Bodleian Library

Additional C.82
Additional D.112

Ashmole 487
Rawlinson A.331
Rawlinson vi.C.12
Tanner 74

San Marino, CA: Henry E. Huntington Library

Ellesmere manuscripts
Francis Bacon Library, Claremont collection

Warminster: Longleat House

Dudley manuscripts

Washington DC: Folger Shakespeare Library

V.a.339
V.b.213, 214

II   CALENDARS AND TRANSCRIPTS OF MANUSCRIPT
SOURCES

Acts of the Privy Council

Acts of the Privy Council of England, n.s. ed. John Roche Dasent (London: HMSO,
    1894–1907)
    vol. 9: *1575–1577* (1894)
    vol. 10: *1577–1578* (1895)
    vol. 11: *1578–1580* (1895)
    vol. 16: *1588* (1897)
    vol. 31: *1600–1601* (1906)
    vol. 32: *1601–1604* (1907)
ed J. V. Lyle (London: HMSO, 1929–1930)
    1617–1619 (1929)
    1619–1621 (1930)
ed. R. F. Menger and P. A. Penfold (London: HMSO, 1960)
    1629 May–1630 May (1960)

Patent Rolls

Calendar of the Patent Rolls Preserved in the Public Record Office: Edward VI, vol. 5: *1547–
    1553* (London: HMSO, 1926)
Calendar of the Patent Rolls Preserved in the Public Record Office: Elizabeth I (London:
    HMSO, 1939 and continuing):
    vol. 7: *1575–1578*, ed. J. H. Collingridge (1982)

vol. 8: *1578–1580*, ed. Margaret Post (1986)
vol. 9: *1580–1582*, ed. Ann Morton (1986)

State Papers – Domestic

Calendar of State Papers, Domestic Series, of the Reigns of Edward VI, Mary, Elizabeth 1547–1580, ed. Robert Lemon (London: Longman et al., 1856)
Calendar of State Papers, Domestic Series, of the Reign of Elizabeth (London: Longman et al., 1865–70):
   Addenda, 1566–1579, ed. Robert Lemon (1865)
   1581–1590, ed. Mary Anne Everett Green (1865)
   1591–1594, ed. Mary Anne Everett Green (1867)
   1595–1597, ed. Mary Anne Everett Green (1869)
   1598–1601, ed. Mary Anne Everett Green (1869)
   1601–1603, with Addenda 1547–1565, ed. Mary Anne Everett Green (1870)
Calendar of State Papers, Domestic Series, of the Reign of James I (London: Longman et al, 1857–9):
   1603–1610, ed. Mary Anne Everett Green (1857)
   1611–1618, ed. Mary Anne Everett Green (1858)
   1619–1623, ed. Mary Anne Everett Green (1858)
   1623–1625, with Addenda 1603–1625, ed. Mary Anne Everett Green (1859)
Calendar of State Papers, Domestic Series of the Reigns of Elizabeth and James I:
   Addenda, 1580–1625, ed. Mary Anne Everett Green (London: Longman et al., 1872)
Calendar of State Papers, Domestic Series, of the Reign of Charles I (London: Longman et al., 1858–9):
   1625–1626, ed. John Bruce (1858)
   1628–1629, ed. John Bruce (1859)

State Papers – Foreign

Calendar of State Papers, Foreign Series, of the Reign of Elizabeth (London: Longman et al.: HMSO, 1880–1936):
   1575–1577, ed. Allan James Crosby (1880)
   1577–1578, ed. Arthur John Butler (1901)
   1578–1579, ed. Arthur John Butler (1903)
   1579–1580, ed. Arthur John Butler (1904)
   January 1581–April 1582, ed. Arthur John Butler (1907)
   May–December 1582, ed. Arthur John Butler (1909)
   January–June 1583 and Addenda, ed. Arthur John Butler (1913)
   July 1583–July 1584, ed. Sophie Crawford Lomas (1916)
   August 1584–August 1585, ed. Sophie Crawford Lomas (1916)
   September 1585–May 1586, ed. Sophie Crawford Lomas (1921)
   June 1586–June 1588, ed. Richard Bruce Wernham (1936)
   July–December 1588, ed. Richard Bruce Wernham (1936)
List and Analysis of State Papers, Foreign Series, Elizabeth I (London: HMSO, 1964):
   vol. 1: *August 1589–June 1590*, ed. Richard Bruce Wernham (1964)

vol. 2: *July 1590–May 1591*, ed. Richard Bruce Wernham (1969)
vol. 3: *June 1591–April 1592*, ed. Richard Bruce Wernham (1980)

State Papers – Ireland

Calendar of the State Papers, Relating to Ireland, of the Reign of James I, 1611–1614, ed. C.W. Russell and John P. Prendergast (London: Longman et al., 1877)

State Papers – Italy

Calendar of State Papers and Manuscripts, Relating to English Affairs, Existing in the Archives and Collections of Venice, and in Other Libraries of Northern Italy (London: HMSO, 1890–1909):
vol. 7: *1558–1580*, ed. Rawdon Brown and G. Cavendish Bentinck (1890)
vol. 9: *1592–1603*, ed. Horatio F. Brown (1897)
vol. 14: *1615–1617*, ed. Allen B. Hinds (1908)
vol. 15: *1617–1619*, ed. Allen B. Hinds (1909)

State Papers – Scotland

Calendar of the State Papers Relating to Scotland and Mary, Queen of Scots 1547–1603 (Edinburgh: HM General Register House/HMSO, 1907–14):
vol. 5: *1574–1581*, ed. William K. Boyd (1907)
vol. 8: *1585–1586*, ed. William K. Boyd (1914)

State Papers – Spain

Calendar of Letters and State Papers, Relating to English Affairs, Preserved Principally in the Archives of Simancas, ed. Martin A. S. Hume (London: HMSO, 1892–4):
vol. 1: *Elizabeth 1558–1567* (1892)
vol. 2: *Elizabeth 1568–1579* (1894)

Other transcripts of manuscript sources

Arber, Edward, ed., *Transcript of the Registers of the Company of Stationers*, 5 vols (London: privately printed, 1875–94)

Aubrey, John, *Aubrey's Brief Lives*, ed. Oliver Lawson Dick (London: Secker & Warburg, 1960)

Bacon, Nathaniel, *The Papers of Nathaniel Bacon of Stiffkey*, 3 vols, ed. A. Hassell Smith, Gillian M. Baker and R.W. Kenny (Norwich: Norfolk Record Society, 1979–90)

Bacon, Nathaniel [the younger], *The Annalls of Ipswiche. The Lawes Customes and Government of the Same*, ed. William H. Richardson (Ipswich: privately printed, 1884)

Bacon, Nicholas, *Sir Nicholas Bacon's Great House Sententiae*, ed. Elizabeth McCutcheon, *English Literary Renaissance Supplements* 3 (Amherst, MA: ELR, 1977)

Bacon, Nicholas, *The Recreations of his Age* (Oxford: Daniel Press, 1903; issued by Leslie Chaundy, 1919)

Bacon, Nicholas, 'On Sir Nicholas Bacon, Lord Keeper; with Extracts from Some of his Unprinted Papers and Speeches', ed. John Payne Collier, *Archaeologia* 36 (1859), 339–48

Beal, Peter, *Index of English Literary Manuscripts*, 2 vols (London: Mansell, 1980)

Bèze, Théodore de, *Correspondance de Théodore de Bèze*, vol. 7 (1566), ed. Hippolyte Aubert, Henri Meylan, Alain Dufour, Claire Chimelli and Mario Turchetti (Geneva: Droz, 1973)

Bèze, Théodore de, *Correspondance de Théodore de Bèze*, vol. 18 (1577), ed. Hippolyte Aubert, Alain Dufour, Béatrice Nicollier and Reinhard Bodenmann (Geneva: Droz, 1995)

Bèze, Théodore de, 'Correspondance de Th. de Bèze (1564–1580). Inventaire', compiled by Alain Dufour and Henri Meylan (Geneva: Musée historique de la Reformation, n.d. [typescript])

Bidwell, William B., and Jansson, Maija, *Proceedings in Parliament 1626*, 4 vols (New Haven: Yale University Press, 1992)

Birch, Thomas, *An Historical View of the Negotiations between the Courts of England, France, and Brussels, From the Year 1592 to 1617* (London: A. Millar, 1749)

Birch, Thomas, *Memoirs of the Reign of Queen Elizabeth, from the Year 1581 till her Death*, 2 vols (London: A. Millar, 1754)

Birch, Thomas, ed., *The Court and Times of James the First; Illustrated by Authentic and Confidential Letters, from Various Public and Private Collections*, rev. Robert Folkestone Williams, 2 vols (London: Henry Colburn, 1848)

Bodley, Thomas, *Reliquiae Bodleianae: or some Genuine Remains of Sir Thomas Bodley* (London: John Hartley, 1703)

Bodley, Thomas, *Trecentale Bodleianum: A Memorial Volume for the Three Hundreth Anniversary of the Public Funeral of Sir Thomas Bodley March 29, 1613* (Oxford: Clarendon Press, 1913)

A Brief Description of a Curious Manuscript in the Collection of the Rev. Dr. Neligan, Entitled A True Historicall Relation of the Conversion of Sir Tobie Matthew, to the Holie Catholic Family, with the Antecedents & Consequents Thereof (n.p.: privately printed, n.d.)

Camerarius, Joachim *see* Languet, Hubert

Carleton, Dudley, *Dudley Carleton to John Chamberlain 1603–1624: Jacobean Letters*, ed. Maurice Lee Jr (New Brunswick, NJ: Rutgers University Press, 1972)

Cary, Robert, *Memoirs of Robert Cary Earl of Monmouth. Written by Himself*, ed. Sir Walter Scott (Edinburgh: James Ballantyne, 1808)

Chamberlain, John, *The Letters of John Chamberlain*, 2 vols, ed. Norman Egbert McClure (Philadelphia: American Philosophical Society, 1939)

Clifford, Anne, *The Diary of Anne Clifford 1616–1619: A Critical Edition*, ed. Katherine O. Acheson (New York: Garland, 1995)

Collier, J. Payne, ed., *The Egerton Papers* (London: Camden Society, 1840, vol. 12)

Collins, Arthur, ed., *Letters and Memorials of State, in the Reigns of Queen Mary, Queen Elizabeth, King James, King Charles the First, Part of the Reign of King Charles the Second, and Oliver's Usurpation*, 2 vols (London: T. Osborne, 1746)

Cooke, Sir Anthony, 'Court Wills – No. 1', ed. Edward J. Sage, *The East Anglian* 1 (1864), 325–7

Copley, Thomas, *Letters of Sir Thomas Copley*, ed. Richard Copley Christie (London: Roxburghe Club, 1897)

Crump, Lucy, tr., *A Huguenot Family in the XVI Century. The Memoirs of Philippe de Mornay Sieur du Plessis Marly Written by his Wife* (London: George Routledge, 1926)

Dalrymple, Sir David, Lord Hailes, *Memorials and Letters Relating to the History of Britain in the Reign of James the First*, 2 vols (Glasgow: Robert & Andrew Foulis: Glasgow, 1762)

Daneau, Lambert, *Lambert Daneau (de Baugency-sur-Loire), Pasteur et Professeur en Théologie 1530–1595: Sa vie, ses ouvrages, ses lettres inédites*, ed. Paul de Félice (Paris: G. Fischbacher, 1881)

Dee, John, *The Private Diary of John Dee*, ed. James Orchard Halliwell (London: Camden Society, 1842)

Devereux, Walter Bourchier, *Lives and Letters of the Devereux, Earls of Essex*, 2 vols (London: John Murray, 1853)

D'Ewes, Simonds, *Extracts from the MS Journal of Sir Simonds D'Ewes, with Several Letters to and from Sir Simonds and his Friends* (London: J. Nichols, 1783)

D'Ewes, Simonds, *The Journals of All the Parliaments during the Reign of Queen Elizabeth, both of the House of Lords and House of Commons*, rev. Paul Bowes (London: John Shirley, 1682)

Dudley, Robert, earl of Leicester, and Hotman, Jean, 'Brieven over het Leycestersche tijdvak uit de papieren van Jean Hotman', ed. R. Broersma and G. Busken Huet, *Bijdgragen en Mededeelingewn van het historisch genootschap* (Amsterdam: Johannes Müller, 1913), 1–271

Dudley, Robert, earl of Leicester, Hotman, François, and Hotman, Jean, 'Correspondance inédite de Robert Dudley, comte de Leycester, et de François et Jean Hotman' ed. P. J. Blak, *Archives du musée Teyler*, ser. 2, vol. 12, pt 2 (Haarlem: Les héritiers Loosjes, 1911), 79–296.

Du Plessis-Mornay, Philippe, *Mémoires et correspondance de Du Plessis Mornay*, ed. A. D. de la Fontenelle de Vandoré and P. R. Auguis, 8 vols (Paris: Treuttel et Wurtz, 1824)

Ellis, Henry, *Original Letters, Illustrative of English History, Including Numerous Royal Letters*, 3rd ser., 4 vols (London: Richard Bentley, 1846)

Emmison, F. G., ed., *Bedfordshire Parish Registers*, vol. 2 (Bedford: County Record Office, 1931)

Fletcher, Reginald J., ed., *The Pension Book of Gray's Inn 1569–1669* (London: Gray's Inn Masters of the Bench, 1901)

Foster, Elizabeth R., ed., *Proceedings in Parliament 1610*, 2 vols (New Haven: Yale University Press, 1966)

Foster, Joseph, ed., *The Register of Admissions to Gray's Inn, 1521–1889* (London: Hansard, 1889)

Foster, Joseph, ed., *Alumni Oxonienses: The Members of the University of Oxford, 1500–1714*, vol. 3 (S–Z) (Oxford: Parker & Co., .n.d.)

Gardiner, Samuel Rawson, ed., *Parliamentary Debates in 1610* (London: Camden Society, 1862)

Gardiner, Samuel Rawson, 'On Four Letters from Lord Bacon to Christian IV. King of Denmark', *Archaeologia* 41 (1867), 219–69

Gardiner, Samuel Rawson, ed., *The Fortescue Papers* (London: Camden Society, 1871, n.s., vol. 1)

Goodman, Godfrey, *The Court of King James the First*, ed. John S. Brewer, 2 vols (London: Richard Bentley, 1839)

Harington, John, *Nugae Antiquae: Being a Miscellaneous Collection of Original Papers, in Prose and Verse*, ed. Henry Harington, new edn, 2 vols (London: J. Wright, 1824)

Harrison, G. B., ed., *A Last Elizabethan Journal: Being a Record of Those Things Most Talked of During the Years 1599–1603* (London: Constable & Co., 1933)

Hartley, T. E., ed., *Proceedings in the Parliaments of Elizabeth*, 3 vols (Leicester: Leicester University Press, 1981–95)

Hatton, Christopher, *Memoirs of the Life and Times of Sir Christopher Hatton, K.G.*, ed. Harris Nicolas (London: Richard Bentley, 1847)

Henri IV of France, *Recueil des lettres missives de Henri IV*, 9 vols: vols 1–7 ed. M. Berger de Xivery (Paris: Imprimerie Royale, 1843–58); *Supplément*, vols 8–9, ed. J. Guadet (Paris: Imprimerie Royale, 1872–6)

Historical Manuscripts Commission, *Second Report of the Royal Commission on Historical Manuscripts*, appendix (London: HMSO, 1871)

Historical Manuscripts Commission, *Calendar of the Manuscripts of the Most Hon. The Marquis of Salisbury, K.G., . . . preserved at Hatfield House, Hertfordshire*, 24 vols (London: HMSO, 1883–1976)

Historical Manuscripts Commission, *Manuscripts of the Earl Cowper, Preserved at Melbourne Hall, Derbyshire*, 3 vols (London: HMSO, 1888–9)

Historical Manuscripts Commission, *Report on Manuscripts in Various Collections* (London: HMSO, 1903)

Historical Manuscripts Commission, *Report on the Manuscripts of Lord de L'Isle & Dudley Preserved at Penshurst Place*, vol. 2, ed. C. L. Kingsford with William A. Shaw (London: HMSO, 1934)

Historical Manuscripts Commission, *Report on the Manuscripts of the Late Reginald Rawdon Hastings, Esq., of The Manor House, Ashby de la Zouch*, vol. 4, ed. Francis Buckley (London: HMSO, 1947)

Historical Manuscripts Commission, *Calendar of the Manuscripts of the Most Honourable the Marquess of Bath, Preserved at Longleat, Wiltshire*, vol. 5: *Talbot, Dudley and Devereux Papers, 1533–1659*, ed. G. Dyfnallt Owen (London: HMSO, 1980)

Holles, John, *Letters of John Holles 1587–1637*, ed. P. R. Seddon, 3 vols (Nottingham: Thornton Society, 1975, vols 31, 35 and 36)

Hotman, François and Hotman, Jean, *Epistolae . . . Ex Bibliotheca Jani Gulielmi Meolii* (Amsterdam: apud Georgium Gallet, 1700)

Hotman, François *see also* Dudley, Robert

Hotman, Jean *see* Dudley, Robert *and* Hotman, François

Howell, T. B., ed., *A Complete Collection of State Trials, and Proceedings for High Treason and other Crimes and Misdemeanours from the Earliest Period to the Year 1783*, 21 vols (London: T. C. Hansard, 1816)

Hughes Clarke, A. W., ed., *The Register of St Clement, Eastcheap and St Martin Ongar*, part 1 (London: Harleian Society, 1937, vol. 67)

James VI and I, *Correspondence of James VI with Sir Robert Cecil and Others in Scotland*, ed. John Bruce (London: Camden Society, vol. 78, 1861)

James VI and I, *Letters of King James VI and I*, ed. G. P. V. Akrigg (Berkeley, CA: University of California Press, 1984)

Jansson, Maija, ed., *Proceedings in Parliament 1614 (House of Commons)* (Philadelphia: American Philosophical Society, 1988)

Jardine, David, ed., *Criminal Trials*, 2 vols (London: Charles Knight, 1832–35)

Journals of the House of Commons. In Anno primo Regni Regis Edwardi Sexti, &c. vol. 1 (n.p., n.d.)

Kitto, J. V., ed., *The Register of St Martin-in-the-Fields London 1619–1636* (London: Harleian Society [vol. 66], 1936)

Laffleur de Kermaingant, P., *Mission de Jean de Thumery sieur de Boissise (1598–1602)*, 2 vols (Paris: Firmin-Didot, 1886)

Languet, Hubert, *Epistolae ad Joachimvm Camerarivm Patrem & Filium*, ed. Ludovicus Camerarius (Leipzig and Frankfurt: Mauritius Georgius Weidmann, 1685)

Lodge, Edmund, *Illustrations of British History, Biography, and Manners, in the Reigns of Henry VIII, Edward VI, Mary, Elizabeth, & James I*, 2nd edn, 3 vols (London: John Chudley, 1838)

Loffelt, A. C., 'A Notice of Bacon', *The Athenaeum*, part 522, no. 2276 (10 June 1871), 720–1

Maitland, S. R., ed., 'Archbishop Whitgift's College Pupils', *The British Magazine* 32 (1847), 361–79, 508–28, 650–6, and 33 (1848), 17–31, 185–97, 445–63

Matthew, A. H., ed., *A True Historical Relation of the Conversion of Sir Tobie Matthew to the Holy Catholic Faith: With the Antecedents and Consequences Thereof* (London: Burns and Oates, 1904)

Matthew, Tobie, *A Collection of Letters* (London: Henry Herringman, 1660)

Middlesex, County of, *Calendar of the Sessions Records*, n.s., vol. 1: *1612–1614*, ed. William Le Hardy (London: Sir Ernest Hart, 1935)

Moor, Revd C., 'Bacon Deeds at Gorhambury', *The Genealogists' Magazine* 7 (1937), 561–74

Morison, Fynes, *An Itenerary Written by Fynes Moryson, Gent. First in the Latine Tongue, and then Translated by him into English* (London: J. Beale, 1617)

Moule, H. J., *Descriptive Catalogue of the Charters, Minute Books and other Documents of the Borough of Weymouth and Melcombe Regis A.D. 1252 to 1800* (Weymouth: Sherren & Son, 1883)

Munby, Lionel M., ed., *Early Stuart Household Accounts* (Hertford: Hertfordshire Record Society, 1986, vol. 2)

Murdin, William, ed., *A Collection of State Papers Relating to Affairs in the Reign of Queen Elizabeth, from the Year 1571 to 1596* (London: William Bowyer, 1759)

Nicholas, Edward, *Proceedings and Debates in the House of Commons in 1620 and 1621*, 2 vols (Oxford: Clarendon Press, 1766)

Nichols, John, ed., *The Progresses and Public Processions of Queen Elizabeth*, rev. edn, 3 vols (London: John Nichols and Son, 1823)

Nichols, John, ed., *The Progresses, Processions, and Magnificent Festivities of King James the First, his Royal Consort and Family*, 4 vols (London: J. B. Nichols, 1828)

Notestein, Wallace, Relf, Frances Helen, and Simpson, Hartley, eds, *Commons Debates 1621*, 7 vols (New Haven: Yale University Press, 1935)

Orridge, B. Brogden, *Illustrations of Jack Cade's Rebellion, from Researches in the Guildhall Records, Together with some Newly-found Letters of Lord Bacon, &c.* (London: John Camde Hotten, 1869)

Parker, Matthew, *Correspondence of Matthew Parker*, ed. John Bruce and Thomas T. Perowne (Cambridge: Parker Society, 1853)

Paulet, Amias, *Copy-book of Sir Amyas Poulet's Letters, Written during his Embassy to France (A.D. 1577). From a MS in the Bodleian Library*, ed. Octavius Ogle (London: Roxburghe Club, 1866)

Paulet, Amias, *The Letter-Books of Sir Amias Poulet, Keeper of Mary Queen of Scots*, ed. John Morris (London: Burns & Oates, 1874)

Pryme, Revd Abraham de la, *Memoirs of Thomas Bushell 'The Recluse of the Calf'*, ed. William Harrison (Douglas: Manx Society, 1878)

Ritchie, John, ed., *Reports of Cases Decided by Francis Bacon, Baron Verulam, Viscount St. Albans, Lord Chancellor of England, in the High Court of Chancery (1617–1621)* (London: Sweet & Maxwell, 1932)

Rymer, Thomas, ed., *Foedera, conventiones, literae, Et cujuscunque generis Acta Publica, inter regis Angliae*, 3rd edn, 10 vols (The Hague: John Neaulme, 1739–45)

Sawyer, Edmund, ed., *Memorials of Affairs of State in the Reigns of Queen Elizabeth and King James I. Collected (chiefly) from the Original Papers of the Right Honourable Sir Ralph Winwood*, 3 vols (London: T. Ward, 1725)

Scrinia Ceciliana: Mysteries of State & Government: in Letters of the Most Famous Lord Burghley, And other Grand Ministers of State: In the Reigns of Queen Elizabeth, and King James. Being a further Additional Supplement of the Cabala (London: G. Bedel & T. Collins, 1663)

Scrinia sacra: Secrets of Empire (London: G. Bedel and T. Collins, 1654)

Sidney, Philip, *Complete Works*, ed. Albert Feuillerat, 4 vols (Cambridge: Cambridge University Press, 1923)

Sidney, Philip and Languet, Hubert, *The Correspondence of Philip Sidney and Hubert Languet*, ed. William Aspenwall Bradley (Boston: Merrymount Press, 1912)

Strype, John, *Annals of the Reformation and Establishment of Religion . . . in the Church of England*, 4 vols (Oxford: Clarendon Press, 1874)

Townshend, Heywood. 'Haywood Townshend's Journals', ed. A. F. Pollard and Marjorie Blatcher, *Bulletin of the Institute of Historical Research* 12 (1934–5), 1–51

Townshend, Heywood, *Historical Collections: or, An Exact Account of the Proceedings of the Four Last Parliaments of Q. Elizabeth* (London: T. Basset, W. Crooke, and W. Cademan, 1680)

Ungerer, Gustav, *A Spaniard in Elizabethan England: The Correspondence of Antonio Pérez's Exile*, 2 vols (London: Tamesis, 1974–6)

Villiers, George, duke of Buckingham, *Letters of the Duke and Duchess of Buckingham, Chiefly Addressed to King James I of England* (Edinburgh: Thomas G. Stevenson, 1834)

Whitelocke, Sir James, *Liber Famelicus* (London: Camden Society, 1858, vol. 70)

Wotton, Henry, *Reliquiae Wottonianae. Or, A Collection of Lives, Letters, Poems; With Characters of Sundry Personages: And other Incomparable Pieces of Language and Art* (London: R. Marriot, G. Bedel and T. Garthwait, 1651)

Wotton, Henry, *The Life and Letters of Sir Henry Wotton*, ed. Logan Pearsall Smith, 2 vols (Oxford: Clarendon Press, 1907)

III EDITIONS OF BACON'S WORKS

Listed in order of date of publication

Essayes. Religious Meditations. Places of perswasion and disswasion (London: Humfrey Hooper, 1597)

Opera Francisci baronis de Vervlamio, vice-comitis Sancti Albani; tomvs primvs: Qui continet De Dignitate & Augmentis Scientiarum Libros IX (London: John Haviland, 1623)

The Essayes or Counsels, Civill and Morall (London: Hanna Barret, 1625)

Certaine Miscellany Works of the Right Honourable, Francis Lo. Verulam, Viscount S. Alban, ed. William Rawley (London: Humphrey Robinson, 1629)

Histoire natvrelle de Mre Francois Bacon, Baron de Verulan, Vicomte de sainct Alban, & Chancelier d'Angleterre (Paris: Antoine de Sommaville & André Sovbron, 1631)

De Proef-Stucken (beschreven in 't Engelsch) van den Wel-Edelen, en Hoogh-Geleerden Heer Franciscus Bacon, in sÿn leven Baron van Verulam, Grave van St. Alban, en Opperste Cancelier van Engelandt, Midtsgaders, sÿn Heylige Meditatien, en de Wÿsheyt der Oude, tr. Peter Boëner (Leiden: Willem Christiaens van der Boxe, 1646)

The Remaines of the Right Honourable Francis Lord Verulam . . . (London: Lawrence Chapman, 1648)

Resuscitatio, Or, Bringing into Publick Light Severall Pieces, of the Works, Civil, Historical, Philosophical, & Theological, Hitherto Sleeping, of the Right Honourable Francis Bacon Baron of Verulam, Viscount Saint Alban . . . *Together, with his Lordships Life*, ed. William Rawley (London: William Lee, 1657)

Opuscula varia posthuma, philosophica, civilia, et theologica, Francisci Baconi, ed. William Rawley (London: R. Daniel, 1658)

Baconiana. Or Certain Genuine Remains of Sir Francis Bacon, ed. Thomas Tenison (London: Richard Chiswell, 1679)

Letters of Sir Francis Bacon, Baron of Verulam, Viscount St Alban, and Lord High Chancellor of England. Written during the Reign of King James the First, ed. Robert Stephens (London: Benjamin Tooke, 1702)

Opera Omnia, 4 vols, ed. John Blackbourne (London: R. Gosling, 1730)

The Philosophical Works of Francis Bacon, 3 vols (London: Knapton et al., 1733)

Letters and Remains of the Lord Chancellor Bacon, ed. Robert Stephens (London: W. Bowyer, 1734)

Letters, Speeches, Charges, Advices &c. of Francis Bacon, Lord Viscount St Alban, Lord Chancellor of England, ed. Thomas Birch (London: Andrew Millar, 1763)

The Works of Francis Bacon, Lord Chancellor of England. A New Edition, ed. Basil Montagu, vol. 16 (London: William Pickering, 1834)

Works, ed. James Spedding, Robert Leslie Ellis and Douglas Denon Heath, 7 vols (London: Longman et al., 1857–9)

Letters and Life, 7 vols, ed. James Spedding (London: Longman, Green, Longman and Roberts, 1861–74)

A Conference of Pleasure, Composed for some Festive Occasions about the Year 1592 by Francis Bacon, ed. James Spedding (London: Longmans, Green, Reader and Dyer, 1870)

The Poems of Francis Bacon, ed. Alexander B. Grosart (London: privately pr. [Miscellanies of The Fullers Worthies' Library], 1870)

Bacon's Essays with Introduction, Notes, and Index, 2 vols, ed. Edwin A. Abbott (London: Longman, Green & Co., 1876)

An Account of the Life and Times of Francis Bacon, ed. James Spedding, 2 vols (Boston: Houghton, Mifflin, & Co., 1880)

The Promus of Formularies and Elegancies, ed. Mrs Henry Pott (London: Longman, Green & Co., 1883)

Bacon's Promus of Formularies and Elegancies, ed. F. B. Buckley and F. A. Herbert, in Edwin Durning-Lawrence, *Bacon is Shakespeare* (London: Gay & Hancock, 1910)

The Essayes or Counsels, Civill and Morall, ed. Michael Kiernan (Oxford: Clarendon Press, 1985)

Francis Bacon's Natural Philosophy: A New Source, a Translation of Manuscript Hardwick 72A with Translation and Commentary, ed. Graham Rees with Christopher Upton, BSHS Monographs Series 5 (Chalfont St Giles: British Society for the History of Science, 1984)

Novum organum with Other Parts of the Great Instauration, ed. Peter Urbach (Chicago and LaSalle: Open Court, 1994)

La Nouvelle Atlantide, tr. Michèle Le Doeuff and Margaret Llasera, ed. Le Doeuff (Paris: Flammarion, 1995)

The Oxford Authors: Francis Bacon, ed. Brian Vickers (Oxford: Oxford University Press, 1996)

The Oxford Francis Bacon, vol. 6: *Philosophical Writings 1611–1618*, ed. Graham Rees (Oxford: Clarendon Press, 1996)

IV   EARLY PRINTED SOURCES (TO 1700) AND LATER EDITIONS

Anon., *A True Report of Sundry Horrible Conspiracies to Have Taken Away the Life of the Queens Maiestie* (London: C. Yetsweirt, 1594)

Anon., *The Maske of Flowers. Presented by the Gentlemen of Graies-Inne* (London: R. Wilson, 1614)

Anon., *The Secret History of K. James I. and K. Charles I.* (1690)

Bacon, Anne, tr. [of John Jewel], *An Apologie or Answere in Defence of the Churche of Englande* (London: Reginald Wolfe, 1563)

Bancroft, Richard, *A Sermon Preached at Paules Crosse the 9. of Februarie, being the first Sunday in the Parleament, Anno. 1588* (London: Gregorie Seton, 1588)

Bancroft, Richard, *A Survay of the Pretended Holy Discipline* (London: J. Wolfe, 1593), ★2ʳ.

Bayly, Thomas, *Witty Apophthegms delivered Severall Times, and upon Severall Occasions, by King James, King Charles, the Marquis of Worcester, Francis Lord Bacon, and Sir Thomas Moore. Collected and Revised* (London: Edward Farnham, 1658)

Bèze, Théodore de, *Psalmorum Davidis et aliorum prophetorum libri quinque* (London: Thomas Vautrollier, 1580)

Bèze, Théodore de, *Chrestiennes méditations*, ed. Mario Richter (Geneva and Paris: Droz and Minard, 1964)

Bèze, Théodore de *see also* Gilbie, Anthony

Bodley, Thomas, *The Life of Sir Thomas Bodley, the Honourable Founder of the Publique Library in the University of Oxford* (Oxford: Henry Hall, 1647)

Bushell, Thomas, *The First Part of Youths Errors* (London, 1628)

Bushell, Thomas, *The Apologie of Thomas Bushell* (Antwerp, 1650)

Bushell, Thomas, *Mr Bushell's Abridgment of the Lord Chancellor Bacon's Philosophical Theory in Mineral Prosecutions* (London, 1659)

Camden, William, *Annales rerum Anglicarum et Hibernicarum regnante Elizabetha*, 3 vols, ed. Thomas Hearne (London: n.p., 1707)

Camden, William, *V. cl. Gulielmi Camdeni et illustrium virorum ad G. Camdenum Epistolae. Cum appendice varii argumenti. Accesserunt Annalium Regni Regis Jacobi I. Apparatus, et Commentarius de antiquitate, dignitate, & officio*, 2 vols (London: Richard Chiswell, 1691)

Camden, William, *The History of the Most Renowned and Victorious Princess Elizabeth, Late Queen of England* (London: M. Flesher, 1688)

Cartwright, Thomas, *The Rest of the Second Replie of Thomas Cartwright: Agaynst Master Doctor Whitgifts Second Answer, Touching the Church Discipline* (n.p.: publisher unknown, 1577)

Cleland, James, *ΗΡΩ-ΠΑΙΔΕΙΑ, Or The Institution of a Young Noble Man* (Oxford: Joseph Barnes, 1607)

Coke, Roger, *A Detection of the Court and State of England during the Four Last Reigns, and the Inter-Regnum*, 2nd edn, 2 vols (London: Andrew Bell, 1694)

C[ooke], A[nne] tr. [of Bernardino Ochino], *Fourtene Sermons . . . Concernyng the Predestinacion and Eleccion of God* (London: John Day, 1550)

C[ooke], A[nne] tr. [of Bernardino Ochino], *Sermons . . . (to the number of 25) Concerning the Predestination and Election of God* (London: John Day, 1570)

Daneau, Lambert, *Opvscvla omnia theologica, ab ipso avthore recognita, & in tres Classes diuisa* (Geneva: Eustace Vignon, 1583)

Daneau, Lambert, *Paratitla in D. Aurelii Augustinii tomos duos* (Geneva: Jac. Stoer, 1578)

Daneau, Lambert. *Commentariorum Lamberti Dancei in prophetas minores Tomus Primus* (Geneva: Eustace Vignon, 1586)

Daneau, Lambert *see also* Stockwood, John

Dekker, Thomas, *The Wonderfull Yeare, 1603* (London: T. Creede, 1603)

Devereux, Robert, earl of Essex, *An Apologie of the Earle of Essex, against Those which Iealovsly, and Maliciovsly, Tax Him to be the Hinderer of the Peace and Qviet of his Covntry* (London: Richard Bradocke, 1603)

Digges, Leonard, *A Geometrical Practise, named Pantometria*, ed. Thomas Digges (London: Henry Bynneman, 1571)

Du Bartas, *The Divine Weeks and Works of Guillaume de Salluste Sieur du Bartas translated by Joshua Sylvester*, 2 vols, ed. Susan Snyder (Oxford: Clarendon Press, 1979)

Du Bartas, *The Works of Guillaume de Saluste Sieur du Bartas: A Critical Edition*, 3 vols, ed. Urban Tigner Holmes, Jr, John Coriden Lyons and Robert White Linker (Chapel Hill, NC: University of North Carolina Press, 1935–40)

Erasmus of Rotterdam, Desiderius, *Education of a Christian Prince*, ed. Lisa Jardine (Cambridge: Cambridge University Press, 1997)

Fuller, Thomas, *The History of the Worthies of England*, 3 vols, ed. P. Austin Nuttall (London: Thomas Tegg, 1840)

Gentillet, Innocent, *Discours contre Machiavel: A New Edition* . . . ed. A. d'Andrea and P. D. Stewart (Florence: Casalini Libri, 1974)

Gentillet, Innocent *see also* Patericke, Simon

Gilbie, Anthony, tr. [of Bèze], *The Psalmes of David, Truly Opened and Explained by Paraphrasis* (London: Henrie Denton, 1581)

Greville, Fulke, Lord Brooke, *Certaine Learned and Elegant Workes* (London: Henry Seyle, 1633)

Holinshed, Raphael, rev. John Stow et al., *Holinshed's Chronicles of England, Scotland and Ireland*, 6 vols (London: J. Johnson et al., 1807–8)

H[owell], J[ames], *Epistolae Ho-Elianae. Familiar Letters Domestic and Forren* (London: Humphrey Moseley, 1645)

Hotman, Jean, *The Ambassador* (London: James Shawe, 1603)

James VI and I, *The Workes of the Most High and Mightie Prince, James* . . . *King of Great Britaine, France and Ireland*, ed. James Montagu (London: Robert Barker and John Bill, 1616)

Jonson, Ben, *Works*, 11 vols, ed. C. H. Herford, Simpson, Percy and Simpson, Evelyn (Oxford: Clarendon Press, 1925–52)

L[enton], F[rancis], *Characterismi: Or, Lentons Leasvres. Expressed in Essayes and Characters* (London: Roger Michell, 1631)

Monings, Edward, *The Landgrave of Hessen his Princelie Receiuing of her Majesties Embassador* (London: R. Robinson, 1596)

Nashe, Thomas, *The First Parte of Pasquils Apologie* (London: J. Charlewood, 1590)

Nashe, Thomas, *Pierce Penilesse his Supplication to the Diuell* (London: Richard Jones, 1592)

Norden, John, *Speculum Britanniae. The First Parte. An Historicall, & Chorographicall Discription of Middlesex* (London: Eliot's Court Press, 1593)

Ochino, Bernardino *see* Cooke, Anne

[Osborn, Francis], *Historical Memoires on the Reigns of Queen Elizabeth and King James* (London: T. Robinson, 1658)

Parr, Richard, *The Life of the Most Reverend Father in God, James Usher* (London: Nathaniel Ranew, 1686)

Patericke, Simon, tr. [of Gentillet], *A Discourse upon the Meanes of Wel Governing and Maintaining in Good Peace, a Kingdome, or other Principalitie* . . . *Against Nicholas Machiavell the Florentine* (London: Adam Islip, 1602)

Pérez, Antonio, *Epistolarum Centuria una* (Paris: n.p., 1600)

Pliny the Younger, *Letters and Panegyrics*, 2 vols, tr. Betty Radice (London: Heinemann [Loeb Classical Library], 1969)

Puttenham, George, *The Arte of English Poesie* (London: Richard Field, 1589)

Rawley, William, ed., *Memoriae honoratissimi Domini Francisci, Baronis de Verulamio, vice-comitis Sancti Albani sacrum* (London: John Haviland, 1626)

Rawley, William, ed. *A Translation of Thirty-two Latin Poems in Honor of Francis Bacon Published by Rawley in 1626* (Boston: privately printed, 1904)

Ridley, Mark, *Magneticall Animadversions* . . . *Upon Certaine Magneticall Advertisements, Lately Published. From Maister William Barlow* (London: Nicholas Oakes, 1617)

Savile, Henry, tr., *The End of Nero and Beginning of Galba. Fower Bookes of the Histories of Cornelivs Tacitvs. The Life of Agricola* (Oxford: Richard Wright, 1591)

Scott, W. ed., *Secret History of the Court of James the First*, 2 vols (Edinburgh: James Ballantyne, 1811)

Stockwood, John, tr. [of Lambert Daneau], *A Frvitfvll Commentarie vpon the Twelve Small Prophets* (Cambridge: John Legate, 1594)

Suetonius, *Vita Plinii Secundi* in *Suetonius*, 2 vols, tr. J. C. Rolfe (London: Heinemann [Loeb Classical Library], 1914)

Twyne, Thomas, *The Garlande of Godly Flowers* (London: William How, 1575?)

Voltaire, François Marie Arouet de, *Lettres philosophiques. Edition critique avec une introduction et un commentaire*, 3 vols, ed. Gustave Lanson (Paris: n.p., 1909)

Walsall, John, *A Sermon Preached at Pauls Crosse . . . 5 October 1578* (London: George Byshop, 1578)

Walton, Isaac, 'Life of Hooker', *The Works of Mr. Richard Hooker*, 2 vols (Oxford: Clarendon Press, 1890), 1: 3–69

Waterhouse, Edward, *Fortescutus Illustratus, or a Commentary On that Nervous Treatise De Laudibus Legum Angliae. Written by Sir John Fortescue* (London: Thomas Dicas, 1663)

W[eldon], Sir A[nthony], *The Court and Character of King James* (London: John Wright, 1650)

W[eldon], Sir A[nthony], *Aulicus Coquinariae* and *Character of King James* in *Secret History of the Court of James the First*, 2 vols, ed. Sir Walter Scott (Edinburgh: James Ballantyne, 1811)

Whetstone, George, *A Mirour for Magestrates of Cyties* (London: Richard Jones, 1584)

Wilcox, Thomas, *A Short, Yet Sound Commentarie: Written on that Woorthie Worke Called; The Prouerbes of Salomon* (London: Thomas Man, 1589)

Wotton, Henry, *A Parallel betweene Robert late Earle of Essex, and George late Duke of Buckingham* (London: n.p., 1641)

V   LATER PRINTED SOURCES

Abbott, Edwin A., *Bacon and Essex: A Sketch of Bacon's Earlier Life* (London: Seely, Jackson, & Halliday, 1877)

Abbott, Edwin A., *Francis Bacon: An Account of his Life and Work* (London: Macmillan, 1885)

Akrigg, G. P. V., *Jacobean Pageant, or, the Court of King James I* (London: Hamish Hamilton, 1962)

Anderson, F. H., *The Philosophy of Francis Bacon* (Chicago: University of Chicago Press, 1948)

Angus, W., *Seats of the Nobility and Gentry in Great Britain and Wales in a Collection of Select Views* (Islington: W. Angus, 1787)

Arensberg, Walter A., *The Secret Grave of Francis Bacon at Lichfield* (San Francisco, 1923)

Arensberg, Walter A., *The Burial of Francis Bacon and his Mother in the Lichfield Chapter House* (Pittsburgh, 1924)

Ashton, H., *Du Bartas en Angleterre* (Paris: Emile Larose, 1908)

Auerbach, Erna, *Nicholas Hilliard* (London: Routledge & Kegan Paul, 1961)

Aylmer, G. E., *The King's Servants: The Civil Servants of Charles I 1625–1642*, rev. edn (London: Routledge & Kegan Paul, 1974)

Baker, J. H., *An Introduction to English Legal History*, 3rd edn (London: Butterworths, 1990)

Barns, Stephen J., 'The Cookes of Gidea Hall', *The Essex Review* 21 (1912), 1–9

Bayley, William D'Oyly, *A Biographical, Historical, Genealogical, and Heraldic Account of the House of D'Oyly* (London: John Bowyer Nichols & Son, 1845)

Beilin, Elaine V., *Redeeming Eve: Women Writers of the English Renaissance* (Princeton, NJ: Princeton University Press, 1987)

Bell, Gary M., *A Handlist of British Diplomatic Representatives, 1509–1688* (London: Royal Historical Society, 1990)

Bergeron, David M., *Royal Family, Royal Lovers: King James of England and Scotland* (Columbia: University of Missouri Press, 1991)

Berkowitz, David Sandler, *John Selden's Formative Years: Politics and Society in Early Seventeenth-century England* (Washington DC: Folger Books, 1988)

Berry, Herbert, 'Chambers, the Bull, and the Bacons', *Essays in Theatre* 7 (1988), 35–42

Bevan, Bryan, *The Real Francis Bacon* (London: Centaur Press, 1960)

Bindoff, S. T., ed., *The House of Commons 1509–1558*, 3 vols (London: History of Parliament Trust, 1982)

Biographia Britannica: or, the Lives of the Most Eminent Persons Who Have Flourished in Great Britain and Ireland, from the Earliest Ages, Down to the Present Times: Collected from the Best Authorities, both Printed and Manuscript, and Digested in the Manner of Mr. Bayle's Historical and Critical Dictionary, 6 vols (London: W. Innys, 1747–66)

Bland, D. S., *A Bibliography of the Inns of Court and Chancery* (London: Selden Society, 1965)

Borgeaud, Charles, *Histoire de l'Université de Genève: L'académie de Calvin, 1559–1798* (Geneva: Georg, 1990)

Boundy, Wyndham S., *Bushell and Harman of Lundy* (Bideford, Devon: Grenville, 1961)

Bowen, Catherine Drinker, *The Lion and the Throne: The Life and Times of Sir Edward Coke (1552–1634)* (Boston: Little, Brown, & Co., 1956)

Bowen, Catherine Drinker, *Francis Bacon: The Temper of a Man* (Boston: Little, Brown & Co., 1963)

Brabazon, James, fifth earl of Verulam, *The Bacon Family: Its Links with Gorhambury, St Michael's, and St Albans 1560–1880* (St Albans: St Albans City Council, 1961)

Bray, Alan, *Homosexuality in Renaissance England* (London: Gay Men's Press, 1982)

Brockwell, Maurice W., 'Bacon and Meautys', *Notes and Queries* 181 (1941), 77

Buisseret, David, *Henry IV* (London: George Allen & Unwin, 1984)

Bunten, A. Chambers, 'Notes on Anthony Bacon's Passports of 1586', *Baconiana* 18 (1925–6), 93–104

Bunten, A. Chambers, *Twickenham Park and Old Richmond Palace, and Francis Bacon Lord Verulam's Connection with Them, 1580–1608* (London: Robert Banks, 1912)

Bunten, A. Chambers, *Life of Alice Barnham (1592–1650)* (London: Page & Thomas, 1919)

Butler, Revd Alban, *The Life of Sir Tobie Matthews* (London: J. P. Coghlan, 1795)

Byrne, M. St Clare, 'The Mother of Francis Bacon', *Blackwood's Magazine* 234 (1934) 758–71

Cecil, Algernon, *A Life of Robert Cecil Earl of Salisbury* (London: John Murray, 1915)

Cobbett, R. S. *Memorials of Twickenham: Parochial and Topographical* (London: Smith, Elder & Co., 1873)

Cogswell, Thomas, 'Underground Verse and the Transformation of Early Stuart Political Culture', in Susan D. Amussen and Mark A. Kishlansky, eds, *Political Culture and Cultural Politics in Early Modern England* (Manchester: Manchester University Press, 1995), 277–300

Collinson, Patrick, 'Sir Nicholas Bacon and the Elizabethan *via media*', *Historical Journal* 23 (1980); 255–73 repr. in his *Godly People: Essays on English Protestantism and Puritanism* (London: Hambledon Press, 1983) 135–54

Cooper, John William, ed., *The Annals of Cambridge*, vol. 5 (Cambridge: Cambridge University Press, 1908)

Coquillette, Daniel, *Francis Bacon* (Stanford, CA: Stanford University Press, 1992)

Cowper, Francis, *A Prospect of Gray's Inn* (London: Stevens & Sons, 1951)

Cross, Claire, *The Puritan Earl: The Life of Henry Hastings, Third Earl of Huntingdon 1536–1595* (London: Macmillan, 1966)

Curtis, Mark H., *Oxford and Cambridge in Transition 1558–1642: An Essay on Changing Relations between the English Universities and English Society* (Oxford: Clarendon Press, 1959)

d'Andrea, Antonio, 'Studies on Machiavelli and his Reputation in the Sixteenth Century', *Medieval and Renaissance Studies* 5 (1961), 214–48

d'Andrea, Antonio, 'The Last Years of Innocent Gentillet: "Princeps Adversariorum Machivaelli"', *Renaissance Quarterly* 20 (1967),12–16

d'Andrea, Antonio, 'The Political and Ideological Context of Innocent Gentillet's Anti-Machiavel', *Renaissance Quarterly* 23 (1970), 397–411

David, Elizabeth, *Harvest of the Cold Months: The Social History of Ice and Ices*, ed. Jill Norman (London: Michael Joseph, 1994)

Dictionary of National Biography, 63 vols (London: Smith, Elder & Co., 1885–1900)

Dimock, Arthur, 'The Conspiracy of Dr Lopez', *English Historical Review* 9 (1894), 441

Dixon, William Hepworth, *Personal History of Lord Bacon from Unpublished Papers* (London: John Murray, 1861)

Dixon, William Hepworth, *The Story of Lord Bacon's Life* (London: John Murray, 1862)

Dodd, A. H., 'Mr Myddelton the Merchant of Tower Street', in S. T. Bindoff, J. Hurstfield and C. H. Williams, eds, *Elizabethan Government and Society: Essays Presented to Sir John Neale* (London: Athlone Press, 1961), 249–81

Douthwaite, William Ralph, *Gray's Inn: Its History & Associations Compiled from Original and Unpublished Documents* (London: Reeves & Turner, 1886)

Droz, Eugénie, *Jacques de Constans, l'ami d'Agrippa d'Aubigné: contribution à l'étude de la poésie protestante* (Geneva: Droz, 1962)

Duke, H. E. and Bernard Campion, *The Story of Gray's Inn* (London: Gray's Inn, 1950)

Du Maurier, Daphne, *Golden Lads: Anthony Bacon, Francis, and their Friends* (London: Victor Gollancz, 1975)

Du Maurier, Daphne, *The Winding Stair: Francis Bacon, His Rise and Fall* (London: Victor Gollancz, 1976)

Eagle, R. L., 'Bacon's Tutor', *Times Literary Supplement*, 23 November 1946, 577

Eagle, Roderick L., 'Bacon's Licence to Travel beyond the Seas: Letters Patent at the Record Office', *Notes and Queries* 195 (1950), 334

Edmond, Mary, *Hilliard and Oliver: The Lives and Works of Two Great Miniaturists* (London: Robert Hale, 1983)

Epstein, Joel J., *Francis Bacon: A Political Biography* (Athens, OH: Ohio University Press, 1977)

Farrington, Benjamin, *The Philosophy of Francis Bacon: An Essay on its Development from 1603 to 1609 with New Translations of Fundamental Texts* (Liverpool: Liverpool University Press, 1964)

Fatio, Olivier, *Méthode et théologie: Lambert Daneau et les débuts de la scolastique réformée* (Geneva: Droz, 1976)

Feingold, Mordechai, *The Mathematicians' Apprenticeship: Science, Universities and Society in England, 1560–1640* (Cambridge: Cambridge University Press, 1984)

Findlen, Paula, *Possessing Nature: Museums, Collecting, and Scientific Culture in Early Modern Literature* (Berkeley, CA: University of California Press, 1994)

Frame, Donald, *Montaigne: A Biography* (London: Hamish Hamilton, 1965)

Frank, Robert G., Jr, *Harvey and the Oxford Physiologists* (Berkeley, CA: University of California Press, 1980)

Fraser, Antonia, *The Gunpowder Plot: Terror and Faith in 1605* (London: Weidenfeld & Nicolson, 1996)

Garde, Noel I., *The Homosexual in History* (New York: Vantage Press, 1964)

Gardiner, Samuel R., *History of England from the Accession of James I to the Outbreak of the Civil War 1603–1642*, 10 vols, (London: Longmans, Green, and Co., 1899–1900)

Gardy, Frédéric (with Alain Dufour), *Bibliographie des oeuvres théologiques, littéraires, historiques et juridiques de Théodore de Bèze* (Geneva: Droz, 1960)

Garrisson, Janine, 'La "Genève française"', in Daniel Ligou, ed., *Histoire de Montauban* (Toulouse: Privat, 1984), ch. 6

Garrisson, Janine, *A History of Sixteenth-century France, 1483–1598: Renaissance, Reformation and Rebellion*, tr. Richard Rex (London: Macmillan, 1995)

Gascoigne, Bamber and Ditchburn, Jonathan, *Images of Twickenham with Hampton and Teddington* (Richmond-upon-Thames: Saint Helena Press, 1981)

Goldschmidt, E. P., 'Nicholas Hillyard as Wood Engraver', *Times Literary Supplement*, 9 August 1947, 403

Gough, J. W., *The Superlative Prodigall: A Life of Thomas Bushell* (Bristol: University of Bristol, 1932)

Green, A. Wigfall, *Sir Francis Bacon* (New York: Twayne, 1966)

Gwyer, John, 'The Case of Lopez', *The Jewish Historical Society of England Transactions* 16 (1952), 163–84

Hamilton, Keith and Langhorne, Richard, *The Practice of Diplomacy: Its Evolution, Theory and Administration* (London: Routledge, 1995)

Hammer, Paul E. J., 'The Uses of Scholarship: The Secretariat of Robert Devereux, Second Earl of Essex, c.1585–1601', *English Historical Review* 109 (1994), 26–51

Hammer, Paul, 'An Elizabethan Spy Who Came in from the Cold: The Return of Anthony Standen to England in 1593', *Bulletin of the Institute of Historical Research*, 65 (1992), 277–9

Handover, P. M., *The Second Cecil: The Rise to Power 1563–1604 of Sir Robert Cecil, Later First Earl of Salisbury* (London: Eyre & Spottiswoode, 1959)

Hardy, Harold, 'Bacon and "The Huddler"', *Notes and Queries* 151 (1926), 39–41

Harrison, G. B., *The Life and Death of Robert Devereux Earl of Essex* (London: Cassell, 1937)

Hasler, P. W., ed., *The House of Commons 1558–1603*, 3 vols (London: History of Parliament Trust, 1981)

Hay, Millicent V., *The Life of Robert Sidney Earl of Leicester (1563–1620)* (Washington DC: Folger Books, 1984)

Haynes, Alan, *Invisible Power: The Elizabethan Secret Services 1570–1603* (Far Thrupp, Glos.: Alan Sutton, 1992)

Headlam, Cecil, *The Inns of Court* (London: Adam & Charles Black, 1909)

Heffner, Ray, 'Essex, the Ideal Courtier', *English Literary History* 1 (1934), 7–36

Heltzel, Virgil B., 'Young Francis Bacon's Tutor', *Modern Language Notes* 63 (1948), 483–5

Herrup, Cynthia, 'The Patriarch at Home: The Trial of the Second Earl of Castlehaven for Rape and Sodomy', *History Workshop Journal* 41 (1996), 1–18

Hervey, Mary F. S., *The Life, Correspondence and Collections of Thomas Howard, Earl of Arundel* (Cambridge: Cambridge University Press, 1921)

Hicks, Leo, 'The Strange Case of Dr William Parry: The Career of an Agent Provocateur', *Studies* 37 (1948), 343–63

Hicks, L., 'The Embassy of Sir Anthony Standen in 1603, Part I', *Recusant History* 5 (1959–60), 91–127

Hill, Christopher, *Intellectual Origins of the English Revolution Revisited* (Oxford: Clarendon Press, 1997)

Hill, L. M., *Bench and Bureaucracy: The Public Career of Sir Julius Caesar, 1580–1636* (Cambridge: James Clarke, 1988)

Houck, J. Kemp, *Elizabethan Bibliographies Supplements*, XV: *Francis Bacon 1926–1966* (London: Nether Press, 1968)

Houston, S. J., *James I* (London: Longman, 1973)

Howarth, David, *Lord Arundel and his Circle* (New Haven: Yale University Press, 1985)

Hughey, Ruth, 'Lady Anne Bacon's Translations', *Review of English Studies* 10 (1934), 211

Hume, Martin, 'The So-Called Conspiracy of Dr Ruy Lopez', *The Jewish Historical Society of England Transactions*, 6 (1912), 32–5

James, Mervyn, *Society, Politics and Culture: Studies in Early Modern England* (Cambridge: Cambridge University Press, 1986)

Jardine, David, *A Narrative of the Gunpowder Plot* (London: John Murray, 1857)

Jardine, Lisa, *Francis Bacon: Discovery and the Art of Discourse* (Cambridge: Cambridge University Press, 1974)

Johnson, Robert C., 'Francis Bacon and Lionel Cranfield', *Huntington Library Quarterly* 23 (1960), 301–20

Kahn, Victoria, 'Reading Machiavelli: Innocent Gentillet's Discourse on Method', *Political Theory* 22 (1994), 539–60

Kahn, Victoria, *Machiavellian Rhetoric: From the Counter-Reformation to Milton* (Princeton, NJ: Princeton University Press, 1994)

Kearney, Hugh, *Scholars and Gentlemen: Universities and Society in Pre-Industrial Britain 1500–1700* (London: Faber, 1970)

Kelley, Donald R., *François Hotman: A Revolutionary's Ordeal* (Princeton, NJ: Princeton University Press, 1973)

Knafla, Louis A., *Law and Politics in Jacobean England: The Tracts of Lord Chancellor Ellesmere* (Cambridge: Cambridge University Press, 1977)

Knecht, R. J., *The French Wars of Religion 1559–1598* (London: Longman, 1989)

Lacey, Robert, *Robert Earl of Essex: An Elizabethan Icarus* (London: Weidenfeld & Nicolson, 1971)

Lafon, Mary, *Histoire d'une ville protestante* (Paris: Amyot, 1862)

Lamb, Mary Ellen, 'The Cooke Sisters: Attitudes toward Learned Women in the Renaissance', in Margaret P. Hannay, ed., *Silent but for the Word: Tudor Women as Patrons, Translators, and Writers of Religious Works* (Kent, OH: 1985), 107–25

Le Bret, H., *Histoire de Montauban*, 2nd edn, 2 vols, rev. and ed. l'abbé Marcellin and Gabriel Ruek (Montauban: Réthare, 1841)

Le Doeuff, Michèle, 'Bacon chez les grands au siècle de Louis XIII', in Marta Fattori, ed., *Francis Bacon: terminologia e fortuna nel XVII secolo* (Rome: Ateneo, 1984)

Lestringant, Frank, 'La Jessée, Jean de (1551–1596)', in Jean-Pierre de Beaumarchais, Daniel Couty and Alain Rey, eds, *Dictionnaire des littératures de langue française*, 3 vols (Paris: Bordas, 1994), vol. 2, 1277–8

Levack, Brian P. *The Civil Lawyers in England 1603–1641: A Political Study* (Oxford: Clarendon Press, 1973)

Levack, Brian P., 'The English Civilians, 1500–1750' in Wilfred Prest, ed., *Lawyers in Early Modern Europe and America* (London: Croom Helm, 1981), 101–28

Lever, Maurice, *Les bûchers de Sodome: Histoire des 'infâmes'* (Paris: Fayard, 1985)

Lockyer, Roger, *Buckingham: The Life and Political Career of George Villiers, First Duke of Buckingham 1592–1628* (London: Longman, 1981)

Lodge, Edmund, *Life of Sir Julius Caesar, Knt.* (London: Robert Wilkinson, 1810)

Loffelt, A. C., 'A Notice of Bacon', *The Athenaeum*, pt 522, no. 2276 (10 June 1871), 720–1

Lysons, Daniel, *The Environs of London*, 4 vols (London: T. Cadell, 1792–6; Supplement, London: T. Cadell & W. Davies, 1811)

Lysons, Daniel, and Lysons, Samuel, *Magna Britannia; being a Concise Topographical Account of the Several Counties of Great Britain*, vol. 1: *Part 1, Containing Bedfordshire* (London: T. Cadell & W. Davies, 1813)

MacCaffrey, Wallace T., *Queen Elizabeth and the Making of Policy, 1572–1588* (Princeton, NJ: Princeton University Press, 1981)

MacCaffrey, Wallace T., *Elizabeth I: War and Politics 1588–1603* (Princeton, NJ: Princeton University Press, 1992)

McIntosh, Marjorie K., 'Sir Anthony Cooke: Tudor Humanist, Educator, and Religious Reformer', *Proceedings of the American Philological Society* 119 (1975), 233–50

Malherbe, Michel and Pousseur, Jean-Marie, eds, *Francis Bacon: Science et méthode* (Paris: J. Vrin, 1985)

Marotti, Arthur, *Manuscript, Print, and the English Renaissance Lyric* (Ithaca, NY: Cornell University Press, 1995)

Martin, Julian, *Francis Bacon, the State, and the Reform of Natural Philosophy* (Cambridge: Cambridge University Press, 1992)

Marwil, Jonathan, *The Trials of Counsel: Francis Bacon in 1621* (Detroit, Michigan: Wayne State University Press, 1976)

Mathew, David, *Sir Tobie Mathew* (London: Max Parrish, 1950)

Mathews, Nieves, *Francis Bacon: The History of a Character Assassination* (New Haven: Yale University Press, 1996)

Matthew, Arnold Harris, and Calthrop, Annette, *The Life of Sir Tobie Matthew: Bacon's alter ego* (London: Elkin Matthews, 1907)

Mattingly, Garrett, *Renaissance Diplomacy* (London: Jonathan Cape, 1955)

Miller, Amos C., *Sir Henry Killigrew: Elizabethan Soldier and Diplomat* (Leicester: Leicester University Press, 1963)

Moir, Thomas L., *The Addled Parliament of 1614* (Oxford: Clarendon Press, 1964)

Morrison, J. H., *The Underhills of Warwickshire: An Essay in Family History* (Cambridge: privately printed at the University Press, 1932)

Moule, H. J., *Descriptive Catalogue of the Charters, Minute Books and other Documents of the Borough of Weymouth and Melcombe Regis AD 1252 to 1800* (Weymouth: Sherrat & Son, 1883)

Mullinger, T. Bass, 'The Relations of Francis Bacon, Lord Verulam, with the University of Cambridge', *Proceedings of the Cambridge Antiquarian Society* 38 (1897), 227–37

Neale, J. E., *Elizabeth I and her Parliaments*, vol. 1: *1559–1581* (London: Jonathan Cape, 1953)

Neale, J. E., *Elizabeth I and her Parliaments*, vol. 2: *1584–1601* (London: Jonathan Cape, 1957)

Noonan, John T., Jr, *Bribes* (Berkeley, CA: University of California Press, 1984)

Notestein, Wallace, *The House of Commons 1604–1610* (New Haven: Yale University Press, 1971)

Nys, Ernest, 'Introduction' to Alberico Gentili, *De legationibus libri tres*, vol. 2, tr. Gordon J. Laing (New York: Oxford University Press, 1924), 11a–37a

Partridge, Charles, 'Edward Bacon', *Notes and Queries* 195 (1950), 459

Pearson, A. F. Scott, *Thomas Cartwright and Elizabethan Puritanism 1535–1603* (Cambridge: Cambridge University Press, 1925)

Peck, Linda Levy, *Northampton: Patronage and Policy at the Court of James I* (London: George Allen & Unwin, 1982)

Peck, Linda Levy, *Court Patronage and Corruption in Early Stuart England* (Boston: Unwin Hyman, 1990)

Pellissier, Georges, *La vie et les oeuvres de Du Bartas* (Paris: Hachette, 1883)

Pérez-Ramos, Antonio, *Francis Bacon's Idea of Science and the Master's Knowledge Tradition* (Oxford: Clarendon Press, 1988)

Plowden, Alison, *The Elizabethan Secret Service* (Hemel Hempstead: Harvester Wheatsheaf, 1991)

Prescott, Anne Lake, 'The Reception of Du Bartas in England', *Studies in the Renaissance* 15 (1968), 144–73

Prest, Wilfrid R. *The Inns of Court under Elizabeth and the Early Stuarts* (London: Longman, 1972)

Prest, Wilfrid R., 'The English Bar, 1550–1700' in Prest, ed., *Lawyers in Early Modern England* (London: Croom Helm, 1981), 65–85

Prestwich, Menna, *Cranfield: Politics and Profits under the Early Stuarts: The Career of Lionel Cranfield Earl of Manchester* (Oxford: Clarendon Press, 1966)

Quinton, Anthony, *Francis Bacon* (Oxford: Oxford University Press, 1980)

Rathé, C. Edward, 'Innocent Gentillet and the First "Anti-Machiavel"', *Bibliothèque d'humanisme et Renaissance* 27 (1965), 186–225

Read, Conyers, *Mr Secretary Walsingham and the Policy of Queen Elizabeth*, 3 vols (Cambridge, MA: Harvard University Press, 1925)

Read, Conyers, *Mr. Secretary Cecil and Queen Elizabeth* (London: Jonathan Cape, 1955)

Read, Conyers, *Lord Burghley and Queen Elizabeth* (London: Jonathan Cape, 1960)

Rees, Graham, 'Bacon's Philosophy: Some New Sources with Special Reference to the *Abecedarium novum naturae*', in Marta Fattori, ed., *Francis Bacon: terminologia e fortuna nel XVII secolo* (Rome: Ateneo, 1984)

Rex, Millicent Barton, *University Representation in England 1604–1690* (London: George Allen & Unwin, 1954)

Ribner, Irving, 'The Significance of Gentillet's Contre-Machiavel', *Modern Languages Quarterly* 10 (1949), 153–7

Rickert, Corinne, 'An Addition to the Canon of Bacon's Writings', *Modern Language Review* 50–1 (1955–6), 71–2

Rossi, Paolo, *Francis Bacon: From Magic to Science*, tr. Sacha Rabinovitch (London: Routledge & Kegan Paul, 1968)

Rowse, A. L., *Ralegh and the Throckmortons* (London: Macmillan, 1962)

Rowse, A. L., 'Bisham and the Hobys', in *Times, Persons, Places: Essays in Literature* (London: Macmillan, 1965), 188–218

Rowse, A. L., *Homosexuals in History: A Study of Ambivalence in Society, Literature and the Arts* (London: Weidenfeld & Nicolson, 1977)

Rowse, A. L., 'The Tragic Career of Henry Cuffe', in *Court and Country: Studies in Tudor Social History* (Brighton: Harvester, 1987), 211–41

Salmon, J. H. M., *Society in Crisis: France in the Sixteenth Century* (London: Ernest Benn, 1975)

Samuel, Edgar Roy, 'Portuguese Jews in Jacobean England', *The Jewish Historical Society of England Transactions* 18 (1958), 171–230

Sarre, A. C., 'The Poulet Family: Governors etc. in Jersey 1550–1600', *Société Jersiaise Annual Bulletin* 17 (1958), 141–9

Schleiner, Louise, *Tudor and Stuart Women Writers* (Bloomington, IN: Indiana University Press, 1994)

Scott-Warren, Jason, 'The Privy Politics of Sir John Harington's *New Discourse of a Stale Subject, Called the Metamorphosis of Ajax*', *Studies in Philology* 93 (1996), 412–42

Sessions, William A., ed., *Francis Bacon's Legacy of Texts: 'The Art of Discovery Grows with Discovery'* (New York: AMS Press, 1990)

Sessions, William A., *Francis Bacon Revisited* (New York: Twayne, 1996)

Shapiro, James, *Shakespeare and the Jews* (New York: Columbia University Press, 1996)

Sharpe, Kevin, 'The Earl of Arundel, his Circle and the Opposition to the Duke of Buckingham', in Kevin Sharpe, ed., *Faction and Parliament* (Oxford: Clarendon Press, 1978), 209–44

Sharpe, Kevin, *Sir Robert Cotton 1586–1631: History and Politics in Early Modern England* (Oxford: Oxford University Press, 1979)

Shaw, William A., ed., *The Knights of England*, 2 vols (London: Sherratt & Hughes, 1906)

Sherman, William H., *John Dee: The Politics of Reading and Writing in the English Renaissance* (Amherst, MA: University of Massachusetts Press, 1995)

Simpson, Alan, *The Wealth of the Gentry 1540–1660: East Anglian Studies* (Chicago and Cambridge: University of Chicago Press and Cambridge University Press, 1961)

Sinfield, Alan, 'Sidney and Du Bartas', *Comparative Literature* 27 (1975), 8–20

Smith, David Baird, 'Jean de Villiers Hotman', *Scottish Historical Review* 14 (1917), 147–66

Smith, A. Hassell, 'The Gardens of Sir Nicholas and Sir Francis Bacon: An Enigma Resolved and a Mind Explored', in Anthony Fletcher and Peter Roberts, eds, *Religion, Culture and Society in Early Modern England: Essays in Honour of Patrick Collinson* (Cambridge: Cambridge University Press, 1994), 125–60

Snow, V. F., 'The Arundel Case 1626', *The Historian* 26 (1964), 323–49

Somerset, Anne, *Unnatural Murder: Poison at the Court of James I* (London: Weidenfeld & Nicolson, 1997)

Stewart, Alan, *Close Readers: Humanism and Sodomy in Early Modern England* (Princeton, NJ: Princeton University Press, 1997)

Stewart, P. D., *Innocent Gentillet e la sua polemica antimachiavellica* (Florence: La Nuova Italia Editrice, 1969)

Stone, Lawrence, *The Crisis of the Aristocracy 1558–1641* (Oxford: Clarendon Press, 1965)

Strong, Roy, 'Nicholas Hilliard's Miniature of Francis Bacon Rediscovered and other Minutiae', *Burlington Magazine* 106 (1964), 337

Sutherland, N. M., *The Huguenot Struggle for Recognition* (New Haven: Yale University Press, 1980)

Thomas, S. G., 'Bacon's Tutors', *Times Literary Supplement*, 25 January 1947, 51

Thomson, Gladys Scott, 'Three Suffolk Figures: Thomas Wolsey; Stephen Gardiner; Nicholas Bacon: A Study in Social History', *Proceedings of the Suffolk Institute of Archaeology and Natural History* 25 (1952) 149–63

Thorne, James, *Handbook to the Environs of London, 1876*, 2 vols (repr. Bath: Adams & Dart, 1970)

Tittler, Robert, *Nicholas Bacon: The Making of a Tudor Statesman* (London: Jonathan Cape, 1976)

Twickenham Corporation/Twickenham and St Margaret's Chamber of Commerce, *The Official Guide to Twickenham*, 4th edn (Cheltenham: J. Burrow, 1927)

Ungerer, Gustav, 'The Printing of Spanish Books in Elizabethan England', *Library* 10 (1965), 177–229

Upton, Anthony F., *Sir Arthur Ingram c.1595–1642: A Study of the Origins of an English Landed Family* (Oxford: Oxford University Press, 1961)

Urbach, Peter, *Francis Bacon's Philosophy of Science: An Account and a Reappraisal* (LaSalle, IL: Open Court, 1987)

Urwick, William, *Nonconformity in Herts* (London: Hazell, Watson & Viney, 1884)

Usher, Roland G., 'Francis Bacon's Knowledge of Law French', *Modern Language Notes* 43 (1919), 28–32

Vickers, Brian, *Francis Bacon and Renaissance Prose* (Cambridge: Cambridge University Press, 1968)

Vickers, Brian, ed., *Essential Articles for the Study of Francis Bacon* (London: Sidgwick & Jackson, 1972)

Vickers, Brian, 'The Authenticity of Bacon's Earliest Writings', *Studies in Philology* 94 (1997), 248–96

Victoria History of the Counties of England, A History of the County of Middlesex, vol. 1, ed. J. S. Cockburn, H. P. F. King and K. G. T. McDonnell (Oxford: Institute of Historical Research, 1969)

Victoria History of the Counties of England, A History of the County of Middlesex, vol. 2, ed. William Page (London: Constable, 1911)

Victoria History of the Counties of England, A History of the County of Middlesex, vol. 3, ed. Susan Reynolds (Oxford: Institute of Historical Research, 1962)

Weaver, F. J. 'Anglo-French Diplomatic Relations 1558–1603' (part 3), *Bulletin of the Institute of Historical Research* 6 (1928–9), 1–9

Webster, Charles, *The Great Instauration: Science, Medicine and Reform 1626–1660* (London: Duckworth, 1975)

Welsby, Paul A., *Lancelot Andrewes 1555–1626* (London: SPCK, 1958)

Whiting, Mary Bradford, 'The Learned and Virtuous Lady Bacon', *The Hibbert Journal* 29 (1930–1), 270–83

Whitney, Charles, *Francis Bacon and Modernity* (New Haven: Yale University Press, 1986)

Wilkinson, Maurice, 'The English on the Gironde in 1592–3', *English Historical Review* 31 (1916), 279–91

Williams, Charles, *Bacon* (London: Arthur Barker, 1933)

Williams, Franklin B., Jr, *Index of Dedications and Commendatory Verses in English Books before 1641* (London: The Bibliographical Society, 1962)

Williams, Owen, 'Bacon's Tutor', *Times Literary Supplement*, 8 February 1947, 79

Williamson, Hugh Ross, *George Villiers First Duke of Buckingham: Study for a Biography* (London: Duckworth, 1940)

Wood, E. R., 'Francis Bacon's "Cousin Sharpe"', *Notes and Queries* 196 (1951), 248–9

Woolf, Daniel R., 'John Selden, John Borough and Francis Bacon's *History of Henry VII*, 1621', *Huntington Library Quarterly* 47 (1984), 47–53

Yates, Frances, *The Art of Memory* (Chicago: University of Chicago Press, 1966)

Young, Alan, *Tudor and Jacobean Tournaments* (London: George Philip, 1987)

Zaller, Robert, *The Parliament of 1621: A Study in Constitutional Conflict* (Berkeley, CA: University of California Press, 1971)

VI UNPUBLISHED DISSERTATIONS

Feil, John P., 'Sir Tobie Matthew and his *Collection of Letters*' (PhD, University of Chicago, 1962)

Freedman, Joyce Treskunof, 'Anthony Bacon and his World, 1558–1601' (PhD, Temple University, 1979)

Laffitte, Susan Cameron Miller, 'The Literary Connections of Sir Thomas Egerton: A Study of the Influence of Thomas Egerton upon Major Writers of Renaissance Literature' (PhD, Florida State University, 1971)

McIntosh, Marjorie Keniston, 'The Cooke Family of Gidea Hall, Essex, 1460–1661' (PhD, Harvard University, 1967)

Sandeen, Ernest R., 'Correspondence of Nicholas Bacon, Lord Keeper' (MA, University of Chicago, 1955)

Index

Index